OPPOSING VIEWPOINTS®

# ADDICTION

Louise I. Gerdes, *Book Editor*

Bruce Glassman, *Vice President*
Bonnie Szumski, *Publisher*
Helen Cothran, *Managing Editor*

San Diego • Detroit • New York • San Francisco • Cleveland
New Haven, Conn. • Waterville, Maine • London • Munich

*For more information, contact*
Greenhaven Press
27500 Drake Rd.
Farmington Hills, MI 48331-3535
Or you can visit our Internet site at http://www.gale.com



**LIBRARY OF CONGRESS CATALOGING-IN-PUBLICATION DATA**

Addiction : opposing viewpoints / Louise I. Gerdes, book editor.
p. cm. — (Opposing viewpoints series)
Includes bibliographical references and index.
ISBN 0-7377-2216-9 (lib. : alk. paper) — ISBN 0-7377-2217-7 (pbk. : alk. paper)
1. Compulsive behavior—United States. 2. Substance abuse—United States. 3. Substance abuse—Government policy—United States. 4. Addicts—United States. I. Gerdes, Louise I., 1953– . II. Opposing viewpoints series (Unnumbered)
HV4998.A32 2005
362.29—dc22 2003067520

Printed in the United States of America

> "Congress shall make no law. . . abridging the freedom of speech, or of the press."

*First Amendment to the U.S. Constitution*

The basic foundation of our democracy is the First Amendment guarantee of freedom of expression. The Opposing Viewpoints Series is dedicated to the concept of this basic freedom and the idea that it is more important to practice it than to enshrine it.

# Contents

# Why Consider Opposing Viewpoints?

*"The only way in which a human being can make some approach to knowing the whole of a subject is by hearing what can be said about it by persons of every variety of opinion and studying all modes in which it can be looked at by every character of mind. No wise man ever acquired his wisdom in any mode but this."*

John Stuart Mill

In our media-intensive culture it is not difficult to find differing opinions. Thousands of newspapers and magazines and dozens of radio and television talk shows resound with differing points of view. The difficulty lies in deciding which opinion to agree with and which "experts" seem the most credible. The more inundated we become with differing opinions and claims, the more essential it is to hone critical reading and thinking skills to evaluate these ideas. Opposing Viewpoints books address this problem directly by presenting stimulating debates that can be used to enhance and teach these skills. The varied opinions contained in each book examine many different aspects of a single issue. While examining these conveniently edited opposing views, readers can develop critical thinking skills such as the ability to compare and contrast authors' credibility, facts, argumentation styles, use of persuasive techniques, and other stylistic tools. In short, the Opposing Viewpoints Series is an ideal way to attain the higher-level thinking and reading skills so essential in a culture of diverse and contradictory opinions.

In addition to providing a tool for critical thinking, Opposing Viewpoints books challenge readers to question their own strongly held opinions and assumptions. Most people form their opinions on the basis of upbringing, peer pressure, and personal, cultural, or professional bias. By reading carefully balanced opposing views, readers must directly confront new ideas as well as the opinions of those with whom they disagree. This is not to simplistically argue that everyone who reads opposing views will—or should—change his or her opinion. Instead, the series enhances readers' understanding of their own views by encouraging confrontation with opposing ideas. Careful examination of others' views can lead to the readers' understanding of the logical inconsistencies in their own opinions, perspective on why they hold an opinion, and the consideration of the possibility that their opinion requires further evaluation.

## Evaluating Other Opinions

To ensure that this type of examination occurs, Opposing Viewpoints books present all types of opinions. Prominent spokespeople on different sides of each issue as well as well-known professionals from many disciplines challenge the reader. An additional goal of the series is to provide a forum for other, less known, or even unpopular viewpoints. The opinion of an ordinary person who has had to make the decision to cut off life support from a terminally ill relative, for example, may be just as valuable and provide just as much insight as a medical ethicist's professional opinion. The editors have two additional purposes in including these less known views. One, the editors encourage readers to respect others' opinions—even when not enhanced by professional credibility. It is only by reading or listening to and objectively evaluating others' ideas that one can determine whether they are worthy of consideration. Two, the inclusion of such viewpoints encourages the important critical thinking skill of objectively evaluating an author's credentials and bias. This evaluation will illuminate an author's reasons for taking a particular stance on an issue and will aid in readers' evaluation of the author's ideas.

It is our hope that these books will give readers a deeper understanding of the issues debated and an appreciation of the complexity of even seemingly simple issues when good and honest people disagree. This awareness is particularly important in a democratic society such as ours in which people enter into public debate to determine the common good. Those with whom one disagrees should not be regarded as enemies but rather as people whose views deserve careful examination and may shed light on one's own.

Thomas Jefferson once said that "difference of opinion leads to inquiry, and inquiry to truth." Jefferson, a broadly educated man, argued that "if a nation expects to be ignorant and free . . . it expects what never was and never will be." As individuals and as a nation, it is imperative that we consider the opinions of others and examine them with skill and discernment. The Opposing Viewpoints Series is intended to help readers achieve this goal.

David L. Bender and Bruno Leone,
Founders

---

Greenhaven Press anthologies primarily consist of previously published material taken from a variety of sources, including periodicals, books, scholarly journals, newspapers, government documents, and position papers from private and public organizations. These original sources are often edited for length and to ensure their accessibility for a young adult audience. The anthology editors also change the original titles of these works in order to clearly present the main thesis of each viewpoint and to explicitly indicate the opinion presented in the viewpoint. These alterations are made in consideration of both the reading and comprehension levels of a young adult audience. Every effort is made to ensure that Greenhaven Press accurately reflects the original intent of the authors included in this anthology.

---

# Introduction

*"Absent a clear definition of addiction, researchers will continue finding it very difficult to determine addiction prevalence rates, etiology, or the necessary and sufficient causes that stimulate recovery."*

*—Howard J. Shaffer, director of the Harvard Medical School Division on Addictions*

Stephen started using heroin when he was fourteen. His parents discovered his heroin use when his grades began to drop, and they sent Stephen to a rehabilitation center. After treatment, Stephen began to use again and became involved in repeated confrontations with the law. At sixteen, Stephen's parents asked him to leave home. Unable to keep a job, Stephen turned to prostitution to obtain money to buy heroin. Despite his estrangement from family and friends, and in spite of the risk of contracting AIDS from needle sharing and prostitution, Stephen continues to use.

Maryann had been married for fifteen years when she began regularly conversing on Internet chat rooms. Soon she was going to bed later and later in order to spend more time chatting, flirting, and occasionally masturbating with an online partner. She felt guilty when she crawled into bed next to her sleeping husband. Each morning she vowed, "Never again." However, the next day she would find herself counting the hours until she could log on again. Although her work and her relationship with her husband have deteriorated, Maryann continues to chat on the Internet late into the night.

While most would consider Stephen an addict, many would not characterize Maryann's behavior as addictive. Indeed, one of the most significant controversies in the addiction debate is whether or not behaviors such as excessive use of the Internet, compulsive sex, or pathological gambling should be considered addictions. Some analysts question whether compulsive behaviors should be lumped together with addictions to substances such as alcohol and heroin. According to Donna Markus, clinical director of AddictionSolutions.com, referring to behaviors as addictive is becoming more common, but professionals have varied views on what should be considered addiction. "Today, it's fairly common to hear the terms 'addict' and 'addiction' applied to a wide variety of behaviors by professionals as well as nonprofessionals," she explains. Nevertheless, she adds, "Although alcohol and other drug addictions have been studied for decades, mental health professionals continue to hold disparate beliefs regarding the etiology and nature of addiction."

In the past, professionals defined addiction as physical dependence on a drug. Craving, increased tolerance, and withdrawal were considered clinical evidence of this dependence. Craving involves an intense desire for the drug, tolerance means that the user needs more and more to achieve the high, and withdrawal is the physical and mental suffering that occurs when drug use is discontinued. Professionals who support this definition of addiction believe that only drugs can induce physiological dependence; thus people can only be addicted to drugs, not behaviors.

As researchers continue to examine addiction and addictive substances, this conception has begun to change. For example, *Science* writer Constance Holden maintains, "Even some seemingly classical addictions don't follow [the traditional] pattern. Cocaine, for example, is highly addictive but causes little withdrawal. And a person who gets hooked on morphine while in the hospital may stop taking the drug without developing an obsession with it." Moreover, director of the Harvard Medical School Division of Addictions Howard J. Shaffer argues, some behaviors seem to induce physiological symptoms. "For example," Shaffer claims, "upon stopping, pathological gamblers who do not use alcohol or other psychoactive drugs often show physical symptoms that appear to be very similar to either narcotics, stimulants, or polysubstance withdrawal."

Advances in neurobiology have also changed traditional conceptions of addiction. Scientists discovered that both drugs and behaviors activate a part of the brain known as the reward center. Drug research revealed that drugs mimic or block the brains neurotransmitters in the reward center and take over the brain's dispensing of the reward—the good feeling people get when they eat or have sex. Psychology professor Alice M. Young explains: "Drugs such as alcohol, nicotine, heroin and cocaine may short-circuit the natural reward pathways that have evolved to ensure that we engage in activities critical to our survival." Thus, in order to get the "reward," the good feeling people often attribute to being high, people must continue to use the drug.

More recently, researchers have found that a habit such as gambling, overeating, excessive sex, or use of the Internet can also hijack the brain's circuitry. According to Stanford University psychologist Brian Knutson, "It stands to reason if you can derange [the brain's] circuits with pharmacology, you can do it with natural rewards too." As a result of this research, some analysts now believe that behaviors can be as addictive as drugs. They contend that the underlying psychological and physiological processes associated with compulsive behaviors and drug abuse are much the same. Markus explains:

> A significant broadening of the range of activities labeled as addiction resulted from research indicating that compulsive behaviors—in addition to the more commonly acknowledged addictive substances—also result in neurochemical changes. . . . In this view, whether the addiction is to food, substances, sex, gambling, other objects or activities, the characteristics of the addictive process are similar.

Despite these recent research findings, many commentators remain reluctant to expand the concept of addiction to include compulsive behaviors. Part of the reason for this is because a precise definition of addiction remains elusive. Shaffer concludes, "Without more clarity and precision, it will remain difficult to distinguish between someone experiencing an overwhelming impulse to act in a self-destructive way and someone who is simply unwilling to control his or her destructive impulses to act." In *Opposing Viewpoints: Addiction*, this and other controversies surrounding the concept of addiction are debated in the following chapters: Is Addiction a Serious Problem? What Factors Contribute to Addiction? What Are the Most Effective Treatments for Addiction? How Should the Government Deal with Addiction? The authors express diverse views about how addiction should be defined.

Chapter 1

# Is Addiction a Serious Problem?

# Chapter Preface

One of many controversies in the addiction field is whether compulsive behaviors such as excessive gambling and overeating should be considered addictions or simply pathological behavior. Even among those mental health experts who are comfortable viewing many behaviors as addictions, there is strong disagreement about whether sexual compulsivity should be viewed as an addiction. This disagreement even extends to sex experts. Clinical psychologist Dennis P. Sugrue writes, "Few topics in the sexology field have galvanized people into opposing camps as stridently as the topics of sex addiction and sexual compulsivity. They are lightening rods in a 20-year-old controversy about the nature and origin of problematic high-frequency sexual behavior."

Psychologist Patrick Carnes, one of the most fervent supporters of the concept of sex addiction, argues that "during the past three decades, professionals have acknowledged that some people use sex to manage their internal distress. These people are similar to compulsive gamblers, compulsive overeaters, or alcoholics in that they are not able to contain their impulses—and with destructive results." Carnes defines sex addiction as any sexually related, compulsive behavior that interferes with normal living and eventually becomes unmanageable. The most recent edition of the *Diagnostic and Statistical Manual of Mental Disorders* (DSM-IV), published by the American Psychiatric Association, describes addictive disorders such as alcoholism and pathological gambling as having three characteristics: a loss of control, a continuation of the behavior or the use of the substance despite adverse consequences, and a preoccupation with the substance or the behavior. Those who believe that sex addiction should be included in the manual as a mental disorder argue that it fits all of these categories. According to Mark Griffith, who writes for *Psychology Review*,

> Like an alcoholic or a pathological gambler, sexual addicts are unable to stop their self-destructive sexual behavior. In fact, sex addicts will often ignore severe emotional, interpersonal, and physical consequences of their behavior. The consequences of excessive sexual behavior are far-reaching and

> can result in losing relationships, family break-ups, difficulties with work, arrests, financial troubles, a loss of interest in things not sexual, low self-esteem and despair. . . . To sex addicts, sex is more important than anything and anyone else and they will engage in the behavior to the neglect of almost everything else.

Other analysts disagree with the premise that excessive sexual behavior is an addiction. According to therapist Marty Klein, publisher of *Sexual Intelligence*, "Most people who self-diagnose as 'sex addicts' aren't compulsive. . . . They're mostly unremarkable people who simply don't like the consequences of their sexual choices—but do not want to deal with the emotional distress that would arise if they made different choices." Another of Klein's concerns is that making sex addiction into a mental disorder implies that sex needs to be controlled, thus declaring sexually healthy people unhealthy. Klein explains:

> The sex addiction movement must . . . inevitably say that people are in danger of becoming addicted and thereby lose their ability to make wholesome choices. We're told that at some point something can happen to healthy people—they can, for example, consume a lot of pornography—and they can become addicted. And so everyone's at risk. The sexual addiction diagnostic criteria make problems of non-problematic experiences, and as a result pathologize a majority of people.

Making unpopular sexual practices into mental disorders is nothing new, maintains Klein. "People who advocated birth control in the 1920s were labeled psychiatrically ill. And we all know that frigidity and homosexuality have been labeled psychiatric diseases," Klein contends. He adds: "Sex addiction falls right into this tradition of 'diagnosing' non-conforming sexual expression as disease."

Whether or not compulsive sex should be classified with substance abuse and other excessive behaviors as an addiction disorder remains controversial. The authors of the viewpoints in the following chapter express their opinions on the nature and scope of addiction.

1

VIEWPOINT

*"The Internet is fueling gambling problems, sex addictions and other forms of compulsive behavior."*

# The Internet Is Fueling Addictions

Brian McCormick

According to Brian McCormick in the following viewpoint, the Internet fuels addictions to sex, gambling, and the Internet itself. The Internet accelerates addictions because of its accessibility, affordability, and anonymity, McCormick claims. Although an increasing number of medical professionals acknowledge that Internet-related addictions are a growing public health problem, contends McCormick, the methods for treating these addicts remains controversial. Brian McCormick is a staff editor for *American Medical News*.

As you read, consider the following questions:

1. What three groups of people access the Internet for sexual gratification, according to research conducted by Al Cooper?
2. In the author's view, what convinced those who treat addicted patients that Internet-related addiction is a problem?
3. In McCormick's opinion, why do most experts say that the tools for treating Internet-related addictions are similar to those used to address other compulsions?

Brian McCormick, "Hooked on the Net," *American Medical News*, vol. 43, June 19, 2000, p. 17. 

The Internet is fueling gambling problems, sex addictions and other forms of compulsive behavior. The burgeoning technology also is raising new treatment issues.

## A Typical Story

Jarvis, 62, says sexual compulsions have been a problem for most of his life. But his problems intensified two years ago when he discovered sexually explicit chat rooms on the Internet.

"I could lose myself for hours or days without ever leaving home," he said. "The level of isolation and separation from real people was jarring. I had an active real life with friends and a job I loved, but I was spending more and more time in an online fantasy world, which I found ultimately to be a very empty, unsatisfying way to live."

According to . . . research findings, Jarvis is one of more than 100,000—and possibly one of more than 2 million—Internet sex addicts. Another million or more may be developing gambling addictions either exclusively or predominantly online, and several hundred thousand may be developing an unhealthy dependence on the Internet itself.

These findings represent the tip of a new and ominous public health threat, one that to date is basically being ignored, according to those who treat Internet-related addictions and compulsions.

## The Cybersex Compulsive

A . . . survey of more than 9,000 Internet users found that 1% of those who visited sex-related sites could be categorically classified as "cybersex compulsives," devoting large amounts of time to the pursuit of sex online and suffering serious consequences as a result. Another 17% were identified as having significant but less severe problems related to sex and the Internet.

Al Cooper, PhD, published the research in a [Spring 2000] special issue of the journal *Sexual Addiction and Compulsivity* devoted to cybersex. His study found three groups of people accessing the Internet for sexual gratification. The first, and largest, were recreational users, for whom it did not seem to be a problem. The second group involved people who already had problems with sexual compulsion that were intensified or exacerbated on the Internet. The third, an at-risk group, were people for whom sexual compulsion would never have been an issue had it not been for the Internet's powerful draw.

Dr. Cooper said that with more than 60 million people on the Internet and at least 20% of that group visiting pornographic sites or engaging in sexually explicit chat, the scope of the problem quickly becomes apparent.

"Using our very conservative definition of a cybersex compulsive, that means at least 120,000 people are suffering from this condition. If the rate of any other disease had gone from virtually zero to 120,000 in five years, it would be declared an epidemic and the full resources of the health system would be brought to bear on it," said Dr. Cooper, clinical director of the San Jose (Calif.) Marital and Sexuality Centre. He also said that while the National Institute of Mental Health is now beginning to look at the issue, the response of the health care community in general has been inadequate.

## An Intense Delivery Device

Those who treat addictions related to the Internet have seen a learning curve among their colleagues. "When I first began dealing with this in 1994, everyone laughed about it. There were even tongue-in-cheek articles about the need for 12-step programs to treat Internet addicts," said Kimberly S. Young, PsyD, who in 1995 created the Center for Online Addiction in Bradford, Pa. "Well, no one is laughing now."

Dr. Young treats people for whom the Internet is a means to access compulsions, such as sex and gambling, as well as those who are dependent on the Internet itself.

For many who treat addicted patients, seeing the impact of the Internet firsthand made believers of them. "I've been treating sexually compulsive people for many years, and I've seen the Internet change the landscape in much the same way crack cocaine did for those who treat drug addicts," said Jennifer Schneider, MD, an internist and addiction medicine specialist in Tucson, Ariz. "The computer is an extremely intense delivery device."

Dr. Cooper agrees that the Internet has "turbocharged"

sexual compulsions for many patients, and he attributes the power of the Internet to what he calls the "Triple A" effect: the accessibility, affordability and anonymity of acting out sexually online.

"My wife doesn't give me everything I want, 24 hours a day, seven days a week, but for those who seek sexual gratification through their computers, the Internet can," said Dr. Cooper. And the relatively low cost compared with other forms of acting out, such as strip clubs, prostitutes or phone sex, also eliminates a barrier.

## The Influence of Internet Anonymity

But the anonymity of virtual sex may provide its biggest boost. "You can be any gender, race, occupation or age you want to be," said John Sealy, MD, medical director of a full-time inpatient recovery center for sexual addiction at Del Amo Hospital in Torrance, Calif.

Those same factors help to explain why compulsive gamblers are also increasingly turning to the Internet, said Kevin O'Neill, deputy director of the Council on Compulsive Gambling of New Jersey Inc. "For compulsive gamblers, this venue—unlike casinos, riverboats, lotteries or any other form of gambling—is not monitored or regulated," he said. That means gamblers often have no upper-end limit on how much they can lose and can spiral down in their addictions more quickly and severely.

The secrecy of Internet gambling also holds allure for these compulsives, who often have a great deal of shame associated with their behavior, O'Neill said. That helps explain why the number of online casinos and other gaming sites went from about 160 to more than 1,000 last year, and how online gambling has become more than a billion-dollar business [in 2000].

Bev, a 54-year-old recovering alcoholic, says she probably always had a problem with gambling. But it got out of hand only after she discovered online casinos in 1998.

When she lost her job a few months later, she devoted most of her waking time to Internet gambling, maxing out three credit cards, cashing in a 401(k), and nearly destroying a 30-year marriage. With the help of a therapist, medication,

Gamblers Anonymous and online support groups, Bev has been able to refrain from gambling since January [2000].

Dr. Sealy said it is the very isolation of the Internet that both appeals to and eventually entraps addicts. "Addiction is based on isolation and intense loneliness," he said. "These online interactions give the addict the illusion of being connected to counter that loneliness and shame, but ultimately as the medium is abused, it only serves to compound the loneliness and the shame."

Other therapists add that the incidence of cross-addiction seems very prevalent among Internet addicts.

"We began as a chemical dependency treatment center, and we saw that one-third of our patients had gambling problems," said Angie Moore, coordinator of addiction and counseling services at the Illinois Institute for Addiction Recovery at Proctor Hospital in Peoria, Ill.

"As we started treating online gambling addicts, we saw that about one-half of them had chemical dependencies, as well," Moore said.

## Treating Internet Addictions

Because it is linked so closely to other addictive behaviors, most experts say the tools for diagnosing and treating Internet-related addictions also are similar to those of other compulsions.

"Patients won't willingly share this information; they have too much shame associated with it," Dr. Sealy said. "Physicians who suspect a problem should ask open-ended questions such as, 'Is there something in your life that feels out of control or that is sapping an inordinate amount of your time and energy?' Most important, doctors need to address this without any hint of shame or judgment. These patients are usually acting out against their own ethics and principles, and they won't open up if they sense the least bit of judgment."

Dr. Schneider adds that for a profession that has repeatedly underdiagnosed and undertreated addiction, changing the average physician's mind-set may be the key to better diagnosis. "Doctors won't know that this is a problem until they know it can be a problem," she said.

Most experts say that, as with other addictions, the preferred treatment includes a combination of therapy and participation in self-help recovery groups. But not all agree with that prescription.

Handelsman. © 1999 by Tribune Media Services. All rights reserved. Reproduced by permission.

"I've found that Internet addicts are not at all receptive to the idea of 12-step recovery groups," Dr. Young said. She has been among the pioneers in another treatment approach, online counseling.

## Logging On for Treatment?

"With the opening of my center, I quickly became the Ann Landers of online therapists," Dr. Young said, "and that eventually evolved into online therapy." For $75 an hour, significantly less than her office rates, Dr. Young will treat patients via computer. But that form of treatment has drawn its own detractors.

"I think that ethically, you need to pick up a phone or see a patient in an office setting," O'Neill said. "In addition to being ethically questionable, I don't think it is particularly effective to treat patients with the very tool through which they are dissociating."

Dr. Sealy insists online therapy has both positive and negative aspects. "Many addicts become so isolated that they have no other way of relating. This may provide a method by which they can reach out and seek help. But recovery needs to be experiential. The patient will inevitably need to interact with a therapist and will likely need to be confronted, and neither of those can be accomplished very well via computer."

The role of the computer in the life of a recovering Internet addict is also controversial. Although many therapists say the increasingly ubiquitous Internet will require most patients to find ways to coexist with their computers, much as compulsive overeaters need to learn to eat moderately, others still counsel abstinence from the Web.

"I realize some people believe in controlled Internet use, but some people believe in controlled drinking for alcoholics; we don't," Moore said. "Once the Internet has become a problem, the risks of exposure vastly outweigh the need for that access."

2

VIEWPOINT

*"[That 6 percent of Internet users are addicts] cannot be confidently applied to Internet users in general."*

# The Threat of Internet Addiction Is Exaggerated

Jacob Sullum

Internet addiction is not a major threat to public health, argues Jacob Sullum in the following viewpoint. Although Internet use, like many pleasurable activities, can for some lead to unhealthy patterns of behavior, claiming that this abuse is an objectively identifiable medical disorder is misleading, Sullum claims. Trying to equate Internet and drug addiction, he asserts, leads people to the conclusion that the problem of Internet addiction is greater than it really is. Jacob Sullum is a senior editor of *Reason*, a magazine that supports individual freedom and opposes big government.

As you read, consider the following questions:

1. According to Sullum, why is psychologist David Greenfield's survey skewed?
2. According to the *Detroit News*, what will happen if Internet addiction is defined as a disorder?
3. In Sullum's opinion, what has Greenfield lost sight of when comparing all pleasurable activities to drug abuse?

Journalists never seem to tire of discovering that human beings remain human even when they go online. From gambling and pornography to fraud and pederasty, the Internet makes everything old new again.

In this category of familiar stories with a cyberspace twist, one of the hardiest topics is Internet addiction, which the news media have been warning us about since 1995. The . . . burst of coverage [in 1999] was generated by a study supposedly showing that 6 percent of Internet users are addicts.

The study, presented at the annual meeting of the American Psychological Association (APA), is based on a survey of visitors to ABCNews.com. Among other things, the survey asked them if they felt preoccupied by the Internet, if they used it to escape problems, if they had trouble reducing their online time, and if they lied about the extent of their Internet use.

Psychologist David Greenfield, who developed the survey based on the American Psychiatric Association's diagnostic criteria for "pathological gambling," identified respondents as addicts if they answered yes to five or more such questions. Of the 17,251 people who filled out the survey, 990 met this definition; hence the widely cited "6 percent."

## A Limited Sample

Contrary to most of the press coverage, however, this figure cannot be confidently applied to Internet users in general, since the sample was limited to people who happened to visit the ABC News site and who were willing to complete the questionnaire. The fact that ABC News posted the survey in conjunction with its own coverage of Internet addiction probably skewed the sample further.

Some people seem to believe that the true incidence of Internet addiction is not 6 percent but zero. A *Detroit News* editorial called the condition "spurious" and observed, "If it can be successfully defined as a disorder, then Internet addiction will be covered by a good many medical insurance policies, and psychologists can expect a tide of Internet-addicted patients to flow into their offices."

It is hard to ignore the fact that the researchers promoting the concept of Internet addiction tend to be entrepreneurs as well as scientists. Greenfield, a West Hartford, Connecticut, therapist, runs a Web site that offers a "Free Virtual Addiction Test" for people who are wondering if they need professional help.

### The Flaws in Internet Addiction Research

The original research into [Internet Addiction Disorder] began with exploratory surveys, which cannot establish *causal* relationships between specific behaviors and their cause. While surveys can help establish descriptions of how people feel about themselves and their behaviors, they cannot draw conclusions about whether a specific technology, such as the Internet, has actually *caused* those behaviors. Those conclusions which are drawn are purely speculative and subjective made by the researchers themselves. Researchers have a name for this logical fallacy, ignoring a common cause. It's one of the oldest fallacies in science, and one still regularly perpetrated in psychological research today.

John M. Grohol, *Internet Addiction Guide*, February 1999.

Psychologist Kimberly Young, who also presented a paper on Internet addiction at the APA meeting, is the founder and CEO of the Center for On-Line Addiction in Bradford, Pennsylvania. She runs the Web site netaddiction.com and offers online counseling to cyberspace junkies at a rate of $55 for each 50-minute session.

But the fact that people make money by "treating" Internet addiction does not mean that the problem is imaginary. After all, no one is forced to ask Greenfield or Young for help in controlling his Internet use.

## An Unhealthy Pattern of Behavior

Some people, by their own judgment, spend too much time online, jeopardizing their work, their health, or their relationships with family and friends. To insist that such a damaging preoccupation is not really an addiction because it does not involve a drug is to insist on an arbitrarily narrow definition that ignores everyday experience.

In real life, people can develop strong attachments to all sorts of things: food, sex, exercise, gambling, shopping, TV, video games. Sometimes these attachments get out of hand.

This is what we mean when we talk about addiction: a pattern of behavior, not a chemical reaction.

When psychiatrists talk about addiction, by contrast, they pretend they are dealing with a precisely defined, objectively verifiable medical disorder. And when Greenfield urges them to recognize Internet addiction as such a disorder, he mimics their biological reductionism.

"The underlying neurochemical changes that occur during any pleasurable act have proven themselves to be potentially addictive on a brain-behavior level," he writes. But notice what this means: Any source of pleasure can be the focus of an addiction.

Greenfield loses sight of the point that drug abuse is simply one form of addiction, instead treating it as a template that all genuine addictions have to match. In his eagerness to show that the Internet is just like a drug, he calls it "potent," emphasizes "tolerance and withdrawal symptoms," and draws an analogy between higher modem speeds and faster routes of drug administration.

"There's a power here that's different from anything we've dealt with before," Greenfield declared at the APA meeting. Here is yet another way in which the Internet resembles drugs: Both inspire exaggeration.

3

VIEWPOINT

*"Most smokers use tobacco regularly because they are addicted to nicotine."*

# Nicotine Addiction Harms Society

National Institute on Drug Abuse

In the following viewpoint the National Institute on Drug Abuse (NIDA) argues that most people smoke tobacco products because they are addicted to nicotine. According to NIDA, research shows that nicotine increases the levels of dopamine in the brain, which triggers feelings of pleasure, thus encouraging users to continue nicotine use. Tobacco smoking is responsible for more than four hundred thousand deaths in the United States each year and $138 billion in health care costs, NIDA claims. NIDA is an agency of the National Institutes of Health.

As you read, consider the following questions:

1. In NIDA's view, how is nicotine absorbed by the body?
2. According to NIDA, what led scientists to believe that nicotine might not be the only psychoactive ingredient in tobacco?
3. What did the 1999 National Household Survey on Drug Abuse reveal about adolescent smoking habits?

National Institute on Drug Abuse, "Nicotine Addiction," www.nida.nih.gov, 2002.

Nicotine, one of more than 4,000 chemicals found in the smoke from tobacco products such as cigarettes, cigars, and pipes, is the primary component in tobacco that acts on the brain. Smokeless tobacco products such as snuff and chewing tobacco also contain many toxins as well as high levels of nicotine. Nicotine, recognized as one of the most frequently used addictive drugs, is a naturally occurring colorless liquid that turns brown when burned and acquires the odor of tobacco when exposed to air. There are many species of tobacco plants; the tabacum species serves as the major source of tobacco products today. Since nicotine was first identified in the early 1800s, it has been studied extensively and shown to have a number of complex and sometimes unpredictable effects on the brain and the body.

Cigarette smoking is the most prevalent form of nicotine addiction in the United States. Most cigarettes in the U.S. market today contain 10 milligrams (mg) or more of nicotine. Through inhaling smoke, the average smoker takes in 1 to 2 mg nicotine per cigarette. There have been substantial increases in the sale and consumption of smokeless tobacco products also, and more recently, in cigar sales.

Nicotine is absorbed through the skin and mucosal lining of the mouth and nose or by inhalation in the lungs. Depending on how tobacco is taken, nicotine can reach peak levels in the bloodstream and brain rapidly. Cigarette smoking, for example, results in rapid distribution of nicotine throughout the body, reaching the brain within 10 seconds of inhalation. Cigar and pipe smokers, on the other hand, typically do not inhale the smoke, so nicotine is absorbed more slowly through the mucosal membranes of their mouths. Nicotine from smokeless tobacco also is absorbed through the mucosal membranes.

## Is Nicotine Addictive?

Yes, nicotine is addictive. Most smokers use tobacco regularly because they are addicted to nicotine. Addiction is characterized by compulsive drug-seeking and use, even in the face of negative health consequences, and tobacco use certainly fits the description. It is well documented that most smokers identify tobacco as harmful and express a desire to reduce or stop using it, and nearly 35 million of them make a serious attempt to quit each year. Unfortunately, less than 7 percent of those who try to quit on their own achieve more than 1 year of abstinence; most relapse within a few days of attempting to quit.

Other factors to consider besides nicotine's addictive properties include its high level of availability, the small number of legal and social consequences of tobacco use, and the sophisticated marketing and advertising methods used by tobacco companies. These factors, combined with nicotine's addictive properties, often serve as determinants for first use and, ultimately, addiction.

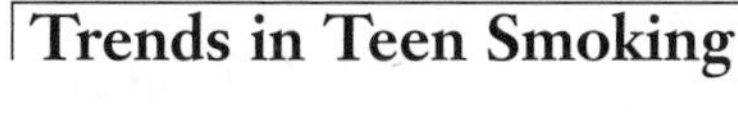
Trends in Teen Smoking

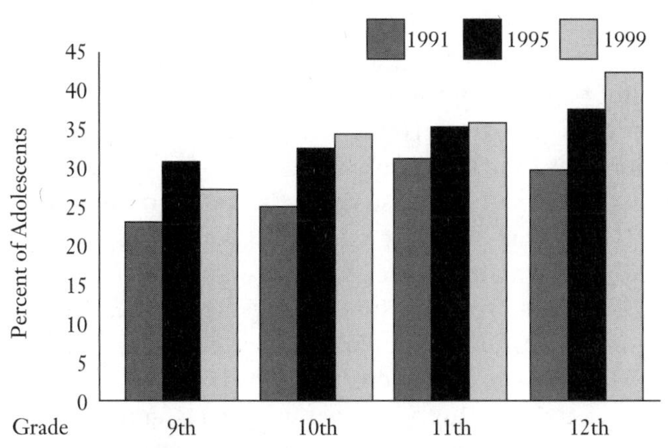


Centers for Disease Control and Prevention, 2000.

## Nicotine and the Brain

Research has shown in fine detail how nicotine acts on the brain to produce a number of behavioral effects. Of primary importance to its addictive nature are findings that nicotine activates the brain circuitry that regulates feelings of pleasure, the so-called reward pathways. A key brain chemical involved in mediating the desire to consume drugs is the neurotransmitter dopamine, and research has shown that nicotine increases the levels of dopamine in the reward circuits. Nicotine's pharmacokinetic properties have been found also to enhance its abuse potential. Cigarette smoking produces a rapid distribution of nicotine to the brain, with drug levels peaking within 10 seconds of inhalation. The acute effects of nicotine dissipate in a few minutes, causing the smoker to continue dosing frequently throughout the day to maintain the drug's pleasurable effects and prevent withdrawal.

What people frequently do not realize is that the cigarette is a very efficient and highly engineered drug-delivery system. By inhaling, the smoker can get nicotine to the brain very rapidly with every puff. A typical smoker will take 10 puffs on a cigarette over a period of 5 minutes that the cigarette is lit. Thus, a person who smokes about 1-1/2 packs (30 cigarettes) daily, gets 300 "hits" of nicotine to the brain each day. These factors contribute considerably to nicotine's highly addictive nature.

Scientific research is also beginning to show that nicotine may not be the only psychoactive ingredient in tobacco. Using advanced neuroimaging technology, scientists can see the dramatic effect of cigarette smoking on the brain and are finding a marked decrease in the levels of monoamineoxidase (MAO), an important enzyme that is responsible for breaking down dopamine. The change in MAO must be caused by some tobacco smoke ingredient other than nicotine, since we know that nicotine itself does not dramatically alter MAO levels. The decrease in two forms of MAO, A and B, then results in higher dopamine levels and may be another reason that smokers continue to smoke—to sustain the high dopamine levels that result in the desire for repeated drug use.

## What Is the Impact of Tobacco Use?

According to the 1999 National Household Survey on Drug Abuse, an estimated 57.0 million Americans were current smokers and 7.6 million used smokeless tobacco, which means that nicotine is one of the most widely abused substances. In addition, in 1998 each day in the United States more than 2,000 people under the age of 18 began daily smoking. According to the Centers for Disease Control and Prevention (CDC), the prevalence of cigarette smoking among U.S. high school students increased from 27.5 percent in 1991 to 36.4 percent in 1997 before declining to 34.8 percent in 1999. NIDA's [National Institute on Drug Abuse] own Monitoring the Future Study, which annually surveys drug use and related attitudes of America's adolescents, also found the prevalence rates for smoking among youth declined from 1999 to 2000. Since 1975, nicotine in the form of cigarettes has consistently been the substance the greatest number of high school students use daily.

The impact of nicotine addiction in terms of morbidity, mortality, and economic costs to society is staggering. Tobacco kills more than 430,000 U.S. citizens each year—more than alcohol, cocaine, heroin, homicide, suicide, car accidents, fire, and AIDS combined. Tobacco use is the leading preventable cause of death in the United States.

Economically, an estimated $80 billion of total U.S. health care costs each year is attributable to smoking. However, this cost is well below the total cost to society because it does not include burn care from smoking-related fires, perinatal care for low-birth-weight infants of mothers who smoke, and medical care costs associated with disease caused by secondhand smoke. Taken together, the direct and indirect costs of smoking are estimated at $138 billion per year.

4

VIEWPOINT

*"The notion that nicotine is an addictive substance lacks reasonable empirical support."*

# The Addictive Properties of Nicotine Are Unproven

Dale M. Atrens

While most people assume that nicotine is addictive, research on nicotine addiction does not support this assumption, argues Dale M. Atrens in the following viewpoint. Nicotine does not meet the criteria that defines addiction, Atrens claims. He maintains, for example, that one element of the Surgeon General's definition for addiction—that addiction takes precedence over other important priorities in the lives of addicts—does not apply to nicotine; most smokers have no problem not smoking in situations where laws prohibit smoking, for example. Atrens, author of *The Neurosciences and Behavior*, is a lecturer in psychobiology at the University of Sydney, in Australia.

As you read, consider the following questions:

1. According to Atrens, what two factors compromise the verbal reports of drug users?
2. What broad behaviors have been labeled "addictions," according to the author?
3. In Atrens's opinion, what is the most serious deficiency in using animal models to study human drug taking?

Dale M. Atrens, "Nicotine as an Addictive Substance: A Critical Examination of the Basic Concepts and Empirical Evidence," *Journal of Drug Issues*, vol. 31, June 9, 2001, pp. 87–114. 

The addiction model has dominated smoking research for over a generation. Tobacco smoke is said to contain numerous agents that cause ill health as well as a powerful addictive drug, nicotine. According to the dominant model, as the nicotine addiction develops, the smoker becomes progressively less able to stop. The essence of the nicotine addiction hypothesis is that smokers are unable to stop because nicotine changes the brain in such a way as to perpetuate its use. More broadly, drug addictions are seen as representing brain dysfunctions. . . .

## A Common View

The 1988 Surgeon General's Report on Smoking and Health states the nicotine addiction viewpoint succinctly:

> Cigarettes and other forms of tobacco are addicting. Nicotine is the drug in tobacco that causes addiction. The pharmacologic and behavioral processes that determine tobacco addiction are similar to those that determine addiction to drugs such as heroin and cocaine. . . .

It is nearly impossible to find a contemporary document on smoking that doesn't mention nicotine addiction as an incontestable point in the first paragraph. Many believe that the recent admissions of tobacco companies constitute further proof that nicotine is addictive. This belief is peculiar since the earlier denials of the tobacco companies were widely held to be false and self-serving. The validity of the nicotine addiction hypothesis is not about admissions, assertions, or concessions; it is about logic and data.

## Questioning the Addiction Model

With sufficient use, certain drugs are said to change the brain in such a way as to make cessation difficult or impossible. Drug users frequently state that they cannot help themselves. The nature of this alleged helplessness remains unclear. Drugs such as opiates and cocaine are clearly very enjoyable, and users often report that such drugs produce intense feelings of pleasure. It is possible that intense pleasure could account for persistent drug use. On the other hand, drugs such as nicotine have only small and variable subjective effects. Although smoking may be pleasant, the effects are not at all comparable to traditional drugs of abuse. Nicotine's lack of potent subjective effects necessitates some other sort of mechanism to account for persistent use. This other mechanism requires a unique pharmacological property, a pleasure-independent ability to lead the user into repeated use. However, at the moment there is no evidence of any neural mechanisms that could mediate such an unprecedented effect.

The most direct form of evidence supporting the belief that drugs induce a form of helplessness in certain users is the verbal reports of the users themselves. That users may not stop is obvious; whether they cannot stop is another matter. The utility of the verbal reports of drug users is compromised by at least two major factors. Drug users, including smokers, tend to suffer from diverse forms of psychopathology. Thus, even with the best of intentions, the fidelity of their verbal reports is uncertain. However, drug users often do not have good intentions. They tend to explain their behavior in a manner that minimizes personal responsibility. This has clear social and legal advantages. Such considerations suggest that the verbal reports of drug users may not be valid explanations of their behavior. Such reports are, at best, pre-scientific data. . . .

The addiction model is counterproductive to the aim of reducing problem drug use. Since its ascendancy there has been little progress made in the treatment of drug taking. In spite of a plethora of theory, research, and application, the success rate for treating common drug problems is so poor that it is rarely mentioned in scientific reports. In contrast, some 50 million Americans alone have quit smoking.

The main reason given by smokers for their failure to stop smoking is that they see themselves as addicted. Smokers are widely portrayed as victims of rogue molecular processes in their brains. As long as smoking is portrayed as an inexorable addictive process, the success of cessation programs will be limited by a self-fulfilling prophecy.

## Defining Addiction

Addiction and related terms have such broad and variable usage that they can mean almost anything. Addiction is used to describe behaviors ranging from injecting heroin and cocaine, to smoking or chewing tobacco, drinking coffee, eating chocolate, shopping, watching television soap operas, and falling in love. There are reports of addiction to water, cardiac defibrillators, carrots, hormone replacement therapy, and numerous other unusual entities. The clinical literature is replete with examples of people who develop unfortunate, even destructive, relationships with a great many substances, objects, events, and people. It is questionable whether these problems are illuminated by invoking the concept of addiction. . . .

Addiction is commonly used to describe drug problems. There can be little objection to such loose everyday use of addiction. The difficulties arise when addiction is used to *explain* drug problems. There is a persistent tendency to confuse description with explanation. There are substantial difficulties even when addiction is used in a descriptive sense. However, there are still greater difficulties when addiction is used to explain persistent drug use. . . .

## Examining the Surgeon General's Definition

The Surgeon General's definition states that "the user's behavior is largely controlled by a psychoactive substance." Whereas nicotine certainly affects behavior, it is questionable whether it can properly be said to control behavior. It has yet to be demonstrated that nicotine can exert more control over behavior than that exerted by any of scores of innocuous substances and events. Moreover, smoking is almost always done along with something else. The fact that smoking enhances a broad range of abilities suggests that the user's behavior is *not* controlled by the substance. In this context the behavioral consequences of nicotine are little different from those of eating a carrot.

Although the Surgeon General stresses that an addiction "takes precedence over other important priorities," this rarely applies to smoking. The overwhelming majority of smokers know when they can and cannot smoke, and they usually find increasingly severe restrictions only a minor nuisance. Certain religions prohibit smoking on the Sabbath, and even the heaviest smokers report no difficulty in observing this rule. It is difficult to imagine a molecular dysfunction of the brain that respects the Sabbath.

The Surgeon General stresses that addictive substances are reinforcing (rewarding). . . . At best, nicotine may be slightly more rewarding than saline. Even under the most carefully contrived circumstances, nicotine is probably no more rewarding than a flash of light or a brief sound. Such feeble reward does not suggest abuse potential. . . .

Next the Surgeon General's definition refers to the substance use continuing: ". . . despite damage to the individual or to society." However, smoking produces no damage in many people and most smokers respond to danger signs by stopping. Few people with clear signs of smoking-related illness persist in smoking; they are not representative of smokers in general.

## An Inadequate Concept

The notion of nicotine addiction suffers from numerous and major conceptual, definitional, and empirical inadequacies. Some reflect general problems with the concept of addiction, whereas others are specific to nicotine.

A recurring source of difficulty for the nicotine addiction hypothesis is the continuing lack of consensus concerning a definition of addiction. Hundreds of definitions have been offered, yet none withstands any scrutiny. Rigorous definitions of addiction clearly exclude nicotine, whereas those that reasonably include nicotine also include so many other substances and events that the notion of addiction becomes trivialized.

Lacking a reasonable definition of addiction, the putative addictiveness of drugs has become a matter of legislative fiat, judicial rulings, and committee edicts. Not surprisingly, which drugs are considered addictive varies markedly over time and in different places. Cannabis was long considered to be the scourge of our youth while tobacco was considered relatively harmless. Recently this position has been reversed. This is not science, but politics.

Self-administration studies, [in which lab animals press a bar to receive a drug or other stimulus] in laboratory species are said to support the view that nicotine, much like heroin and cocaine, is powerfully reinforcing. However, nicotine self-administration doesn't remotely approach the vigor or reliability of that supported by drugs such as cocaine and heroin. The strongest reinforcing effects of nicotine in laboratory species are less than those of innocuous reinforcers such as light, sound, sugar, or salt.

Moreover, nicotine self-administration requires doses that are far higher than humans ever encounter. These effects may well represent monoaminergic effects of high nicotine doses. There are no reports of nicotine self-administration in laboratory species at doses even approaching those self-administered by humans. It is unjustified to use weak and inconsistent reinforcement effects obtained with high intravenous doses in laboratory species as evidence for human abuse potential.

Perhaps the most serious deficiency in using animal models to study human drug taking is that animals do not seem to get 'hooked' on any substance. This is particularly true of nicotine. It is difficult to show any rewarding effects of nicotine in laboratory species, let alone the powerful effects associated with drugs of abuse. It is possible that drug abuse is a uniquely human phenomenon.

### What Is the Active Ingredient in Smoke?

It is not universally accepted . . . that nicotine is the active ingredient in tobacco smoke. The authors of the widely respected "Merck Manual" say only that it is "probably" the active ingredient. If, in fact, the anti-smokers finally succeed in getting the tobacco companies to remove the nicotine from cigarettes, we will finally find out the truth. My own bet is that a cigarette without nicotine will probably be almost as satisfying as one with nicotine. The active ingredient in smoke is smoke.

Lauren A. Colby, *In Defense of Smokers*, 1999.

Like the data from animal experimentation, the data on nicotine reinforcement in humans do not suggest that nicotine has abuse potential. There are no credible demonstrations in humans that nicotine is any more reinforcing than many other substances and events that have no abuse potential. The subjective effects of nicotine suggest a drug that is pleasant, nothing more. In this crucial respect, nicotine contrasts markedly with reference drugs such as cocaine and heroin that consistently produce strong feelings of euphoria.

## Addiction Is Not a Brain Disease

There have been attempts to lend credibility to the notion of addiction by describing it as a brain disease. However, there is little evidence for such a view. There is no special brain state associated with nicotine use. Although nicotine has diverse effects on the brain, none has any significant potential to perpetuate nicotine use. Moreover, the neural effects of nicotine and other putatively addictive drugs are indistinguishable from those produced by many relatively harmless substances and everyday experiences.

Nicotine has effects on dopaminergic transmission that, in certain respects, resemble those of cocaine or heroin. However, almost anything that alters arousal alters dopaminergic transmission. Such neurochemical effects should not be interpreted as a correlate of addiction. The fact that some of the effects on dopamine transmission may be restricted to the shell of the nucleus accumbens is interesting, but irrelevant to whether nicotine or anything else is addictive.

The finding that dopamine may be involved in the effects of nicotine and reinforcement processes lends no support to the notion that nicotine is addictive. The dopamine hypothesis of reinforcement remains an intensely debated issue in which the theory, methodology, and empirical findings are all disputed. Claims to the contrary notwithstanding, none of the many variants of the dopamine theory has, as yet, any implications for human drug use. There is no justification for making the major leap from the poorly understood neural sequelae of reinforcement in laboratory species to the still more poorly defined and understood notion of addiction in humans.

The effects of nicotine, like those of virtually every other drug, psychoactive or not, show a degree of tolerance. It is questionable whether this ubiquitous phenomenon says anything about abuse potential. It certainly does not distinguish nicotine from many other innocuous substances.

Nicotine use may sometimes produce withdrawal effects. However, many drugs with no abuse potential produce withdrawal effects that are much more dramatic than those produced by nicotine. Conversely, many drugs with substantial abuse potential produce little in the way of withdrawal effects. Additionally, nicotine withdrawal effects last for no more than a few weeks, whereas relapse potential may last for years. The fact that withdrawal and relapse potential have such different temporal characteristics indicates that they cannot be causally related.

In summary, apart from numerous conceptual and definitional inadequacies, the notion that nicotine is an addictive substance lacks reasonable empirical support. There are so many and such grossly conflicting findings that adhering to the nicotine addiction thesis is only defensible on political, not scientific, grounds. More broadly, addiction may have some use as a description of certain types of behavior, but it fails badly as an explanation of such behaviors.

It is commonly assumed that questioning the addiction hypothesis is to condone and even advocate drug use. Such an assumption is incorrect. In order to develop effective treatments for drug problems, it is necessary to escape from the unproductive ideology that is currently dominant. Abandoning the concept of addiction is a step in this direction.

5

VIEWPOINT

*"Legalized gambling destroys individuals and families, increases crime and ultimately costs society far more than the government makes."*

# Compulsive Gambling Is a National Concern

Tom Grey

In the following viewpoint Tom Grey argues that compulsive gambling has become a national epidemic. Once illegal in all states but Nevada, legalized gambling has grown as governments have come to see the revenues they receive from state-sponsored and state-sanctioned gambling as a means to balance state budgets and promote economic growth, claims Grey. However, gambling addiction destroys individuals and their families as well as increases crime in communities that have legalized gambling, Grey maintains. The price society pays for compulsive gambling, he argues, far outweighs any revenue governments may gain from it. Grey, a Methodist minister, is executive director of the National Coalition Against Legalized Gambling.

As you read, consider the following questions:

1. What effect did legalization of riverboat casinos have in Iowa, according to Grey?
2. What impact does pathological gambling have on families, in the author's view?
3. According to Earl Grinols, what percentage of a casino's revenues comes from gambling addicts?

Tom Grey, "An Epidemic of Gambling," *Family Voice*, July/August 1999, pp. 16–19.

Just 18 years old, Bob Hafemann won $500 from an Oregon lottery scratch ticket. He became a regular lottery player, but Bob seemed to have his gambling under control—until Oregon introduced video poker in 1992. Though he earned $45,000 a year, Bob began borrowing money to feed his gambling habit. Then he sold his possessions and stopped paying all his bills but the rent. Utterly destroyed by video gambling, Bob took his own life at age 28. "The gambling addiction completely changed who he was," said Bob's sister.

Legalized gambling not only changes individuals, it changes society. We destroyed Bob—and millions of others—because our governments push a highly addictive activity: gambling. Governments spend millions of dollars warning us about narcotics, alcohol and tobacco, and the campaigns have been effective.

But today, gambling is the fastest growing addiction in America. According to [a June 1999] report of the National Gambling Impact Study Commission (NGISC), about five million pathological and problem gamblers live in America. An additional fifteen million risk developing this addiction.

Besides individuals, state governments have become addicted to the revenues derived from casinos, slot machines, keno and lotto. So instead of warning citizens, many governments exploit them. Ignoring the social costs of gambling, they think the cash will help balance their budgets.

## A Gambling Boom

In 1977, every state except Nevada prohibited commercial gambling casinos. Only 13 states had lotteries. Native American casinos didn't exist. All together, Americans wagered about $17 billion on legal commercial gambling.

Between 1976 and 1988, Atlantic City legalized casinos, and the number of state lotteries more than doubled. By 1994, 21 new states had legalized gambling casinos, and slot or video poker machines were authorized at racetracks and bars in 10 states.

*Americans wagered over $600 billion on legal gambling last year—an astonishing 3,500 percent increase in just two decades.*

Since mid-1994, anti-gambling activists have nearly halted the expansion of gambling. But the damage has been done.

For 10 years, lawmakers have forgotten why gambling was considered a "vice." But the growth in gambling has sparked research. Today, considerable evidence demonstrates that legalized gambling destroys individuals and families, increases crime and ultimately costs society far more than the government makes.

Gambling addiction is just as real and tragic as alcohol or drug addiction. The American Psychiatric Association and the American Medical Association both recognize pathological (or "compulsive") gambling as a mental disorder.

Experts say that pathological gambling is closely linked to the accessibility and acceptability of gambling. Like alcoholism, only a small percentage of Americans are susceptible. But more legalized gambling exposes more of those prone to addiction. Fast-paced gambling, like casinos and video gambling, also maximizes addiction.

In Iowa, the 1991 legalization of riverboat casinos more than tripled addiction. A study released in 1995 found that 5.4 percent of the state's adults were pathological or problem gamblers—compared to only 1.7 percent before riverboats came.

Just four years after Louisiana legalized casinos and slot machines, a study found that 7 percent of adults had become addicted. In Minnesota, as 16 Indian casinos opened across the state, the number of Gamblers Anonymous groups shot up from 1 to 49.

## The Nature of the Problem

Pathological gamblers lose all their money. Then they run up credit card debt. They sell or pawn possessions and beg for loans.

The average Gamblers Anonymous member will have lost all his money and accumulated debts from $35,000 to $92,000 before he seeks treatment. Thousands file bankruptcy. Many commit suicide.

Pathological gambling rarely affects just one person. Families lose savings, college and retirement funds. They suffer foreclosed mortgages. Under the stress, many problem gamblers commit domestic and child abuse. After casinos came to the Mississippi Gulf Coast, domestic violence

## The Increase in Lottery and Casino Gambling

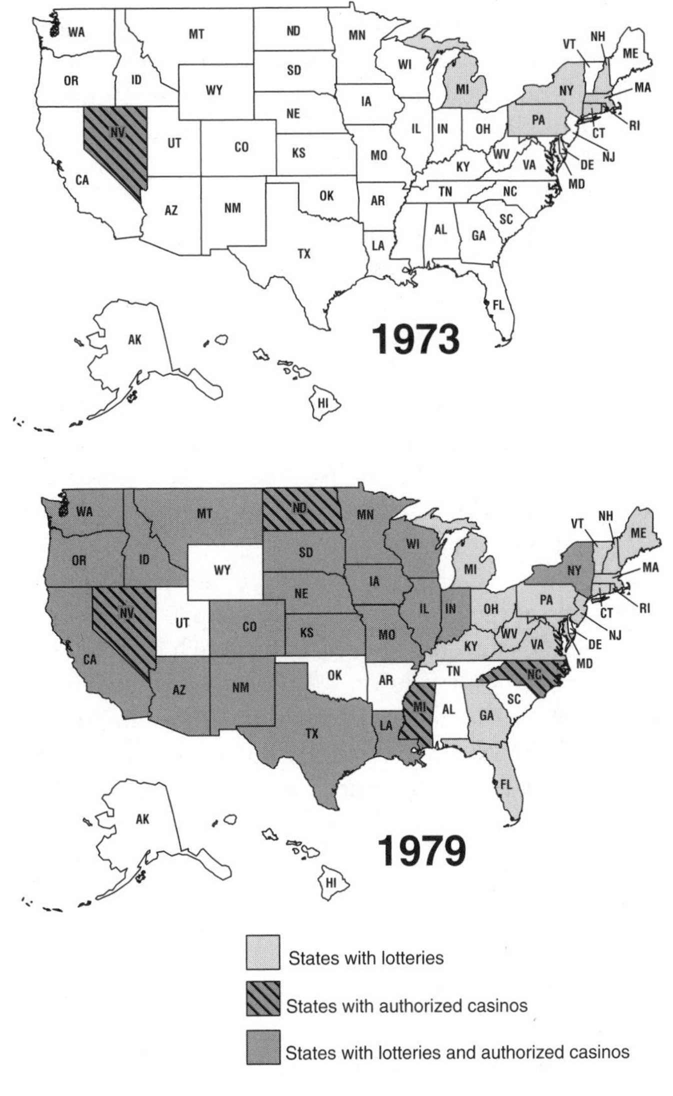


*National Gambling Impact Study Commission Report*, June 18, 1999.

increased 69 percent. An estimated 37 percent of all pathological gamblers have abused their children.

Many studies support the link between gambling and crime. But less publicized is how gambling addiction turns people into criminals. More than half of all pathological gamblers will commit crimes—embezzlement, tax evasion, fraud—to pay off debts.

The Florida Office of Planning and Budgeting researched projected costs of legalizing casino gambling in the state. The largest potential government expense came from incarcerating new gamblers who turn to crime. According to the study, this "could cost Florida residents *$6.08 billion* [emphasis added]."

The managers of gambling establishments who see these addicts daily should understand.

In Atlantic City, for example, after pathological gamblers lose their cash and empty their ATM accounts, they walk outside to sell their valuables.

About three dozen "Cash for Gold" stores operate near the boardwalk casinos. How many thousands of people are needed each year to keep three dozen "Cash for Gold" stores in business? And why don't the Atlantic City casinos try to help these customers?

Before the U.S. House Judiciary Committee, Professor Earl Grinols of the University of Illinois presented evidence that the casinos depend on addicts for much of their profits. These gamblers represent only 4 percent of adults, but they may account for as much as 52 percent of a casino's revenues.

Similarly, the NGISC's study estimates that 51 percent of all state lottery revenues come from just 5 percent of lottery players.

## Gambling Politics

As dreams of prosperity evaporated, state and local citizen groups sprang up to oppose gambling's spread. In 1994, they created the National Coalition Against Legalized Gambling (NCALG).

The members of NCALG span the political spectrum, with activists in every state. They battle gambling's expansion because it harms individuals, families, businesses and society. Despite furious efforts by gambling promoters, [few states have] legalized casinos or slot machines.

*The political tide is turning.*

[In the summer of 1999], the National Gambling Impact Study Commission issued its report: gambling is out of control. The Commission condemned nearly every type of gambling considered in Congress and state legislatures.

The Commission urged state lotteries to stop preying on the poor. And it challenged Congress to stop Internet gambling, ban gambling "cruises to nowhere," and scrutinize tribal gambling operations.

The report clearly states that gambling is not just recreation. It is addictive and potentially destructive. In fact, the Commission called on schools from elementary levels through college to teach and warn students of gambling's dangers.

Will America continue to belittle the epidemic of gambling addiction? Or will we finally acknowledge that it has become a public health emergency?

All bets are off.

6 VIEWPOINT

*"People who have visited casinos and played the lottery have seen that misery and damnation don't necessarily follow."*

# The Dangers of Compulsive Gambling Are Exaggerated

Steve Chapman

In the following viewpoint Steve Chapman refutes claims that legalized gambling is destroying lives and corrupting American communities. For example, those who oppose gambling claim that legalized gambling increases suicide and crime rates, Chapman claims. He asserts, however, that these claims are unfounded; while suicide and crime rates may have risen in some states that have legalized gambling, they have decreased in others, suggesting other factors may be responsible for the increases. Moreover, most people who patronize gambling establishments gamble responsibly; in fact, he argues, only 1.6 percent of American adults will be become gambling addicts. Chapman is a columnist for the *Chicago Tribune*.

As you read, consider the following questions:

1. According to Chapman, what percentage of American adults will become pathological gamblers?
2. How does Chapman refute the argument that gambling depletes the local economy?
3. How does Chapman refute the assumption that gamblers are being fooled?

[Conservative columnist] William Safire and [*New York Times* columnist] Frank Rich hail from opposite ends of the political spectrum, but on the subject of gambling, you could barely squeeze a poker chip between them. Safire preaches his immovable conviction "that casino operators are predators; that state-sponsored lotteries make a mockery of public policy; that politicians who are on the take from gambling interests are wallowing in the occasion of sin." Counterpoint, Frank? ". . .The stench of influence-peddling suffuses some state governments where gambling rules. In the Midwest, riverboat casinos can be an economic boon but sometimes suck local retail businesses dry. Statistics suggest that crime, domestic abuse and alcoholism rise in gambling's wake—while the poor most conspicuously get poorer."

Legal gambling brings out the latent puritan in many Americans. The right detests gambling because it promises something for nothing. The left hates it because it enriches corporations by emptying the pockets of the gullible lower classes. Republican right leader Ralph Reed and the more-liberal-than-thou Harvard political scientist Michael Sandel condemn it, as do [consumer advocate] Ralph Nader and [family values advocate] Gary Bauer.

Everyone seems to detest legal gambling—everyone, that is, except the public. Once regarded as a low habit, gambling is now generally treated as wholesome entertainment in all states but two. Americans spend nearly $51 billion a year on various games of chance—twice as much as they spend on movies, plays, operas, and spectator sports combined.

But gambling's place at the table is threatened by the puritans, who've used their political muscle to help establish a National Gambling Impact Study Commission. They hope its June 1999 report will prove their claims that gambling wrecks lives, stimulates crime, saps local economies, mercilessly exploits human weakness, and sustains itself through bribery and corruption. A review, then, and a brief refutation of their best arguments.

People Become Addicted to Gambling: The critics warn of an exploding epidemic of addicted gamblers, but a recent study by researchers at Harvard Medical School's Division on Addictions argues against this notion. An estimated 1.6

percent of American adults will become pathological gamblers, compared with 6.2 percent who will succumb to drug addiction and 13.8 percent who will become alcoholics. A study published [in 1997] claimed that the legalization of casinos causes an increase in suicide rates. Indeed, Nevada's suicide rate is the highest in the country, double the national average. But New Jersey, home of Atlantic City, enjoys the lowest rate. Mississippi, the South's gambling Mecca, falls slightly below the national average.

Legal Gambling Fosters Crime: Exhibit A for the prosecution is Atlantic City, which went from being No. 50 among American cities in crimes per capita to being No. 1 after the arrival of casinos. This increase fails to account for the city's huge influx of tourists, who on any given day outnumber residents by more than 2-to-1. As noted in a study by University of Maryland Professor Peter Reuter, homicides barely increased at all, despite the influx of outsiders, and assaults rose only about as fast as the average daily population. The real increases have come in robbery and aggravated assaults. Elsewhere, though, it's impossible to detect any consistent relationship between the existence of casinos and the prevalence of lawlessness. Jeremy Margolis, who headed the Illinois State Police when the state introduced 13 riverboat casinos, has testified that "crime has not been a problem." Looking at rural Colorado, Texas A&M scholar Patricia Stokowski found that with the arrival of casinos, "the likelihood of becoming a crime victim in Gilpin County has decreased."

Legal Gambling Depletes the Local Economy: Economists normally extol anything that allows consumers to satisfy their preferences, but several members of the profession depict casinos as the enemy of prosperity. Earl Grinols of the University of Illinois excoriates them as "a shell game, attracting dollars from one person's pocket to another and from one region to another." Another view holds that life for the casinos means death for restaurants, car dealers, hardware stores, and other wholesome businesses unless legal gambling attracts massive numbers of new tourists.

But these are the wrong measures of the economic value of gambling establishments. Existing businesses are threatened when a new business comes to town, whether it's Nordstrom or a shoe repair shop. No economist with ambitions for tenure would dream of dismissing a business as a "shell game" merely because its revenue diverts revenue from other businesses.

**A Lack of Evidence**

There is no evidence that gamblers are any more likely than nongamblers to forsake responsibility. Indeed, one Swedish study found no relationship between gambling and crime, marital instability, or "the degree of participation in community activities." In another survey, the economist Reuven Brenner of McGill University notes that there is "little evidence to support the view that the majority of gamblers squander their money recklessly, whether it is money spent on stakes or money earned from winnings."

Guy Calvert, *Policy Analysis*, June 18, 1999.

Legal Gambling Causes Corruption: Casino operators are portrayed as the Typhoid Marys [people from whom something undesirable spreads] of political corruption, the usual evidence being their lavish bankrolling of politicians. But of the 16 industries that gave "soft money" to the two major political parties in 1996, the gambling industry ranked 16th, according to the ultrafastidious Center for Responsive Politics.

Casino owners are right to take a greater-than-average interest in the workings of government. 1) Until recently, their industry was illegal almost everywhere. 2) They cannot operate without hard-to-get government licenses. 3) Their many enemies want to legislate them out of existence.

As long as we're talking about corruption and exploitation, we should not forget that the wickedest gambling sharpies don't live in Las Vegas but in the state capitals, where the lotteries are headquartered. The lotteries' pitiful payout—about half of all money wagered, compared with 92 percent or so at your average casino—rightly draws cries of outrage. If the critics were interested in remedying the lotteries, they'd have the states repeal their monopolies on these games and let the market compete away the excess profits.

Whose Life Is It, Anyway? Gambling's opponents never tire of reciting statistics and anecdotes to suggest that the costs of legalized gambling dwarf any possible benefits. But they fail to count the central benefit—the diversion and pleasure it provides to millions of people. Until 1978, casinos were accessible only to people with the means to travel to Las Vegas. The relaxation of prohibitionist laws has brought them within easy reach of most of the American public, and the public has voted for them with its feet. The overwhelming majority of these patrons gamble responsibly and impose no burden on their fellow citizens. They treat games of chance as exactly that—games.

Yet critics insist on portraying gamblers as a pitiable class of suckers, enslaved by fantasies of unearned wealth. It's hard to see why. No one accuses movie theaters or gardening-supply outlets of ruthlessly exploiting the weaknesses of clients who turn over their money only because they lack the self-control to refuse. Most people who patronize the lottery, the track, or the slot machines end up poorer, with nothing to show for the transaction—which is also true of people who eat in restaurants and attend concerts. To incurable bluenoses, gambling is an infuriating scam. But why assume gamblers are being fooled? It's more reasonable to assume that they know they will probably lose but are happy to take that chance for 1) the pleasure of playing and 2) the chance of coming out ahead.

In the end, that's a decision they ought to be free to make, unimpeded by moralists and social reformers who think ordinary people cannot be trusted to look after their own interests. If gambling were the grim scourge portrayed by its opponents, it would not have gone from a contemptible vice to an innocent diversion in a single generation. People who have visited casinos and played the lottery have seen that misery and damnation don't necessarily follow, either for themselves or for surrounding communities. Gambling has become a widespread pastime for the simple and unassailable reason that it adds to the sum of human happiness. That's reason enough to leave it alone.

# Periodical Bibliography

The following articles have been selected to supplement the diverse views presented in this chapter.


| | |
|---|---|
| Dan Allsup | "Gambling's Dark Side," *American Legion*, June 2002. |
| American Medical Association | "Underage Drinkers' Risk of Brain Damage," *USA Today Magazine*, February 2003. |
| Karen Asp | "Addicted to Sweat," *American Fitness*, November 1999. |
| Steven Belenko et al. | "Substance Abuse and the Prison Population," *Corrections Today*, October 1998. |
| B. Bower | "Youthful Nicotine Addiction May Be Growing," *Science News*, September 22, 2001. |
| Susan Brink | "When Being First Isn't Best," *U.S. News & World Report*, May 7, 2001. |
| Thomas E. Broffman | "Why Women Gamble: The Causes and Treatment," *Counselor*, August 2001. |
| Beth Fontenot | "Consuming Disorders," *Priorities for Health*, 1999. |
| Mark Griffith | "Addicted to Love? The Psychology of Sex Addiction," *Psychology Review*, November 2001. |
| Jerome D. Levin | "Sexual Addiction," *National Forum*, Fall 1999. |
| Mary Lord | "Drinking: Here's Looking at You, Kids," *U.S. News & World Report*, April 1, 2002. |
| Michelle Meadows | "Prescription Drug Use and Abuse," *FDA Consumer*, September 2001. |
| Eric Metcalf | "A Web of Addictions: Internet Obsessions Could Hurt Your Loved Ones Financially, Emotionally, and Physically," *Better Homes and Gardens*, May 2003. |
| Norbert R. Myslinkski | "Addiction's Ugly Face," *World & I*, December 1999. |
| National Gambling Impact Study Commission | "The Gambling Debate," *Christian Social Action*, September 1999. |
| Ronald M. Pavalko | "Problem Gambling," *Phi Kappa Phi Journal*, Fall 1999. |
| Monica Preboth | "NIAA Report on Prevention of College Drinking," *American Family Physician*, June 15, 2002. |

Robert R. Selle — "Alcoholism's Nemesism," *World & I*, June 2000.

Mary Sojourner — "Squandering Our Kids' Inheritance," *High Country News*, January 18, 1999.

S. Alex Stalcup — "High-Intensity Drugs," *Professional Counselor*, February 1999.

Patricia D. Sweeting and Joan L. Weinberg — "Gambling: The Secret Invisible Addiction," *Counselor*, December 2000.

Chapter 2

# What Factors Contribute to Addiction?

# Chapter Preface

The relationship between teen alcohol use and adult alcohol addiction is subject to heated debate. Some analysts claim that there is a direct correlation between teen alcohol use and adult alcoholism; thus they suggest that teen alcohol policies should emphasize abstinence. Others maintain that alcohol addiction is the result of multiple factors, not just teenage drinking. They claim that teen alcohol use is a normal part of adolescent culture and disagree with abstinence policies.

A 1998 study conducted by Bridget F. Grant and Deborah A. Dawson of the National Institute on Alcohol Abuse and Alcoholism (NIAAA) revealed that young people who begin drinking before age fifteen are four times more likely to become addicted to alcohol as adults. Organizations and activists nationwide began to use such statistics to promote abstinence. A good example is prevention specialist Kay Provine, of the Hazeldon Foundation, a nonprofit organization that provides rehabilitation, education, and prevention services in the field of chemical dependency. "As soon as the study came out," says Provine, "I made a bar graph to show the correlation between early drinking and alcoholism." According to Provine, "It is so effective for parents to see something this concrete. Every year you can delay kids from using alcohol, you are buying them time."

Other commentators, even those from NIAAA, question whether the NIAAA study constitutes concrete evidence that teen alcohol use leads to adult alcoholism. When the NIAAA report was released, NIAAA director Enoch Gordis was careful to note, "We don't know what causes this extraordinary association between early drinking and later alcohol dependence." Moreover, in a June 2000 report, the same authors, Grant and Dawson, concluded, "A complex set of factors introduces individuals to alcohol and produces variations in alcohol use and abuse over the life course. Factors include psychosocial and neurobiological mechanisms as well as influences from the larger society."

Addiction author Stanton Peele, who opposes abstinence messages, points to research that draws a different conclusion about the relationship between teen alcohol use and later alcoholism. Research conducted by Harvard psychiatrist George Vaillant found that children in cultures that teach responsible drinking are less likely to develop problems with alcohol as adults than in cultures that emphasize complete abstinence. According to Peele,

> Ironically, in the United States today, we follow the method of alcohol education found least successful in the Vaillant study. That is, alcohol is grouped with illicit drugs, and children are taught that abstinence is the only answer. Yet children are aware that most adults drink, and many drink alcohol themselves on the sly. Moreover, drinking will be legal and widely available to them within a few short years. Clearly, many young people find the abstinence message confusing and hypocritical.

Commentators such as Peele who oppose teaching abstinence contend that drinking is an inevitable part of adolescent development. According to professor Rutger Engels, "Occasional drinking may be a manifestation of developmentally appropriate experimentation." In fact, Engels asserts, most teens in Western societies drink, which implies that "drinking is not only a socially acceptable behavior but also normative. Youngsters who do not drink are exceptional." Since most teens have experimented with alcohol, Engels reasons, they are likely to have had positives experiences that contradict the antidrinking messages. Engels concludes, "Therefore, health education that aims to discourage adolescents from drinking will have limited effects."

Whether or not teen alcohol use leads to alcohol addiction remains controversial. The authors of the viewpoints in the following chapter express their opinions on the factors that contribute to addiction.

1

VIEWPOINT

*"The majority of the biomedical community now considers addiction, in its essence, to be a brain disease."*

# Addiction Is a Brain Disease

Alan I. Leshner

Addiction is a biobehavioral disorder—a brain disease that leads to compulsive behaviors that in turn have negative health consequences for the addict, asserts Alan I. Leshner in the following viewpoint. Although addicts first voluntarily choose to use drugs, claims Leshner, research shows that their brains become altered by drug use, and most are unable to stop without medical help. Unfortunately, he argues, old ideas about the nature of addiction—that addicts are simply too weak willed to quit—keep people from seeing addiction as a chronic illness much like other brain diseases such as Alzheimer's that affect behavior. Leshner is director of the National Institute on Drug Abuse at the National Institutes of Health.

As you read, consider the following questions:

1. In Leshner's opinion, why are physical withdrawal symptoms not that important from both clinical and policy perspectives?
2. In addition to addiction, what other diseases are influenced by voluntary behavior patterns, in the author's view?
3. According to Leshner, what is one major reason why efforts to prevent drug use are so vital to the nation's drug strategy?

Alan I. Leshner, "Addiction Is a Brain Disease," *Issues in Science and Technology*, vol. 17, Spring 2001, pp. 75–80. 

The United States is stuck in its drug abuse metaphors and in polarized arguments about them. Everyone has an opinion. One side insists that we must control supply, the other that we must reduce demand. People see addiction as either a disease or as a failure of will. None of this bumper-sticker analysis moves us forward. The truth is that we will make progress in dealing with drug issues only when our national discourse and our strategies are as complex and comprehensive as the problem itself.

A core concept that has been evolving with scientific advances over the past decade is that drug addiction is a brain disease that develops over time as a result of the initially voluntary behavior of using drugs. The consequence is virtually uncontrollable compulsive drug craving, seeking, and use that interferes with, if not destroys, an individual's functioning in the family and in society. This medical condition demands formal treatment.

## Changes in the Brain

We now know in great detail the brain mechanisms through which drugs acutely modify mood, memory, perception, and emotional states. Using drugs repeatedly over time changes brain structure and function in fundamental and long-lasting ways that can persist long after the individual stops using them. Addiction comes about through an array of neuroadaptive changes and the laying down and strengthening of new memory connections in various circuits in the brain. We do not yet know all the relevant mechanisms, but the evidence suggests that those long-lasting brain changes are responsible for the distortions of cognitive and emotional functioning that characterize addicts, particularly including the compulsion to use drugs that is the essence of addiction. It is as if drugs have highjacked the brain's natural motivational control circuits, resulting in drug use becoming the sole, or at least the top, motivational priority for the individual. Thus, the majority of the biomedical community now considers addiction, in its essence, to be a brain disease: a condition caused by persistent changes in brain structure and function.

This brain-based view of addiction has generated substantial controversy, particularly among people who seem able to think only in polarized ways. Many people erroneously still believe that biological and behavioral explanations are alternative or competing ways to understand phenomena, when in fact they are complementary and integratable. Modern science has taught that it is much too simplistic to set biology in opposition to behavior or to pit willpower against brain chemistry. Addiction involves inseparable biological and behavioral components. It is the quintessential biobehavioral disorder.

Many people also erroneously still believe that drug addiction is simply a failure of will or of strength of character. Research contradicts that position. However, the recognition that addiction is a brain disease does not mean that the addict is simply a hapless victim. Addiction begins with the voluntary behavior of using drugs, and addicts must participate in and take some significant responsibility for their recovery. Thus, having this brain disease does not absolve the addict of responsibility for his or her behavior, but it does explain why an addict cannot simply stop using drugs by sheer force of will alone. It also dictates a much more sophisticated approach to dealing with the array of problems surrounding drug abuse and addiction in our society.

## The Essence of Addiction

The entire concept of addiction has suffered greatly from imprecision and misconception. In fact, if it were possible, it would be best to start all over with some new, more neutral term. The confusion comes about in part because of a now archaic distinction between whether specific drugs are "physically" or "psychologically" addicting. The distinction historically revolved around whether or not dramatic physical withdrawal symptoms occur when an individual stops taking a drug: what we in the field now call "physical dependence."

However, 20 years of scientific research has taught that focusing on this physical versus psychological distinction is off the mark and a distraction from the real issues. From both clinical and policy perspectives, it actually does not matter very much what physical withdrawal symptoms occur. Physical dependence is not that important, because even the dramatic withdrawal symptoms of heroin and alcohol addiction can now be easily managed with appropriate medications. Even more important, many of the most dangerous and addicting drugs, including methamphetamine and crack cocaine, do not produce very severe physical dependence symptoms upon withdrawal.

### The Need for a Medical Model

Whether addiction is a disease or merely a choice, the utility of the medical model is needed to address resultant risks to public and individual health. A careful review of this growing body of scientific literature should offer hope that real solutions are possible. All other models for addressing drug dependence have, to date, proven to be costly failures, and doctors are not going to ignore viable treatment options for healing those suffering with drug dependence. Defining addiction as a choice only abdicates our responsibility for seeking health and true healing for our patients and, instead, leaves crushed lives dehumanized by a chronic relapsing condition with no hope for cure. As every doctor knows, "Remember to do some good" should quickly follow the first rule to "do no harm."

John H. Halpern, *Psychiatric Times*, October 2002.

What really matters most is whether or not a drug causes what we now know to be the essence of addiction: uncontrollable, compulsive drug craving, seeking, and use, even in the face of negative health and social consequences. This is the crux of how the Institute of Medicine, the American Psychiatric Association, and the American Medical Association define addiction and how we all should use the term. It is really only this compulsive quality of addiction that matters in the long run to the addict and to his or her family and that should matter to society as a whole. Compulsive craving that overwhelms all other motivations is the root cause of the massive health and social problems associated with drug addiction. In updating our national discourse on drug abuse, we should keep in mind this simple definition: Addiction is a brain disease expressed in the form of compulsive behavior. Both developing and recovering from it depend on biology, behavior, and social context.

It is also important to correct the common misimpression

that drug use, abuse, and addiction are points on a single continuum along which one slides back and forth over time, moving from user to addict, then back to occasional user, then back to addict. Clinical observation and more formal research studies support the view that, once addicted, the individual has moved into a different state of being. It is as if a threshold has been crossed. Very few people appear able to successfully return to occasional use after having been truly addicted. Unfortunately, we do not yet have a clear biological or behavioral marker of that transition from voluntary drug use to addiction. However, a body of scientific evidence is rapidly developing that points to an array of cellular and molecular changes in specific brain circuits. Moreover, many of these brain changes are common to all chemical addictions, and some also are typical of other compulsive behaviors such as pathological overeating.

Addiction should be understood as a chronic recurring illness. Although some addicts do gain full control over their drug use after a single treatment episode, many have relapses. Repeated treatments becoming necessary to increase the intervals between and diminish the intensity of relapses, until the individual achieves abstinence.

## A Similarity to Other Brain Diseases

The complexity of this brain disease is not atypical, because virtually no brain diseases are simply biological in nature and expression. All, including stroke, Alzheimer's disease, schizophrenia, and clinical depression, include some behavioral and social aspects. What may make addiction seem unique among brain diseases, however, is that it does begin with a clearly voluntary behavior—the initial decision to use drugs. Moreover, not everyone who ever uses drugs goes on to become addicted. Individuals differ substantially in how easily and quickly they become addicted and in their preferences for particular substances. Consistent with the biobehavioral nature of addiction, these individual differences result front a combination of environmental and biological, particularly genetic, factors. In fact, estimates are that between 50 and 70 percent of the variability in susceptibility to becoming addicted can be accounted for by genetic factors.

Over time the addict loses substantial control over his or her initially voluntary behavior, and it becomes compulsive. For many people these behaviors are truly uncontrollable, just like the behavioral expression of any other brain disease. Schizophrenics cannot control their hallucinations and delusions. Parkinson's patients cannot control their trembling. Clinically depressed patients cannot voluntarily control their moods. Thus, once one is addicted, the characteristics of the illness—and the treatment approaches—are not that different from most other brain diseases. No matter how one develops an illness, once one has it, one is in the diseased state and needs treatment.

Moreover, voluntary behavior patterns are, of course, involved in the etiology and progression of many other illnesses, albeit not all brain diseases. Examples abound, including hypertension, arteriosclerosis and other cardiovascular diseases, diabetes, and forms of cancer in which the onset is heavily influenced by the individual's eating, exercise, smoking, and other behaviors.

## The Environmental Cues

Addictive behaviors do have special characteristics related to the social contexts in which they originate. All of the environmental cues surrounding initial drug use and development of the addiction actually become "conditioned" to that drug use and are thus critical to the development and expression of addiction. Environmental cues are paired in time with an individual's initial drug use experiences and, through classical conditioning, take on conditioned stimulus properties. When those cues are present at a later time, they elicit anticipation of a drug experience and thus generate tremendous drug craving. Cue-induced craving is one of the most frequent causes of drug use relapses, even after long periods of abstinence, independently of whether drugs are available.

The salience of environmental or contextual cues helps explain why reentry to one's community can be so difficult for addicts leaving the controlled environments of treatment or correctional settings and why aftercare is so essential to successful recovery. The person who became addicted in the home environment is constantly exposed to the cues conditioned to his or her initial drug use, such as the neighborhood where he or she hung out, drug-using buddies, or the lamppost where he or she bought drugs. Simple exposure to those cues automatically triggers craving and can lead rapidly to relapses. This is one reason why someone who apparently overcame drug cravings while in prison or residential treatment could quickly revert to drug use upon returning home. In fact, one of the major goals of drug addiction treatment is to teach addicts how to deal with the cravings caused by inevitable exposure to these conditioned cues.

## The Implications of Addiction as a Disease

Understanding addiction as a brain disease has broad and significant implications for the public perception of addicts and their families, for addiction treatment practice, and for some aspects of public policy. On the other hand, this biomedical view of addiction does not speak directly to and is unlikely to bear significantly on many other issues, including specific strategies for controlling the supply of drugs and whether initial drug use should be legal or not. Moreover, the brain disease model of addiction does not address the question of whether specific drugs of abuse can also be potential medicines. Examples abound of drugs that can be both highly addicting and extremely effective medicines. The best-known example is the appropriate use of morphine as a treatment for pain. Nevertheless, a number of practical lessons can be drawn from the scientific understanding of addiction.

It is no wonder addicts cannot simply quit on their own. They have an illness that requires biomedical treatment. People often assume that because addiction begins with a voluntary behavior and is expressed in the form of excess behavior, people should just be able to quit by force of will alone. However, it is essential to understand when dealing with addicts that we are dealing with individuals whose brains have been altered by drug use. They need drug addiction treatment. We know that, contrary to common belief, very few addicts actually do just stop on their own. Observing that there are very few heroin addicts in their 50s or 60s, people frequently ask what happened to those who were heroin addicts 30 years ago, assuming that they must have quit on their own. However, longitudinal studies find that only a very small fraction actually quit on their own. The rest have either been successfully treated, are currently in maintenance treatment, or (for about half) are dead. Consider the example of smoking cigarettes: Various studies have found that between 3 and 7 percent of people who try to quit on their own each year actually succeed. Science has at last convinced the public that depression is not just a lot of sadness; that depressed individuals are in a different brain state and thus require treatment to get their symptoms under control. The same is true for schizophrenic patients. It is lime to recognize that this is also the case for addicts.

## Accepting Personal Responsibility

The role of personal responsibility is undiminished but clarified. Does having a brain disease mean that people who are addicted no longer have any responsibility for their behavior or that they are simply victims of their own genetics and brain chemistry? Of course not. Addiction begins with the voluntary behavior of drug use, and although genetic characteristics may predispose individuals to be more or less susceptible to becoming addicted, genes do not doom one to become an addict. This is one major reason why efforts to prevent drug use are so vital to any comprehensive strategy to deal with the nation's drug problems. Initial drug use is a voluntary, and therefore preventable, behavior.

Moreover, as with any illness, behavior becomes a critical part of recovery. At a minimum, one must comply with the treatment regimen, which is harder than it sounds. Treatment compliance is the biggest cause of relapses for all chronic illnesses, including asthma, diabetes, hypertension, and addiction. Moreover, treatment compliance rates are no worse for addiction than for these other illnesses, ranging from 30 to 50 percent. Thus, for drug addiction as well as for other chronic diseases, the individual's motivation and behavior are clearly important parts of success in treatment and recovery.

2

VIEWPOINT

*"The contention that addiction is a disease is empirically unsupported."*

# Addiction Is Not a Disease

Jeffrey A. Schaler

In the following viewpoint Jeffrey A. Schaler argues that addiction is a behavior, not a disease. He asserts that people voluntarily choose to consume drugs and alcohol, despite the health and social consequences. Evidence that drug use has both physical and behavioral effects, he maintains, does not mean that the physical effects of drug use cause the behavioral effect—addiction. Moreover, claims Schaler, the fact that faith-based programs such as Alcoholics Anonymous are the best treatment for addiction supports the conclusion that addiction is an ethical problem, not a disease. Schaler, professor at Johns Hopkins University in Baltimore, Maryland, is author of *Addiction Is a Choice*.

As you read, consider the following questions:

1. What are some of the ways addicts monitor their rate of drug consumption, in Schaler's opinion?
2. What did P.A. Garris, M. Kilpatrick, and M.A. Bunin discover actually triggered dopamine release as a result of their research on dopamine and the reward process in mice?
3. According to Schaler, what is the potential harm of psychotherapy as a treatment for addiction?

Jeffrey A. Schaler, "Addiction Is a Choice," *Psychiatric Times*, vol. 19, October 2002. 

Is addiction a disease, or is it a choice? To think clearly about this question, we need to make a sharp distinction between an activity and its results. Many activities that are not themselves diseases can cause diseases. And a foolish, self-destructive activity is not necessarily a disease.

With those two vital points in mind, we observe a person ingesting some substance: alcohol, nicotine, cocaine or heroin. We have to decide, not whether this pattern of consumption causes disease nor whether it is foolish and self-destructive, but rather whether it is something altogether distinct and separate: Is this pattern of drug consumption itself a disease?

## Addiction Is a Behavior

Scientifically, the contention that addiction is a disease is empirically unsupported. Addiction is a behavior and thus clearly intended by the individual person. What is obvious to common sense has been corroborated by pertinent research for years.

The person we call an addict always monitors their rate of consumption in relation to relevant circumstances. For example, even in the most desperate, chronic cases, alcoholics never drink all the alcohol they can. They plan ahead, carefully nursing themselves back from the last drinking binge while deliberately preparing for the next one. This is not to say that their conduct is wise, simply that they are in control of what they are doing. Not only is there no evidence that they cannot moderate their drinking, there is clear evidence that they do so, rationally responding to incentives devised by hospital researchers. Again, the evidence supporting this assertion has been known in the scientific community for years.

My book *Addiction Is a Choice* was criticized in a recent review in a British scholarly journal of addiction studies because it states the obvious. According to the reviewer, everyone in the addiction field now knows that addiction is a choice and not a disease, and I am, therefore, "violently pushing against a door which was opened decades ago." I'm delighted to hear that addiction specialists in Britain are so enlightened and that there is no need for me to argue my case over there.

In the United States, we have not made so much progress. Why do some persist, in the face of all reason and all evidence, in pushing the disease model as the best explanation for addiction?

## The Relationship Between Mind and Body

I conjecture that the answer lies in a fashionable conception of the relation between mind and body. There are several competing philosophical theories about that relation. Let us accept, for the sake of argument, the most extreme "materialist" theory: the psychophysical identity theory. Accordingly, every mental event corresponds to a physical event, because it is a physical event. The relation between mind and the relevant parts of the body is, therefore, like the relation between heat and molecular motion: They are precisely the same thing, observed in two different ways. As it happens, I find this view of the relation between mind and body very congenial.

However, I think it is often accompanied by a serious misunderstanding: the notion that when we find a parallel between physiological processes and mental or personality processes, the physiological process is what is really going on and the mental process is just a passive result of the physical process. What this overlooks is the reality of downward causation, the phenomenon in which an emergent property of a system can govern the position of elements within the system. Thus, the complex, symmetrical, six-pointed design of a snow crystal largely governs the position of each molecule of ice in that crystal.

Hence, there is no theoretical obstacle to acknowledging the fact that thoughts, desires, values and other mental phenomena can dominate bodily functions. Suppose that a man's mother dies, and he undergoes the agonizing trauma we call unbearable grief. There is no doubt that if we examine this man's bodily processes we will find many physical changes, among them changes in his blood and stomach chemistry. It would be clearly wrong to say that these bodily changes cause him to be grief-stricken. It would be less misleading to say that his being grief-stricken causes the bodily changes, but this is also not entirely accurate. His knowledge of his mother's death (interacting with his prior beliefs and values) causes his grief, and his grief has blood-sugar and gastric concomitants, among many others.

### The Problem with the Brain-Disease Model

Labeling addiction a chronic and relapsing brain disease is mere propaganda. By downplaying the volitional dimension of addiction, the brain-disease model detracts from the great promise of strategies and therapies that rely on sanctions and rewards to shape self-control. And by reinforcing a dichotomy between punitive and clinical approaches to addiction, the brain-disease model devalues the enormous contribution of criminal justice to combating addiction. The fact that many, perhaps most, addicts are in control of their actions and appetites for circumscribed periods of time shows that they are not perpetually helpless victims of chronic disease. They are the instigators of their own addiction, just as they can be the agents of their own recovery.

Sally L. Satel, *Public Interest*, Winter 1999.

There is no dispute that various substances cause physiological changes in the bodies of people who ingest them. There is also no dispute, in principle, that these physiological changes may themselves change with repeated doses, nor that these changes may be correlated with subjective mental states like reward or enjoyment.

## Examining the Dopamine Hypothesis

I say "in principle" because I suspect that people sometimes tend to run away with these supposed correlations. For example, changes in dopamine levels have often been hypothesized as an integral part of the reward/reinforcement process. Yet research shows that dopamine in the nucleus accumbens does not mediate primary or unconditioned food reward in animals. According to [J.D.] Salamone, the theory that drugs of abuse turn on a natural reward system is simplistic and inaccurate: "Dopamine in the nucleus accumbens plays a role in the self-administration of some drugs (i.e., stimulants), but certainly not all."

[P.A.] Garris, [M. Kilpatrick, and M.A. Bunin] reached similar conclusions: "Dopamine may therefore be a neural substrate for novelty or reward expectation rather than reward itself." They concluded:

> [T]here is no correlation between continual bar pressing during [intracranial self-stimulation] and increased dopaminergic neurotransmission in the nucleus accumbens . . . our results are consistent with evidence that the dopaminergic component is not associated with the hedonistic or 'pleasure' aspects of reward. . . . Likewise, the rewarding effects of cocaine do not require dopamine; mice lacking the gene for the dopamine transporter, a major target of cocaine, will self-administer cocaine. However, increased dopamine neurotransmission in the nucleus accumbens shell is seen when rats are transiently exposed to a new environment. The increase in extracellular dopamine quickly returns to normal levels and remains there during continued exploration of the new environment . . . dopamine release in the nucleus accumbens is related to novelty, predictability or some other aspects of the reward process, rather than to hedonism itself.

Perhaps, then, some people have been too ready to jump to conclusions about specific mechanisms. Be that as it may, chemical rewards have no power to compel—although this notion of compulsion may be a cherished part of clinicians' folklore. I am rewarded every time I eat chocolate cake, but I often eschew this reward because I feel I ought to watch my weight.

## An Ethical Problem

Experience with addiction treatment must surely make us even more dubious about the theory that addiction is a disease. The most popular way of helping people manage their addictive behavior is Alcoholics Anonymous (AA) and its various 12-step offshoots. Many observers have recognized the essentially religious nature of AA. The U.S. courts are increasingly regarding AA as a religious activity. In *United States v Seeger* (1965), the U.S. Supreme Court stated that the test to be applied as to whether a belief is religious is to enquire whether that belief "occupies a place in the life of its possessor parallel to that filled by the orthodox belief in God" in religions more widely accepted in the United States. This requirement is met by members of AA and other secular programs that help people with addictive behaviors and encourage their members to turn their will and lives over to the care of a supreme being. What kind of disease is this for which the best available treatment is religion? Clinical applications are based on explanations for why the behavior occurs. An activity based on a religious belief masquerading as a clinical form of treatment tells us something about what the activity really is—an ethical, not medical, problem in living.

What passes as clinical treatment for addiction is psychotherapy, which essentially consists of various forms of conversation or rhetoric. One person, the therapist, tries to influence another person, the patient, to change their values and behavior. While the conversation called therapy can be helpful, most of the conversation that occurs in therapy based on the disease model is potentially harmful. This is because the therapist misleads the patient into believing something that is simply untrue—that addiction is a disease, and, therefore, addicts cannot control their behavior. Preaching this falsehood to patients may encourage them to abandon any attempt to take responsibility for their actions.

The treatment of drug effects, at the patient's request, is well within the domain of medicine; what passes as evidence for the theory that addiction is a disease is merely clinical folklore.

3

VIEWPOINT

*"Marijuana is a 'gateway' drug that has enabled millions of Americans to proceed toward a miserable lifetime of drug addiction."*

# Marijuana Is a Gateway to Other Addictive Drugs

Kenneth M. Sunamoto

Marijuana use leads to the use of other illicit drugs, claims Kenneth M. Sunamoto in the following viewpoint. According to Sunamoto, the use of marijuana and other illicit drugs such as heroin and cocaine are connected because they all act on brain areas that produce dopamine—a neurotransmitter that enables people to feel good. Moreover, marijuana itself has many adverse effects on users, including physical dependence and the loss of short-term memory and psychomotor control. Sunamoto is a family physician with a special interest in addiction treatment.

As you read, consider the following questions:

1. What did Sunamoto and his staff discover from a review of the histories of severe addicts that they were trying to help?
2. In the author's opinion, in what ways does abstinence from marijuana resemble getting off heroin?
3. According to Sunamoto, what evidence shows that the genetic changes that occur as a result of marijuana use are transferred to subsequent generations?

I am appalled by many of the comments being made about marijuana, within the context of legalizing medical marijuana. Yet I do not recall any inclusion of the scientific evidence that is accumulating as to the detrimental effects of marijuana.

I have personally worked for many years in the substance abuse field. On a daily basis, I see hardcore drug addicts desperately trying to recover from their severe addictions, mostly to heroin. It has destroyed their lives.

The staff and I make monumental efforts to help these individuals, with the discussion often based on "how to get them to stop." And when we review their histories, their substance abuse often includes the use of alcohol, tobacco and marijuana in their early years.

Marijuana, in fact, often has been characterized as the "gateway" drug that leads to further illicit drug use and addictions like heroin.

## Examining the Evidence

In fact, sociological studies in high schools have shown that teens who use tobacco and alcohol have a 200 times greater likelihood of going on to illicit drugs such as heroin.

New scientific evidence is very clear that marijuana acts on the Mu opiate receptor sites, the same area of the brain stimulated by morphine. Heroin, after it is injected intravenously, is broken down into morphine, which stimulates the opiate receptor sites of the brain, resulting in the "high" that heroin addicts achieve.

Furthermore, it has been scientifically proven that opiates like heroin stimulants—such as cocaine, alcohol and nicotine—all act on the same area of the brain producing dopamine. Dopamine is the neurotransmitter that enables us to feel good, and is increased by marijuana.

Marijuana, unfortunately, often is characterized as being a "safe" drug. Yet its potency has grown tremendously with the selective breeding techniques boosting the active ingredient, delta-90-tetrahydrocannabinol.

The resulting physical dependence developed from chronic marijuana use will cause a much more severe abstinence syndrome when marijuana use ceases. Abstinence from marijuana may duplicate the classic "cold turkey" syndrome of getting off heroin, with symptoms including insomnia, nausea, agitation, irritability, depression and tremor.

The adverse effect of marijuana causing major havoc in our schools is its effect on learning. Short-term memory loss can be severe. The ability to learn is often impaired.

Sybrick. © 1997 by *Funny Times*. Reproduced by permission.

Recent research on the detrimental effects of drugs has been focusing more on the genetic effects of marijuana. Most studies have been concerned with the effects of illicit drug use by a pregnant mother on her unborn child.

Only a few studies have been conducted on prospective fathers. One of the most interesting involves mice exposed to marijuana.

A radioactive-isotope was attached to the marijuana, which was inhaled by the mice. This isotope could be clearly visualized with specialized instruments on the head of the sperm. It was noted that the sperm of the mice had a significant increase in the incidence of "two-headed" sperm.

The sons of these mice had a significant increase in the incidence of "two-headed" sperm as well.

This is evidence that genetic changes occur as a result of marijuana use and are genetically transferred to subsequent generations.

The effect of marijuana on psychomotor tasks is enormous. Motor vehicle accidents are prevalent when drivers are intoxicated by marijuana. The effect of recreational use of marijuana has been characterized as equivalent to .07–.10 percent blood alcohol levels. These levels are consistent with a DUI conviction in many states.

As a member of the American Society of Addiction Medicine, I have attended meetings with thousands of physicians nationwide dedicated to the fight against drug addiction. We are united in fighting the disease of drug addiction, which is so prevalent in society.

We have debated the use of marijuana in the population of outpatient addiction centers that most of us were involved in. The vast majority of the physicians felt that marijuana greatly prevented the recovery of many addicts from drug addiction.

Marijuana is a "gateway" drug that has enabled millions of Americans to proceed toward a miserable lifetime of drug addiction and suffer many severe health consequences. It is not harmless.

4

VIEWPOINT

*"Most people who try marijuana do not use it regularly and never try hard drugs."*

# Marijuana Is Not a Gateway to Other Addictive Drugs

Mitch Earleywine

In the following viewpoint Mitch Earleywine contends that most people who try marijuana never use hard drugs. Moreover, evidence shows that some who use hard drugs such as heroin did not use marijuana first, which means marijuana could not have caused them to use these drugs, he concludes. Lying to America's youth about marijuana leads them to question other information about the dangers of drugs and risks to their health and well being, he argues, even if that information is true. Earleywine, a professor of psychology at the University of Southern California, is author of *Understanding Marijuana.*

As you read, consider the following questions:

1. According to Earleywine, how many Americans who try marijuana never touch heroin?
2. According to the author, what determines the first drug users will select?
3. What substances do some teens choose to use if they believe that marijuana leads to hard drugs, in Earleywine's opinion?

Gateway theory suggests that marijuana is the first step toward painful drug addiction. Many fans of the theory think that marijuana creates an urge for hard drugs the way eating salt makes people thirsty. Two facts prove that the gateway theory is patently false. Perpetuating this lie is also incredibly dangerous.

## Most Marijuana Users Do Not Touch Hard Drugs

We all may know heroin addicts who smoked marijuana, which may lead us to think that marijuana and heroin go together. But we forget the 83 million Americans who tried marijuana and never touched heroin. The chances of regularly using hard drugs after trying marijuana are small. In fact the chances of regularly using marijuana are small.

Data from the 2001 National Household Survey on Drug abuse show that if you've ever tried marijuana in your life, your chance of using other drugs in the last month is:

1 in 7 for marijuana
1 in 12 for any other illicit drug
1 in 50 for cocaine
1 in 208 for crack
1 in 677 for heroin

You're more likely to flip a coin nine times and get all 'heads' than become a regular user of heroin after trying marijuana.

In short, most people who try marijuana do not use it regularly and never try hard drugs.

Again, we all may know heroin addicts who used marijuana first. Nevertheless, research shows plenty of people, especially those with drug problems, use hard drugs before marijuana. One study showed that 39% of drug abusers started with a drug other than marijuana.

Users tend to start with whatever drug is most available. In neighborhoods filled with crack dealers, people could start with crack. But crack is not the gateway to marijuana use. Allen Ginsberg, the legendary 'Beat' poet, used heroin before marijuana. But heroin is not the gateway, either. Obviously, if marijuana use doesn't happen first, it can't cause hard drug use.

Even if every heroin addict used marijuana first, that fact

alone would not prove that marijuana caused heroin addiction. They all ate bread before their heroin addiction, but nobody has called bread the gateway drug. (At least not yet.) Marijuana doesn't cause hard drug use. People may wonder, "What's the harm in scaring teens with this little white lie, especially if it keeps them away from drugs?" Like all lies, this one catches up later. Teens who believe that marijuana leads to hard drugs end up using substances with markedly worse effects. I've had clients and students explain: "We heard pot led to heroin, so we just sniffed glue." Inhalants cause more problems than marijuana ever will, including brain damage and death.

## The Common-Factor Model

Another explanation [for the link between marijuana and hard-drug use] has been suggested: Those who use drugs may have an underlying propensity to do so that is not specific to any one drug. There is some support for such a "common-factor" model in studies of genetic, familial, and environmental factors influencing drug use. The presence of a common propensity could explain why people who use one drug are so much more likely to use another than are people who do not use the first drug. It has also been suggested that marijuana use precedes hard-drug use simply because opportunities to use marijuana come earlier in life than opportunities to use hard drugs. The DPRC [Drug Policy Research Center] analysis offers the first quantitative evidence that these observations can, without resort to a gateway effect, explain the strong observed associations between marijuana and hard-drug initiation.

Drug Policy Research Center, 2002.

In addition, the gateway lie leads to hard drugs in unexpected ways. When kids try marijuana, they realize that the propaganda they've heard is untrue. They don't shoot their friends with handguns, wake up pregnant, or support terrorism. They soon suspect that other drug information is false. The teachers who said that marijuana leads to hard drugs were wrong. Why believe it when they say that crack is addictive?

The gateway lie costs us our credibility. Marijuana does not lead teens to hard drugs, but lying to them about it does.

5

VIEWPOINT

*"We might find the root cause of addiction in our genetic makeup."*

# Genetic Factors Contribute to Addiction

Ernest P. Noble

Some people may have a genetic predisposition to drug addiction, argues Ernest P. Noble in the following viewpoint. Noble claims that people with a gene variant, which researchers have nicknamed the "pleasure-seeking" gene, may turn to drugs to increase their levels of dopamine—a neurotransmitter that enables people to feel good. Understanding the nature of this gene, Noble contends, can lead to more effective treatment options. Noble is a professor of psychiatry and director of the Alcohol Research Center at the University of California, Los Angeles, Neuropsychiatric Institute and Hospital.

As you read, consider the following questions:

1. How did people view addiction through most of the twentieth century, in Noble's opinion?
2. In the author's view, what did research show was different about the brain tissue of those with the "pleasure-seeking" gene compared to the brain tissue of those without it?
3. According to Noble, how can addicts with a genetic predisposition to drug addiction be differentiated from those who simply developed a bad habit?

Why would a talented and successful actor like Robert Downey Jr. repeatedly risk his career for the sake of a drug-induced high?

For many addicts like Downey, the answer may lie not in their upbringing or the company they keep, but in their genetic makeup.

And for drug users whose DNA plays a role in their habit, clinicians need to turn their attention to new treatment options that address the genetics of addiction.

Downey's very public yet personal struggle is a familiar story to millions of Americans who struggle with addiction. A quarter of the U.S. adult population is hooked on alcohol, cocaine, nicotine, amphetamines or some other substance.

Through most of the 20th century, we viewed addiction largely as the product of a flawed upbringing or bad character. Addicts deserved punishment, not sympathy.

## The "Pleasure-Seeking" Gene

Studies comparing the lifestyles and habits of twins and adopted children first suggested that addictive behavior has a hereditary component. We began to consider the possibility that we might find the root cause of addiction in our genetic makeup. A major breakthrough in understanding the genetics of addiction came in 1990, when researchers first linked a gene called DRD2—later nicknamed the "pleasure-seeking" gene—to severe alcoholism.

UCLA [University of California at Los Angeles] studies of brain tissue showed that individuals with the "A1 variation" of the DRD2 gene have significantly fewer dopamine receptors in pleasure centers of the brain.

The findings suggest that many addicts use drugs, which increase brain dopamine levels, to compensate for the deficiency in their neurological pleasure system.

Subsequent studies linked the A1 variation of the DRD2 gene to cocaine, amphetamine, heroin and nicotine addiction.

What does this all mean? It means simply that people with this genetic trait are much more susceptible to addiction. In addition, they are more likely to fall prey to the most severe forms of addiction. In fact, data show that while only 10% of the general population in the United States has the

A1 variation of the DRD2 gene, it is found in about half of addicts.

## Reexamining Treatment Options

Meanwhile, the implications for treatment programs are becoming increasingly clear. A UCLA study of heroin addicts published [in the summer of 2000] showed that a high percentage of heroin users who respond poorly to traditional addiction treatment programs have the troublesome A1 variation of the DRD2 gene.

And a recent study of alcoholics showed that patients with the same "pleasure-seeking" trait responded well to treatment with a nonaddictive drug that stimulates the dopamine receptors.

These findings demand that clinicians rethink treatment options for the millions of drug-users who are genetically predisposed to addiction.

The implications carry additional weight in California, where voter-approved Proposition 36 will divert tens of thousands of addicts a year from the criminal justice system into treatment.

---

### Studying the Role of Genes

Why do some people become addicts while others do not? Why can some teenagers take a drink of alcohol and not crave more while others know from the instant of their first drink that alcohol is going to cause them problems for the rest of their life?

The most obvious reasons is that the susceptibility to addictive behaviors is an inborn or genetic trait. Studies of the frequency of alcoholism in children of alcoholics adopted away from their alcoholic parents at birth provide some of the most powerful evidence that our genes play an important role in the development of subsequent alcoholism.

Dr. Donald Goodman was one of the pioneers in this field. On the basis of such an adoption study he found that the frequency of alcoholism, in adopted-out sons of alcoholic fathers, was just as great when they were placed with non-alcoholic parents as with alcoholic parents. This meant that this form of alcoholism was predominantly a genetic disorder.

David E. Comings, *Addiction & Recovery*, November/December 1991.

---

A simple cheek cell test of DNA can help differentiate hard-core, genetic addicts from those who developed bad habits while socializing with bad crowds.

Drug abusers with a genetic propensity toward addiction typically require one of a growing number of innovative prescription drug therapies to beat their habit. Those without the gene more often respond best to counseling that addresses environmental factors that led to their drug abuse.

The more we know about why the body craves drugs and the more we put that knowledge to use, the more successful we will be in mitigating the heavy toll that drug addiction takes on individuals, families and our society.

VIEWPOINT 6

*"Addiction is a chronic, progressive, and sometimes fatal disorder with both genetic and environmental roots."*

# Genetic and Environmental Factors Contribute to Addiction

Judy Shepps Battle

In the following viewpoint Judy Shepps Battle claims that both genetic and environmental factors determine whether a person will develop an addiction. According to Battle, twin studies show that the children of addicts are more likely to become addicts themselves; however, environmental factors such as living in a poor, urban neighborhood also increase the likelihood that children will become addicts. One of the most important environmental factor is home life; people who come from loving, structured families are less likely to succumb to addiction, Battle maintains. Prevention programs designed to counteract environmental factors may provide potential addicts with the skills they need to escape addiction, she concludes. Battle, president of Write Action Inc., an organization devoted to helping writers promote positive social change, writes on spirituality and addiction.

As you read, consider the following questions:

1. How much money is spent annually in the United States on medical and social issues related to addiction, as cited by Battle?
2. According to Battle, what survival tools did successful adults from at-risk backgrounds use to keep from becoming addicts?

Addiction is a chronic, progressive, and sometimes fatal disorder with both genetic and environmental roots. It is a compulsion that drives an individual to continue to behave in a way that is harmful to self and loved ones, despite an intense desire to halt that behavior. It is a disease of "more"—an active addict needs an increasing amount of substance to get high and is unable to cease usage without painful withdrawal symptoms. This is true whether the addictive substance is a drug—such as alcohol, tobacco, marijuana, cocaine, or heroin—or a behavior, such as gambling or sexual promiscuity.

Addiction is not confined to any economic, social, racial, religious, occupational, or age group. Addicts are not visually identifiable; it is impossible to pick out an alcoholic, drug addict, or the people who enable addictive behavior (co-dependents) from a gallery of photographs.

Alcohol, tobacco, and other drug abuse is costly. More than $275 billion dollars are spent annually in the United States on medical and social issues related to addiction. This averages out to nearly $1000 per person, whether or not that person uses drugs, because these costs include related crime, loss of work time, medical expenses from health-related injuries or illnesses, property damage, and treatment.

There is no known cure for addiction. Relapse is a part of the disease and may be triggered in a variety of environmental and emotional ways. Life-long monitoring is necessary, yet with appropriate identification, treatment, and self-care, an addict can live a productive substance-free life.

We know that addiction runs in families, but how is it transmitted? Are we born with an "addiction gene" or with an "addictive personality," or are we taught addictive behavior by our family and society? This classic question of nature vs. nurture is answered with a qualified "both."

## The Genetic Causes

There is evidence that heredity plays an important part in increasing the likelihood of developing active addiction to illicit drugs, alcohol, and tobacco.

Researchers have compared alcoholism rates of adoptees born to alcoholic parents with those born to nonalcoholic parents. One study found higher alcoholism rates (two to three times higher) in sons whose natural parents were alcoholics than in sons whose natural parents were nonalcoholics. If we assume that the children studied were adopted by families with equal addiction rates, we can also assume that genetic factors play a significant role. Unfortunately, these studies could not rule out the effect of environment on their subjects.

## The "Self-Medicating" Hypothesis

According to psychiatrists who have studied psychodynamic causes of drug addiction, the motivation to use psychoactive substances can often be traced to critical passages early in life. Says Edward J. Khantzian, a Harvard psychiatrist and author of the "self-medicating" hypothesis of drug addiction, many substance-dependent people who make it into therapy show a profound inability to calm and soothe themselves when stressed. The ability to self-regulate mood—to maintain psychic homeostasis—is a task learned between the ages of 1 and 3, when a toddler normally internalizes such a function from caring parents. Mothers, and no doubt many fathers, of frequent drug users have been described as "relatively cold, unresponsive and underprotective." Regarding their children's accomplishments, they send a very mixed message: They're pressuring and overly interested in their children's performance, yet rarely offer them encouragement.

Eating disorders, which are considered addictions and primarily affect women, offer a clear illustration of the self-regulation mechanism gone haywire. If the inability to soothe oneself is due to a distant or rejecting parent, compulsive eating is an attempt to make up for the loss, to construct a substitute attachment to a nurturing parent, with a primitive form of self-medication—food—one of the few things (in addition to love) that can calm a distressed child.

Michael Segell, "Big Mystery: What Causes Addiction?" MSNBC.com, 2003.

Twin studies offer more convincing evidence. Monozygotic (identical) twins share an identical genetic makeup while dizygotic (fraternal) twins share, on average, only 50 percent of genetic similarities. When we look at pairs of twins who have been raised together the variable of "environment" is controlled (not a factor).

Studies of mate twins find that identical twins have 50 to 200 percent greater rates of alcoholism than fraternal twins.

The abuse of sedatives, stimulants, cocaine, and opiates also follows this pattern and is associated with genetic predisposition.

## The Environmental Factors

Although both adoption and twin studies indicate that genetic factors contribute to a predisposition for addiction, they do not tell the entire story. Environmental factors can increase the risk for developing addiction or assist in the development of resiliency skills that protect an individual from beginning to use addictive substances.

Many professionals focus primarily on environmental risk factors as determinants of a child's vulnerability to substance use and other behavioral health problems. These include demographics (geography, economics, crime rate, quality of schools) and familial factors (genetics, family addiction, family parenting skills).

A child from an urban, poor neighborhood with a high crime rate and poor school system is more likely to begin substance use than his demographic opposite. Having a family history of addiction, living with active addicts, and being inadequately parented also increases the risk of using and abusing substances.

## The Tools of Prevention and Treatment

But not all kids from these high-risk environments become casualties. When we study characteristics of successful adults who come from at-risk backgrounds it is found that these adults have developed certain strengths (resiliency factors) that become survival tools.

Basic resiliency factors involve self-esteem and sound decision-making skills. Many school systems have developed curricula to foster this quality, but the primary garden of resiliency is the family.

Findings consistently show that the more adolescents feel a mix of unconditional love and loving boundaries (also called "loving control" or "loving autonomy"), the less likely they are to experience substance abuse and related problems.

Most critically, the longer initiation into substance use is delayed, the less likely addiction will result.

There is a saying that we cannot choose our family but we can choose our friends. Similarly, we have little ability to change genetic inheritance but we can support school and community prevention programs that effectively delay first use of alcohol and drugs and strengthen resiliency in at-risk youth.

If we couple this prevention effort with providing adequate treatment resources for those already addicted (and their families), we will begin to create a solid foundation for an addiction-free society.

# Periodical Bibliography

The following articles have been selected to supplement the diverse views presented in this chapter.


| | |
|---|---|
| Joseph A. Califano | "It's All in the Family," *America*, January 15, 2000. |
| Amal Chandra | "Addiction Is a Virus from Outer Space," *Genre*, November 1999. |
| Michael D. Clark | "Choice and Responsibility in Recovery from Addiction," *Counselor*, February 1999. |
| Anthony Daniels | "Cold Turkey Is No Worse than Flu," *New Statesman*, April 9, 1999. |
| Caroline Eick | "Tapping the Core," *Counselor*, August 1998. |
| Michael Fitzpatrick | "Addiction Addicts," *Spiked*, March 13, 2001. |
| Ronald Kotulak | "Everyone Is Genetically Vulnerable to Addiction," *Seattle Times*, April 4, 1999. |
| Donna Markus | "Of Addiction and Accountability," *Networker*, July/August 2000. |
| Norbert R. Myslinkski | "Addiction and the Brain," *World & I*, November 1999. |
| Eric J. Nester and David Landsman | "Learning About Addiction from the Genome," *Nature*, February 15, 2001. |
| Kim Pittaway | "Is Addiction a Choice?" *Chatelaine*, June 2000. |
| Wendy Richardson | "The Link Between ADHD and Addiction," *Counselor*, April 1999. |
| Jeff Riggenbach | "Hooked on Addiction," *Liberty*, September 2000. |
| Ted Roberts | "I Never Dream of Nicotine," *Ideas on Liberty*, May 2003. |
| Chris Sandvick | "Recovery Is Addict's Responsibility," *Counselor*, October 1998. |
| Sally L. Satel | "The Fallacies of No-Fault Addiction," *Public Interest*, Winter 1999. |
| Marc A. Schuckit and Thomas C. Jefferson | "New Findings in the Genetics of Alcoholism," *JAMA*, May 26, 1999. |
| Steven Stocker | "Finding the Future Alcoholic," *Futurist*, May 2002. |
| Jacob Sullum | "High Road: Is Marijuana a 'Gateway'?" *Reason*, March 2003. |

| | |
|---|---|
| Jacob Sullum | "H: The Surprising Truth About Heroin and Addiction," *Reason*, June 2003. |
| Robert A. Wascher | "Marijuana: A Gateway Drug?" *Jewish World Review*, January 23, 2003. |
| Alice M. Young | "Addictive Drugs and the Brain," *National Forum*, Fall 1999. |

Chapter 3

# What Are the Most Effective Treatments for Addiction?

# Chapter Preface

One of many controversies in the addiction treatment debate is whether treatment for drug addicts who have been convicted of minor, nonviolent drug-related crimes should be provided in lieu of incarceration. Public attitudes toward this issue have moved in cycles. In the 1960s and 1970s, many Americans came to see drug addiction as a medical problem, and in consequence, the public concluded that treatment for drug addiction would be more effective than punishment. However, in 1979 the National Academy of Sciences reported that few of these treatment programs had a lasting positive impact, and many addicts eventually ended up in prison. Moreover, during the 1980s and early 1990s, Americans, believing crime was on the rise, favored aggressive anticrime and antidrug polices. As a result, addiction rehabilitation programs declined, and policies such as mandatory minimum sentences, which increased the sentencing times for many drug offenses, increased. As prisons became overpopulated (with no corresponding decline in drug use), American attitudes once again began to change. In 1996 the citizens of Arizona passed a treatment in lieu of incarceration initiative, and in 2000 California followed suit. While some claim these initiatives will reduce prison overpopulation and prevent the inequitable punishment of drug addicts, others think these policies must be approached with caution.

Those who support treatment in lieu of incarceration argue that implementing these policies will alleviate prison overpopulation and inequities in the criminal justice system created by aggressive anticrime laws such as mandatory minimum sentences. In the past twenty years, the incarceration rate in U.S. prisons has increased 385 percent. According to William D. McColl and Opio Sokoni of the Drug Policy Alliance, an organization working to end the war on drugs and promote new drug policies, "Much of this growth was caused by the increase in imprisonment of drug offenders. From 1987 to 1997 the number of people entering prison . . . for drug offenses increased 11-fold." Moreover, they argue, mandatory minimum sentences have created absurd criminal justice outcomes. McColl and Sokoni assert, for example, that "some low-level, nonviolent drug defendants face more severe sentences than violent offenders convicted of rape or manslaughter."

Martin Y. Iguchi, a researcher at the RAND Drug Policy Research Center, agrees that efforts to deter drug use have overloaded the criminal justice system. He argues, however, that as a solution to this problem, treatment programs in lieu of incarceration have several drawbacks. He maintains, for example, that there are a limited number of treatment slots available at any given time, and mandatory treatment in lieu of incarceration will use up most if not all of these slots. Iguchi cautions, "We do not want someone who is voluntarily seeking treatment to be deprived of that opportunity because the slot has been filled with an individual mandated to receive treatment." Iguchi also warns that the policy could be abused if prosecutors instead of judges manage the drug courts that administer these programs. "Some public defenders and defense attorneys," he explains, "have voiced concern that prosecutors may be tempted to offer access to drug court only to those individuals who are 'cooperative.'" Such policies, he argues, use treatment as a weapon rather than a tool, which defeats the purpose of the program—to help all nonviolent drug addicts recover and stay out of prison.

Whether or not treatment in lieu of incarceration is effective continues to be fervently disputed. The authors of the viewpoints in the following chapter express their opinions on other controversial treatment options.

1

VIEWPOINT

*"The 12-step-oriented programs were not only cost-efficient, they were also effective."*

# Twelve-Step Programs Are an Effective Treatment for Addiction

Krista Conger

In the following viewpoint Krista Conger, who represents the Office of Communications and Public Affairs for the Stanford Medical Center, claims that a study conducted by the center found that the twelve-step approach to addiction treatment is less expensive and more effective than cognitive-behavioral approaches. Twelve-step approaches (such as Alcoholics Anonymous) emphasize seeking spiritual help for substance-abuse problems, Conger maintains, while cognitive-behavioral programs teach coping skills. According to Conger, the study suggests that twelve-step treatment approaches save money because patients seek self-help rather than medical help upon release from treatment centers. Moreover, nearly 46 percent of those in twelve-step programs remained sober one year after discharge, she claims. Conger writes for *Stanford Medicine* and *Stanford Report.*

As you read, consider the following questions:

1. In Conger's view, what has happened to funding for substance abuse treatment programs nationwide in recent years?
2. How might treatment programs around the United States benefit from the study's conclusions, in Conger's opinion?

Krista Conger, "Study Points Out Value of 12-Step Groups in Treating Substance Abuse," *Stanford Report*, May 23, 2001. 

Inpatient substance abuse treatment programs emphasizing the spiritually oriented "12-step" approach to addiction save money and promote abstinence more effectively than treatment programs that emphasize practical coping skills, say medical school researchers. Graduates from the 12-step-oriented programs slice their long-term health care costs by more than half by turning to community-based self-help groups rather than to professional mental health services for support in the year after discharge, say the researchers. They are also significantly more likely to remain abstinent in the year following their treatment.

"Groups like Alcoholics Anonymous and Narcotics Anonymous are taking a huge burden off of the health care system," said Keith Humphreys, PhD. "We found that addiction treatment programs are more effective and less expensive when they link patients to spiritually based self-help groups."

Humphreys, assistant professor of psychiatry and behavioral science [at Stanford University], is the lead author of the study published in the May [2001] issue of *Alcoholism: Clinical and Experimental Research*. Humphreys is also the associate director of the Program Evaluation and Resource Center at the Veterans Affairs Palo Alto Health Care System in Menlo Park, Calif.

Although one-quarter of all deaths in this country are caused by alcohol, tobacco or illegal drugs, funding for substance abuse treatment programs nationwide has decreased dramatically in recent years, Humphreys said. "Most mental health treatment professionals are being asked to do more and more with less and less," he said. He and co-author Rudolf Moos, PhD, investigated whether free, community-based support groups could stand in for professional mental health treatment, reducing health care costs without compromising patient outcome.

## Comparing Treatment Programs

Humphreys studied 1,774 low-income, substance-dependent men who had been enrolled in inpatient substance abuse treatment programs at 10 Department of Veteran Affairs medical centers around the country. Five of the programs strongly emphasized the 12-step approach to addiction, a spiritually oriented philosophy that urges individuals to take responsibility for their actions and ask for help from God in conquering their dependency. These programs frequently hold Alcoholics Anonymous or Narcotics Anonymous meetings on-site, and refer to the "Big Book," an inspirational text that complements the 12 steps.

### The Twelve Steps

1. We admitted we were powerless over alcohol, that our lives had become unmanageable.
2. Came to believe that a Power greater than ourselves could restore us to sanity.
3. Made a decision to turn our will and our lives over to the care of God *as we understood Him.*
4. Made a searching and fearless moral inventory of ourselves.
5. Admitted to God, to ourselves, and to another human being the exact nature of our wrongs.
6. Were entirely ready to have God remove all these defects of character.
7. Humbly asked Him to remove our shortcomings.
8. Made a list of all persons we had harmed, and became willing to make amends to them all.
9. Made direct amends to such people wherever possible, except when to do so would injure them or others.
10. Continued to take personal inventory and when we were wrong promptly admitted it.
11. Sought through prayer and meditation to improve our conscious contact with God *as we understood Him*, praying only for knowledge of His will for us and the power to carry that out.
12. Having had a spiritual awakening as the result of these steps, we tried to carry this message to alcoholics, and to practice these principles in all our affairs.

Alcoholics Anonymous, 2001.

The remaining five programs used an approach called cognitive-behavioral therapy that concentrates on teaching individuals coping skills to avoid relapse. These programs, which emphasized a medical and scientific approach to addiction treatment, spent only about 7 percent of treatment time discussing the 12-step approach. The men in the study were evenly divided between the two types of programs.

Humphreys paired up men from the two programs whose mental health care costs in the year preceding treatment were similar. He then compared the mental health care costs between the men in the year following discharge. He found that the total mental health care costs for men enrolled in cognitive-behavioral programs were about $4,700 higher than those for men enrolled in 12-step-oriented programs, even though their starting values were similar.

The cost difference was attributed to the increased likelihood of men enrolled in the 12-step-oriented approach to attend meetings of community-based self-help groups after discharge while also being less likely to seek help from traditional medical professionals to avoid relapsing.

The 12-step-oriented programs were not only cost-efficient, they were also effective—nearly 46 percent of the men in these programs were abstinent one year after discharge, compared to 36 percent of those treated in cognitive-behavioral programs. This may be due in part to strong endorsements from staff members at the 12-step-oriented programs who are more likely to be recovering addicts.

"They tend to be people who really believe in the approach they're teaching," said Humphreys. "They are more likely to say, 'I can help you overcome your cocaine addiction, because I overcame one.'" Once the patients of these programs are discharged, they can call on self-help group members and sponsors they met during their treatment, creating a mutual support network that can in some ways mirror the support provided by professional counselors.

The study suggests that it may be beneficial for treatment programs around the United States to incorporate more of the 12-step philosophy into their substance abuse therapies, and to increase their efforts to link patients with community-based self-help groups after discharge.

"In the current health care climate, a clinical strategy that reduces the ongoing health care costs of substance abuse patients by 64 percent while also promoting good outcome deserves serious attention," Humphreys and Moos concluded in the paper.

2

VIEWPOINT

*"The view that one can only recover via the moral improvement of the 12 steps is doing more harm than good."*

# Twelve-Step Programs Are Inadequate to Treat Addiction

Maia Szalavitz

By rejecting all alternative treatment options, twelve-step treatment programs such as Alcoholics Anonymous prevent some people from getting the help they need, argues Maia Szalavitz in the following viewpoint. These programs emphasize faith in God over scientific fact, she maintains, and thus reject empirically proven treatments for addiction. For example, Szalavitz claims, twelve-step programs reject the use of medication by alcoholics suffering from diseases such as depression despite the scientifically proven relief medication can provide. Moreover, argues Szalavitz, twelve-step programs support punitive drug policies that contradict their claim that addiction is a disease, not a sin. Szalavitz, a science journalist, is the author of *Recovery Options: The Complete Guide.*

As you read, consider the following questions:

1. According to Szalavitz, what has happened to the twelve-step movement since the 1980s and 1990s?
2. What happened during the last five years of the author's experience in a twelve-step recovery program?
3. In Szalavitz's opinion, how do twelve-step treatment providers characterize addiction to secure support from the drug-war establishment?

Maia Szalavitz, "Breaking Out of the 12-Step Lockstep," *Washington Post*, June 9, 2002, p. B03. 

In the 1980s and '90s, 12-step programs like Alcoholics Anonymous [AA] were the gold standard for addiction treatment. Even among the non-addicted, they had become an accepted part of American culture. In Tim Robbins's 1992 film, *The Player*, the title character attended AA meetings not because he drank too much but because that's where the deals were being made. In 1995, *New York* magazine suggested that single women attend AA to meet men.

But today, the recovery movement—with its emphasis on childhood victimization, lifetime attendance at 12-step groups and complete abstinence from all psychoactive substances—has fallen from pop culture favor. "There was a time when it was almost the 'in thing' to say you were in recovery," says William White, author of *Slaying the Dragon*, a history of addiction treatment. Thankfully, that is no longer the case.

*Vogue*, *Elle* and the *New York Times Magazine* have recently run articles critical of the recovery movement. The "addictions" section of the bookstore—once taking up several bookcases in superstores—has shrunk to a few shelves, with a growing proportion of critical books. By the late '90s, the number of inpatient rehab facilities offering treatment centered on the 12-step process was half what it had been earlier in the decade. And AA membership, which grew explosively from the late '70s through the late '80s, has held steady at about 2 million since 1995.

## Examining 12-Step Contradictions

Still, it is difficult to say goodbye to an organization and philosophy that may have helped save my life. Between the ages of 17 and 23, I was addicted to cocaine and then heroin. For the next 12 years, I was an often enthusiastic participant in 12-step recovery. Eventually, however, it became difficult to imagine defining myself for the rest of my life in relation to behavior that had taken up so few years of it.

During my last five years in the program, I had become increasingly uncomfortable with what it presented as truth: the notion, for example, that addiction is a "chronic, progressive disease" that can only be arrested by 12-stepping. The more research I did, the more I learned that much of what I had been told in rehab was wrong. And yet, I'd indisputably gotten better. Once an unemployed, 80-pound wreck, I had become a healthy, productive science journalist. That science part, however, became the root of my problem with a model based on anecdote as anodyne.

The 12-step model has always been rife with contradiction. Its adherents recognize, for example, that addiction is a disease, not a sin. But their treatment isn't medical; it's praying, confession and meeting. And while they claim that the belief in a "God of your understanding" on which the program rests is spiritual, not religious, every court that has ever been asked whether ordering people into such programs violates the separation of church and state has disagreed with the "non-religious" label.

So why have the contradictions come to the fore now? For me, the first step came in 2000 when I wrote about New York's Smithers Addiction Treatment and Research Center and its attempts to modernize treatment. Its director, Alex DeLuca, saw that options needed to be expanded beyond AA. Guided by DeLuca, Smithers began publishing studies funded by the National Institute on Alcoholism and Alcohol Abuse showing that adding treatment options, including support for moderation rather than abstinence, was effective.

## Protesting Evidence-Based Options

However, when a group of people in recovery learned that those options included moderation, they protested, and DeLuca was fired. Imagine cancer or AIDS patients demonstrating against evidence-based treatment offering more options. This deeply distressed me, as did AA's religious aspects. In any other area of medicine, if a physician told you the only cure for your condition was to join a support group that involves "turning your will and your life" over to God (AA's third step), you'd seek a second opinion.

The insistence on the primacy of God in curing addiction also means that treatment can't change in response to empirical evidence. Which leaves us with a rehab system based more on faith than fact. Nowhere is this clearer than in the field's response to medication use. The National Institute on Drug Abuse is pouring big bucks into developing "drugs to fight drugs" but, once approved, they sit on the shelves because many rehab facilities don't believe in medication. Until 1997, for example, the well-known rehab facility Hazelden refused to provide antidepressants to people who had both depression and addiction.

### A Treatment Monopoly

The AA [Alcoholics Anonymous] 12-step industry maintains a virtual monopoly over the nation's recovery programs. Though AA 12-step programs are open to all who wish to participate, they remain surprisingly antagonistic to partnering with medical scientists—this in spite of AA cofounder Bill Wilson's recognition nearly 50 years ago that the "discoveries of the psychiatrists and biochemists have vast implications for us alcoholics."

Manijeh Nikakhtar and Louis F. Markert, *Family Practice News*, July 15, 2001.

Those who promote just one means of recovery are right to find medication threatening. When I finally tried antidepressants, after years of resisting "drugs" because I'd been told they might lead to relapse, my disillusionment with the recovery movement grew. Years of groups and talking couldn't do what those pills did: allow me not to overreact emotionally, and thus to improve my relationships and worry less. I didn't need to "pray for my character defects to be lifted" (AA's 6th and 7th steps)—I needed to fix my brain chemistry.

This is not to say that I didn't learn anything through recovery groups. The problem is their insistence that their solutions should trump all others. Many recovering people now use medication and groups both—but within the movement there is still an enormous hostility toward this and a sense that people on medications are somehow cheating by avoiding the pain that leads to emotional growth.

## Questionable Motives

Another contradiction in the notion of 12-step programs as a medical treatment shows up in the judicial system. Logically, if addiction were a disease, prison and laws would have no place in its treatment. However, to secure support from the drug-war establishment, many 12-step treatment providers argue that addiction is a disease characterized by "denial"—

despite research showing that addicts are no more likely to be in denial than people with other diseases, and that most addicts tell the truth about their drug use when they won't be punished for doing so.

Because of "denial," however, many in-patient treatment providers use methods that would be unheard of for any other condition: restrictions on food and medications, limits on sleep, hours of forced confessions and public humiliation, bans on contact with relatives and, of course, threats of prison for noncompliance.

If these programs wanted what was best for their patients, they would support measures to fund more treatment and divert people from jail. Watching famous 12-steppers such as Martin Sheen fight against California's Proposition 36, which mandates treatment rather than punishment for drug possession, was the final straw for me.

If their argument is that people won't attend treatment without the threat of prison, how do they explain all the alcoholics they treat? How, for that matter, do they explain that 12-step programs were started by volunteers? Their opposition only makes sense in the context of a view of addicts as sinners, not patients.

The view that one can only recover via the moral improvement of the 12 steps is doing more harm than good. It is supporting bad drug policy, preventing people from getting the treatment they need and hampering research.

Yet it is important not to dismiss 12-step programs entirely. They provide a supportive community and should be recommended as an option for people with addictions. Let evidence-based research determine how people are treated medically for drug problems.

3

VIEWPOINT

*"God, religion and spirituality are key factors for many in prevention and treatment of substance abuse and in continuing recovery."*

# Spirituality Can Help Those Trying to Recover from Addiction

National Center on Addiction and Substance Abuse

People of all ages who attend religious services and who consider religious beliefs important are less likely to abuse alcohol or drugs, according to a study summarized in the following viewpoint. Conducted by the National Center on Addiction and Substance Abuse (CASA) at Columbia University in New York City, the study analyzed research from a variety of sources and concluded that spiritual faith is an important element in substance-abuse treatment. These results, CASA maintains, should encourage cooperation among the clergy, the medical community, and treatment providers to provide faith-based programs for patients struggling with addiction.

As you read, consider the following questions:

1. According to the authors of the CASA study, what percentage of clergy members recognized substance abuse as an important issue among family members in their congregations?
2. In the opinion of the authors of the CASA study, what should physicians and substance-abuse treatment specialists discuss with patients?

National Center on Addiction and Substance Abuse, *So Help Me God: Substance Abuse, Religion, and Spirituality*. New York: National Center on Addiction and Substance Abuse at Columbia University, 2001. 

Ninety-five percent of Americans profess a belief in God. For many individuals, religion and spirituality are important components of prevention and treatment of substance abuse and of successful recovery. One has only to listen to the voices of recovery to hear how eloquently they speak about the role of religion or spirituality in their own healing process.

## A Spiritual Connection

CASA's [National Center on Addiction and Substance Abuse] research has identified an important connection between spiritual and religious practices and lower risk of substance abuse:

- CASA's annual teen surveys have consistently demonstrated that adolescents who attend religious services are less likely to report substance use.
- CASA's study, *Under the Rug: Substance Abuse and the Mature Woman* revealed that 91 percent of woman over the age of 59 who did not identify themselves as religious consumed alcohol compared with 64 percent who identified themselves as Catholic and 52 percent who identified themselves as Protestant. Similarly, mature women who say they are not religious are more likely to be current smokers (45 percent) than those who are Catholic (25 percent) or Protestant (21 percent).
- Roughly one-third of prison inmates participates in religious activities and those who do so have been found to exhibit lower rates of recidivism.
- CASA's CASASTART (Striving to Achieve Rewarding Tomorrows) parent program found that participating children had less past month drug use, delinquency and other problems, and that the most frequently attended activities were those sponsored by religious organizations.

## A Source of Hope

These findings and experience have led CASA to explore . . . the link between God, religion and spirituality and substance abuse prevention, treatment and recovery, and how to better exploit any such link. By examining recent findings in practice and research with respect to the role of religion and spirituality in dealing with substance abuse and by listening to the voices of recovery, CASA aims to draw attention to a powerful source of hope for many affected by this disease.

As part of this two-year study, CASA conducted two unprecedented surveys: one, asking presidents of schools of theology and seminaries about their perceptions of the extent of substance abuse problems and the formal training and coursework offered in this subject; the other, asking clergy in the field their perspective of these problems among their congregations and what training they had received in this area.

CASA conducted its own special analyses of three national data sets: *1998 National Household Survey on Drug Abuse;* CASA's Back to School Surveys—*Back to School 1999—National Survey of American Attitudes on Substance Abuse V: Teens and Their Parents* and *National Survey of American Attitudes on Substance Abuse VI: Teens;* and the General Social Survey. CASA undertook an extensive review of more than 300 publications that examine the link between spirituality, religiousness and substance abuse and addiction. Finally, CASA looked at a wide range of programs that incorporate spiritual or religious components in their prevention or treatment programs.

Most data and research on the link between substance abuse and religion and spirituality are limited to the Protestant and Catholic religions and to a lesser extent the Jewish faith. Unfortunately, we were unable to find any significant information in Islam, Buddhism or Hinduism.

## Summarizing

Key Findings

- God, religion and spirituality are key factors for many in prevention and treatment of substance abuse and in continuing recovery.
- Adults who do not consider religious beliefs important are more than one and one-half times likelier to use alcohol and cigarettes, more than three times likelier to binge drink, almost four times likelier to use an illicit drug other than marijuana and more than six times likelier to use marijuana than adults who strongly be-

lieve that religion is important.

- Adults who never attend religious services are almost twice as likely to drink, three times likelier to smoke, more than five times likelier to have used an illicit drug other than marijuana, almost seven times likelier to binge drink and almost eight times likelier to use marijuana than those who attend religious services at least weekly.
- Teens who do not consider religious beliefs important are almost three times likelier to drink, binge drink and smoke, almost four times likelier to use marijuana and seven times likelier to use illicit drugs than teens who strongly believe that religion is important.
- Teens who never attend religious services are twice as likely to drink, more than twice as likely to smoke, more than three times likelier to use marijuana and binge drink and almost four times likelier to use illicit drugs than teens who attend religious services at least weekly.
- Children who strongly believe that religion is important report learning more about the risks of drugs. When discussing drugs with their parents, 63.5 percent of teens who strongly believe religion is important feel they learned a lot about the risks of drugs; only 41 percent who believe religion is not important feel they learned a lot.
- College students with no religious affiliation report higher levels of drinking and binge drinking than those of either Catholic or Protestant religious affiliation.
- Ninety-four percent of clergy members—priests, ministers and rabbis—recognize substance abuse as an important issue among family members in their congregations and almost 38 percent believe that alcohol abuse is involved in half or more of the family problems they confront.
- Only 12.5 percent of clergy completed any coursework related to substance abuse while studying to be a member of the clergy and only 25.8 percent of presidents of schools of theology and seminaries report that individuals preparing for the ministry are required to take courses on this subject.

## Presidents of Schools of Theology Rate Importance of Substance Abuse

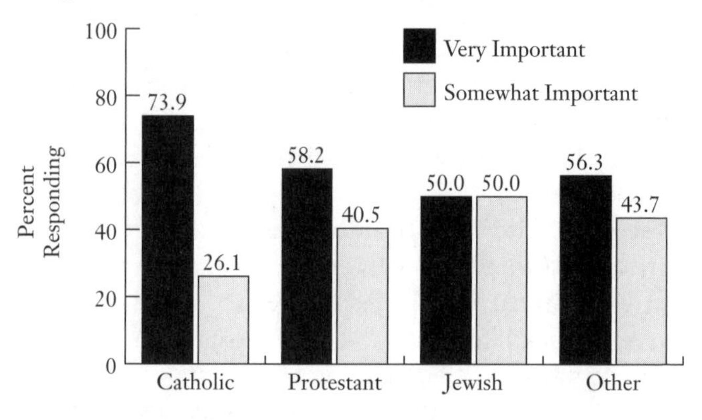


CASA Presidents' Survey, 2001.

- Only 36.5 percent of clergy report that they preach a sermon on substance abuse more than once a year; 22.4 percent say they never preach on the subject.
- Seventy-nine percent of Americans believe that spiritual faith can help people recover from disease and 63 percent think that physicians should talk to patients about spiritual faith. One study found that 99 percent of family physicians are convinced that religious beliefs can heal and 75 percent believe that prayers of others can promote a patient's recovery. However, 74 percent of psychiatrists disapprove of praying with a patient; only 37 percent say they would pray with a patient even if provided with scientific evidence that doing so would improve patient progress. Only 57 percent would recommend that a patient consult with a member of the clergy.
- Individuals who attend spiritually-based support programs, such as 12-Step programs of Alcoholics Anonymous [AA] and Narcotics Anonymous [NA], in addition to receiving treatment are more likely to maintain sobriety. Individuals in successful recovery often show greater levels of faith and spirituality than individuals who relapse.

Despite these facts, spirituality and religion are often

overlooked as relevant factors in preventing and treating substance abuse and addiction.

Each religious and spiritual tradition has it own unique beliefs, commitments and rituals to bring to bear to minimize substance abuse and to aid recovery. To take advantage of the potentially positive benefits of religion and spirituality to prevent substance abuse and help individuals, CASA recommends a series of steps to combine the resources of religion and spirituality with those of science and medicine in order to enhance the prevention and treatment of substance abuse and to strengthen and maintain recovery:

## The Next Step for Clergy

- Protestant, Catholic, Rabbinical and other schools of theology and seminaries should train clergy to recognize the signs and symptoms of substance abuse and know how to respond, including referral to treatment and strategies for relapse prevention. These schools should provide basic educational and clinical knowledge of the short and long term effects of tobacco, alcohol and other drugs and educate their students about ways to incorporate prevention messages both formally and informally into their work. They should educate their students about the co-occurrence of mental health and other problems (such as domestic violence and child abuse) and substance abuse. These schools should include courses related to substance abuse in degree requirements and provide in-service training for current clergy.
- Clergy members who have completed their formal training should take advantage of additional substance abuse training in order to be knowledgeable about the topic. Resources include: local public substance abuse treatment agencies, private licensed substance abuse professionals, substance abuse professional organizations such as the National Association of State Alcohol and Drug Agency Directors (NASADAD), federal resources such as the National Institute on Drug Abuse and the National Institute on Alcohol Abuse and Alcoholism, the U.S. Department of Health and Human Services Substance Abuse and Mental Health Services

Administration and its Centers for Substance Abuse Prevention and Substance Abuse Treatment.

- Members of the clergy should preach about substance abuse issues and informally include messages about the problem throughout their organization's programs, services and counseling. Even religions with assigned readings and themes for sermons can incorporate messages about substance abuse as examples and prayers for those addicted in their services. Recognizing that substance abuse affects individuals and families in all congregations, clergy can inform their members with prevention messages, and help connect members of their community to needed intervention and treatment resources and, as many presently do, open their facilities to AA and NA meetings.
- Members of the clergy should reach out to treatment programs to offer spiritual support to individuals who desire such assistance. Clergy can help educate treatment providers of the promising effects of spirituality and religion in recovery. Clergy should learn about treatment programs in their communities. By building this relationship, clergy will know who to refer members to for treatment and know how to support referrals from treatment providers of clients seeking to deepen their spiritual life.

Participants in recovery may have great needs for spiritual guidance. Individuals struggling to recover may feel abandoned by God or alienated from God or the religious community. Clergy can help recovering individuals navigate these issues and benefit from a connection to a loving God and religious community.

## The Future of Treatment

For many individuals, spirituality and religiousness can be important companions to recovery and maintaining sobriety.

- Physician and other health professions training programs should educate physicians and treatment specialists to understand that many patients desire spiritual help as complements to medical treatment, and the research documenting the benefits of spirituality and religiousness to physical and mental health.

- Physicians and substance abuse treatment specialists should discuss patients' spiritual needs and desires and, where appropriate, refer clients to clergy or spiritually-based programs to support their recovery.
- Substance abuse treatment providers (physicians and other health clinicians) should establish working relationships with local clergy members not only to educate clergy members about substance abuse but also to better respond to patients needs and desires for a spiritual complement to their recovery regimen.
- More research is needed to evaluate the efficacy and increase the effectiveness of faith-based prevention initiatives and treatment programs, develop better ways of measuring adolescent spirituality and religiousness and document pathways through which religion and spirituality work to prevent substance abuse and aid in recovery.

4

VIEWPOINT

*"With the number of non-religious adults increasing . . . , it is imperative to find ways to reach this group with [substance-abuse] education and treatment options which they can accept."*

# The Importance of Spirituality in Addiction Recovery Is Exaggerated

Kevin Courcey

According to Kevin Courcey in the following viewpoint, research claiming that religious faith helps keep Americans from abusing drugs and alcohol is flawed. He claims that such studies, which are funded by groups working to make religion more central to American society, inflate the number of religious believers, create misleading categories that distort the results, and exaggerate the severity of alcohol abuse. Despite claims by these researchers, the number of nonbelievers is growing nationwide, Courcey claims; developing nonreligious-based treatment options for those individuals will become increasingly important. Courcey is a registered nurse at Humboldt County Mental Health in Eureka, California.

As you read, consider the following questions:

1. In Courcey's opinion, why is the American Religious Identification Survey, conducted by the City University of New York, more objective than the Gallup Poll?
2. According to the author, how did the CASA study define alcohol abuse?

In a report published in November of 2001, Columbia University's Center on Addiction and Substance Abuse (CASA) reviewed the statistics on religiosity and substance abuse in adults and teens. They also "conducted an unprecedented survey of attitudes and experiences" of members of the clergy about their perceptions of substance abuse problems in their congregations, and their preparedness to deal with those problems. In a summary statement, CASA President Joseph Califano Jr., former head of Health, Education and Welfare under [former president] Jimmy Carter, writes:

> The key finding of this two-year study is this: if ever the sum were greater than the parts it is in combining the power of God, religion and spirituality with the power of science and professional medicine to prevent and treat substance abuse and addiction. A better understanding by the clergy of the disease of alcohol and drug abuse and addiction among members of their congregations and a better appreciation by the medical profession, especially psychiatrists and psychologists, of the power of God, religion and spirituality to help patients with this disease hold enormous potential for prevention and treatment of substance abuse and addiction that can help millions of Americans and their families.

The study emphasizes that we are a country of "believers"; that 95% of us believe in God, 92% are affiliated with an established religion, "In God We Trust" is emblazoned on our currency, *etc.* They boldly assert that non-believers are more prone to substance abuse:

> Adults who never attend religious services are almost twice as likely to drink, three times likelier to smoke, five times likelier to use illicit drugs other than marijuana, seven times likelier to binge drink and almost eight times likelier to use marijuana than adults who attend religious services weekly or more.

These are horrifying statistics. It would seem that non-believers are a bunch of low-life scum who are half in the bag most of the time on any of a half-dozen different legal and illegal drugs, while religious folks are content to go to church several times a week and spend their free time volunteering at their local homeless shelters.

But perhaps a closer look at this research is in order.

As those of you who are familiar with this genre of research might have guessed, this research was funded by the

Templeton Foundation. The Templeton Foundation's stated goat is: "By promoting collaboration and clinical research into the relationship between spirituality and health and documenting the positive medical aspects of spiritual practice, the Foundation hopes to contribute to the reintegration of faith into modern life." Notice that the Foundation is only interested in funding research that documents the positive medical effects of religion and spirituality. This puts significant pressure on the researchers to "mine the data" until they can come up with positive findings.

Singled out for his contribution to this research was David Larson, M.D., President of the International Center for the Integration of Health and Spirituality (formerly called the National Institute for Health Care Research). The Templeton Foundation funds Larson's spirituality and health research ventures at roughly $3–4 million per year. The CASA study also frequently cites Templeton-funded researchers Harold Koenig and Michael McCullough to bolster their claims for the positive effects of religion on health.

The Bodman Foundation also helped fund this research. Like the Templeton Foundation. this group also has a conservative, religious viewpoint, and is known for funding religious homeless programs, school-choice/voucher research, sexual abstinence-only programs, welfare-to-work reform, and faith-based solutions to drug abuse, teen pregnancy, and youth violence. It was at the request of the Bodman Foundation that this research was undertaken.

## Evaluating the Data

CASA used several data sets to generate their figures. Much of their religious affiliation and religious belief data was obtained from surveys done by the Gallup Poll. This organization has been accused of slanting their survey questions over the years to inflate the apparent number of religious believers in the country. For example, what started out in the '50s as "Do you believe in the God of the Bible?" has devolved into questions about belief in a "universal spirit" or "animating force."

Fortunately [in 2001], the City University of New York repeated their American Religious Identification Survey (ARIS).

ARIS surveyed over 50,000 households about their religious beliefs, affiliation with specific denominations, church attendance, *etc.* Since the ARIS survey was not funded by religious organizations, its data are more objective and designed to elicit a deeper understanding of religious belief in America. In fact, ARIS specifically changed the wording of the question they used to ascertain religious identification, adding the phrase "if any" to make the question "What is your religion, if any?" They did this because they felt that previous surveys (such as those used by Gallup) had subtly influenced respondents to choose a religion by not offering an alternative. Whether as a result of this change, or reflecting a major shift away from belief in the population, they found that the number of people choosing "none" or "no religion" has more than doubled since 1990. While the ARIS survey did not investigate substance abuse, it does give us a more reliable reference paint to evaluate the claims for religious belief and participation made by the CASA study, which based its data primarily on the more limited General Social Survey, and data supplied by Gallup.

## The Claims and Proposed Solutions

The CASA report can be summarized as follows:

We are a nation of believers and our faith is very important to us.

Religious faith and practice has a prophylactic effect against substance abuse.

Religious faith and practice can be essential in recovery from substance abuse.

Non-believers abuse substances at significantly higher rates.

The clergy believe substance abuse is a big problem.

The clergy is unprepared to deal with substance abuse problems.

The medical establishment, especially mental health professionals, are unreasonably reluctant to use religious interventions with clients.

The clergy therefore need to be trained on how to handle substance-abuse problems, and should preach about this topic from the pulpit.

The clergy should contact local treatment centers in order to offer their services to the clients there, and to educate the providers on the "promising effects" of religious counseling on substance-abuse treatment.

Physicians should recognize that many clients desire spiritual help, and should refer them to spiritually based treatment programs.

The report makes it obvious that in order to cut down on teen drug use, parents should impress upon our youth the importance of religion and make sure they attend religious services at least weekly. The report also stresses the need to provide religious treatment options to all clients with substance-abuse problems. It is implied that intervention strategies that do not incorporate God and religion are likely to fail.

This focus fits well with the Tempteton goal of "reintegrating" faith into our lives, and they are more than willing to impose that goal on a vulnerable population seeking treatment for addiction.

## The Art of Skewing a Survey

Several methods were used to skew the results of this survey. First, the figures used for religious identification and practice were inflated. While the CASA report repeatedly states that 95% of Americans believe in God, and that 92% of us are affiliated with a specific religion, the 2001 ARIS survey shows this to be false. The percentage of American adults who self identify with a specific religion has dropped to 81%. Of those who do claim a religious affiliation, 40% stated that neither they nor their family members attend services. The ARIS survey also found that 14% of those surveyed chose "no religion." This means that a substantial majority of the adults in this country either profess no religion, or have so little interest in organized religion that neither they nor their family members go to services. This fatally undercuts the argument that the way to curb drug abuse is to train clergy. Why expend resources addressing the problem where, according to their data, it is least prevalent? This would be equivalent to saying that since syphilis is concentrated in the South, and living on the West coast seems to have a prophylactic effect against contracting syphilis, we should better educate medical professionals in the west on how to treat syphilis.

*'It's a side-effect from giving up booze.'*



Why would CASA use inflated figures for religious belief? In order to project the image of a huge, receptive client base for religiously oriented intervention services, of course. This would then be used to justify funneling taxpayer funds to these faith-based groups. But aren't they simultaneously saying that the religious are less likely to abuse substances? Yes, but for them there is no contradiction in saying that the non-religious are more likely to abuse substances so we should train the clergy to treat them. One need only recall that the goal of the Templeton Foundation is to reintegrate faith into American life. This approach is not as concerned with appropriately treating an illness as it is with bringing the wayward sheep back into the fold.

Their approach is likely doomed to failure, in any case. When Templeton funded Dale Matthews to do research evaluating Christian prayer for arthritis sufferers in conservative Florida, they were unable to recruit sufficient volunteers to carry out their research design. A public demand for religiously oriented healthcare interventions is not going to materialize just because Templeton and CASA would like it to happen.

## Using Arbitrary Definitions

The second method used to skew this survey was arbitrarily defining the groups to be studied. If one's goal were to show the religious to be a relatively healthy norm, while non-believers are shown to be a drug-abusing fringe group, you would need to artificially expand the religious group and restrict the non-believer group to achieve this end.

In order to expand the "religious" category, the concept of being "spiritual" was added to it. This is how the CASA group defined spirituality for the purposes of this report:

> Spirituality, on the other hand, is a deeply personal and individualized response to God, a higher power or an animating force in the world. One does not have to engage in religious rituals, belong to a church or even believe in God to be spiritual . . . Identifying proxies for spirituality is more difficult because of its highly individual and personal nature. Such proxies include the extent of prayer or meditation, importance individuals attach to their spiritual life and personal statements linked to purpose in life and hope for the future.

People can be declared Atheists, yet if they have a positive outlook on life, *i.e.* have decided their life has meaning and purpose, and they hope to make the world a better place, this survey would count them as "religious or spiritual."

By creating such a positive and all-inclusive definition of what constitutes "religious or spiritual," the group that remains, the vehemently "non-religious," becomes an extremely depressed and negative sub-group of the population. In almost every case, this study compares this small, negativistic subgroup to those who attend church weekly or more often, and to whom religious belief is very important. I would submit that few Americans fall into either of these groups.

The ARIS survey tells us that 14% of the adult population is non-religious and at least another 40% don't attend services. You would expect the CASA "non-religious" group to reflect these percentages. However, when the CASA survey compares alcohol use among those who think religion is very important *versus* those who strongly disagree that religion is important, the CASA survey admits that this "non-religious" comparison group represents only 3% of the population. The data are further skewed because the respondents are not asked if they feel religion in general is important or not, but are asked whether they feel their religious views are important. Even totally secular Atheists would be likely to answer that they felt their religious views are important; so, once again, the remaining group who feel strongly that their own religious views are unimportant is a very negativistic subgroup, and are expressing views consistent with the low self-esteem and negative self-image that often accompanies substance abuse. By crafting this subgroup for its comparisons, the CASA survey guarantees that the more positive and inclusive "religious" group will have lower rates of substance abuse.

## Distorting Use and Abuse

The third clue that this report is distorting its findings is found in how they defined the problem. The report is full of statements that seem to reflect serious health problems. For example: "Adults who never attend religious services are almost twice as likely to drink as those who attend religious services weekly or more often," and "91% of women over age 59 who do not identify themselves as religious consume alcohol." Yes, both sentences are about alcohol use, and contain fancy scientific and statistical jargon, but what are they really talking about here? *The definition of alcohol abuse in this case is having had one drink in the past month*. Even your humble author can admit to having had a glass of wine with dinner at least once in the past month. I don't feel this represents a national health crisis worthy of statistical analysis.

A more disturbing statistic is CASA's claim that 24% of those who never attend religious services reported having five or more drinks on one occasion in the past month.

However, in a footnote, the researchers note that many of these problem drinkers could be college students, especially those in fraternities. They also admit that while those who have little or no interest in religion drink alcohol and party more frequently than their religious peers, *the rates of alcoholism do not differ between the groups.*

A final fatal flaw in this report is the fact that no multivariate analysis was done. When assessing the relationship between any two variables, say alcohol consumption and religious belief, you must ascertain if you are actually measuring something other than the target variable. For example, if you are looking at the relationship between church attendance and alcohol consumption, you might find that those who attend church drink less than those who do not. If your goal was to belittle those who are non-believers, you would probably stop right there and publish your report. But if you are interested in a deeper understanding of the issue, you would subject your data to multivariate analysis—and what you might find is that it is not that people who attend church drink less, it is people who are married drink less. The fact that married people tend to be churchgoers is interesting, but it is unrelated to the original research question.

According to the ARIS survey, non-believers have a high rate of being single or unmarried. Analysis might have shown that the seemingly high rate of substance abuse in the CASA non-believer category was actually related to the group's marital status, rather than having anything to do with their lack of religious belief. A similar confounding variable is age. The ARIS survey notes that over one-third of the non-religious are between 18 and 29 years of age. Experimentation with drugs and alcohol tends to occur at this age. Sometimes discovering how much alcohol is the right amount entails repeated episodes of finding out how much is too much. Multivariate analysis might have shown that it was the relative youth of the non-believer group that was the critical variable, not their religious beliefs. But the CASA researchers did no such analysis.

Like every Templeton-funded research project before it, this latest report suffers from researcher bias. From the title "So Help Me God," to the fact that "God" as an actual entity is consistently cited as important to addicts' treatment (rather than a "belief in God") this report exhibits a religious, rather than scientific, slant on the research. It used inflated figures for religious belief, arbitrarily created misleading categories to skew the results, and in many cases exaggerated the severity of the issues being studied. Its conclusions are misleading and biased toward faith-based solutions.

Do some people benefit from religiously based substance abuse programs such as AA [Alcoholic Anonymous] and NA [Narcotics Anonymous]? Of course. They are helpful to many, and should be continued. Should priests, pastors and rabbis learn more about substance abuse and its treatment? Yes. Educating all community leaders on substance abuse issues and treatment is a good idea.

But it is a significant violation of the public trust when a University research center compromises its research in order to appease a funding organization, especially when subsequent public policy decisions could affect peoples' lives. Where the CASA report specifically fails the public is in not demanding more non-religious interventions for drug and alcohol abuse. It is difficult to find rational, non-religious alternatives to AA and NA Rescue Missions are often sponsored by religious organizations. And while I disagree with the CASA report on the extent to which this problem affects the non-believer population, substance abuse is a problem in our society, and with the number of non-religious adults increasing dramatically (more than doubling in the past ten years), it is imperative to find ways to reach this group with education and treatment options which they can accept. The vast majority of adults in this country are not going to be reached by having sermons on substance abuse preached from the pulpit since they are not going to be in church in the first place. In Oregon, Washington, Idaho and Wyoming the non-religious are now the largest denomination in the state. We need to spend more of our resources on secular alternatives to religiously based support and treatment options—not only for addiction, but also for the homeless, the hungry, pregnant teens, and at-risk youth. No one should be forced to pray or profess a belief in a higher power, in order to receive a meal, obtain medical treatment, or join a support group to maintain sobriety. It is simply un-American.

5

VIEWPOINT

*"A National Institutes of Health (NIH) consensus development panel concluded that methadone maintenance is the most effective treatment for opioid addiction."*

# Methadone Maintenance Is an Effective Treatment for Heroin Addiction

Sharon Stancliff

Because heroin addiction is a physiological condition that alters the brain's chemistry, simply abstaining is difficult for heroin addicts, claims Sharon Stancliff in the following viewpoint. An effective alternative to abstinence, she argues, is long-term methadone maintenance. According to the author, methadone, an opiate drug administered to addicts in order to eliminate their craving for heroin, has no significant adverse side effects and can reduce the risk addicts will become infected with the human immunodeficiency virus (HIV) from unclean needles. Stancliff is the medical director of the Harlem East Life Plan Methadone Maintenance Treatment Program in New York City.

As you read, consider the following questions:

1. According to Stancliff, what changes have scientists observed in the brain chemistry of heroin addicts?
2. In the author's view, why do many patients have no access to methadone maintenance treatment?
3. Why do heroin addicts sometimes require a great deal of education about the benefits of methadone treatment, in the author's view?

The development of addiction remains poorly understood, but evidence now supports the proposition that opioid addiction has a physiologic basis influenced by both genetics and the environment. Much addiction research has focused on an apparent "reward pathway" of the mesolimbic system, where opioid-mediated dopamine pathways help to generate the positive-feedback system that supports species-sustaining activities such as eating and procreation. The central role of endogenous opioids to this system suggests the mechanism by which the drive to administer exogenous opioids can become as intense as the drives for food and sex.

Changes that have been observed in association with chronic administration of opioids include physical atrophy of dopamine-producing neurons in the ventral tegmental area.[1] Such changes may account for some of the aversive symptoms of opioid withdrawal. It is theorized that neuroadaptations to chronic drug exposure may also lead to the long-term anhedonia[2] that many opioid users experience and may explain why sustained abstinence is so difficult for many users.

## An Effective Treatment

In 1997, a National Institutes of Health (NIH) consensus development panel concluded that methadone maintenance is the most effective treatment for opioid addiction. Methadone is initiated at 20 to 40 mg and gradually increased until the patient reports clinical comfort and urine screens are free of other opioids. Most studies suggest that patients generally require a methadone dosage of 60 to 120 mg per day to stop using and craving heroin, although some patients respond to lower dosages and others require much higher dosages.

Methadone maintenance is a long-term therapy. The majority of patients who discontinue methadone relapse to heroin use, and no factors reliably predict which opioid-dependent patients may do well without pharmacotherapy. Long-term methadone treatment has no major adverse effects. Constipation and increased sweating are the most common side effects, and they tend to diminish over time. Be-

1. part of the midbrain that releases dopamine, a chemical that stimulates the positive reinforcement or reward center 2. the absence of pleasure or the ability to experience it

cause methadone can be used safely during pregnancy, it is the treatment of choice in opioid-dependent pregnant women. Physicians need to be aware of methadone's interactions with other drugs and should be alert for information about possible interactions as new medications are introduced.

## An Effective Treatment for Heroin Addiction

Methadone is to heroin users what nicotine skin patches are to tobacco smokers. Both deliver "addictive" drugs—albeit drugs that pose virtually no health risks—in a form designed to reduce associated harms to consumers and others. Both have proven effective in reducing more dangerous forms of drug consumption. Both are readily integrated with most living styles. Consumed orally or transdermally, neither provides addicts with much of the effect on mood or cognition that is experienced with injected heroin or smoked cigarettes. But both are potentially available in other forms—injections, nasal sprays, and inhalers—that may be more effective for some users.

Ethan Nadelmann and Jennifer McNeely, *Public Interest*, Spring 1996.

Studies have found that persons on methadone maintenance are three to six times less likely to become infected with the human immunodeficiency virus (HIV), even if they continue to use drugs. One study compared heroin addicts who were receiving methadone maintenance treatment with heroin addicts who were not receiving this treatment. Follow-up of HIV-negative patients over 18 months showed seroconversion rates of 3.5 percent among those who remained on methadone versus 22 percent among those who were not treated with methadone. Heroin addicts who are already infected with HIV also benefit from methadone treatment. One study found that HIV-positive patients with a history of heroin addiction who were receiving methadone maintenance were less likely to be hospitalized than their counterparts who were not taking methadone.

Regulations require frequent attendance at methadone programs, and the number of methadone maintenance spots is highly restricted. Many patients are required to attend six to seven days per week, and only after three years can patients who are considered to be socially rehabilitated decrease their attendance to weekly. Thus, many patients have no access to treatment, and others are deterred by the strict regulations. The NIH Consensus Report stated, "The unnecessary regulations of methadone maintenance therapy and other long-acting opiate agonist[3] treatment programs should be reduced, and coverage for these programs should be a required benefit in public and private insurance programs." In March 2001, the federal regulations were modified, allowing more liberal take-home privileges. Each state has the option of adopting these regulations.

As [L.L.] Krambeer [W. von McKnelly Jr., W.F. Gabrielli, Jr., and E.C. Penick] note in their article on methadone therapy, which appears in [the June 15, 2001], issue of *American Family Physician*, there is a move toward a greater role for office-based prescribing, also termed "office-based opioid therapy." In New York City, a highly successful pilot project has been operating for more than 15 years. A federal waiver allows stable patients to participate in "medical maintenance" through monthly visits to a primary care physician, from whom they receive methadone in addition to regular medical care.

Until office-based prescribing becomes common, primary care physicians can play a supportive role in methadone therapy. Because methadone use is highly stigmatized, opioid addicts may require a great deal of education about the benefits of this treatment. Because misconceptions about methadone are widespread, it may be helpful to include family members in educational efforts. Krambeer and associates suggest that patients become involved in Narcotics Anonymous (NA); however, NA and other similar programs often consider methadone maintenance to be contrary to recovery. In becoming knowledgeable about methadone as a treatment for opioid dependence, the primary care physician can play an important role in bringing this highly effective modality to its full potential.

3. a chemical that combined with a cell receptor can reproduce a physiological reaction typical of a naturally occurring substance

VIEWPOINT 6

*"Methadone is not the answer."*

# Methadone Maintenance Programs Are Abused by Heroin Addicts

I.E. Hawksworth

In the following viewpoint, originally published as a letter addressed to the editor of the *Abbotsford Times*, I.E. Hawksworth, a former addict who works with heroin addicts in prison, argues that methadone is not the answer to the problem of heroin addiction. Many on the methadone program, which administers methadone to addicts in order to eliminate their craving for heroin, continue to use heroin, he claims. He also contends that many addicts abuse the methadone program by doing whatever it takes, including submitting other people's urine for testing, to get enough methadone to induce a high. Rather than support a system that promotes addiction, Hawksworth maintains, money should be spent on programs that build an addict's self-worth.

As you read, consider the following questions:

1. According to Hawksworth, why would addicts only use half the dose of methadone they were given at a clinic?
2. In the author's view, what policies contradict the belief that methadone stops criminals from doing crime?
3. What other program, in addition to methadone, encourages abuse by the addicts who use it, in Hawksworth's opinion?

I used heroin for many years of my life, as well as many other drugs. I knew many people on the methadone program. Whenever I was sick and could not find heroin, I would go down to the methadone clinic and wait until someone came out with a "carry" [take-home supply of methadone] and buy their methadone at $1 per milligram, 50 milligrams for $50.

## A Long List of Abuses

Some friends would get on the program, get their doses raised every week until they were on the maximum dose. Depending on what doctor they were seeing, that maximum could be anywhere from 120 mg to 250 mg.

Once they were at the maximum they would then bring themselves down without letting their doctors know. They would only be using half of what they were given and sell the rest.

When they had to drink the full dose in front of the pharmacist, they would leave the drug store, stick their fingers down their throat and purge so they would not overdose on the high dose.

Most of the people I knew also continued using while on the methadone program, and in order to beat the urine analysis they would have someone urinate in a cup, hand that in, and the test result would be clean. They would actually buy someone else's urine. People in this community are led to believe that methadone stops criminals from doing crime. If that is true, why is it that they have the policy in place, that when someone on the methadone program ends up with such serious charges that they are sentenced to do jail time, they are automatically given their methadone in jail?

From the other side the frustration I felt was working with people in prison applying for parole. A lot of the prisoners were told that they would not receive parole unless they went on the methadone program, even after being drug free. Methadone is the worst drug to detox from. It is so severe that even the licensed detox centres will not even attempt the process without the individual being down to a minimum of 30 mg per day, which is a very low dose. When looking into the institutions that give methadone out to the prisoners, I know people that actually vomit methadone up after drinking it and then someone actually drinking that to reach the high.

### The Madness of Methadone

Addicts like Scott P. contend that what clinics say they do and what is actually carried out by clinic administrators are two different things. "Methadone is probably the worst thing that can be given to somebody because you're saying it's okay to get high."

He claims that during his two years on a methadone program he never stopped using heroin, which was repeatedly revealed in urine test. . . . Most clients, he maintains, abuse the system. "I think the people like me were in the majority. I know people who were on three clinics at once."

Scott P. was eventually detoxed (he claims in four days), went through the prolonged painful withdrawal from methadone—consisting of convulsions, constant vomiting and bone aches—and went back to full-time heroin addiction to a much greater extent. He lived like this until he entered Springfield's Marathon House [in Massachusetts] two years ago, where he completed their one-year program and remains active in a 12-step program.

Keith Sikes, *Valley Advocate*, January 5, 1995.

In my opinion methadone is not the answer. Spend the money on opening a detox facility, . . . as well as more treatment facilities, recovery homes and safe homes for follow-up recovery.

When the needle exchange opened in Vancouver [Canada], I used to go around to the back alleys and pick up the old used needles and bring them in to exchange. After hours I could sell them for $2 a piece and use the money to get another fix. Fifty needles was $100.

When I had drugs and the needle exchange was not open, I used whatever needle was available. It didn't matter to me who used it before me. If I had bleach, I would rinse it; if not, I just cleaned it with water.

When I was looking to score drugs, I knew that a dealer would be not too far away from the exchange. When I was selling drugs, I knew that I could sell near the exchange. It didn't matter to me at the time that the police station was right across the street.

When you are wired out on drugs, your self-esteem is so low that you don't care if you live or die. Let's work on building the self-worth and start saving lives. Treatment works. Let's stick with what works. Drug addicts do recover, when led in the right direction.

7

VIEWPOINT

*"Some problem drinkers can be trained to control their intake."*

# Some Problem Drinkers Can Drink in Moderation

Sally L. Satel

Some problem drinkers are not alcoholics and can learn to control their intake of alcohol, claims Sally L. Satel in the following viewpoint. Proponents of abstinence-only programs refuse to admit that there is a distinction between alcoholics and problem drinkers, and they erroneously claim that all problem drinkers who reject abstinence are simply in denial about their alcoholism; however, research shows that some problem drinkers can in fact drink in moderation, maintains Satel. To force problem drinkers to choose abstinence, she argues, denies many people the treatment they need. Dr. Satel, a psychiatrist who works in a Washington methadone clinic, is author of *PC, M.D.: How Political Correctness Is Corrupting Medicine.*

As you read, consider the following questions:

1. In Satel's view, what two events rekindled the controversy about treatment approaches that allow for some controlled drinking?
2. According to the U.S. government's National Household Survey, what is the working definition of the heavy drinker?
3. In the author's opinion, what are the warning signs that a problem drinker has crossed the line into alcoholism?

Sally L. Satel, "Learning to Say 'I've Had Enough,'" *New York Times*, July 14, 2000. 

Can people who drink too much be taught to control their alcohol consumption? Unthinkable, say mainstream treatment organizations like the Betty Ford Center and Hazelden, which have long insisted on total abstinence.

Now controversy about a treatment approach that allows for some controlled drinking has flared again. [Early in July 2000], in Washington State, . . . a leading proponent of this option, Audrey Kishline, pleaded guilty to killing two people while driving drunk. She is the founder of Moderation Management, set up in 1993 as an alternative to the abstinence-only Alcoholics Anonymous. Then Alex DeLuca, the director of the respected Smithers Addiction Treatment and Research Center in New York City, resigned after failing to persuade his clinic to offer some alternative to total abstinence.

The case of Ms. Kishline may argue strongly against the idea, but some problem drinkers can be trained to control their intake. The difficulty is in figuring out which ones.

The working definition of the heavy drinker, according to the government's National Household Survey, is the consumption of five or more drinks on a single occasion, five or more times within a month. This kind of use, excessive as it is, doesn't make someone an alcoholic. A heavy drinker could be a college student who drinks to the point of getting sick on Saturday nights but keeps up his grades and football practice. Or an employee who drinks a bottle of wine alone at night but never misses a deadline.

Call these people "problem drinkers"—but not alcoholics. It is possible, but far from guaranteed, that they will become full-blown alcoholics, drinking compulsively despite serious consequences like deteriorating job performance and withdrawal symptoms.

The distinction between the problem drinker and the alcoholic, while not razor sharp, exists—but hard-core opponents of the drinking-in-moderation policy don't want to acknowledge it. To them, you are either an alcoholic or not. Virtually no treatment program will accept a patient who rejects abstinence as a goal. And counselors tend to engage in double-think: if the patient says he's an alcoholic, he is; if he refuses to admit he has a problem, he's an alcoholic "in denial" and headed toward the gutter.

But there are data that contradict this view. The "Handbook of Alcoholism Treatment Approaches," a textbook for clinicians, provides evidence that some problem drinkers can successfully control their consumption. Admittedly, this approach only works when the risks are relatively low. If an individual has crossed the line, admittedly fuzzy, into alcoholism, then the risks of allowing someone to have an occasional drink or two become too high.

## The Advantages of Moderation Programs

By the time people reach serious stages of alcohol dependency, changing drinking becomes more difficult, and treatment is usually costly. MM [Moderation Management] believes that this situation needs to be remedied in the interest of public health and human kindness with early intervention and harm reduction programs. Moderation programs are less costly, shorter in duration, less intensive, and have higher success rates than traditional abstinence-only approaches.

Moderation Management, 2001.

The warning signs that the line has been crossed are a history of domestic violence, suicide attempts, missed work, neglected children—an "unmanageable" life in the words of Alcoholics Anonymous. Ms. Kishline must have known that the risks for her were too high because she had quit Moderation Management and joined Alcoholics Anonymous . . . several months before the fatal accident.

Advocates of total abstinence are afraid that some people will use the Moderation Management option as an excuse to drink. But the majority of problem drinkers, let alone alcoholics, have already rejected abstinence, Surveys from Alcoholics Anonymous indicate that its annual dropout rates average around 75 percent.

True, some doctors worry that sober recovering alcoholics will start to think that moderate drinking is O.K. and try it. The task for the therapist is to have the patient think hard about why he wants to sabotage so much. Some drinkers will never lose hope that they can one day enjoy alcohol minus the devastation, but the chances for relapse are reduced if we are adamant that controlled drinking is not an option for everybody.

At the same time, intolerance of moderate drinking also has a price.

"If some problem drinkers are told by treatment professionals that their choice is abstinence or no treatment, they will take nothing, and the opportunity to help is lost," says Jon Morgenstern, director of alcohol treatment research at the Mount Sinai School of Medicine in New York City.

So, the choice is rather stark. Admit that some problem drinkers aren't alcoholics, and help them learn how to drink moderately. Or insist on abstinence for those with even mild drinking problems—and drive millions of people away who need help.

VIEWPOINT 8

*"Moderation management is nothing but alcoholics covering up their problem."*

# Problem Drinkers Cannot Drink in Moderation

Mike Harden

In the following viewpoint Mike Harden maintains that problem drinkers cannot drink in moderation. The author cites, for example, the case of Audrey Kishline, who pled guilty to vehicular homicide in the drunk-driving deaths of a father and daughter. According to the author, Kishline was the leading proponent of Moderation Management, a program developed to help problem drinkers learn to drink in moderation. Kishline herself concluded that the program was simply a way for alcoholics to hide their problem, the author claims. Harden is a *Columbus Dispatch* columnist.

As you read, consider the following questions:

1. What analogy does Tom Pepper use to explain why controlled drinking is impossible for those with alcoholic drinking patterns?
2. According to Harden, what motivated Kishline to seek a less rigid way to address drinking issues?
3. For whom is Kishline's Moderation Management program intended, in Harden's view?

Six years ago, the mere mention of author Audrey Kishline's book *Moderate Drinking* was enough to set the alcohol-treatment community on edge all the way from Manhattan to Maui.

"I met the lady and debated her on television before," said Dr. Tom Pepper, medical director of Talbot Hall, Ohio State University's alcohol and chemical dependency treatment center.

Kishline was a proponent of the notion that problem drinkers could teach themselves to drink socially once again by following her "nine steps toward moderation and balance."

## A Controversial Plan

Her book, subtitled *The Moderation Management Guide for People Who Want to Reduce Their Drinking*, made her a much-sought-after subject for talk shows. *Psychology Today* showcased her controversial plan in a cover article that appeared after publication of *Moderate Drinking*. Kishline argued that self-imposed behavior modification techniques are sufficient to corral unmanaged drinking patterns. She said such techniques spare individuals the ordeal of treatment and lifelong consignment to an abstinence-based recovery program.

"I don't know of any credible organization or publication that recommends controlled drinking for people with alcoholic drinking patterns," Pepper said. "You can make a pickle out of a cucumber, but you can't make a cucumber out of a pickle. Controlled drinking is that attempt to unpickle the cucumber."

Kishline believed otherwise. She suggested that her personal experiences with the 12-step program of Alcoholics Anonymous had left her wanting for a less rigid way to address drinking issues. Promotional copy heralding publication of her book noted, "Based on her own unsatisfactory experience with abstinence-based programs, Kishline offers inspiration and a step-by-step program to help individuals avoid the kind of drinking that detrimentally affects their lives."

Her Web site for Moderation Management explained, "MM is intended for problem drinkers who have experienced mild-to-moderate levels of alcohol-related problems."

Jill Reese, a Talbot Hall staff member, has observed attempts to make social drinkers of people with significant alcohol-related problems. "I've worked in this field for 20 years, and I've never met anybody who could pull it off."

### No Way Back for Alcoholics

*John Schwarzlose, president, Betty Ford Center:* The reason we have movements like Moderation Management is because of the confusion that is overwhelming about alcohol and alcoholism in our society. In reality, there is well-defined criteria that distinguishes between the abuse of alcohol and alcoholism.

Once someone is addicted to alcohol, is an alcoholic, there is a change, an alteration, of the neurochemistry of the brain. And you cannot go back once you've become addicted to that drug.

John Schwarzlose, CNN.com, July 10, 2000.

After basking in the talk-show limelight, Kishline faded from public controversy and—so it seemed—became less a thorn in the side of alcohol-treatment experts.

## A Tragic Awakening

Not many days ago [on June 20, 2000], however, she was the subject of a news release prepared by the National Council on Alcoholism and Drug Dependence. The release was issued on the day Kishline, 43, was scheduled to go to trial on two counts of vehicular manslaughter in Washington state.

According to police reports and news accounts, Kishline on March 25 [2000] was driving her pickup truck in the wrong direction on Washington's I-90. She struck a vehicle driven by Richard Davis of Yakima County.

Davis was killed instantly. His 12-year-old daughter, LaSchell, died before reaching the hospital.

Kishline's blood-alcohol level was measured at 0.26 following the crash, a reading which—in Washington—is more than three times the legal limit. She was hospitalized briefly for chest and facial injuries.

Two months before the fatal crash, Kishline apparently had experienced second thoughts about her personal issues with alcohol. She announced on her Web site that she was stepping down as Moderation Management's spokeswoman and giving up moderation drinking for abstinence.

Kishline wept as she pleaded guilty on Thursday [June 29, 2000] to two counts of vehicular homicide in the deaths of Davis and his daughter. Kishline's lawyer told a Seattle journalist that his client is "extremely remorseful" and that she had carried photographs of the two crash victims with her at an alcohol treatment center.

Sources said Kishline conceded that "moderation management is nothing but alcoholics covering up their problem."

That admission doesn't come as news to Tom Pepper or Jill Reese any more than it does to the National Council on Alcoholism and Drug Dependence.

Would that the price of Kishline's awakening were consequences that only she had to deal with.

# Periodical Bibliography

The following articles have been selected to supplement the diverse views presented in this chapter.


| | |
|---|---|
| David Farabee | "Addicted to Treatment," *Forbes*, December 23, 2002. |
| Steve Friedman | "One More Round: Can an Alcoholic Who's Been Sober for 17 Years Leap Off the Wagon into the Risky Realm of Moderation?" *Men's Health*, May 2003. |
| Keith Humphreys | "Can Addiction-Related Self-Help/Mutual-Aid Groups Lower Demand for Professional Substance Abuse Treatment?" *Social Policy*, Winter 1998. |
| Linda Davis Kyle | "Alternative Treatments for Addictions: Promises and Perils," *Counselor*, August 1999. |
| David Lewis | "Drug-Assisted Addiction Treatment: Stop the Discrimination," *Brown University Digest of Addiction Theory and Application*, December 2000. |
| Charles Marwick | "Treatment Works for Substance Abusers," *JAMA*, October 7, 1998. |
| Sharon O'Hara | "Injecting Hope," *Community Care*, May 2, 2002. |
| Tara Parker-Pope | "Kicking the Habit (Sort of): New Theory Lets Smokers Smoke, Alcoholics Drink," *Wall Street Journal*, July 2, 2002. |
| Stanton Peele | "Drunk with Power: The Case Against Court-Imposed 12-Step Treatments," *Reason*, May 2001. |
| Stanton Peele | "Everything in Moderation: The Debate over Alcohol: Is One Too Many?" *Star Ledger*, August 13, 2000. |
| Richard Sadovsky | "Public Health Issue: Methadone Maintenance Therapy," *American Family Physician*, July 15, 2000. |
| Gerald D. Shulman | "Addiction Treatment 'Success' Is Killing Us," *Behavioral Health Management*, September/October 2002. |
| Harold Sloves | "Drug Treatment for Drug Addiction: Surmounting the Barriers," *Behavioral Health Management*, July 2000. |

| | |
|---|---|
| Abraham J. Twerski | "Comic Relief: Cartoons Can Often Succeed Where Therapists Fail," *Professional Counselor*, April 1998. |
| Lawrence Matthew Ventline | "Faith Communities Have Powerful Influence in Confronting Addictions," *Counselor*, October 2002. |
| Clare Wilson | "Fixed Up: When Nothing Else Works, Heroin Addicts Should Be Prescribed the Drug They Crave," *New Scientist*, March 30, 2002. |

Chapter 4

# How Should the Government Deal with Addiction?

# Chapter Preface

State-sponsored lotteries and the controversy over their impact are nothing new in the United States. In fact, an English lottery supported the first American settlement in Jamestown, Virginia, in 1612. Despite opposition by those colonists who saw gambling as a dangerous activity that encouraged immoral behavior, all thirteen original colonies held lotteries to raise revenue. By 1894, however, gambling was considered a corrupting influence and was banned in most states. The tide turned once again in 1964 when the citizens of New Hampshire, who paid no sales or income tax, approved a state-sponsored lottery to raise funds needed for education. The idea of using lotteries to raise state revenues slowly spread among the states, and by December 2002, thirty-nine states had sponsored lotteries. One of several arguments against these lotteries is that they promote addictive gambling. Those who subscribe to this view argue that all people are vulnerable to compulsive gambling; thus the promotion of state-sponsored lotteries should be regulated. Others believe that the benefits derived from state lotteries outweigh the harm to a minority of gamblers who do so compulsively.

Those who support state-sponsored lotteries argue that compulsive gamblers constitute a minority of those who choose to gamble. A Harvard Medical School study found that only 1.6 percent of gamblers were considered "clinically disordered," which supports this assumption. Moreover, supporters claim, lotteries generate substantial income for the states that sponsor them. In 1999 total U.S. lottery sales totaled $3.7 billion. States use this lottery revenue to benefit their citizens in a variety of ways. In California, lottery funds support education and in Colorado, funds are used to preserve wildlife and open space. Lottery advocates conclude that the benefits to the people of states that vote to accept lotteries outweigh the risk to the few.

Opponents contend that compulsive gambling is a vulnerability common to everyone, and state-sponsored lotteries take advantage of these natural weaknesses. Valerie C. Lorenz, an expert on pathological gambling, believes that the reintroduction of the lottery has made Americans more accepting of gambling, thus facilitating the legalization of other gambling activities and encouraging a supply of future gamblers. The outcomes for compulsive gamblers and their families can be devastating. "They become so out of control," Lorenz maintains. "When someone drinks too much, at some point they pass out. If someone gambles to the point of being out of control, they will try to win it back. They chase their losses, and in a 48-hour period the losses can become huge."

Those hoping to protect these vulnerable citizens argue that state governments must discontinue their predatory advertising practices. According to the authors of *National Issues Forums*, states spend $370 million a year on advertising campaigns to coax the most vulnerable people into buying lottery tickets. In Washington State, the authors reveal for example, lottery ads coincide with the delivery of Social Security and welfare checks. In one poverty-stricken Chicago neighborhood, the authors write, a billboard reads, "This Could Be Your Ticket Out." According to business professor Julian Simon, this behavior is not only reprehensible, but hypocritical:

> Government nowadays is not only willing to profit from people's betting, but also to promote it. This is extraordinarily sinful, in my view. What the government formerly hunted down with the police and courts when done privately, it now not only tolerates but actively engenders—simply because government and officials benefit. Even worse are the diabolical devices appealing to the fantasies of have-nots with the hope of huge hits. If there ever was a get-rich-quick scam, this is it—perpetrated by government. All in the "public interest," of course.

Whether or not state lotteries and the advertising used to promote them encourage addictive gambling is controversial. The authors of the viewpoints in the following chapter examine whether or not the government should intervene to reduce the problem of addiction.

1

VIEWPOINT

*"Congress must act now to clearly and unequivocally ban Internet gambling."*

# Internet Gambling Should Be Banned

Richard Blumenthal

In the following viewpoint Connecticut's attorney general, Richard Blumenthal, claims that Internet gambling interests take advantage of gambling addicts, who find it easier to hide their addiction by using the Internet as opposed to more traditional gambling methods, such as buying lottery tickets. Blumenthal argues that Congress should prohibit all Internet gambling and the use of financial instruments—such as credit and debit cards—when used to finance online gambling. By granting law enforcement broad powers to prosecute those who violate these laws, Blumenthal contends, the government can send a clear message that the United States will not tolerate Internet gambling.

As you read, consider the following questions:

1. In addition to taking advantage of gambling addicts, what are some of the other problems associated with Internet gambling, in Blumenthal's view?
2. In the author's opinion, what would prohibiting the use of financial instruments such as credit and debit cards prevent online gambling businesses from seeking?
3. What legislative proposals does Blumenthal include when he says Internet bans must admit no exceptions?

Richard Blumenthal, testimony before the Senate Committee on Banking, Housing and Urban Affairs, Washington, DC, March 18, 2003.

Use of the Web to place bets on the starting date of a war with Iraq speaks volumes about the sordid, despicable nature of an unregulated, faceless, nameless Internet gambling industry. Internet gambling is growing. Beginning with the first internet gambling website in 1995, the industry has exploded—Bear, Stearns estimates—to more than $8 billion in revenues in 2002.

Now, without delay, clear and specific federal measures are vital to add deterrent strength to current general prohibitions. State and federal law enforcement authorities have the historic opportunity and obligation to work together and halt the ongoing abuse.

## The Threat of Internet Gambling

Internet gambling threatens the integrity of our athletic and sports institutions—from college basketball to professional football. It turns homes into betting parlors and lures bettors with pop-up advertising. If bettors finally stop playing—typically after losing thousands of dollars or maybe even after seeking counseling for gambling addiction—the industry barrages them with personal emails.

A 2002 study by the University of Connecticut found that Internet gamblers are most likely to develop signs of problem gambling. The anonymity of Internet gambling makes it easier for problem gamblers to conceal their activity. These addicted gamblers do not have to explain the hours spent at a casino or OTB [Off Track Betting] parlor or face a store owner every day while purchasing hundreds of dollars in instant lottery tickets.

## A Need for Federal Laws

Congress must act now to clearly and unequivocally ban Internet gambling. There are a number of federal laws—including the Federal Wire Act, 18 USC 1084,—that provide a legal basis for prosecuting Internet gambling web sites located within the United States. In fact, several years ago, a successful prosecution was upheld involving the use of the Internet for sports betting: *U.S. v. Cohen*, 260 F.3d 68 (2nd Cir. 1999). The presence of these laws has been enough to prevent any organization from establishing a gambling web site based in our country. There is still a need for Congress to make the prohibition clear and unassailable.

Congress should enact provisions prohibiting the use of credit cards, debit cards, checks and other financial instruments for the purposes of Internet gambling. As in our battle against money laundering and terrorism, we must take steps to eradicate the financial infrastructure for this illegal activity. If federal law prohibits the use of credit cards and other financial instruments for Internet gambling, financial institutions are in a stronger position to reject any charge from such sources.

### A Threat to the Nation

Problem gambling results in broken families, bankruptcy, crime and higher rates of suicide. Unlike "traditional" gambling, Internet gambling comes right into our homes, and thus carries an even greater ability to hurt a wider segment of the population. . . .

Illegal Internet gambling has reached epidemic proportions. Increasingly, it is putting our youth at greater risk, exacerbating pathological gambling, and opening the door for fraud and money laundering. It is a threat to our nation and must be stopped.

Spencer Bachus, "Don't Bet on It," http://bachus.house.gov, October 1, 2002.

In fact, Citibank, Discover, American Express, PayPal and others have already announced that they will not accept charges from online gambling facilities. A federal law would ensure full industry-wide compliance with this common sense policy. It would also prevent any on-line gambling business from seeking a court order for such payments. Without American dollars flowing through our credit card and debit card facilities, Internet gambling companies will be stunted if not stifled.

## A Broad Application

Any new federal law must include federal and state enforcement provisions as well as criminal and civil sanctions. Because of the international and interstate nature of the Internet, federal criminal and civil enforcement is critical to the success of a law prohibiting Internet gaming and the use of credit and debit cards. States also must have enforcement authority. Many federal consumer protection laws include authorization for state attorneys general to bring civil actions against violators of federal law. This state enforcement role often meaningfully supplements federal enforcement efforts and leads to greater compliance with the law's provisions.

Finally, any ban on Internet gambling and the use of financial instruments in furtherance of such gambling must be clear and broad, admitting no exceptions. I oppose legislative proposals authorizing the use of the Internet for state sanctioned gambling. These exceptions would almost certainly encourage states to use the Internet for state lotteries, OTB and other gaming. These exceptions swallow the rule, leading to the use of credit card and debit cards to fund purchases of state lottery tickets and for other state gambling.

Currently, no state, except for California's Off Track Betting game, uses the Internet for state gaming. Few states allow use of credit and debit cards to pay for state lottery tickets and other games. An exception may create more problems by encouraging people to play on the Internet and use credit or debit cards to fund excessive gambling, creating crushing personal debt and tragedy.

Congress should take the simple, straightforward approach: prohibit all online gambling and prohibit the use of credit and debit cards and other financial instruments for Internet gambling.

VIEWPOINT 2

*"A ban on Internet gambling violates our natural and Constitutional rights."*

# Internet Gambling Should Not Be Banned

Fred E. Foldvary

According to Fred E. Foldvary in the following viewpoint, individuals should be free to choose whether or not they want to gamble on the Internet without interference by the government. Claims that Internet gambling funds terrorism and threatens American consumers—used to garner support for a ban on Internet gambling—are exaggerated, he claims. Moreover, Foldvary argues, to ban Internet gambling would give the government the power to invade people's privacy and interfere with free enterprise. Fred E. Foldvary is senior editor of *Progress Report*, a libertarian publication.

As you read, consider the following questions:

1. In Foldvary's opinion, what would have been the effect of including an antigambling provision in an anti-terrorist bill?
2. What does the wide popularity of gambling indicate, in the author's view?
3. According to Foldvary, on what should an effective Internet gaming policy focus?

Fred E. Foldvary, "Keep Internet Gambling Legal," *Progress Report*, March 24, 2003. 

The gambling industry, or "gaming" as they like to call it, has become a major player in the Internet. While real-estate–based casinos offer a lot of hardware such as slot machines, roulette wheels, and card tables, gambling is essentially a mental construct. The money that is exchanged is basically numbers, the vehicles such as cards and wheels are images that can be electronic, and the communication can now be digital. So gambling, like music and text, is well suited to doing business on the Internet.

Whereas many U.S. State governments ban gambling, other than their own lottery monopolies, the Internet has no real location, so online gambling slips by orthogonal to State and federal laws. Now some State legislators and Representatives in Congress are seeking to prohibit Internet gaming. Congressman James Leach of Iowa has been trying to enact his Unlawful Internet Gambling Funding Prohibition Act. The bill would make it illegal to send funds electronically for illegal online gambling.

## Attempts to Ban Internet Gambling

The September 11 [2001], terrorist attacks have become for some an excuse to increase government power. Leach slipped his bill into an anti-terrorist bill. The excuse is that illegal Internet gambling web sites may have been used for money laundering by organized crime, and also, "Islamic" extremists have used money laundering in connection with their attacks. Leach combined these activities to allege that terrorists use Internet gambling to launder money.

But the FBI as well as the CIA have stated that there is no evidence that Islamic terrorists have had any connection with Internet gaming. The Senate voted for an anti-terrorist bill that did not include any prohibition of online gambling or its use of funds. The inclusion of the anti-gambling provisions would have complicated the bill unnecessarily at a time of crisis.

Representative Frank Wolf of Virginia has also called for bans on Internet gaming. According to I. Nelson Rose's article "Politics and the Law of Gambling" in the Spring 2002 *Gambling Times*, Wolf stated, "Gambling is beginning to destroy and fundamentally corrupt this country." Is he crying wolf?

At the State level, in California, Assemblyman Dario Frommer is pushing AB1229, a bill to ban Internet gambling in the State. If it becomes illegal for any resident in the State to gamble on the Internet, how is this supposed to be enforced? Is the State government to spy and monitor all Internet messages coming into and out of the State? The bill passed the State Assembly 61-2 but has so far not been passed by the California Senate. *Gambling Times* reports that their telephone calls to him have been ignored.

## Spying on Private Computers

Assuming you were gambling on the Internet, how would the government ever know about it? For the government to know about such personal, consensual behavior requires spying. And that's what anti-gambling legislation would require. Banks and Internet Service Providers would be drafted into the role of snooper, sifting all financial transactions. The notion of government mandating surveillance of private computers is repugnant.

Clyde Wayne Crews, "Should Washington Ban Internet Gambling?" CNSNews.com, June 10, 2002.

One wonders what great problem these bills are trying to solve. Gambling does have its problems, including fraud and addiction, but the wide popularity of gambling indicates that most folks do not abhor it as some horrible sin or a great threat to national security.

## The Dangers of Prohibition

A ban on Internet gambling violates our natural and Constitutional rights. If you are not allowed to indulge in gambling even inside your own home, then the government voids your property rights to your home as well as your right to spend your money as you wish. To enforce the law, the State would have to be given the power to intrude into your private conversations and financial dealings. Our rights have already been severely eroded as it is.

If there is a problem with fraud or other consumer protection, that can well be handled without a complete prohibition. And to the extent that online gambling takes away business from landed gaming places, the answer is that competition is not and should not be a tort or crime.

This is not to say that gambling is any wonderful thing. I personally think folks should have more productive and more wholesome ways of spending their time and money. But that's my personal taste. As a libertarian, I don't favor forcing anyone's personal preferences on others.

Life has enough risks and gambles without adding to them. But if folks like the thrill of taking chances with their money, to forcibly prevent them from doing so is an assault on their dignity as adult human beings with minds and values of their own. Whatever troubles exist with gaming, the best policy is to focus directly on the problem and not the medium or an activity that many indulge in without problems.

A ban on Internet gambling is not just a big-government nanny-state meddling with a recreational preference, but also a trade barrier, an intervention on enterprise, an assault on an industry. Shame on those legislatures who ignorantly wield their power against individual choice. They are the problem, not the gamblers.

3

VIEWPOINT

*"Legalizers overstate the social costs of [illegal drug] prohibition, just as they understate the social costs of legalization."*

# Drug Laws Decrease Addiction

John P. Walters

In the following viewpoint John P. Walters argues that the prohibition of illegal drugs protects public health. Walters refutes the claim that prisons are flooded with innocent drug users, maintaining that most of those imprisoned are violent drug offenders. Walters also contests claims that legalization has worked in Europe, pointing out that Dutch decriminalization of marijuana has increased use by 300 percent. According to Walters, drugs, not drug laws, create problems for addicts and society. Walters is director of the National Office of Drug-Control Policy.

As you read, consider the following questions:

1. In Walters's opinion, what is the softest spot in the reasoning of legalizers?
2. In 1998 how much did American drug abuse cost, in the author's view?
3. According to Walters, what percentage of the child welfare caseload involves caregivers who abuse substances?

John P. Walters, "Don't Legalize Drugs," *Wall Street Journal*, July 19, 2002. 

The charge that "nothing works" in the fight against illegal drugs has led some people to grasp at an apparent solution: legalize drugs. They will have taken false heart from news from Britain, . . . where the government acted to downgrade the possession of cannabis to the status of a non-arrestable offense.

According to the logic of the legalizers, it's laws against drug use, not the drugs themselves, that do the greatest harm. The real problem, according to them, is not that the young use drugs, but that drug laws distort supply and demand. Violent cartels arise, consumers overpay for a product of unknown quality, and society suffers when the law restrains those who "harm no one but themselves."

Better, the argument goes, for the government to control the trade in narcotics. That should drive down the prices (heroin would be "no more expensive than lettuce," argues one proponent), eliminate violence, provide tax revenue, reduce prison crowding, and foster supervised injection facilities.

Sounds good. But is it realistic? The softest spot in this line of reasoning is the analogy with alcohol abuse. The argument goes roughly like this: "Alcohol is legal. Alcohol can be abused. Therefore, cocaine should be legal." Their strongest argument, by contrast, is that prohibition produces more costs than benefits, while legalized drugs provide more benefits than costs.

## The Social Costs

But legalizers overstate the social costs of prohibition, just as they understate the social costs of legalization. Take the statistic that more than 1.5 million Americans are arrested every year for drug crimes. Legalizers would have us believe that otherwise innocent people are being sent to prison (displacing "true" criminals) for merely toking up. But only a fraction of these arrestees are ever sentenced to prison. And there should be little question that most of those sentenced have earned their place behind bars.

Some 24% of state prison drug offenders are violent recidivists, while 83% have prior criminal histories. Only 17% are in prison for "first time offenses," while nominal "low-level" offenders are often criminals who plea-bargain to escape more serious charges. The reality is that a high percentage of all criminals, regardless of the offense, use drugs. In New York, 79% of those arrested for any crime tested positive for drugs.

**Americans Spent $63 Billion on Illegal Drugs**

Americans' overall spending on illegal drugs was an estimated $63.2 billion in 1999, a decline of $5.2 billion, or 7.6 percent, since 1997. Spending on cocaine dropped the most—by nearly $5 billion.

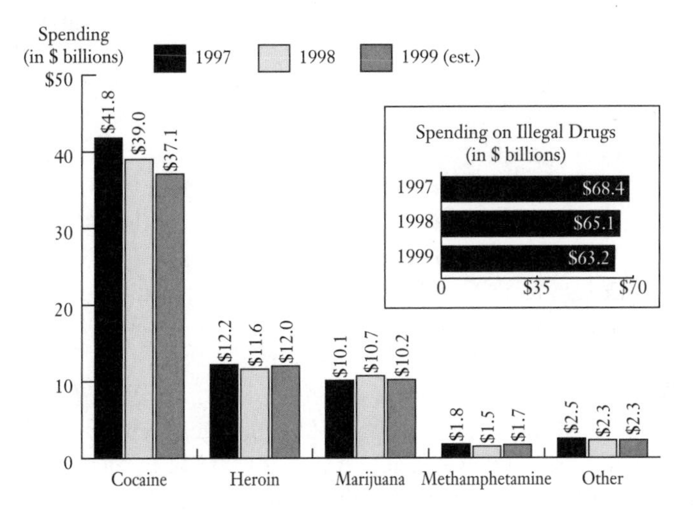


Office of National Drug Control Policy, 1999.

Drug abuse alone cost an estimated $55 billion in 1998 (excluding criminal justice costs), and deaths directly related to drug use have more than doubled since 1980. Would increasing this toll make for a healthier America? Legalization, by removing penalties and reducing price, would increase drug demand. Make something easier and cheaper to obtain, and you increase the number of people who will try it. Legalizers love to point out that the Dutch decriminalized marijuana in 1976, with little initial impact. But as drugs gained social acceptance, use increased consistently and sharply, with a 300% rise in use by 1996 among 18–20 year-olds.

Britain, too, provides an instructive example. When British

physicians were allowed to prescribe heroin to certain addicts, the number skyrocketed. From 68 British addicts in the program in 1960, the problem exploded to an estimated 20,000 heroin users in London alone by 1982.

## Raising Questions

The idea that we can "solve" our complex drug problem by simply legalizing drugs raises more questions than it answers. For instance, what happens to the citizenship of those legally addicted? Will they have their full civil rights, such as voting? Can they be employed as school bus drivers? Nurses? What of a woman, legally addicted to cocaine, who becomes pregnant? Should she be constrained by the very government that provides for her habit?

Won't some addicts seek larger doses than those medically prescribed? Or seek to profit by selling their allotment to others, including minors? And what about those promised tax revenues—how do they materialize? As it is, European drug clinics aren't filled with productive citizens, but rather with demoralized zombies seeking a daily fix. Won't drugs become a disability entitlement?

Will legalization eliminate violence? The *New England Journal of Medicine* reported in 1999 on the risks for women injured in domestic violence. The most striking factor was a partner who used cocaine, which increased risk more than four times. That violence is associated not with drug laws, but with the drug. A 1999 report from the Department of Health and Human Services showed that two million children live with a parent who has a drug problem. Studies indicate that up to 80% of our child welfare caseload involves caregivers who abuse substances. Drug users do not harm only themselves.

Legalizers like to argue that government-supervised production and distribution of addictive drugs will eliminate the dangers attributed to drug prohibition. But when analyzing this "harm reduction" argument, consider the abuse of the opiate OxyContin, which has resulted in numerous deaths, physicians facing criminal charges, and addicts attacking pharmacies. OxyContin is a legally prescribed substance, with appropriate medical uses—that is, it satisfies those conditions legalizers envision for cocaine and heroin. The point is clear: The laws are not the problem.

Former Sen. Daniel Patrick Moynihan observed that drugs place us in a dilemma: "We are required to choose between a crime problem and a public health problem." Legalization is a dangerous mirage. To address a crime problem, we are asked to accept a public health crisis. Yet if we were to surrender, we would surely face both problems—intensified.

4

VIEWPOINT

*"Government regulation can result in harmful unintended consequences to the consumers of potentially addictive substances."*

# Drug Laws Increase Addiction

Adam Gifford

According to Adam Gifford in the following viewpoint, attempts to regulate addictive substances actually exacerbate problems associated with addiction. Gifford claims that regulation cannot alter the biological fact that when addicts are cut off from customary doses of an abused substance, their bodies will force them to find a substitute drug; thus when governments prohibit a drug, addicts find other, sometimes more harmful drugs of unknown quality and concentration. Gifford concludes that regulating addictive substances harms public health rather than improves it. Adam Gifford is a professor of economics at California State University at Northridge.

As you read, consider the following questions:

1. In Gifford's opinion, how is the activation of the reinforcement area of the brain by psychotropic substances different from activation by food?
2. How does the "set-point mechanism" operate in human smokers, in the author's view?
3. According to Gifford, what are some of the policy tools a state can use to regulate the consumption of a psychotropic substance?

Adam Gifford, "The Unintended Consequences of Regulating Addictive Substances," *Cato Journal*, vol. 18, Fall 1999, pp. 301–11. 

Former Food and Drug Commissioner David Kessler, former Surgeon General C. Everett Koop, and a legion of others argue that significant government regulation is needed to protect consumers from nicotine, which has been shown to be addictive, and from smoking, which increases the risk of lung cancer, heart disease, and a host of other health problems. The biology and the economics of addiction, however, suggest that government regulation can result in harmful unintended consequences to the consumers of potentially addictive substances. . . .

## The Motivation-Reinforcement System

Reinforcement of behavior depends on a goal-directed arousal system in the brain that is responsible for learning at a basic level, and this learning involves the creation of memories necessary for the survival of individuals and species. . . .

This motivational system allows creatures from bees to humans to take the measure of their environment in a very specific and sophisticated fashion. When an animal finds and consumes a good, a value—in economic terms, a marginal value—becomes attached to an internal representation of that good. This value is based on the ability of a good to enhance the fitness of an individual—that is, to increase the likelihood that an individual will survive and procreate. Furthermore, associations will be created between the good, its value, and characteristics such as location, complementary goods, and other environmental cues. In this example, the location where the good was found will be stored in memory, subject to recall when the animal seeks the good in the future. The associated goods and cues are used by the animal to predict when and where the primary reinforcing good can be found. Since the probability of finding a good in this same location in the future is uncertain, the motivational system enables the animal to form expectations about the probability of finding it there in the future. Expectations about associated or complementary cues and about the ability of a good to enhance fitness are formed and stored during a learning process, and the values attached to these expectations motivate behavior and generally allow the animal to organize that behavior in an efficient manner. The addictive properties of certain substances are a result of their effects on the motivation-reinforcement system.

## Activating Reinforcement Systems

Addictive substances are defined as those that activate these reinforcing systems. However, the activation of the reinforcement area of the brain by psychotropic substances is generally different from its activation by ordinary reinforcing goods such as food. Food, for example, is only reinforcing when an animal is hungry—only a hungry animal will seek a location where, from past experience, it expects to find food. Addictive substances seem to be much more capable of reinforcement effects, independent of the animal's internal state. Also, the value assigned to an ordinary good reflects its expected ability to enhance the animal's fitness. The values assigned to potentially addictive goods may exceed the value that measures the ability of the good to satisfy these requirements.

The associated or complementary goods and cues by themselves will begin to activate the motivational area of the brain; they become conditioned reinforcers. These associations can be positive, as with the association of a good bottle of wine with a fine meal. The associations can also be adverse, such as when smoking and drinking alcohol become associated, making it difficult to quit one activity without quitting the other. Similarly, the sight of the needle used to inject heroin can become associated by reinforcement with the effects of the drug itself, so that simply seeing a needle can stimulate craving for the drug. And an associated location or social environment, for example, back alley needle sharing, can even become a sought-after aspect of the consumption of heroin.

## The Set-Point Mechanism

In a recent set of experiments [S.H.] Ahmed and [G.F.] Koob (1998) found that rats allowed to self-administer cocaine "regulated their intoxication around some endogenous reference or 'hedonic set point.'" The initial consumption history, in part, determined the level of the set point. Animals given longer initial access periods to the drug escalated use over time and reached a higher set point then those with shorter access. For both low- and high-set-point animals "decreasing the [concentration of each] dose produced an increase in cocaine self-infusions," so that the rats could attain their set-point concentration levels in response to the diminished concentration of each dose. [According to M.L. Pianezza, E.M. Sellers, and R.F. Tyndale,] the same response has been seen in human smokers, where "dependent smokers adjust their smoking to maintain constant blood and brain nicotine concentrations."

Asay. © by *Colorado Springs Gazette Telegraph*. Reproduced by permission of Chuck Asay.

What the set-point response suggests for cigarette regulation is that if regulation mandated lower nicotine levels in cigarettes, individuals would simply adjust their smoking behavior to return their blood and brain nicotine concentrations to their set-point level by increasing the volume and depth of inhalations or the number of cigarettes smoked in a given period of time. The extent to which the smoker uses one or both of these methods to maintain nicotine concentration levels will depend on, among other factors, the economic costs of each method. Both methods will increase the harmful effects of smoking resulting from the absorption of nitrosamines, collectively referred to as tars, and from the absorption of carbon monoxide. Ironically, then, one of the results of reducing the nicotine levels in cigarettes is a potential increase in the injurious effects of smoking caused by tars and other harmful substances. It seems that this effect could, in part, be alleviated by reducing nitrosamine levels. However, it is primarily the tars that give cigarettes their taste and, in dependent smokers, that taste becomes associated with the pleasure of smoking by the reinforcing effects of nicotine. Like needle sharing, the associated taste becomes a feature of smoking sought after for its own sake. Consequently, reduced-tar cigarettes are not popular with smokers. In fact, it is possible that a set point for tar concentrations could result from the association effects of reinforcement. . . .

## The Benefits of Addictive Substances

An often implicit assumption of those who argue in favor of the government regulation of addictive substances is that their consumption yields few or no benefits to the consumer. Though most economists reject this conclusion, I want to mention a few of the known biological benefits derived from consuming various psychotropic substances. One of the effects of many of these substances, including alcohol, barbiturates, heroin, tobacco, and marijuana, is that they reduce anxiety. Further, alcohol reduces inhibitions, and while this effect can sometimes result in trouble, by reducing social anxiety it probably increases the enjoyment of many individuals in certain social settings. Reduced cognitive activity is an effect related to the consumption of various psychotropic substances, and another suggested effect on individuals is short-term "myopia for the future."

All of these effects can be considered beneficial if not carried to the extreme, since they allow the individual a temporary respite from social anxieties and other cares, and they probably explain why most societies past and present have their equivalent of the six pack or glass of wine.

Interestingly, some substances can be said to increase cognitive ability by increasing alertness. Since some minimum level of alertness is necessary for rationality, substances like nicotine, caffeine, and even cocaine taken in small doses yield utility by increasing alertness and thus could be said actually to enhance rational thought. Of course, in larger doses cocaine can make users feel more rational and powerful than they actually are, and this can create problems. One of the interesting aspects of smoking is that there is evidence that it enhances memory formation and may be useful in enhancing the memories of Alzheimer's patients. Smoking may also result in a lower incidence of Parkinson's disease and can relieve some of its symptoms.

## The Effects of Regulatory Policy

When the state makes the decision to regulate the consumption of a psychotropic substance, it has several policy tools it can use. It can use taxes, including taxes set so high that they drive legal provision to zero; it can use outright prohibition; and finally it can turn to a modern innovation—it can allow and encourage the use of the legal system to sue the legal producers of addictive substances out of the market. Increasing the "cost" of the legal consumption and production of potentially addictive substances by the various regulatory means will result in substitutions along several margins. . . .

A few examples will serve to illustrate the perverse effects of the state's attempt to regulate addictive substances. In 1644 the emperor of China banned the smoking of tobacco, which resulted in many Chinese smokers switching to opium. The Harrison Narcotics Act of 1914 made it illegal in the United States to sell or use opium, morphine, or cocaine. As a result many opium addicts switched to the more highly addictive heroin, which was not covered by the act. Crack cocaine, introduced as a cheaper alternative to regular cocaine in the 1980s, partly in response to the increases in street prices brought about by the War on Drugs, "is probably the most effective reinforcer of all available drugs" [says N.R. Carlson]. The search for possible legal substitutes for various psychotropic drugs led to the introduction of so-called designer drugs. In 1992 a contaminated batch of these designer drugs resulted in several individuals developing the symptoms of severe Parkinson's disease—the victims froze up and could not talk or move. And in the second half of the

19th century, high taxes on whisky in the United States led many individuals to substitute opium and hashish. Obviously, attempts to regulate along one margin simply lead to a shift to another, and often the substitute product is a more highly concentrated form than the one it replaced and thus potentially more harmful. Furthermore, a potential effect of the consumption of substances with higher concentration levels of their active ingredient will be a higher set point than would otherwise be the case, and, as a result, regulation may increase the average severity of the addiction problem for users of potentially addictive substances.

In sum, prohibition results in substitutions along several margins, most of which, when coupled with biology effects, work in the opposite direction of the goal of reducing harmful outcomes. Prohibition has adverse effects that complicate the addiction problem. By increasing concentrations, it increases the reinforcing strength of substances and thus is more likely to lead to naïve users quickly becoming addicted and increase the severity of the addiction resulting from increasing the set point. Also, variations in the quality and concentration increase the difficulty of the learning problem faced by naive users—for example, unanticipated variations in concentration can lead to fatal overdoses.

5

VIEWPOINT

*"[Efforts to prevent alcohol-related problems must] include public policy changes that would include . . . regulating the advertising."*

# Regulating Alcohol Advertising Will Reduce Alcohol Abuse

Jean Kilbourne

To prevent the problems associated with alcohol abuse, alcohol advertising must be regulated, argues Jean Kilbourne in the following viewpoint. In order to appeal to their best customers—alcoholics—beverage companies promote alcohol abuse by creating myths that alcohol improves life when in fact alcohol addiction destroys lives, she contends. The alcohol industry, Kilbourne maintains, should not be allowed to make alcohol use appear harmless because such myth-making impedes efforts to educate the public about the real dangers of alcohol abuse. Jean Kilbourne, EdD, is the author of *Can't Buy My Love: How Advertising Changes the Way We Think and Feel* (Simon & Schuster, 2000) and the creator of several award-winning films, including the "Killing Us Softly: Advertising's Image of Women" series.

As you read, consider the following questions:

1. According to Kilbourne, what would happen to the alcohol industry's gross revenue if alcoholics were to stop drinking?
2. Why is the college market particularly important to the alcohol industry, in the author's view?
3. In Kilbourne's opinion, what is at the heart of the alcoholic's dilemma and denial?

Alcohol is the most commonly used drug in the United States. It is also one of the most heavily advertised products in the United States. The alcohol industry generates more than $65 billion a year in revenue and spends more than $3 billion on advertising. The advertising budget for one beer—Budweiser—is more than the entire federal budget for research on alcoholism and alcohol use. Unfortunately, young people and heavy drinkers are the primary targets of the advertisers.

There is no conclusive proof that advertising increases alcohol consumption. The research is clear that, in addition to parents and peers, alcohol advertising and marketing have a significant impact on youth decisions to drink.

The alcohol industry claims that it is not trying to create more or heavier drinkers. It says that it only wants people who already drink to switch to another brand and that they want them to drink the new brand in moderation. But this industry-wide claim does not hold up under scrutiny. An editorial in *Advertising Age* concluded: "A strange world it is, in which people spending millions on advertising must do their best to prove that advertising doesn't do very much!"

About a third of Americans choose not to drink at all, a third drink moderately, and about a third drink regularly. Ten percent of the drinking-age population consumes over 60 percent of the alcohol. This figure corresponds closely to the percentage of alcoholics in society. If alcoholics were to recover (i.e., to stop drinking entirely), the alcohol industry's gross revenues would be cut in half.

## Who Are the Industry's Targets?

Recognizing this important marketing fact, the alcohol industry deliberately devises ads designed to appeal to heavy drinkers. Most advertising is directed toward promoting brand loyalty and increasing usage. Obviously, the heavy users of any product are the best customers. However, when the product is a drug, the heavy user is often an addict. And any time an addict recovers, someone loses money, whether it is the pusher on the corner or the pusher in the boardroom.

If every adult in America drank according to the federal guidelines of what is low-risk drinking (which is no more than two drinks a day for a man and no more than one drink a day for a woman), alcohol industry sales would be cut by 80%. Although the alcohol companies claim they want people to drink "responsibly," the truth is that "responsible" drinking would destroy them.

These statistics show how important the heavy drinker is to the alcohol industry. Modern research techniques allow the producers of print and electronic media to provide advertisers with detailed information about their readers, listeners, and viewers. Target audiences are sold to the alcohol industry on a cost per drinker basis.

One example of how magazines sell target audiences appeared in *Advertising Age*, the major publication of the advertising industry. *Good Housekeeping* advertised itself to the alcohol industry as a good place to reach women drinkers, proclaiming "You'll catch more women with wine than with vinegar. She's a tougher customer than ever. You never needed *Good Housekeeping* more."

## The Youth Market

The young audience is also worth a great deal to the alcohol industry. *Sport* magazine promoted itself to the alcohol industry as a conduit to young drinkers with an ad in *Advertising Age* stating, "What young money spends on drinks is a real eye-opener."

Social learning theory suggests that repeated exposure to modeled behavior can result in behavioral change. The impact of modeling on young people is particularly important given the widespread use of such celebrities as rock stars, television personalities, and athletes in alcohol ads. Alcohol ads feature only very healthy, attractive, and youthful-looking people. Advertising is a powerful educational force in American culture, one that promotes attitudes and values as well as products.

The "Seventh Special Report to the US Congress on Alcohol and Health" found evidence that early positive expectations about alcohol were strong predictors of drinking behavior in adolescence. "Children at highest risk were most likely to have strong expectancies of social enhancement and to believe that alcohol improves cognitive and motor functioning."

## The Ad Campaigns

What more powerful source of these early expectancies is there in a culture than alcohol advertising? Indeed, one of the functions of advertising is to induce these early expectancies. According to an editorial in *Advertising Age*, "Quite clearly, the company that has not bothered to create a favorable attitude toward its product before the potential customer goes shopping hasn't much of a chance of snaring the bulk of potential buyers."

No wonder ads feature characters with special appeal to children. The Spuds MacKenzie [dog] . . . reportedly has been licensed by Anheuser-Busch to the makers of some 200 consumer products, including stuffed animals, dolls, T-shirts, posters, and mugs. In one Christmas ad campaign, Spuds appeared in a Santa Claus suit, promoting 12-packs of Bud Light beer. In another ad he is cavorting with ninjas, drawing on the popularity of the Teenage Mutant Ninja Turtles movie. "Heavy Metal," proclaims one Budweiser ad featuring a six-pack hardly an ad designed for the middle-aged crowd.

Many alcohol ads play on the theme that drinking is the primary ritual into adulthood in our society. Others turn soft drinks into alcoholic drinks, often in a way that scoffs at the idea of a soft drink standing alone (e.g., an ad for a wine cooler says, "Sick of soft drinks? Here's thirst aid.") In 2001 the alcohol industry introduced 130 new spirits, 46 new beers, and 103 new wines. Many of these were sweet products clearly designed to appeal to new drinkers, i.e. young people. These included chocolate and raspberry beer, gelatin shots, hard cider, hard lemonade, liquor popsicles, and drinks with alcohol premixed with milk, cola, jello, and ice cream.

Recent studies have found that alcohol ads are far more likely to appear in youth-oriented magazines and radio programs than in those aimed at adults. As a result, young people see more ads for beer than for jeans, sneakers, or gum. In addition, many films, especially those appealing to young people, include paid placements of cigarettes and alcohol.

The average age at which people begin drinking is 13. The most recent federal survey of school children found that 16.6% of eighth graders reported having been drunk at least once in the past year. By the tenth grade, that number is almost 40%. Children who begin drinking before the age of 15 are four times more likely to develop alcohol dependence than those who wait until the age of 21. Recent evidence indicates that alcohol damages the brains of young people and that the damage may be irreversible.

Youthful drinking is frequently characterized by high-risk heavy drinking, making youngsters a lucrative market for alcohol producers. Underage drinkers account for 12% of all alcohol sales. The most widely used illegal drug in America by far is beer. Junior and senior high school students alone drink over a billion cans of beer a year, spending almost $500 million.

The college market is particularly important to the alcohol industry not only because of the money the students will spend on beer today, but because they may develop drinking habits and brand allegiances for a lifetime. As one marketing executive said, "Let's not forget that getting a freshman to choose a certain brand of beer may mean that he will maintain his brand loyalty for the next 20 to 35 years. If he turns out to be a big drinker, the beer company has bought itself an annuity." This statement undercuts the industry's claim that it does not target advertising campaigns at underage drinkers since today almost every state prohibits the sale of alcohol to people under 21 years old and the vast majority of college freshmen are below that age. . . .

## Creating Myths About Alcohol Use

Advertising does not cause alcoholism. Alcoholism is a complex illness and its etiology is uncertain. But alcohol advertising does create a climate in which abusive attitudes toward alcohol are presented as normal, appropriate, and innocuous. One of the chief symptoms of alcoholism is denial that there is a problem. It is often not only the alcoholic who denies the illness but also his or her family, employer, doctor, etc. Alcohol advertising often encourages denial by creating a world in which myths about alcohol are presented as true and in which signs of trouble are erased or transformed into positive attributes.

One of the primary means of creating this distortion is through advertising. Most advertising is essentially myth-making. Instead of providing information about a product, such as its taste or quality, advertisements create an image of the product, linking the item with a particular lifestyle which may have little or nothing to do with the product itself. According to an article on beer marketing in *Advertising Age*, "Advertising is as important to selling beer as the bottle opener is to drinking it. . . . Beer advertising is mainly an exercise in building images." Another article a few months later on liquor marketing stated that "product image is probably the most important element in selling liquor. The trick for marketers is to project the right message in their advertisements to motivate those motionless consumers to march down to the liquor store or bar and exchange their money for a sip of image."

## The Normalization of Alcohol Use

The AMA [American Medical Association] long has focused on how alcohol advertising affects young people, who, studies show, typically will see 100,000 beer commercials before reaching age 18. These ads are a major contributor to the "normalization" of alcohol use by children and youth—a phenomenon that has reached epidemic proportions. About 11 million Americans younger than 21 drink, and nearly half of them drink to excess. Boys usually try alcohol for the first time at just 11 years old, while the average first-drink age for American girls is 13.

American Medical Association, Amednews.com, February 24, 2003.

The links are generally false and arbitrary but we are so surrounded by them that we come to accept them: the jeans will make you look sexy, the car will give you confidence, the detergent will save your marriage.

Advertising spuriously links alcohol with precisely those attributes and qualities such as happiness, wealth, prestige, sophistication, success, maturity, athletic ability, virility, creativity, sexual satisfaction, and others, that the use of alcohol destroys. For example, alcohol is often linked with romance and sexual fulfillment, yet it is common knowledge that alcohol use can lead to sexual dysfunction. Less well known is the fact that heavy drinkers and alcoholics are seven times more likely than the general population to be separated or divorced.

Image advertising is especially appealing to young people who are more likely than adults to be insecure about the image they are projecting. Sexual and athletic prowess are two of the themes that dominate advertising aimed at young people. A television commercial for Miller beer featured Danny Sullivan, the race car driver, speeding around a track with the Miller logo emblazoned everywhere. The ad implies that Miller beer and fast driving go hand in hand. A study of beer commercials funded by the American Automobile Association found that they often linked beer with images of speed, including speeding cars.

"It separates the exceptional from the merely ordinary." This advertising slogan for Piper champagne illustrates the major premise of the mythology that alcohol is magic. It is a magic potion that can make you successful, sophisticated, and sexy; without it you are dull, mediocre, and ordinary. The people who are not drinking champagne are lifeless replicas of the happy couple who are imbibing. The alcohol has rescued the couple, resurrected them, restored them to life. At the heart of the alcoholic's dilemma and denial is this belief, this certainty, that alcohol is essential for life, that without it he or she will literally die or at least suffer. This ad and many others like it present the nightmare as true, thus affirming and even glorifying one of the symptoms of the illness.

## Distorting the Dangers

Such glorification of the symptoms is common in alcohol advertising. "Your own special island," proclaims an ad for St. Croix rum. Another ad offers Busch beer as "Your mountain hide-a-way." Almost all alcoholics experience intense feelings of isolation, alienation, and loneliness. Most make the tragic mistake of believing that alcohol alleviates these feelings rather than exacerbates them. The two examples above distort reality in much the same way the alcoholic does. Instead of being isolated and alienated, the people in the ad are in their own special places.

The rum ad also seems to be encouraging solitary drinking, a sign of trouble with alcohol. There is one drink on the tray and no room for another. Although it is unusual for solitary drinking to be shown (most alcohol ads feature groups or happy couples), it is not unusual for unhealthful attitudes toward alcohol to be presented as normal and acceptable.

The most obvious example is obsession with alcohol. Alcohol is at the center of the ads just as it is at the center of the alcoholic's life. The ads imply that alcohol is an appropriate adjunct to almost every activity from love-making to white-water canoeing. An ad for Puerto Rican rums says, "You know how to make every day special. You're a white rum drinker." In fact, less than 10 percent of the adult population makes drinking a part of their daily routine.

There is also an emphasis on quantity in the ads. A Johnnie Walker ad features 16 bottles of scotch and the copy, "Bob really knows how to throw a party. He never runs out of Johnnie Walker Red." Light beer has been developed and heavily promoted not for the dieter but for the heavy drinker. The ads imply that because it is less filling, one can drink more of it.

Thus the ads tell the alcoholic and everyone around him that it is all right to consume large quantities of alcohol on a daily basis and to have it be a part of all of one's activities. At the same time, all signs of trouble and any hint of addiction are conspicuously avoided. The daily drinking takes place in glorious and unique settings, such as yachts at sunset, not at the more mundane but realistic kitchen tables in the morning. There is no unpleasant drunkenness, only high spirits. There are never any negative consequences. Of course, one would not expect there to be. The advertisers are selling their product and it is their job to erase any negative aspects as well as to enhance the positive ones. When the product is a drug that is addictive to one out of ten users, however, some consequences go far beyond product sales.

Western culture as a whole, not just the advertising and alcohol industry, tends to glorify alcohol and dismiss the problems associated with it. The "war on drugs," as covered by newspapers and magazines in this country, rarely includes the two major killers, alcohol and nicotine. It is no coincidence that these are two of the most heavily advertised products. The use of all illicit drugs combined accounts for about 14,000 deaths a year. Alcohol is linked with over 100,000 deaths annually. Cigarettes kill a thousand people every day.

A comprehensive public health effort is needed to prevent alcohol-related problems. Such an effort must include education, media campaigns, increased availability of treatment programs and more effective deterrence policies. It must also include public policy changes that would include raising taxes on alcohol, putting clearly legible warning labels on the bottles, and regulating the advertising.

The kind of public education essential to solving our major drug problem is probably not possible until the media no longer depend on the goodwill of the alcohol industry. For this reason alone, we need some controls on alcohol. One doesn't even have to enter into the argument about whether such advertising increases consumption. At the very least, it drastically inhibits honest public discussion of the problem in the media and creates a climate in which alcohol use is seen as entirely benign.

6

VIEWPOINT

*"Restrictions on [alcohol] advertising will not reduce or eliminate misuse."*

# Regulating Alcohol Advertising Will Not Reduce Alcohol Abuse

Advertising Association

In the following viewpoint the Advertising Association, a federation of trade bodies representing advertising and promotional marketing industries in Great Britain, argues that restrictions on alcohol advertising will not reduce alcohol abuse. The association claims that no studies have established a causal connection between alcohol advertising and increased consumption. In fact, the association maintains, countries that have imposed bans have actually seen an increase in teen alcohol consumption. According to the association, alcohol advertising is not designed to increase overall consumption but to encourage consumers to switch brands.

As you read, consider the following questions:

1. In the Advertising Association's view, what are some of the causal factors related to alcohol abuse?
2. What had been happening to alcohol consumption in France before the implementation of the Loi Evin in 1991, according to the author?
3. How are organizations that portray restrictions on advertising as a panacea for the problems associated with alcohol mistaken, in the association's opinion?

Advertising Association, "Alcohol Advertising," www.adassoc.org.uk, December 2000. 

In spite of the proven success of advertising regulation and the responsible attitude of the advertising industry, there is criticism about alcohol advertising, especially in relation to its presumed impact on consumption and abusive consumption. Such criticism is, more often than not, based on a lack of understanding about the role of advertising and confusion between "brand advertising" and "generic advertising".

In general, companies advertise their own brands in order to increase the overall market share of their brands alone and to protect that market share against brand switching by consumers. Brand advertising, of the type seen in the alcoholic drinks market sector, is a tool of competition between brands, not a means to ensure overall increases in total consumption of a product type.

Moreover, there is no relationship between responsible brand advertising in the alcoholic drinks sector and the misuse of the product itself. The causal factors related to alcohol abuse are many. They include social, economic, demographic and perhaps genetic influences upon which brand advertising has little or no impact. Restrictions on advertising will not reduce or eliminate misuse as the experience of countries in which bans have been imposed shows. According to a paper entitled "The Drinking Revolution: Building a Campaign for Safer Drinking", published by Alcohol Concern in 1987: "There is little or no evidence that advertising increases total consumption of alcohol as against increasing a particular product's share of the market."

Per capita consumption of alcohol is lower today in Europe than it has been for most of the past three centuries. In addition, the UK [United Kingdom] actually has lower rates of "officially recorded" consumption than almost any ether country in Western Europe, other than the Scandinavian countries and Iceland, where high taxes and national alcohol policies have led to very high levels of unrecorded consumption. France, where an ad ban has been in place since 1991, continues to have a very high level of alcohol consumption and is in second place in the Western Europe per capita alcohol consumption league.

The US Federal Trade Commission's (FTC) Bureaux of Consumer Protection & Economics undertook a review of the available literature on alcohol advertising and consumption in 1985. This extensive government survey of the literature concerning the general effects of advertising reached conclusions that were further confirmed by similar FTC appraisals directed specifically at the alcoholic drinks sector. The review of evidence concluded that: "The large majority of such studies found little or no effect of advertising on total industry demand."

## Reviewing the Studies

A study by [B.] Chiplin, [B.] Sturgess and [J.H.] Dunning in 1981 also concluded that: "It remains unproven that advertising has led to any marked increase in aggregate demand in general, or in the demand for . . . alcohol . . . It must be recognised that advertising could well be the wrong target in seeking to curtail consumption of products such as . . . alcohol. . . . It does appear that so far there is little convincing support for the argument that changes in total consumption of these products are caused by advertising."

A more recent independent review of the available literature carried out by [J.E.] Calfee and [C.] Scheraga in 1989 concluded that: "Econometric and laboratory research in the US, Canada and the UK have not revealed advertising to have a significant effect on alcohol consumption. The same is true of survey research which confirms the powerful role of social factors such as the attitudes and behaviour of parents and peers."

The authors go on to say that: "The data shows that social forces other than prices and income were bringing about a strong reduction in demand for alcoholic beverages and that advertising did nothing to ward off this trend."

One study, published in 1981, has been quoted by many observers as demonstrating a link between advertising and consumption. This study was [C.] Atkin & [M.] Block: "Content and Effects of Alcohol Advertising", National Technical Information Service (USA) 1981. However, in April 1992, Dr Block submitted evidence to a US Senate Subcommittee which included the following reference to his 1981 study: "This study does not demonstrate that exposure to alcohol advertising causes consumption of alcohol that would not otherwise occur. . . . Most importantly, from my review of the scientific literature, I can find no persuasive evidence that advertising causes non-drinkers to start drinking or that advertising causes drinkers to become abusers . . . if anything the advertisements we studied would reinforce only moderate consumption. . . ."

Although these remarks referred to the findings of Dr Block from US sources, many of the ads described were produced by advertisers and agencies who market and advertise the same or similar brands in Europe and follow similar self-regulatory codes.

## The French Connection

Many organizations calling for tighter restrictions on alcoholic drinks advertising cite the example of France as providing substantiation for their arguments.

Per capita alcohol consumption in France had peaked during the mid 1950s. The decline that followed was halted briefly in the early 1970s only to resume even more strongly in the later part of that decade. It should be noted that in spite of this decline, France continues to have one of the highest rates of alcohol consumption in Europe. At first these reductions in French consumption were driven by the increased availability of clean drinking water. Then changing lifestyles took over. Adults began to drop the habit of drinking liqueurs after dinner. Younger consumers gradually abandoned the traditional French preference for wine with every meal and adopted the more international preference for beer, soft drinks and "lighter products" generally.

In 1991 the French Government implemented the Loi Evin with the explicit purpose of reducing the health costs of alcohol abuse. The law severely restricts alcoholic drinks advertising.

The downward slide in consumption continued through 1994 virtually as it had in the fifteen years before the Loi Evin was enacted, despite the fact that advertising declined precipitously after the law was passed.

In 1997, John E Calfee (Resident Scholar at the American Enterprise Institute for Public Policy Research, Washington DC) revisited the issue of advertising and consumption in his book entitled "Fear of Persuasion: A New Perspective on Advertising and Regulation". Calfee examined the situation within France and concluded that: "Statistical analysis confirmed that advertising has had no discernible effect in increasing French total alcohol consumption above what it would otherwise have been. Of course market shares have shifted (wine's share has fallen dramatically for example) and advertising is presumably a factor in those shifts. But advertising has had no detectable effect in the deeper issue of how much drinking occurs overall."

### Should the Government Restrict Advertising of Alcoholic Beverages?

As a psychiatrist, scientist, and former architect of the national effort to prevent alcohol problems, it was my job to seek out the best science, both biomedical and behavioral. Today, a heated debate swirls around the issue of restricting alcohol advertising on TV. Assorted opponents who argue that advertising contributes to alcohol-related problems—especially among young people—are way off base.

When I consider the pros and cons of alcohol advertising and its alleged effect on problem drinking, I find myself asking the crucial question: Where in the name of science is there proof that alcohol advertising is bad for society? Shouldn't there be some science to say it's so?

[In 1996] I was asked to write a review for the *New England Journal of Medicine* on how advertising affects alcohol use. I did not find *any* studies that credibly connect advertising to increases in alcohol use (or abuse) or to young persons taking up drinking.

Morris E. Chafetz, *Priorities*, 1997.

More recently, a new survey of alcohol consumption in France by the French Health Education Authority has found that French teenagers are actually smoking and drinking more per year since 1991, the year in which the ban on alcohol and tobacco advertising was introduced. Furthermore, since the imposition of the Loi Evin, a competitive new market for low priced high strength own label beer has emerged. This category (now sold in supermarkets and apparently drunk by those "seeking inebriation") increased by no less than 33% between 1991 and 1996. Over the same period, alcohol consumption by teenagers has actually increased—the opposite of what was intended. . . .

## Current Regulation Is Enough

Independent, academic research based on statistical evidence and taking into account prices, incomes, sales and ad-spend illustrates that, at most, advertising has a statistically insignificant effect on consumption. There is little or no overall impact on total category consumption as a result of brand advertising. This would reinforce the argument put forward by the advertising industry that in a mature market such as alcoholic drinks, advertising is targeted to reinforce brand identity, offset brand-switching and maintain market share rather than encourage greater levels of overall consumption across the category.

Evidence from countries in which advertising bans have been imposed show that, contrary to the arguments put forward by some lobbying organizations, these bans have little or no effect on reducing consumption, particularly among target groups such as young people.

The current regulatory structures in the UK are working well and are regularly reviewed to take into account perceived problems and changes in public opinion. Responsible advertising is the norm in the alcoholic drinks sector and compliance with existing regulations is high.

Those organizations that continue to portray restrictions on advertising as a panacea for the problems associated with alcohol misuse, whilst undoubtedly well-intentioned, are mistaken in their belief that restricting legitimate freedom of speech is a credible addition or alternative to a logical anti-misuse strategy.

# Periodical Bibliography

The following articles have been selected to supplement the diverse views presented in this chapter.


| | |
|---|---|
| Richard Amberg | "Addicted to Lotteries," *Insight*, September 20, 1999. |
| Tom Bell | "Internet Gambling: Impossible to Stop, Wrong to Outlaw," *Regulation*, Winter 1998. |
| Joseph A. Califano | "It's All in the Family," *America*, January 15, 2000. |
| Guy Calvert | "Gambling and the Good Society," *World & I*, July 2000. |
| Mary H. Cooper | "Drug Policy Debate," *CQ Researcher*, July 28, 2000. |
| Thomas A. Hemphill | "Harmonizing Alcohol Ads: Another Case for Industry Self-Regulation," *Regulation*, Spring 1998. |
| Robert Higgs | "We're All Sick, and Government Must Heal Us," *Independent Review*, Spring 1999. |
| Michael deCourcy Hinds | "Gambling: Is It a Problem? What Should We Do?" *National Issues Forums*, 1998. |
| James Kilpatrick | "Gambling Is Bad, but Freedom Is Good," *Conservative Chronicle*, January 13, 1999. |
| Joe Loconte | "Killing Them Softly," *Policy Review*, July/August 1998. |
| Davis Masci | "Preventing Teen Drug Use," *CQ Researcher*, March 15, 2002. |
| William D. McColl | "The Politics of Drug Issues," *Counselor*, October 2000. |
| Max Pappas | "Betting on IT," *Foreign Policy*, July/August 2003. |
| Bill Stronach | "Alcohol Advertising Must Be Curtailed to Change Attitudes to Drinking," *Online Opinion*, July 3, 2003. |
| Eric A. Voth | "America's Longest 'War,'" *World & I*, February 2000. |

# For Further Discussion

## Chapter 1

1. Brian McCormick claims that the Internet has made it easier for addicts to act out their compulsive behaviors. Jacob Sullum agrees that the Internet can lead to compulsive behaviors but argues that the Internet is not like a drug; therefore, he asserts, making comparisons between compulsive Internet activity and excessive drug use leads to an exaggeration of the problems associated with Internet use. How does each author view the nature of addiction? How is this reflected in their arguments? Explain, citing from the viewpoints.
2. The National Institute on Drug Abuse argues that nicotine is a highly addictive substance. Dale M. Atrens claims that this assumption—that nicotine is addictive—is widespread, yet it is not supported by research. Does Atrens's analysis of the research convince you that nicotine is not addictive? Why or why not?
3. Tom Grey claims that compulsive gambling is a serious problem. Steve Chapman maintains that opposition to gambling is based on faulty assumptions. What evidence do the authors use to support their views? Based on their use of evidence, whose argument do you find more persuasive and why?

## Chapter 2

1. Alan I. Leshner argues that addiction is a disease that should be treated as a medical problem. Jeffrey A. Schaler claims that addiction is a voluntary behavior that should not be treated like a medical problem. To support his view, Schaler contends that research showing that drug and alcohol use generates electrochemical changes in the brain does not prove that future drug use is therefore involuntary. Is the failure to prove a direct connection between electrochemical changes and future drug use sufficient to convince you that addiction should not be treated as a medical problem? Explain why or why not.
2. Kenneth M. Sunamoto cites research to support his view that marijuana leads to the use of other illicit drugs. Mitch Earleywine also cites evidence to support his argument that marijuana does not lead to the use of other illicit drugs. Which author's use of evidence do you find more persuasive? Explain, citing from the text.
3. Ernest P. Noble argues that understanding the gene that predisposes some people to drug addiction may lead to more effective

addiction treatments. Judy Shepps Battle agrees that genetics play a part in drug addiction, but she claims that environmental factors should be addressed in order to prevent and treat addiction. Which approach do you think would be more effective to treat addiction? Explain, citing from the viewpoints.

**Chapter 3**

1. Krista Conger maintains that twelve-step programs are more likely to lead to abstinence than are cognitive-behavioral programs that teach coping skills. Maia Szalavitz does not dispute that twelve-step programs are effective for some people, but she argues that the treatment community's emphasis on these programs discourages those who might require more medically based treatment options. Based on the evidence these authors provide, do you think health care practitioners should emphasize twelve-step programs at the exclusion of other treatments? Explain, citing from the texts.
2. Do you agree with Kevin Courcey's assessment of the study conducted by the National Center on Addiction and Substance Abuse? Why or why not?
3. Sharon Stancliff argues that methadone is an effective treatment for heroin addiction. I.E. Hawksworth claims that heroin addicts abuse methadone programs and recommends different treatment strategies. Stancliff is a physician and director of a methadone maintenance treatment program while Hawksworth is a former addict. How does knowing the authors' backgrounds affect your evaluation of their arguments?
4. Sally L. Satel and Mike Harden use different terms to define people who have problems with alcohol. How does the way each author describes these people differ? How do the differences reflect their respective stances on the merits of moderation?

**Chapter 4**

1. Richard Blumenthal sees the Internet gambling industry as an unsavory business that takes advantage of vulnerable addicts. Fred E. Foldvary, on the other hand, sees the industry as a traditional business trying to compete for the dollars of willing consumers. How is the way these authors view the Internet gambling industry reflected in their viewpoints?
2. In defense of laws prohibiting use of illegal drugs, John P. Walters argues that drugs, not the laws that prohibit them, hurt addicts, their families, and society. Adam Gifford argues that when governments try to regulate drugs, addicts simply adapt their

behavior to maintain their addiction or shift to other, possibly more dangerous, substances. Based on the evidence these authors provide, do you think prohibition of drugs protects or harms addicts? Explain, citing from the texts.

3. Jean Kilbourne argues that alcohol advertising should be regulated because it misleads alcoholics—the alcohol industry's best customers—into believing that alcohol is a benign substance that makes life better, when in fact, alcohol can be deadly. The Advertising Association argues that no causal connection has been established between increased alcohol consumption and alcohol advertising. Do you agree that in order to justify the regulation of alcohol advertising a causal connection between alcohol ads and increased consumption must be proven? Explain.

# Organizations to Contact

The editors have compiled the following list of organizations concerned with the issues debated in this book. The descriptions are derived from materials provided by the organizations. All have publications or information available for interested readers. The list was compiled on the date of publication of the present volume; names, addresses, phone and fax numbers, and e-mail and Internet addresses may change. Be aware that many organizations take several weeks or longer to respond to inquiries, so allow as much time as possible.

**Addiction Resource Guide**
PO Box 8612, Tarrytown, NY 10591
(914) 725-5151 • fax: (914) 631-8077
e-mail: info@addictionresourceguide.com
website: www.addictionresourceguide.com

The Addiction Resource Guide is a comprehensive online directory of addiction treatment facilities, programs, and resources. The Inpatient Treatment Facility directory provides in-depth profiles of treatment facilities. The resources directory is a comprehensive listing of links for laypeople and professionals.

**Alcoholics Anonymous (AA)**
Grand Central Station, PO Box 459, New York, NY 10163
(212) 870-3400 • fax: (212) 870-3003
website: www.aa.org

Alcoholics Anonymous is a worldwide fellowship of sober alcoholics, whose recovery is based on twelve steps. AA requires no dues or fees and accepts no outside funds. It is self-supporting through voluntary contributions of members and is not affiliated with any other organization. AA's primary purpose is to carry the AA message to the alcoholic. Its publications include the book *Alcoholics Anonymous* (more commonly known as the Big Book) and the pamphlets *A Brief Guide to Alcoholics Anonymous*, *Young People and AA*, and *AA Traditions—How It Developed.*

**American Council on Science and Health (ACSH)**
1995 Broadway, 2nd Fl., New York, NY 10023-5860
(212) 362-7044 • fax: (212) 362-4919
e-mail: acsh@acsh.org • website: www.acsh.org

ACSH is a consumer education group concerned with issues related to food, nutrition, chemicals, pharmaceuticals, lifestyle, the environment, and health. It publishes the quarterly newsletter *Pri-*

*orities* as well as the booklets *The Tobacco Industry's Use of Nicotine as a Drug* and *A Comparison of the Health Effects of Alcohol Consumption and Tobacco Use in America.*

**Canadian Centre on Substance Abuse (CCSA)**
75 Albert St., Suite 300, Ottawa, ON K1P 5E7 Canada
(613) 235-4048 • fax: (613) 235-8101
e-mail: info@ccsa.ca • website: www.ccsa.ca

Established in 1988 by an act of Parliament, the CCSA works to minimize the harm associated with the use of alcohol, tobacco, and other drugs by sponsoring public debates on this issue. It disseminates information on the nature, extent, and consequences of substance abuse and supports organizations involved in substance abuse treatment, prevention, and educational programming. The center publishes the newsletter *Action News* six times a year.

**Canadian Foundation for Drug Policy (CFDP)**
70 MacDonald St., Ottawa, ON K2P 1H6 Canada
(613) 236-1027 • fax: (613) 238-2891
e-mail: eoscapel@fox.nstn.ca • website: www.cfdp.ca

Founded by several of Canada's leading drug policy specialists, the CFDP examines the objectives and consequences of Canada's drug laws and policies. When necessary, the foundation recommends alternatives that it believes would make Canada's drug policies more effective and humane. The CFDP also disseminates educational material.

**Canadian Foundation on Compulsive Gambling (CFCG)**
**Responsible Gambling Council**
505 Consumers Rd., Suite 801, Toronto, ON M2J 4V8 Canada
(416) 499-9800 • 1-888-391-1111 • fax: (416) 499-8260
e-mail: infosource@cfcg.org • website: www.cfcg.org

CFCG conducts research into compulsive gambling and supports public awareness programs designed to prevent gambling-related problems. On its website, the CFCG provides a library of articles and research reports, links to treatment resources, and recent news about gambling issues.

**Drug Enforcement Administration (DEA)**
2401 Jefferson Davis Hwy., Arlington, VA 22301
website: www.usdoj.gov/dea

The DEA is the federal agency charged with enforcing the nation's drug laws. The agency concentrates on stopping the smuggling and distribution of narcotics in the United States and abroad. It publishes the *Drug Enforcement Magazine* three times a year.

**The Lindesmith Center–Drug Policy Foundation (TLC-DPF)**
4455 Connecticut Ave. NW, Suite B-500, Washington, DC 20008-2328
(202) 537-5005 • fax: (202) 537-3007
e-mail: information@drugpolicy.org
website: www.lindesmith.org

The Lindesmith Center–Drug Policy Foundation seeks to educate Americans and others about alternatives to current drug policies on issues including adolescent drug use, policing drug markets, and alternatives to incarceration. TLC-DPF also addresses issues of drug policy reform through a variety of projects, including the International Harm Reduction Development (IHRD), a response to increased drug use and HIV transmissions in eastern Europe. The center also publishes fact sheets on topics such as needle and syringe availability and drug education.

**Moderation Management (MM)**
c/o HRC, 22 W. 27th St., New York, NY 10001
(212) 871-0974 • fax: (212) 213-6582
e-mail: mm@moderation.org • website: www.moderation.org

Moderation Management is a recovery program and national support group for people who have made the decision to reduce their drinking and make other positive lifestyle changes. MM empowers individuals to accept personal responsibility for choosing and maintaining their own recovery path, whether moderation or abstinence. It offers the book *Responsible Drinking, A Moderation Management Approach for Problem Drinkers*, as well as other suggested reading material, including books, pamphlets, and guidelines regarding drinking in moderation.

**Narcotics Anonymous (NA)**
World Services Office, PO Box 9999, Van Nuys, CA 91409
(818) 773-9999 • fax: (818) 700-0700

Narcotics Anonymous, comprising more than eighteen thousand groups worldwide, is an organization of recovering drug addicts who meet regularly to help each other abstain from drugs. It publishes the monthly *NA Way Magazine* and annual conference reports.

**National Center on Addiction and Substance Abuse at Columbia University (CASA)**
633 3rd Ave., 19th Floor, New York, NY 10017-6706
(212) 841-5200
website: www.casacolumbia.org

CASA is a private, nonprofit organization that works to educate the public about the hazards of chemical dependency. The organization supports treatment as the best way to reduce chemical dependency. It produces publications describing the harmful effects of alcohol and drug addiction and effective ways to address the problem of substance abuse. Its reports include the "National Survey of American Attitudes on Substance Abuse," "Research on Drug Courts," and "So Help Me God: Substance Abuse, Religion and Spirituality."

**National Coalition Against Legalized Gambling (NCALG)**
110 Maryland Ave. NE, Room 311, Washington, DC 20002
(800) 664-2680 • (307) 587-8082
e-mail: ncalg@ncalg.org • website: www.ncalg.org

NCALG is an antigambling organization that seeks to educate the public, policy makers, and media about the social and economic costs of gambling. On its website, NCALG provides news of recent legislation and current and archived issues of the NCALG quarterly newsletter.

**National Council on Alcoholism and Drug Dependence (NCADD)**
20 Exchange Pl., Suite 2902, New York, NY 10005
(212) 269-7797 • fax: (212) 269-7510
e-mail: national@ncadd.org • website: www.ncadd.org

NCADD is a volunteer health organization that helps individuals overcome addictions, develops substance abuse prevention and education programs for youth, and advises the federal government on drug and alcohol policies. It operates the Campaign to Prevent Kids from Drinking. Publications include brochures and fact sheets such as "Youth, Alcohol and Other Drugs."

**National Council on Sexual Addiction and Compulsivity (NCSAC)**
PO Box 725544, Atlanta, GA 31139
(770) 541-9912 • (770) 541-1566
e-mail: ncsac@mindspring.com • website: www.ncsac.org

The goal of the NCSAC is to promote acceptance of the diagnosis of sexual addiction and sexual compulsivity. NCSAC provides up-to-date research and information on sexual addiction for addicts and professionals who work with people struggling with sexual addiction and compulsion. Publications include *Sexual Addiction and Compulsivity: The Journal of Treatment and Prevention* and the *NCSAC Newsletter*. Its website provides papers and articles on sexual addiction.

**National Institute on Alcohol Abuse and Alcoholism (NIAAA)**
Willco Building
6000 Executive Blvd., Bethesda, MD 20892-7003
(301) 496-4000
e-mail: niaaaweb-r@exchange.nih.gov
website: www.niaaa.nih.gov

NIAAA supports and conducts biomedical and behavioral research on the causes, consequences, treatment, and prevention of alcoholism and alcohol-related problems. The institute disseminates the findings of this research to the public, researchers, policy makers, and health care providers. The NIAAA publishes pamphlets, reports, the quarterly journal *Alcohol Research & Health* (formerly *Alcohol Health & Research World)*, and *Alcohol Alert* bulletins.

**National Institute on Drug Abuse (NIDA)**
U.S. Department of Health and Human Services
6001 Executive Blvd., Room 5213, Bethesda, MD 20892
(301) 443-1124
e-mail: information@lists.nida.nih.gov
website: www.nida.nih.gov

NIDA supports and conducts research on drug abuse—including the yearly Monitoring the Future survey—in order to improve addiction prevention, treatment, and policy efforts. It publishes the bimonthly *NIDA Notes* newsletter and a catalog of research reports and public education materials.

**Office of National Drug Control Policy (ONDCP)**
Drug Policy Information Clearinghouse
PO Box 6000, Rockville, MD 20849-6000
(800) 666-3332 • fax: (301) 519-5212
e-mail: ondcp@ncjrs.org
website: www.whitehousedrugpolicy.gov

The Office of National Drug Control Policy formulates the government's national drug strategy and the president's antidrug policy and coordinates the federal agencies responsible for stopping drug trafficking. Its reports include "National Drug Control Strategy, 2002" and "Get It Straight! The Facts About Drugs."

**Rational Recovery**
Box 800, Lotus, CA 95651
(530) 621-2667
e-mail: icc@rational.org • website: www.rational.org/recovery

Rational Recovery is a national self-help organization that offers a cognitive rather than spiritual approach to recovery from alcoholism. Its philosophy holds that alcoholics can attain sobriety without depending on other people or a "higher power." It publishes materials including the bimonthly *Journal of Rational Recovery* and the book *Rational Recovery: The New Cure for Substance Addiction.*

**Secular Organization for Sobriety (SOS)**
SOS National Clearinghouse, The Center for Inquiry—West
4773 Hollywood Blvd., Hollywood, CA 90026
(323) 666-4295 • fax: (323) 666-4271
e-mail: sos@cfiwest.org
website: www.secularhumanism.org/sos

SOS is an alternative recovery method for alcoholics or drug addicts who are uncomfortable with the spiritual content of twelve-step programs. SOS takes a secular approach to recovery and maintains that sobriety is a separate issue from religion or spirituality. Its publications include the books *How to Stay Sober: Recovery Without Religion* and *Unhooked: Staying Sober and Drug Free* as well as the *SOS International Newsletter.*

**Stanton Peele Addiction Website**
website: www.peele.net

Stanton Peele has been investigating and writing about addiction since 1969. His approach to addiction revolutionized thinking on the subject by suggesting that addiction is not limited to narcotics and that addiction is a pattern of behavior that is best understood by examining an individual's relationship with his or her world. Peele is also a well-known opponent of the American medical model of treating alcohol and drug abuse. Peele has written numerous books and articles in support of his position, many of which are available on his website, including *The Nature of Addiction* and *The Politics and Persecution of Controlled Drinking and Drug Use.*

# Bibliography of Books


Caroline Jean Acker — *Creating the American Junkie: Addiction Research in the Classic Era of Narcotic Control.* Baltimore: Johns Hopkins University Press, 2002.

Rachel Green Baldino — *Welcome to Methadonia: A Social Worker's Candid Account of Life in a Methadone Clinic.* Harrisburg, PA: White Hat Communications, 2001.

Terry Burnham — *Mean Genes: From Sex to Money to Food, Taming Our Primal Instincts.* Cambridge, MA: Perseus, 2000.

Patrick Carnes — *In the Shadows of the Net: Breaking Free of Compulsive Online Sexual Behavior.* Center City, MN: Hazeldon, 2001.

Rosalyn Carson-Dewitt and Joseph W. Weiss, eds. — *Drugs, Alcohol, and Tobacco: Learning About Addictive Behavior.* New York: MacMillan Reference Books, 2003.

Rod Colvin — *Prescription Drug Addiction: The Hidden Epidemic.* Omaha, NE: Addicus Books, 2001.

Al Cooper — *Cybersex: The Dark Side of the Force.* Philadelphia: Brunner-Routledge, 2000.

Carlo C. DiClemente — *Addiction and Change: How Addictions Develop and Addicted People Recover.* New York: Guilford Press, 2003.

Robert L. Dupont and Betty Ford — *The Selfish Brain: Learning from Addiction.* Washington, DC: Hazeldon Information Education, 2000.

Jon Elster and Ole-Jørgen Skog, eds. — *Getting Hooked: Rationality and Addiction.* New York: Cambridge University Press, 1999.

Stanley D. Glick and Isabelle M. Maisonneuve, eds. — *New Medications for Drug Abuse.* New York: New York Academy of Sciences, 2000.

Marcus Grant and Jorge Litvak, eds. — *Drinking Patterns and Their Consequences.* Washington, DC: Taylor & Francis, 1998.

Jonathan Gruber — *Is Addiction "Rational"?: Theory and Evidence.* Cambridge, MA: National Bureau of Economic Research, 2000.

Glen Hanson, Peter Venturelli, and Annette E. Fleckenstein, eds. — *Drugs and Society.* Boston: Jones and Bartlett, 2001.

Philip B. Heymann and William N. Brownsberger, eds. — *Drug Addiction and Drug Policy: The Struggle to Control Dependence.* Cambridge, MA: Harvard University Press, 2001.

James A. Inciardi and Lana D. Harrison, eds. *Harm Reduction: National and International Perspectives*. Thousand Oaks, CA: Sage, 2000.

Denise B. Kandel, ed. *Stages and Pathways of Drug Involvement: Examining the Gateway Hypothesis*. New York: Cambridge University Press, 2002.

Little Hoover Commission *For Our Health and Safety: Joining Forces to Defeat Addiction*. Sacramento: Little Hoover Commissions, 2003.

David F. Musto *The American Disease: Origins of Narcotic Control*. New York: Oxford University Press, 1999.

Stanton Peele *The Diseasing of America: How We Allowed Recovery Zealots and the Treatment Industry to Convince Us We Are Out of Control*. San Francisco: Jossey-Bass, 1999.

Stanton Peele *The Meaning of Addiction: An Unconventional View*. San Francisco: Jossey-Bass, 1998.

Jeffrey A. Schaler *Addiction Is a Choice*. Chicago: Open Court, 2000.

Jennifer P. Schneider *Cybersex Exposed: Simple Fantasy or Obsession?* Center City, MN: Hazeldon, 2001.

Paul Slovic, ed. *Smoking: Risk, Perception, and Policy*. Thousand Oaks, CA: Sage, 2001.

Jacob Sullum *For Your Own Good: The Anti-Smoking Crusade and the Tyranny of Public Health*. New York: Free Press, 1998.

Glenn D. Walters *Addiction Concept: Working Hypothesis or Self-Fulfilling Prophecy?* New York: Pearson Higher Education, 1998.

Martin Weegmann and Robert Cohen, eds. *The Psychodynamics of Addiction*. London: Whurr, 2002.

Patsy Westcott *Why Do People Take Drugs?* Austin: Raintree Steck-Vaughn, 2001.

William L. White *Slaying the Dragon: The History of Addiction Treatment and Recovery in America*. Bloomington, IL: Chestnut Health Systems, 1998.

Kimberly S. Young *Caught in the Net: How to Recognize the Signs of Internet Addiction—and a Winning Strategy for Recovery*. New York: J. Wiley, 1998.

Kimberly S. Young *Tangled in the Web: Understanding Cybersex from Fantasy to Addiction*. Bloomington, IN: 1st Books, 2001.

# Index

NORTHEASTERN SICILY
*Pages 158–191*

Aeolian Islands

Messina

NORTHEASTERN SICILY

CATANIA

Enna

ERN

Caltanissetta

SOUTHERN SICILY

Syracuse

RAGUSA

SOUTHERN SICILY
*Pages 132–157*

0 kilometres 250

0 miles 20

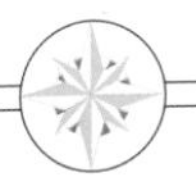

EYEWITNESS TRAVEL

# SICILY

EYEWITNESS TRAVEL

# SICILY

LONDON, NEW YORK,
MELBOURNE, MUNICH AND DELHI
www.dk.com

Produced by Fabio Ratti
Editoria Libraria e Multimediale, Milan, Italy
PROJECT EDITOR Giovanni Francesio
EDITOR Elena Marzorati
SECRETARY Emanuela Damiani
DESIGNERS STUDIO Matra–Silvia Tomasone, Lucia Tirabassi
MAPS Oriana Bianchetti

Dorling Kindersley Ltd
PROJECT EDITOR Fiona Wild
DTP DESIGNERS Maite Lantaron, Lee Redmond
PRODUCTION David Proffit
MANAGING EDITORS Fay Franklin, Louise Bostock Lang
MANAGING ART EDITOR Annette Jacobs
EDITORIAL DIRECTOR Vivien Crump
ART DIRECTOR Gillian Allan
PUBLISHER Douglas Amrine

CONTRIBUTORS
Fabrizio Ardito, Cristina Gambaro
Additional tourist information by Marco Scapagnini

ILLUSTRATORS
Giorgia Boli, Silvana Ghioni, Alberto Ipsilanti, Nadia Viganò

ENGLISH TRANSLATION Richard Pierce

Reproduced by Colourscan (Singapore)
Printed and bound by L. Rex Printing Company Limited, China

First American Edition, 2000
09 10 9 8 7 6 5 4 3 2

Published in the United States by DK Publishing,
375 Hudson Street, New York, New York 10014

**Reprinted with revisions 2001, 2003, 2005, 2007, 2009**



Published in Great Britain by Dorling Kindersley Limited.

A CATALOGING IN PUBLICATION RECORD IS AVAILABLE FROM THE LIBRARY OF CONGRESS.

ISSN 1542-1554

ISBN 978-0-75666-121-2

THROUGHOUT THIS BOOK, FLOORS ARE REFERRED TO IN ACCORDANCE WITH EUROPEAN USAGE, I.E., THE "FIRST FLOOR" IS THE FLOOR ABOVE GROUND LEVEL.

*Front cover main image: View of Castello di Falconara, Butera*

**We're trying to be cleaner and greener:**

- we recycle waste and switch things off
- we use paper from responsibly managed forests whenever possible
- we ask our printers to actively reduce water and energy consumption
- we check out our suppliers' working conditions – they never use child labour

**Find out more about our values and best practices at www.dk.com**

**The information in this DK Eyewitness Travel Guide is checked regularly.**

Every effort has been made to ensure that this book is as up-to-date as possible at the time of going to press. Some details, however, such as telephone numbers, opening hours, prices, gallery hanging arrangements and travel information are liable to change. The Publishers cannot accept responsibility for any consequences arising from the use of this book, nor for any material on third party websites, and cannot guarantee that any website address in this book will be a suitable source of travel information.
We value the views and suggestions of our readers very highly. Please write to: Publisher, DK Eyewitness Travel Guides, Dorling Kindersley, 80 Strand, London WC2R 0RL, Great Britain.

◁ **The Temple of Hera in the Valle dei Templi at Agrigento**

# CONTENTS

**Female bust sculpted in the 5th century BC *(see pp30–31)***

**Backcloth, Museo delle Marionette in Palermo *(see pp50–51)***

Castellammare del Golfo *(see p96)*, one of many fishing villages on the Sicilian coast



## SICILY AREA BY AREA

Ancient theatre mask, Museo Eoliano *(see p190)*



## TRAVELLERS' NEEDS

A cheese vendor at Catania's open-air market *(see pp222–3)*



## SURVIVAL GUIDE



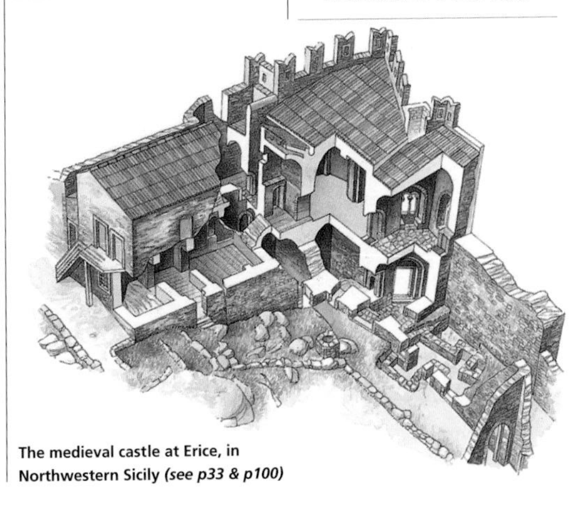

The medieval castle at Erice, in Northwestern Sicily *(see p33 & p100)*

# HOW TO USE THIS GUIDE

This guide will help you to get the most out of your visit to Sicily. It provides detailed practical information and expert recommendations. *Introducing Sicily* maps the island and sets Sicily in its historic, artistic, geographical and cultural context. *Palermo Area by Area* and the four regional sections describe the most important sights, with maps, floor plans, photographs and detailed illustrations. Restaurant and hotel recommendations are described in *Travellers' Needs* and the *Survival Guide* has tips on everything from transport to hiring a surfboard.

## PALERMO AREA BY AREA

The historic centre of the city has been divided into two areas, East and West, each with its own chapter. *Further Afield* covers peripheral sights. All sights are numbered and plotted on the *Area Map*. The detailed information for each sight is easy to locate as it follows the numerical order on the map.

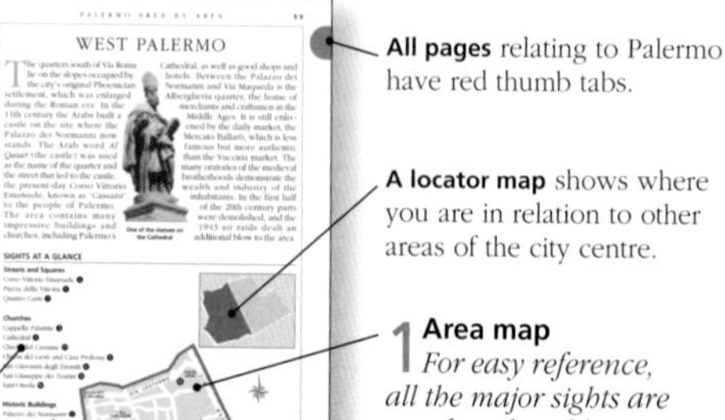

**All pages** relating to Palermo have red thumb tabs.

**A locator map** shows where you are in relation to other areas of the city centre.

**1 Area map**
*For easy reference, all the major sights are numbered and located on this map.*

**Sights at a Glance** lists the chapter's sights by category: Churches and Cathedrals, Historic Buildings, Museums, Streets and Squares, Parks and Gardens.

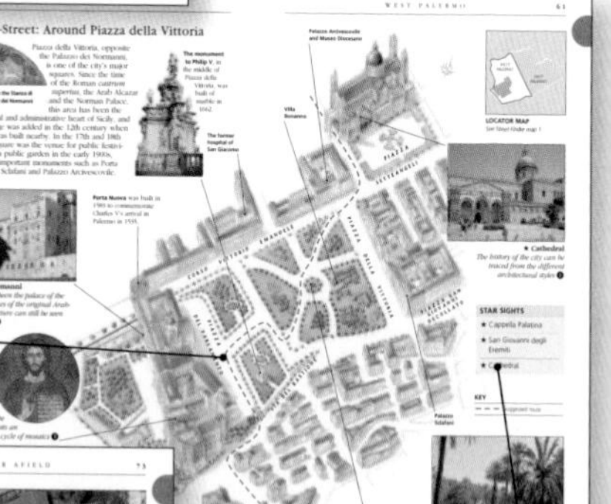

**2 Street-by-Street Map**
*This gives a bird's-eye view of the key areas in each chapter.*

**A suggested route** for a walk is shown in red.

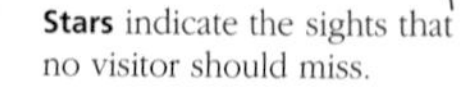

**Stars** indicate the sights that no visitor should miss.

**3 Detailed Information**
*The sights in Palermo are described individually. Addresse[s], telephone numbers, opening hou[rs] and admission charges are also provided. Map references refer t[o] the* Street Finder *on pp78-9.*

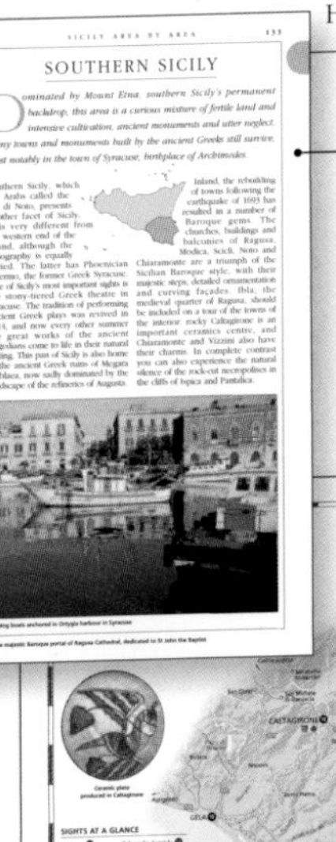

## 1 Introduction

*The landscape, history and character of each region is described here, showing how the area has developed over the centuries and what it has to offer to the visitor today.*

## SICILY AREA BY AREA

Apart from Palermo, Sicily has been divided into four regions, each with a separate chapter. The most interesting towns, villages and sights to visit are numbered on a *Regional Map*.

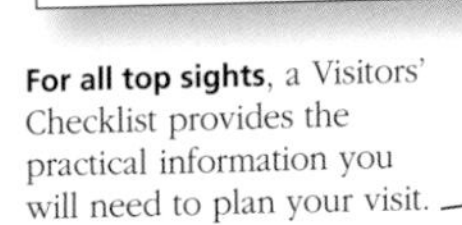

**Each area** can be identified by its own colour coding.

## 2 Regional Map

*This shows the road network and gives an illustrated overview of the whole region. All the interesting places to visit are numbered and there are also useful tips on getting to, and around, the region by car and by public transport.*

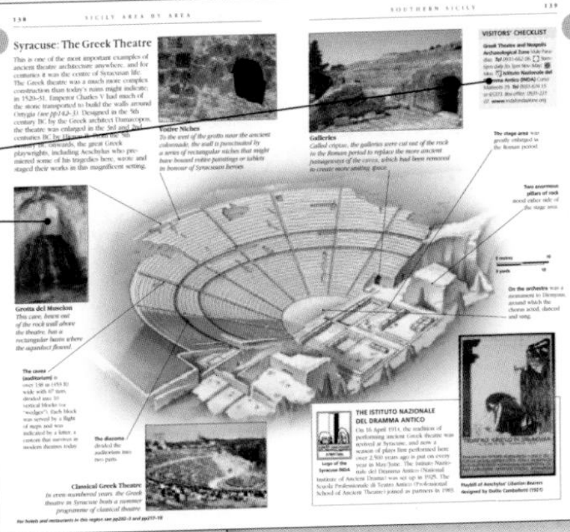

**For all top sights**, a Visitors' Checklist provides the practical information you will need to plan your visit.

## 3 Sicily's top sights

*These are given two or more full pages. Historic buildings are dissected to reveal their interiors. The most interesting towns or city centres are shown in a bird's-eye view, with sights picked out and described.*

## 4 Places of Interest

*All the important towns and other places to visit are described individually. They are listed in order, following the numbering on the* Regional Map. *Within each town or city, there is detailed information on important buildings and other sights. The* Road Map *references refer to the inside back cover.*

# INTRODUCING SICILY

# DISCOVERING SICILY

Off the toe of the Italian peninsula in the far south, the sun-baked island of Sicily has wonderful surprises in store for visitors. Active volcanoes light up the night sky, and windswept uplands punctuated by riots of wildflowers contrast with picture-postcard Mediterranean fishing villages. Imposing ancient temples and fortresses left by waves of occupiers vie for attention with glorious beaches on distant islands. Then there are the chaotic cities with their colourful markets, the museums crammed with priceless antiquities, and the joyous festivals that punctuate the Sicilian calendar year, creating memorable occasions for outsiders. These two pages detail the highlights of each region.

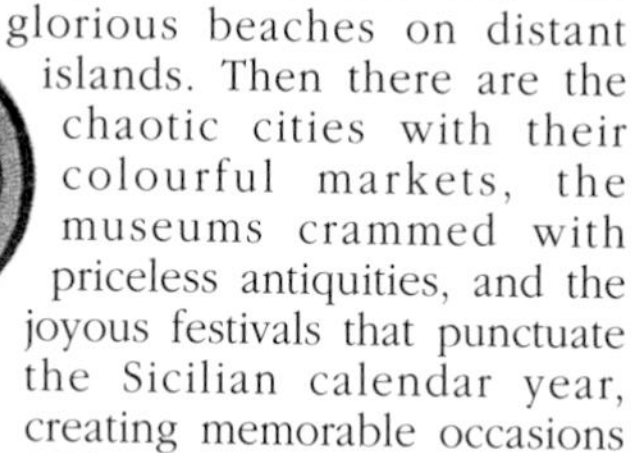

Preserved Roman mosaic

Olive stall at Vucciria market, Palermo

## PALERMO

- **Piazza della Vittoria area**
- **Colourful markets**
- **Monreale cathedral**
- **Cripta dei Cappuccini**

The island's capital city is renowned for its fascinating blend of Arabic, Norman and Baroque architecture, as well as its unbelievably chaotic traffic. Visits are best on foot or by local transport. Off **Piazza della Vittoria** *(see pp60–1)* with its relaxing gardens is the 12th-century **Cappella Palatina** *(see pp62–3)*, an inspiring place to start before moving on to the lively **Vucciria** *(see p56)* and **Ballarò** *(see p69)* outdoor markets, feasts for all the senses. Well-stocked art galleries alternate with shady parks such as the wonderful **Orto Botanico** *(see p75)*, where beautiful tropical plants are clearly at home in the warm Sicilian climate. One unmissable highlight a short distance out of town is the cathedral at **Monreale** *(see pp76–7)*, a unique masterpiece of Byzantine art with glittering mosaics and a cool Moorish-style courtyard. A rather different style of art, that of embalming, is on display at the **Cripta dei Cappuccini** *(see p74)*. Intriguing, but definitely not for the faint-hearted, the catacombs host an army of the deceased, many in skeletal shape.

## NORTHWESTERN SICILY

- **Archaeological site of Selinunte**
- **Stunning Egadi islands**
- **Hilltop town of Erice**
- **Medieval Cefalù**

Arguably Sicily's top archaeological site, the ancient port of **Selinunte** *(see pp104–7)* and its cluster of Hellenic temples occupies a beautiful seafront position on the westernmost coast. The nearby port of **Trapani** *(see p102)* is the gateway to the divine **Egadi islands** *(see p108)* where islanders transport visitors by boat around the idyllic bays and isolated beaches.

Back on the mainland, the hilltop town of **Erice** *(see pp100–1)* boasts pretty paved streets, exquisite almond pastries and superb views. Nature lovers will appreciate the **Riserva dello Zingaro** *(see p97)*, a pristine stretch of mountainous coastline broken up by inviting coves and home to typical Mediterranean flora.

A hydrofoil trip north from Palermo takes you to the rocky volcanic island of **Ustica** *(see p109)*, its turquoise waters and underwater caves a haven for scuba divers. No visitor should miss the atmospheric medieval town of **Cefalù** *(see pp88–91)*, a warren of narrow streets and a landmark cathedral in the shadow of a limestone promontory.

A view of the dramatic coast from Riserva dello Zingaro

The rocky coastline of Lampedusa, Pelagie islands

## SOUTHWESTERN SICILY

- **Roman mosaics at Piazza Armerina**
- **Agrigento's Valle dei Templi**
- **Volcanic Pelagie islands**

Any visit to this wild southwestern region of Sicily should begin with a visit to the ruined Roman villa at **Piazza Armerina** *(see pp129–31)*, which contains simply exquisite, beautifully preserved mosaics depicting scenes of hunting and the life of the well-to-do.

The Greek temple complex at **Agrigento** *(see pp114–15)* is also a highlight, though its proximity to busy roads detracts somewhat from its appeal. By contrast, the atmospheric archaeological site of **Morgantina** *(see p128)* is set in lovely rolling countryside, away from modern civilization. The town of **Sciacca** *(see pp118–19)* is worth a visit for its spa facilities and vast views from Monte San Calogero. To really get away from it all, take a ferry to the isolated, volcanically formed islands of **Pantelleria** *(see p124)* and **Lampedusa** *(see p125)*.

## SOUTHERN SICILY

- **Baroque towns of Noto and Ragusa**
- **Majolica tiles at Caltagirone**
- **Greek theatre at Syracuse**

The ornate style of Sicilian Baroque architecture can be admired in a fascinating series of towns across the south of Sicily. Completely rebuilt in a new location after a devastating earthquake in the 1600s, **Noto** *(see pp144–7)* with its stone churches makes for a memorable visit, as does **Ragusa** *(see pp150–51)*.

Marvellous ceramics from a tradition that dates back to Arab times are the main draw in the hilly town of **Caltagirone** *(see pp154–5)*, which boasts a unique staircase studded with colourful majolica tiles. The lovely seafront city of **Syracruse** *(see pp136–43)* has many sightseeing attractions, not least its position on a high, rocky peninsula that juts out into the sea, and the intriguing maze of streets that make up the Ortygia district. Its archaeological site is also rewarding, with a Greek theatre carved into the hillside that continues to host live theatrical performances during the summer.

Adventurous visitors should make a point of visiting the Monti Iblei hinterland and the steep gorges at **Pantalica** *(see p157)*, accessible on foot or horseback.

The delightful town of Ragusa, famous for its Baroque architecture

## NORTHEASTERN SICILY

- **Awesome Mount Etna**
- **Charming Taormina**
- **The Aeolian Islands**

This slice of Sicily is dominated by volcanoes of all shapes and sizes. **Mount Etna** *(see pp170–3)* towers to incredible heights and is visible from much of Sicily, often providing live firework shows from its summit craters.

Ruins of the Greek Theatre at Taormina, with imposing Mount Etna in the background

Accessible all year round thanks to good roads and a high-altitude cable-car, it is always popular. At its feet is the bustling if rather run-down city of **Catania** *(see pp162–5)*, worth a visit for its lively fish market and Baroque cathedral.

No-one should miss the pretty town of **Taormina** *(see pp176–80)*, which spreads across steep flowered hillsides high above the sparkling Ionian coast. The town boasts a spectacular outdoor Greek theatre and perfect views of Etna.

The far-flung **Aeolian Islands** *(see p188–91)* offer countless delights to the hordes of visitors who arrive each summer. The largest island in this marvellous windswept archipelago is Lipari, which makes a good base for exploring its more remote neighbours. Stromboli, with its on-going minor eruptions, can be admired from a boat and the ruins of a prehistoric village can be found on Filicudi.

# Putting Sicily on the Map

Sicily is the largest region in Italy (25,708 sq km, 9,923 sq miles) and the third most highly populated with more than five million inhabitants. The terrain is mostly hilly – the plains and plateaus make up only 14 per cent of the total land area. The most interesting features of the mountain zones are the volcanoes, especially Mount Etna, which is the largest active volcano in Europe. The longest river is the Salso, which is 144 km (89 miles) long. Besides Sicily itself, the Region of Sicily includes other smaller islands: the Aeolian Islands, Ustica, the Egadi Islands, Pantelleria and the Pelagie Islands. Palermo is the Sicilian regional capital, and with its population of almost 650,000 is the fifth largest city in Italy after Rome, Milan, Naples and Turin.

Palermo, Italy's fifth largest city

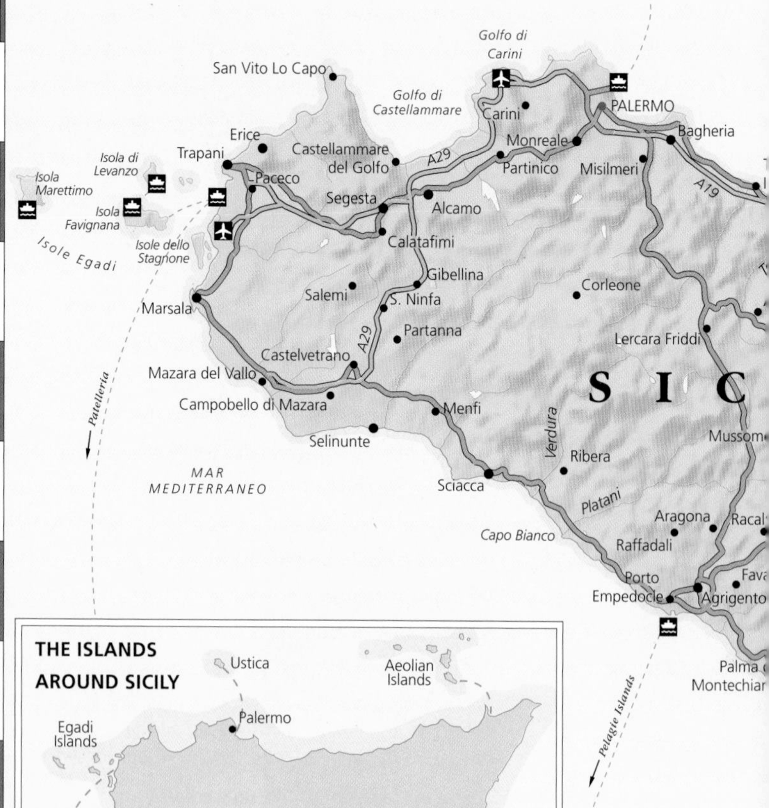


The carnival at Acireale, one of the most colourful in Sicily

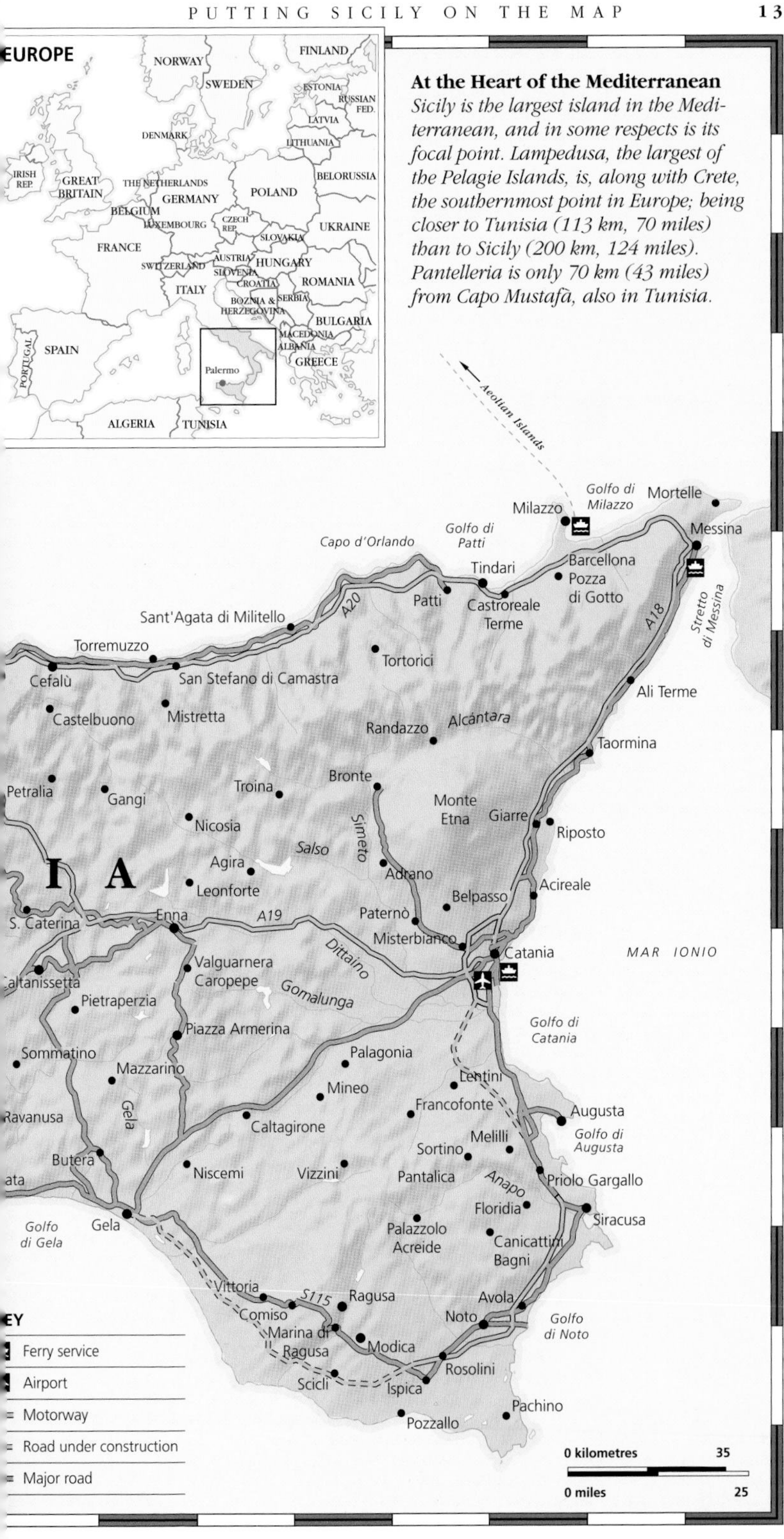


**At the Heart of the Mediterranean**
*Sicily is the largest island in the Mediterranean, and in some respects is its focal point. Lampedusa, the largest of the Pelagie Islands, is, along with Crete, the southernmost point in Europe; being closer to Tunisia (113 km, 70 miles) than to Sicily (200 km, 124 miles). Pantelleria is only 70 km (43 miles) from Capo Mustafà, also in Tunisia.*

D IOANNE CERDA
DVCE SICILIÆ PROREGE

# A PORTRAIT OF SICILY

*Sicilian shores are washed by three different seas, and this is reflected in the island's ancient name for Sicily: "Trinacria", the three-cornered island. Each part of the island has its own history, its own character, creating a varied and complex whole. Yet over the centuries Sicily has acquired a sense of unity and identity.*

Sicily's history can be traced back more than 2,000 years, during which time it has been dominated by many different rulers, from the Greeks to the Romans, Byzantines and Arabs, from the Normans to the Spanish. Each succeeding culture left a mark on the island and may perhaps help to explain aspects of the modern Sicilian character. This diverse inheritance manifests itself in a curious combination of dignified reserve and exuberant hospitality.

The Easter Week procession in Enna

The western side of the island, which is centred upon Palermo, is historically considered to be of Punic-Arab influence. The eastern side was once the centre of Magna Graecia, with its coastal towns of Messina, Catania and Syracuse. This difference may be discerned in the speech of local people: the "sing-song" dialect of Palermo as opposed to the more clipped accent of Catania and Syracuse. Accent differences are still noticeable, although they have moderated to some degree over the centuries. There are east-west economic and social differences as well as linguistic ones.

However, the island's long, eventful and tortuous history has not been the only factor influencing its life and inhabitants. Few places have been so affected by their climate and topography: in Sicily the

The rural landscape of the Sicilian interior, until recently characterized by its large estates

◁ Messina's Fontana del Nettuno (Fountain of Neptune), a traditional starting point for a tour of the island

Livestock raising, one of the mainstays of the economy in the Sicilian interior

temperature is 30°C (86°F) for six months of the year, and when the sun disappears, destructive torrential rains can take its place. The Sicilian climate is one of extremes and can sometimes even be cruel; it has shaped the island's extraordinary landscape which, as the Sicilian novelist Tomasi di Lampedusa described it, includes the hell of Randazzo and, just a few miles away, the paradise of Taormina. Then there are splendid verdant coasts everywhere, with the arid interior a stone's throw away, marvellous towns overlooking the sea and villages perched on hilltops surrounded by inhospitable, barren uplands. An aerial view of this unique island offers a spectacle that is at once both magnificent and awe-inspiring.

Villagers observing passers-by

## ECONOMY AND SOCIETY

The historic, geographic and climatic differences in Sicily have produced a complex and varied society. Yet Sicilians have a strong sense of identity and for centuries made their unique nature a point of honour (in a spirit of independence they used to call the rest of Italy "the continent"). Today this society is at a crossroads between tradition and modernity, much more so than other Mediterranean regions. Sicilian society is attempting to reconcile newer lifestyles and outlooks with deeply rooted age-old customs.

A watermelon seller in Palermo

One of the poorest regions in Italy, Sicily has had to strive for a more streamlined and profitable economy against the resistance of the ancient *latifundia* (feudal estate) system, just as the fervent civic and democratic spirit of the Sicilian people clashes with what remains of Mafia mentality and practice.

The criminal organization known to all as the Mafia is one of Sicily's most notorious creations. Sociologists and criminologists both in Italy and abroad have tried to define the phenomenon without success. Is it a criminal structure that is simply stronger and more efficiently

An outdoor café on the island of Lampedusa

organized than others, partly because of the massive emigration in the early 20th century, which took many Sicilians to the other side of the ocean? Or is it an anti-government movement whose leaders have played on the strong feelings of independence and diversity, which have always characterized Sicily? Is the Mafia the tool of the remaining large estate owners, who once dominated the island and are determined to retain power? Or is it perhaps a combination of all the above factors, which have found fertile soil in the innate scepticism and pessimism of the Sicilians? Whatever the answer may be, eliminating the Mafia is one of Sicily's greatest challenges. After the early 1990s, which saw the deaths of several anti-Mafia figures, there is a new spirit abroad and the tide now seems to be turning in favour of the new Sicily.

### ART AND CULTURE

For more than 2,000 years, Sicily has inspired the creation of artistic masterpieces, from the architecture of Magna Graecia to the great medieval cathedrals, from the paintings of Antonello da Messina to the music of Vincenzo Bellini, and from the birth of Italian literature under Frederick II to the poets and novelists of the 19th and 20th centuries. Sadly, this glorious artistic heritage is not always well cared for and appreciated. Noto, near Syracuse, provides one example. This splendid town was built entirely of tufa in the early 1700s and is one of the great achievements of Sicilian Baroque architecture. Today Noto is falling to pieces (the Cathedral collapsed in 1996), and the material used to build the town makes any restoration a difficult task. This mixture of splendour and decay, or as Gesualdo Bufalino, the acute observer of his land, once said, "light and lamentation", is typical of Sicily today. However, the creation of new nature reserves, renewed interest in preserving historic centres, and initiatives such as extended church opening hours, are all causes for cautious optimism in the future.

Renato Guttuso, View of Bagheria (1951)

# Sicily's Geology, Landscape and Wildlife

Typical Sicilian landscape consists of coast and sun-baked hills. The irregular and varied coastline is over 1,000 km (620 miles) long, or 1,500 km (931 miles) if the smaller islands are included. The island's geological make-up is also quite varied, with sulphur mines in the centre and volcanic activity in the east. Sicily's many volcanoes, in particular Mount Etna (the largest in Europe), have created a landscape that is unique in the Mediterranean.

### SICILIAN FAUNA

**Painted frog**

Sicily has preserved a variety of habitats in its large nature reserves, the most famous of which is the Mount Etna National Park. These parks are home to a wide range of species, some of which are endangered, including wildcats, martens and porcupines. The birdlife includes the rare golden eagle.

### RUGGED COASTS AND STACKS

**Vanessa butterfly**

The Sicilian coastline is steep and rugged, particularly along the Tyrrhenian sea and the northern stretch of the Ionian, where there are many peninsulas, river mouths, bays and rocky headlands. It is also characterized by stacks, steep-sided pillars of rock separated from the coastal cliffs by erosion.

**The sawwort *Serratula cichoriacea*** *is a perennial found along these coastlines.*

**Astroides calycularis** *is an alga that thrives in the shaded cliff areas.*

### SANDY COASTLINES

**Flamingo**

Around the Trapani area the Sicilian coast begins to slope down to the Mozia salt marshes, followed by uniform and sandy Mediterranean beaches. This type of coastline continues along the Ionian side of Sicily, where there are marshy areas populated by flamingoes. These birds can be seen nesting as far inland as the Plain of Catania.

**The dwarf palm**, *called* scupazzu *in Sicilian dialect, is a typical western Mediterranean plant.*

**The prickly pear** *is an example of an imported plant that was initially cultivated in gardens and then ended up crowding out the local flora.*

**All kinds of coleoptera**, *including this shiny-backed carabid beetle, can be found in Sicily. In the Mount Etna area alone, 354 different species have been identified.*

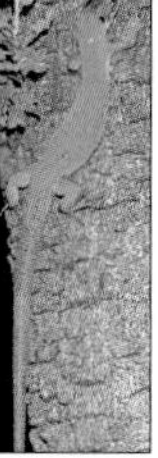

**The reptile family** *is represented by numerous species, ranging from various types of snake to smaller creatures such as this green lizard, which is well known for its shiny skin and sinuous body.*

**Foxes** *were at one time rare in Sicily, but in recent years they have been spotted near towns foraging for food among household refuse.*

**Martens** *love to roam in the woods around Mount Etna. Weasels and ferrets can also be found in Sicily.*

## THE INTERIOR

Green woodpecker

Sicily's hinterland has not always looked the way it does today. Maquis once carpeted areas that, except for a few stretches far from the towns, are arid steppes today. As a result, apart from grain, which has always been the island's staple, the flora is not native, originating in North Africa or the Italian mainland. Birds like the woodpecker can be seen.

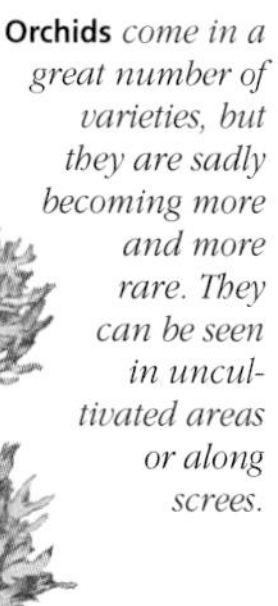

**Orchids** *come in a great number of varieties, but they are sadly becoming more and more rare. They can be seen in uncultivated areas or along screes.*

**The vegetation** *in the interior often looks like this: quite low-growing and with brightly coloured flowers.*

## VOLCANIC AREAS

A falcon, an Etna raptor

Volcanic zones, particularly around Mount Etna, are very fertile and yield rich vegetation: from olive trees growing on mountain slopes to the pines, birch and beech that thrive at 2,000 m (6,560 ft). Higher up grows the milk vetch, forming spiky racemes. Above 3,000 m (9,840 ft) nothing grows. Raptors can often be seen circling.

**Moss and lichens** *cover the walls of houses on the slopes of Mount Etna, which are built using volcanic sand.*

**Cerastium** *and Sicilian soapwort flourish on the Mediterranean uplands.*

# Architecture in Sicily

Hygeia, 3rd century BC

Three periods have shaped much of Sicilian architecture. The first was the time of Greek occupation, when monumental works (especially temples and theatres) were built. Aesthetically they were often equal to, and in some cases superior to, those in Greece itself. The medieval period witnessed the fusion of the Byzantine, Arab and Norman styles in such buildings as the Duomo at Monreale near Palermo. Last came the flowering of Baroque architecture in the 17th–18th centuries. The style was so individual that it became known as Sicilian Baroque.

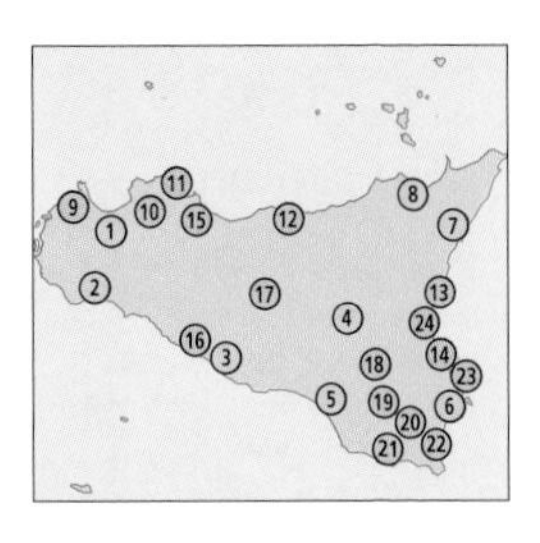

**LOCATOR MAP**

- Classical architecture
- Medieval architecture
- Baroque architecture

## STYLES OF CLASSICAL GREEK TEMPLE

The earliest version of the Greek temple consisted of a rectangular chamber housing the statue of a god. Later, columns were added and the wooden elements were replaced by stone. There were three Greek architectural orders: the Doric, Ionic and Corinthian, in chronological order. They are easily distinguished by the column capitals. The temples built in Sicily displayed an experimental, innovative nature compared with those in Greece.

**The Doric Temple** *The Doric temple stood on a three-stepped base. The columns had no base, were thicker in the middle and tapered upwards, and the capital was a rectangular slab. Other elements were the frieze with its alternating metopes and triglyphs, and the triangular pediment.*

**The Ionic Temple** *The differences between the Ionic and Doric styles lay in the number of columns and in the fact that Ionic columns rest on a base and their capitals have two volutes, giving the appearance of rams' horns.*

**The Corinthian Temple** *The Corinthian temple featured columns that were more slender than in the Ionic temple, and the elaborate capitals were decorated with stylized acanthus leaves.*

**The column shafts** were tapered upwards.

**Triangular pediment**

**The metopes** could be decorated.

**Doric capital**

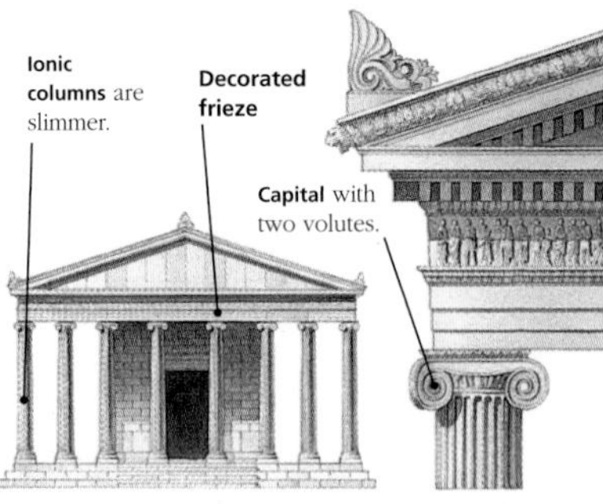


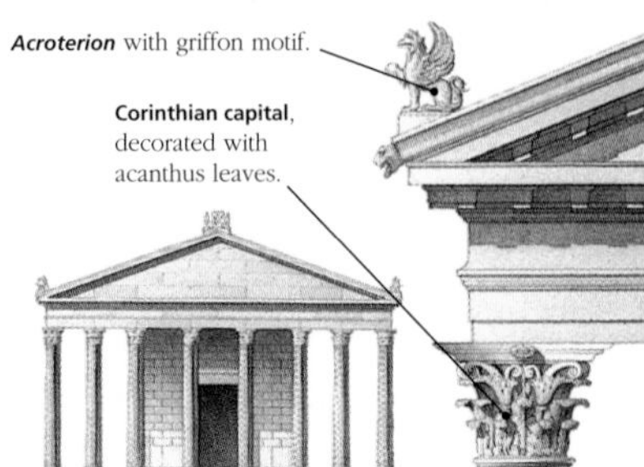


## CLASSICAL ARCHITECTURE

① Segesta *p98*
② Selinunte *pp104–6*
③ Valle dei Templi (Agrigento) *pp116–17*
④ Morgantina *pp128–9*
⑤ Gela *p153*
⑥ Syracuse *pp136–43*
⑦ Taormina *pp176–80*
⑧ Tindari *p186*

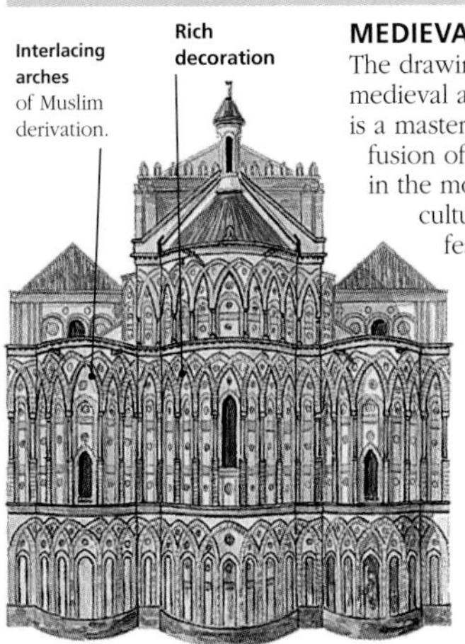


## MEDIEVAL CHURCHES

The drawings illustrate two of the greatest achievements of medieval architecture in Sicily. The Duomo of Monreale *(left)* is a masterpiece from the Norman period, with a splendid fusion of Byzantine, Arab and Norman figurative elements in the mosaics in the interior. A similar fusion of styles and cultures can be seen in the exterior architectural features. The Cathedral in Cefalù *(below)* also dates from the Norman period and, like Monreale, has beautiful mosaics. Its austere and stately quality is created by Romanesque elements such as the two lateral towers.

**The windows,** double and single lancet, make the towers look lighter.

**Romanesque side towers**

**Interlacing arches**

**The Gothic portal** is under a 15th-century narthex.

## MEDIEVAL ARCHITECTURE

⑨ Erice *pp100–1*
⑩ Monreale *pp76–7*
⑪ Palermo *pp42–75*
⑫ Cefalù *pp88–91*
⑬ Catania *pp162–5*
⑭ Syracuse *pp136–43*

## BAROQUE CHURCHES

After the 1693 earthquake the towns of eastern Sicily were almost totally rebuilt. Spanish-influenced Baroque was combined with Sicilian decorative and structural elements (convex church façades and impressive flights of steps), giving rise to an original, innovative style. Two great examples are shown here: the Cathedral in Syracuse *(left)* and the Basilica di San Giorgio in Ragusa *(below)*. The architect was GB Vaccarini (1702–1769), who also rebuilt Catania.

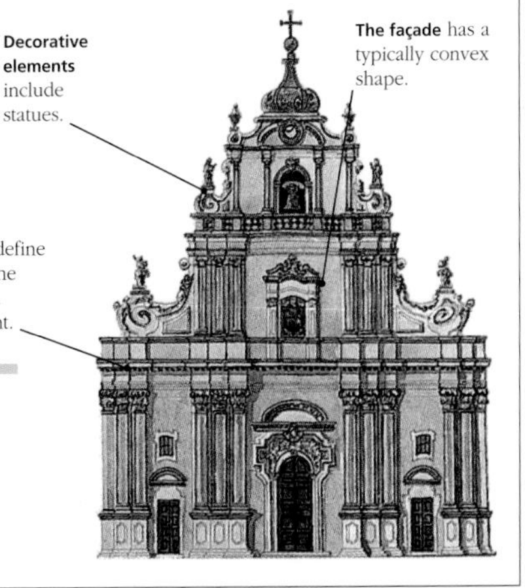


## BAROQUE ARCHITECTURE

⑮ Palermo *pp42–75*
⑯ Agrigento *pp114–15*
⑰ Caltanissetta *p126*
⑱ Caltagirone *pp154–5*
⑲ Ragusa *pp150–51*
⑳ Modica *p152*
㉑ Scicli *p149*
㉒ Noto *pp144–7*
㉓ Syracuse *pp136–43*
㉔ Catania *pp162–5*

# Sicilian Literature and Art

Luigi Pirandello, 1934 Nobel Prize winner

In the history of Sicilian art and literature there have been periods of tremendous creativity and others when little of note was produced. In the field of literature, the 13th-century Sicilian school of lyric poetry, 19th-century *verismo* or realism and Luigi Pirandello's novels and plays scale the heights of Italian and European literary production. In the field of art, Sicily has produced such great artists as Antonello da Messina, one of the great figures in 15th-century rationalism and portraiture, and the modern painter Renato Guttuso.

## WRITERS

Metope from Temple E in Selinunte: Artemis and Acteon

Only fragments remain of Greek Sicilian literary works. Unlike other artistic fields such as architecture, Siceliot (ancient Greek-Sicilian) literature is indistinguishable from the local production, as both were the expression of the same religious, cultural and civic milieu. Apart from Pindar, who dedicated lyric poems to Syracuse and Agrigento, the names of two Siceliot poets have survived. Stesichorus, who lived in Catania in the 7th–6th century BC, "achieved great fame in all Hellas" according to Cicero, leaving a few fragments written in the Homeric style. Theocritus, a Syracusan who lived in the 4th–3rd centuries BC, created the genre of pastorals, short poems on bucolic or mythological subjects. Another important figure in the Greek context was the historian Diodorus Siculus (1st century BC).

The first known figure in medieval Sicilian literature is the Arab poet 'Ibn Hamdis, who was born in Syracuse in 1055 and was forced to leave the island while still young. He wrote moving verses filled with nostalgia for the land of his youth.

In the 13th century, the first school of lyric poetry in Italy developed at the court of Emperor Frederick II and his successor Manfred. It later became known as the Sicilian School. Among the key figures were Jacopo da Lentini, Pier della Vigna, Stefano Pronotaro, Rinaldo d'Aquino and Guido delle Colonne. Their love poetry took up the themes of Provençal lyric poetry but were written in vernacular Italian instead of Latin. Their psychological penetration and the stylistic and metric innovations led to the invention of the sonnet. After this period of splendour, Sicilian literature declined, as did conditions generally in Sicily. This literary "drought" lasted throughout the Renaissance and Baroque periods, and the only author of note at this time is Antonio Veneziano (born in Monreale in 1543), a poet who wrote in the local dialect and left a collection of love poems. The 18th century was another fallow period for literary production, and it was not until the mid-1800s that there was a rebirth of Sicilian literature. The writers Giovanni Verga and Federico De Roberto became the mainspring of the realistic novel, *verismo*. This style of writing was an extreme and, to a certain extent, more refined version of French naturalism, as embodied in the work of Emile Zola.

Guidebook by Federico De Roberto

Giovanni Verga was born in Catania in 1840. After producing work in a late Romantic vein, in the 1870s he was drawn to French naturalism by creating his so-called "poetic of the defeated", in which he set out to depict the hardship of contemporary social reality. He began with short stories set in a rural context (the first was *Nedda*, 1873), which were followed by his masterpieces, the novels *I Malavoglia* (The House by the Medlar Tree, 1881) and *Mastro Don Gesualdo* (1889), which both depict the immutable Sicilian society of the time. The former – a truly innovative work from a stylistic and linguistic standpoint – is the story of a family of fishermen at Aci Trezza who, after a short-lived period of relative well-being, plunge into a life of poverty and suffering. *Mastro Don Gesualdo* narrates the rise on the social

Giovanni Verga, author of *I Malavoglia* (1881)

scale and existential drama of a workman *(mastro)* who, thanks to his marriage, becomes a "Don". These two novels were part of Verga's planned *ciclo dei vinti* (cycle of the defeated), which was to have consisted of five novels; but the author left the project unfinished.

In the same vein as Verga were two other Sicilian writers, Luigi Capuana (1839–1915) and, more importantly, Federico De Roberto (1861–1927), who wrote *I Viceré* (The Viceroys, 1894), about a 19th-century aristocratic family in Catania.

The literature of Sicily continued to be at the forefront in the 20th century. The first half was dominated by Luigi Pirandello (1867–1936), who won the Nobel Prize for Literature in 1934. In his novels (such as *The Late Mattia Pascal*, 1904), nearly 300 short stories, plays *(see p25)* and essays he combines wit with a lucid and sometimes ruthless vision of reality.

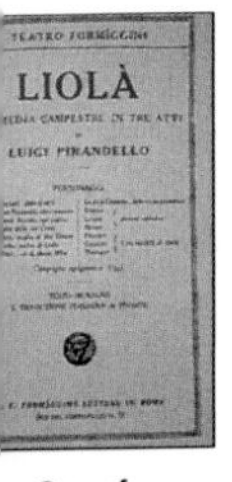
TEATRO FORMIGGINI
LIOLÀ
LUIGI PIRANDELLO

One of Pirandello's earliest plays

Among the many noteworthy post-war Sicilian writers are the "hermetic" poet Salvatore Quasimodo (1901–68), author of the collection of poems *Ed è subito sera* (And Suddenly it's Evening, 1942). He won the Nobel Prize in 1959. Giuseppe Tomasi di Lampedusa (1896–1957), wrote *Il Gattopardo* (The Leopard, 1958; *see p122*), a vivid portrait of feudal Sicily, later made into a film, and Leonardo Sciascia (1921– 89), wrote novels and essays painting a penetrating, lively portrait of post-war Sicily.

Leonardo Sciascia (1921–89)

Renato Guttuso, *Boogie-woogie* (1953 – 4)

## ARTISTS

Until the Renaissance, Sicilian art was basically decorative. During the Greek period probably the best painting was produced in the 7th century BC, when Siceliot vase painters stopped imitating the mainland models and adopted a fresh, eclectic style that combined and elaborated upon the original Greek red-figure ware motifs. The only known artist was Zeuxis, and this only through literature, not his works. The Roman period distinguished itself for some fine wall paintings, in which wax-derived colours were applied, fused into a layer and then fixed onto the wall with heat. The decorative arts in the Middle Ages in Sicily were dominated by mosaics. Among earlier fine works in this medium are the mosaics of the late Roman period at Piazza Armerina and those in the Cappella Palatina in Palermo and Cefalù Cathedral, which are a magnificent combination of Byzantine, Arab and Norman motifs and stylistic elements. Sicilian art reached a peak during the Renaissance, thanks to artists such as Giuffrè (15th century), Quartarano (1484–1501), the unknown author of *Trionfo della morte* (The Triumph of Death), and, last but by no means least, to the genius of Antonello da Messina (1430–79), one of the greatest Renaissance portraitists and exponents of figurative rationalism, who was active throughout Italy.

Although Sicily was one of the favourite subjects of the great European landscape artists, from the 17th to the 19th century the island produced only one important painter, Pietro Novelli, known as "the man from Monreale" (1603–47).

In the 20th century, the painter Renato Guttuso (1912–87) took up his artistic heritage in a realistic vein, becoming one of Italy's leading artists.

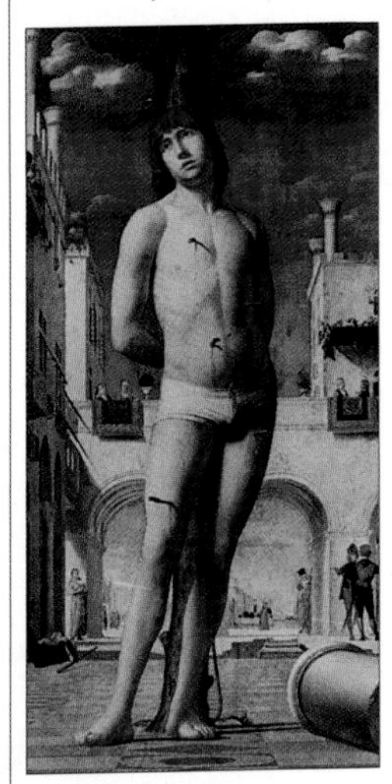

Antonello da Messina, *St Sebastian* (1476)

# Cinema and Theatre in Sicily

Anyone who witnesses the colour of Carnival in Sicily, or the bustle of the Vucciria market in Palermo, will appreciate that Sicily is a theatrical place in its own right. The reasons perhaps lie in the turbulent history of the place. One thing is certain: the island has been a source of inspiration for both theatre and cinema, providing subjects from peasant life to the decadent aristocracy and the Mafia, and producing world-famous playwrights, such as the late Luigi Pirandello, and award-winning films.

Burt Lancaster as the Prince of Salina in *Il Gattopardo* (1963)

## SICILIAN CINEMA

The first Sicilian to forge a successful career in the seventh art was probably the playwright Nino Martoglio, who in 1914 directed *Sperduti nel Buio* (Lost in the Dark), a film set in Naples, and edited with a highly original technique. Shortly afterwards, in 1919, Pirandello also wrote two screenplays, *Pantera di Neve* (Snow Panther) and *La Rosa* (The Rose), followed by *Acciaio* (Steel) in 1933. The great playwright and the directors of the films experienced difficulties, however, and the results were not entirely successful. After World War II Sicilian cinema and films set in Sicily reached a peak. In 1948 Luchino Visconti produced *La Terra Trema*, a loose adaptation of Giovanni Verga's *I Malavoglia* *(see p169)*. The Milanese director returned to the island in 1963 to film *Il Gattopardo* (The Leopard), based on the novel of the same name by Tomasi di Lampedusa *(see p122)* and starring Burt Lancaster, Alain Delon and Claudia Cardinale.

In the same period, the Palermitan director Vittorio De Seta, following some fascinating documentaries on Sicily, directed a feature film set in Sardinia, *Banditi a Orgosolo* (Bandits at Orgosolo, 1961), and Neapolitan director Francesco Rosi made *Salvatore Giuliano* (1961), the story of the famous Sicilian bandit, acclaimed as "the greatest film on southern Italy". That same year Pietro Germi shot another famous film in Sicily: *Divorzio all'Italiana*, (Divorce – Italian Style), with Marcello Mastroianni and Stefania Sandrelli. Roman director Elio Petri made another important film about the island in the 1960s: *A Ciascuno il Suo* (To Each His Own, 1967), an adaptation of Leonardo Sciascia's novel of the same name *(see p23)*. The 1970s and 1980s produced a number of films about the Mafia, while Sicilian filmmaker Giuseppe Tornatore directed *Cinema Paradiso*, set in Palazzo Adriano *(see p120)*, which won an Academy Award as the best foreign film of 1990.

Neon sign of the *Nuovo Cinema Paradiso* in Giuseppe Tornatore's award-winning film

## CINEMA AND THE MAFIA

Marlon Brando as Don Corleone in *The Godfather*

Since the end of World War II the Mafia has been a favourite subject for film. (However, there is a distinction between Italian-made and Hollywood films.) The most distinguished Mafia films made in Italy are Francesco Rosi's *Salvatore Giuliano*; *Il Giorno della Civetta* (Mafia), adapted from Leonardo Sciascia's novel *(see p23)* directed by Damiano Damiani, who also made *Confessione di un Commissario di Polizia al Procuratore della Repubblica* (1971), and Elio Petri's *A Ciascuno il Suo* (To Each His Own, 1967). Last, the Mafia is also the subject of two films by Giuseppe Ferrara, *Il Sasso in Bocca* (1969) and more recently *Cento Giorni a Palermo* (A Hundred Days in Palermo, 1983), the tragic story of the Carabiniere general Dalla Chiesa, who was killed by the Mafia *(see p36)*. Any number of Hollywood movies have been made about the Mafia, though they are almost always set in the US. The most famous is the Academy Award-winning film *The Godfather* (1972), directed by Francis Ford Coppola and starring Marlon Brando and Al Pacino.

## SICILIAN THEATRE

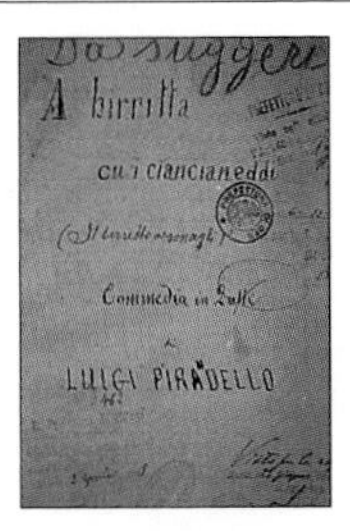
A birritta
cu i ciancianeddi
LUIGI PIRANDELLO

The original script of *Il Berretto a Sonagli* by Pirandello (1917)

Sicilian theatre is most closely identified with Luigi Pirandello (1867–1936), but there is also a rich tradition of theatre in Sicilian dialect. This theatre form dates from the Middle Ages, but its greatest interpreters were active in the late 19th century. Popular actors included Giuseppe Rizzotto (*I Mafiusi de la Vicaria*, The Mafiosi of the Vicariate, 1863) and Giovanni Grasso, and playwright Nino Martoglio, who in 1903 founded the Grande Compagnia Drammatica Siciliana. Luigi Pirandello also began his theatre career with comedies in dialect such as *Il Berretto a Sonagli* (1917), but he gained international renown in the 1920s with his plays written in Italian. In 1921 he wrote *Six Characters in Search of an Author* and, the following year, *Henry IV*. In these plays, probably his greatest, Pirandello deals with the themes that made him world-famous: the relationship between illusion and reality, existential hypocrisy and the need to find a profound identity.

Sicilian playwright Nino Martoglio (1870–1921)

### THE OPERA DEI PUPI

Sicilian puppets, now sought after by antique dealers

*Pupi* are large Sicilian rod puppets. They date from the 1600s but became a huge success only in the late 1800s. The traditional "puppet opera" stories narrate the adventures of Charlemagne and his paladins, but there are also more modern topics revolving around Garibaldi and King Vittorio Emanuele. Famous puppeteers included Greco, who was based in Palermo, and the Grasso family from Catania, renowned craftsmen in their own right.

## CLASSICAL THEATRE IN SICILY

Ancient theatre in Sicily can boast a great genius as its adoptive father, since Aeschylus (525–456 BC), who is regarded as the inventor of Greek tragedy, spent long periods in Sicily and died here. A number of his works were first produced in Syracuse *(see pp138–9)*. Sicily was therefore well acquainted with, and assimilated, the subject matter of Greek theatre: freedom versus destiny, the sense of divine power and human suffering, the anguish of the tragedies and excoriating, bitter satire of the comedies. Classical theatre declined with the fall of the western Roman Empire, and it was not until the 20th century that the great tragedies were again performed in Sicily. In 1913, Count Mario Tommaso Gargallo and his fellow Syracusans, including archaeologist Paolo Orsi *(see pp140–41)* decided to champion the production of Aeschylus' *Agamemnon*. The premiere was held on 16 April 1914 and since then, with the exception of wartime, the Greek Theatre in Syracuse, one of the most beautiful in the world, has remained a venue for ancient theatre – thanks to the efforts of the Istituto Nazionale del Dramma Antico (National Institute of Ancient Drama, *see p139*). Many famous theatre personalities have participated in these productions over the years, including poets Salvatore Quasimodo *(see p23)* and Pier Paolo Pasolini as translators, and the actors Giorgio Albertazzi and Vittorio Gassman.

Programme of the Istituto Nazionale del Dramma Antico, set up in 1925

# THE HISTORY OF SICILY

Hercules killing a deer

The most striking aspect of Sicilian history is the enormous influence of all the different peoples who have colonized the island. Even the Sicani, Elymi and Siculi, the first populations to leave traces of their cultures in Sicily, came from other parts of the Mediterranean. They were followed by the Carthaginians and then by the Greeks, under whom Sicily saw its first real period of great splendour. Greek domination ended in 212 BC with the siege of Syracuse, in which the great inventor Archimedes was killed. For the next six centuries, the island became the bread basket of the Roman Empire and during this period acquired a social system that was to be its distinguishing characteristic for centuries. After the fall of the Roman Empire and the barbarian invasions, Sicily was ruled by the Byzantines. The island was then conquered by the Arabs, under whom it became one of the most prosperous and tolerant lands in the Mediterranean. The next rulers were the Normans, who laid the foundations for the splendid court of Frederick II in Palermo. A long period of decadence coincided with the dwindling of the Middle Ages. The Angevins, Aragonese and Bourbons in turn took power in Sicily, but these dynasties exploited the island and treated it like a colony instead of improving life for the people there. Giuseppe Garibaldi's expedition in 1860 paved the way for the unification of Italy. Despite initial neglect by the central Italian government, Sicilians were finally given control of their own affairs. Yet many long-standing economic and social problems still need to be tackled and resolved, in particular, the continuing presence of the Mafia in Sicily.

Sicily in a 1692 print showing its three provinces: Val di Demona, Val di Noto, Val di Mazara

◁ Pietro Novelli, *St Benedict Offering the Book of the Order*, San Castrense Monreale (16th century)

# The Conquerors of Sicily

Because of its strategic position in the middle of the Mediterranean, Sicily has always been fought over by leading powers. Its history is therefore one of successive waves of foreign domination: Greek tyrants, Roman proconsuls and barbarian chieftains, then the Byzantines, Arabs and Normans, the Hohenstaufen monarchs, the Angevin and Aragonese dynasties, the Spanish viceroys and then the Bourbons, the last foreign rulers in Sicily before Italy was unified.

**5th century BC** Battles for supremacy in Sicily between the Greek and Punic colonies

**Cleandros** initiates the period of tyrannical rule in Gela

**Hippocrates** succeeds Cleandros and extends Gela's dominion

**Agathocles**, king of Syracuse (317–289 BC)

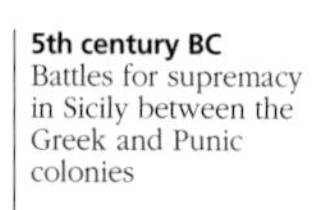

**King Pyrrhus** at Syracuse (280–275 BC)

**Hieron II** (265–215 BC)

**Verres** becomes the Roman governor in 73–71 BC and is notorious for his corrupt rule

**Genseric**, chief of the Vandals, conquers Sicily in AD 440

**Justinian I**, the Byzantine emperor, annexes Sicily in AD 535

| 600 BC | 400 | 200 | AD 1 | 200 | 400 | 6 |
|---|---|---|---|---|---|---|
| GREEKS | | ROMANS | | | BARBARIANS A | |
| 600 BC | 400 | 200 | AD 1 | 200 | 400 | 6 |

**Gelon** conquers Syracuse in 490 BC

**Theron** tyrant in Agrigento in 488 BC

**Ducetius**, last king of the Siculi, dies in 440 BC

**The Peloponnesian War** (431–404 BC), brings an attack on Syracuse by the Athenian army, who are later defeated

**Dionysius the Elder** becomes tyrant of Syracuse in 405 BC and rules for 38 years

**Dionysius the Younger** succeeds his father in 368 BC

**Timoleon** restores democracy in Syracuse in 339 BC

**The Romans** conquer Sicily definitively in 212 BC

**Diocletian** divides the Roman Empire in AD 285. Sicily remains part of the Western Empire

**Odoacer** and the Ostrogoths conquer Sicily in AD 491. He is succeeded by **Theodoric**

## ARTISTS AND SCIENTISTS

In at least two significant periods, artists and scientists played a leading role in the long and eventful history of Sicily. The outstanding figure was Archimedes, born in Syracuse in 287 BC and on intimate terms with the ruler Hieron II. Thanks to the ingenious machines of war he invented, the city was able to resist Roman siege for three years (215–212 BC). Another great moment in Sicilian history came when the court of Frederick II in Palermo became known for its artists, poets and architects in the 1300s. Palermo became a leading centre for intellectuals.

**Archimedes, the great Syracusan scientist**

**Frederick II**, emperor from 1216, is King of Sicily from 1197 to 1250, the year of his death. He moved his court to Palermo

**Tancred** (1190–94)

**William I** (1154–66)

**Roger I**, the Norman lord, conquers Sicily in 1091 after a war lasting 30 years

**Charles I of Anjou** wrests the throne of Sicily from Manfred. He dies in 1285.

**Charles II** succeeds his father Charles I but in 1288 is forced to cede Sicily to **Peter III of Aragón**, who had occupied the island in 1282

**James II of Aragón** (1286–96)

**Frederick II of Aragón** (1296–1337)

**Peter II of Aragón** (1337–41)

**Louis of Aragón** (1341–55)

**The viceroys** (above, Severino Filangieri) govern Sicily for the Spanish sovereigns until 1713

**Ferdinand** (1759–1825) unifies the kingdoms of Naples and Sicily in 1816

**Ferdinand II** (1830–59) is the last Bourbon ruler in Sicily

| 800 | 1000 | 1200 | 1400 | 1600 | 1800 |
|---|---|---|---|---|---|

ARABS | NORMANS | ANGEVINS AND ARAGONESE | BOURBONS | SAVOY

| 800 | 1000 | 1200 | 1400 | 1600 | 1800 |
|---|---|---|---|---|---|

**Roger II** (1105–1154)

**William II** (1166–89)

**The Arabs** begin their invasion of Sicily in 827 and conquer the island in 902

**Henry VI**, emperor and son of Barbarossa, conquers Sicily in 1194. He dies in 1197

**Manfred**, the natural son of Frederick II, rules Sicily until 1266

**Frederick III of Aragón** (1355–77), whose death triggers a period of struggle and strife that brings about the end of the Kingdom of Sicily

**Duke John of Pegnafiel**, son of Ferdinand of Castille, begins the viceroyalty period in 1412. This system of rule lasts for three centuries

**Vittorio Amedeo II of Savoy** acquires Sicily in 1713 through the Peace of Utrecht, ceding it to the **Habsburgs of Austria** in 1718

**Charles III of Spain** acquires Sicily from Austria in 1735 and governs until 1759

**Vittorio Emanuele II of Savoy** becomes the first king of a unified Italy. Sicily forms a part of the new kingdom, having voted for annexation following Garibaldi's conquest of the island in 1860

# Prehistoric and Ancient Sicily

Female bust (470–460 BC)

When Greek colonists arrived in Sicily in the 8th century BC, in the east they found the Siculi – a Mediterranean population that had been there since 2,000 BC – and the Phoenicians to the west. The former were soon assimilated, while the latter were ousted after the Battle of Himera (480 BC). This marked the beginning of Greek supremacy and the height of the Magna Graecia civilization, which ended in 212 BC with the Roman conquest of Syracuse. Roman Sicily saw the rise of large feudal estates and the imposition of taxes. Christianity began to spread in the 3rd–4th centuries AD.

GREEK COLONIZATION OF THE MEDITERRANEAN

## MYTHS AND GODS

Magna Graecia adopted the religion of the mother country while adding local myths and legends. Mount Etna was seen as the home of Hephaestus, the god of fire, whom the Romans identified with Vulcan. Homer chose the island of Vulcano, in the Aeolians, as the workplace of this fiery god of blacksmiths. At Aci Trezza on the Ionian Sea, a group of stacks is known as "the islands of the Cyclops", since it was believed that they were the boulders Polyphemus hurled against Ulysses in the famous episode in Homer's *Odyssey*.

Zeus, the supreme Greek deity

## VOYAGE TO SICILY

The ships the Greeks used for the dangerous trip to Sicily were called triremes. These galleys were about 35 m (115 ft) long, were faster and more agile than the Phoenician vessels and travelled about 100 km (62 miles) per day. They were manned by a crew of 200 and were equipped for transport and battle.

**The double oar** on the stern was used as a rudder.

**Stern**

**Mother Goddess**
*This intense limestone statue, an archetype of femininity, dates from the middle of the 6th century BC and is in the Museo Archeologico of Syracuse* (see pp140–41).

## TIMELINE

**1600 BC** | **1300 BC** | **1000 BC** | **800 BC** | **600 BC**

**1500 BC** Contacts between Aeolian and Cretan and Minoan cultures

**1270–1000 BC** First period of Siculan civilization

**1000–850 BC** Second period of Siculan civilization

**850–730 BC** Third period of Siculan civilization

**8th century BC** Greeks colonize east, Phoenicians west. *Panormos* (Palermo) founded

**730–650 BC** Fourth period of Siculan civilization

**733 BC** Dorians from Corinth found Syracuse

**729 BC** *Katane* (Catania) founded

**628 BC** Selinunte founded

**413 BC** Athenian invasion led by Nicias and Alcibiades a total failure

**480 BC** Battle of Himera: Greeks defeat Carthaginians

*The goddess Athena*

**The Roman Villas**
*Roman dominion in Sicily brought about the spread of* latifundia *(large feudal estates) and landowners' villas such as the Villa del Casale* (see pp130–31), *whose mosaics were preserved thanks to a flood that buried them for centuries.*

### WHERE TO SEE ANCIENT SICILY

Almost every Sicilian town of any size has an archaeological museum. The most interesting prehistoric ruins are to be found in the islands, particularly the Aeolians *(see pp188–91)*, while the few Punic remains are on display in the museums. The main Greek sites include Segesta *(see p98)*, Selinunte *(see pp104–6)*, Syracuse *(see pp136–43)*, the Valle dei Templi at Agrigento *(see pp116–17)* and Morgantina *(see pp128–9)*. One of the best preserved Roman sites is the ancient villa at Piazza Armerina *(see pp129–31)*.

**4th-century BC crater**

**A trireme** drew only about 60 cm (24 in).

**The spur** was used to destroy the oars on enemy vessels.

**The third rank** of oars (hence "trireme" or three oars), was on an external deck jutting out from the hull. Everything was carefully calculated so that the 170 oar movements were synchronized.

**Prehistoric Village**
*Remains of settlements dating from the beginning of the first millennium BC lie all over Sicily. However, the first populations who left traces in Sicily (Sicani, Elymi and Siculi) were not native people.*

*Aeschylus, the great Greek tragedian who was also active in Syracuse*

**AD 293** The emperor Diocletian makes Sicily *regio suburbicaria*, or directly dependent on Rome

**AD 325** Christianization of the Syracuse area

**AD 535** Sicily becomes part of Justinian's Eastern Roman Empire

200 | AD 1 | AD 200 | 400 | 600

**212 BC** Syracuse conquered by Romans. Sicily loses its autonomy

*Female clay bust*

**AD 440** During the barbarian invasions of Italy the Vandals led by Genseric conquer Sicily

**AD 491** The Ostrogoths under Odoacer take Sicily from the Vandals

**AD 600** Christianization of all of Sicily

# Medieval Sicily

Coin with imperial coat of arms

The frequent Arab raids became in 827 a real campaign to conquer Sicily, which ended successfully in 902. Arab dominion coincided with the rebirth of the island after the decadence of the final years of Byzantine rule. In 1061 the Christian crusade began, the Normans conquering Sicily 30 years later. The Kingdom of Sicily was established in 1130 and reached its zenith with the splendour of Frederick II's court. In 1266 the Angevin dynasty took power, followed by the Aragonese, initiating a long period of decline in which powerful feudal landowners ruled the island.

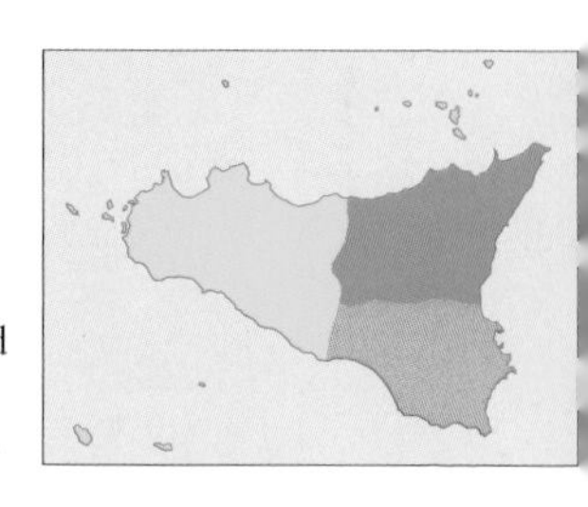

**THE ARAB REGIONS OF SICILY**

- *Val Demone*
- *Val di Noto*
- *Val di Mazara*

**Tancred**
*The natural son of Roger III of Puglia, Tancred was appointed king of Sicily by the feudal barons in 1190. He was the last Norman to rule Sicily. When he died, the emperor Henry VI, son of Barbarossa and father of Federico II, ascended the throne.*

**Sicily under Arab Rule**
*During the century of Arab dominion Sicily was the richest and most tolerant land in the Mediterranean. The governing administration was reorganized and the arts and culture flourished to an exceptional degree, as can be seen in this decorated coffer.*

**The poor and ill** are spared.

**The dog** leads the man in the night of death.

## TIMELINE

**725** Worship of sacred images is prohibited. The possessions of the Sicilian church are confiscated by the patriarchate in Constantinople

**831** Palermo becomes capital of the Arab emirate

**902** Taormina surrenders, Arab conquest completed

**1091** After 30 years fare, Sicily is once Christian land thanks Norman

700

*The Virgin of Odigitria, Lentini*

800

**827** Arab conquest of Sicily begins

900

*Coin with Arab inscriptions*

**1038–1043** Eastern Sicily is temporarily reconquered by Byzantium

1000

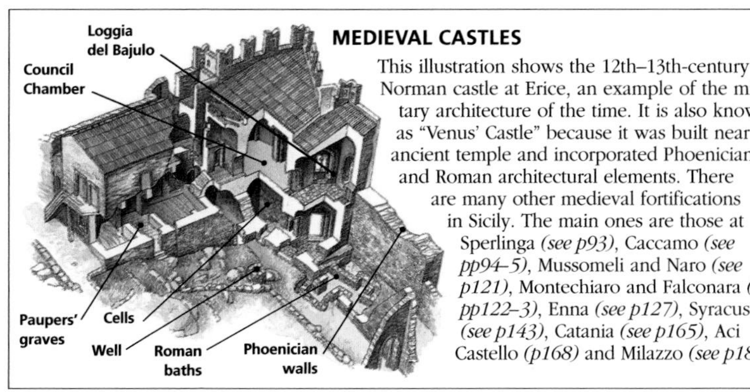


## MEDIEVAL CASTLES

This illustration shows the 12th–13th-century Norman castle at Erice, an example of the military architecture of the time. It is also known as "Venus' Castle" because it was built near an ancient temple and incorporated Phoenician and Roman architectural elements. There are many other medieval fortifications in Sicily. The main ones are those at Sperlinga *(see p93)*, Caccamo *(see pp94–5)*, Mussomeli and Naro *(see p121)*, Montechiaro and Falconara *(see pp122–3)*, Enna *(see p127)*, Syracuse *(see p143)*, Catania *(see p165)*, Aci Castello *(p168)* and Milazzo *(see p187)*.

**Death** strikes with bow and arrows, like a horseman of the Apocalypse.

**A lady** maintains her proud attitude.

**The rich and powerful** are killed with arrows.

## THE TRIUMPH OF DEATH

This mid-15th-century fresco, painted and kept in Palermo *(see pp52–3)*, drew inspiration from the Apocalypse: Death is a horseman armed with bows and arrows who kills the rich and spares the poor. These symbolic "triumphs" were common in medieval iconography.

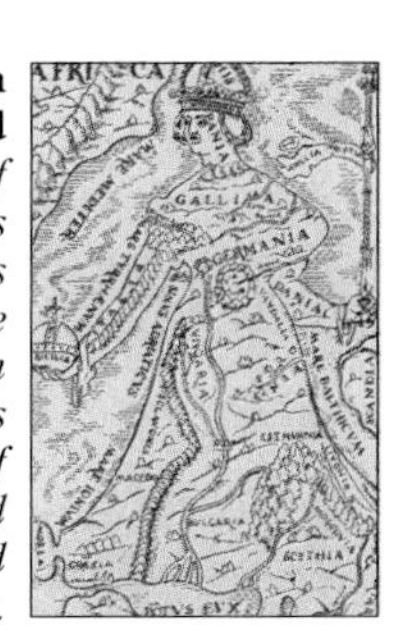

**Representation of the World**

*After the conquest of Sicily, the Normans and Hohenstaufens assimilated the culture of the Arabs, as can be seen in this representation of the world, executed in the Norman period by an Arab artist.*

### WHERE TO SEE MEDIEVAL SICILY

Besides the castles *(see above)*, do not miss the Cappella Palatina in Palermo *(see pp62–3)*, Monreale Cathedral *(see pp76–7)*, and the towns of Cefalù *(see pp88–91)* and Erice *(see pp100–1)*, including their cathedrals. Despite some rebuilding, the many villages that have preserved their Arab town planning layout are also interesting sites.

*The tiara of Constance of Aragón, Frederick II's wife*

**1194** Henry VI conquers Sicily and makes it part of his empire

**1282** The Sicilian Vespers revolt overthrows the Angevin rulers and Peter of Aragón becomes the new king

**1415** Ferdinand of Castile sends his first viceroy, Giovanni di Pegnafiel, to Sicily

00 | 1200 | 1300 | 1400

**1130** er II is owned ing of Sicily. rmo is capital

**1250** The death of the emperor Frederick II marks the end of Sicily's most glorious period

**1265** Charles of Anjou crowned King of Sicily by the Pope

**1302** The Peace of Caltabellotta sanctions the independence of the Kingdom of Sicily

**1377** Under Maria of Aragón war breaks out among the feudal landowners, which leads to the union of the Kingdom of Sicily and the Kingdom of Aragón

# From Spanish Rule to Unified Italy

Painter Pietro Novelli (1603 – 47)

In 1415 Sicily became an Aragonese province ruled by a viceroy. The island's economic and cultural decadence continued, partly because the Jews were driven away. A series of revolts was subdued with the help of the Pope's Holy Office. There was a slight recovery after the devastating earthquake of 1693, which destroyed eastern Sicily. After brief periods of Savoyard and Austrian dominion, in 1735 Sicily passed to the Bourbons, in constant battles with the land barons. In 1814 the island became a province of the Kingdom of Naples; popular unrest led to Garibaldi's 1860 expedition and union with the burgeoning Kingdom of Italy. The late 1800s were marked by banditry and poverty in the rural areas.

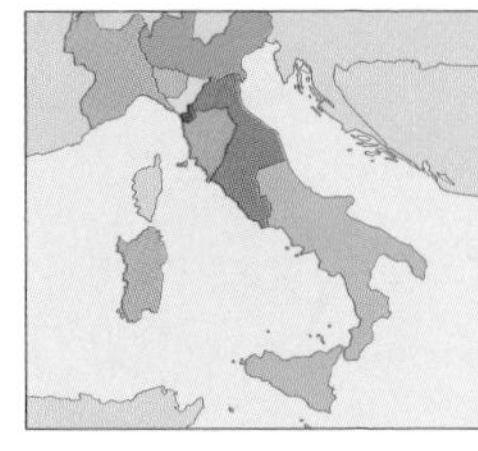

**THE STATES OF ITALY**

- *Kingdom of Two Sicilies*
- *Papal States*
- *Grand Duchy of Tuscany*
- *Habsburg Empire*
- *Kingdom of Sardinia*
- *Duchy of Modena*
- *Duchy of Parma-Piacenza*

**The 1693 Earthquake**
*On the night of 9 January 1693, Mount Etna burst into life. Two days later, "the Earth was rent from its bowels", as the historian Di Blasi said. The earthquake, seen above in a print of the time, levelled 23 towns, including Catania, Noto and Lentini.*

**Nino Bixio** was immortalized in Giovanni Verga's short story Libertà *(see p174)*.

**Many volunteers** joined Garibaldi's 1,000 Red Shirts.

**Giuseppe Garibaldi**, a socialist, set off for Sicily despite Cavour's initial opposition.

## TIMELINE

**1415** First year of the Viceroyalty, which ends in 1712

**1442** Alfonso V unites the crowns of Sicily and Naples, thus founding the Kingdom of Two Sicilies

**1458** Alfonso V dies and Sicily is again ruled by Spain

1450 | 1500 | 1550 | 1600

**1535** Emperor Charles V visits Sicily

**1571** The harbour in Messina houses the Christian fleet that later wins the Battle of Lepanto against the Ottomans

**1649** Palerm

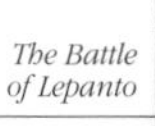

*The Battle of Lepanto*

**The Revolt of Messina**
*This print depicts the 1848 insurrection at Messina. The city was bombarded by Ferdinand, afterwards known as "re Bomba", or "king Bomb".*

**The Sulphur Mines**
*After the unification of Italy, sulphur mining began in the Sicilian interior. Children were employed for their small size and agility.*

**The Baroque Period**
*This stucco work (c.1690) in Palermo* (see pp56–7) *by Giacomo Serpotta represents* The Battle of Lepanto *and is a marvellous example of the style that became known as "Sicilian Baroque".*

## GARIBALDI INVADES SICILY

On 11 May 1860, a thousand volunteers led by Giuseppe Garibaldi (1807–82) landed in Marsala to conquer the Kingdom of the Two Sicilies. They succeeded in this incredible feat, taking Palermo, then Messina and lastly Naples by storm.

**Composers and Authors**
*In the 19th century, cultural life flourished in Sicily. The leading figures at this time were writer Giovanni Verga (1840–1922) and composer Vincenzo Bellini (1801–35), seen in this portrait.*

*The Sicilian Parliament*

**1674** Revolt in Messina

**1693** A disastrous earthquake destroys most of eastern Sicily

1700

**1713** With the Peace of Utrecht, Sicily is ceded first to Vittorio Amedeo II of Savoy and then (1720) to the Habsburgs

**1735** The Spanish Bourbons become new rulers of Sicily

1750

**1759** Sicily taken over by the Kingdom of Naples

1800

**1812** The Sicilian Parliament sanctions an English-type constitution

**1820** First uprisings

**1848** The entire island hit by revolts, especially Messina

1850

**1860** Garibaldi's Red Shirts invade in May. In October the people vote to merge with Kingdom of Italy

*Giovanni Verga*

# Modern Sicily

The new century began with the catastrophic 1908 quake in Messina. For the most part excluded from the process of modernization, Sicily was a living contradiction: its splendid cultural life as opposed to poverty, backwardness and the spread of the Mafia which, despite all attempts to curb its activities, had become a veritable state within a state. However, thanks to the perseverance and courage of public servants and growing public awareness of the problem, the Mafia seems to be less powerful than before.

**1943** After heavy bombardment, the Allies land in Sicily on 10 July and take it in 38 days

**1901** Many people wounded during clashes between police and workmen

**1908** The night of 28 December marks the greatest disaster in 20th-century Sicily: a quake totally destroys Messina and kills 100,000 persons

**1920** The farmers rebel against the landowners. At Ribera the Duke of Bivona is kidnapped

**1936** Luigi Pirandello dies in Rome

**1937** Popular Catanian actor Angelo Musco dies

**1941** Syracusan novelist Elio Vittorini publishes *Conversation in Sicily*

**1950** The bandit Giuliano is betrayed by his cousin Gaspare Pisciotta and killed

| 1900 | 1910 | 1920 | 1930 | 1940 |
|---|---|---|---|---|

| 1900 | 1910 | 1920 | 1930 | 1940 |
|---|---|---|---|---|

**1902** Heavy autumn rainfall triggers a tragic flood in southern Sicily, especially in Modica, in which 300 people lose their lives

**1901** Famous statesman from Agrigento, Francesco Crispi, dies

**1919** Don Luigi Sturzo, from Caltagirone, founds the Partito Popolare and becomes its leader. After World War II the party is renamed Democrazia Cristiana

**1921** At Rome, Luigi Pirandello directs the première of his famous play *Six Characters in Search of an Author*

**1922** Giovanni Verga dies in Catania

**1923** Mount Etna eruption in June destroys towns of Catena and Cerro, barely missing Linguaglossa and Castiglione. The king and Mussolini inspect the damage

**1930** Mussolini sends prefect Cesare Mori to try to suppress the Mafia

**1934** Pirandello wins Nobel Prize for Literature

**1945** The founder of the the Sicilian Separatist Movement, Finocchiaro, is arrested

**1947** Salvatore Giuliano's bandits shoot demonstrators: 11 dead, 56 wounded

**1987** In a trial in Palermo hundreds of Mafiosi are condemned to a total of 2,600 years in prison. The verdict is based on the confessions of Tommaso Buscetta

**1983** Thanks to a sophisticated system of controlled explosions, a lava flow from Mount Etna is deviated for the first time

**1982** Communist deputy Pio La Torre is killed by the Mafia

**1966** A landslide at Agrigento, perhaps caused by illegal building construction, leaves 10,000 people homeless

**957**
ebellion in
cciardone
rison in
alermo

**1995** After years in hiding, top Mafia boss Totò Riina is arrested

**1984** The former mayor of Palermo, Vito Ciancimino, is arrested

**1968** A huge quake in northwestern Sicily claims over 400 victims

**2006** After 43 years on the run, Mafia godfather Bernardo Provenzano is arrested in Sicily

| 1960 | 1970 | 1980 | 1990 | 2000 |
|---|---|---|---|---|



| 1960 | 1970 | 1980 | 1990 | 2000 |
|---|---|---|---|---|



**1959** Poet Salvatore Quasimodo, born in Modica, wins Nobel Prize for Literature, the second Sicilian to do so in less than 20 years

**1972** In May a plane crashes near Punta Raisi, the Palermo airport, and 115 persons are killed. In December, Mafia boss Tommaso Buscetta is arrested; he is the first Mafioso to cooperate with Italian justice

**2002** In February the euro replaced the lira as the only legal tender

**958** Giuseppe Tomasi
di Lampedusa's novel
*'l Gattopardo*, published
posthumously, is great
success

**July 1992** Paolo Borsellino, the magistrate who worked with Falcone, is assassinated in Palermo

**1971** Another eruption of Mount Etna. In Palermo, the Mafia kills Public Prosecutor Pietro Scaglione

**1968** Clashes between farm labourers and police at Avola cause 2 deaths

**1982** Carabiniere general Carlo Alberto Dalla Chiesa, new prefect of Palermo, is assassinated

**May 1992** Judge Giovanni Falcone, for years a huge thorn in the side of the Mafia, is killed in an ambush near Capaci

**1980** A DC9 crashes near Ustica, with 81 victims. The cause of the accident has never been explained

# SICILY THROUGH THE YEAR

Sicilians say that Sicily has the most beautiful sky in the world; certainly the island enjoys more than 2,000 hours of sunshine per year, more than any other part of Europe. The climate is generally mild, but it can get hot in high summer. In 1885 the temperature rose to 49.6° C (121.3° F), the highest ever recorded in Italy. However, winters can be cold, especially inland, and Mount Etna remains snow-capped into the spring. A land of ancient customs and deep-rooted beliefs, Sicily has preserved most of its traditional celebrations, almost all of them religious in nature.

The Trinacria, ancient symbol of Sicily

## SPRING

Spring generally begins early in Sicily, although the weather can be quite unpredictable and patterns vary from year to year. In areas with orchards the air is filled with the scent of spring blossoms, and early flowers make this a particularly lovely time for visiting ancient sites. This is also the season with the greatest number of feast-days, processions and festivals *(sagre)*. Almost all these events are linked with the celebration of Easter.

The Sfilata dei Misteri, which takes place on Good Friday in Trapani

Festa della Crocifissione (Feast of the Crucifixion) procession, Calatafimi

## APRIL

**Sagra della Ricotta e del Formaggio** (cheeses), Vizzini.
**Sagra del Carciofo** (artichokes), Cerda, Palermo.

## EASTER WEEK

**Celebrazione dei Misteri** *(all week)*, Enna. The Stations of the Cross celebrations and processions all week long.
**Festa del Pane** (bread) *(all week)*, San Biagio dei Platani and Agrigento. Bread sculpture and decoration.
**Giorni della Pena** *(Wed, Thu, Fri)*, Caltanissetta. "Days of suffering and grief", with impressive processions.
**Maundy Thursday Procession**, Marsala. A kilometre of masked figures.
**Festa della Crocifissione** *(Fri)*, Calatafimi, Trapani.
**Il Cristo Morto** *(Fri)*, Partanna, Trapani. The Crucifixion is re-enacted.
**Processione dei Misteri** *(Fri)*, Trapani. Groups of statues and hooded men commemorate Christ's sacrifice in the Procession of Mysteries, which lasts for 20 hours.
**Ballo dei Diavoli** *(Sun)*, Prizzi, Palermo. Masked men perform the "devils' dance", which symbolizes the struggle between good and evil.

## MAY

**International Windsurfing Championship**, Mondello and Palermo.
**Classic Theatre**, alternate years at Syracuse and Segesta.
**Settimana delle Egadi**, island of Favignana. The traditional *mattanza* tuna fishing method is celebrated.
**L'Infiorata**, Noto. The streets are filled with images and words created with flowers.
**Sagra della Ricotta** *(24 May)*, Sicilian cheese, celebrated at Mussomeli near Caltanissetta.

Christ's crucifixion re-enacted at Partanna, Trapani

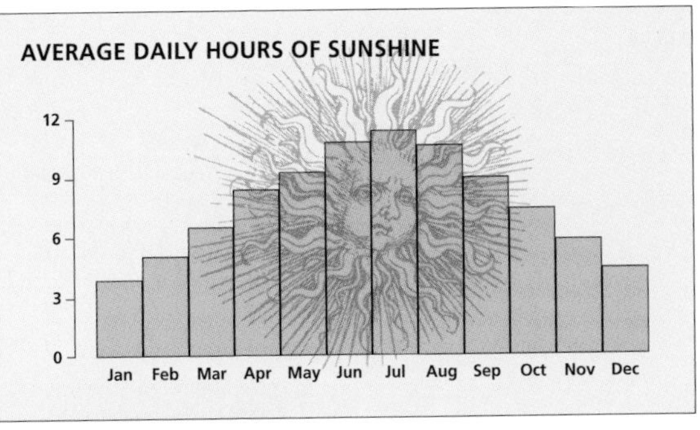


**Sunshine**
*Sicily has the highest average hours of sunshine in the whole of Europe. As the chart shows, the sunniest time is from May to September. In the autumn and winter months it may be cold and rainy.*

The Pepper Festival at Sutera

## SUMMER

Sports, summer vacations, many important musical events, folk celebrations and food festivals characterize the long summer in Sicily.

The weather does, however, get extremely hot in certain places on the island, particularly inland but occasionally even in coastal areas.

## JUNE

**Fiera Campionaria** *(first two weeks)*, Palermo. A samples fair for the Mediterranean countries, with exhibitions and meetings.
**Rappresentazioni Pirandelliane** *(Jun–Aug)*, Agrigento. Luigi Pirandello's home town is the venue for theme theatre events.
**Sagra delle Fragole e dei Frutti di Bosco** (fruits), Maletto sull'Etna, Catania.
**Taormina Arte** *(Jun–Aug)*. Cultural events at the Greek Theatre, with leading figures from the entertainment world.

## JULY

**Festa di Santa Rosalia** *(9–14 Jul)*, Palermo. Six days of festivities in honour of the city's patron saint, who, according to legend, saved Palermo from the terrible plague of 1624.
**Festa di San Giuseppe** *(last week)*. Terrasini, Palermo. St Joseph is honoured with a procession of fishing boats bearing the saint's statue. Fried fish for everybody in the main square.
**Festa di San Giacomo** *(24 and 25 July)*, Caltagirone. The town's long ceramic stairway is decorated with lighted candles representing assorted figures and scenes.
**International Cinema, Music, Theatre and Dance Festival** *(Jul–Aug)*, Taormina. An important international festival that forms part of the Taormina Arte series of events.

## AUGUST

**Festa della Spiga** *(1–10 Aug)*, Gangi, Palermo. An entire week of games, parades and spectacles.
**Festa della Burgisi** *(1–15 Aug)*, Palermo countryside. Festival dedicated to the goddess Demeter, symbolising man's labour and the fruits of the earth.
**Festa della Castellana** *(first Sun)*, Caccamo. An all-women feast that re-enacts the period when the lords – and grand ladies – of the castle ran the town.
**Palio dei Normanni** *(13–14 Aug)*, Piazza Armerina. Historical re-enactment in period costume of various tests of courage on horseback, in honour of the great Norman king, Roger I.
**Processione della Vara and Cavalcata dei Giganti** *(15 Aug)*, Messina. Gigantic statues of the founders of Messina, Mata and Grifone, are paraded through the streets, followed by a float bearing a huge, elaborate triumphal cart and tableau called the "Vara".
**Sagra della Mostarda** (mustard), Regalbuto, Enna.
**Sagra del Pane** (bread) *(last Sun in Aug)*, Monterosso Almo, Ragusa.
**Sagra del Pomodoro *"Seccagno"*** (tomatoes), Villalba, Caltanissetta. Celebration of one of the island's most commonly and successfully grown products.

The statues of Mata and Grifone at Messina

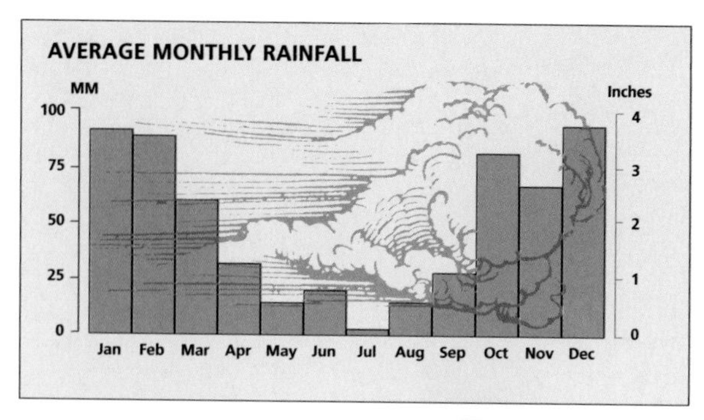


**Rainfall**
*As the chart shows, in the six months from April to September there is very little rain. In autumn, by contrast, violent storms are common throughout the island, raising the average rainfall.*

## AUTUMN

This season begins late in Sicily, as September and often October continue sunny and warm. In autumn you can see many of the characteristic festivals celebrating local produce, such as grapes, and the theatre, classical music, opera and the football (soccer) season all resume their annual cycle.

## SEPTEMBER

**International Medieval and Renaissance Music Week**, Erice. A celebration of ancient music.
**International Tennis Tournament**, Palermo.
**Sagra del Peperone** (peppers), Sutera, Caltanissetta.
**Sagra dell'Uva** (grapes), Vallelunga, Caltanissetta; Roccazzo and Chiaramonte Gulfi, Ragusa.
**Festa della Madonna della Luce** *(17–18 Sep)*, Mistretta, Messina. The symbolic dance of two armed giants and the Madonna della Luce procession.
**Festa di San Vincenzo** Aragona, Agrigento. Masked revellers go in procession through the town.
**Bellini Festival**, Catania. Organized by the city opera company.
**Vini dell'Etna**, Milo sull'Etna, Catania. Exhibition and sale of the wines made from grapes grown on the slopes of Mount Etna.
**Efebo d'Oro International Prize** *(end Sep–early Oct)*, Agrigento. A prize is awarded to the best film adaptation of a novel.

Statue for the Festa di San Vincenzo, at Aragona

## OCTOBER

**Coppa degli Assi**, Palermo. Grand Prix of horsemanship at the Parco della Favorita.
**Sagra del Miele** (honey) *(first Sun in Oct)*, Sortino, Syracuse.
**Sagra del Pesco** (peaches), Leonforte, Enna.
**Extempora**, Palermo. An important and fascinating antiques fair.
**Festival di Morgana** *(Oct–Nov)*, Palermo. An international marionette workshop of the Opera dei Pupi, held at the Museo Internazionale delle Marionette, with plays and exhibits.
**Festival sul Novecento**, Palermo. First held in 1997, the 20th-Century Festival attracts media people, leading artists, writers and film directors.
**Ottobrata**, Zafferana Etnea, Catania. Every Sunday in October, in this village close to Mount Etna, the main square is filled with stalls selling produce and articles made by local craftsmen.

Ballet performances, staged at the theatres in Catania and Palermo

### PUBLIC HOLIDAYS IN SICILY

**New Year's Day** (1 Jan)
**Epiphany** (6 Jan)
**Easter Sunday and Monday**
**Liberation Day** (25 Apr)
**Labour Day** (1 May)
**Ferragosto** (15 Aug)
**All Saints' Day** (1 Nov)
**Immaculate Conception** (8 Dec)
**Christmas** (25 Dec)
**Santo Stefano** (26 Dec)

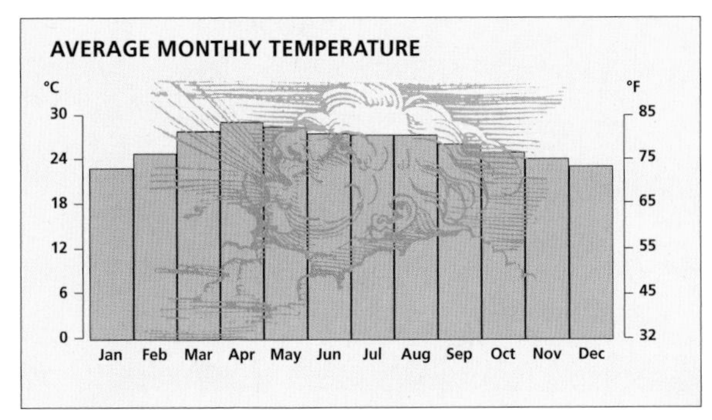


**Temperature**
*From May to September the average temperature is rarely below 20° C (68° F), and, except for very unusual weather, it is seldom below 10° C (50° F) any other month. July and August may see peaks of more than 40° C (104° F).*

## NOVEMBER

**Religious Music Week**, Monreale. Another great musical event, which takes place in Monreale's splendid medieval abbey.

## WINTER

Winter in Sicily is usually cool and often rainy, and may not be the ideal season to visit the interior and the larger towns. In February you might see one of the many Carnival festivities held throughout the island, which are famous for their originality and the enthusiastic participation of the local people. There are also a limited number of events in January.

The Madonna del Soccorso, celebrated at Sciacca in February

## DECEMBER

**Handicrafts Fair**, Palermo. In Piazza Politeama, an exhibition of handicrafts from all over the island. **Rassegna di Studi Pirandelliani**, Agrigento. This workshop is important for all Pirandello scholars. It includes lectures and productions of his plays.
**Festa di Santa Lucia** *(13 Dec)*, Syracuse. On the saint's feast day, her statue is taken out in a public procession and is then placed on public exhibition for eight days.

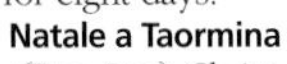

**Natale a Taormina** *(Dec–Jan)*. Christmas fair with street theatre and gospel music.

## JANUARY

**Festa di San Sebastiano** Acireale, Catania. On 20 Jan the saint's statue is taken from his church on an elaborately decorated wooden float and borne in a procession in front of a huge crowd.

The carnival at Acireale, considered one of the most colourful in Sicily

The Festa del Mandorlo in Fiore, Valle dei Templi at Agrigento

## FEBRUARY

**Festa della Madonna del Soccorso**, Sciacca.
**Festa del Mandorlo in Fiore** (Festival of the Almond Tree in Bloom), Agrigento. The arrival of spring is celebrated in the Valley of Temples. At the same time there is the **Folklore Festival**, which for more than 50 years has featured folk music and dance from all over the world.
**Festa di Sant'Agata** *(3–5 Feb)*, Catania. The city is filled with "strangers" who invoke the saint's protection, while Catanians, dressed only in "sackcloth", bear her statue in an impressive procession.
**Carnival**, Acireale. Allegorical floats, a colourful atmosphere and huge crowds.
**Carnival**, Sciacca. Together with Acireale, the most famous carnival in Sicily.
**Sagra della Salsiccia, del Dolce e della Trota** (sausage, pastries and trout), Palazzolo Acreide, Syracuse.

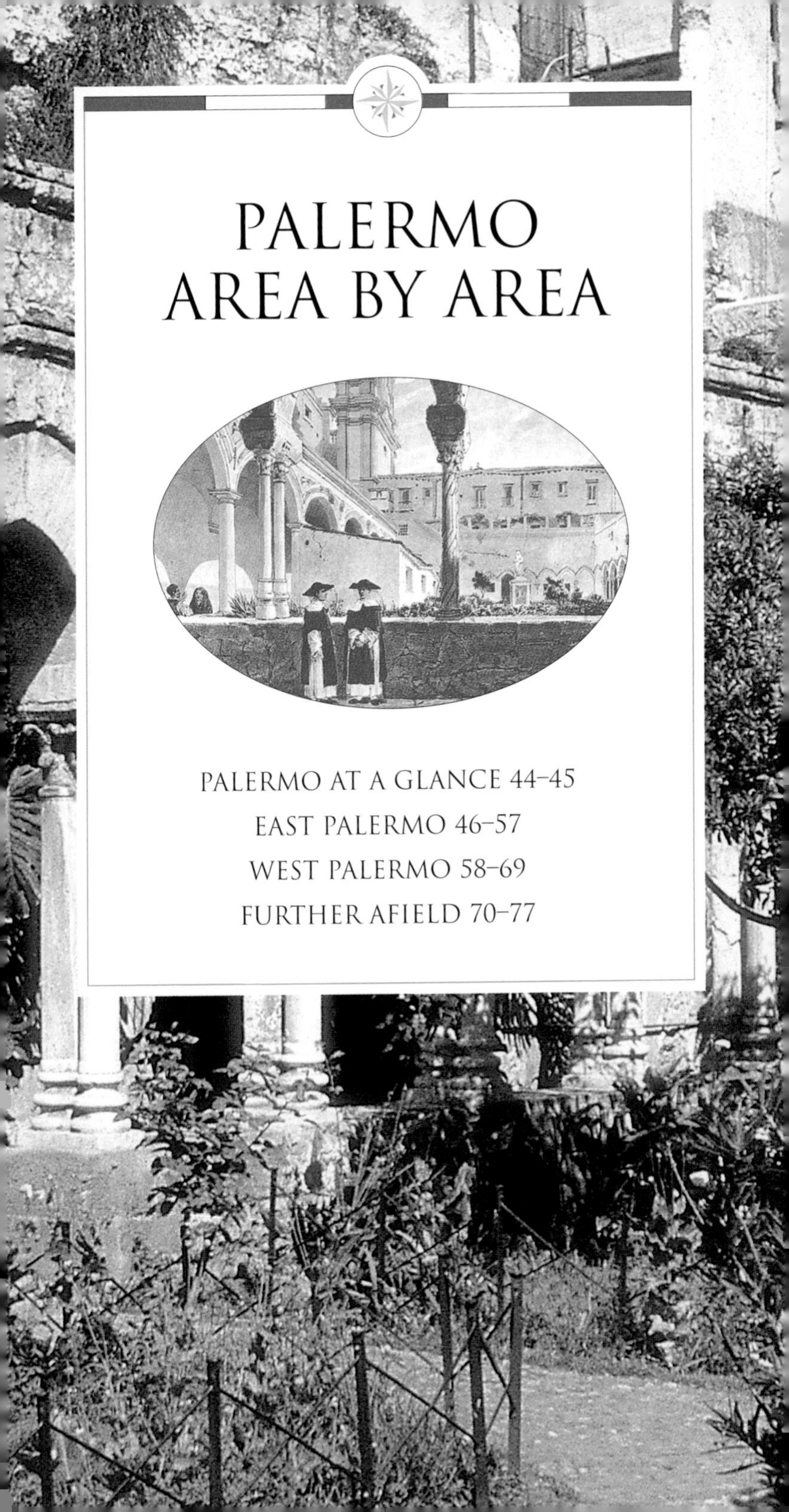

# PALERMO AREA BY AREA

# Palermo at a Glance

The capital of Sicily is built along the bay at the foot of Monte Pellegrino. Palermo owes its name to the sea: it was originally called *Panormos*, or "port", in Phoenician times. The town prospered under the Romans, but its golden age was under Arab domination, when it rivalled Cordoba and Cairo in beauty. Later, Palermo became the capital of the Norman kingdom. Today very little remains of the fabulous city of bygone times, but the Middle Eastern influence can still be seen in the architecture of the churches, the many alleys in the old town and the markets. The other age of splendour, which left a lasting mark on the city's civic and religious buildings, was the Baroque period (17th–18th centuries). Palermo suffered badly in the massive bombardments of 1943 and was then rebuilt chaotically, the result of political corruption and the Mafia. Recently things have taken a turn for the better.

**The Oratorio del Rosario di Santa Cita** *(or Santa Zita), with its stuccoes by Giacomo Serpotta, is a splendid example of Baroque ornamentation* (see pp56–7).

WEST PALERMO
*(see pp58–69)*

**The Palazzo dei Normanni**, *of Arab origin, has superb mosaic and fresco decoration. It became the royal palace under the Normans* (see p64).

**The Cappella Palatina**, *a masterpiece of Norman art, is covered with Byzantine-influenced mosaics representing scenes from the Bible* (see pp62–3).

0 metres 350

0 yards 350

◁ The cloister of San Giovanni degli Eremiti *(pp64–5)*

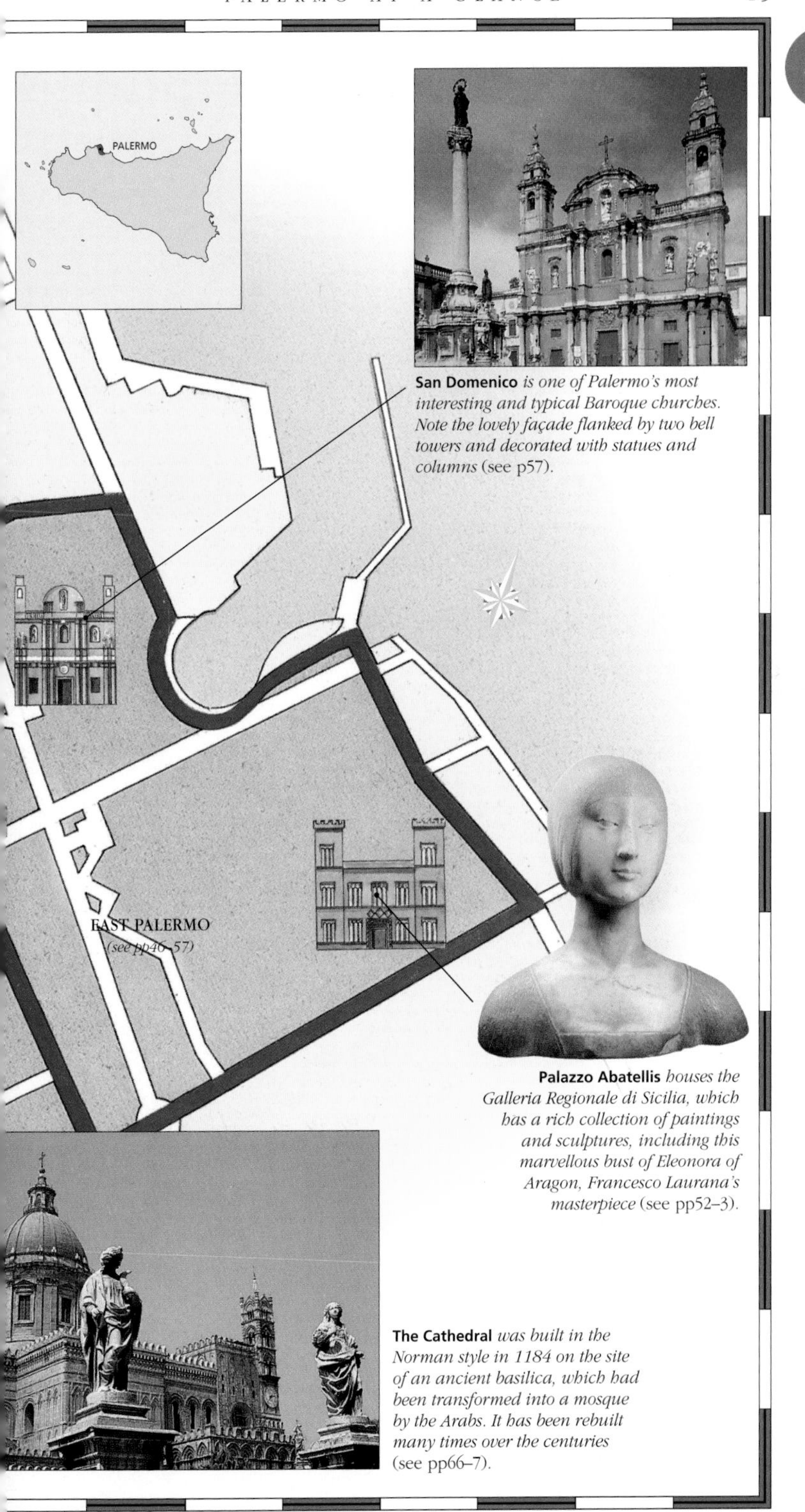


**San Domenico** *is one of Palermo's most interesting and typical Baroque churches. Note the lovely façade flanked by two bell towers and decorated with statues and columns* (see p57).

**Palazzo Abatellis** *houses the Galleria Regionale di Sicilia, which has a rich collection of paintings and sculptures, including this marvellous bust of Eleonora of Aragon, Francesco Laurana's masterpiece* (see pp52–3).

**The Cathedral** *was built in the Norman style in 1184 on the site of an ancient basilica, which had been transformed into a mosque by the Arabs. It has been rebuilt many times over the centuries* (see pp66–7).

IC XC
ΕΓΩ ΕΙΜΙ ΤΟ ΦΩϹ ΤΟΥ ΚΟϹΜΟΥ · Ο ΑΚΟΛΟΥΘΩΝ ΕΜΟΙ ΟΥ ΜΗ ΠΕΡΙΠΑΤΗϹΗ ΕΝ ΤΗ ϹΚΟΤΙΑ ΑΛΛ ΕΞΕΙ ΤΟ ΦΩϹ ΤΗϹ ΖΩΗϹ
Ο ΑΡΧ ΓΑΒΡΙΗΛ

# EAST PALERMO

Between Via Maqueda and the sea lie the old Arab quarters of Palermo, with their maze of narrow streets and blind alleys. This area includes the Kalsa quarter (from the Arabic *al-Halisah*, or the Chosen), which was built by the Arabs in the first half of the 10th century as the seat of the Emirate, the government and the army. During the Norman era it became the sailors' and fishermen's quarter. It was badly damaged in World War II, and many parts are still being restored. Most of the Aragonese monuments, dating from the late Middle Ages and the Renaissance, are in the Kalsa. The focal point is Piazza Marina, for a long time the heart of city life and seat of the Aragonese court and the Inquisition courtroom. Via Maqueda opens onto Piazza Pretoria, the civic heart of Palermo, with Palazzo delle Aquile, Santa Caterina and San Giuseppe dei Teatini. West of Corso Vittorio Emanuele is Castellammare, with the Vucciria market and the Loggia quarter near the port, where Catalan, Pisan and Genoese communities once lived.

**Statue of the Fontana Pretoria**

## SIGHTS AT A GLANCE

**Museums and Galleries**
Museo Archeologico Regionale 14
Museo Internazionale delle Marionette 4
*Palazzo Abatellis pp52–3* 2

**Historic Buildings**
Palazzo delle Aquile 8
Palazzo Mirto 5

**Streets and Squares**
Piazza Marina 1

**Churches**
La Gancia 3
La Magione 12
La Martorana 10
Oratorio del Rosario di San Domenico 18
Oratorio del Rosario di Santa Cita 16
San Cataldo 11
San Domenico 17
San Francesco d'Assisi 6
Santa Caterina 9
Santa Maria dello Spasimo 13

**Markets**
Mercato della Vucciria 15

**Monuments**
Fontana Pretoria 7

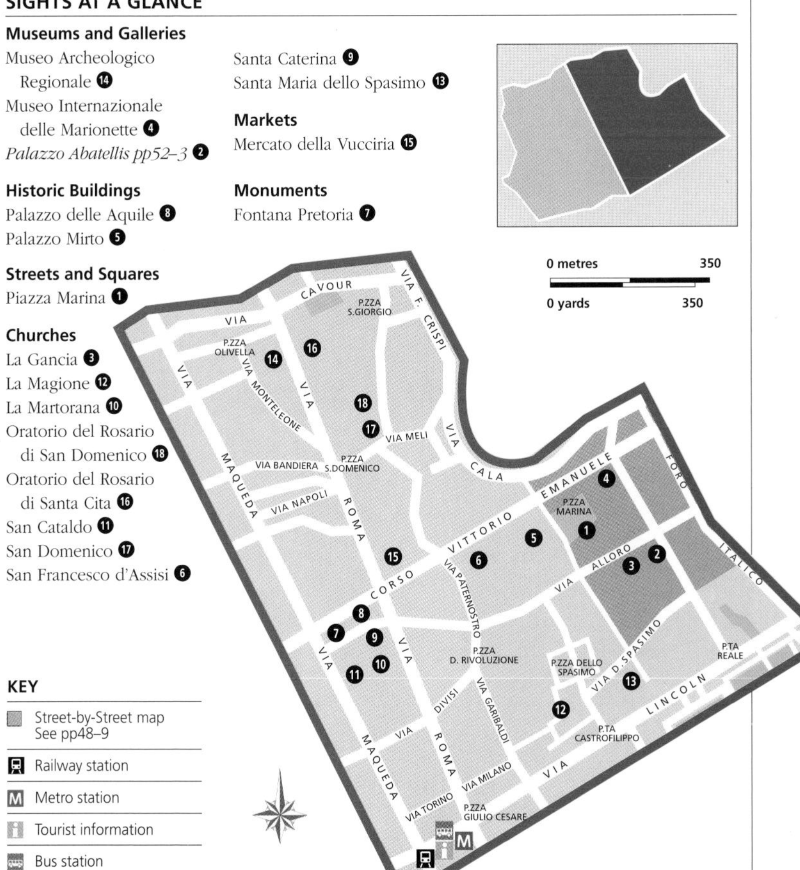


◁ **Christ Pantocrator in the mosaic decoration on the cupola of La Martorana (12th century)**

# Street-by-Street: Around Piazza Marina

Poster for the Museodelle Marionette

The main square in Old Palermo lies at the edge of the Kalsa quarter. From the Middle Ages onwards it was used for knights' tournaments, theatre performances, markets and public executions. On the occasion of royal weddings, such as the marriage of Charles II and Marie Louise in 1679, impressive shows were put on in specially built wooden theatres. The square's irregular four sides are flanked by such monuments as Palazzo Steri-Chiaramonte, Palazzo del Castillo, Palazzo della Zecca, San Giovanni dei Napoletani, Palazzo della Gran Guardia, Santa Maria della Catena, Palazzo Galletti and Palazzo Villafiorita. In the middle is the Giardino Garibaldi, shaded by enormous fig trees.

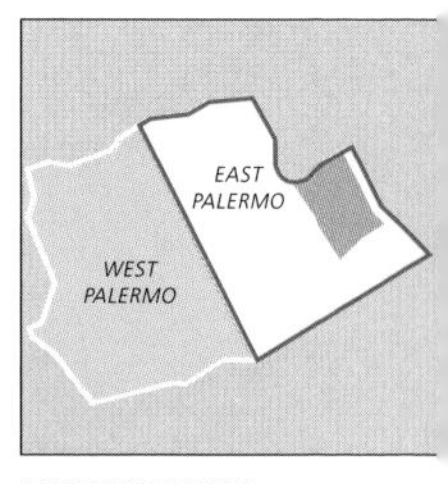


**LOCATOR MAP**

*See Street Finder map 1, 2*

**Santa Maria della Catena** (early 16th century) owes its name to the chain (*catena*) across the mouth of the city harbour. A broad stairway leads to the beautiful three-arched porch of this Catalan Gothic church.

CORSO VITTORIO EMANUELE

PIAZZA MARINA

Santa Maria dei Miracoli

**Piazza Marina**

*This is one of the largest squares in Palermo. Once part of the harbour, but long since silted up and reclaimed, its central garden is home to massive* ficus magnolioides *trees, with strange, exposed roots* ❶

***For hotels and restaurants in this area see p198 and p212***

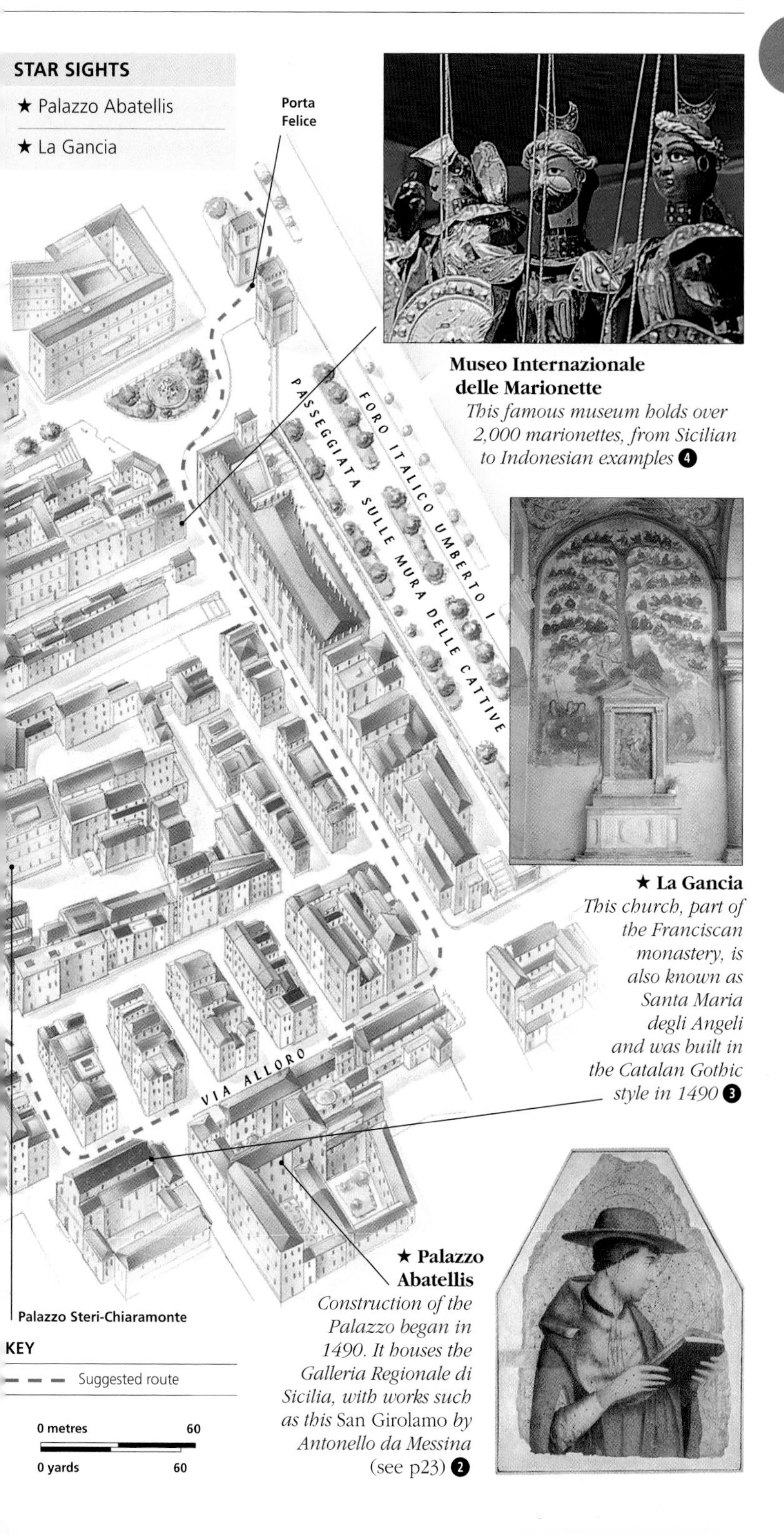


**Museo Internazionale delle Marionette**
*This famous museum holds over 2,000 marionettes, from Sicilian to Indonesian examples* ❹

**★ La Gancia**
*This church, part of the Franciscan monastery, is also known as Santa Maria degli Angeli and was built in the Catalan Gothic style in 1490* ❸

**★ Palazzo Abatellis**
*Construction of the Palazzo began in 1490. It houses the Galleria Regionale di Sicilia, with works such as this* San Girolamo *by Antonello da Messina* (see p23) ❷

The Giardino Garibaldi, in the middle of Piazza Marina

## Piazza Marina ❶

**Map** 2 E3

This square is one of the largest in Palermo. It lies on what was once the southern side of the natural harbour. In the middle of Piazza Marina is the **Giardino Garibaldi**, designed in 1863 by GB Basile and planted with *Ficus magnolioides*, a species of fig tree, which are now enormous. The garden is surrounded by a cast-iron fence decorated with bows and arrows, rabbits and birds. Inside are a fountain and busts of Risorgimento figures, including Benedetto De Lisi's monument to the Italian leader Garibaldi.

The most important building in Piazza Marina is **Palazzo Steri-Chiaramonte**, built in 1307 by Manfredo Chiaramonte, a member of one of Sicily's most powerful families. In the Middle Ages the Chiaramonte family controlled most of the island. The name "Steri" comes from *Hosterium*, or fortified building, as most patrician mansions were just that during the turbulent period of Norman and Hohenstaufen rule. Built in the Gothic style with Arab and Norman influences, the palazzo has an austere façade. The portal is decorated with a double arched lintel of ashlars and a series of double and triple Gothic lancet windows with multicoloured inlay. When the new Aragonese rulers arrived in 1392, Andrea Chiaramonte was beheaded right in front of Palazzo Steri. It later became the palace of the Aragonese kings and then of the viceroys. In the 17th century it housed the Inquisition courtroom, or Holy Office, where suspected heretics were interrogated and often tortured. Later, Palazzo Steri-Chiaramonte became the city court of law. The courtyard is open to the public and palazzo are available.

Across the square is the Renaissance **Santa Maria dei Miracoli** (1547). On the corner of Via Vittorio Emanuele is the Baroque **Fontana del Garraffo** designed by Paolo Amato, a fountain with three shell-shaped basins supported by dolphins' heads. At the northeastern corner is the church of **San Giovanni dei Napoletani** (1526–1617), with a trapezoidal portico.

## Palazzo Abatellis ❷

*See pp52–3.*

The Gothic portal of La Gancia, with bas-relief on the arch

## La Gancia ❸

Via Alloro 27. **Map** 2 E3. ***Tel*** *091-616 52 21. ◯ 9:30am–noon, 3–6pm Mon–Sat; 10am–12:30pm Sun.*

This church was built in 1485 and dedicated to Santa Maria degli Angeli. The façade is decorated with two Spanish-Gothic portals. The aisleless nave in the interior has 16 side chapels, a multi-coloured marble floor and a wooden patterned ceiling. In the Baroque period, stucco decoration was added by the sculptor Giacomo Serpotta. The choir, in a separate room near the church's entrance, has a fine late-16th-century organ. The panels dating from 1697 show Franciscan saints painted by Antonio Grano.

Palermitan marionette from the theatre of Francesco Sclafani

## Museo Internazionale delle Marionette ❹

Via Butera 1. **Map** 2 E3. ***Tel*** *091-328 060. ◯ 9am–1pm, 3:30–6:30pm Mon–Fri; 9am–1pm Sat.* **Shows** *5:30pm Tue, Fri (winter only).* **www**.museomarionettepalermo.it

This museum boasts one of the world's main collections of puppets, marionettes and shadow puppets. In the first room are the great schools of marionettes, from the Catania style to those of Liège, Naples and Brussels. The second room has a collection of figures belonging to puppeteers from

**Stage backdrop in the Museo delle Marionette depicting knights errant**

Palermo, Castellammare del Golfo, Alcamo and Partinico. Among the stage scenery here is *Charlemagne's Council* and *Alcina's Garden*. The international section includes Chinese shadow theatre puppets, Thai *hun krabok*, Vietnamese, Burmese and Rajasthan marionettes, and Javanese *wayang* figures, as well as animated figures from Oceania and Africa. The theatre of puppeteer Gaspare Canino di Alcamo has backcloths showing the feats of Orlando; most productions of the *Opera dei Pupi* (puppet opera) featured the exploits of Charlemagne's knights errant.

The museum also organizes the Festival di Morgana (usually in October) which features puppet operas from around the world, all performed in Italian.

## Palazzo Mirto ❺

Via Merlo 2. **Map** 2 D3. ***Tel*** *091-616 75 41.* ◯ *Apr–Oct: 9am– 6:30pm Mon–Sat, 9am–1pm Sun & hols.*

This is a splendid example of a centuries-old nobleman's mansion that has miraculously preserved its original furnishings. Palazzo Mirto was built in the 18th century on to pre-existing 15th- and 16th-century architectural structures. The palazzo passed from the aristocratic Des Puches family to the equally noble Filangeri, who lived here until 1980, when the last heir donated it to the Region of Sicily. An 18th-century portal with the coat of arms of the Filangeri family leads to the courtyard, where a majestic marble stairway takes you to the piano nobile. Here there is a series of elegantly furnished drawing rooms. The first of these is the Sala degli Arazzi (Tapestry Hall), with mythological scenes painted by Giuseppe Velasco in 1804, then there is the "Chinese" room, and lastly the so-called Baldachin Salon with late 18th-century allegorical frescoes. The furniture and other furnishings date from the 18th and 19th centuries. Some rooms overlook a courtyard garden dominated by a theatrical Rococo fountain flanked by two aviaries.

**Coat of arms of Palazzo Mirto**

## San Francesco d'Assisi ❻

Piazza San Francesco d'Assisi. **Map** 2 D3. ***Tel*** *091-616 28 19.* ◯ *8am–noon, 4–6:30pm Mon–Sun.*

This 13th-century church has retained its medieval aspect despite the numerous alterations it has undergone. Built in the early 13th century together with the Franciscan monastery, it was destroyed by Frederick II soon afterwards when he was excommunicated by the Pope. In 1255, work on the new church began, reaching completion only in 1277. The 15th and particularly the 16th centuries witnessed additions and alterations; for example, the wooden roof was replaced and the presbytery was enlarged.

After the 1943 bombardments the church was restored to its original state. The austere façade has a large rose window and Gothic portal, while the interior boasts many noteworthy works of art, including sculptures by Giacomo Serpotta *(see p35)* and Antonello Gagini. The side chapels house funerary stelae and sarcophagi.

The fourth chapel in the left-hand aisle is the Cappella Mastrantonio, with one of the first Renaissance works in Sicily, the portal by Francesco Laurana. Behind the high altar is a wooden choir built in 1520, as well as 17th-century paintings of the *Resurrection*, *Ascension* and *Mission*.

**The drawing rooms in Palazzo Mirto, still with their original furniture**

# Palazzo Abatellis ❷

This Catalan Gothic building, which now houses the 16 rooms of the Galleria Regionale della Sicilia, has an austere air. The elegant doorway leads to the large courtyard, which has a portico on the right side and a stairway to the upper floors. On the ground floor is one of its most famous works, the *Triumph of Death* fresco (located in the former chapel) as well as a fine collection of statues by Antonello Gagini and Francesco Laurana. The first floor has noteworthy late medieval crucifixes including one by Pietro Ruzzolone (16th century), and paintings by Antonello da Messina. The most interesting work by a foreign artist is the *Malvagna Triptych* by Jan Gossaert (known as Mabuse). The museum is closed for restoration until 2010/11.

**★ Annunciation**
*This is perhaps the best-known work by the great Antonello da Messina (1430–79). It is a masterful and exquisite example of 15th-century figurative rationalism and the artist's fusion of Northern and Italian painting.*

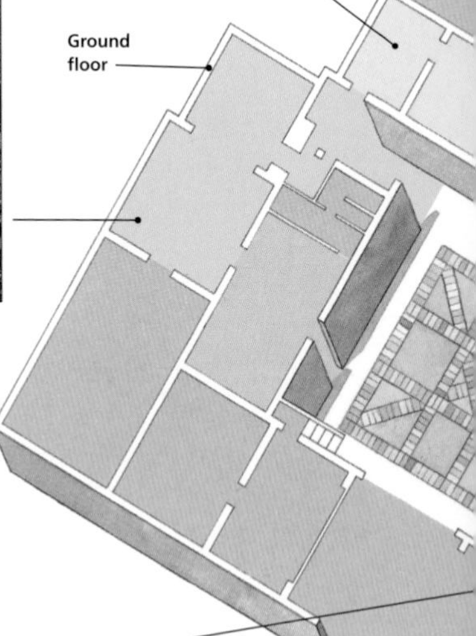


**The "Laurana Room"** houses the great sculptor's famous Bust of Eleonora of Aragon *(see p45)*.

**★ The Triumph of Death**
*Among the sculptures in this room, is a fine medieval fresco by an unknown artist, portraying Death in the guise of a knight shooting his bow* (see pp32–3).

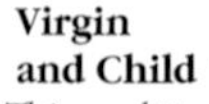

**Virgin and Child**
*This sculpture group, attributed to Domenico Gagini (ca. 1420–1492) comes from the Basilica di San Francesco d'Assisi in Palermo* (see p51). *Note the delicate treatment of the Virgin's features.*

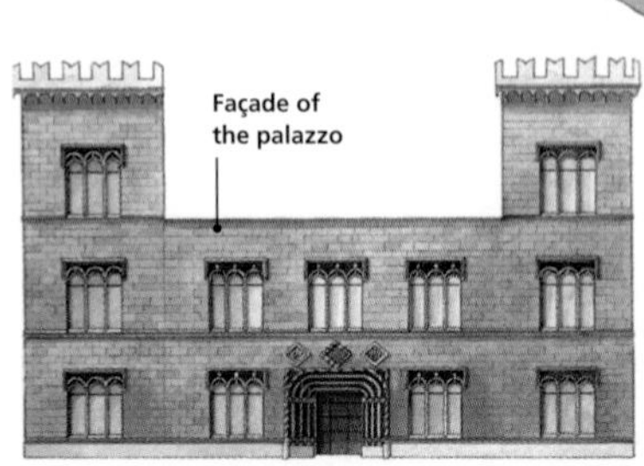

**Façade of the palazzo**

**The Malvagna Triptych**
*This work by the Flemish artist Mabuse (1478–1532) portrays the Virgin and Child among angels and saints.*

## VISITORS' CHECKLIST

Via Alloro 4. **Map** 2 E3. ***Tel*** *091-623 00 11.* *The museum is currently closed for restoration, call for further information.*

**Wooden Crucifix**
*Palermo artist Pietro Ruzzolone (15th–16th century) painted the Crucifixion (seen above) on the front and the risen Christ on the reverse.*

**First floor**

**Portrait of a Youth**
*This work is attributed to Antonello Gagini (1478–1536), son of Domenico, and was once part of a statue of San Vito in the Palermo church of the same name. The facial features reveal the influence of Laurana.*

**KEY**

- 12th-century carvings
- 14th–15th-century sculptures
  14th–16th-century majolicas
- 5th–16th-century sculptures and paintings
- 13th–16th-century paintings
- non-exhibition space

**Ticket office**

## HISTORY OF THE PALAZZO

Palazzo Abatellis was designed in 1490–95 by Matteo Carnalivari for Francesco Abatellis, the city's harbour-master and magistrate, who wanted to live in a luxurious mansion as befitted his social status. He died without leaving an heir, and the mansion was taken over by the Benedictine order and then by the Region of Sicily. It was damaged in the 1943 bombings and then restored by architect Carlo Scarpa.

**The loggia**

## STAR SIGHTS

★ The Triumph of Death

★ Annunciation by Antonello da Messina

The Fontana Pretoria, once called "the fountain of shame" because of its statues of nude figures

## Fontana Pretoria 7

Piazza Pretoria. **Map** 1 C3.

Located in the middle of Palermo's most intriguing square, this fountain is on a slightly higher level than Via Maqueda. It was designed in 1552–55 by Tuscan sculptor Francesco Camilliani for the garden of a Florentine villa and was later installed in Piazza Pretoria. The concentric basins are arranged on three levels, with statues of mythological creatures, monsters, tritons, sirens and the four rivers of Palermo (Oreto, Papireto, Gabriele, Maredolce). Because of the nude statues it was known as "the fountain of shame".

A statue on the Fontana Pretoria

## Palazzo delle Aquile 8

Piazza Pretoria. **Map** 1 C3. ***Tel*** *091-740 2249.* *9am–1:30pm, 3–7pm Mon–Fri, 9am–1pm Sat.*

Its proper name is Palazzo Senatorio, or Palazzo del Municipio, but it is commonly called "delle Aquile" because of the four eagles *(aquile)* decorating the exterior and the portal. Now the town hall, it is Palermo's major civic monument, although its original 16th-century structure was radically altered by 19th-century restoration. However, a statue of Santa Rosalia by Carlo Aprile (1661) still lies in a niche on the top of the façade. At the entrance, a grand staircase with a coffered ceiling takes you to the first floor and various public rooms: the Sala delle Lapidi, Sala dei Gonfaloni and Sala Rossa, which is also known as the Mayor's Hall.

## Santa Caterina 9

Piazza Bellini. **Map** 1 C3. *Dec–Mar: 9:30am–1pm; Apr–Nov: 9:30am–1pm, 3:30–7pm.*

The church of the Dominican monastery of Santa Caterina is a splendid example of Sicilian Baroque art, despite the fact that both buildings originated in the 14th century.

The main features of the late Renaissance façade (the present church was built in 1580–96) are its double stairway and the statue of St Catherine (Caterina) in the middle of the portal. The large cupola was built in the mid-18th century. The interior is a blaze of decoration, with marble inlay, sculpture pieces, stuccoes and frescoes. In the chapel to the right of the transept is a fine statue of Santa Caterina, sculpted by Antonello Gagini in 1534.

## La Martorana 10

Piazza Bellini 3. **Map** 1 C4. ***Tel*** *091-616 16 92.* *Apr–Oct: 9:15am–1pm, 3:30–7pm Mon–Sat, 8:30–9:45am, 11:45am–1pm Sun; Nov–Mar: 9:15am–1pm, 3:30–5:30pm Mon–Sat, 8:30–9:45am, 11:45am–1pm Sun.*

Santa Maria dell'Ammiraglio is called La Martorana in memory of Eloisa della Martorana, who founded the nearby Benedictine convent. Built in 1143 on a Greek cross plan, it was partly altered and enlarged in the Baroque period. The 16th-century façade is also Baroque. This unique church combines Norman features and decoration with those of later styles.

The portal on the Baroque façade of La Martorana

*For hotels and restaurants in this area see p198 and p212*

You enter the church by the bell tower, whose dome was destroyed in the 1726 earthquake and never replaced. The Baroque interior is decorated with stuccoes and enamelwork. The bay vaulting has striking frescoes, in particular Olivio Sozzi's *Glory of the Virgin Mary* (1744). The original church was decorated with 12th-century mosaics, perhaps made by the same craftsmen who worked in the Cappella Palatina. The cupola shows *Christ Pantocrator Surrounded by Angels* *(see p46)*, on the tambour are *The Prophets* and *The Four Evangelists*; figures of saints are on the arches, and on the walls are an *Annunciation*, *The Nativity* and *The Presentation at the Temple*. The marble and mosaic choir partition, inlaid pavement, and lapis lazuli tabernacle are also of note.

## San Cataldo ⓫

Piazza Bellini 3. **Map** 1 C4. ***Tel*** *091-616 16 92* ◯ *daily; times vary.*

San Cataldo was the chapel of a palazzo built by Maio of Bari, William I's admiral, in the 12th century. It now belongs to the Order of Knights of the Holy Sepulchre. It has kept the linear Arab-Norman style, with three red domes raised above the wall, the windows with pointed arches and the battlement decoration. Inscriptions with quotations from the Koran can still be seen. The interior has no decoration except for the mosaic-patterned floor. In the middle of the nave is a series of Arab arches supported by ancient columns, above which are three domes with conical vaults.

**San Cataldo, with its characteristic Arab architectural elements**

## La Magione ⓬

Via Magione 44. **Map** 2 D4. ***Tel*** *091-617 05 96.* ◯ *8:30am–noon, 4–6:30pm Mon–Sat; 8am–1pm Sun.* **Cloister & Chapels** ◯ *Nov–Mar: 9:30am– 6:30pm Mon–Sat, 9:30am-1pm Sun; Apr–Oct: 9am–7pm Mon–Sat, 9am–1:30pm Sun & hols.*

Founded by Matteo d'Aiello in the mid-1100s, La Magione became the mansion of the Teutonic Knights from 1197 to 1492. The church was frequently rebuilt and was then damaged in the bombings of 1943. Careful restoration has revived its original Norman features. A Baroque portico, with marble columns and statues, affords access to a garden. The Teutonic Knights' coat of arms can be seen on the tympanum. The façade has three doorways with double arched lintels and convex rustication, a series of blind arches and windows. Pointed arches run along the length of the nave. A double row of columns leads to the apses, which are decorated with interlaced arches.

## Santa Maria dello Spasimo ⓭

Via dello Spasimo. **Map** 2 E4. ***Tel*** *091-616 14 86.* ◯ *8am–8pm daily.*

**The roofless interior of Santa Maria dello Spasimo**

Santa Maria dello Spasimo lies in the heart of the Kalsa quarter. It was founded in 1506 by the monks of Santa Maria di Monte Oliveto and was dedicated to the Virgin Mary grieving before Christ on the Cross, subject of a painting by Raphael in 1516, which is now in the Prado Museum in Madrid. Santa Maria was the last example of Spanish Gothic architecture in the city. The cells and courtyards of the monastery were built around the church and in 1536 the complex, at that time outside the city walls, was incorporated into a rampart, so that it now looks like a watchtower.

The church was bought by the city and became, in turn, a theatre, warehouse, hospice and hospital, while all the time falling into a state of neglect. A few years ago, the Spasimo area was redeveloped and transformed into a cultural centre for exhibitions and concerts. Performances are held inside the church, part of which no longer has a roof.

One of the rooms in the Museo Archeologico Regionale

## Museo Archeologico Regionale ⓮

Piazza Olivella 24. **Map** 1 C2. ***Tel*** *091-611 67 05.* *8:30am–1:15pm, 3–6:15pm Tue–Fri, 8:30am–1:15pm Sat–Sun.*

The Archaeological Museum is housed in a 17th-century monastery and holds treasures from excavations across the island. The entrance leads to a small cloister with a fountain bearing a statue of Triton. The former cells contain finds such as the large Phoenician sarcophagi in the shape of human beings (6th–5th centuries BC) and the *Pietra di Palermo*, a slab with a hieroglyphic inscription (2900 BC). On the first floor there is a display of Punic inscriptions and objects, as well as terracotta and bronze sculpture, including a fine 3rd-century BC ram's head. On the second floor is the Sala dei Mosaici, with mosaics and frescoes from digs at Palermo, Solunto and Marsala. The large cloister houses Roman statues, slabs and tombstones. At the end of the cloister are three rooms with the marvellous pieces taken from the temples at Selinunte; these include a lovely leonine head from the Temple of Victory and the valuable metopes from other temples. Those from Temple C represent *Helios's Chariot, Perseus Helped by Athena while Killing the Gorgon* and *Heracles Punishing the Cercopes*; the metopes from Temple E are *Heracles Fighting the Amazons, Hera and Zeus on Mount Ida, Actaeon Attacked by Dogs in the Presence of Artemis* (see p22) and *Athena Slaying the Giant Enceladus.*

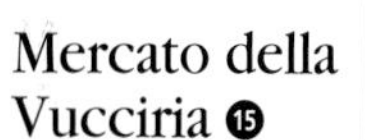

**Roman head, Museo Archeologico**

## Mercato della Vucciria ⓯

Piazza Caracciolo and adjacent streets. **Map** 1 C3.

This is Palermo's most famous market, immortalized by Renato Guttuso in his painting *La Vucciria (see p222).* The name derives from *Bocceria nuova*, the "new market" built for the sale of vegetables, to distinguish it from *Bocceria veccia*, which was in Piazza Sant'Onofrio and sold meat. Today, this outdoor marketplace trades not only in vegetables, dried fruit and preserves, but also sells other foods such as cheese, fish and meat, amid a tumult of colours, sounds and smells reminiscent of the souks in North Africa. The Vucciria is especially impressive at sunset, when the atmosphere is heightened by a thousand lights. There are stalls that prepare octopus or will do skewered giblets for you on the spot. Another speciality is boiled spleen, also used for making *ca' meusa* bread, the locals' favourite snack. To get to the market, from Piazza San Domenico take Via Maccheronai, once the colourful pasta-producing area, where freshly made pasta was hung out to dry.

## Oratorio del Rosario di Santa Cita ⓰

Via Valverde 3. **Map** 1 C2. ***Tel*** *091-332 779.* *9am–1pm Mon–Sat (ring for admittance).*

Founded in 1590 by the Society of the Rosary, this was one of the city's richest oratories. A marble staircase opens onto a cloister and then goes up to an upper loggia decorated with marble busts, and to the vestibule, with portraits of the Superiors of the Society. The Oratory (which has recently been restored) is an example of Giacomo Serpotta's best work

**The Mercato della Vucciria, Palermo's colourful open-air market**

**The Baroque façade of San Domenico**

*(see p35)*, a lavish display of Baroque decoration, its fusion of putti volutes, statues, floral elements and festoons creating an amazing theatrical atmosphere. The *Battle of Lepanto* sculpture group *(see p35)* is spectacular. On the sides of the tribune are statues of Esther and Judith, while the altarpiece is Carlo Maratta's *Madonna of the Rosary* (1695). Along the walls there are seats with mother-of-pearl inlay, and the floor is made of red, white and black marble.

**Detail of stucco-work, Santa Cita**

## San Domenico ⓱

Piazza San Domenico. **Map** 1 C3. ***Tel*** *091-589 172.* ◯ *9am–noon Tue–Sat, 5–7pm Sat & Sun.* **Cloister** ◯ *9am–1pm Tue-Sat, by appointment.*

This basilica, which belongs to the Dominican monastery, has been rebuilt many times over the past six centuries. The most drastic alteration was in 1640, when Andrea Cirincione tore down part of the cloister to enlarge the church. In 1724, when Piazza San Domenico was remodelled, the façade was rebuilt and is now animated by the fusion of curves on the one hand, and jutting columns and statues, niches and twin bell towers on the other. The interior has a typical Latin cross plan with two aisles and a deep semicircular dome. The total lack of decoration serves to heighten the elegance of the architecture. In contrast, the chapels, used since the 19th century as the burial place for the city's most illustrious personages, are quite richly decorated. The third chapel is the tomb of the Oneto di Sperlinga family and has multicoloured marble funerary monuments, a statue of St Joseph by Antonello Gagini, and stucco- and putti-decorated walls. The altar in the transept is adorned with lateral volutes and bronze friezes, while the 18th-century high altar is made of marble and decorated with semi-precious stones.

## Oratorio del Rosario di San Domenico ⓲

Via dei Bambinai. **Map** 1 C2. ◯ *9am–1pm Mon–Sat.*

Behind San Lorenzo, in the Vucciria market area, is the Oratory of San Domenico, founded at the end of the 16th century by the Society of the Holy Rosary. Two Society members were painter Pietro Novelli and sculptor Giacomo Serpotta, who left the marks of their genius on this elegant monument.

The black and white majolica floors fit in well with the tumult of figures of great ladies, knights and playful putti. These form a kind of frame for the statues of Christian virtues by Giacomo Serpotta and the paintings representing the mysteries of the Rosary. The latter were executed by Pietro Novelli and Flemish artists, while the altarpiece, *Madonna of the Rosary with St Dominic and the Patronesses of Palermo,* was painted by Anthony Van Dyck in 1628. In the middle of the vault is Novelli's *Coronation of the Virgin.*

**Van Dyck's fine canvas stands behind the Oratorio altar**

# WEST PALERMO

The quarters south of Via Roma lie on the slopes occupied by the city's original Phoenician settlement, which was enlarged during the Roman era. In the 11th century the Arabs built a castle on the site where the Palazzo dei Normanni now stands. The Arab word *Al Qasar* (the castle) was used as the name of the quarter and the street that led to the castle, the present-day Corso Vittorio Emanuele, known as "Cassaro" to the people of Palermo. The area contains many impressive buildings and churches, including Palermo's Cathedral, as well as good shops and hotels. Between the Palazzo dei Normanni and Via Maqueda is the Albergheria quarter, the home of merchants and craftsmen in the Middle Ages. It is still enlivened by the daily market, the Mercato Ballarò, which is less famous but more authentic than the Vucciria market. The many oratories of the medieval brotherhoods demonstrate the wealth and industry of the inhabitants. In the first half of the 20th century parts were demolished, and the 1943 air raids dealt an additional blow to the area.

One of the statues on the Cathedral

## SIGHTS AT A GLANCE

**Streets and Squares**
Corso Vittorio Emanuele 6
Piazza della Vittoria 1
Quattro Canti 7

**Churches**
Cappella Palatina 3
Cathedral 5
Chiesa del Carmine 11
Chiesa del Gesù and Casa Professa 9
San Giovanni degli Eremiti 4
San Giuseppe dei Teatini 8
Sant'Orsola 10

**Historic Buildings**
Palazzo dei Normanni 2
Teatro Massimo 12

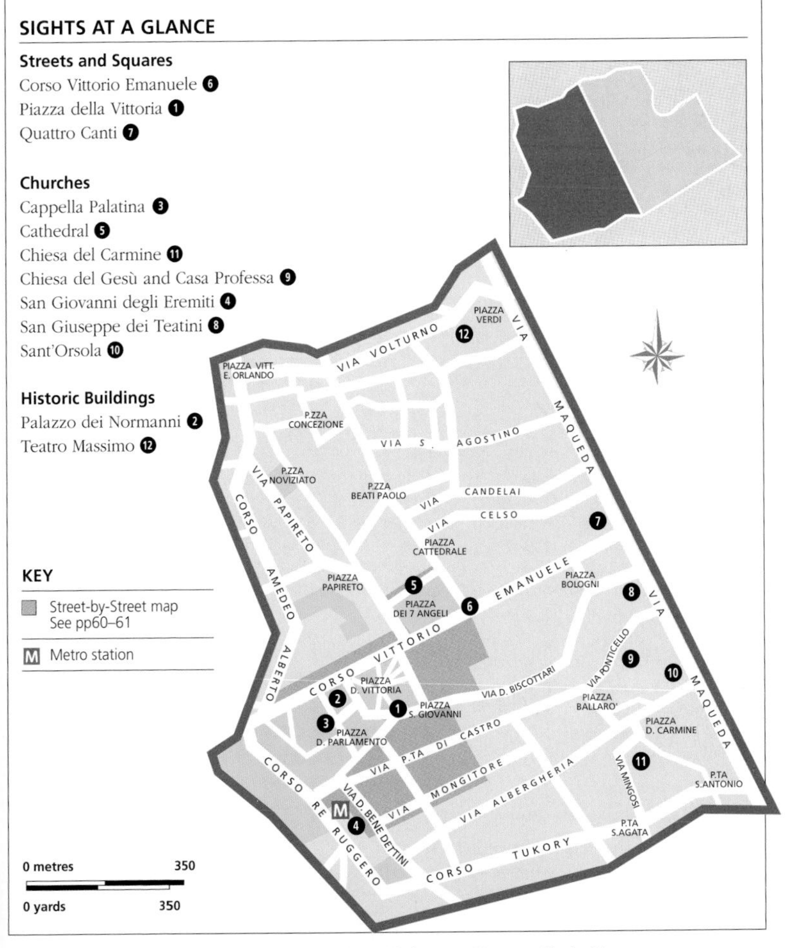


**KEY**

Street-by-Street map See pp60–61

M Metro station

0 metres 350

0 yards 350

◁ **The Atlantes at Porta Nuova, the city gate built in 1583 in honour of Emperor Charles V**

# Street-by-Street: Around Piazza della Vittoria

Mosaic lunette in the Stanza di Ruggero, Palazzo dei Normanni

Piazza della Vittoria, opposite the Palazzo dei Normanni, is one of the city's major squares. Since the time of the Roman *castrum superius*, the Arab Alcazar and the Norman Palace, this area has been the military, political and administrative heart of Sicily, and religious prestige was added in the 12th century when the Cathedral was built nearby. In the 17th and 18th centuries the square was the venue for public festivities. It became a public garden in the early 1900s, surrounded by important monuments such as Porta Nuova, Palazzo Sclafani and Palazzo Arcivescovile.

**The monument to Philip V**, in the middle of Piazza della Vittoria, was built of marble in 1662.

**The forme hospital o San Giaco**

**Porta Nuova** was built in 1583 to commemorate Charles V's arrival in Palermo in 1535.

**Palazzo dei Normanni**
*This has always been the palace of the city's rulers. Traces of the original Arab-Norman architecture can still be seen on the exterior* ❷

**★ Cappella Palatina**
*Founded in 1130 by the Norman king Roger II, the chapel boasts an extraordinary cycle of mosaics* ❸

**★ San Giovanni degli Eremiti**
*This church, surrounded by a luxuriant garden, is one of the most important monuments in Palermo, partly because of its Arab architecture* ❹

*For hotels and restaurants in this area see p198 and pp212–13*

**LOCATOR MAP**
*See Street Finder map 1*

**★ Cathedral**
*The history of the city can be traced from the different architectural styles* ❺

**STAR SIGHTS**

- ★ Cappella Palatina
- ★ San Giovanni degli Eremiti
- ★ Cathedral

**KEY**

– – – Suggested route

**Piazza della Vittoria**
*This huge square is entirely occupied by the palm trees and well-tended gardens around Villa Bonanno* ❶

# Cappella Palatina ❸

Detail of a mosaic in the interior

Founded in 1132 by Roger II *(see pp28–9)*, the Cappella Palatina with its splendid mosaics is a jewel of Arab-Norman art. The basilica has two side aisles and three apses, granite columns dividing the nave. The walls are decorated with Biblical scenes. On the cupola is the image of Christ Pantocrator surrounded by angels, while the niches house the Four Evangelists. Old Testament kings and prophets are on the arches, Christ blessing the faithful dominates the middle apse, and the transept walls bear scenes from the Gospel. Other important features are the wooden ceiling, a masterpiece of Muslim art, and the marble pulpit and candelabrum. The overall harmony of the design, and the perfection of the details, make this a unique monument.

**★ The Central Apse**
*In the middle is Christ blessing faithful; below him are archangels.*

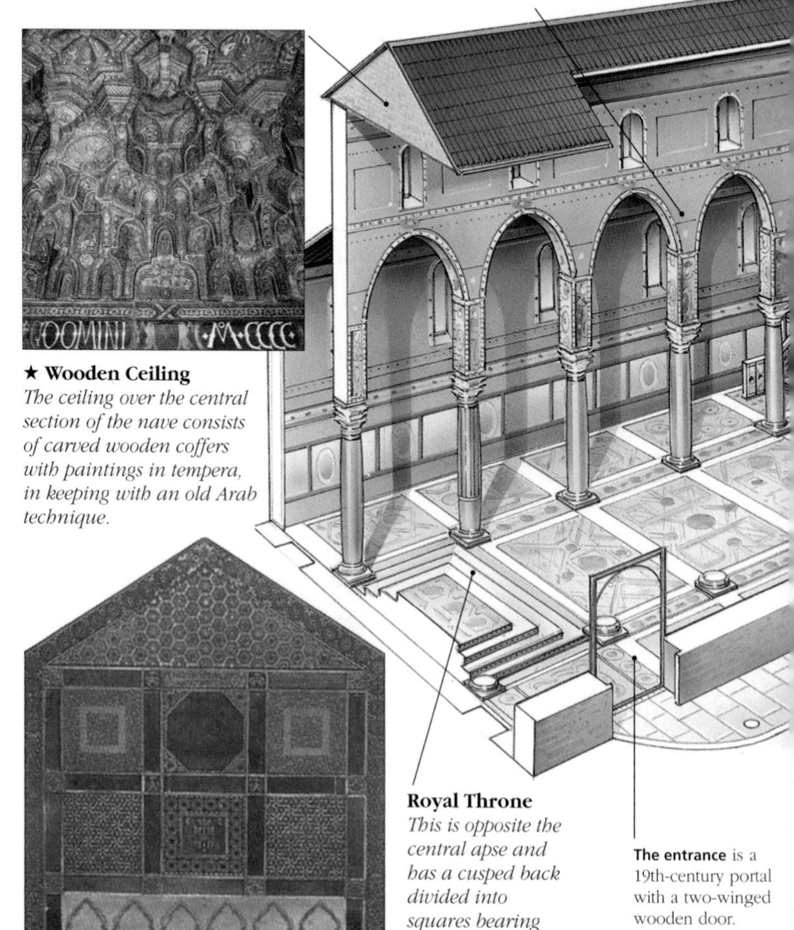

**★ Wooden Ceiling**
*The ceiling over the central section of the nave consists of carved wooden coffers with paintings in tempera, in keeping with an old Arab technique.*

**Royal Throne**
*This is opposite the central apse and has a cusped back divided into squares bearing the Aragonese coat of arms.*

**The entrance** is a 19th-century portal with a two-winged wooden door.

**★ Christ Pantocrator**
*In the middle of the cupola is this glory of mosaic decoration, the figure of Christ Pantocrator, holding a closed book. Around him is the Greek text from the Book of Isaiah.*

**VISITORS' CHECKLIST**

Piazza Indipendenza.
**Map** 1 A5. ***Tel*** *091-626 28 33.*
*8:30am–noon, 2–5pm Mon–Sat; 8:30am–12:30pm Sun.*

**Candelabrum**
*Made entirely of white marble, this beautiful candelabrum is the oldest Romanesque work of art in Sicily. Four lions devouring animals decorate the base, while there are interlaced floral and human motifs along the shaft. On the top are three slender figures supporting the disc that held the Easter candle.*

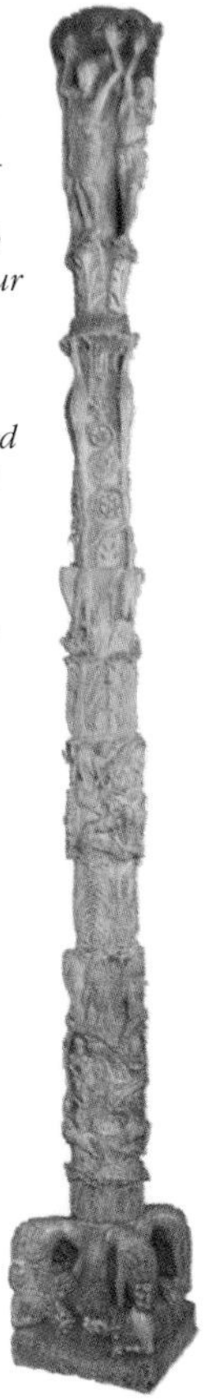

**The side apse** is decorated with images of St Paul and the Virgin Mary.

**The Crypt**
*This lies under the presbytery. It is built on a square plan and was probably King Roger's original chapel. Sacred objects and works of art such as this Byzantine school Madonna and Child are now kept here.*

**STAR FEATURES**

- ★ Wooden Ceiling
- ★ The Central Apse
- ★ Christ Pantocrator

Piazza della Vittoria, with Palazzo dei Normanni in the background

## Piazza della Vittoria ❶

This square is completely occupied by the **Villa Bonanno** garden. In the middle is the **Teatro Marmoreo** fountain, built in honour of Philip V, with statues of the continents partly under this ruler's dominion (Europe, America, Asia and Africa). Archaeological digs have unearthed Roman villas and mosaics; the finds are in the Museo Archeologico Regionale *(see p56)* and the Sala dell'Orfeo pavilion. Among the palazzi and churches facing the square are the Baroque **Cappella della Soledad**, with multi-coloured marble and stucco decoration, and the former hospital of **San Giacomo** (now the Bonsignore barracks), with the lovely Norman **Santa Maria Maddalena** in the interior.

## Palazzo dei Normanni ❷

Piazza Indipendenza. **Map** 1 A5. ***Tel*** *091-626 28 33.* ☐ *8:30am–noon, 2–5pm Mon–Tue & Thu–Sat; 8:30am–12:30pm Sun & hols.*

The Arabs built this palace over the ruins of a Roman fort in the 11th century. The following century it was enlarged and became the royal palace of the Norman king Roger II, with Arab architects and craftsmen building towers and pavilions for the king and his retinue. Not much is left of the Norman age, partly because the palace was abandoned when Frederick II left his Palermo court. The Spanish viceroys preferred to use the more modern Palazzo Steri. The present-day appearance of the palace, now the seat of the Sicilian Regional Assembly, dates back to alterations made in the 16th and 17th centuries. The entrance is in Piazza Indipendenza. After a short walk uphill, you enter the Maqueda courtyard, built in 1600 with three rows of arcades and a large staircase leading to the first floor and the Cappella Palatina *(see pp62–3)*, one of the few remaining parts from the Norman period. The royal apartments, which now house the Sicilian Parliament, are on the second floor (visits only with a guard). The most interesting room is the Sala di Re Ruggero, the walls and arches of which are covered with 12th-century mosaics with animal and plant motifs in a naturalistic vein that probably reveals a Persian influence: centaurs, leopards, lions, deer and peacocks. The vault has geometric motifs and medallions with owls, deer, centaurs and lions. The tour ends with the Chinese Room, frescoed by Giovanni and Salvatore Patricolo, and the Sala Gialla, with tempera decoration on the vaults.

## Cappella Palatina ❸

*See pp62–3.*

## San Giovanni degli Eremiti ❹

Via dei Benedettini 18. **Map** 1 A5. ***Tel*** *091-651 50 19.* ● *for restoration.*

Built in 1132 for Roger II *(see pp28–9)* over the foundation of a Benedictine monastery that had been constructed in 581 for Pope Gregory the Great, San Giovanni degli Eremiti displays

King Roger's Hall in Palazzo dei Normanni, showing the mosaics

The five typically Arab domes on San Giovanni degli Eremiti

a clearly Oriental influence. It was built by Arab-Norman craftsmen and labourers, and their work is at its most striking in the red domes and cubic forms.

The delightful garden of citrus trees, pomegranate, roses and jasmine leads to the ruins of the monastery, a small cloister with twin columns and pointed arches *(see pp42–3)*.

The cross-plan interior has an aisleless nave ending in the presbytery with three apses. The right-hand apse is covered by one of the red domes, while above the left-hand one is a fine bell tower with pointed windows and a smaller red dome on top.

## Cathedral ❺

*See pp66–7.*

## Corso Vittorio Emanuele ❻

This is the main street in the heart of Palermo, which lies on the Phoenician road that connected the ancient city and the seaside. The locals call it "Cassaro", from the Arab *al Qasar* or castle, to which the road led. In the Middle Ages it was the most important artery in the city, but in the 1500s it became an elegant street. In that period the street was extended to the sea, and two city gates were built: **Porta Felice** to the north and **Porta Nuova** to the south, next to Palazzo dei Normanni. It was called Via Toledo during the Spanish period. The stretch between Porta Nuova and the Quattro Canti boasts several patrician mansions. On the western side is the former hospital of San Giacomo, now the Bonsignore barracks; the Baroque **Collegio Massimo dei Gesuiti**, the present Regional Library; **Palazzo Geraci**, a Baroque residence rebuilt in the Rococo style; and the 18th-century **Palazzo Tarallo della Miraglia**, restored as the Hotel Centrale. On the eastern side are **San Salvatore**, a lovely Baroque church with an elliptical plan and lavish decoration, and **San Giuseppe dei Teatini**. Just beyond Vicolo Castelbuono is **Piazza Bologna**, which has several Baroque buildings.

## Quattro Canti ❼

Piazza Vigliena. **Map** 1 C3.

The intersection of Corso Vittorio Emanuele and Via Maqueda is Palermo's most fashionable square. Quattro Canti dates from 1600, when the new town plan was put into effect and the city was divided into four parts, called *Mandamenti*: the northeastern *Kalsa* section, the southeastern one of Albergheria, Capo to the southwest and Castellammare or Loggia in the southeast. The piazza is rounded, shaped by the concave façades of the four corner buildings (hence the name) with superimposed architectural orders – Doric, Corinthian and Ionic. Each façade is decorated with a fountain and statues of the *Mandamenti* patron saints, of the seasons and of the Spanish kings.

One of the façades making up the corners of the Quattro Canti

# Cathedral ❺

Dedicated to Our Lady of the Assumption, the Cathedral stands on the site of an Early Christian basilica, later a mosque. It was built in 1179–85 but, because of frequent rebuilding and alterations, very little of the original structure remains. In the late 1700s the nave was widened and the central cupola was added. The original Norman structure can be seen under the small cupolas with majolica tiles, with the typical arched crenellation decoration on the wall tops. The exterior of the apses has maintained its original character with its interlaced arches and small columns. As a result of the mixture of styles, the right-hand side forms a kind of "carved history" of the city. Opposite the façade, on the other side of the street, is the medieval campanile. The tiara of Constance of Aragón *(see p3 and p33)* is kept here.

**One of the statues that decorate the Cathedral**

**Cupolas with Majolica Tiles**
*The small cupolas were built in 1781 over the side chapels, the addition of which drastically changed the Cathedral's original plan.*

**Arab Inscription**
*Various parts of the former mosque were retained in the Cathedral, such as this passage from the Koran inscribed on the left-hand column of the southern portico.*

**★ Catalan Gothic Portico**
*The work of Antonio Gambara (1430), the portico has three pointed arches and a Gothic tympanum with Biblical scenes and the city coat of arms in bas-relief.*

**The portal** was built in the 1400s and is decorated with a two-winged wooden door with a mosaic of the Virgin Mary above.

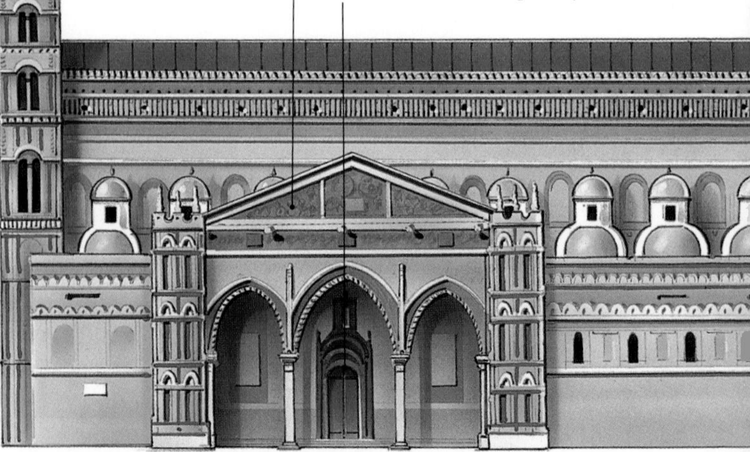

The Cappella di Santa Rosalia, patron saint of Palermo

Middle section of the nave, with statues by Antonello Gagini

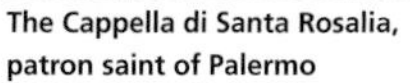

## THE INTERIOR OF THE CATHEDRAL

Alterations carried out in the 18th century gave the interior a Neo-Classical look. Of the many chapels, the most important are the first two on the right-hand side of the nave with the imperial tombs, and the chapel of Santa Rosalia, where the saint's remains are in a silver coffer on the altar.

### VISITORS' CHECKLIST

Corso Vittorio Emanuele. **Map** 1 B4. ***Tel*** *091-334 373.* *104.* *9:30am–5:30pm Mon–Sat (9:30am–1:30pm Nov–Feb), 8am–1:30pm, 4:30–6pm Sun & hols.* *9:30am–5:30pm Mon–Sat.*

**★ Towers with Gothic Double Lancet Windows**
*The slender Gothic turrets with their lancet windows were added to the 12th-century Norman clock tower in the 14th–15th centuries.*

### STAR SIGHTS

- ★ Catalan Gothic Portico
- ★ Towers with Double Lancet Windows

**The cupola**, in Baroque style, was added in the late 1700s to a design by Ferdinando Fuga.

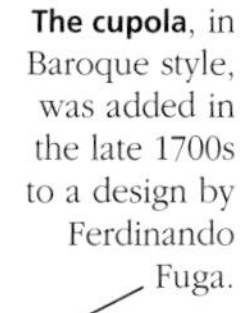

**The arched crenellation motif** characteristic of Norman architecture runs along the right side of the Cathedral.

**The exterior of the apses**, decorated with interlaced arches, is the best preserved part of the original design.

The lavishly decorated Baroque interior of the Chiesa del Gesù

## San Giuseppe dei Teatini ❽

Piazza Pretoria. **Map** 1 C4. ***Tel*** *091-331 239.* ◯ *Sep–Jul: 7:30am–noon, 5:30–8pm Mon–Sat; 8:30am–1pm, 6–8pm Sun. Aug–Jun: 7:30–11am, 6–8pm Mon–Sat; 8:30am–noon, 6–8pm Sun.*

The Theatine congregation spared no expense in the construction of this church (1612–45). Despite the fact that the façade was finished in 1844 in Neo-Classical style, the church exudes a Baroque spirit, beginning with the cupola covered with majolica tiles. The two-aisle nave is flanked by huge columns, the ceiling is frescoed and the walls are covered with polychrome marble decoration. On either side of the entrance are two marble stoups held up by angels.

The chapels are richly decorated with stucco and frescoes, and the high altar is made of semiprecious stone.

## Chiesa del Gesù and Casa Professa ❾

Piazza Casa Professa. **Map** 1 C4. ***Tel*** *091-606 71 11.* ◯ *8–11:30am, 5–6:30pm daily.*

This church perhaps represents the peak of Baroque art in Palermo. The late 16th-century façade was one of the sets for the film *Il Gattopardo (see p24)*. Work on the decoration began in 1597 and was interrupted permanently when the Jesuits were expelled in 1860. The grandiose interior is entirely covered with marble inlay – walls, columns and floor – in a profusion of forms and colours, blending in well with the fine stuccoes of Giacomo Serpotta *(see p35)*, the imitation bas-relief columns, and the various decorative motifs. The pulpit in the middle of the nave was the work of the Genoese school (1646). To the right of the church is the western section of the Casa Professa, with a 1685 portal and an 18th-century cloister affording access to the City Library.

## Sant'Orsola ❿

Via Maqueda. **Map** 1 C4. ◯ *8:30–11am. Oratory visits by request only.*

Sant'Orsola was built in the early 17th century by the Society of St Ursula, known as "Dei Negri" because of the dark habits the members wore during processions. The late Renaissance façade is decorated with figures of souls in Purgatory and angels. Three skulls lie on the architrave. The aisleless interior is an example of a light-filled Baroque church, with deep semicircular chapels linked by galleries. The vault over the nave is decorated with the fresco *The Glory of St Ursula* and two medallions depicting Faith and Charity. The painting *The Martyrdom of St Ursula* by Pietro Novelli *(see p23)* is in the second chapel on the right, while frescoes of scenes of the saint's life are on the vault. Another work by Novelli, *Madonna with the Salvator Mundi*, is in the sacristy. From the sacristy there is access to the Oratorio di Sant'Orsola, decorated with 17th-century paintings and stucco sculpture.

The 18th-century cloister of the Casa Professa

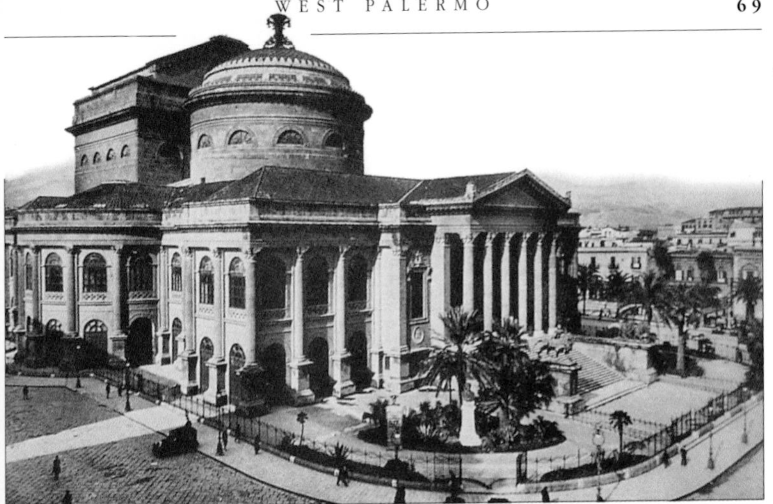

**An old commemorative postcard of the Teatro Massimo, Palermo's opera house**

## Chiesa del Carmine ⓫

Via Giovanni Grasso 13a.
**Map** 1 C5. ***Tel*** *091-651 20 18.*
*9–10:30am. Outside these hours, ring bell for admittance.*

This church, seat of the Carmelite friars, dates from the 1600s. It lies on a much higher level than the nearby Mercato del Ballarò and is topped by a cupola covered with multicoloured majolica tiles supported by four Atlantes. The interior is dominated by an altar resting on pairs of spiral columns decorated with stuccoes by Giuseppe and Giacomo Serpotta (1683) of scenes from the life of Mary. The painting by Pietro Novelli *(see p23)*, *The Vision of Sant' Andrea Corsini*, is also worth a look.

**The cupola with polychrome majolica tiles, Chiesa del Carmine**

## Teatro Massimo ⓬

Piazza Giuseppe Verdi. **Map** 1 B2. ***Tel*** *091-605 35 15.* *for visits: 10am–2:30pm Tue–Sun (not during rehearsals).* **www**.teatromassimo.it

The recently reopened Teatro Massimo is one of the symbols of Palermo's rebirth. Designed in 1864 by Giovanni Battista Filippo Basile, it was finished in 1897. In order to make room for it, the city walls of Porta Maqueda, the Aragonese quarter, San Giuliano convent and church, and the Chiesa delle Stimmate di San Francesco and its monastery, were all demolished. Its 7,700 sq m (9,200 sq yd) make it one of the largest opera houses in Europe. The theatre now boasts five rows of boxes, a lavishly decorated gallery and a ceiling frescoed by Ettore Maria Bergler and Rocco Lentini. The entrance, with its Corinthian columns, is also monumental in style.

### GUIDED TOURS OF THE MERCATO BALLARÒ

The Albergheria is one of the poorest and most run-down quarters in the old town, but it is also one of the most intriguing. Guided tours are organized by the San Francesco Saverio parish church and by the agency **Albergheria Viaggi**. The neighbourhood children, accompanied by bilingual guides for foreigners, will take you on the same itinerary once used by those making the Grand Tour. The first stop is the bell tower of San Francesco Saverio, a typical example of Sicilian Baroque, with a view of the cupolas and rooftops of Palermo. Then you will be able to observe how the local carob sweets are made and to see one of the last remaining decorators of authentic Sicilian carts, Pippino La Targia, at work. This tour also allows you to see monuments normally closed to the public, such as the 17th-century Oratorio del Carminello. But the highlight is the Mercato di Ballarò, one of the best markets in the city, a vivid combination of colours, smells and lively atmosphere.

**Detail of a mural in the Albergheria quarter**

**Albergheria Viaggi**
Piazza San Francesco Saverio.
**Map** *1 B5.* ***Tel*** *091-651 85 76.*

# FURTHER AFIELD

The destruction of the 16th-century defensive ramparts took place in the late 1700s, but it was only after the unification of Italy that Palermo expanded westwards past the city walls, which involved making new roads and demolishing old quarters. The heart of town shifted to Piazzas Verdi and Castelnuovo, where the Massimo and Politeama theatres were built. This expansion also meant the disappearance of most of the lovely Arab-Norman gardens and parks the rulers had used for hunting and entertainment. Only a few, such as Castello della Zisa, have remained. At this time, "Greater Palermo" was created – an area that now includes Mondello and Monreale Cathedral.

**Capital of a column at Monreale**

## SIGHTS AT A GLANCE

**Galleries and Museums**
Galleria d'Arte Moderna 6
Museo Etnografico Pitrè 4

**Historic Buildings**
Castello della Zisa 8
La Cuba 9
Palazzina Cinese 3
Ponte dell'Ammiraglio 14
Teatro Politeama 5

**Churches**
Cripta dei Cappuccini 7
*Monreale Cathedral pp76–7* 15
San Giovanni dei Lebbrosi 13
Santo Spirito 12

**Parks and Gardens**
Orto Botanico 11
Parco della Favorita 2
Villa Giulia 10

**Beaches**
Mondello 1

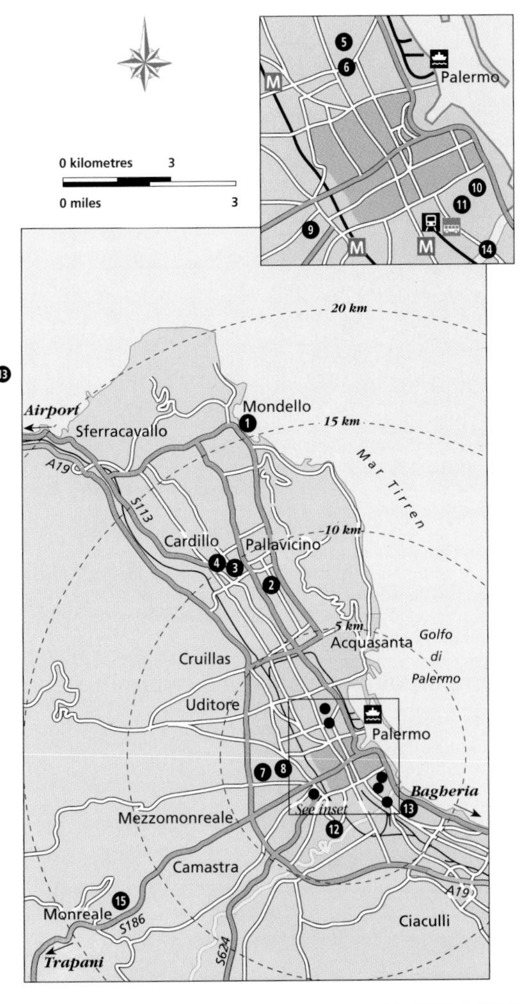


**KEY**
- Historic centre
- Urban area
- Motorway (Highway)
- Major road
- Minor road
- Railway line
- Railway station
- Ferry
- Metro station
- Bus station

◁ **Cloister of the original Benedictine monastery next to Monreale Cathedral (12th century)**

The lively fishing harbour at Mondello, filled with boats

## Mondello ❶

10 km (6 miles) north of Palermo.

A favourite with Palermitans, Mondello beach lies a short distance from the centre of the town, between the rocky promontories of Monte Pellegrino and Monte Gallo.

Mondello was once a small village of tuna fishermen, centred around a 15th-century square tower, but in the last 70 years it has become a residential area immersed in greenery. Mondello's golden age was at the turn of the 19th century, when a kind of garden-city was founded and well-to-do Palermitans had lovely Art Nouveau villas built here. The Kursaal bathhouse, built on piles in the sea a few yards from the beach, also dates from this period. Designed by Rudolph Stualket in the Art Nouveau style, it is decorated with mythological figures and sea monsters. Mondello is a popular town, perhaps even more on summer evenings, when the city dwellers come to escape from the heat and dine in one of the many fish and seafood restaurants lining the road in the old fishing quarter.

## Parco della Favorita ❷

Viale Ercole, Viale Diana.

This large public park, which is unfortunately in a state of neglect, extends for almost 3 km (2 miles) behind Monte Pellegrino. It was originally a hunting reserve, but King Ferdinand I *(see p29)* turned it into a garden in 1799, when he fled to Palermo with his retinue after being forced into exile from Naples by Napoleon's troops. The park has two large roads. Viale Diana, which goes to Mondello, is intersected by Viale d'Ercole, at the end of which is a marble fountain with a statue of Hercules, a copy of the famous *Farnese Hercules* that the king had wanted for himself in his court at Naples.

Most of the park is occupied by sports facilities (tennis courts, pools, stadium and racetrack). On the edge of the park there are many villas built in the 18th century as summer residences for the Sicilian nobility. The most interesting are the Villa Sofia, now a hospital; Villa Castelnuovo, an agricultural institute; and Villa Niscemi, mentioned in di Lampedusa's novel *The Leopard (see p23)*, now the venue for cultural activities.

## Palazzina Cinese ❸

Via Duca degli Abruzzi. ***Tel*** *091-740 48 85.* ● *for restoration.*

The extravagant façade of the Palazzina Cinese

At the edge of the Parco della Favorita is the "little Chinese palace", the summer residence of Ferdinand I and his wife Maria Carolina during their period of exile in Sicily.

### SANCTUARY OF SANTA ROSALIA ON MONTE PELLEGRINO

Period print of Santa Rosalia's float

On Monte Pellegrino, which dominates the city, is the Sanctuary dedicated to Santa Rosalia, the patron saint of Palermo. The daughter of the Duke of Sinibaldo, Rosalia decided to lead the life of a hermit in a cave. Five centuries after her death in 1166, the discovery of her remains coincided exactly with the end of the plague that had struck the city. Since then the saint has been venerated twice a year: on 11–15 July a triumphal float with her remains is taken in a procession through the city, and on 4 September the same procession goes to the Sanctuary. This was built in 1625; it consists of a convent and the saint's cave, filled with ex-votos.

It was designed by Venanzio Marvuglia in 1799 (it seems that the king himself had a hand in the design) and entertained such illustrious guests as Horatio Nelson and his wife, Lady Hamilton.

The Palazzina Cinese was the first example of eclectic architecture in Palermo, a combination of Chinese decorative motifs and Gothic, Egyptian and Arab elements. Overall it is an extravagant work, exemplified by details such as the repetition of bells in the shape of a pagoda on the fence, the cornices and the roof. The interior is equally flamboyant: Neo-Classical stuccoes and paintings are combined with 18th-century chinoiserie, scenes of Chinese life and Pompeiian painting.

Aerial view of the Neo-Classical Teatro Politeama

## Museo Etnografico Pitré ❹

Via Duca degli Abruzzi.
***Tel*** *091-740 48 93.* ● *for restoration.*

The Ethnographic Museum, next to the Palazzina Cinese, has a collection of about 4,000 exhibits, documenting Sicilian life, traditions and folk art. The first rooms feature local embroidery and weaving and are followed by sections on traditional costumes and rugs. A great many display cases contain ceramics and glassware, as well as a fine collection of oil lamps. A further section displays traditional Sicilian carts, late 19th-century glass painting, and carts and floats dedicated to Santa Rosalia. The Sala del Teatrino dell' Opera dei Pupi has on display a number of rod puppets, which are traditional characters in Sicilian puppet opera, as well as playbills decorated with scenes taken from the puppeteers' works. The Sala dei Presepi features more than 300 nativity scenes, some by the 18th-century artist Giocanni Matera.

Entrance to the Museo Pitré, devoted to Sicilian folk art and customs

## Teatro Politeama ❺

Piazza Ruggero VII. **Map** 1 B1.
***Tel*** *091-324 594 (box office 091-588 001).*

This historic theatre is in the heart of modern-day Palermo, at the corner of Via Ruggero VII and tree-lined Viale della Libertà, the city's "outdoor living room". The Neo-Classical building was designed in 867–74 by Giuseppe Damiani Almeyda. The façade is a triumphal arch whose attic level is decorated with sculpture crowned by a chariot. While the Teatro Massimo was closed, the Politeama was the centre of the city's cultural life. It still plays host to some operatic and theatrical performances (Nov–May).

## Galleria d'Arte Moderna ❻

Via Filippo Turati 10. **Map** 1 B1.
***Tel*** *091-588 951.* ○ *9:30am–6:30pm Tue–Sun.*

The Gallery of Modern Art has been on the top floor of the Teatro Politeama since 1910. It contains a collection of works of art by 19th- and 20th-century sculptors and painters, the majority from Southern Italy. The best known are Renato Guttuso, Felice Casorati, Carlo Carrà, Fausto Pirandello, Domenico Purificato and Emilio Greco.

## Cripta dei Cappuccini 7

Via Cappuccini. ***Tel*** *091-212 117.* *9am–noon daily (3–5:30pm Apr–Oct).*

The catacombs of the Convento dei Cappuccini contain the bodies – some mummified, others in the form of skeletons – of the prelates and well-to-do citizens of Palermo. They are divided according to sex, profession and social standing, wearing their best clothes, some of which are moth-eaten. Visitors can see the cells where the corpses were put to dry. At the end of the stairway is the body of the first friar "buried" here, Fra' Silvestro da Gubbio, who died in 1599. In 1881, interment in the catacombs ceased, but on display in the Cappella dell'Addolorata is the body of a little girl who died in 1920 and was so skilfully embalmed that she seems asleep. In the cemetery behind the catacombs is the tomb of Giuseppe di Lampedusa.

**Embalmed body in the crypt**

## Castello della Zisa 8

Piazza Zisa 1. ***Tel*** *091-652 02 69.* *9am–6:30pm Mon–Sat, 9am–1pm Sun.* **Museo d'Arte Islamica** *9am–6:30pm Mon–Sat (to 6pm Nov–Mar), 9am–1pm Sun & hols.*

This remarkable palace, built in 1165–67, once overlooked a pond and was surrounded by a large park with many streams and fish ponds. Sadly, the Zisa Castle now stands in the middle of an ugly fringe area of Palermo. After years of neglect, the castle has now been restored and once again merits the name given to it by the Arabs – *aziz*, or splendid. The handsome exterior gives the impression of a rectangular fortress; the blind arcades, which once enclosed small double lancet windows, lend it elegance. Two square towers stand on the short sides of the castle.

On the ground floor is the Sala della Fontana (Fountain Hall), one of the rooms with a cross plan and exedrae on three sides. The cross vault above is connected to the side recesses by means of a series of *muqarnas* (small stalactite vaults typical of Arab architecture). Along the walls is a fine mosaic frieze. Water gushing from the fountain runs along a gutter from the wall to the pavement and then pours into two square fish ponds. The air vents channelled the warm air towards the Sala della Fontana, where it then became cooler. On the second floor, the palace houses a fine collection of Islamic art.

## La Cuba 9

Corso Calatafimi 100. ***Tel*** *091-590 299.* *9am–6:30pm daily.*

William II ordered this magnificent Fatimite-style Norman palace to be built in 1180. It too stood in a large park, the Genoardo, surrounded by an artificial pond, and served as a pavilion in which to spend the hot afternoons. This palace was so famous that Boccaccio used it as the setting for one of the tales in the *Decameron* (Day 5, no 6).

The rectangular construction acquires rhythm and movement from the pointed blind arcading. The interior ran around an atrium that may have been open to the air. The recesses under the small towers originally would have housed fountains.

## Villa Giulia 10

Via Abramo Lincoln.

Despite its name, the Villa Giulia is not a house but an impressive Italianate garden designed in 1778 outside the city walls by Nicolò Palma and then enlarged in 1866. It was named after Giulia Avalos Guevara, wife of the viceroy, and was the city's first public park. Its square plan is divided by roads decorated with statues, such as the marble image of the "Genius of Palermo" and the statues representing *Glory Vanquishing Envy* and *Abundance Driving Out Famine*. The roads converge centrally in an area with four Pompeiian-style niches by Giuseppe Damiani Almeyda decorated with frescoes in great need of restoration.

**The distinctive Fatimite architecture of La Cuba, used by Boccaccio as the setting for one of the tales in the *Decameron***

***For hotels and restaurants in this region see pp198–9 and pp213–14***

San Giovanni dei Lebbrosi, built in the Arab-Norman style

## Orto Botanico ⓫

Via Abramo Lincoln 2B. **Map** 2 E4. ***Tel*** *091-623 82 41.* ◯ *Apr, Oct: 9am–6pm; May, Sep: 9am–7pm; Jun–Aug: 9am–8pm; Nov–Mar: 9am–5pm.* **www**.ortobotanico.palermo.it

The Botanical Garden was laid out in 1785 and has attained international fame thanks to the wealth and range of its plant species: palm trees, bamboo, dracaenas, various cacti, euphorbias, spiny kapok trees with bottle-shaped trunks, pineapples and huge tropical plants. One of the marvels is a 150-year-old *Ficus magnolioides* fig tree with aerial roots. The Neo-Classical *Gymnasium* (now a museum), library and herbaria are by the entrance, a pond with waterlilies and papyrus is in the centre, and glass-houses line both sides.

## Santo Spirito ⓬

Via Santo Spirito, Cimitero di Sant'Orsola. ***Tel*** *091-422 691.* ◯ *8am–noon daily.* ● *Wed, Aug.*

Inside the Sant'Orsola Cemetery, this Norman church was founded by Archbishop Gualtiero Offamilio in 1178. It is also known as the "Chiesa dei Vespri" because, on 31 March 1282, at the hour of Vespers, a Sicilian uprising against the Angevin rulers *(see p33)* began right in front of the church. Simple and elegant, like all Norman churches, Santo Spirito has black volcanic stone inlay on its right side and on the apse. The two-aisle nave with three apses is bare but full of atmosphere. The wooden ceiling has floral ornamentation and there is a fine wooden crucifix over the high altar.

## San Giovanni dei Lebbrosi ⓭

Via Cappello 38. ***Tel*** *091-475 024.* ◯ *9:30–11am, 4–6pm Mon–Sat; 9–11am Tue.*

One of the oldest Norman churches in Sicily lies in the middle of a luxuriant garden of palms. SanGiovanni dei Lebbrosiwas founded in 1071 by Roger I and, in 1119, a lepers' hospital was built next to it, hence its name. It was most probably constructed by Arab craftsmen and workers, as can be seen in the pointed arches crowned by arched lintels (also visible in San Giovanni degli Eremiti, *see pp64–5;* and San Cataldo, *see p55).* The façade has a small porch with a bell tower above. Inside the church there are three apses and a ceilingwith trusses. Digs to the right of the church have unearthed remains of the Saracen Yahia fortress, which once defended southeastern Palermo.

## Ponte dell'Ammiraglio ⓮

Via dei Mille.

The Admiral's Bridge used to span the Oreto river before the latter was diverted. It is made of large cambered blocks of limestone resting on twelve pointed arches, five of them no more than small openings in the imposts. This beautiful and amazingly well-preserved bridge was built in 1113 by George of Antioch, Roger II's High Admiral (the *ammiraglio* of the name), but is now a rather incongruous sight, isolated without a river.

The impressive pointed arches of the 12th-century Ponte dell'Ammiraglio

# Monreale Cathedral ⓯

Capital in the cloister

Dominating the Conca d'Oro, the Cathedral of Monreale is the pinnacle of achievement of Arab-Norman art. It was founded in 1172 by William II and a Benedictine monastery was built next to it. The cathedral is famous for its remarkable interior with the magnificent gold mosaics representing episodes from the Old Testament. The cloister *(see p70)* has pointed Arab arches with geometric motifs, and scenes from the Bible are sculpted on the capitals of the 228 white marble twin columns.

**★ Christ Pantocrator**
*The church, with a Latin cross plan, is dominated by the 12th–13th-century mosaic of Christ in the middle apse.*

**Exterior of the Apse**
*With its interlaced marble and tufa arches and multicoloured motifs, the exterior of the apse is the apogee of Norman decoration.*

**The royal tomb** of William II, sculpted in white marble, is next to the tomb of William I in a corner of the transept.

**The bronze door by Barisano da Trani** (1179), on the northern side, is under the porch designed by Gian Domenico and Fazio Gagini (1547–69).

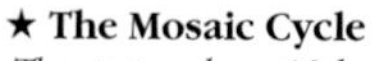

**★ The Mosaic Cycle**
*The stupendous 12th–13th-century mosaics occupy the entire nave and the aisles, the choir and the transepts. They illustrate scenes from the New and Old Testaments.*

**★ Cloister**
*This masterpiece of Norman art has 228 small double columns with varied decoration culminating in the highly elaborate capitals supporting the arches of Arab inspiration.*

## VISITORS' CHECKLIST

*AMAT 309, 389, 809, 8/9.* **Cathedral** (Piazza Duomo). ***Tel*** *091-640 44 13.* *Apr–Oct: 8am–6pm Mon–Sat; Nov–Mar: 8am–12:30pm Mon–Sat, 8–10am, 3:30–5:30pm Sun.* (**tour of roof** only). **Cloister** (Piazza Guglielmo il Buono). ***Tel*** *091-640 44 03.* *9:30am– 6:30pm daily.*

**A wing of the original monastery** lies over the southern portico.

**Arab-inspired fountain**

**Columns**
*The cloister columns were made by skilled craftsmen from throughout Southern Italy. This carved detail shows Adam and Eve.*

**18th-century portico**, flanked by two bell towers.

**Bronze Door on the Portal**
*This lovely door by Bonanno da Pisa (1185) has 42 elaborately framed Biblical scenes and other images. The lion and griffon were Norman symbols.*

**STAR FEATURES**

- ★ The Mosaic Cycle
- ★ Christ Pantocrator
- ★ Cloister

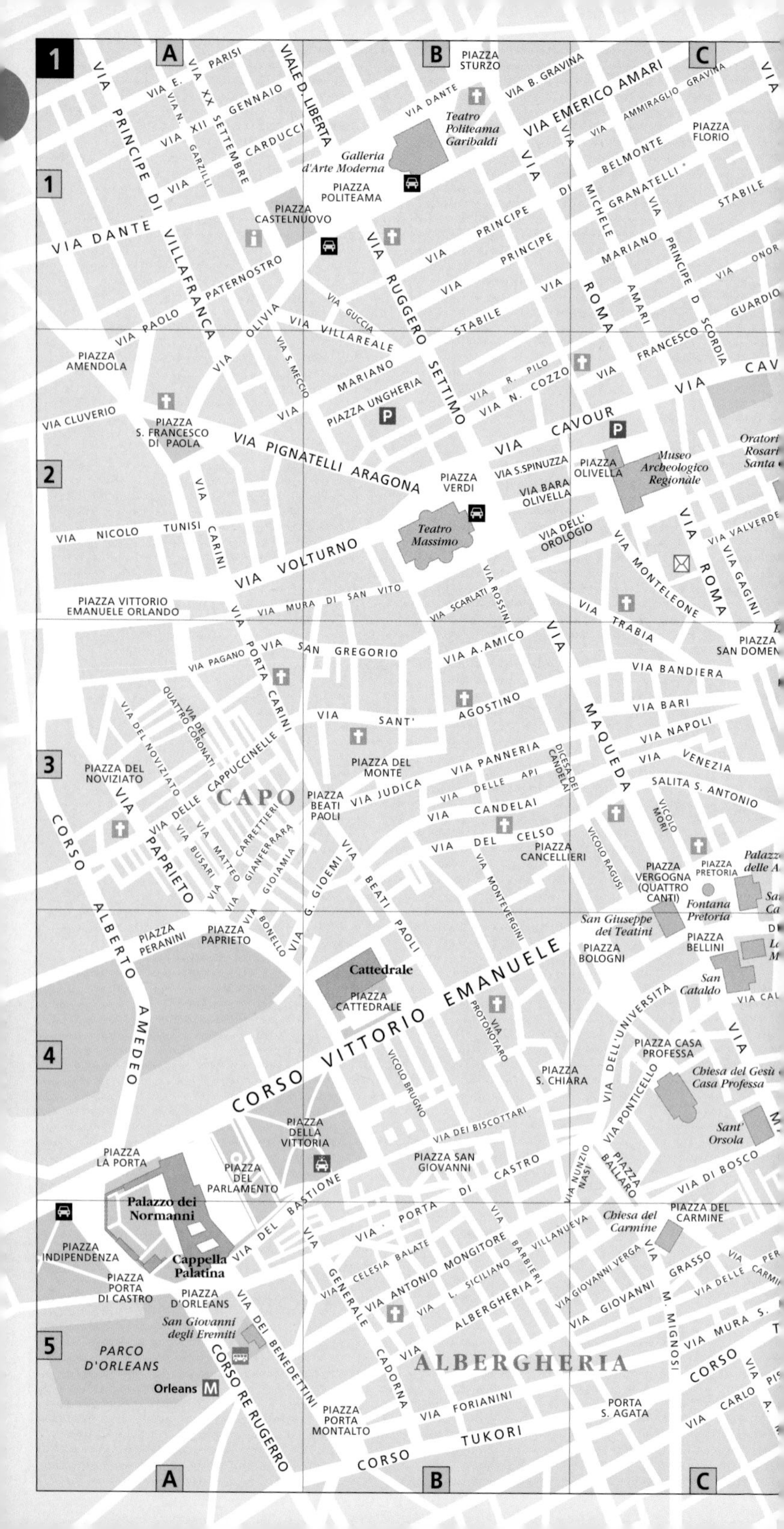
1
A
B
C
Piazza Sturzo
Teatro Politeama Garibaldi
Galleria d'Arte Moderna
Piazza Politeama
Piazza Castelnuovo
Piazza Florio
Via Dante
Via Principe di Villafranca
Viale d. Libertà
Via Emerico Amari
Via Roma
Via Ruggero Settimo
Via Mariano Stabile
Piazza Amendola
Piazza S. Francesco di Paola
Via Pignatelli Aragona
Piazza Ungheria
Via Cavour
Piazza Verdi
Teatro Massimo
Piazza Olivella
Museo Archeologico Regionale
Via Volturno
Piazza Vittorio Emanuele Orlando
Via Maqueda
Piazza San Domenico
Piazza del Noviziato
Capo
Piazza Beati Paoli
Piazza del Monte
Piazza Cancellieri
Piazza Vergogna (Quattro Canti)
Piazza Pretoria
Fontana Pretoria
San Giuseppe dei Teatini
Piazza Bologni
Piazza Bellini
San Cataldo
Piazza Peranini
Piazza Papireto
Cattedrale
Piazza Cattedrale
Corso Vittorio Emanuele
Corso Alberto Amedeo
Piazza Casa Professa
Chiesa del Gesù Casa Professa
Piazza S. Chiara
Sant' Orsola
Piazza della Vittoria
Piazza La Porta
Piazza del Parlamento
Piazza San Giovanni
Palazzo dei Normanni
Cappella Palatina
Piazza Indipendenza
Piazza Porta di Castro
Piazza d'Orleans
San Giovanni degli Eremiti
Chiesa del Carmine
Piazza del Carmine
Parco d'Orleans
Orleans
Albergheria
Corso Re Rugerro
Piazza Porta Montalto
Porta S. Agata
Corso Tukori
Via Porta di Castro
Via dei Benedettini
2
3
4
5

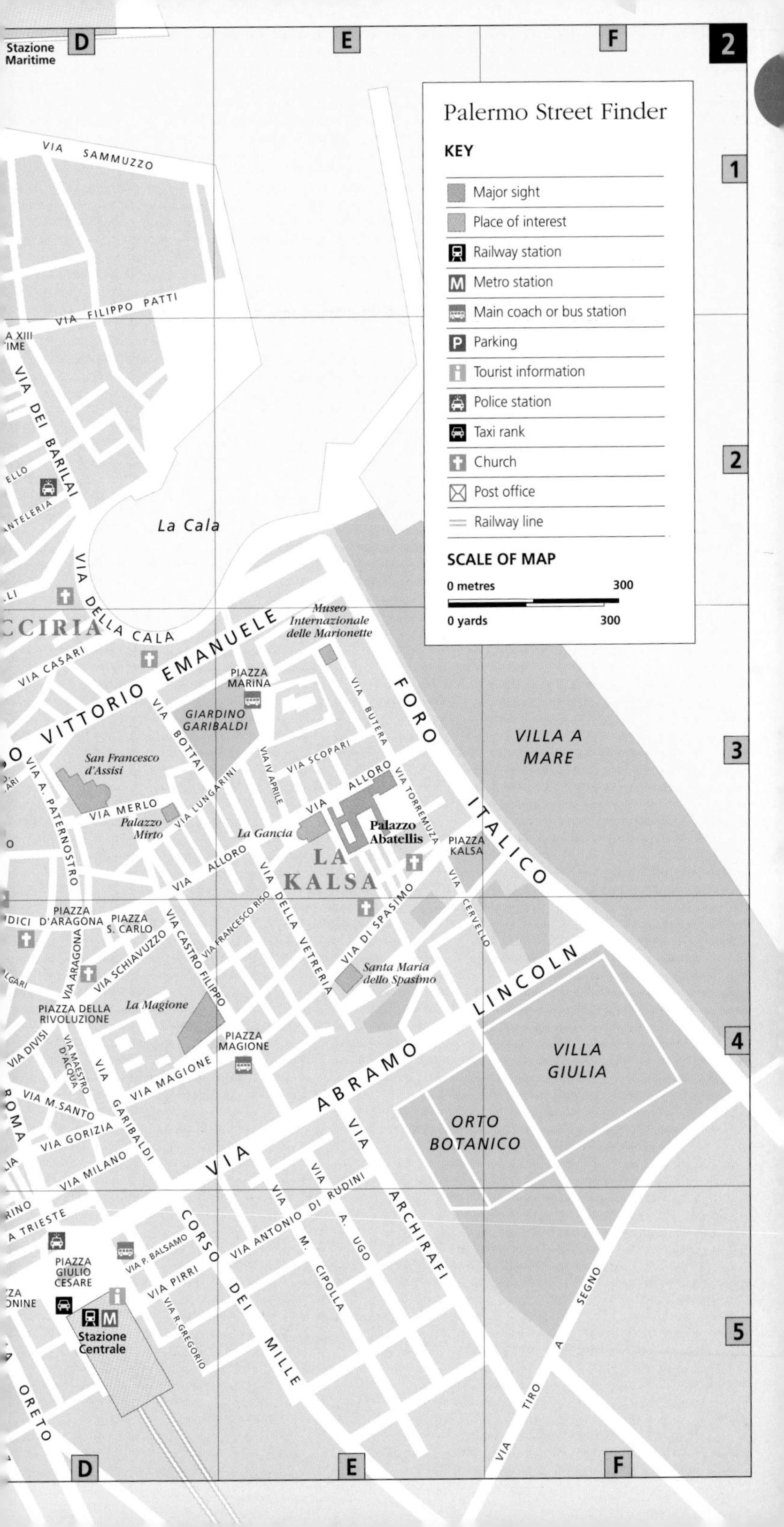
Palermo Street Finder
KEY
Major sight
Place of interest
Railway station
Metro station
Main coach or bus station
Parking
Tourist information
Police station
Taxi rank
Church
Post office
Railway line
SCALE OF MAP
0 metres
300
0 yards
300
Stazione Maritime
La Cala
Museo Internazionale delle Marionette
PIAZZA MARINA
GIARDINO GARIBALDI
San Francesco d'Assisi
Palazzo Mirto
La Gancia
Palazzo Abatellis
LA KALSA
PIAZZA KALSA
VILLA A MARE
Santa Maria dello Spasimo
La Magione
PIAZZA MAGIONE
PIAZZA D'ARAGONA
PIAZZA S. CARLO
PIAZZA DELLA RIVOLUZIONE
VILLA GIULIA
ORTO BOTANICO
PIAZZA GIULIO CESARE
Stazione Centrale
VIA SAMMUZZO
VIA FILIPPO PATTI
VIA DEI BARILAI
VIA DELLA CALA
VIA CASARI
VITTORIO EMANUELE
VIA BOTTAI
VIA BUTERA
FORO ITALICO
VIA SCOPARI
VIA IV APRILE
VIA ALLORO
VIA TORREMUZA
VIA A. PATERNOSTRO
VIA MERLO
VIA LUNGARINI
VIA DELLA VETRERIA
VIA CERVELLO
VIA DI SPASIMO
VIA FRANCESCO RISO
VIA CASTRO FILIPPO
VIA SCHIAVUZZO
VIA ARAGONA
VIA DIVISI
VIA MAESTRO D'ACQUA
VIA MAGIONE
VIA M.SANTO
VIA GORIZIA
VIA GARIBALDI
VIA MILANO
VIA ABRAMO LINCOLN
VIA ANTONIO DI RUDINI
VIA M. CIPOLLA
VIA A. UGO
ARCHIRAFI
CORSO DEI MILLE
VIA P. BALSAMO
VIA PIRRI
VIA R. GREGORIO
VIA TIRO A SEGNO
ORETO
ROMA
A TRIESTE
D
E
F
1
2
3
4
5

# SICILY AREA BY AREA

# Sicily at a Glance

There are few places in the Mediterranean that can equal Sicily's striking landscapes and colourful history. There are noticeable differences between the eastern part of the island, culturally of Greek origin, and the Phoenician and Arab western side. However, Sicily is not simply an east and a west side – every village and town has its own unique story. Within a few kilometres of each other you may find splendid luxuriant coastline and arid, sun-parched hills, just as you can pick out different layers of civilization side by side or overlapping one another. It is not that unusual to see Greek, Arab, Norman and Baroque influences in the same site, sometimes even in the same building.

**The Chiesa Matrice in Erice** (see pp100–1), *built in the 14th century, is a good example of Arab-Norman religious architecture.*

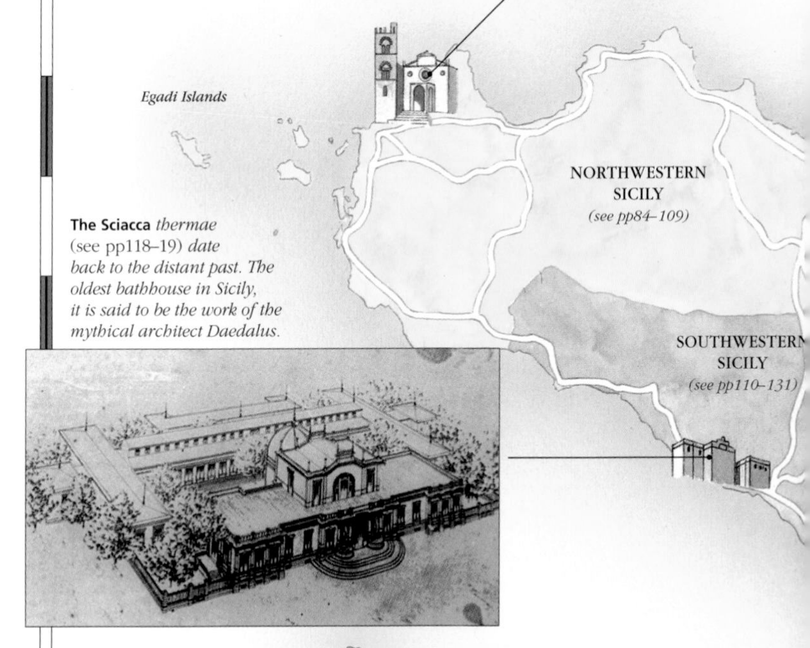


**The Sciacca** *thermae* (see pp118–19) *date back to the distant past. The oldest bathhouse in Sicily, it is said to be the work of the mythical architect Daedalus.*

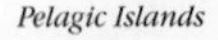

**The Castello di Lombardia at Enna** (see p127) *is one of the most important medieval fortifications in Sicily.*

◁ **Classical Greek theatre at Taormina, the second-largest of its kind in Sicily**

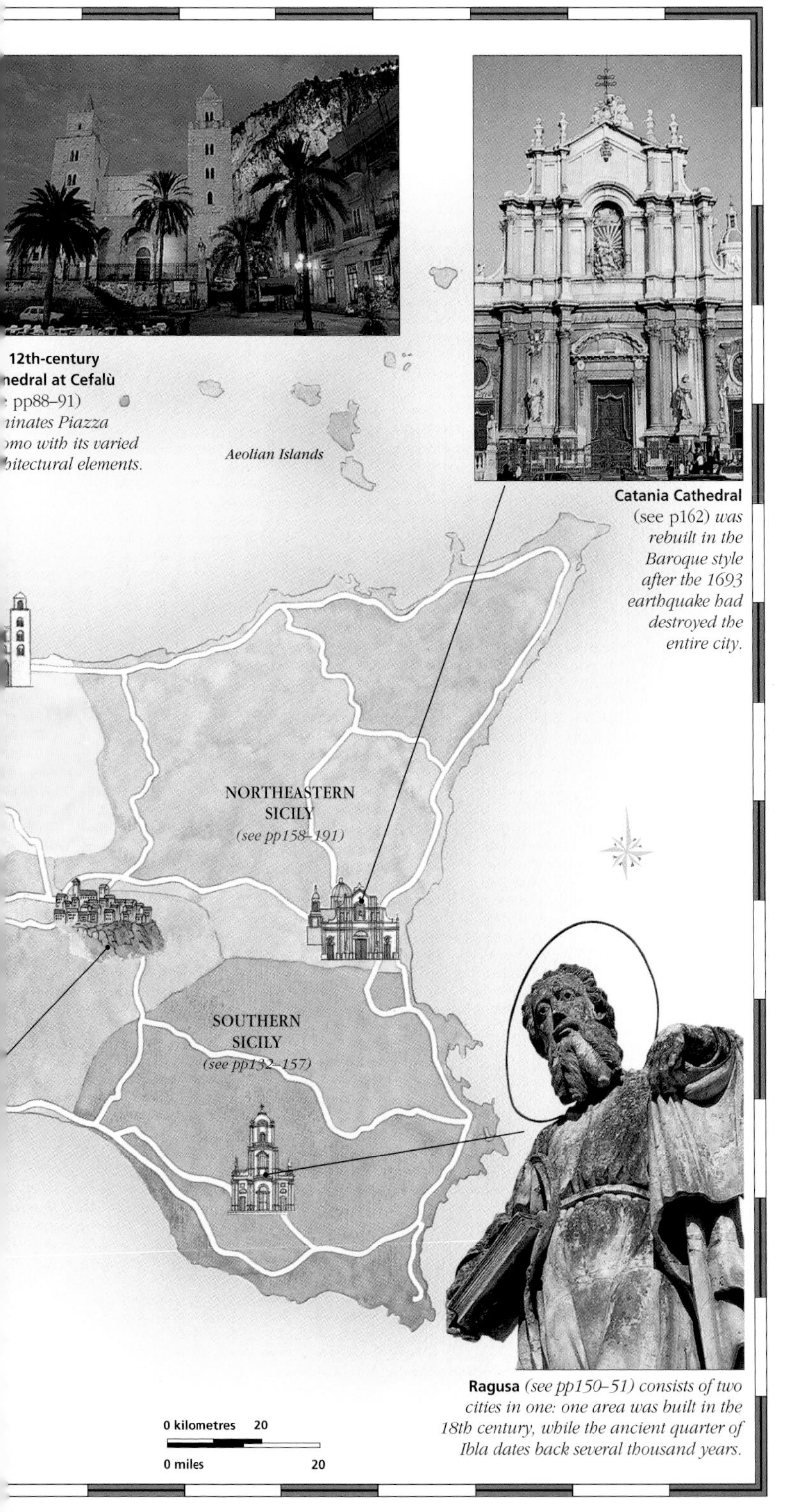


**12th-century**
**nedral at Cefalù**
pp88–91)
*inates Piazza*
*omo with its varied*
*hitectural elements.*

**Catania Cathedral** (see p162) *was rebuilt in the Baroque style after the 1693 earthquake had destroyed the entire city.*

**Ragusa** *(see pp150–51) consists of two cities in one: one area was built in the 18th century, while the ancient quarter of Ibla dates back several thousand years.*

# NORTHWESTERN SICILY

*Over the centuries, this area of Sicily has been particularly. exposed to influences from different colonizing civilizations. The Phoenicians settled in Mozia and founded harbour towns at Palermo and Solunto. They were followed by the Greeks and then the Arabs, who began their conquest of the island at Marsala.*

These cultures are still very much alive in the names of the towns and sights, in the architecture, and in the layout of the towns from Marsala to Mazara del Vallo. But, unfortunately, northwestern Sicily is also one of the areas most affected by the scourges of uncontrolled property development and lack of care for the environment. Examples of this are the huge area of unattractive houses between Palermo and Castellammare, which have disfigured what was one of the most fascinating coastlines in Sicily, and the squalidly reconstructed inhabited areas in the Valle del Belice, destroyed by the 1968 earthquake. However, there are other towns pursuing a policy of preserving and reassessing their history. Erice is one of these; its medieval architecture and town plan have been preserved, and many of the churches have been converted into art and culture centres, instead of being left in a state of neglect. The same holds true for Cefalù, Nicosia, Sperlinga and the two Petralias. There is also a good deal of unspoiled scenery besides the nature reserves. The areas around Trapani and Belice are fascinating, as are the rugged valleys in the interior, characterized by villages perched on the top of steep cliffs with breathtaking views. Other beautiful sights include the Egadi Islands and Ustica.

**The Palazzina Pepoli at Erice, converted into a villa in the 19th century**

◁ **Typical Sicilian scenery: in the background is the Monte Cofano promontory near San Vito Lo Capo**

# Exploring Northwestern Sicily

With the magnificent ruins of Segesta, Selinunte, Solunto and Mozia, this area is full of archaeological fascination. The splendid medieval towns of Cefalù and Erice are also worth a visit in themselves. In the interior there are villages where time seems to have stood still, especially in the Madonie mountains. For those who prefer natural history, there are the crystal-clear waters of Ustica and the Egadi Islands, the Riserva Naturale Marina and the Riserva Naturale dello Zingaro between Scopello and San Vito Lo Capo.

A windmill and outbuilding in the salt marshes near Trapani

One of the statues on Caccamo Cathedral

**KEY**

- Motorway
- Major road
- Secondary road
- Minor road
- Main railway
- Minor railway

0 kilometres 20

0 miles 10

***SEE ALSO***

• ***Where to Stay*** pp199–201

• ***Where to Eat*** pp214–16

## SIGHTS AT A GLANCE

Alcamo 13
Caccamo 10
Castel di Tusa 2
Castellammare del Golfo 14
Castelvetrano 24
*Cefalù pp88–91* 1
*Erice pp100–1* 19
Gangi 6
Gibellina 17
Marsala 21
Mazara del Vallo 25
Mozia 22
Nicosia 4
Petralia Soprana 8
Petralia Sottana 7
Piana degli Albanesi 12
Polizzi Generosa 9
Salemi 18
Santo Stefano di Camastra 3
*Segesta p98* 16
*Selinunte pp104–6* 23
Sperlinga 5
Solunto 11
Trapani 20

**Islands**

Egadi Islands 26
Ustica 27

**Tour**

Riserva dello Zingaro 15

## GETTING AROUND

Northwestern Sicily has a very good road network. Toll-free *autostrada* (motorway) A29 links Palermo with Mazara del Vallo, while a connecting road goes to Trapani. Travelling eastwards, A20 now goes to Messina, and a toll is charged. The main roads along the coast and in the Valle del Belice are good, while those leading to the villages at the foot of the mountains are winding and slow and, in the winter, may be covered with snow or ice. There are frequent trains between Messina and Palermo, less frequently to Trapani, Marsala and Mazara. The bus network connects the main towns and smaller and more remote villages.

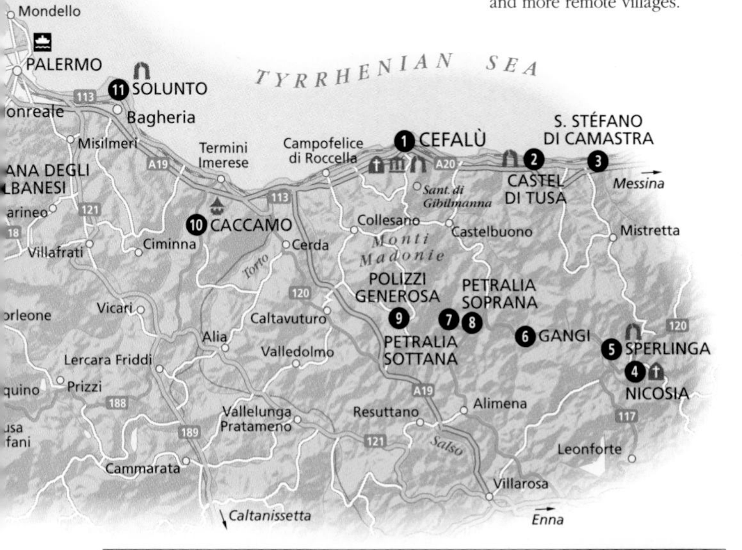

**The theatre at Segesta, on the top of Monte Barbaro, set in an extraordinary landscape. As with all Greek theatres, the scenery formed part of the stage set**

# Street-by-Street: Cefalù ❶

*Tonnaio Vase, Museo Mandralisca*

Founded on a steep promontory halfway between Palermo and Capo d'Orlando, Cefalù has retained its medieval appearance around the Norman cathedral, which was built by Roger II in the 12th century. The narrow streets of the city centre are lined with buildings featuring elaborate architectural decoration. There are also numerous churches, reflecting the town's status as a leading bishopric. The fishermen's quarter, with its old houses clustered along the seafront, is very appealing, as is the long beach with fine sand, considered to be one of the most beautiful stretches on the northern coast.

**★ Cathedral**
*Oversized compared with the rest of the city, this masterpiece of Norman art contains magnificent mosaics in the interior.*

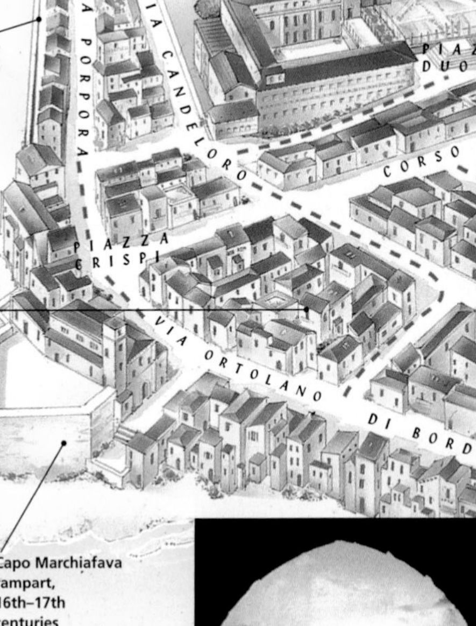


**Seventeenth-century fortifications**

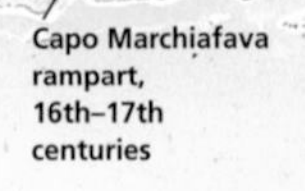

**Capo Marchiafava rampart, 16th–17th centuries**

**The Streets of Cefalù**
*The layout of the city is basically a grid plan crossed horizontally by Corso Ruggero and Via Vittorio Emanuele and intersected by alleys of medieval origin.*

**Porta Marina**
*This striking city gate overlooking the sea is a Gothic arch. It is the only one remaining of the four that originally pierced the city wall, affording access to Cefalù.*

**KEY**

— — — Suggested route

**Chiesa del Purgatorio**
*Most of Cefalù's many churches date from the 17th century. The Chiesa del Purgatorio (1668), on Corso Ruggero, has a richly decorated Baroque doorway at the top of a double stairway.*

## VISITORS' CHECKLIST

**Road map** D2. 14,000. Falcone e Borsellino. FS Messina–Palermo line (091-616 18 06; 091-892 021). AAST, Corso Ruggero 77 (0921-421 050). Sat. Processione del Venerdì Santo (Good Friday Procession); Cefalù Incontri (Jul, Aug, Sep); Festa di San Salvatore (2–6 Aug); Le Città del Cinema (Oct); Vecchia Strina (31 Dec).

**★ Museo Mandralisca**
*This museum was founded by Enrico Piraino, the Baron of Mandralisca, and has a wide range of precious works of art, such as this 4th-century BC tragic mask.*

**Medieval Fountain**
*This recently restored medieval stone fountain was used for washing clothes until a few years ago.*

## STAR SIGHTS

★ Cathedral

★ Museo Mandralisca

## Exploring Cefalù

Cefalù is mentioned for the first time in 396 BC in an account by Diodorus Siculus, but the city is more famous for its medieval monuments. Piazza Garibaldi (where you have to leave the car) is a good starting point for a walk around the town. Follow Corso Ruggero to reach the open space of Piazza Duomo, home to one of Sicily's most splendid cathedrals.

**The medieval façade of the Cathedral of Cefalù**

### Piazza Duomo

This lively square, dominated by the sheer mass of the **Cathedral** and the steep **Rocca**, is the heart of Cefalù. It is surrounded by buildings constructed in different styles. On the southern side are the **Oratorio del Santissimo Sacramento; Palazzo Maria**, which was most probably Roger II's *Domus Regiae (see p29)*, decorated with an ogee portal and a Gothic window; and **Palazzo Piraino**, with its late 16th-century ashlar door. To the north, the square is bordered by the **Seminario** and the **Palazzo Vescovile**, while to the west is the **Palazzo del Municipio** (Town Hall), which incorporates the former **Santa Caterina monastery**.

### Cathedral

Piazza Duomo. ***Tel*** *0921-922 021.* *9am–12:30pm, 2:30–6pm daily.* *9am–1pm, 3–7pm daily.*

Cefalù Cathedral is one of Sicily's major Norman monuments. Building began in 1131 under Roger II. When he died work continued in fits and starts. The façade has two rows of blind arcades set over the three-arch outer narthex and is flanked by two masssive bell towers with single and double lancet windows. On the right-hand side you can see the interlaced arch motifs of the three side apses. The nave is divided by arches supported by marble columns. The wooden ceiling, with its painted beams, bears an obvious Islamic influence, while the presbytery is covered with splendid mosaics. On high in the apse is the figure of Christ Pantocrator with the Virgin Mary, Archangels and the apostles; on the choir walls are saints and prophets, while cherubs and seraphim decorate the vault. A door on the northern aisle leads to the lovely cloister, long closed for restoration.

**Statue of a bishop, Cefalù Cathedral**

### Corso Ruggero

This avenue goes all the way across the old town, starting from **Piazza Garibaldi**, where the **Porta di Terra** city gate once stood. A few steps on your left is **Palazzo Osterio Magno**, built in the 13th and 14th centuries, according to legend, as the residence of the Ventimiglia family. Almost opposite, a modern building houses the remains of the ancient Roman road. Visits can be made from 9am to 4:30pm. Continuing to the right, you will come to **Piazzetta Spinola**, with **Santo Stefano** (or Delle Anime Purganti), the Baroque façade of which is complemented by an elegant double staircase.

### Museo Mandralisca

Via Mandralisca 13. ***Tel*** *0921-421 547.* *9am–7pm daily.*
**www**.museomandralisca.it

This museum was founded by Enrico Piraino, the Baron of Mandralisca, in the 19th century and includes fine archaeological, shell and coin collections. It also houses an art gallery and a library with over 9,000 historic and scientific works, including incunabulae, 16th-century books and nautical charts.

Among the most important paintings are the *Portrait of a Man* by Antonello da Messina, *View of Cefalù* by Francesco Bevilacqua, *Christ on Judgment Day* by Johannes De Matta (mid-1500s), and a series of icons on the second

**Medieval fishermen's dwellings lining the seafront**

Antonello da Messina, *Portrait of an Unknown Man* (1465)

floor. Archaeological jewels include a late Hellenistic mosaic and a 4th-century BC krater with a figure of a tuna fish cutter. A curiosity exhibit is the collection of patience (solitaire) playing cards made out of precious materials.

**Via Vittorio Emanuele**

This street runs along the seafront, separated by a row of medieval houses facing the bay. Under one of these is the famous **Lavatoio**, the stone fountain known as *U' Ciuni*, or river, which was mentioned by the writer Boccaccio and was used for washing clothes until a few years ago. A stairway leads to the basin where water gushes from holes on three walls. The lovely **Porta Marina** is the only remaining city gate of the four that once afforded access to the town. It leads to the colourful fishermen's quarter, where scenes were shot for the film *Cinema Paradiso* *(see p120)*.

**La Rocca**

From Piazza Garibaldi a path halfway up the hill offers a fine view of the old town and the sea and leads to the ruins of the fortifications (most probably Byzantine) and the prehistoric sanctuary known as the **Tempio di Diana**, a megalithic construction with a portal dating from the 9th century BC. On the top of the Rocca are the ruins of a 12th–13th-century castle.

**Environs**

On the slopes of Pizzo Sant' Angelo is the **Santuario di Gibilmanna**, a sanctuary built in the 17th and 18th centuries and the most popular pilgrimage site in Sicily. The former convent stables house the **Museo dell' Ordine**, the museum of the Capuchin friars with paintings, sculpture and vestments. The most interesting pieces are crêche figures, enamelled reliquaries, a 16th-century alabaster rosary, and a white marble Pietà by the local sculptor Jacopo Lo Duca, a pupil of Michelangelo.

A 16th-century statuette, Santuario di Gibilmanna

## Castel di Tusa ❷

**Road map** D2. *3,600.* FS *0921-334 325.* *0921-334 332.*

This beautiful swimming resort is dominated by the ruins of a 14th-century castle. The characteristic alleys with old stone houses and villas converge in the central square, which is paved with stone. To get to the little port you must go under the railway arches. The banks of the nearby Tusa River have been turned into an outdoor gallery with works by contemporary artists, including sculptor Pietro Consagra. Only a few miles away are the **Ruins of Halaesa Arconidea**.

**Ruins of Halaesa Arconidea**

3 km (2 miles) on the road to Tusa.
**Tel** *0921-334 796.* *9am–2 hrs before sunset.*

On a hill covered with olive trees and asphodels are the ruins of the city of Halaesa Arconidea, a Greek colony founded in 403 BC, which prospered until it was sacked by the Roman praetor Verres. Excavations have started and you can see the Agora, remains of cyclopean walls and a Hellenistic temple. Near the archaeological site is the **Monastery of Santa Maria della Palate**.

Ruins of the Hellenistic temple of Halaesa, amid olive trees and asphodels

## Santo Stefano di Camastra ❸

**Road map** D2. *5,200.*
FS *Messina–Palermo.*
*Town hall (0921-331 127 or 331 181). Easter Week.*

This town facing the Tyrrhenian Sea is one of the leading Sicilian centres for the production of ceramics. All the local craftsmen have their wares on display: vases, jugs, cornices and tiles with period designs such as those used in the **Villa Comunale**. In the centre of town stands the **Chiesa Madre**, or San Nicolò, with a Renaissance doorway and late 18th-century stucco decoration in the interior.

## Nicosia ❹

**Road map** D3. *15,100.*
*129 km (80 miles) from Catania, 44 km (27 miles) from Enna.*
*Town hall, Piazza Garibaldi (0935-672 11 11). Easter Week,* O' Scontro *(Easter), Macaroni Festival (May), Palio (2nd week Aug), Nicosia da Vivere Festival (Jul–Sep).*

Sprawled over four hills, Nicosia is dominated by the ruins of an Arab-Norman castle. Originally a Byzantine settlement, the town was repopulated in the Norman era by Lombard and Piedmontese colonists, who have left traces of their local dialects. The many churches and patrician mansions are a sign of the town's former splendour. Narrow streets and alleys run up the hills, often providing spectacular panoramic views.

**The Villa Comunale, Santo Stefano di Camastra, with a tiled altar**

**Piazza Garibaldi** is the heart of Nicosia, with the Gothic **San Nicolò Cathedral** and old buildings, including the current Town Hall. The **Salita Salomone** steps lead to Romanesque **San Salvatore**. There is a fine view of the old town from the porch. The church has a series of sundials which, according to tradition, were once used as the town's "clocks". **Via Salomone**, lined with aristocratic palazzi, leads up to **Santa Maria Maggiore**, just under the castle rock. The doorway is decorated with pagan statues of Jove, Venus and Ceres. In the interior is Charles V's throne, in memory of the emperor's visit here in 1535, a gilded marble altarpiece by Antonello Gagini and a crucifix known as *Father of Mercy*. From here you can go up to the **Castle**, with its Norman drawbridge and the remains of the keep. At the foot of the castle is the Norman **Basilica of San Michele**, with its austere apses and majestic 15th-century bell towers.

**Detail of the ceiling of the Nicosia Cathedral**

### Cathedral

Piazza Garibaldi.
*Call 0935-638 139 for details.*

The cathedral is dedicated to the town's patron saint, San Nicolò. It was founded in the 14th century and partially rebuilt in the 19th century. What remains of the original structure are the 14th-century façade with porticoes running along the left-hand side and the bell tower with three sections, each distinguished by a different style, from Arab to Romanesque. The rebuilt interior has a crucifix attributed to Fra Umile de Petralia and a font by Antonello Gagini, while the choir was carved out of solid walnut by local artists. The vault, frescoed in the 19th century, conceals a fine Norman truss ceiling decorated in brilliant colours with scenes from the lives of the saints, hunting scenes, images of wild animals, a number of human heads, stylized flowers and geometric decorative motifs.

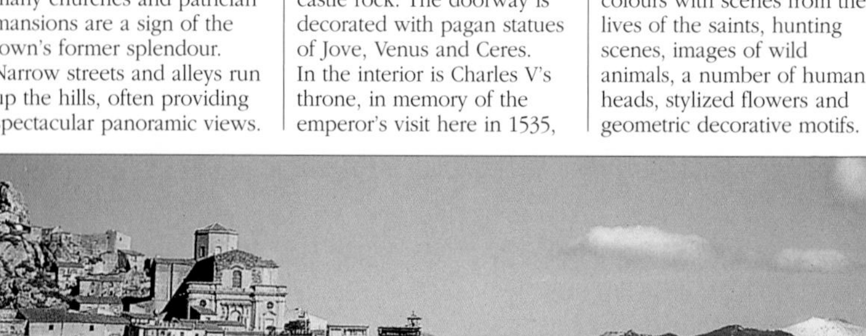

**Nicosia, perched on a hill and once crucial to the area's defensive network**

*For hotels and restaurants in this region see pp199–201 and pp214–16*

Panoramic view from the Norman castle at Sperlinga (c.1100)

## Sperlinga 5

**Road map** D3. *1,100.* *47 km (29 miles) from Enna.* *Town hall, Via Umberto I (0935-643 025 or 643 177).* *Sagra del Tortone (16 Aug).*

Sperlinga seems to have been pushed against a spectacular rock face, its parallel streets on different levels connected by steps. In the eastern section, right up against the sandstone cliff, numerous troglodytic cave dwellings have been carved out. Until recently many of them were inhabited.

### Norman Castle

Via Castello. ***Tel*** *0935-643 119.* *10am–1pm, 2–5pm daily.* **Museum** *10am–1pm, 3:30–8pm daily.*

Sperlinga's castle was built by the Normans under Roger I around the year 1100 on the top of an impregnable rock face. It was later reinforced by Frederick II. It is linked with the Sicilian Vespers revolt *(see pp32–3)*, when it was the last refuge of the Angevin rulers, who managed to resist attacks for a year. The events are commemorated by an inscription carved in the vestibule: *Quod Siculis placuit sola Sperlinga negavit* ("Sperlinga alone denied the Sicilians what they desired").

The numerous chambers in the castle make it a veritable stone labyrinth. The entrance hall, the Grotta delle Guardie (Guards' Grotto), is now an ethnographic museum with examples of cave dwellings and everyday work tools and objects. After passing through the second gate and crossing the Sala Riunioni, or assembly hall, you will find the stables, the prisons and the foundry (hewn entirely out of the rock). In the middle of the cliff is **San Domenico di Siria**, the nave of which has three side niches; next to this are the rooms used as a kitchen with the remains of two wood-burning ovens. Steep stairs lead to the top of the rock with magnificent views.

## Gangi 6

**Road map** D3. *8,100.* *51 km (32 miles) from Cefalù.* *Pro Loco, Cortile Ospedale 4.* *Sagra della Spiga (2nd Sun Aug).*

This town lies on the southwestern slope of Monte Marone, facing the Nebrodi and Madonie mountains. The birthplace of painters Gaspare Vazano and Giuseppe Salerno has retained its medieval character, with winding streets and steps connecting the different levels. The towering **Chiesa Madre** has a 14th-century bell tower and a lovely *Last Judgment* by Salerno, inspired by Michelangelo's painting in the Sistine Chapel.

## Petralia Sottana 7

**Road map** D3. *3,800.* *98 km (61 miles) from Palermo.* *Town hall, Corso Agliata (0921-684 311).* *Ballo della Cordella dance (1st Sun after 15 Aug).*

This village is perched on a rock 1,000 m (3,300 ft) up, and nestled at the foot of the tallest peaks in the Madonie mountains. Petralia Sottana is laid out around **Via Agliata**, which ends in **Piazza Umberto I**, opposite the **Chiesa Madre**. The late Gothic church was partially rebuilt in the 1600s. Inside is a fine wooden triptych, *The Virgin Mary and Child between Saints Peter and Paul*. An arch connects the bell tower with the **Santissima Trinità**, which has a marble altarpiece by Domenico Gagini.

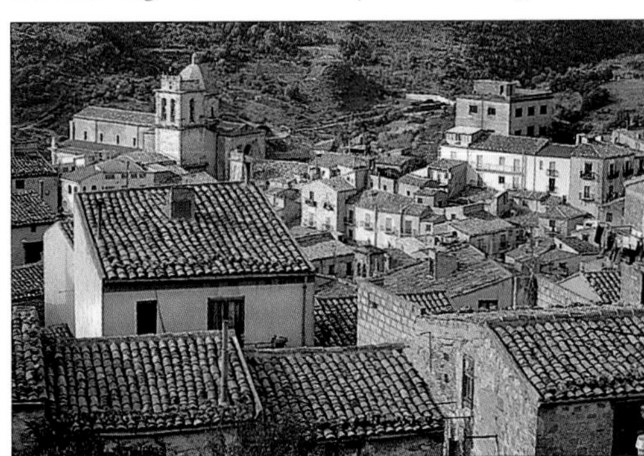
Petralia Sottana, in the middle of the verdant Valle dell'Imera

Petralia Soprana, the highest village in the Madonie mountains

## Petralia Soprana ❽

**Road map** D3. *3,900.* *104 km (65 miles) from Palermo.* *Town hall (0921-641 050).*

The highest village in the Madonie mountains lies on a plateau 1,147 m (3,760 ft) above sea level, where the panoramic view ranges from the Nebrodi hills to the volcanic cone of Mount Etna. Petralia Soprana was an extremely important Greek and Phoenician city. Under Roman dominion ancient "Petra" was one of the largest wheat-producing *civitates* in the Empire. The city became *Batraliab* after the Arab conquest and a powerful defensive stronghold under the Normans. Later, the two Petralias (Soprana and Sottana) were taken over by noble families.

The village has preserved its medieval layout, with narrow paved streets, old stone houses, patrician residences and churches. The old **Chiesa Madre**, dedicated to Saints Peter and Paul and rebuilt in the 14th century, stands in an attractive square with a 17th-century double-column colonnade designed by the Serpotta brothers. In the interior is the first crucifix by Fra' Umile Pintorno (1580–1639), who also painted many other crucifixes throughout the island. **Santa Maria di Loreto** was built in the 18th century over the remains of a castle; it has a cross plan and the façade is flanked by two decorated bell towers.

## Polizzi Generosa ❾

**Road map** D3. *4,700.* *93 km (58 miles) from Palermo.* *Pro Loco, Via Mistretta 18 (0921-649 018).*

On the western slopes of the Madonie mountains, this village grew up around an ancient fortress rebuilt by the Normans. Among its many churches is the **Chiesa Madre**, with a fine 16th-century altarpiece, *Madonna and Child among Angels and Saints* by an unknown Flemish artist and a relief by Domenico Gagini (1482). A small museum shows the natural history of the area.

**Environs**

From Polizzi, ascend to Piano Battaglia, part of the nature reserve, with footpaths in summer and ski runs in winter.

Coat of arms of a noble family of Caccamo

## Caccamo ❿

**Road map** C2. *8,700.* *48 km (30 miles) from Palermo.* *Town hall, Piazza Duomo (091-810 32 48).* *Sat.* *Agricultural and gastronomic show (Dec–Jan), Investiture of the Chatelaine (Aug).*

Caccamo lies under the castellated walls of its **Norman castle**, in a lovely setting of softly rolling hills only 10 km (6 miles) from the Palermo-Catania motorway. The town is laid out on different levels, with well maintained roads that open onto pretty squares. The most appealing of these is **Piazza Duomo**, with the **Chiesa Matrice** dedicated to San Giorgio, flanked by statues and two symmetrically arranged Baroque buildings: the **Oratorio della Compagnia del Sacramento** and the **Chiesa delle Anime Sante del Purgatorio**. The former was built by the Normans but was enlarged in the 17th century. Its richly decorated interior has a font by Gagini and his workshop. Not far away are the **Annunziata**, with twin bell towers, **San Marco** and **San Benedetto alla Badia**. The last is perhaps the loveliest of the three, with its Baroque stucco and majolica decoration, and a colourful floor depicting a ship sailing on the high seas, guarded by angels.

Interior of the impregnable Norman castle at Caccamo

*For hotels and restaurants in this region see pp199–201 and pp214–16*

**The *Gymnasium* at Solunto, with its Doric columns intact**

### Norman Castle

*by appointment 9am–1pm, 4–8pm. Tel 091-814 92 52 or 810-32 48.*

This formidable Norman castle is truly impregnable. It was built on the top of a steep rock overlooking the valley and is protected by a series of walls. The first entranceway on the lower floor leads to a broad stairway flanked by castellated walls; this leads to the second entrance, where the guardhouse once stood. After crossing a drawbridge, you will find another door that leads to the inner courtyard. Through this you can reach the famous Sala della Congiura (Conspiracy Hall), so named because it was here in 1160 that the Norman barons hatched a plot against William I. The panoramic views from the large western terrace are breathtaking.

## Solunto ⓫

**Road map** C2. FS *Santa Flavia–Solunto–Porticello.* *091-904 557.* *9am–4:30pm Tue–Sat (to 6:30pm in summer), 9am–1pm Sun & hols.* *Mon.*

The ruins of the city of Solunto lie on the slopes of Monte Catalfano in a stupendous site with a beautiful panoramic view of the sea. Solunto was one of the first Phoenician colonies in Sicily and was mentioned, together with Palermo and Mozia, by the Greek historian Thucydides. In 254 BC it was conquered by the Romans. By the 2nd century AD the city had been largely abandoned, and it was later almost destroyed by the Saracens. At the entrance there is a temporary exhibition (until the new museum is finished) with finds from the various digs, which began in 1826 and are still under way.

Solunto follows a traditional layout. The path leading to the site takes you to Via dell'Agorà, with a fired-brick pavement and gutters for drainage. This street makes a right angle with the side stairs, which mark off the blocks of buildings *(insulae)*. Six Doric columns and part of the roof of one of these, the *Gymnasium*, are still standing. Other *insulae* have mosaic floors and plastered or even painted walls. At the eastern end is the Agora, with workshops, cisterns to collect rainwater and a theatre with the stage area facing towards the sea.

**Panoramic view of Solunto**

### THE VILLAS IN BAGHERIA

In the 18th century, Bagheria was the summer residence of Palermo's nobility, who built luxurious villas surrounded by orange groves as retreats from the torrid heat of the capital. Prince Ettore Branciforti built the first, Villa Barbera, in 1657, followed by other aristocrats such as the Valguarnera and Gravina families. The most famous is the recently restored Villa Palagonia (091-932 088; www.villapalagonia.it), decorated with hundreds of statues of monsters and mythological figures. Visitors can see the Salone degli Specchi (Hall of Mirrors), where balls were held, and the frescoed Room of the Labours of Hercules. The villas eventually proved too costly to keep and were either abandoned or put to other uses. When the gardens were destroyed to make room for ugly housing units, the villas lost most of their fascination.

**Façade of Villa Palagonia, the most famous villa in Bagheria**

**"Monster" at the Villa Palagonia**

Typical Piana degli Albanesi costumes

## Piana degli Albanesi ⓬

**Road map** B2. *6,200.*
*Pro Loco, Via Kastrota 207 (091-856 10 59). Santa Maria Odigitria (Tue after Pentecost, 2 Sep).*

During the expansion of the Ottoman Empire in the Balkans, many groups of Albanians *(Albanesi)* fled to Italy. At the end of the 15th century, John II allowed an Albanian community to settle in this area, which originally took the name of Piana dei Greci, because the inhabitants belonged to the Greek Orthodox Church. The place was renamed Piana degli Albanesi in 1941. The town is famous for its colourful religious festivities, such as those during Epiphany and Easter. Try to catch the celebrations in honour of the patron saint Santa Maria Odigitria, which are followed by traditional folk festivities.

**Piazza Vittorio Emanuele**, in the heart of town, is home to the Municipio (Town Hall) and the Orthodox church of **Santa Maria Odigitria**, which has a beautiful iconostasis in the interior. Opposite the parish church is the oldest church in Piana degli Albanesi, **San Giorgio**, which was altered in the mid-1700s. Along the avenue named after the Albanian national hero, Giorgio Kastriota Skanderbeg, is the cathedral, **San Demetrio**. As is customary in Orthodox churches, the apses are closed off by the iconostasis. On the vault is a fresco representing the Apostles, Christ and the four Orthodox patriarchs. Near the town is an artificial **lake** created by a dam built in the 1920s, containing 32 million cubic metres (1,129.6 million cu ft) of water.

## Alcamo ⓭

**Road map** B2. *44,000.*
*FS Palermo–Trapani line. Town hall, Piazza Ciullo (0924-590 111).*

During the Arab period the fortress of *Manzil Alqamah* was built as part of this area's defensive network. The town of Alcamo developed later, and between the 13th and 14th centuries centred around the Chiesa Madre and the castle, which has been restored. In recent decades, population growth has led to the expansion of the town and the demolition of parts of the old city walls. In Piazza Ciullo is **Sant'Oliva**, built in 1723 over an earlier church, while the nearby **Chiesa del Rosario** boasts late 15th-century frescoes. Facing Piazza della Repubblica is **Santa Maria del Gesù**, with the so-called Greek Madonna altarpiece (1516), showing the Madonna with the Counts of Modica. But the most important church here is the **Chiesa Madre,** founded in 1332. Its Baroque façade, overlooking Piazza IV Novembre, has a 14th-century bell tower with double lancet windows, and many paintings and sculptures can be seen in the chapels.

## Castellammare del Golfo ⓮

**Road map** B2. *15,000.*
*FS Palermo–Trapani. Town hall, Via Alcide de Gasperi 6 (0924-30217)*

This town was the Greek port for Segesta and Erice, and then an Arab fortress. It became an important trading and tuna-fishing centre in the Middle Ages. In the heart of the town, on an isthmus, is the **Aragonese Castle**, and the old picturesque streets of the medieval quarter known as *castri di la terra*. On Via Garibaldi is the **Chiesa Madre**, frequently rebuilt in the 1700s and 1800s.

**Castellammare del Golfo, on the Tyrrhenian Sea, a leading port town in the Arab-Norman period**

# Riserva dello Zingaro ⓯

Twenty kilometres (12 miles) from Erice, along the coast going towards Palermo, is the Riserva dello Zingaro, a nature reserve of about 1,600 ha (3,950 acres) sloping down to the sea. It is a paradise for birds, especially for raptors such as Bonelli's eagles, peregrine falcons and kites, and even, in recent years, golden eagles.

**San Vito lo Capo ①**
North of the reserve is this impressive promontory plunging into the sea.

**Grotta dell'Uzzo ②**
Human skeletons over 12,000 years old have been found in this grotto.

SAN VITO LO CAPO ①
MONTE ACCI
829 m, 2,720 ft
MONTE PASSO DEL LUPO
868 m, 2,847 ft
Contrada Acci
⑥
Contrada Uzzo
Ficarella
②
PIZZO AQUILA
759 m, 2,490 ft
Contrada Sughero
③
MONTE SPEZIALE
913 m, 2,994 ft
Contrada Pianello
PIZZO DEL CORVO
415 m, 1,360 ft
PIZZO PASSO DEL LUPO
610 m, 2,000 ft
④
Contrada Scardina
SCOPELLO ⑤
MONTE SCARDINA
680 m, 2,230 ft

**Portella Mandra Nuova ⑥**
A typical village 700 m (2,296 ft) above sea level.

**Grotta del Sughero ③**
Animals such as foxes, rabbits and porcupines live in these caves.

**Contrada Capreria ④**
Punta di Capreria, one of the loveliest parts of the reserve, lies in this area.

**KEY**

- Negotiable road
- Path
- Viewpoint

## TIPS FOR WALKERS

**Road map** C2.
***Tour length:*** *there are four marked footpaths. The shortest one (6 km/4 miles) goes from Scopello to Tonarella dell'Uzzo, taking about 2 hrs 20 mins. The longest is 19 km (12 miles) and takes about 9 hrs. The reserve can also be explored on horseback.*
**www.**riservazingaro.it

**Baglio di Scopello ⑤**
Scopello is a farming hamlet that grew up around an 18th-century fort.

0 kilometres 2

0 miles 1

# Segesta ⑯

According to legend, the ancient capital of the Elymians was founded on the rolling green hills of the Castellammare del Golfo area by exiles from Troy. Segesta was constantly at war with Selinunte and was frequently attacked. Yet the majestic Doric temple has miraculously survived sacking and the ravages of time, and stands in splendid and solemn isolation on the hill facing Monte Barbaro. The city of Segesta was built above the temple on the top of the mountain. Here lie the ruins of some buildings and the well-preserved 3rd-century BC theatre, where ancient Greek plays are performed every other summer.

### VISITORS' CHECKLIST

**Road map** B2. *0924-952 356.* *32 km (20 miles) from Trapani.* *Trapani-Palermo (coach to theatre).* *9am–4pm daily (to 5pm Nov–Mar).* *Classical theatre (Jul–Aug alternate years).*

**The Temple**
*Built in the 5th century BC, the temple is still well preserved; 36 Doric columns support the pediments and entablatures.*

**Panorama**
*Ancient Segesta and the beautiful setting create an atmospheric scene.*

**Interior of the Temple**
*The lack of architectural elements in the interior has led scholars to believe that the construction was interrupted by the war with Selinunte.*

**The Theatre**
*The Segesta theatre is a semicircle with a diameter of 63 m (207 ft) hewn out of the top of Monte Barbaro. A curious feature is that the stage area faces north, probably to allow a view of the hills and sea.*

## Gibellina 17

**Road map** B3. 5,000.
89 km (55 miles) from Trapani.
Town hall, Piazza XV Gennaio
0924-67877). Oresteia (classical
theatre, biennial, summer).

In 1968 a terrible earthquake destroyed all the towns in the Valle del Belice and the vicinity, including Gibellina. The new town was rebuilt, after years of bureaucratic delay, in the Salinella zone about 20 km (12 miles) from the original village. Thirty years after the event, the new Gibellina already seems old and rather sad. However, it is worth visiting because, thanks to the cooperation of contemporary architects and artists, the area has been enriched with many works of art, including a huge sculpture, *Stella* (Star) by Pietro Consagra, the city gate and symbol of Gibellina Nuova. Other attractions are the **Torre Civica Carillon**, a tower in Piazza del Municipio, and the **Centro Culturale**, the cultural centre built over the remains of the 17th-century **Palazzo Di Lorenzo**.
Lastly, be sure to visit the **Museo Antropologico-Etnologico**, with everyday objects and tools illustrating local folk customs, and, above all, the **Museo Civico d'Arte Contemporanea**.

The town of Salemi, dominated by its impressive medieval castle

**Museo Civico d'Arte Contemporanea**
Via Segesta. **Tel** 0924-67428.
8:30am–1:30pm daily.
This museum contains works by artists such as Fausto Pirandello, Renato Guttuso, Antonio Sanfilippo and Mario Schifano.

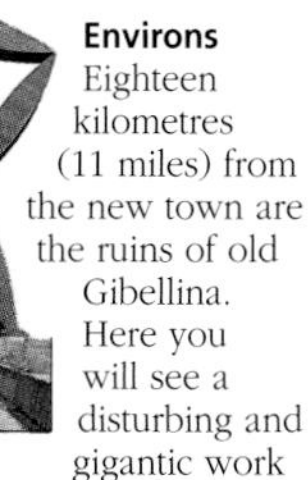
The Star of Gibellina, by Pietro Consagra

**Environs**
Eighteen kilometres (11 miles) from the new town are the ruins of old Gibellina. Here you will see a disturbing and gigantic work of land art by Alberto Burri, who covered the ruins with a layer of white cement. The cracks cutting through this white expanse, known as *Burri's Crevice*, follow the course of the old streets, creating a labyrinth.

The so-called *Burri's Crevice* covering part of the ruins of old Gibellina

## Salemi 18

**Road map** B3. 12,500. 95 km (59 miles) from Palermo. Town hall, Piazza Lampiasi Ignazio (0924-982 233). Sat. San Giuseppe (Mar).

This agricultural town in the Valle del Delia dates from ancient times (it was probably the Halicyae mentioned by Diodorus Siculus). Despite the 1968 earthquake, the Arab town plan has remained, with a jumble of narrow streets at the foot of the three towers of the **Castle**. Here, on 14 May 1860, Garibaldi proclaimed himself ruler of Sicily in the name of King Vittorio Emanuele II *(see pp34–5)*. The castle was built in the 12th century by Frederick II and rebuilt in 1210.

In the old town, interesting sights are **Sant'Agostino** with its large cloister and the 17th-century **Collegio dei Gesuiti**, which houses the **Chiesa dei Gesuiti**, the **Oratorio del Ritiro** and the city museums, in particular the **Museo Civico d'Arte Sacra**.

**Museo Civico d'Arte Sacra**
Collegio dei Gesuiti. **Tel** 0924-982 376.
9am–1pm, 4–6pm Tue–Fri; 9am–1pm, 3–7pm Sat.
This museum of religious art has sculptures by Domenico Laurana and Antonello Gagini *(see p21)*, 17th-century paintings and wooden Baroque sculpture. The Risorgimento section features objects commemorating Garibaldi's feats.

# Erice ⓳

Sign for an art gallery in Erice

The splendid town of Erice, perched on top of Monte San Giuliano, has very ancient origins, as is shown by the cult of the goddess of fertility, Venus Erycina. Laid out on a triangular plan, the town has preserved its medieval character, with fine city walls, beautifully paved streets, stone houses with decorated doorways, small squares and open spaces with numerous churches – including the medieval Chiesa Matrice – many of which have recently become venues for scientific and cultural activities.

### Cyclopean walls

These extend for 700 m (2,296 ft) on the northern side of the town, from Porta Spada to Porta Trapani.

The lower part of the wall, with its megalithic blocks of stone, dates back to the Phoenician period; the letters *beth, ain, phe* of the Phoenician alphabet are carved in it. The upper part and the gates were built by the Normans. The **Porta Spada** gate owes its name to the massacre of the local Angevin rulers during the Sicilian Vespers (*spada* means sword) *(see pp32–3)*. Nearby are **Sant'Antonio Abate** and **Sant'Orsola**. The latter houses the 18th-century "Mysteries", sculptures borne in procession on Good Friday.

### Castello Pepoli e Venere

Via Conte Pepoli. ***Tel*** *0923-869 388.*
*9am–1 hour before sunset daily.*

This Norman castle was built on an isolated rock over the ruins of the **Temple of Venus Erycina**. Entrance is gained via a tower, the only remaining original part of the castle, with Ghibelline castellation. It was used as a prison and watchtower. Above the entrance, with its pointed arch, is a plaque with the coat of arms of the Spanish Habsburgs, surmounted by a 14th-century double lancet window. Inside are a sacred well and the ruins of the Temple of Venus Erycina, a Phoenician house and a Roman bath. The castle is the starting point of a system of fortifications including the **Torri del Balio**, formerly the headquarters of the Norman governor. Further down, on a ledge over the Pineta dei Runzi pine forest, is the **Torretta Pepoli** *(see p85)*, built as a hunting lodge in 1872–80 and one of the symbols of Erice. In front of the castle are the 19th-century public gardens, **Giardini del Balio**, which link this zone with the eastern side of Erice.

The Norman castle, built on the site dedicated to Venus Erycina in ancient times

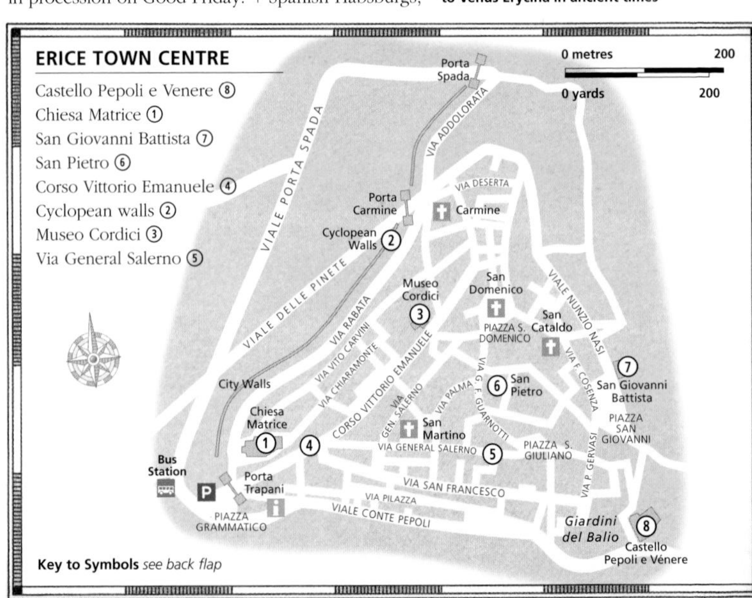

The austere exterior of the Chiesa Matrice in Erice

### Chiesa Matrice

Piazza Matrice. ***Tel*** *0923-869 123.*
*10am–1pm, 3–6pm.*

This church is dedicated to Our Lady of the Assumption. It was built in 1314. The austere façade has a portico with pointed arches surmounted by a beautiful rose window; it faces the detached campanile with double lancet windows, which was built in 1312 as a lookout tower. The interior was drastically restored in 1865, and little remains of its original look.

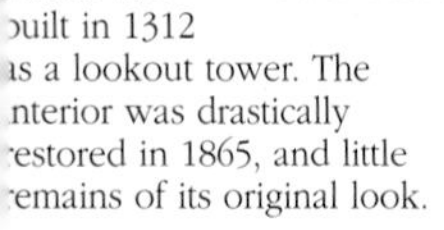

### Corso Vittorio Emanuele

The Corso, the main street in Erice, begins at **Porta Trapani**, one of the three gates through the massive city walls, and goes uphill. The street is lined with Baroque patrician residences and tempting pastry shops selling local specialities. To the left is **San Salvatore**, which once had a monastery annexe and boasts a 15th-century portal. At the end of the Corso, formerly called Via Regia, is **Piazza Umberto I**, redesigned in the 19th century, and the **Palazzo del Municipio** (town hall), which houses the **Museo Comunale Cordici**.

### Museo Cordici

Piazza Umberto I. ***Tel*** *0923-502 148.*
*8am–2pm Mon–Fri (also 2:30–5:30pm Mon & Thu).*

This museum features finds from the necropolis, coins, terracotta items and a small head of Venus. Some rooms also exhibit vestments and old paintings and sculpture such as the *Annunciation*, a marble group by the artist Antonello Gagini.

### San Pietro

Via Filippo Guarnotti.

Founded in the 14th century in the middle of Erice, this church was rebuilt in 1745, and a fine Baroque portal added. The nearby convent is now one of the bases for the **Centro di Cultura Scientifica Ettore Majorana**. This centre, founded in the early 1960s to honour the brilliant Sicilian scientist who died in mysterious circumstances before World War II, runs courses and conferences on various subjects, from medicine to mathematical logic. The centre makes use of abandoned buildings such as the former convents of San Domenico, San Francesco and San Rocco.

Plaque commemorating the Sicilian scientist Ettore Majorana

### Via General Salerno

This street, with its noble palazzi, connects **Corso Vittorio Emanuele** with the castle area. Immediately to the left is **San Martino**, a Norman church with a Baroque portal and interior, where there is a fine 17th-century wooden choir. The sacristy takes you to the **Oratorio dei Confrati del Purgatorio**, built in Rococo style, with a carved altar decorated with gilded stucco. Further along the street is **San Giuliano**, which looks over a square made even more spectacular by the pink colour of the façade. The church was begun in 1080 by Roger I but was radically altered in the 1600s. It was closed when the vault caved in on the central section of the nave; now restored, it is used as a cultural and artistic centre.

## VISITORS' CHECKLIST

**Road map** A2. *25,000.*
*16 km (9 miles) from Trapani.*
*0923-869 673.* *Mon.*
*Processione dei Misteri (Good Friday), International Week of Medieval and Renaissance Music (Jul), Estate Ericina (Jul, Aug), International Musical Instruments Show.*

An example of the lovely paved streets in Erice

### San Giovanni Battista

Piazzale San Giovanni.
***Tel*** *0923-869 171.*
*only for events.*

This white-domed church is probably the oldest in Erice, despite the many alterations that have changed its appearance. The last refurbishing phase took place in the 1600s, when the nave was totally rebuilt. The church is now used only as an auditorium, but interesting works of art remain. These include the statue of St John the Baptist by Antonio Gagini and the 14th-century frescoes moved here from the deconsecrated church of Santa Maria Maddalena.

### Environs

On the slopes of Monte San Giuliano, in the restored Baglio Cusenza, is the **Museo Agroforestale**, with an exhibition of farm equipment. Old ploughs, presses, barrows and a limestone millstone are on display in the courtyard.

### Museo Agroforestale

Località San Matteo
***Tel*** *0923-869 532.* *8:30am–2pm Mon–Sat, 9am–5pm Sun.*

Boats anchored in the large port of Trapani

## Trapani ⓴

**Road map** A2. *70,000.* *Vincenzo Florio a Birgi (0923-842 502). FS 0923-540 416. 0923-871 922. Via San Francesco d'Assisi (0923-545 511). Thu. Processione dei Misteri (Good Friday).*

The town was built on a narrow, curved promontory (hence the name, which derives from the Greek word *drepane*, or sickle) that juts out into the sea opposite the Egadi Islands. In ancient times Trapani was the port town for Erice *(see pp100–1)*. It flourished under the Carthaginians and languished under the Vandals, Byzantines and Saracens. The economy has always been linked to the sea and reached its peak in the 1600s and 1700s with shipyards and tuna fishing. The town now extends beyond the promontory to the foot of Monte San Giuliano and the edge of the salt marshes.

### Museo Pepoli

Via Conte Agostino Pepoli 200. ***Tel*** *0923-553 269. 9am–1:30pm Tue–Sat; 9am–12:30pm Sun & hols.*

This museum was opened in 1906 in the former Carmelite monastery, thanks to Count Agostino Pepoli, who donated his private collection. A broad polychrome marble staircase leads to the first floor, which has archaeological finds, 12th–18th century Sicilian painting, jewellery and ceramics. The art produced in Trapani is interesting: wooden 16th-century angels, an 18th-century coral and alabaster nativity scene, jewellery, clocks with painted dials, tapestries with coral and majolica from Santa Maria delle Grazie.

### Via Garibaldi

This is the street that leads to the old town. It begins in **Piazza Vittorio Veneto**, the heart of the city with **Palazzo d'Ali**, now the Town Hall. The street is lined with 18th-century patrician residences such as **Palazzo Riccio di Morana** and **Palazzo Fardella Fontana**. Almost directly opposite the 1621 Baroque façade of **Santa Maria d'Itria** are the steps leading to **San Domenico**, built in the 14th century and restructured in the 18th. In the interior is the sarcophagus of Manfred, natural son of Frederick II *(see p29)*.

### Corso Vittorio Emanuele

This is the main street in the old town, lined with late Baroque buildings and **San Lorenzo Cathedral,** which has a fine portico. The main features of the interior are the painted ceiling, stucco decoration and, in the right-hand altar, a *Crucifixion* attributed to Van Dyck.

### Santuario di Maria Santissima Annunziata

Via Conte Agostino Pepoli. ***Tel*** *0923-539 184. winter: 7am–noon, 4–7pm including hols; summer 7am–noon, 4–8pm (7am–1pm, 4–8pm hols). 8 & 9am, 6pm.* **www**.madonnaditrapani.com

Known as the Madonna di Trapani, this church was built by the Carmelite fathers in 1224. The portal and part of the rose window are the only original elements remaining, as the rest of the church is Baroque, thanks to the restoration effected in 1714. Inside are the Cappella dei Pescatori, the Cappella dei Marinai, and

### THE SALT MARSHES

Windmills, used for draining water from the basins

The Stagno and Trapani salt marshes were exploited in antiquity and reached the height of their importance in the 19th century, when salt was exported as far away as Norway. The long periods of sunshine (five or six months a year) and the impermeable nature of the land made these marshes very productive, although activity has declined in the last 20 years. At one time, windmills supplied energy for the Archimedes screws used to take water from basin to basin; some of them have now been restored. At Nubia the Museo delle Saline (Salt Marsh Museum) is now open, and the Stagnone area will soon become a fully fledged nature reserve. The seawater will be protected from pollution, and the age-old tradition of salt extraction will survive.

A workman at the Stagnone salt marsh

ell tower of the Santuario
lell'Annunziata in Trapani

he Cappella della Madonna
li Trapani with the *Madonna*
*ind Child* by Nino Pisano,
one of the most important
Gothic sculptures in Sicily.

**Chiesa del Purgatorio**
*'ia San Francesco d'Assisi. **Tel** 0923-21321. 10am–noon Tue, 10am–noon, 5–7pm Fri (10am–noon, 4–7pm daily in Lent; 9am–midnight Jul & Aug).*
This church is well known
because it houses unusual
18th-century wooden statues
with precious silver decoration
representing the Stations of
the Cross *(Misteri)*. At 2pm on
Good Friday, they are carried
n a 24-hour procession, a
ritual dating from the 1700s.

**Museo di Preistoria**
*Torre di Ligny. **Tel** 0923-223 00. 9:30am–12:30pm (also 4–6:30pm Nov–Mar; 9am–midnight Jul & Aug).*
At the tip of the peninsula, the
**Torre di Ligny** (1671) affords a
fine view of the city and its
port. The tower is now used
as an archaeological museum,
with objects from the Punic
Wars and from the shipwrecks
that occurred on the ancient
trade routes, and amphoras
used to carry wine, dates and
garum, a prized fish sauce.

**Museo del Sale**
*Via delle Saline, Contrada Nubia, Paceco. **Tel** 0923-867 442. 9am–7pm daily. **WWF Reserve Tel** 0923-867 700.*
From Trapani to Marsala
the coast is lined with salt
marshes. The area is now a
WWF nature reserve, a unique
habitat for migratory birds.
The landscape, with its salt
marshes and windmills (three
of which can be visited), is
striking. A museum illustrates
the practice of salt extraction.

## Marsala 21

**Road map** *A3. 85,000. 124 km (77 miles) from Marsala and 31 km (19 miles) from Trapani. 0923-714 097. Tue. Maundy Thursday procession.*

Sicily's largest wine-producing centre was founded by the colonists from Mozia who survived the destruction of the island by Dionysius of Syracuse in 397 BC. It then became a major Carthaginian city, but in the first Punic War it was conquered by the Romans, who made it their main Mediterranean naval base. The city plan is basically Roman, other quarters being added by the Arabs, who conquered the city in 830 and made it a flourishing trade centre. **Piazza della Repubblica**, bounded by **Palazzo Senatorio** and the **Cathedral**, dedicated to St Thomas of Canterbury, is the heart of town. The Cathedral was founded by the Normans and completed in the 1900s. It boasts sculptures by the Gaginis and their school. Behind the apse is the **Museo degli Arazzi Fiamminghi**, with eight 16th-century Flemish tapestries depicting Titus' war against the Hebrews. They were donated by Philip II of Spain to the Archbishop of Messina and later taken to Marsala Cathedral.

**Museo degli Arazzi Fiamminghi**
*Chiesa Madre, Via G Garaffa 57. **Tel** 0923-216 295. 9am–1pm, 4–6pm. Mon.*

**Museo Archeologico**
*Via Capo Lilibeo 34. **Tel** 0923-952 535. 9am–1:30pm daily (also 4–6:30pm Wed, Fri–Sun).*
This archaeological museum features prehistoric and ancient finds from local digs, including the mosaics from the Roman ruins at Capo Boeo and a 3rd-century-BC Punic shipwreck.

## Mozia 22

**Road map** *A2–3. from Trapani and Marsala (dawn to sunset). APT di Trapani (0923-712 598).* **Museum** *9am–7pm daily (to 3pm Nov–May).*

The prosperous Phoenician city of Mozia was built on the island of San Pantaleo, a very short distance from the shores of Sicily. The ancient site is linked with Joseph Whitaker, the son of an English wine merchant who made his fortune from Marsala wine. He became owner of the island in the early 1900s, began archaeological digs in 1913, and founded a museum that houses the statue of the "young man from Mozia". You can also visit the dry docks, which, together with those in Carthage, are the most ancient in the Mediterranean.

Punic head, Mozia museum

Ruins of the northern gate on the island of Mozia, destroyed in 397 BC

# Selinunte ㉓

Attic vase found in Selinunte

The ruins of Selinunte, overlooking the sea, are among the most striking archaeological sites in the Mediterranean and a supreme example of the fusion of Phoenician and Greek culture. Founded in the 7th century BC by colonists from Megara Hyblaea, Selinunte soon became a powerful city with flourishing trade and artistic activity. A rival to Segesta and Mozia, it was destroyed by Carthage in 409 BC and largely forgotten. Excavations (still under way in the oldest parts of the Selinunte ruins) have brought to light eight temples with colossal Doric columns, as well as a fortification system.

**★ Temple C (580–550 BC**

*Decorated with metopes no kept in Palermo, this was th largest and oldest temple on th acropolis, dedicated t Heracles or Apollo*

**Temple A (480–470 BC)**, perhaps dedicated to Leto.

Sanctuary of Malophoros

Ruins of ancient city

**Temple D (570 –550 BC)** w perhaps dedicat to Aphrodite.

Car park

**Temple O (480 – 470 BC)**, sacred to Artemis.

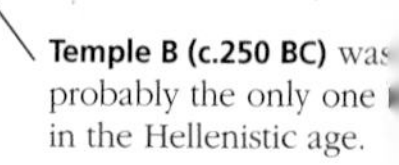

**Temple B (c.250 BC)** was probably the only one in the Hellenistic age.

**★ Acropolis**

*This was the hub of public life. It centred around two main streets that divided it into four quarters protected by a wall 1,260 m (4,132 ft) long*

**★ Temple E (490–480 BC)**
*This temple, located at the top of an eight-stepped base (crepidoma), was partly rebuilt in the 1960s. It was probably sacred to Hera and is considered one of the finest examples of Doric architecture in Sicily.*

## VISITORS' CHECKLIST

**Road map** B3.
✈ *Palermo Punta Raisi (Falcone Borsellino).* 🚌 *Castelvetrano.* ℹ *0924-46277 or 46251.* ◯ *9am–7pm (to 5pm in winter).* 

**Temple F (560–530 BC)** was dedicated to Athena and is the most ancient temple on the eastern hill. Sadly it is totally in ruins.

**The harbour area** lay at the junction of the Cotone river and the road connecting the Acropolis to the eastern hill.

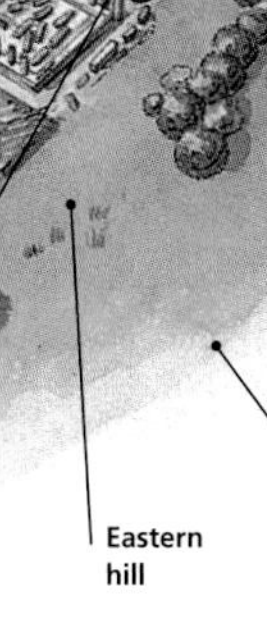

**Entrance and car park**

**Eastern hill**

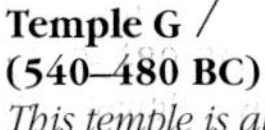

**Temple G (540–480 BC)**
*This temple is also completely in ruins but is still an important monument because, at 6,120 sq m (65,850 sq ft), it was one of the largest temples in antiquity. It reached a height of 30 m (98 ft) when complete.*

## STAR FEATURES

- ★ Acropolis
- ★ Temple
- ★ Temple E

0 metres 130

0 yards 130

## Exploring Selinunte

You will need at least two hours to visit the archaeological site of Selinunte. The excavated area is divided into four zones, starting off from the east: the eastern hill with its group of temples; the Acropolis; the ancient city; and the Sanctuary of Malophoros. Besides its great cultural interest, the surrounding landscape is very beautiful, and there are lovely views of the sea.

**The metopes of Temple C are now in Palermo museum** ***(see p56)***

### Acropolis

This lies on a bluff right over the sea, between the Selino river to the west and the Gorgo Cotone river to the east. Their mouths once formed the city harbour, now silted up. The Acropolis was surrounded by colossal stone walls 3 m (10 ft) high, with two gates, the larger one on the northern side. This area contained the public buildings and temples, all facing east. From the southern end, the first places are the sparse ruins of **Temples O and A,** close together and much alike. This similarity is perhaps due to the fact that they were both dedicated to Castor and Pollux. There were originally 6 columns along the short sides and 14 on the longer ones. Further on you come to the small Hellenistic **Temple B**, which was perhaps dedicated to Empedocles, the philosopher and scientist from Agrigento who may have supervised the drainage operations in the area. **Temple C** is the most ancient on the Acropolis. It was dedicated to Apollo and had 6 columns on the short sides and 17 on the long ones. The pediment was decorated with superb metopes, three of which are now kept in the Museo Archeologico in Palermo *(see p56)*.

**Hellenistic vases, Museo Archeologico, Palermo** ***(see p56)***

In 1925–6, 14 columns on the northern side and on part of the architrave were reconstructed. Seeing these among the other blocks of massive columns placed here and there around the ancient sacred precinct is quite an impressive sight.

**Temple D** is also reduced to a state of fragmentary ruins. The Acropolis area was divided by two main perpendicular streets, which can be reached by means of stone steps.

### The eastern hill

The sacred precinct has remains of three temples set parallel to one another at the entrance to the archaeological zone. In ancient times it was surrounded by an enclosure. The partially reconstructed **Temple E** was built in the pure Doric style. An inscription on a votive stele found in 1865 shows that it was dedicated to Hera (Juno). Its 68 columns still support part of the trabeation.

**The bronze ephebus, Selinunte**

An eight-step stairway leads to **Temple F**, the smallest and most badly damaged of the three. It was built in the

**Temple E, one of the best examples of Doric architecture in Sicily**

The Collegio dei Gesuiti at Mazara del Vallo, home to the Museo Civico

archaic style, surrounded by 36 columns which were more than 9 m (29 ft) high. The vestibule had a second row of columns, and the lower part of the peristyle was enclosed by a wall.

The size of **Temple G** was 110.36 by 50.10 m (362 by 164 ft). Today it is only a huge mass of stones, in the middle of which stands a column, which was restored in 1832. It was dedicated to Apollo, but its construction was never completed.

**The Ancient City**
On the Collina di Manuzza hill north of the Acropolis, the ancient city has been the subject of archaeological excavations only in recent years. After the destruction of the city in 409 BC, this ancient part was used as a necropolis by those inhabitants who remained.

**Malophoros Sanctuary**
Situated west of the Selino river, about a kilometre (half a mile) away from the Acropolis, the Malophoros Sanctuary is extremely old and perhaps was founded even before the city itself.

The main building in this sanctuary is enclosed by walls and was dedicated to a female divinity, Malophoros (meaning "bearer of pomegranate"), the goddess of fertility, many statuettes of whom have been found in the vicinity. According to experts, the sanctuary was a stopping point on the long, impressive funeral processions making their way to the Manicalunga necropolis.

## Castelvetrano ㉔

**Road map** B3. *30,300.* *73 km (45 miles) from Trapani, 110 km (68 miles) from Palermo.* *APT, c/o Museo Civico (0924-904 932).* *Tue.* *Funzione dell'Aurora (Easter).*

The centre consists of three linked squares. The main one is **Piazza Garibaldi**, where the mainly 16th-century **Chiesa Madre** has an interesting medieval portal. Inside are stuccoes by Ferraro and Serpotta, and a *Madonna* by the Gagini school. By the church are the **Municipio** (Town Hall), the **Campanile** and the Mannerist **Fontana della Ninfa**. Close by is the **Chiesa del Purgatorio**, built in 1624–64, its façade filled with statues, and the neo-Doric **Teatro Selinus** (1873).

**Environs**
At **Delia**, 3.5 km (2 miles) from town, is Santa Trinità, a church built in the Norman period.

## Mazara del Vallo ㉕

**Road map** A3. *50,000.* *50 km (31 miles) from Trapani, 124 km (77 miles) from Palermo.* *Piazza Santa Veneranda 2 (0923-941 727).* *Wed.* *Festino di San Vito (Aug).*

Facing the Canale di Sicilia, at the mouth of the Mazarò river, the town, a colony of Selinunte, was destroyed in 409 BC by the Carthaginians, passed to the Romans and then became a prosperous city under the Arabs, who made it the capital of one of the three "valleys" into which they split Sicily *(see p32)*. In 1073 Mazara was conquered by Roger I; he convened the first Norman Parliament of Sicily here.

In **Piazza Mokarta** remains of the castle can be seen. Behind this is the **Cathedral**, of medieval origin but rebuilt in 1694. It houses the *Transfiguration*, a sculpture group by Antonello Gagini. The left side of the Cathedral closes off Piazza della Repubblica, with the façade of the **Seminario dei Chierici** and the **Palazzo Vescovile**. On Lungomare Mazzini you will see the **Collegio dei Gesuiti**, seat of the **Museo Civico** and can enter the old Arab town.

**Museo Civico**
Via Garibaldi 50. ***Tel*** *0923-940 266.* *8:30am–2pm Mon–Sat.*
The former Collegio dei Gesuiti, with its Baroque door with four telamons, contains archaeological finds, sculpture and medieval paintings.

Mazara del Vallo, one of the most important fishing harbours in Italy

# Egadi Islands 26

**Road map** A2. 4,700. *from Trapani (Siremar: 0923-545 455).* *Consorzio Turistico Egadi, Largo Marina 14, Favignana (0923-922 121); APT Trapani (0923-545 511).* **www**.isoleegadi.it

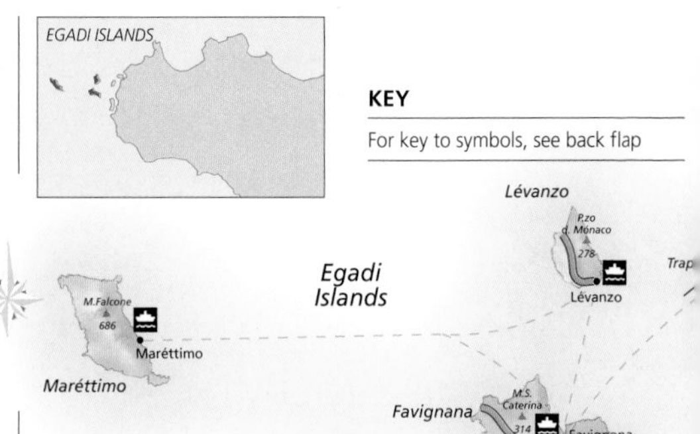


The Sicilian islands of Favignana, Levanzo and Marettimo were connected to mainland Sicily 600,000 years ago. As the sea level gradually rose, the links were submerged, slowly changing the islands into an archipelago in the centre of the Mediterranean. The islands are now popular as places for vacations and swimming as they are easily reached from Trapani.

**A stretch of the Favignana coastline**

### Favignana

This island has two distinct parts. The eastern side is flat, with pastureland and farmland, while the other half is craggy and barren. In the middle is the small town of **Favignana**, which was rebuilt in the 1600s over its original medieval layout. Sights worth visiting are the **Chiesa Matrice** (dedicated to the Immaculate Conception), the buildings constructed during the height of the tuna fishing industry and the 19th-century **Villino Florio**, which is now the Town Hall. The so-called **Bagno delle Donne** (Ladies' Bath), a Roman bath with traces of mosaics, is worth a look.

The boat tour of the island is to be recommended. It departs from the port and visits **Punta Faraglione, Punta Ferro** and **Punta Sottile**, where there is a lighthouse. It continues to the small islands of **Galera** and **Galeotta, Punta Fanfalo** and **Punta Calarossa**, where there are heaps of tufa from the island quarries. The tour ends here, taking you back to the port.

### Levanzo

The smallest of the Egadi Islands has a wilder aspect than Favignana: the tall, rocky coastline is dominated by a cultivated plateau. There is only one small village, **Cala Dogana**, and the landscape is barren and desolate, interrupted here and there by the green maquis vegetation. A series of footpaths crosses the island and provides very pleasant walks to the beautiful **Cala Tramontana** bay.

Northwest of Cala Dogana is the **Grotta del Genovese**, which can be reached on foot in about two hours or by boat. The grotto has a series of carved Palaeolithic drawings of human figures, animals and idols, some in a rather naturalistic style, others rendered more schematically.

### Marettimo

The rugged, mountainous and varied landscape of Marettimo, the first island in the group to break off from the mainland, is very striking. The paths crossing the island – there are no roads or hotels here – will introduce you to a world of limestone pinnacles and caves leading up to Monte Falcone (686 m, 2,250 ft). The island has many rare plant species that grow only here – caused by the long isolation of Marettimo – as well as some introduced moufflon and boar. The **Punta Troia fort** housed a Bourbon penal colony where the Risorgimento hero, Guglielmo Pepe, was held for three years. Not far from the tiny village of Marettimo there are some ancient Roman buildings and, in the vicinity, a small Byzantine church.

**The little harbour at Cala Dogana, the only village in Levanzo**

*For hotels and restaurants in this region see pp199–201 and pp214–16*

The Grotta Azzurra, a major attraction on boat tours around Ustica

# Ustica 27

**Road map** B1. *1,200. from Palermo (Siremar: 091-582 403); in summer from Naples (Ustica Lines: 081-251 4721). Palermo Punta Raisi 091-591 663. Pro Loco di Ustica (091-844 91 90; open Jun–Sep); APT Palermo (091-583 847).*

Ustica is the result of ancient volcanic eruptions: its name derives from the word *usta* (burned) and the land is made up of sharp black volcanic rock, which lends it its unique appearance. The emerged part of the gigantic submerged volcano, about 49 km (30 miles) from the Sicilian coast, is only 8.6 sq km (3.32 sq miles), but its extremely fertile lava terrain is ideal for the cultivation of grapes, wheat and vegetables. The steep and rocky coasts and the landscape of the island make it an ideal spot for underwater sports. Because of the importance of the sea beds, the first **Marine Reserve** in Italy was established here on 12 November 1986; it is run by the local authorities. The park is divided into three sections, and the degree of protection ranges from total (from Caletta to Cala Sidoti) to partial. Guided tours are organized by the Marine Reserve itself, and in July the island plays host to a series of international skin- and scuba-diving programmes. A particularly interesting underwater excursion is the one that starts off at **Punta Gavazzi**, with what could be described as an archaeological diving tour of the ancient Roman amphorae, old anchors, and traces of the passage of sailors since the beginning of human history in this part of the sea.

The village of **Ustica** is dominated by the **Capo Falconara** promontory, where the Bourbon rulers built a little fort offering a splendid view as far as the Sicilian coast. Ustica was founded in the mid-1700s and is still inhabited. Local life revolves around Piazza Umberto I, where there is a whitewashed parish church. Age-old human presence on the island is visible in a number of interesting sites, such as the prehistoric village of **Faraglioni** and the Phoenician tombs at **Falconara**, which were used at different times by the Greeks, the Romans and the Byzantines.

The main feature of a boat tour of the island is the great number of underwater caves in the rocky coastline: the **Grotta Azzurra**, whose large caverns are preceded by an imposing natural arch, the **Grotta delle Colonne**, with a cliff of the same name, and the **Grotta Blasi, Grotta dell'Oro** and **Grotta delle Barche** (where fishermen used to moor their boats during storms), are only a few of the many caves to be seen.

Underwater exploration around the island of Ustica

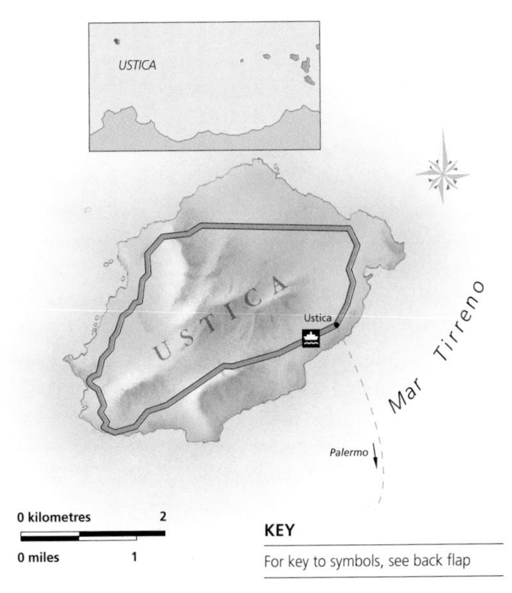


**KEY**

For key to symbols, see back flap

# SOUTHWESTERN SICILY

*This corner of Sicily is only a stone's throw from North Africa. The landscape is varied, much of it hilly or mountainous, with rugged cliffs along parts of the coast and arid, barren plateaus inland. The Greeks built classically beautiful temples at Agrigento, and the Romans left an extensive villa at Piazza Armerina, saved for posterity by being buried under mud for centuries.*

Along the coast, steep craggy cliffs alternate with flatter, stretches of sand. This southern shore was a favourite landing place for travellers plying the Mediterranean, with their ships putting in at places like Agrigento, Eraclea and Sciacca.

Agrigento became an important Greek centre, and an entire valley of temples still remains as evidence of their skills. Some are still in good condition 2,000 years later. The mud-preserved Roman mosaics at the Villa del Casale at Piazza Armerina are in marvellous condition and provide an excellent picture of Roman life.

The land rises away from the sea to become soft, rolling htills and then, quite abruptly, rugged mountains. Rivers may emerge for only a few weeks each year. Around the towns of Enna and Caltanissetta lies the stony heart of the island, exploited for its sulphur mines and quarries for centuries. Inland, Southwestern Sicily is a totally different world from the coast. Towns like Enna seem to perch precariously on hilltops. Many of the people of these rather isolated towns have retained a deep-seated religious faith, which is expressed in the colourful processions held during Easter Week *(see p126)*. The flatter land and slopes nearer to the sea were once the domain of ancient feudal estates with their olive and orange groves, vividly described in Giuseppe di Lampedusa's novel *The Leopard*. This, perhaps the most truly "Sicilian" part of Sicily, was also the birthplace of the great Italian writer Pirandello.

**A boar being captured in one of the fine hunting scene mosaics in the Villa del Casale, at Piazza Armerina**

**◁ The beautifully preserved Temple of Concord (c.430 BC) in the valley of the Temples at Agrigento**

# Exploring Southwestern Sicily

A good starting point for a visit to this corner of Sicily is Agrigento, as it is within easy reach of the eastern coast, with Palma di Montechiaro and Licata, and the western coast, moving towards Megara and Sciacca. Major communications routes travel into the interior towards Caltanissetta and Enna on the one hand and, westwards, into the hinterland towards Palermo. From the port at Agrigento there is a regular boat service to the islands of Lampedusa and Linosa.

Bust of Persephone found at Aidone, near Enna

**GETTING AROUND**

You can visit the sights of Agrigento by public transport if you choose to, but if you want to see the interior you will need a car. The main roads in this area are the SS189 Agrigento–Palermo, the SS640 to Caltanissetta (from Caltanissetta to Enna it becomes the SS117b and returns to the coast via Piazza Armerina and Gela) and lastly the SS115, which runs along the entire southwestern coastline of Sicily.

For additional map symbols *see back flap*

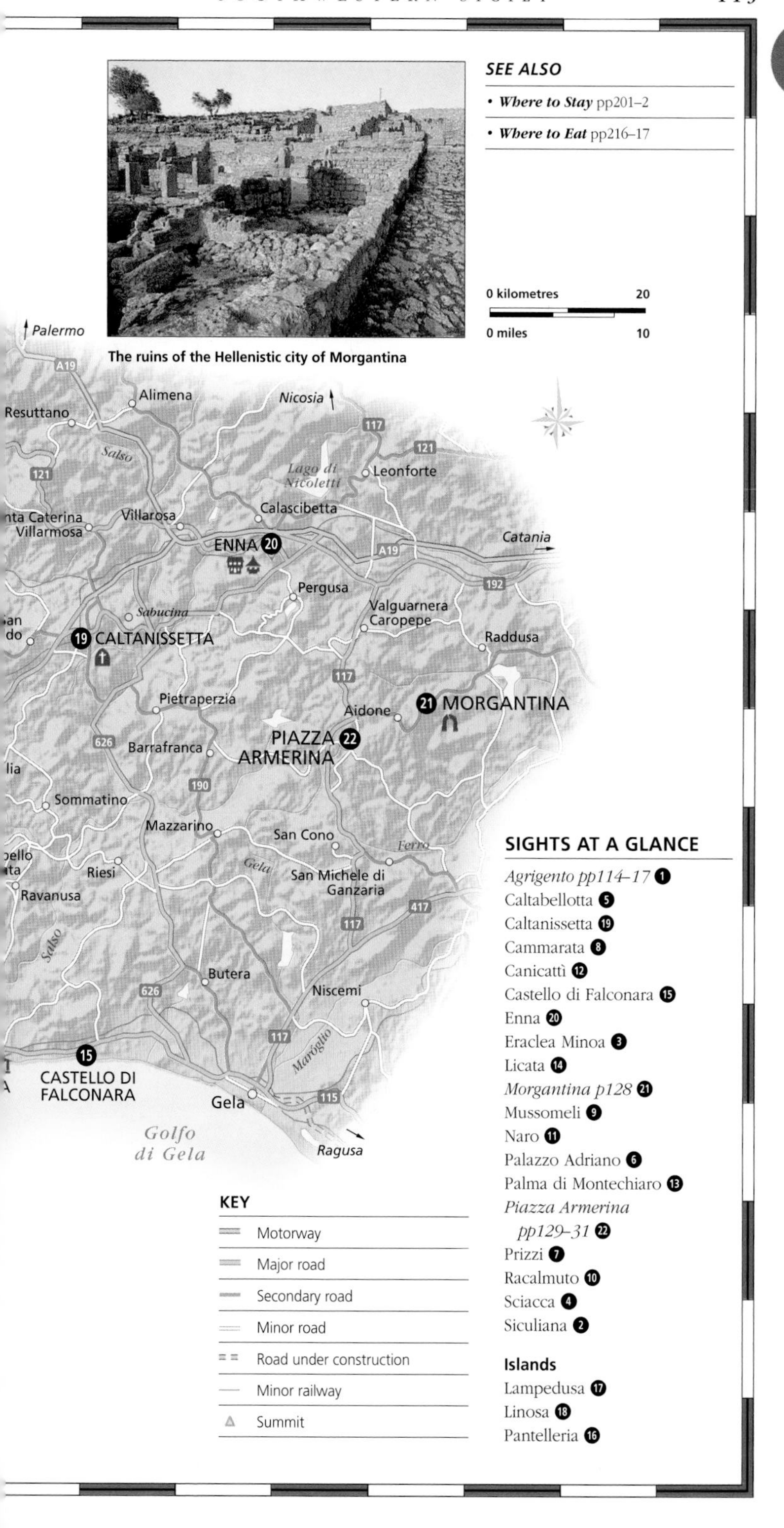


The ruins of the Hellenistic city of Morgantina

### SEE ALSO


- ***Where to Stay*** pp201–2
- ***Where to Eat*** pp216–17


## SIGHTS AT A GLANCE



### KEY

- Motorway
- Major road
- Secondary road
- Minor road
- Road under construction
- Minor railway
- Summit

# Agrigento ❶

Detail of San Nicola, Museo Archeologico

There are two main sights in Agrigento: the magnificent remains of the Greek colony in the Valle dei Templi *(see pp116–17)* and the rocky hill where the medieval town was built. The city of Akragas was founded by the Greeks, then conquered by the Romans in 210 BC, who gave it the name of Agrigentum. During a period of barbarian invasions the town moved from the valley to the rock. It was then ruled by the Byzantines and for some time by the Arabs, whose dominion came to an end with the Normans in 1087.

## VISITORS' CHECKLIST

**Road map** C4. *57,500. Palermo. 0922-616 18 06. AAPT (0922-401 352).* **Valle dei Templi** ***Tel*** *0922-497 226. 8:30am–7pm.* **Museo Archeologico** ***Tel*** *0922-401 565. 9am–7:30pm Tue–Sat, 9am–1:30pm Mon & hols.*

Façade of Agrigento Cathedral (11th century)

### Cathedral and Museo Diocesano

Piazza Don Minzoni. ***Tel*** *0922-241 81.* **Museo Diocesano** ***Tel*** *0922-401 352. daily.*

Agrigento's cathedral was founded in the 12th century and subsequently enlarged and altered, as can be seen in some of the exterior details. For example, the bell tower has a series of Catalan-Gothic single lancet windows, while others are in the original style.

Inside is the Cappella di San Gerlando, named after the bishop who founded the church, with an elegant Gothic portal. The ceiling features both painted and coffered sections, dating from the 16th and 17th centuries respectively. A curious acoustic phenomenon, known as the *portavoce*, takes place in the chapel: if you stand under the apse, you can clearly hear the whispering of people at the other end of the nave, 80 m (262 ft) away.

The **Museum** has some Roman sarcophagi and a series of frescoes taken from the Cathedral walls in 1951.

### Teatro Pirandello

Piazza Pirandello. ***Tel*** *0922-203 91.* www.teatropirandello.it

Founded in 1870 and originally called Teatro Regina Margherita, the Teatro Pirandello was renamed after the Agrigento-born playwright *(see p22 & p25)*. Part of the Town Hall, it was designed by Dionisio Sciascia, and the decoration was executed by Palermo architect Giovanni Basile.

### Museo Civico

Piazza Pirandello. ***Tel*** *0922-597 198. Mon.*

The city museum, which is located in the old Convento degli Agostiniani, opposite the Municipio (Town Hall), contains a collection of paintings from the 14th to the 18th century and medieval sculpture.

### San Lorenzo

Piazza del Purgatorio. *daily.*

Little remains of this church (also known as Chiesa del Purgatorio), which was rebuilt in the Baroque style in the 1600s. The two-stage façade has an interesting portal flanked by two large spiral columns and a large bell tower. Both interior and exterior have a series of allegorical statues representing the Christian Virtues, executed in the early 1700s by Giuseppe and Giacomo Serpotta, and a *Madonna of the Pomegranate* attributed to Antonello Gagini.

Near the church, under a stone lion, is the Ipogeo del Purgatorio (Hypogeum of Purgatory), a network of underground conduits built

## AGRIGENTO

Cathedral and Museo Diocesano ①
Convento di Santo Spirito ⑤
Museo Archeologico Nazionale ⑦
Museo Civico ③
Piazza Vittorio Emanuele ⑥
San Lorenzo ④
Teatro Pirandello ②
*Valle dei Templi (see pp116–17)* ⑧

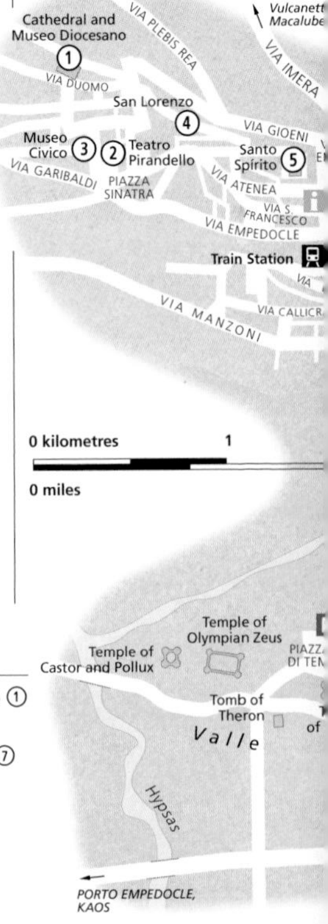

The arched coupled windows in the Convento di Santo Spirito (1295)

in the 5th century BC by the Greek architects to supply water to the various quarters of the city.

### Convento di Santo Spirito

Salita Santo Spirito. *daily.*

This abbey complex is of ancient origin. The church and adjacent Cistercian monastery were founded in the 13th century by the Countess Prefoglio of the powerful Chiaramonte family. They were altered several times, particularly the façade, which, however, still maintains a Gothic portal and rose window. For many centuries the church was the most important in the Agrigento area and was known as the Badia Grande. In the 18th century the nave was decorated with lavish and fantastic stuccowork that mirrors the shapes of the church; the motif is also developed in sculpted panels.

Next to the church is the monastery, now city property, where the cloister is well worth a visit. The impressive chapterhouse is lined with Gothic arcades.

Key to Symbols *see back flap*

### Piazza Vittorio Emanuele

This large, lively, traffic-filled square connects the old town of Agrigento with the more recently built part, which developed during the 19th century. The two areas, Girgenti to the west and Rupe Atenea to the east, were once separated by a valley that was filled in during the late 19th century, blocking what was traditionally known as "Empedocles' opening", through which the north wind passed, cooling the valley below.

### Environs

Towards the sea is the parish of Kaos, worth visiting to see the **Birthplace of Luigi Pirandello**, the house of the great dramatist and novelist *(see pp22–5)*. The winner of the 1934 Nobel Prize for Literature once lived here; it is now a museum. The urn containing Pirandello's ashes can be found in a crack in a rock next to an old fallen pine, facing the sea.

Nearby, **Porto Empedocle** is an important outlet for the mining activity in the interior. In the old harbour is the Bastione di Carlo V (Rampart of Charles V), while there is a constant bustle of fishing boats around the more industrialized area.

Heading north from Agrigento and turning off SS189 at the Comitini crossroads, two kilometres (one mile) of dirt road to the south takes you to a place famous for a curious geological phenomenon: little volcano-shaped cones known as the **Vulcanetti di Macalube** emit methane gas bubbles and brackish mud in a lunar landscape made sterile by this pseudo-volcanic activity.

### Museo Archeologico Regionale

Contrada San Nicola. ***Tel*** *0922-401 565.* *9am–7:30pm Tue–Sat, 9am–1pm Mon, Sun & hols.*

Part of the Convento di San Nicola and located in a panoramic spot that affords beautiful views over the Valley of the Temples *(see pp116–17)*, this interesting archaeological museum shows material recovered from several excavations around Agrigento.

Among the items on display are a remarkable Attic vase, the Crater of Dionysus, and the marble statue of a young athlete known as the Ephebus of Agrigento.

### Birthplace of Pirandello

Contrada Kaos, SS 115. ***Tel*** *0922-511 826.* *9am–1pm, 2–7pm daily.*

The eerie landscape of the Vulcanetti di Macalube

# Valle dei Templi

Agrigento was founded in 581 BC by colonists from Gela, who named the town Akragas *(see p30)*. Yet only a century later the population had grown to 200,000 and the Greek poet Pindar described it as "the fairest city inhabited by mortals". It was ruled briefly by the Carthaginians. The Valley of Temples is the site of the main temples (dedicated to Olympian Zeus, Heracles, Concord and Hera), minor shrines (Sanctuary of the Chthonic Divinities) and the Archaeological Museum.

The Ephebus of Agrigento

**Sanctuary of the Chthonic Divinities (6th–5th century B**

*A shrine dedicated to Demeter a Persephone (also known as Kore with altars and sacred precincts.*

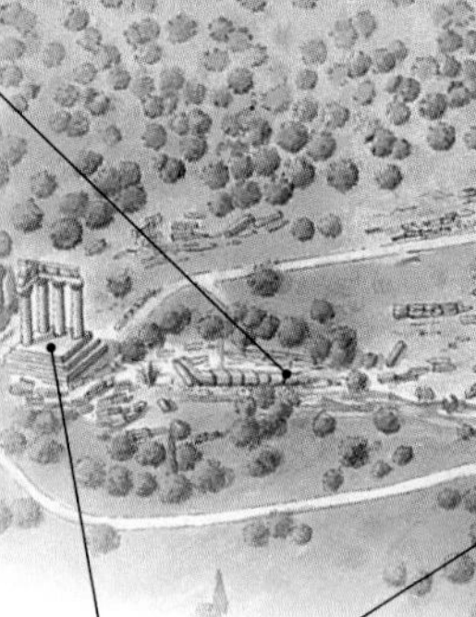


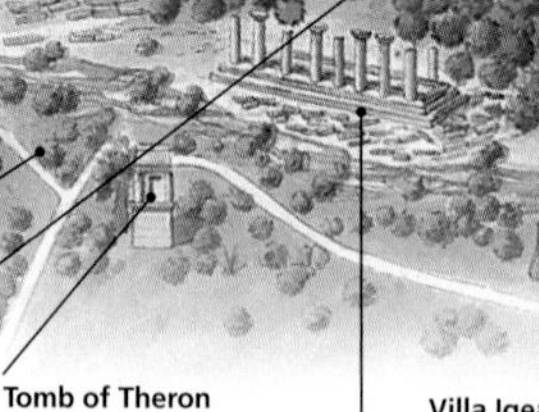

**Temple of Olympian Zeus (5th century BC)**

*Only fragmentary ruins remain of this temple, except for this Telamon now on display in the Museo Archeologico.*

**Temple of Castor and Pollux (5th century BC)**

*The four surviving columns, a symbol of the Valley of Temples, were restored in the 19th century.*

**Temple of Heracles (6th century BC)**

*These eight columns, put back in place in 1924, belonged to the oldest temple dedicated to the hero worshipped by both the Greeks and Romans (as Hercules). The archaic Doric structure has an elongated rectangle plan.*

**★ Museo Archeologico**
*The Archaeological Museum was opened to the public in 1967. The 13 rooms display objects ranging from prehistoric times to the early Christian period, including pieces from the Classical era.*

## EARLY CHRISTIAN CATACOMBS

The niches, hewn along the floors and walls

The Valle dei Templi is famous for its splendid monuments of the Magna Graecia civilization, but it also has Early Christian ruins. The Ipogei of Villa Igea (also known as the Grotta di Frangipane), between the Temple of Heracles and the Temple of Concord, were cut out of the rock to house the bodies of the first Christians here. A series of niches, closed off by stone slabs, alternated with chapels that still bear traces of wall paintings.

**The Hellenistic-Roman quarter** is all that remains of the large post-Classical age settlement.

**Rock sanctuary of Demeter**

**★ Temple of Hera (5th century BC)**
*This well-preserved temple was restored in Roman times. Note the northern colonnade with its architrave.*

**Line of fortifications**

**★ Temple of Concord (5th century BC)**
*With its 34 columns, this is one of the best preserved Doric temples in the world, partly thanks to alterations made in the 4th century AD, when it became a Christian basilica. It was restored to its original classical form in 1748.*

0 metres 200
0 yards 200

### STAR FEATURES

- ★ Museo Archeologico
- ★ Temple of Concord
- ★ Temple of Hera

## Siculiana ❷

**Road map** C4. 5,100. *from Palermo and Trapani to Castelvetrano, then* *Town hall, Piazza Kennedy (0922-815 105).*

The present-day town of Siculiana was built on the site of an Arab fort destroyed by the Normans in the late 11th century. The new lords – the Chiaramonte family from Agrigento – rebuilt the fortress in the 1300s and it was altered several times afterwards. Despite all the changes, Siculiana has retained some Arab features.

In central Piazza Umberto I is the Baroque **Chiesa Madre**, dedicated to San Leonardo Abate, dominating the square at the top of a flight of steps. In the old centre, divided into large blocks, you can glimpse entrances to courtyards and alleys, which were once part of the covered Arab town.

Siculiana, built on a hill during Arab rule

The archaeological site at Eraclea Minoa, close to the rocky shore

## Eraclea Minoa ❸

**Road map** B4.
**Digs** *Cattolica Eraclea.* ***Tel*** *0922-846 005.* *9am–1 hr before sunset.*

This ancient settlement was founded during the Mycenaean age and then developed by Spartan colonists who arrived in the 6th century BC and gave it its present name. After being fought over by Agrigento and Carthage, Eraclea became a Roman colony. Today it is a stone's throw from the craggy coast jutting out into the sea. Eraclea is a wonderful combination of a lovely setting and atmospheric ruins. The **theatre** is well preserved – excavations began in the 1950s – and hosts special performances of Greek theatre, although the overall impression is marred somewhat by the plastic used to protect it in bad weather. All around the theatre are the ruins of the ancient city with its defence system, as well as some necropolises.

## Sciacca ❹

**Road map** B3. *40,000.* *from Palermo and Trapani.* *AAST, Corso Vittorio Emanuele 84 (0925-21182 or 22744); AAR Terme di Sciacca, Via Agatocle 2 (0925-961 111).*
**www**.aziendaturismosciacca.it

From a distance, Sciacca seems to be overwhelmed by Monte San Calogero, with its thermal waters and steam vapours, which have made the town famous over the centuries. Although the hot springs had been used since prehistoric times, Sciacca was founded as a mere military outpost for Selinunte during the interminable warfare with the city of Agrigento, and was called *Thermae Selinuntinae* (Selinunte baths) by the Romans. It developed rapidly under Arab rule (Sciacca derives from *as-saqah*) and many traces of their culture can be seen in the old Rabato and Giudecca-Cadda quarters, with their blind alleys and maze of roofed courtyards.

### THE ORANGES OF RIBERA

Orange decoration for the festival

The real home of orange-growing is the plain around Mount Etna, but oranges play an important role in the southwestern corner of Sicily, too. At Ribera, an agricultural town where the statesman Francesco Crispi was born *(see p36)*, they grow a special type of navel orange that was brought to Sicily from America by emigrants returning home. These enormous and delicious oranges are celebrated in an annual orange festival during which the public gardens are filled with sculptures made of fruit. A short distance from Ribera, the impressive ruins of the Poggio Diana castle tower above the wooded gullies of the Verdura river.

Locally grown oranges, still harvested by hand in this area

'he rusticated façade of the Catalan-Gothic Palazzo Steripinto

'he town was further fortified •y the Normans, who quickly ecognized its strategic nportance in controlling ,ne trade routes. Much ought over in the years that ollowed, the town was ortified again and again, in ›articular against the assault ›f Charles I of Valois.

In the middle of town is **'alazzo Steripinto**, built in :atalan-Gothic style in 1501 vith a rusticated façade. The ·hurch of **Santa Margherita** ,as a splendid Gothic portal; ıote the bas-relief sculpture ı the lunette representing ;anta Margherita, the Arch- ıngel Gabriel, Our Lady of he Assumption and saints :alogero and Maddalena. )o not miss the cloister of he former **Convent of San ·rancesco** and the unfinished 3aroque façade of the **Chiesa ıel Carmine**, with its 14th- :entury rose window. In :entral Piazza Don Minzoni ;tands the **Cathedral**, dedica- :ed to Santa Maria Maddalena. 't was rebuilt in 1656, but ·etains three Norman apses.

However, the main ıttractions in Sciacca are Monte San Calogero and its :hermal pools. From the large square at the summit, with :he sanctuary dedicated to the :vangelist San Calogero, who ın the 5th century eliminated pagan rites in the mountain caves, the panorama is breathtaking. The summit is almost 400 m (1,312 ft) high, and on a clear day there is a :ommanding view from Capo Bianco to Capo Lilibeo, with the limestone ridge of Caltabellotta in the background and Pantelleria island before you. The older spas are on the slopes of the mountain, while new ones have been built closer to the seaside.

Sciacca is also known for its ceramics, which were mentioned in antiquity by Diodorus Siculus. Local production thrived during the period of Arab rule, and another golden age came in the 16th century. The tradition is being maintained today by the local craftsmen.

## Caltabellotta ❺

**Road map** B3. 5,300.
*Town hall, Piazza Umberto I 1 (0925-951 013).*

Visible from most of the hilly area of Sciacca, the rocky crest of Caltabellotta (950 m, 3,116 ft) has been inhabited for millennia, as can be seen in the many ancient necropolises and hypogea. The site was fortified at different stages until the arrival of the Arabs, who gave the castle its definitive form, calling it *Kal'at–at–al ballut* (rock of the oak trees). The county capital, Caltabellotta witnessed the signing of peace between Charles I of Valois and Frederick II of Aragon in 1302 *(see pp28–9)*, who took over the whole of Sicily. Perched on the ridge above the houses of the Torrevecchia quarter are the ruins of the **Norman castle** and **San Salvatore**, while on the other side of the rock is the **Chiesa Madre**, now being restored, founded by Roger I to celebrate his victory over the Arabs. On the western slope, the **Hermitage of San Pellegrino**, which consists of a monastery and a chapel, dominates the city.

**Sculpture at the Hermitage of San Pellegrino**

The town of Caltabellotta at the foot of Monte Castello

The façade of San Nicolò, in the upper part of Palazzo Adriano

## Palazzo Adriano ❻

**Road map** C3. *2,800.*
*Pro Loco, Piazza Umberto I (091-834 9911).*

Almost 700 m (2,296 ft) above sea level, on the ridge of Cozzo Braduscia, is Palazzo Adriano, founded in the mid-15th century by Albanian refugees who fled from the Turkish conquerors. Central Piazza Umberto I boasts two important churches: Greek Orthodox **Santa Maria Assunta**, built in the 16th century and then rebuilt (the interior has a lovely iconostasis and an icon of Our Lady of the Assumption); and **Santa Maria del Lume**, which is Catholic and was founded in the 18th century. In the middle of the square, bordered by **Palazzo Dara**, now the Town Hall, and **Palazzo Mancuso**, there is a lovely octagonal fountain sculpted in 1607. Further up the hill, in the oldest part of Palazzo Adriano, the red dome of the 15th-century **San Nicolò** overlooks the alleyways of this quarter, which were built around the castle that stood here before the town was founded.

## Prizzi ❼

**Road map** C3. *6,900.*
*Town hall, Piazza Francesco Crispi (091-834 50 45).*

The slopes of wind-blown Mount Prizzi overlooking the surrounding valleys have been inhabited since ancient times. There was once a fortified Arab town here, but present-day Prizzi mostly reflects the influence of the Middle Ages. The maze of alleys winding up the slopes to the summit (960 m, 3,149 ft) is crowned by the ruins of the medieval castle. Along the narrow streets you will see **San Rocco**, a large stretch of open space with **Santa Maria delle Grazie**, and the 18th-century **Chiesa Madre** dedicated to St George and bearing a fine statue of the Archangel Michael.

## Cammarata ❽

**Road map** C3. *7,000.*
FS *from Palermo & Agrigento.*
*Town hall (0922-907 211).*

The earliest historic records for this town date from the Norman period, when Roger I donated the fief to Lucia de Cammarata. The **Chiesa Madre**, San Nicolò di Bari, and the **Dominican monastery**, whose church was rebuilt in the 1930s, are all worth a visit. But the fascination of Cammarata lies in the overall layout: a labyrinth of alleys and steps – narrow or wide, depending on the natural slope of the rock – offering an unforgettable view of the valleys below this medieval hill town.

### CINEMA PARADISO

In 1990 the film *Cinema Paradiso* by the Sicilian director Giuseppe Tornatore *(see p24)* won an Oscar for the best foreign film. The film tells the story of the arrival of cinema (the "Nuovo Cinema Paradiso") in an isolated village in Sicily and the effect the big screen has on the main character, a young boy. *Cinema Paradiso* was filmed in the streets and squares of Palazzo Adriano and used many of the locals as extras, conferring fame on the village. The weeks the film unit and the inhabitants of Palazzo Adriano spent working together are commemorated on a majolica plaque on a corner of Piazza Umberto I.

The plaque commemorating the filming of *Cinema Paradiso*

The characteristic stone trough at Piazza Fontana, in Racalmuto

## Mussomeli ⓽

**Road map** C3. *11,700.* *0934-961 111 or 951 192.* **Castello Manfredano** *Summer: 9:30am–noon, 3:30–6pm Tue–Sun; winter: 9:30am–noon Sat & Sun.*

In the 14th century, Manfredi III Chiaramonte founded the town of Mussomeli and the large fortress that still towers over what has since become a large agricultural centre. The **castle**, called Manfredano or Chiaramontano in honour of its founder and built over the remains of a Hohenstaufen fortification, was altered in the 15th century by the Castellar family. It has a second walled enclosure in the interior as well as the Sala dei Baroni, with noteworthy portals. From the outer walls there are panoramic views of the valleys and hills of the interior of the island.

## Racalmuto ⓾

**Road map** C4. *10,300.* *from Catania and Palermo (via Caltanissetta).* *Comune di Racalmuto (0922-948111).*

The town of Racalmuto (the name derives from the Arab *rahalmut*, or destroyed hamlet) was founded by Federico Chiaramonte (head of the powerful Sicilian Chiaramonte family) over an existing fortification. For centuries the growth of the town went hand in hand with the development of various monastic orders (Carmelite, Franciscan, Minor and Augustines), but the place still bears traces of the typical Arab layout marked by courtyards and alleys. For centuries Racalmuto thrived on the mining of rock salt and sulphur. The town is also the birthplace of author Leonardo Sciascia *(see p23)* . Today it is a famous agricultural centre, especially known for its dessert grapes.

In the middle of town, in Piazza Umberto I, is the 17th-century **Chiesa Madre dell'Annunziata**, its interior decorated with lavish stucco, as well as **San Giuseppe** and the ruins of the 13th-century **Chiaramonte castle** (closed to the public). Steps lead to Piazza del Municipio, with the **Santa Chiara Convent**, now the Town Hall, and the **Teatro Regina Margherita**, founded in 1879 by Dionisio Sciascia. Further up the hill, at the far end of the steps is the **Sanctuary of Santa Maria del Monte**, where an important annual festival is held on 11–14 July. Inside the sanctuary is a statue of the Virgin Mary from 1503. Other churches worth visiting are the Carmelites' (with canvases by Pietro D'Asaro), the Itria and San Giuliano, which was once the chapel of the **Sant'Agostino Convent**. A short walk from the centre takes you to **Piazza Fontana**, with a stone drinking trough, and, further along, Piazza San Francesco, where there is the monastery complex of the Conventual friars, rebuilt in the 1600s.

## Naro ⓫

**Road map** C4. *8,800.* *Pro Loco (0922-953 011).*

Naro lies on a hill in the middle of a water-rich area. Its name derives from ancient Greek and Arab origins – the Greek word for river is *naron*, and *nahr* is the Arab translation of the same.

A "resplendent" royal city during the reign of Frederick II Hohenstaufen, it was fortified at different times. Besides the Baroque churches and the remains of monasteries, there are the ruins of the medieval **Chiaramonte castle**, which is always closed, 14th-century Santa Caterina and the 16th-century Chiesa Madre.

The Chiaramonte castle at Naro, built in the 14th century

The 15th-century Castello di Montechiaro, overlooking the sea

## Canicattì 12

**Road map** C4. 32,000.
*Town hall (0922-856 738).*

The large agricultural town of Canicattì owes its fame to the production of dessert grapes (a festival in celebration is held each autumn). Known to Arab geographers as *al-Qattà*, this town became a part of documented Sicilian history in the 14th century, when it was registered as the fief of the Palmieri family from Naro. The late 18th century marked a period of prosperity and growth under the Bonanno family, who commissioned numerous buildings and public works.

In the centre of town are the ruins of the **Castello Bonanno** and the **Torre dell'Orologio**, rebuilt in the 1930s. Economic prosperity is confirmed by the many churches – **San Diego**, rebuilt in the Baroque period with stucco decoration; the **Chiesa del Purgatorio**, with a statue of the Sacred Heart; the **Chiesa del Carmelo**, rebuilt in the early 20th century with funds donated by the local sulphur mine workers – and civic works such as the **Fountain of Neptune** and the recent **Teatro Sociale**. The **Chiesa Madre** is dedicated to San Pancrazio. It was rebuilt in the early 20th century. The new façade is the work of Francesco Basile and among its many interesting sculptures and paintings is the *Madonna delle Grazie*, sculpted in the 16th century in Byzantine style. Along the main street in the upper town there are three monasteries.

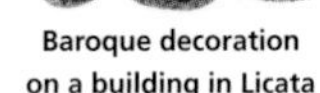

Baroque decoration on a building in Licata

## Palma di Montechiaro 13

**Road map** C4. 21,500.
*Town hall (0922-799 111).*

Founded in 1637 by Carlo Tomasi, the Prince of Lampedusa, Palma owes its name to the palm tree on the coat of arms of the De Caro family, relatives of the Tomasi. The town was the property of the Tomasi di Lampedusa family up to the early 19th century, but the family name became really famous only after the publication of the novel *Il Gattopardo (The Leopard)* in 1958.

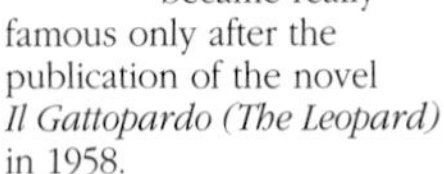

Palma was created with a town plan, partly the inspiration of the 17th-century astronomer Giovanni Battista Odierna, and loosely based on that of Jerusalem. The layout revolves around **Piazza Provenzani**, with the church of **Santissimo Rosario** and a Benedictine monastery. Further up is the monumental stairway leading to Piazza Santa Rosalia, with the **Chiesa Madre**, built in the late 1600s with an impressive two-stage façade flanked by twin bell towers. On Sundays and holidays this square is the hub of city life.

A walk through town reveals a number of interesting Baroque buildings.

### *IL GATTOPARDO*

Giuseppe Tomasi di Lampedusa (1896–1957)

Tomasi di Lampedusa's famous novel *(see pp23–4)* was a great success when it was published posthumously in 1958, selling over 100,000 copies. It was later made into a highly acclaimed film by Luchino Visconti. The novel was published thanks to the efforts of novelist Giorgio Bassani, who met Tomasi di Lampedusa in 1954, three years before he died. Most of the novel is set in Palermo, but there are recognizable descriptions of the villages and landscape in this part of Sicily, with which the author had strong bonds.

A typical square in Licata

A few miles away, not far from the sea, are the evocative ruins of **Castello di Montechiaro**, founded, according to tradition, by Federico III Chiaramonte. Although it is now closed for restoration, it is worthwhile visiting the site of this 15th-century castle because of the wonderful views of the coastline from its walls.

## Licata ⓮

**Road map** C4. 35,000.
FS *from Syracuse, Palermo & Catania, via Caltanissetta (0922-774 122).* *Town hall (0922-868 111).*

Licata is one of the chief market garden towns in southern Sicily. It was built in the Greek period – according to tradition it was founded by the tyrant of Agrigento, Phintias, in 280 BC and was named after him – and under Roman dominion became the port for the shipment of local produce. Evidence of the town's former wealth can be seen in the many rock-hewn Byzantine churches. After the period of Arab rule, in 1234 Frederick II made it part of the public domain, building fortresses which over the centuries have disappeared (Castel Nuovo was destroyed by the Turks at the end of the 1561 siege). Licata again became a part of history on 10 July 1943, when Allied troops landed nearby and advanced northwards in their conquest of Italian territory.

The centre of town life is Piazza Progresso, where there is the art deco **Municipio** or Town Hall, designed in 1935 by Ernesto Basile, which houses some interesting art works, including a statue of the *Madonna and Child* and a 15th-century triptych. Also worth visiting is the **Museo Archeologico**, which has exhibits of prehistoric artifacts from the Palaeolithic to the Bronze Age, archaic Greek (particularly funerary objects) and Hellenistic archaeological finds, and a series of medieval statues representing the Christian virtues. Along Corso Vittorio Emanuele, which leads towards the coast, there are some patrician mansions such as **Palazzo Frangipane**, which has an 18th-century façade decorated with reliefs. On the Corso you can also see the **Chiesa Matrice di Santa Maria la Nova**, which, according to local legend, the Turks tried to burn down in 1553. Founded in the 1500s, it houses a 16th-century crucifix and a 17th-century Flemish Nativity scene. The harbour is almost exclusively given over to fishing boats since the decline of sulphur mining drastically decreased its industrial importance.

**Museo Archeologico**
Via Dante, Badia di Licata. ***Tel*** *0922-772 602.* *8am–8pm Mon–Sat, 8am–1pm Sun.*

## Castello di Falconara ⓯

**Road map** D4. *by appt only.*
***Tel*** *0934-347 929.*
**www**.castellodifalconara.it

Not far from Licata, on the road towards Gela, is the village of Falconara, famous most of all for the impressive castle towering above the sea from the top of a rocky bluff. The Castello di Falconara was built in the 15th century. It is usually closed, but you can make an appointment to view with the custodian.

Towards Licata is the Salso river, the second largest in Sicily. Its name derives from the many outcrops of rock salt that make its waters salty (*salso* means saline). The river flows through the Sommatino plateau and down a series of gullies before meandering across the coastal plains.

Castello di Falconara, constructed in the 15th century, set among greenery at the water's edge

## Pantelleria ⓰

**Road map** A5. *7,800.*
*Town hall (0923-695 011); Pro Loco (0923-911 838).*
**www**.pantelleria.it

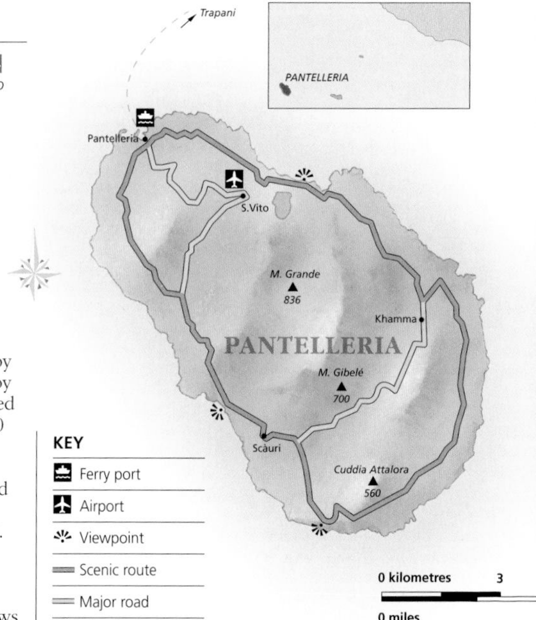


Pantelleria, the largest island off the Sicilian coastline, is also closer to the Tunisian coast (Capo Mustafà is 70 km or 44 miles away) than to Capo Granitola in Sicily (100 km, 62 miles). Despite this isolation, Pantelleria was colonized by the Phoenicians and then by the Greeks. It was controlled by the Arabs for almost 400 years (in fact, its name derives from *Bent el-Rhia*, "daughter of the wind") and was then conquered and fortified in 1123 by Roger I. Since that time its history has run in parallel to the vicissitudes of Sicily.

The strong wind that blows here all year round has forced the inhabitants to protect their plants and kitchen gardens with enclosures and walls, and to prune the olive trees so that they grow almost horizontally, close to the ground. Wind is also responsible for a typical style of building called *dammuso*, a square, whitewashed peasant's house with walls almost 2 m (6 ft) thick and tiny windows in order to provide the best insulation. Water is scarce on the island, so the roofs of these homes are shaped to collect rainwater. The coastal road is 45 km (28 miles) in length; it starts at the town of Pantelleria and goes past the **archaeological zone of Mursia** (with a series of megalithic structures called *sesi* in local dialect) and then goes up to high ground. The main sights here are **Punta Fram, Cala dell'Altura** and **Punta Tre Pietre**, where another road takes you to the village of **Scauri**. The coast is steep and craggy with some inlets (like the **Balata dei Turchi**, a favourite landing place for Saracen pirates, or the lovely **Cala Rotonda**) up to the **Punta Tracino** promontory– with a striking rock formation in front of it – which separates the **Tramontana** and **Levante inlets**. After the village of Gadir and the lighthouse at Punta Spasdillo the road descends to the **Cala Cinque Denti** inlet or the **Bagno dell'Acqua** hot springs and then back to its starting point. The town of **Pantelleria**, at the foot of the **Barbacane Castle**, was almost destroyed by Allied bombings in World War II. Life revolves around **Piazza Cavour** and the new **Chiesa Madre**, both facing the sea. Renting a bicycle is a very pleasant way of getting to know the island and the local way of life, as well as the handicrafts, the famous *Moscato passito* dessert wine and the locally grown capers.

**Walled gardens on Pantelleria**

**Arco dell'Elefante, one of the most beautiful spots in Pantelleria**

Baia dei Conigli in Lampedusa, where the rare sea turtle still survives

## Lampedusa ⓱

**Road map** B5. *(with Linosa) 5,200.* *0922-970 588.* *APT Agrigento (0922-401 352); Consorzio Albergatori 35° Parallelo (0922-971 906); Pro Loco (0922-971 390).* *22 Sep.* **www**.lampedusa.it

The largest island in the Pelagie (the archipelago that includes Linosa and the small island of Lampione), Lampedusa is 200 km (124 miles) from Sicily and 150 km (93 miles) from Malta. The Greek name *Pelaghiè* reflects their chief characteristic – isolation in the middle of the sea. Inhabited for a little more than a century – from the time Ferdinand II of Bourbon sent a group of colonists and prisoners there – Lampedusa was soon deforested, which in turn brought about the almost total degradation of the soil and any possibility of cultivating it. Human settlements have also led to a dramatic decrease in local fauna, and the Baia dei Conigli nature reserve was set up to create a safe refuge for sea turtles *(Caretta caretta)*. The island's main beaches are **Cala Maluk, Cala Croce, Baia dei Conigli, Cala Galera** and **Cala Greca**, and diving is one of the many popular sports. Near the town of **Lampedusa** (almost completely destroyed in 1943) is the **Madonna di Lampedusa Sanctuary**, where on 22 September the Bourbon takeover is commemorated.

## Linosa ⓲

**Road map** B5.
*(with Lampedusa) 5,200.* *APT Agrigento (0922-401 352); Consorzio Albergatori 35° Parallelo (0922-971 906).*

Ancient Aethusa, 40 km (25 miles) from Lampedusa, is a small volcanic island where life centres around the village of Linosa, with its brightly coloured houses. Thanks to the naturally fertile volcanic soil, agriculture thrives on the island. One of the best ways of exploring Linosa is by leaving the road behind and rambling around the craters and the fenced-in fields.

Entrance to a house in Linosa

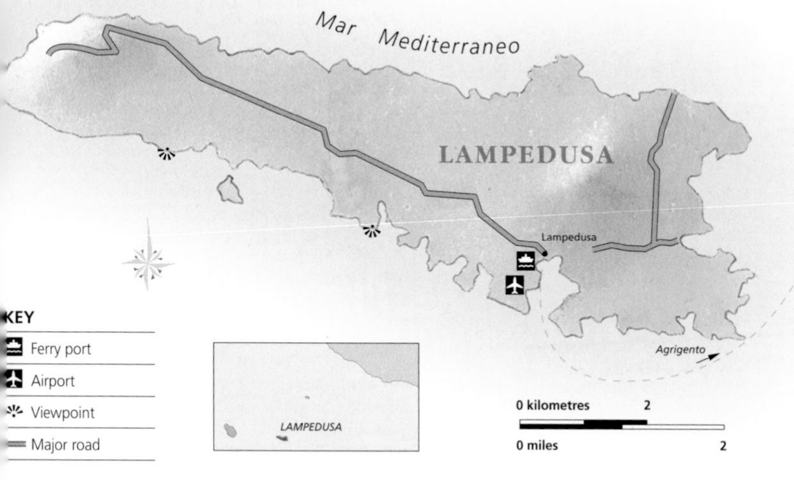

## Caltanissetta ⓳

**Road map** D3. 61,000. FS *from Catania & Palermo (095-532 719).* *Corso Vittorio Emanuele 109 (0934-530 403).* **www**.aapit.cl.it

The Baroque façade of San Sebastiano, completed in the 1800s

One of the earliest traces of a settlement in this area is the **Badia di Santo Spirito**, a Norman abbey commissioned by Roger I and his wife Adelasia in the late 11th century and consecrated in 1153. It is still one of the most interesting sights in Caltanissetta and its immediate vicinity. In common with other hill towns in the interior, Caltanissetta was surrounded by medieval walls and then expanded towards the monasteries, built around the city from the 15th century on. The centre of a thriving mineral-rich area, it became prosperous after the unification of Italy thanks to the **sulphur and rock salt mines**. It was during this period that the look of the town changed with the construction of buildings and public works. In the heart of town, in Piazza Garibaldi, are the Baroque **San Sebastiano** and the **Cathedral** (dedicated to Santa Maria la Nova and San Michele). A brief walk down Corso Umberto I will take you to **Sant'Agata** – or Chiesa del Collegio – built in 1605 for the Jesuits of Caltanissetta, next to their seminary. The rich decoration inside includes a marble statue of *St Ignatius in Glory* on the left-hand transept altar, the altarpiece *San Francesco Saverio* in a side chapel and a canvas of the *Martyrdom of Sant'Agata*. Not far from the **Castello di Pietrarossa**, probably a former Arab fortress, is the **Museo Archeologico**, where the sections are given over exclusively to archaeology and to modern art.

The **Museo Mineralogico, Paleontologico e della Zolfara** established by the local Mineralogy School, has a fine and extensive collection of minerals and fossils.

**Badia di Santo Spirito**
***Tel*** *0934-566 596.*
*9am–12:30pm, 4–7pm daily.*

**Museo Archeologico**
Via Colajanni 3. ***Tel*** *0934-259 36.*
*9am–1pm, 3:30–7pm daily.*
*last Mon of month.*

**Museo Mineralogico**
***Tel*** *0934-591 280.*
*9am–1pm Mon–Sat.*

The Badia di Santo Spirito, one of the major Norman churches in Sicily

### Environs

About 5 km (3 miles) along the main road to Enna is the site of the ancient city of **Sabucina**, where you can see a prehistoric village and cave tombs dating from the 12th–10th centuries BC. The city became a Greek colony, but subsequently declined and was later abandoned.

### EASTER WEEK

In the interior of Sicily the celebrations of the *Misteri*, or statues of the Stations of the Cross, during Easter Week, are of the greatest importance. At Enna they begin on Palm Sunday. For four days, the 15 city confraternities take part in processions through the streets to the Cathedral; on Good Friday a huge torchlit procession bears the statue of the Madonna of the Seven Griefs, the Reliquary of Christ's Thorn and the Dead Christ's Urn through the city; then on Easter Sunday the Resurrected Christ and the Virgin Mary statues meet in Piazza Duomo. At Caltanissetta, celebrations begin on Wednesday with the Procession of the Holy Sacrament, followed by the representatives of the 11 city confraternities. On Maundy Thursday the large statues of the Passion of Christ are taken through the city and on Good Friday the Passion of the Black Christ ends the celebrations.

Part of the colourful Easter Week celebrations

**Sabucina**

*el 0934-566 982. ◯ 9am–1pm, :30–7pm daily.*

**The Sulphur Mines**

*Ente Parco Minerario Floristella, rottacalda (0935-958 105).*

or centuries the Floristella ılphur field was one of the ıost important sources of 'ealth in the Sicilian hinter-ınd. Mining activity ceased ı 1988 and the mines are losed to the public, but now 'ork is under way to turn ıis yellow-stained land into mining park. Extraction eached its height during the 9th century – when Palazzo ennisi, the residence of ıe mine owners, was built.

## :nna ⓴

**oad map** D3. *30,000.* **FS** *from atania and Palermo (0935-500 91 0).* **i** *AAPIT, Via Roma 411 (0935-28 288); AST, Piazza Colaianni 6 935-500 875).* **www**.apt-enna.com

mountain town – at 931 m 3,054 ft) the highest rovincial capital in Italy – ı antiquity Enna was first ireek, then Carthaginian and nally Roman. It remained a yzantine stronghold even fter the Arab conquest of 'alermo, and was then onquered by general Al-ıbbas Ibn Fadhl in 859 and 'as wrested from the Muslims nly in 1087. From that time it 'as repeatedly fortified around ıe strongholds of Castello di Lombardia and Castello Vecchio (present-day Torre di Federico). The defensive walls, no longer visible, were the basis of the city's plan, while all the principal sites of religious and civic power were constructed on what is now Via Roma. Because of its altitude, Enna has a climate unique in the interior of Sicily and even during summer the temperature is pleasant.

nna Cathedral, built in the 15th entury and rebuilt after a fire

**The Castello di Lombardia, built over an Arab fortification**

The town's exceptional position means splendid views. Going up Via Roma, you first come to Piazza Vittorio Emanuele, site of **San Francesco d'Assisi**, the only original part of which is the fine 15th-century bell tower. In Piazza Colajanni you will see the façade of **Palazzo Pollicarini**, which has many Catalan Gothic features on the side next to the stairway, as well as the former church of **Santa Chiara**.

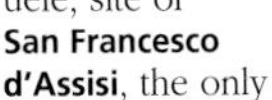

**The "Madonna's Crown", Museo Alessi in Enna**

In 1307 Eleonora, wife of Frederick II of Aragon, founded the **Cathedral** of Enna. The building was destroyed by fire in the mid-1400s and subsequently rebuilt. A fine 16th-century doorway – with a bas-relief depicting *St Martin and the Beggar* – leads to the Latin cross interior with two aisles. The cathedral is richly decorated with an assortment of statues and paintings.

Just past the Gothic apse are the rooms housing the **Museo Alessi**, which includes the Cathedral Treasury with its candelabra and vestments, a fine collection of coins and an art gallery featuring *St John the Baptist*, part of a 16th-century wooden triptych.

Almost directly opposite the entrance of the Museo Alessi is the **Museo Archeologico**, with a fine display of prehistoric, Greek and Roman archaeological items found in the city, in the area around and near Lake Pergusa. But the pride and joy of Enna are its two fortresses. The **Castello di Lombardia**, built by the Hohenstaufens and altered in the Aragonese era, is one of the grandest in Sicily. A tour here includes the three courtyards, the Torre Pisana and the Rocca di Cerere. In the public gardens is the octagonal **Torre di Federico II**, the only remaining part of the original defences.

**Museo Alessi**
*Tel 0935-503 165. ◯ 8am–8pm.*

**Museo Archeologico**
*Tel 0935-528 100. ◯ 9am–1 hr before sunset.*

**Castello di Lombardia**
*Tel 0935-500 962. ◯ 8am–8pm.*

**Torre di Federico II**
*◯ 9am–7pm.*

# Morgantina ㉑

Situated about 4 km (2 miles) from Aidone, the ancient city of Morgantina was founded by the Morgeti, a population from Latium who settled here around 1000 BC. The city was then occupied by Greek colonists. Its golden age, when the city was a strategic trade centre between the north and south of Sicily, was in the Hellenistic and Roman periods. From the top of the hill visitors have a fine view of what remains of the theatre, the city streets and the agora, all set in lovely countryside. Whole sections of the city may be closed for digs.

**The Gymnasiur**
*This was a large area fc athletic exercises, with bath (in the photo), dressin rooms and rooms wit equipment for the athlete:*

## RECONSTRUCTION OF MORGANTINA

This drawing shows the city as it appeared around 300 BC. The reconstruction is based on studies made by archaeologists from Princeton University in the United States.

**Residential quarter**

**Colonnade *(stoa)***

**This area** was filled with the workshops of craftsmen, mostly ceramicists.

**Sanctuary of Demeter and Persephone**

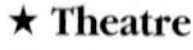

**★ Theatre**
*Constructed at the end of the 4th century BC, the theatre at Morgantina was carved out of the slope of a hill and could seat about a thousand spectators.*

**★ A**
*Unusually, the agora, or forum divided into two parts, one above the linked by a trapezoidal, 14-step stair*

0 metres 50

0 yards 50

## VISITORS' CHECKLIST

**Road map** D4. *AAST, Piazza Armerina, Via Muscara Generale.* ***Tel*** *0935-680 201.*
**Morgantina archaeological site** ***Tel*** *0935-879 55.*
*9am–1 hr before sunset.*

**The Market**
*This lay in the middle of the upper agora. Above is the* tholos, *a round structure which had a number of different functions.*

**Street Paving**
*In the eastern residential quarter, the remains of the paved street leading out of the city walls are still visible.*

## STAR FEATURES

★ Theatre

★ Agora

# Piazza Armerina ㉒

**Road map** D4. *21,000.* *AAST, Piazza Armerina, Via Muscara Generale.* ***Tel*** *0935-680 201.* *Palio dei Normanni (13–14 Aug).*

In the middle of an area inhabited since the 8th century BC, Piazza Armerina developed in the Middle Ages, a period marked by frequent clashes between the local population – strongly influenced by the centuries of Arab domination – and the Latin conquerors. After the huge devastation wrought in the 12th century by battles between these two factions, Piazza Armerina was recreated around the Colle Mira hill (in the middle of the present-day Monte quarter) and was populated by a colony of Lombards from Piacenza. A new, massive defensive wall system was built in the late 14th century, but the city soon spread well beyond this into the surrounding hills and slopes.

In the heart of town is a large **Aragonese Castle**, built by King Martin I in the late 14th century, whose massive towers dominate the **Cathedral**. Dedicated to Our Lady of the Assumption, the Cathedral is flanked by the campanile of another church which had been built on the same site in the 14th century. Inside, look out for the choir, built in 1627, and a wooden crucifix painted in the late 15th century. The Cathedral also affords access to the small **Museo Diocesano**, which has vestments, monstrances and reliquaries on display. Elsewhere in the town are many other interesting attractions. **Piazza Garibaldi** is the heart of town life, boasting the Baroque **Palazzo del Senato** and two palatial mansions belonging to the barons of Capodarso. The whole of the historic centre deserves further exploration on foot, through charming medieval alleys, steps and lanes.

Not far from town, at the end of Via Tasso, is the **Chiesa del Priorato di Sant'Andrea**, founded in 1096 and then acquired by the Knights of the Order of the Holy Sepulchre. This magnificent example of Sicilian Romanesque architecture has a commanding view over a valley. Do not miss seeing the series of 12th- to 14th-century frescoes in the interior (visits are allowed only on Sundays, when mass is celebrated).

The Cathedral at Piazza Armerina, with its 14th-century bell tower

View of Piazza Armerina, which developed around the Colle Mira hill

# Piazza Armerina: Villa del Casale

Autumn, from the Hall of the Seasons

This famous villa was part of a 3rd-4th century AD estate, and is one of the most fascinating attractions in archaeologically rich Sicily. The exceptionally beautiful mosaics that decorated every one of the rooms of the landowner's apartments have been preserved through the centuries, thanks to a flood that buried them in mud in the 12th century. The villa was discovered in the late 19th century. A logical sequence for a visit to the site is as follows: the thermae, the large peristyle, the long corridor with hunting scenes and, lastly, the owners' private apartments.

Peristyle

**The circus hall** was decorated with mosaics depicting a chariot race.

**★ Frigidarium**
*The cold bath room is decorated with mosaics depicting mythical sea creatures: nereids, tritons and cherubs.*

**The calidarium** (sauna) still has the supports of the raised thermae floor.

**Tepidarium**

**Semi-circular latrine**

**The atrium** was really a colonnaded courtyard with Ionic capitals.

**Entrance**

## THE DISCOVERY OF THE VILLA

The first archaeological digs in the area were carried out at the end of the 19th century and were resumed in 1929 and 1935. But it was the 1950–60 excavations that made the major discoveries, and these brought fame to the Villa del Casale. Perfectly preserved by a layer of mud caused by a flood many centuries ago, the mosaics are now being restored. Visitors today may come across expert archaeologists working on the tesserae of what have been called "the most exceptional Roman mosaics in the world".

The exterior of the Villa del Casale

## STAR FEATURES

- ★ Frigidarium
- ★ Hall of the Female Gymnasts in Bikinis
- ★ Corridor with Hunting Scenes
- ★ The Myth of Arion

*For hotels and restaurants in this region see pp201–2 and pp216–17*

**★ Corridor with Hunting Scenes**
*This passageway contains splendid mosaics representing wild game hunting. Ferocious beasts such as boar and lions are being loaded onto ships after capture.*

## VISITORS' CHECKLIST

**Road map** D4. *AAST, Piazza Armerina, Via Muscara Generale (0935-680 201).* **Villa Romana del Casale** ***Tel*** *0935-680 036.* *10am–5pm Tue–Sun.* *Mon.* **www.** villaromanadelcasale.it

**Northern Area**
*The vestibule in the private apartments of the villa has a large mosaic depicting Ulysses and Polyphemus.*

0 metres 10
0 yards 10

**★ The Myth of Arion**
*In the colonnaded semicircular atrium the mosaic shows Arion saved by a dolphin and surrounding him are female figures, sea creatures and cupids.*

Aqueduct

**★ Hall of the Female Gymnasts in Bikinis**
*The ten gymnasts seen in the mosaics in this hall are a rare and precious record of the Roman fashions of the time.*

**Triclinium**
*The mosaics in the dining room feature the Labours of Hercules and other mythological subjects.*

# SOUTHERN SICILY

*Dominated by Mount Etna, southern Sicily's permanent backdrop, this area is a curious mixture of fertile land and intensive cultivation, ancient monuments and utter neglect. Many towns and monuments built by the ancient Greeks still survive, most notably in the town of Syracuse, birthplace of Archimedes.*

Southern Sicily, which the Arabs called the Val di Noto, presents another facet of Sicily. It is very different from the western end of the island, although the topography is equally varied. The latter has Phoenician Palermo, the former Greek Syracuse. One of Sicily's most important sights is the stony-tiered Greek theatre in Syracuse. The tradition of performing ancient Greek plays was revived in 1914, and now every other summer the great works of the ancient tragedians come to life in their natural setting. This part of Sicily is also home to the ancient Greek ruins of Megara Hyblaea, now sadly dominated by the landscape of the refineries of Augusta.

Inland, the rebuilding of towns following the earthquake of 1693 has resulted in a number of Baroque gems. The churches, buildings and balconies of Ragusa, Modica, Scicli, Noto and Chiaramonte are a triumph of the Sicilian Baroque style, with their majestic steps, detailed ornamentation and curving façades. Ibla, the medieval quarter of Ragusa, should be included on a tour of the towns of the interior: rocky Caltagirone is an important ceramics centre, and Chiaramonte and Vizzini also have their charms. In complete contrast you can also experience the natural silence of the rock-cut necropolises in the cliffs of Ispica and Pantalica.

Fishing boats anchored in Ortygia harbour in Syracuse

◁ The majestic Baroque portal of Ragusa Cathedral, dedicated to St John the Baptist

# Exploring Southern Sicily

An excellent starting point for any visit to Sicily's southern tip is Syracuse, with its exceptional artistic and cultural heritage. It lies about 60 km (37 miles) from Catania airport and is a two-hour drive from Messina, along a scenic route with the Ionian Sea to your left and Mount Etna to your right. Other popular sights in this area are the old cities in the interior – those in Val di Noto (Caltagirone, Modica, Noto, Palazzolo Acreide, Ragusa and Scicli, along with Militello Val di Catania and Catania itself) have all been named UNESCO World Heritage sites. The mountains conceal an impressive testimony to the ancient history of southern Sicily in the crevices of Pantalica, Ispica and Lentini.

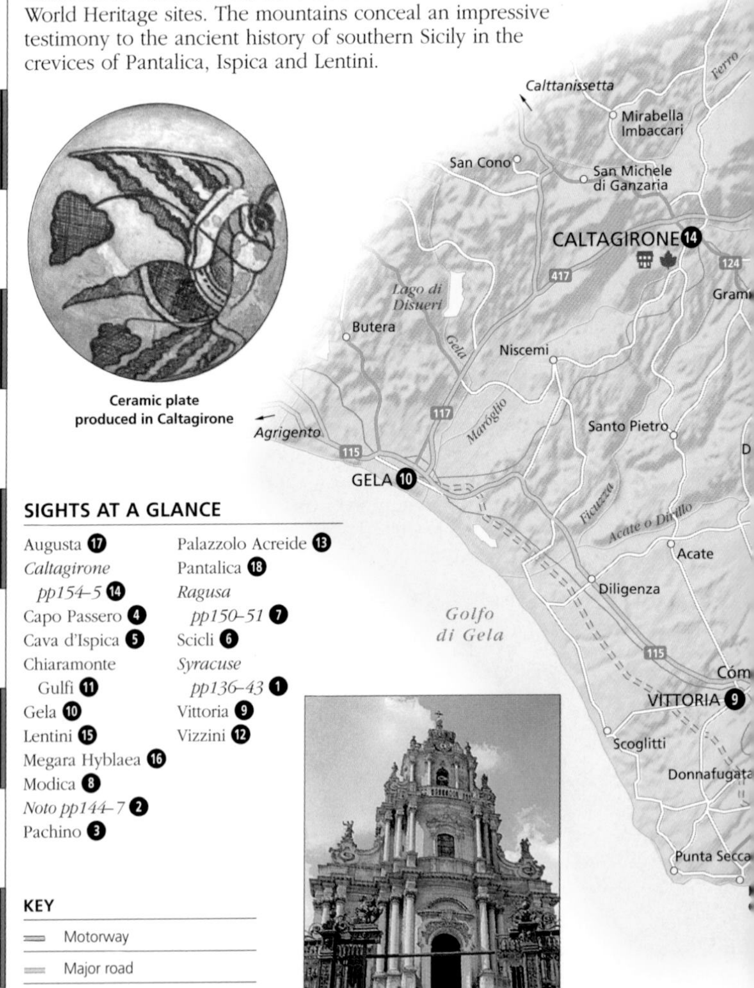


**Ceramic plate produced in Caltagirone**

## SIGHTS AT A GLANCE

Augusta 17
*Caltagirone pp154–5* 14
Capo Passero 4
Cava d'Ispica 5
Chiaramonte Gulfi 11
Gela 10
Lentini 15
Megara Hyblaea 16
Modica 8
*Noto pp144–7* 2
Pachino 3
Palazzolo Acreide 13
Pantalica 18
*Ragusa pp150–51* 7
Scicli 6
*Syracuse pp136–43* 1
Vittoria 9
Vizzini 12

## KEY

- Motorway
- Major road
- Secondary road
- Minor road
- Road under construction
- Main railway
- Minor railway

**The Baroque façade of the Basilica di San Giorgio in Ragusa**

*SEE ALSO*

- ***Where to Stay*** pp202–3
- ***Where to Eat*** pp217–18

## GETTING THERE

There are two ways of getting to the interior of southern Sicily. You can either take road SS115 connecting Syracuse and Gela – passing through Noto, Ispica, Modica and Ragusa – opting for detours if you wish, or go up to Catania and follow motorway A19 to Enna, or A18 to Syracuse. Syracuse can also be reached by train.

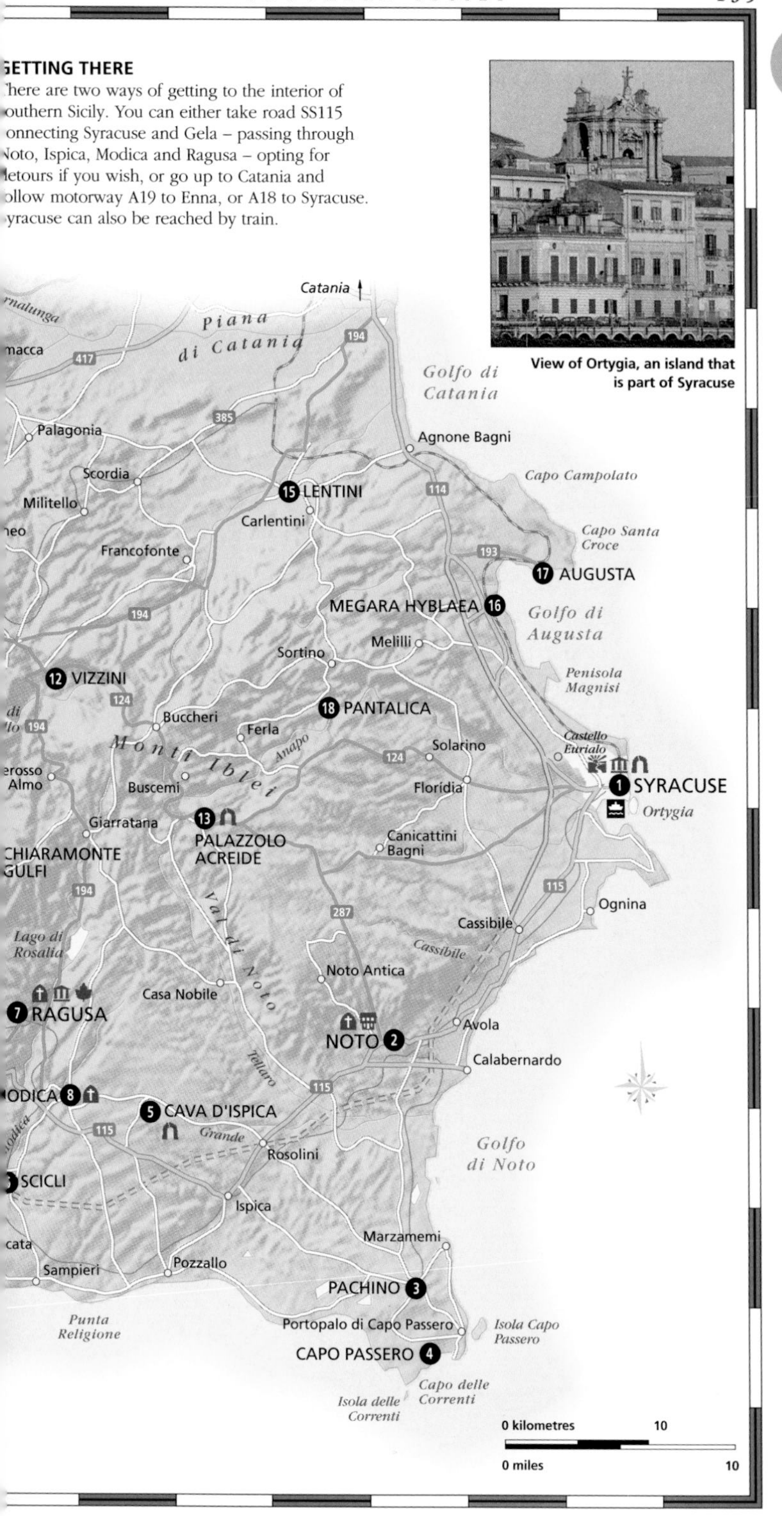


View of Ortygia, an island that is part of Syracuse

# Syracuse ❶

Goddess, Museo Archeologico

For 27 centuries the city of Syracuse, in modern Italian, Siracusa, has been of great economic and cultural importance. From the prehistoric populations to the Corinthians who founded the Greek city, to the introduction of Baroque architecture, the history of Syracuse is an open book, clearly visible in many streets and buildings. The Greek theatre survives in good condition, and you can still see the stone quarries, or Latomie, which provided stone for many of the ancient monuments, but also served as prisons.

### The Neapolis Archaeological Zone

Viale Paradiso. ***Tel*** *0931-66206.*
*9am–3pm daily (to 6pm Jun–Oct).*
*Mon.*

The Neapolis Archaeological Zone was established in 1955 with the aim of grouping the antiquities of Syracuse within one site, enabling visitors to make an uninterrupted tour of the city's most remote past. Not far from the ticket office for the park is medieval **San Nicolò dei Cordari**, built over a reservoir *(piscina)* cut out of the rock, which was used for cleaning the nearby Roman amphitheatre.

### Greek Theatre

*See pp138–9.*

### Latomie

A huge hollow separates the theatre area and the southern section of the archaeological site. This is the area of the Latomie – stone quarries – from which Syracuse architects extracted millions of cubic metres of stone for building. The enormous caves were also used as prisons for centuries. The Ear of Dionysius (**Orecchio di Dioniso**), is one of the most impressive

Entrance to the Orecchio di Dioniso, in the Latomie area

quarries. According to legend, thanks to the extraordinary acoustics of this cave, the local tyrant Dionysius could hear the whispers of his most dangerous prisoners and take

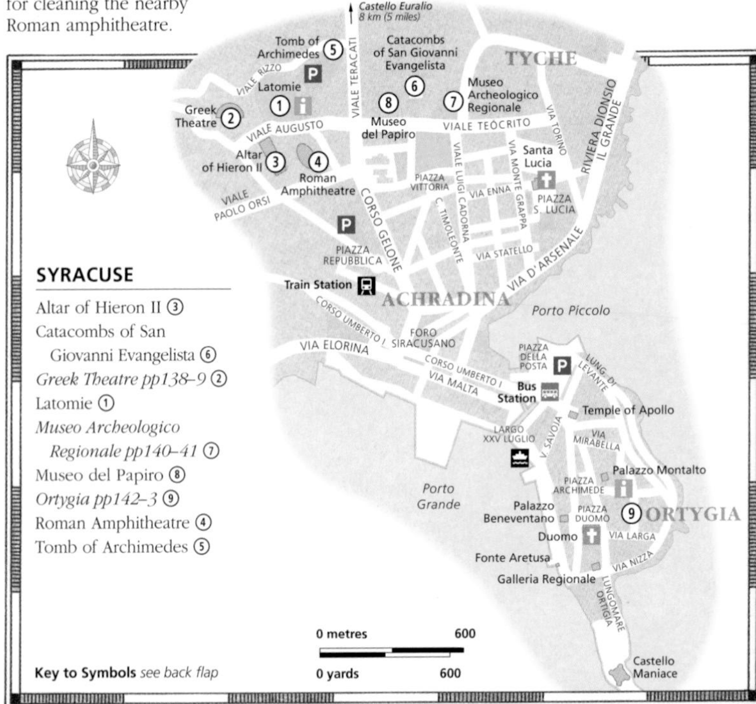

The large Grotta dei Cordari, the most interesting of the Latomie caves

due precautions. There are other huge adjacent caves, such as the **Grotta dei Cordari**, which until recently was used by local rope makers *(cordari)*, the **Latomia Intagliatella** and the **Latomia Santa Venera**.

### Tomb of Archimedes

In the northwestern corner of the Neapolis site there is an area that was used as a burial ground until the Hellenistic era. This is known as the **Necropoli Grotticelli**. One of the largest tombs here is traditionally called the **Tomb of Archimedes**. Archimedes was a native of Syracuse and one of the greatest scientists in antiquity *(see p28)*.

### Altar of Hieron II and Roman Amphitheatre

These lie on the other side of the road that cuts the Neapolis area in two. Although only the foundations remain of the **Altar of Hieron II**, its impressive size (198 x 23 m, 649 x 75 ft) is clear. This monument was dedicated to Zeus and was used for public sacrifices, in which as many as 400 bulls were put to death at one time.

A huge public work undertaken in the early years of the Empire, the **Roman Amphitheatre** (outer diameter, 140 x 119 m, 459 x 390 ft) is only slightly smaller than the Arena in Verona. The walls in the interior were part of the underground section, used to house the stage scenery. Beneath the tiers were corridors through which the gladiators and wild beasts entered the arena.

## VISITORS' CHECKLIST

**Road map** F4. *123,000.* *from Messina, Naples, Rome, Milan, Turin (0931-464 467).* *AAPT (0931-481 200); AAST (0931-462 711). SAIS (0931-662711).* *13 Dec, Santa Lucia; first Sunday in May, Santa Lucia delle Quaglie.*
**www**.apt-siracusa.it

### Museo Archeologico Regionale

*See pp140–41.*

### Catacombs of San Giovanni Evangelista

Viadi San Giovanni. ***Tel*** *0931-646 94.* *Apr–Oct: 9:30am–noon, 2:30–4:30pm; May–Jun: 9:30am–1pm, 2:30–5:30pm; Jul–Aug: 9:30am–1:30pm, 2:30-6pm.*

This underground complex – which dates back to 360–315 BC – housed hundreds of loculi, or rooms, which were used to bury the followers of the new Christian religion in Roman times.

The main gallery of the catacombs leads to a series of round chapels that still bear traces of frescoes.

### Museo del Papiro

Viale Teocrito 66. ***Tel*** *0931-616 16.* *9am–2pm.* *Mon.*

This museum is devoted to the *Cyperus papyrus* plant. The largest European colony of the papyrus plant thrives on the banks of the Ciane river near Syracuse.

The stepped base of the Altar of Hieron II, giving an idea of the impressive size of the original sacrificial site

# Syracuse: The Greek Theatre

This is one of the most important examples of ancient theatre architecture anywhere, and for centuries it was the centre of Syracusan life. The Greek theatre was a much more complex construction than today's ruins might indicate; in 1520–31, Emperor Charles V had much of the stone transported to build the walls around Ortygia *(see pp142–3)*. Designed in the 5th century BC by the Greek architect Damacopos, the theatre was enlarged in the 3rd and 2nd centuries BC by Hieron II. From the 5th century BC onwards, the great Greek playwrights, including Aeschylus who premiered some of his tragedies here, wrote and staged their works in this magnificent setting.

**Votive Niches**
*To the west of the grotto near the ancie colonnade, the wall is punctuated by a series of rectangular niches that mig have housed votive paintings or tablets in honour of Syracusan heroes.*

**Grotta del Museion**
*This cave, hewn out of the rock wall above the theatre, has a rectangular basin where the aqueduct flowed.*

**The *cavea* (auditorium)** is over 138 m (453 ft) wide with 67 tiers, divided into 10 vertical blocks (or "wedges"). Each block was served by a flight of steps and was indicated by a letter, a custom that survives in modern theatres today.

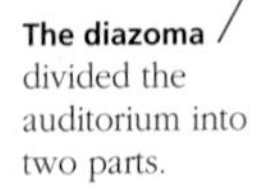

**The diazoma** divided the auditorium into two parts.

**Classical Greek Theatre**
*In even-numbered years, the Greek theatre in Syracuse hosts a summer programme of classical theatre.*

## VISITORS' CHECKLIST

**Greek Theatre and Neapolis Archaeological Zone** Viale Paradiso. ***Tel*** *0931-662 06.* *9am–6pm daily (to 3pm Nov–May).* *Mon.* **Istituto Nazionale del Dramma Antico (INDA)** Corso Matteotti 29. ***Tel*** *0931-487 200. Box office: 0931-487 248.* **www**.indafondazione.org

**Galleries**
*Called* criptae, *the galleries were cut out of the rock in the Roman period to replace the more ancient passageways of the* cavea, *which had been removed to create more seating space.*

**The stage area** was greatly enlarged in the Roman period.

**Two enormous pillars of rock** stood either side of the stage area.

0 metres 10
0 yards 10

**On the orchestra** was a monument to Dionysus, around which the chorus acted, danced and sang.

Logo of the Syracuse INDA

## THE ISTITUTO NAZIONALE DEL DRAMMA ANTICO

On 16 April 1914, the tradition of performing ancient Greek theatre was revived at Syracuse, and now a season of plays first performed here over 2,500 years ago is put on every year in May/June. The Istituto Nazionale del Dramma Antico (National Institute of Ancient Drama) was set up in 1925. The Scuola Professionale di Teatro Antico (Professional School of Ancient Theatre) joined as partners in 1983.

**Playbill of Aeschylus' *Libation Bearers* designed by Duilio Cambellotti (1921)**

# Syracuse: Museo Archeologico Regionale

6th–5th-century BC theatre mask

Founded in 1967 (and opened to the public in 1988), in order to establish a proper home for the enormous quantity of material excavated from digs throughout southeastern Sicily, the Regional Archaeological Museum is divided into three main sections with over 18,000 pieces on display. The museum is named after the eminent archaeologist Paolo Orsi, head of the Antiquities Department of Sicily from 1888, who was instrumental in fostering interest in the island's past and was personally responsible for many important excavations and discoveries. The collections named after him have been reorganized since the museum moved from its Ortygia site.

**★ Funerary Statue**
*This came from the digs at Megara Hyblaea, dating from 560–550 BC. The inscription on the right thigh shows it was dedicated to the physician Sambroditas.*

Syracuse

Megara Hyblaea

Chalcidian colonies

Protohisto

Prehistory

Prehistory

Prehistory

## GUIDE TO THE MUSEUM

*The museum is divided into three sections. Section A features the geological history of Sicily and then the prehistoric, protohistoric and Siculan cultures. Section B is given over to the Greek colonies, and includes the Landolina Venus and the friezes from the Temple of Apollo. Last, Section C has material from the subcolonies founded by the Syracusans in 663–598 BC and from digs in the Hellenized towns in the interior. Finds from Gela and Agrigento complete the exhibition.*

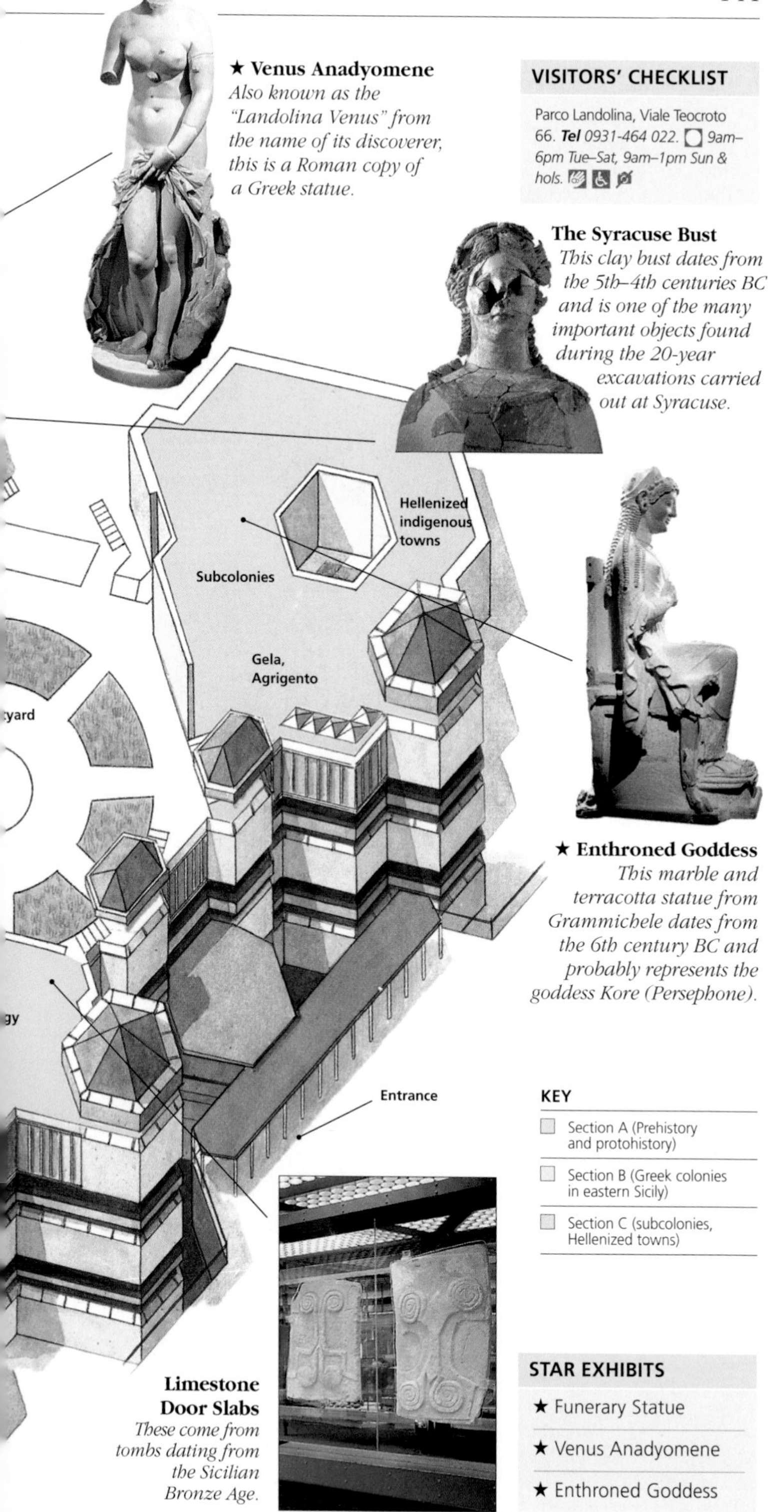


**★ Venus Anadyomene**
*Also known as the "Landolina Venus" from the name of its discoverer, this is a Roman copy of a Greek statue.*

**VISITORS' CHECKLIST**

Parco Landolina, Viale Teocroto 66. ***Tel*** *0931-464 022.* ◯ *9am–6pm Tue–Sat, 9am–1pm Sun & hols.*

**The Syracuse Bust**
*This clay bust dates from the 5th–4th centuries BC and is one of the many important objects found during the 20-year excavations carried out at Syracuse.*

**★ Enthroned Goddess**
*This marble and terracotta statue from Grammichele dates from the 6th century BC and probably represents the goddess Kore (Persephone).*

**KEY**

- Section A (Prehistory and protohistory)
- Section B (Greek colonies in eastern Sicily)
- Section C (subcolonies, Hellenized towns)

**Limestone Door Slabs**
*These come from tombs dating from the Sicilian Bronze Age.*

**STAR EXHIBITS**

- ★ Funerary Statue
- ★ Venus Anadyomene
- ★ Enthroned Goddess

# Syracuse: Exploring Ortygia

The island of Ortygia has always been the focal point of Syracuse. A stronghold until the end of the 19th century, it separates the city's two harbours (connected by the dock canal). Ortygia (in Italian, Ortigia) is now linked to the mainland by the Umbertino bridge. The town's long history is visible in many buildings, going back as far the 6th-century BC Temple of Apollo.

### Lungomare di Levante

This is the promenade that overlooks the **Porto Piccolo**, or small port, and is still the maritime heart of town. By going southwards along the promenade you reach **Spirito Santo**, with an 18th-century façade dramatically facing the sea. This church was the seat of the Holy Spirit Confraternity, hence its name.

### Temple of Apollo

A good part of Piazza Pancali, as you enter Ortygia, consists of the ruins of the Temple of Apollo, which were discovered in 1860 inside the old Spanish barracks. The temple was built in the early 6th century BC, which makes it the oldest extant Doric temple in Western Europe. It is of an imposing size – 58 x 24 m (190 x 79 ft). On the top step of the base, an inscription to Apollo provides proof that the building was dedicated to the god. Over the centuries the temple has served as a Byzantine church, a mosque, again a Christian church under the Normans, and a military stronghold.

### Palazzo Greco

On Corso Matteotti, an avenue created by demolition during the Fascist era, only one old building has survived: Palazzo Greco, founded in the mid-14th century and now serving as the home of the Istituto Nazionale del Dramma Antico *(see p139)*. It has a lovely Gothic double lancet window and a loggia.

### Palazzo Beneventano del Bosco

Piazza Duomo is home to Palazzo Beneventano del Bosco, built in 1779 by architect Luciano Alì. The façade, with its doorway supporting a lovely balcony, is an impressive sight. The interior is also interesting; a broad staircase leads up to the private apartments filled with Venetian furniture, where Admiral Horatio Nelson and King Ferdinand III of Bourbon once stayed.

**Façade of Palazzo Beneventano del Bosco, opposite the Cathedral**

### Duomo

Piazza Duomo. ***Tel*** *0931-65328.*
*7:30am–8pm.*

In Piazza Duomo, next to the **Palazzo del Senato**, now the Town Hall, is the city's Cathedral, built in 1728–53. It was designed by Andrea Palma, and incorporates an ancient Temple of Minerva, which in turn had been built over the site of a 6th-century BC monument, which Gelon had dedicated to Athena. The intact ancient structures can be best seen by skirting the outer northern side of the church, where a series of massive columns from the temple are clearly visible. Initially a temple, and then a Christian

**Decorative coat of arms on the Duomo façade**

**The ruins of the Temple of Apollo, in the heart of Ortygia**

*For hotels and restaurants in this region see pp202–3 and pp217–18*

The Baroque façade of the Duomo, designed by Andrea Palma (1728–53)

hurch, the building became Muslim mosque and finally glorious example of Sicilian aroque religious architec- ire. The Duomo contains a 3th-century font, Norman ra mosaics, and many fine aintings and sculptures. The acristy has 16 wooden choir alls carved in 1489.

### Galleria Regionale i Palazzo Bellomo

*a Capodieci. **Tel** 0931-695 11 r 653 43. 9am–7pm Tue–Sat, am–1:30pm Sun.*

his museum, housed in ie **Parisio** and **Bellomo** alazzi, has both interesting rchitecture (much of the riginal Hohenstaufen onstruction still stands) and rtworks on display. The first ooms contain medieval and enaissance sculpture. The ourtyard, decorated with oats of arms, leads to the rst floor, with the jewel of ie collection, Antonello a Messina's *Annunciation* 1474, *see p23*). In the next oom is a display of Christmas ribs. The exhibition ends ith Arab and Sicilian eramics and jewels.

### Fonte Aretusa

On Largo Aretusa, facing the **Porto Grande**, the waters of this spring still gush just as they did in Greek times. According to the myth made famous by Pindar and Virgil, Arethusa was a nymph transformed into a spring by the goddess Artemis.

### San Filippo Apostolo

In the heart of the Giudecca– the Jewish quarter of Syracuse – is **San Filippo Apostolo**, which was built over the old synagogue. In the crypt you can still see the basin of holy water in which the Jewish women purified themselves.

### Palazzo Margulensi-Montalto

A stone's throw from central **Piazza Archimede**, with the 19th-century **Fountain of Artemis**, a walk along Via Montalto takes you to Palazzo Margulensi-Montalto, one of the most interesting medieval buildings in Syracuse. Built in 1397, this palazzo still features some original elements: the Gothic windows of the façade supported by spiral columns, the staircase and the arcade.

### Castello Maniace

***Tel** 0931-464 420 8:30am–1:30pm Mon–Sat, 9:30am–1:30pm Sun & hols.*

This castle is on the southern tip of Ortygia, where tradition says the temple of Hera and the villa of the Roman governor once stood. It was built by Frederick II in the 1200s and over the centuries had various functions: royal residence, fortress and even storehouse. The name derives from the Byzantine general Maniakes, who took the city from the Arabs.

### Environs

On the hill overlooking the city is the main work of military architecture in the Greek world, the **Castello Eurialo** (currently being restored), built by Dionysius the Elder in 402 BC to protect Syracuse. Two rock-cut moats and a tower protected the fortress on the eastern side, a 15-m (49-ft) keep was built in the middle of the fortification, and the towers overlooked the sea.

**Castello Eurialo**
Frazione Belvedere, 8 km (5 miles) from Syracuse. ***Tel** 0931-711 773. 9am–6pm daily (to 5pm in winter, to 7pm in summer).*

The ruins of the extensive Castello Eurialo

# Street-by-Street: Noto ❷

Sculpture in the Cathedral

Throughout the 18th century, following the terrible earthquake of 1693, the ruined town of Noto became an enormous construction site run by prominent architects such as Rosario Gagliardi, Vincenzo Sinatra and Antonio Mazza. Today Noto's magnificent Baroque architecture is unique in Sicily, despite an unmistakable air of decay. However, substantial restoration work started after the town was named a UNESCO World Heritage site. Soon, Noto's Baroque buildings will be revealed in all their glory.

**Palazzo Nicolaci**

**Montevergine church**

**Palazzo Astuto** lies behind the Cathedral.

**★ Cathedral**
*Dedicated to San Nicolò, the Cathedral looks down on three flights of steps. The cupola collapsed in 1996.*

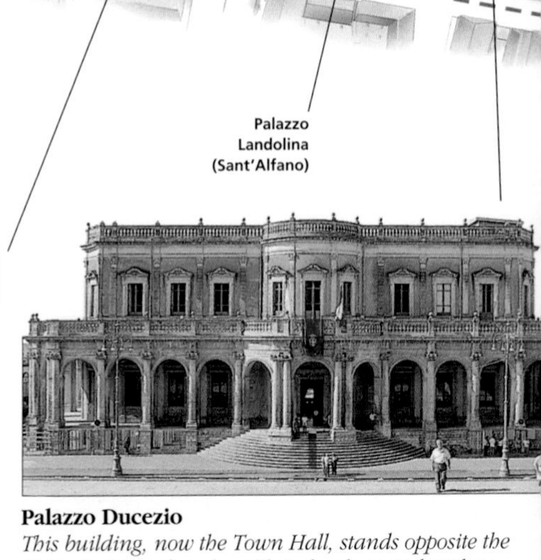


**Palazzo Landolina (Sant'Alfano)**

**★ San Carlo al Corso**
*Formally called San Carlo Borromeo, this church contains paintings and frescoes attributed to Carasi.*

**Palazzo Ducezio**
*This building, now the Town Hall, stands opposite the Cathedral. The façade, with its lovely round arches, has been described as "a triumph of columns".*

For hotels and restaurants in this region see pp202–3 and pp217–18

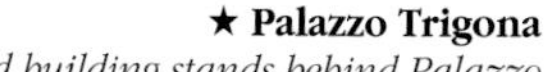

**★ Palazzo Trigona**

*This splendid building stands behind Palazzo Vescovile. Curved balconies decorate the façade and some rooms were frescoed by Antonio Mazza.*

## VISITORS' CHECKLIST

**Road map** E5. 23,000. Catania Fontanarossa (80 km, 50 miles). FS from Syracuse (0931-464 467). Azienda Provinciale Turismo, Piazza XXIV Maggio (0931-573 779). (0931-835 201 or 835 005). 3rd Sun May: flower festival.

**The Salvatore convent** belonged to nuns from noble families in the 18th century.

**San Francesco**

*A Baroque staircase leads to this church, which has a Latin cross interior and an aisleless nave.*

**Museo Civico**

**Santa Chiara**

*The church was designed by Rosario Gagliardi. It is built on an oval plan and is richly decorated. This 19th-century altarpiece of San Benedetto and Santa Scolastica is by the Palermo artist Lo Forte.*

**KEY**

– – – Suggested route

## STAR SIGHTS

- ★ Cathedral
- ★ San Carlo al Corso
- ★ Palazzo Trigona

0 metres 70

0 yards 70

# Exploring Noto

The heart of the town is the main avenue, modern Viale Marconi, which becomes Corso Vittorio Emanuele at the monumental Porta Reale (or Ferdinandea) city gate, and passes through Piazza XXIV Maggio, Piazza Municipio (a good starting point for a visit) and Piazza XXX Ottobre. Steps lead to the upper town, with marvellous views of the landscape around.

**The Cathedral prior to 1996**

**The Cathedral after the collapse**

### Cathedral

In the winter of 1996, a loud rumble signalled the collapse of the Cathedral cupola, leaving a noticeable scar in the heart of Noto. It was a great loss to Sicilian Baroque art. The church was originally completed in 1776, and dedicated to San Nicolò. It stands at the end of a spectacular three-flight staircase designed by Paolo Labisi, the façade bearing twin bell towers and a bronze portal. The interior has a wealth of frescoes and other decoration, especially in the side chapels. The Cathedral has now been brought back to its former splendour following restoration.

### Palazzo Ducezio

*Tue–Sun.*

This palazzo, which stands opposite the Cathedral, was built in 1746 by Vincenzo Sinatra. The façade is decorated with an impressive series of columns. In the interior, which now houses the town hall offices, there is a huge drawing room decorated in the French Louis XV style, with gold and stucco decorative elements and a fine fresco on the vault by Antonio Mazza.

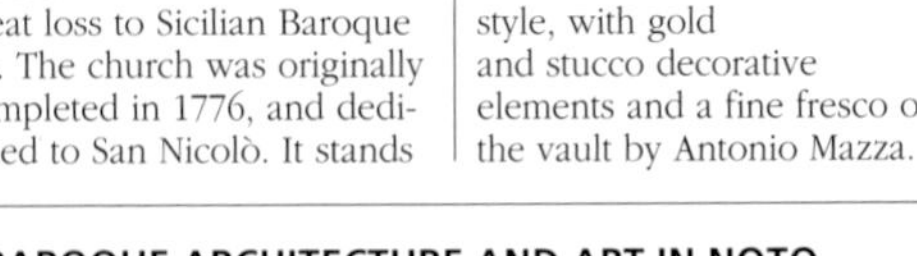

**Statue on the Cathedral façade**

### Museo Civico

Corso Vittorio Emanuele 34. ***Tel*** *0931-836 462.* *9am–1pm, 3:30–7:30pm Tue–Sun.*

The Civic Museum (some rooms of which are closed for restoration) features ancient and medieval material from the old town, Noto Antica, and from many nearby places.

### San Francesco

*8:30am–12:30pm, 4:30–6:30pm.*

On the wide stretch of Piazza XXX Ottobre, a monumental stairway leads to San Francesco, which was once part of a convent, and is now a high school. The church, with fine stucco decoration, was built in the mid-18th century and has some paintings of interest as well as a wooden statue of the Virgin Mary (1564), which probably came from one of the churches in the old town, Noto Antica.

### Palazzo Trigona

*to the public.*

This palazzo is perhaps the most "classically" Baroque building in Noto. The façade with its curved balconies blends in with the adjacent religious and civic buildings, in line with the schemes of the architects who rebuilt Noto. The drawing rooms of the palazzo were frescoed by Antonio Mazza.

## BAROQUE ARCHITECTURE AND ART IN NOTO

After the devastating 1693 earthquake, a programme of reconstruction was introduced throughout eastern Sicily in the early 18th century. The architects entrusted with this task elaborated upon the achievements of 17th-century Baroque architecture and adopted recurrent features that can still be seen in the streets of Noto. The façades of both churches and civic buildings became of fundamental importance in the hands of these men. Some of them, like Rosario Gagliardi, who designed the churches of Santa Chiara, Santissimo Crocefisso and San Domenico in Noto, were originally craftsmen themselves. Their skills can be seen in the great attention paid to decorative detail in façades and balconies. Rebuilding made the large monastery complexes – which together with the mansions of the landed gentry were the economic and social backbone of 18th- and 19th-century Noto – even more grandiose than before. In 2002 Noto and other Baroque towns were named World Heritage sites by UNESCO.

**An 18th-century Baroque balcony on Palazzo Nicolaci in Noto**

### San Carlo

long Corso Vittorio Emanele, San Carlo (also called hiesa del Collegio because f the attached former Jesuit ıonastery) has a slightly onvex façade with three evels – Doric, Ionic and orinthian. The impressive atin cross plan interior is ecorated with frescoes.

### San Domenico

ooking over Piazza XXIV laggio, the church of San Domenico is part of a group f buildings that includes the **ominican Convent**, worth isiting because of its plendid entrance with a host f friezes. Like other buildings f this kind, the convent was bandoned after the elimination of all congregational rders, decreed by the Italian overnment in 1866. The ovely façade of the church, vith its convex central part, as designed by the architect osario Gagliardi. The portal ives way to a rounded hurch interior, which is rowned by five cupolas ith fine stucco decoration.

he convex façade of San omenico, designed by Gagliardi

### Palazzo Nicolaci illadorata

*10am–1pm, 3pm–1 hr before ınset.*

On nearby Via Nicolaci, one of loto's most striking streets, is alazzo Nicolaci del Principe i Villadorata. The façade has x balconies supported by orbels which are decorated – ı keeping with the pure

Palazzo Landolina, former residence of the Norman Sant'Alfano family

Baroque style – with complex wrought-iron work and grotesque and mythological figures: lions, sirens, griffons and cherubs. The interior is interesting because of the fresco decoration in the lavish rooms, the most striking of which is the Salone delle Feste (Hall of Festivities). The palazzo will soon house the **Biblioteca Comunale**, or City Library (currently on Via Cavour), founded in the mid-19th century, with many old volumes and the architects' original designs for Noto.

### Palazzo Landolina

To the right of the Cathedral is the 19th-century **Palazzo Vescovile** (Bishop's Palace), while to the left is Palazzo Landolina, residence of the marquises of Sant' Alfano, an old and powerful family of the Norman aristocracy. Once past the elegant Baroque façade you enter a courtyard where two sphinxes flank the stairway leading to the main floor and frescoed rooms.

### Chiesa del Crocefisso

In the heart of Noto Alta, at the end of a stairway that begins at Piazza Mazzini, is this church, built at the end of the street that leads upwards from Piazza Municipio and the Cathedral. The façade – designed by Gagliardi but never finished – has a large Baroque door. The Latin cross plan interior boasts a magnificent Renaissance statue by Francesco Laurana, known as the *Madonna della Neve* (Madonna of the Snow, 1471) which miraculously survived the earthquake. At the end of the left-hand aisle is Cappella Landolina. The Romanesque statues of lions also come from the old town. The church is surrounded by palazzi, convents and churches. Among others, the façades of **Sant'Agata**, the **Badia della Santissima Annunziata** and **Santa Maria del Gesù** are well worth a longer look.

Detail of Baroque decoration

The unfinished façade of the Chiesa del Crocefisso in the upper town, Noto Alta

The road leading to Pachino, one of the most important agricultural towns in southern Sicily

## Pachino ❸

**Road map** E5. 22,000. *Pachino Town Hall (0931-803 111).*

The town of Pachino, founded in 1758 by the princes of Giardineli and populated by a few dozen families, has evolved into a large agricultural and wine-producing centre. Despite inroads made by modern architecture, there are still some traces of the original town plan: a series of courtyards and alleys reveals an Arab influence.

Pachino is also synonymous with a variety of small red tomato used for sauces and salads, which has become familiar throughout the country (it has even acquired DOC status). Besides the *pachini* tomatoes, the area – close to the sea and seaside resorts – is famous for the production of red wine.

## Capo Passero ❹

**Road map** E5.

Fishing boats on the beach at Capo Passero

At the southern tip of Sicily, on the Capo Passero headland, lies the small town of **Portopalo di Capo Passero**, a centre for agricultural produce and fishing. Portopalo, together with the nearby town of **Marzamemi**, has in recent years become a popular summer tourist spot.

Just off the coast is the small island of **Capo Passero**, which, because of its strategic position, has always been considered an excellent observation point. Proof is provided by the 17th-century watchtower, which replaced a series of military installations and fortifications, some of which were of ancient origin.

The southernmost point on the headland is **Capo delle Correnti**. Opposite the point a lighthouse stands on an island called **Isola delle Correnti**. Near here – or more precisely, close to Portopalo – Allied troops landed on 10 July 1943 with the aim of establishing a bridgehead on Sicily.

North of Portopalo you can see a tuna fishery *(tonnara)* and a fish processing plant. In nearby Marzamemi the town also grew up around a tuna fishery and the residence of the noble Villadorata family, who are still the proprietors of the local *tonnara*.

The waters of the central Mediterranean are still populated by large schools of tuna fish which migrate annually. Enticed towards the *tonnara,* the fish become trapped in a complicated network of tuna fishing nets. Tuna caught using this traditional method is prized and considered highly superior to tuna caught out on the open sea, because the method of killing (which involves very rapid loss of blood) seems to enhance the flavour of the meat.

Portopalo di Capo Passero, a fairly recent tourist attraction

*For hotels and restaurants in this region see pp202–3 and pp217–18*

Byzantine fresco in the Ipogeo di San Michele, in the Cava d'Ispica gorge

## Cava d'Ispica ❺

**Road map** E5. *Access from SS115 from Ispica to Modica, right-hand turn-off at Bettola del Capitano, follow the branch for 5.5 km (3.5 miles) as far as the Cavallo d'Ispica mill.* FS *Syracuse–Ispica (0931-464 467).* ***Tel*** *0932-771 667.* *Apr–Oct: 9am–7pm Mon–Sat, varies Sun; Nov–Mar: 9am–1:30pm Mon–Sat.*

An ancient river carved the Cava d'Ispica out of the rock and the gorge has developed into an open-air monument. The sides of the canyon are perforated with the tombs of a necropolis, places of worship, and cave dwellings where religious hermits went through mystical experiences. It was an Egyptian hermit, Sant'Ilarione, who initiated the monasticism in the canyon, which was used only as a burial site in antiquity.

New, improved access has made it possible to visit the **Larderia Necropolis**, although since the establishment of a new enclosure, it is much more difficult to gain an overall idea of the complex of caves that have made Cava d'Ispica such a world-famous attraction for decades. While the Larderia necropolis is an impressive network of catacombs (there is also a small museum), not far from the entrance you can visit – on request – the **Ipogeo di San Michele**, a cave with a Byzantine fresco of the Madonna, or the small Byzantine church of **San Pancrati**, set in a claustrophobically narrow enclosure. Despite the difficult terrain, the unfenced part of the gorge is also well worth visiting. Every step of the way you will be well rewarded for the strenuous climb.

## Scicli ❻

**Road map** E5. *25,200.* FS *from Syracuse (0931-464 467).* *from Noto.* *Pro Loco, Via Castellana 2 (0932-932 782).* *Festa delle Milizie: last Sun in Jun.*

The town lies at the point where the Modica river converges with the valleys of Bartolomeo and Santa Maria la Nova. Scicli, a UNESCO World Heritage site, once played a major role in controlling communications between the coast and the uplands. It was an Arab stronghold and then became a royal city under the Normans. It was totally rebuilt after the 1693 earthquake, and Baroque streets, façades and churches emerged from the devastated town.

For visitors arriving from Modica along the panoramic San Bartolomeo valley, the first stop is San Bartolomeo followed by the new town centre, built on the plain after the old hill town was abandoned. In the centre is the church of **Santa Maria la Nova**, rebuilt several times and now with Neo-Classical features, **Palazzo Beneventano** with its Baroque motifs, the former **Convent of the Carmelites** and the adjoining **Chiesa del Carmine**. Lastly is the **Chiesa Madre**, in Piazza Italia. This has a papier mâché statue – the Madonna dei Milici – depicting the Virgin Mary on horseback subduing two Turks, which represents the famous 1091 battle between Christians and Arabs. Higher up are the ruins of **San Matteo**, the old cathedral, at the foot of the ruined **castle** built by the Arabs.

Santa Maria la Nova, at Scicli, rebuilt in the Neo-Classical style

# Ragusa ❼

Baroque decoration, Duomo

This ancient city was founded as Hybla Heraia when the Siculi moved into the interior to escape from the Greek colonists. Ragusa, a UNESCO World Heritage site, is divided into two communities: new Baroque Ragusa, built on the plateau after the 1693 earthquake, and quiet, atmospheric Ibla, which is linked to the modern town by a rocky crest. A visit to Ragusa therefore involves two stages.

The Duomo of Ibla in the heart of the old town

**Exploring Ragusa**
The new town was designed to suit the needs of the emerging 17th-century landed gentry as opposed to the old feudal nobles, who preferred to stay entrenched in old Ibla. It was laid out on an octagonal plan, the result of detailed planning following the earthquake of 1693.

**Cathedral**
Piazza San Giovanni. *8am–noon, 4–7pm daily.*
This splendid cathedral was built between 1706 and 1760 in the middle of the new town. It replaced a smaller building that had been hastily erected after the earthquake of 1693.

The low and broad façade is an excellent example of Sicilian Baroque, with a lovely monumental portal *(see p132)* and fine sculptures of St John the Baptist, to whom the cathedral is dedicated, the Virgin Mary and St John the Evangelist. There is also an impressive porticoed terrace and a massive cusped bell tower.

The ornate Baroque interior has a Latin cross plan with two side aisles and fine stucco decoration.

**Museo Archeologico Ibleo**
Via Natalelli. ***Tel*** *0932-622 963.*
*9am–1:30pm, 4–7:30pm daily.*
The Archaeological Museum is divided into six sections and is devoted to the cultures that have dominated the province of Ragusa. The first section has prehistoric finds from Modica, Pantalica and Cava d'Ispica. The second one is given over to Kamarina, the Syracusan subcolony founded on the banks of the Ippari river on a coastal site not far from present-day Vittoria. Kamarina once enjoyed important trade links with ancient Ibla. Among the displays here are the statue of a warrior, the bronzes of Kamarina and Attic vases, all recovered during the recent excavations at Kamarina, organized and sponsored by the Syracuse Archaeological Office. The third section of the museum features the Siculi cultures, followed by an exhibit of Hellenistic finds – especially from Scornavacche, a very important trade and caravan centre – including an interesting reconstruction of a potter's oven. The fifth section focuses on the Roman epoch, while the last one illustrates the growth of this area in the Byzantine age, with finds from the ancient port of Caucana.

**Santa Maria delle Scale**
This church stands at the top of a flight of 340 steps connecting Ibla and Ragusa, hence the name, *scale* meaning stairs. Santa Maria delle Scale was built in the

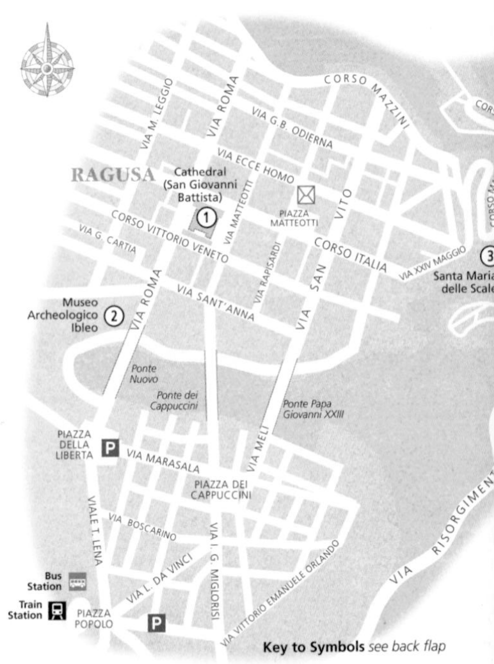


Key to Symbols *see back flap*

4th century over a Norman onvent and was rebuilt after ie 1693 earthquake. The riginal Gothic doorway nd external pulpit of the ampanileare still intact.

**xploring Ibla**

he hill of Ibla has probably een inhabited since the rd millennium BC and is ch in history. However, in ecent years its economic nportance has waned ompared with the "new" own of Ragusa.

**Duomo (San Giorgio)**

he Cathedral stands t the top of a stairway nat begins at **Piazza uomo**, the real centre f Ibla. It was built ver the foundations of an Nicolò, which was lestroyed by the 1693 arthquake. The new hurch was designed y Rosario Gagliardi nd built in 1738–75. he huge façade is mmediately striking, vith its three tiers f columns which, ogether with the ertical lines of the monu- nental stairway leading to ne church, accentuate the ertical thrust of the building. n impressive Neo-Classical cupola dominates the nave. The interior contains a series of paintings from different periods (including a 16th-century *Enthroned Madonna and Child)* and 13 stained-glass windows.

**Circolo di Conversazione**

If you go down Corso XXV Aprile, you will see the Neo-Classical Circolo di Con- versazione (Conversation Club), on your left. This private club has a plush Neo-Classical interior, steeped in the atmo- sphere of 19th-century Ibla.

Statue of San Giuseppe

**San Giuseppe**

Also along Corso XXV Aprile, at Piazza Pola, is the Baroque **San Giuseppe**, which is in many ways similar to the Duomo, San Giorgio, and for this reason is also attributed to the architect Gagliardi. The oval-shaped interior has a large cupola decorated with Sebastiano Lo Monaco's fresco *Glory of St Benedict*. After leaving this church, turn down Corso XXV Aprile and you will come to a fascinating series of monuments. First there are the ruins of the Norman church of Santa Maria la Nova. Then there is San Francesco all'Immacolata, built over Palazzo Chiaramonte and incorporating its Gothic portal. Last is **San Giorgio Vecchio**, for the most part destroyed by the 1693 earthquake. A splendid Catalan-Gothic portal survives – its lunette has a bas-relief of St George killing the dragon and, above, the eagles from the House of Aragon coat of arms.

**Giardino Ibleo**

This delightful 19th-century public garden has a fine view of the area. It also contains a number of churches, such as San Giacomo and the Chiesa dei Cappuccini. The former was built in the 14th century and restructured in the 1600s, when it was given a Baroque slant. The Chiesa dei Cappuccini has a simple aisleless nave and contains some interesting 15th-century altarpieces, including one by Pietro Novelli.

**VISITORS' CHECKLIST**

**Road map** E5. *67,500.* *from Syracuse (0931-464 467).* *Piazza Stazione (0932-623 440).* *AAPIT, Via Bocchieri 33 (0932-221 511 or 663 094).* **www**.ragusaturismo.it

**The façade of San Giuseppe, with its Corinthian columns**

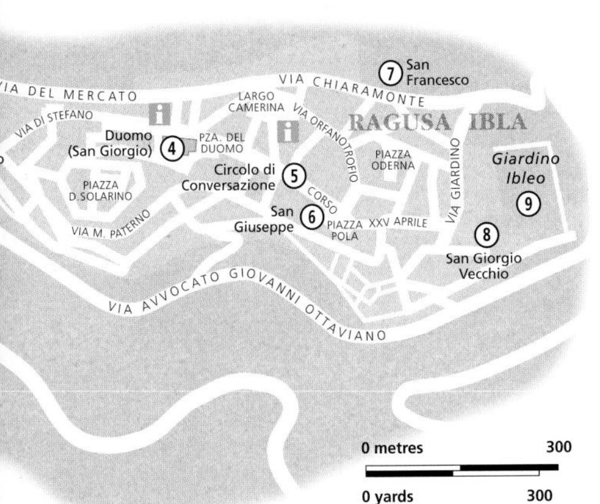


**RAGUSA AND IBLA**

Cathedral (San Giovanni Battista) ①
Circolo di Conversazione ⑤
Duomo (San Giorgio) ④
Giardino Ibleo ⑨
Museo Archeologico Ibleo ②
San Francesco ⑦
San Giorgio Vecchio ⑧
San Giuseppe ⑥
Santa Maria delle Scale ③

**The Duomo at Modica, a remarkable example of Sicilian Baroque**

# Modica ❽

**Road map** E5. *52,500.* **FS** *from Syracuse (0931-464 467).* **i** *Pro Loco, Via Maccalle' (0932-763 459).*

Inhabited since the era of the Siculi culture, Modica (a UNESCO World Heritage site) rebelled against Roman rule in 212 BC and, thanks to its strategic position, became one of the most important towns in medieval and Renaissance Sicily. Peter I of Aragon made it capital of an area that roughly corresponds to the present-day province of Ragusa, and it was later ruled by the Chiaramonte and Cabrera families. Perched on the rocky spurs dominating the large "Y" formed by the confluence of the Janni Mauru and Pozzo dei Pruni rivers, Modica grew, occupying the valley where the rivers were filled in after a disastrous series of floods.

Modica Alta is built on the hill and is connected to the lower town, Modica Bassa, via flights of steps. Some of these are monumental, such as the 250-step flight built in the 19th century which descends from San Giorgio. Alleys and lanes evoke the walled town, which from 844 to 1091 was an important Arab city known as *Mohac*.

**Sculpture on Corso Umberto I**

### Duomo (San Giorgio)

It is worthwhile making the effort to climb up the hill to see the Cathedral. It is dedicated to St George and was built by Count Alfonso Henriquez Cabrera on the site of a 13th-century church which had been destroyed by an earthquake. The magnificent façade (which, because of its similarity to several churches in Noto, is attributed to the architect Rosario Gagliardi) rises upwards elegantly with three ranks of columns. In the interior are ten 16th-century wooden panels with scenes from the New Testament.

**Corso Regina Margherita**, the main street in Modica Alta, has many fine 19th-century palazzi.

### Santa Maria di Betlem

By going up the road following one branch of the confluence of the valley rivers, now called Via Marchesa Tedeschi, you will come across the façade of Santa Maria di Betlem, a 16th-century church which was rebuilt after the 1693 earthquake. At the end of the right-hand aisle is the beautiful Cappella del Sacramento, a splendid example of late Gothic-Renaissance architecture. It was commissioned by the Cabrera family.

### Corso Umberto I

The many interesting churches and buildings along the city's main street include the former **Monastero delle Benedettine** (a convent for Benedictine nuns now used as a courthouse), the 19th-century **Teatro Garibaldi**, the 18th-century **Palazzo Tedeschi, Santa Maria del Soccorso** and **Palazzo Manenti**, whose corbels are decorated with figures of all kinds: knights with plumes in their hats, lovely girls and grotesque monsters.

### San Pietro

Also on Corso Umberto I is a flight of Baroque **monumental steps**, flanked by statues of the Apostles, which leads to the entrance of **San Pietro**. This church was built after the 1693 earthquake on the site of a 14th-century church. The two-aisle interior has a number of paintings and statues. The *Madonna dell'Ausilio*, a Gagini-school statue, stands in the second chapel in the right-hand aisle.

**San Pietro stands at the top of a monumental Baroque staircase**

### Museo Civico

Largo Mercè. ***Tel*** *0932-945 081.* *9am–1pm Mon–Sat.*

Craftsmen and their tools are featured in this ethnographic museum, with workshops reconstructed in the cells of the former monastery of the Mercedarian friars. You can make an appointment to see the various local artisans (saddle-makers, smiths, basket weavers, shoemakers and stone-cutters) demonstrating their ancient skills.

***For hotels and restaurants in this region see pp202–3 and pp217–18***

The ruins of the Greek walls at the Capo Soprano headland, Gela

## Vittoria ❾

**Road map** D5. *54,300.*
*Pro Loco (0932-992 953).*

Founded by Vittoria Colonna in 1603, this agricultural town lies on the plain between the Ippari and Dirillo rivers. In the central Piazza del Popolo are the **Teatro Comunale** (1877) and **Santa Maria delle Grazie**, a Baroque church built after the disastrous 1693 earthquake.

## Gela ❿

**Road map** D4. *72,000.* FS *from Syracuse (0931-464 467).* *AAST (0931-911 423).* **Fortifications at Capo Soprano** ***Tel*** *0933-554 964.* *9am–1 hr before sunset.* **Museo Archeologico Comunale** ***Tel*** *0933-912 626.* *9am–1pm, 3–7:30pm.* *last Mon of month.* *(combined with excavations.)* **Acropolis excavations** *9am–1 hr before sunset.*

According to Greek historian Thucydides, Gela was founded in 688 BC. In the 6th century BC its inhabitants founded Agrigento. Extending over two slopes – the present-day **Acropolis** and the **Capo Soprano** area – the town was revived, after a long period of abandonment, by Frederick II. Today Gela is marred by ugly buildings, industrial plants and a strong anti-Mafia military presence. However, there are the archaeological sites: a long stretch of Greek fortifications built by Timoleon at Capo Soprano and the sacred precinct and ancient Temple of Athena on the **Acropolis**, all good introductions to a visit to the **Museo Archeologico**.

## Chiaramonte Gulfi ⓫

**Road map** E4. *8,100.*

This town was founded by Manfredi Chiaramonte, the Count of Modica, on the steep slopes of a rise and then developed towards the valley. The **Chiesa del Salvatore** and **Matrice Santa Maria la Nova** are in the centre, while the **Madonna delle Grazie Sanctuary** is on the outskirts.

## Vizzini ⓬

**Road map** E4. *7,000.*
*Town hall (0933-968 211).*

The fascination of Vizzini lies in the small streets and alleys of the old town, which has preserved its atmosphere and town plan – increasingly rare in Sicily because of modern urban growth. Also worth a look is the fine architecture of the **Chiesa Madre di San Gregorio** with its Gothic portal, taken from the destroyed Palazzo di Città.

## Palazzolo Acreide ⓭

**Road map** E4. *9,000.*
*Town hall (0931-875 841).*

Originally named Akrai, this town, a UNESCO World Heritage site, has some important Baroque churches and buildings – the **Chiesa Madre di San Nicolò, Palazzo Zocco** and the 18th-century **Chiesa dell'Annunziata**. However, the most interesting sight is the peaceful plain with the **excavations of Akrai**.

A Baroque balcony in the centre of Palazzolo Acreide

### Excavations at Akrai

2 km (1.2 miles) from the centre. ***Tel*** *0931-881 499.* *9am–1 hr before sunset (Nov–Apr: 9–1pm, 3:30–5pm).*
This area was inhabited in 664 BC, when the city was founded by the Syracusans. A small **theatre** stands by the entrance. The **acropolis** contains an **agora**, two **latomie** (the Intagliata and Intagliatella quarries, *see p136*), the ruins of the **Temple of Aphrodite** and the so-called **Santoni**, 12 rock-hewn statues representing the goddess Cybele.

The theatre at Palazzolo Acreide: the colony dates back to the early 7th century BC

# Caltagirone ⓮

Ceramic tile on Ponte San Francesco

In the history of this city (a UNESCO World Heritage site), built between the Erei and Iblei hills, there is one element of continuity – ceramics production. Prehistoric pottery has been found on the hills around the Arab *Cal'at Ghiran* ("castle of vases"). The local potters were world famous in the Middle Ages, and the tradition is maintained today.

San Giuliano, displaying some 20th-century architectural features

**Exploring Caltagirone**
It is pleasant exploring Caltagirone on foot, walking around the streets and squares, pausing at the local craftsmen's workshops. There is quite a difference in altitude between the lower part and the hill of Santa Maria del Monte, so plan your visit with this in mind.

**Piazza Municipio**
The former Piano della Loggia – now Piazza Municipio – is the heart of the city, where the main streets converge. In the piazza are the **Town Hall** and **Palazzo Senatorio**, formerly the city theatre, now home to the Galleria Sturzo.

**Duomo di San Giuliano**
The Cathedral is in Piazza Umberto I. The exterior of the church, dedicated to San Giuliano, has a long history: first it was Norman, then Baroque, and was rebuilt in the 20th century (the façade in 1909, the bell tower in 1954). In the interior is a 16th-century wooden crucifix. By going down Via Roma towards the **San Francesco bridge** – you will come to an open space with the old Bourbon prison and the church of **Sant'Agata**.

**Museo Civico**
Via Roma. ***Tel*** *0933-31590.*
*9:30am–1:30pm, 4–7pm Tue & Fri–Sun.*
This museum in the former 17th-century Bourbon prison has prehistoric, Greek and Roman material, sculptures and ceramics from the 1500s to the present.

**San Francesco d'Assisi**
The Ponte San Francesco, decorated with typical coloured tiles, leads to the church of San Francesco d'Assisi, which was founded in the 12th century and rebuilt in Baroque style after the 1693 earthquake.

**Giardino della Villa**
The public gardens can be reached by going down Via Roma. The park was designed in the mid-1800s by Giovanni Battista Basile, and the long balustrade and the bandstand are richly decorated with coverings of ceramic tiles.

**Museo della Ceramica**
Viale Giardini Pubblici. ***Tel*** *0933-58418.* *9am–6:30pm.*
From the Belvedere del Teatrino, in Giardino della Villa, you can visit the Ceramics Museum. There are Bronze Age pots and Greek, Hellenistic and Roman kraters and figurines. The Middle Ages are represented by Arab vases and Sicilian pieces. The collection also has more recent pharmacy jars and glazed vases with religious figures.

**Santa Maria del Monte Stairway**
Once back in the centre of town, one of the most impressive sights is the monumental Santa Maria del Monte

Ponte San Francesco in Caltagirone

Coloured majolica tiles, decorating every step of this staircase

staircase, with its 142 steps decorated with majolica tiles. The flight of steps was built in 1608 to link the seat of religious power – the Cathedral – with that of civic power, the **Palazzo Senatorio**.

During the feast day of San Giacomo (24 July) *(see p39)* the entire flight of stairs is illuminated with thousands of lamps, skilfully arranged to create interesting patterns of lighting effects.

## VISITORS' CHECKLIST

**Road map** D4. 37,500. *from Catania and Gela (095-532 719). AAST, Volta L Libertini 3 (0933-538 09). 24 Jul, Festa di San Giacomo.*

### Santa Maria del Monte

At the top of the stairway is the former Cathedral of Caltagirone, built in the mid-1500s and then rebuilt after the 1693 earthquake. A slender bell tower, designed by Natale Bonaiuto, was also added. A castle once stood at the top of the hill. Today, in an area that was once heavily fortified, can be found the **Sant'Agostino Convent** and **San Nicola**, both constructed in the 18th century.

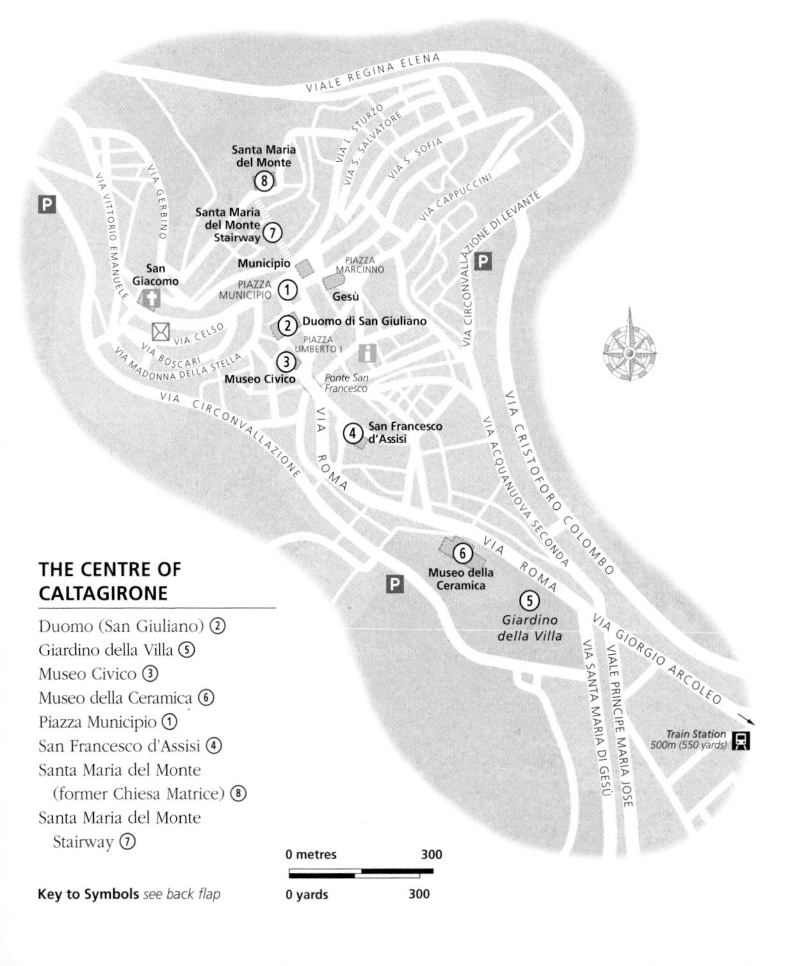


## THE CENTRE OF CALTAGIRONE

Duomo (San Giuliano) ②
Giardino della Villa ⑤
Museo Civico ③
Museo della Ceramica ⑥
Piazza Municipio ①
San Francesco d'Assisi ④
Santa Maria del Monte (former Chiesa Matrice) ⑧
Santa Maria del Monte Stairway ⑦

**Key to Symbols** *see back flap*

The Cathedral of Lentini, dedicated to Sant'Alfio, in Piazza Duomo

## Lentini ⓯

**Road map** E4. 23,700. *from Catania, Syracuse & Messina (095-532 719). APT Siracusa (0931-481 200 or 464 255); Pro Loco Lentini, Piazza Duomo (095-941 433).*
**Museo Archeologico**: Via Museo **Tel** *095-832 962 for restoration; call ahead for up-to-date information.*
**Digs at Leontinoi**: *9am–1 hr before sunset, daily. Good Friday "Scesa e Cruci"; 1st week of May: Festival of orange trees in bloom.*

An ancient Siculan city originally named *Xuthia*, Lentini was conquered by the Chalcidians in 729 BC and fought against neighbouring Syracuse with the support of Athens. Defeated and then occupied by the Romans, the city went into a period of decline. In the Middle Ages it became an important agricultural centre. The local museum has finds from the ancient city, especially from the Siculan and Greek epochs. The digs at ancient Leontinoi, at the edge of town in the Colle Castellaccio area, can be reached via the ancient Porta Siracusana city gate. The various walls testify to the city's battle-worn history, and there are a number of ancient burial grounds inside the archaeological precinct.

## Megara Hyblaea ⓰

**Road map** F4. *Augusta station. APT Siracusa (0931-481 200 or 464 255). 8:30am–1 hr before sunset.*

One of the first Greek colonies in Sicily was founded in 728 BC here at Megara. According to legend, the founders were the followers of Daedalus, who had escaped from Crete. Unfortunately, today the site is surrounded by the oil refineries of Augusta and in such squalid surroundings it is difficult to visit the ruins of the ancient city with a sense of atmosphere. The Megara colonists who founded Megara Hyblaea were soon at war with Syracuse and Leontinoi, and a century later founded the city of Selinunte, in western Sicily *(see pp104–5)*. You should be able to see the ruins of the Hellenistic walls, the Agora quarter, and the remains of some temples, baths and colonnades. The excavations were led by the eminent archaeologist Paolo Orsi and the École Française of Rome. Information display boards will help you to get orientated.

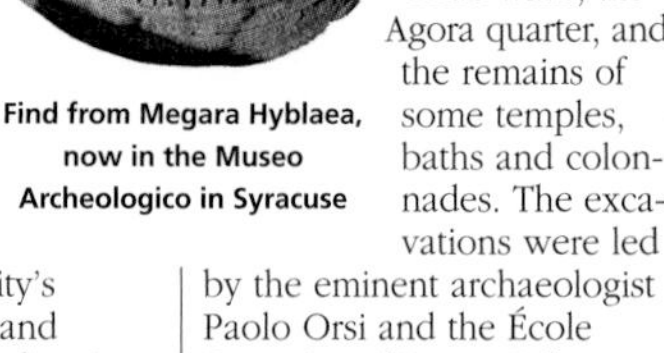

Find from Megara Hyblaea, now in the Museo Archeologico in Syracuse

Ruined foundations in the ancient Greek colony of Megara Hyblaea, founded in the 8th century BC

The Porta Spagnola in Augusta (1681), the old city gate

## Augusta ⓱

**Road map** F4. 34,000. from Catania, Syracuse, Messina (0931-994 100). *APT Siracusa (0931-481 200 or 464 255); Augusta town hall (0931-521 269).*

Augusta was founded on an island by Frederick II as a port protected by a castle. Under the Aragonese the city was constantly at war with Turkish and North African pirates. It was almost totally destroyed by the 1693 earthquake. In the early 1900s the city expanded and became a major petrochemical port, and this drastically changed the landscape. You enter the old town through the **Porta Spagnola** city gate, built by the viceroy Benavides in 1681, next to which are the ruins of the old walls. In the centre, the Baroque **Chiesa delle Anime Sante**, the **Chiesa Madre** (1769) and the **Museo delle Armi** (Arms Museum) are worth a look.

## Pantalica ⓲

**Road map** E4 (19 km, 12 miles from Ferla, 45 km, 28 miles from Syracuse).

Rock-cut tombs, dwellings and temples line the steep walls of the limestone gorges at the confluence of the Bottiglieria and Anapo rivers. Pantalica was the heart of the ancient kingdom of Hybla which, in its heyday, used Syracuse as its port. The city was conquered by the Greeks when the coastal colonies became powerful in the 8th century BC, and Pan-talica became important again during the early Middle Ages, when Arab invasions and constant wars led the locals to seek refuge in its inaccessible canyons. The cave-dwellings and hermitages date from this period, as do the ruins of a settlement known as the "Byzantine village".

View of the steep gorges surrounding the necropolis of Pantalica

### A WALK THROUGH PANTALICA

This archaeological site – the largest necropolis in Sicily – covers a large area, but the steep gorges mean there are few roads, and the only practical way of getting around is on foot. About 9 km (5 miles) from Ferla stands the Filiporto Necropolis, with more than 1,000 tombs cut out of the cliffs. Next is the North Necropolis; the last place to park is near the *Anaktoron*, the megalithic palace of the prince of ancient Hybla dating from the 12th century BC. The road ends 1 km (half a mile) further on. From this point, one path goes down to the Bottiglieria river, where steep walls are filled with rock-cut caves, and another takes you to the so-called "Byzantine village", the rock-hewn church of San Micidiario and the other necropolises in this area. It is not advisable to try to go to Pantalica from Sortino (the northern slope); it is an extremely long walk.

The North Necropolis at Pantalica

# NORTHEASTERN SICILY

*Thanks to the presence of Mount Etna, the Ionian coast of Sicily has often had to deal with violent volcanic eruptions. One of the most devastating was in 1669, when the molten lava even reached Catania and the sea. The lava flows have formed Etna's distinctive landscape, and flowers, putti and festoons of black lava now adorn many churches and buildings in Catania and Aci Castello.*

In 734 BC the first colonists from Greece landed on this coast and founded Naxos, the first of a series of powerful colonies in Sicily that gave rise to a period of prosperity and cultural sophistication. However, volcanic eruptions and devastating earthquakes have destroyed almost all traces of the splendid Greek cities in this area, with the exception of the ancient theatre in Taormina, which was rebuilt in the Roman era. The panoramic position, mild climate and wealth of architectural beauty have made this coast a favourite with visitors. The first of these were people who undertook the Grand Tour in the 1700s and made their first stop at Messina, just as many modern travellers do. In summer, the Ionian coast is crowded because of the beauty of its beaches and sea. But it is also fascinating in the winter, when the top of Mount Etna is covered with snow and the citrus orchards are heavy with fruit, or in spring, when the air is filled with the scent of orange blossoms and flower gardens in bloom. Another part of northeastern Sicily worth visiting is the archipelago of the unique Aeolian Islands, of volcanic origin.

The old harbour at Catania, still crowded with fishing boats

◁ The awe-inspiring sight of an erupting Mount Etna at night

# Exploring Northeastern Sicily

The pearl of the Ionian coast is Taormina, famous for its stupendous panoramic views, but this area has many other fascinating sights too – from the fishing villages of Aci Trezza and Aci Castello to the Baroque splendour of Catania, as well as Mount Etna, the largest active volcano in Europe. You can go up to the edge of its awesome crater by jeep or on foot, or visit the villages on its black lava slopes with the quaint Ferrovia Circumetnea trains. Those who prefer the seaside can visit the beaches of the Aeolian Islands, which also offer unique scenery with volcanic soil and maquis vegetation.

**The ravine of the Alcantara River near Taormina**

## SIGHTS AT A GLANCE

Aci Castello 9
Acireale 11
Aci Trezza 10
Adrano 7
Agira 6
Bronte 14
Capo d'Orlando 24
Castiglione di Sicilia 20
*Catania pp162–5* 1
Centuripe 4
Giardini Naxos 19
Giarre 17
Linguaglossa 16
Mascalucia 8
*Messina pp182–5* 21
Milazzo 25
Motta Sant'Anastasia 2
*Mount Etna pp170–73* 13
Paternò 3
Patti 23
Randazzo 15
Regalbuto 5
*Taormina pp176–80* 18
Tyndaris 22
Zafferana Etnea 12

**Islands**

*The Aeolian Islands pp188–91* 26

**KEY**

- Motorway
- Major road
- Secondary road
- Minor road
- Main railway
- Minor railway
- Summit

**The Monastery of Santa Lucia at Adrano, on the slopes of Etna**

**For additional map symbols** *see back flap*

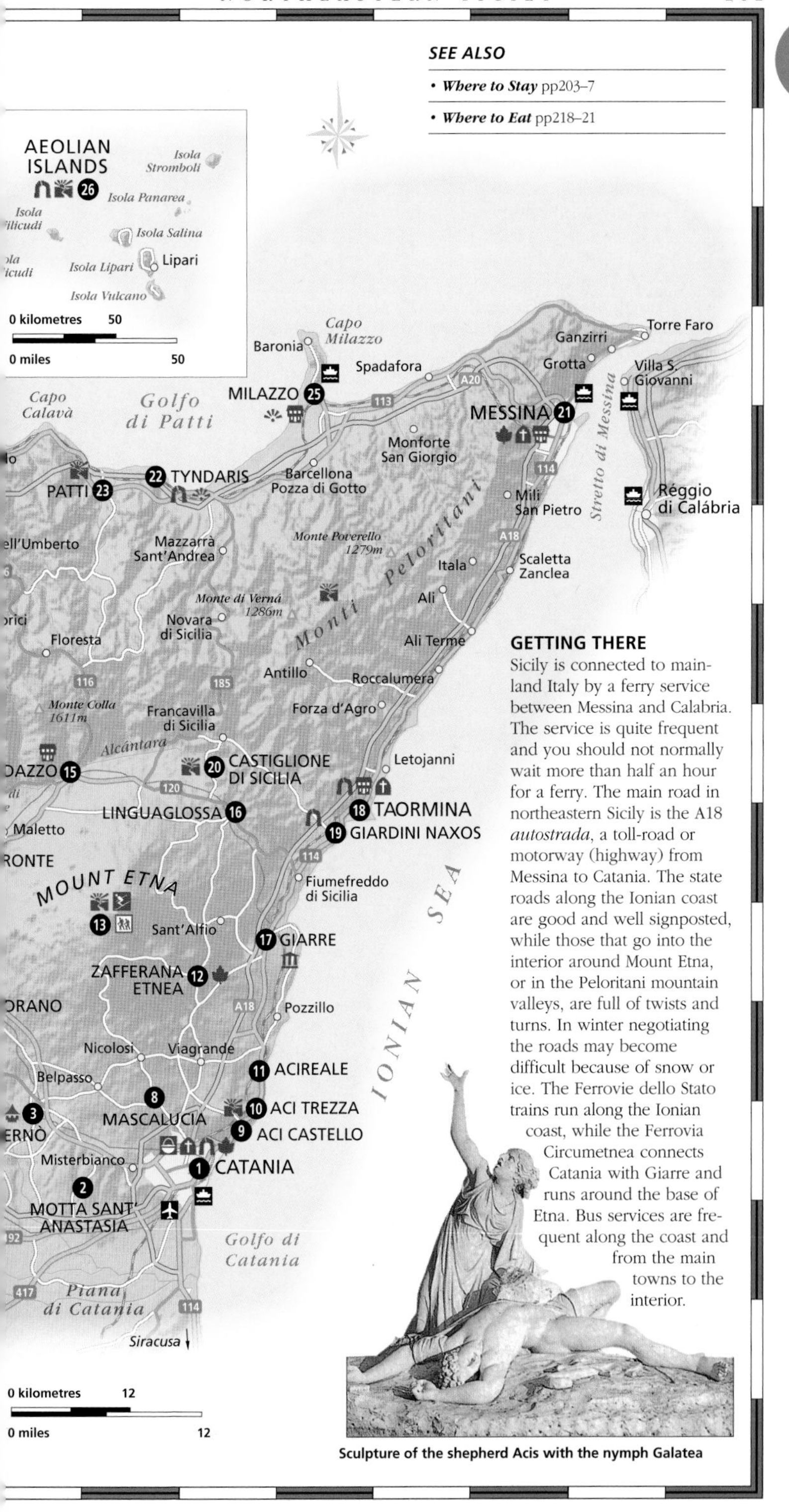


### SEE ALSO


- ***Where to Stay*** pp203–7
- ***Where to Eat*** pp218–21


### GETTING THERE

Sicily is connected to mainland Italy by a ferry service between Messina and Calabria. The service is quite frequent and you should not normally wait more than half an hour for a ferry. The main road in northeastern Sicily is the A18 *autostrada*, a toll-road or motorway (highway) from Messina to Catania. The state roads along the Ionian coast are good and well signposted, while those that go into the interior around Mount Etna, or in the Peloritani mountain valleys, are full of twists and turns. In winter negotiating the roads may become difficult because of snow or ice. The Ferrovie dello Stato trains run along the Ionian coast, while the Ferrovia Circumetnea connects Catania with Giarre and runs around the base of Etna. Bus services are frequent along the coast and from the main towns to the interior.

**Sculpture of the shepherd Acis with the nymph Galatea**

# Catania ❶

Situated between the Ionian Sea and the slopes of Mount Etna, Sicily's second city (a UNESCO World Heritage site) has always had a close relationship with the volcano, and most of the city's buildings are made from black lava. According to the historian Thucydides, the city was founded in 729 BC by Greek colonists from Chalcis *(see p156)*. Since then it has been flooded with lava and shaken by earthquakes, most radically in 1693, when it was razed to the ground. Catania today is the result of 18th-century rebuilding: broad, straight streets and large, unevenly shaped squares, a precaution against earthquakes.

**The Fontana dell'Elefante**

## CATANIA TOWN CENTRE

Badia di Sant'Agata ④
Castello Ursino ⑩
Cathedral ③
Museo Civico Belliniano ⑤
Museo Verga ⑪
Palazzo Biscari ①
Pescheria ⑦
Piazza Duomo ②
Roman Theatre ⑨
San Nicolò all'Arena ⑫
Teatro Bellini ⑥
Via Cruciferi ⑧
Via Etnea ⑬

### Palazzo Biscari

Via Museo Biscari, Via Dusmet. ***Tel*** *095-715 2508 or 321 818.* ☐ *by appt.* **www**.palazzobiscari.com

This is the largest private palazzo in 18th-century Catania. Construction was begun by Prince Paternò Castello on an embankment of the 16th-century city walls. Work continued for nearly a century and involved some of the leading architects of the time. The most interesting side of the building faces Via Dusmet, with a large terrace decorated with putti, telamons and garlands sculpted by Antonino Amato. The building is partly private and partly used as city administrative offices.

### Piazza Duomo

The heart of city life lies at the crossing of Via Etnea and Via Vittorio Emanuele. The square boasts many fine Baroque buildings: **Palazzo del Municipio** (the Town Hall), the former **Chierici Seminary**, the **Cathedral** and **Porta Uzeda**, the city gate built in 1696 to connect Via Etnea with the port area. In the middle is the **Fontana dell'Elefante**, a well-known fountain sculpted in 1736 by Giovanni Battista Vaccarini. On a pedestal in the basin is an elephant made of lava, on the back of which is an Egyptian obelisk

**Key to Symbols** *see back flap*

## VISITORS' CHECKLIST

**Road map** E3. *313,000.* *Aeroporto Fontanarossa (at Fontanarossa) (095-340 505).* *Piazza Giovanni XXIII (095-532 719).* *AST, Via Luigi Sturzo 220 (095-746 1096 or 840 000 323).* *AAPT, Via Cimarosa 12 (095-730 6222).* *(antiques) Sun am in Piazza Carlo Alberto; (coins) Largo Paisiello.* *Feb: Festa di Sant'Agata, Jul–Sep: Catania Musica Estate; Aug–Sep: International Jazz Festival; Oct: symphony and chamber music concerts.* **www**.apt.catania.it

**Entrance to the lovely 18th-century Palazzo Biscari**

with a globe on top. The latter, a late Roman sculpture, has become the city's symbol.

### Cathedral

Piazza Duomo. ***Tel*** *095-320 044.* *9am–1pm, 4:30–7:30pm daily.* *8, 10, 11:30am & 6pm.*

The principal church in Catania is dedicated to the city's patron saint, Sant'Agata. It still has its three original Norman apses and transept. The façade, with two tiers of columns, is fully Baroque thanks to the design of GB Vaccarini, who also designed the left-hand side of the Cathedral.

The majestic interior has a cupola, a tall transept and three apses with lovely columns. On the second pilaster to the right is the **Tomb of Vincenzo Bellini**; on the first one to the left, a 15th-century stoup. A door in the right-hand transept leads to the Norman Cappella della Madonna, with the remains of various Aragonese rulers.

### Badia di Sant'Agata

Via Vittorio Emanuele II. *7:30am–noon Mon–Sat; 4–7:30pm Sun.*

This masterpiece of Catanian Baroque architecture was built in 1735–67 and designed by Giovanni Battista Vaccarini. The façade is a play of convex and concave surfaces. The octagonal interior, a triumph of Rococo decoration, is equally impressive.

### Museo Civico Belliniano

Piazza San Francesco 9. ***Tel*** *095-715 05 35.* *9am–1:30pm Tue–Sat, 9am–1pm Sun.* *1 Jan, 1 May, 25 Dec.*

Vincenzo Bellini's birthplace *(see p35)* is now a museum with mementos, autographed scores, musical instruments and models of scenes from some of his operas.

TEATRO BELLINI

**Detail of the façade of Teatro Bellini**

### Teatro Bellini

Via Perrotta 12. ***Tel*** *095-730 61 11.* *Oct–Jun.*

Named after the Catania-born composer Vincenzo Bellini, this theatre attracts praise from both critics and the public for its high-quality performances.

**The Baroque façade of Catania Cathedral, dedicated to Sant'Agata**

The lively Mercato della Pescheria (fish market) in Catania

### Pescheria

Situated at the beginning of Via Garibaldi, the **Fontana dell'Amenano** fountain is fed by the waters of the underground Amenano river, which also forms a pool in the Roman theatre. Sculpted in 1867, the fountain is the focal point of a colourful fish market, the **Mercato della Pescheria**, which occupies the nearby streets and small squares every morning. The smells and atmosphere of the market are reminiscent of North Africa and the Middle East. At the end of Via Garibaldi is the monumental **Porta Garibaldi** city gate, built of limestone and lava in 1768 to celebrate the wedding of Ferdinand IV of Sicily.

### Via Cruciferi

This street is lined with lavishly decorated Baroque palazzi and churches. The road begins at **Piazza San Francesco**, with the Baroque **San Francesco d'Assisi**. In the interior are the so-called *candelore*, carved and gilded wooden constructions which symbolize the various artisans' guilds in the city. Every February the *candelore* are carried in procession as part of the impressive celebrations honouring Sant'Agata, the city's patron saint. Outside the church is the **Arco di San Benedetto**, an arch connecting the fine **Badia Grande** abbey, designed by Francesco Battaglia, and the **Badia Piccola**, attributed to Giovanni Battista Vaccarini. To the left is **San Benedetto**, where the wooden portal carries scenes of the life of St Benedict, and **San Francesco Borgia**, at the top of a double flight of steps flanked by the former **Jesuit College**. Opposite stands **San Giuliano**, a masterpiece of Catanian Baroque architecture designed by Vaccarini.

### Roman Theatre

Via Vittorio Emanuele 226.
***Tel*** *095-715 05 08.*
*9am–1:30pm, 2:30–5pm daily.*

Built of limestone and lava on the southern slope of the acropolis, the theatre had a diameter of 87 m (285 ft) and could seat 7,000 people. Although there was probably a Greek theatre on this site once, the present ruins are all Roman. The theatre was badly damaged in the 11th century, when Roger I authorized the removal of the marble facing and limestone blocks for use as building material for the cathedral. What remains of the theatre today are the cavea, the edge of the orchestra and part of the backstage area of the theatre. Next to the theatre is the small semicircular **Odeion**, made of lava and used mainly for competitions in music and rhetoric. It had a seating capacity of 1,500. The entrance to the Odeion is near the top tiers of seats in the Roman theatre.

### Castello Ursino

Piazza Federico di Svevia. ***Tel*** *095-345 830.* *9am–1pm, 3–7pm Mon–Sat.* *Sun & hols.*

This castle (currently closed for restoration) was built in 1239–50 by Riccardo da Lentini for Frederick II and is one of the few vestiges of medieval Catania.

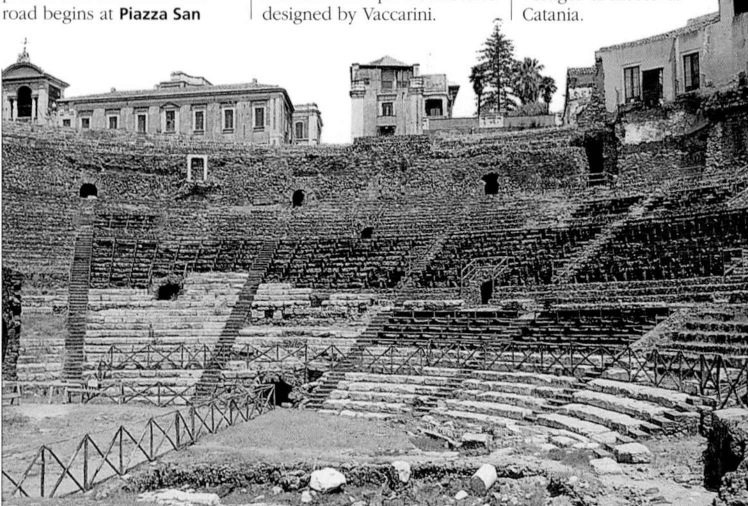

The Roman theatre in Catania, now completely surrounded by buildings

*For hotels and restaurants in this region see pp203–7 and pp218–21*

Castello Ursino, one of the rare medieval buildings in Catania

The Castello Ursino originally stood on a promontory overlooking the sea and was part of a massive defence system that once included the Motta, Anastasia, Paternò and Adrano castles. Castello Ursino is square, with four corner towers, and was rebuilt in the mid-1500s. On the eastern side of its exterior, above a large window, a five-pointed star with a cabalistic meaning is visible. In a niche on the façade, the Swabian eagle seizing a lamb with its claws is the symbol of Hohenstaufen imperial power. In the inner courtyard, where the kings of Aragon administered justice, there is a display of sarcophagi, columns and other pieces.

The upper rooms house the interesting **Museo Civico**, which has a fine art gallery with important works such as *The Last Judgement* by Beato Angelico, *The Last Supper* by the Spanish painter Luis de Morales, *St John the Baptist* by Pietro Novelli *(see p23)* and a dismantled polyptych by Antonello Saliba of the *Madonna and Child* taken from Santa Maria del Gesù.

### Home and Museum of Giovanni Verga

Via Sant'Anna 8. ***Tel*** *095-71 50 598.* *9am–1pm, 3–5:30pm Tue–Fri, 9am–1pm Sat, Sun.*

The apartment where the great Sicilian author Giovanni Verga lived for many years and died in 1922 is on the second floor of a 19th-century building. The house contains period furniture and personal mementos. At the entrance are displayed reproductions of manuscripts, the originals of which are at the Biblioteca Universitaria Regionale di Catania. The library in Verga's house boasts over 2,500 books from the author's collection, ranging from works by the Italian Futurist Marinetti to the Russian author Dostoevsky. The bedroom is quite simple, with a bed, a dressing table, a wardrobe and portraits of Verga painted by his grandson Michele Grita.

San Nicolò, intended to be the largest church in Sicily

### San Nicolò l'Arena

Piazza Dante. ***Tel*** *095-312 366.* *9am–1pm daily (also 3–6pm Tue & Thu).*

San Nicolò was built on the site of a Benedictine monastery damaged in the 1669 eruption. After collapsing in the 1693 earthquake, the church was rebuilt in the 1700s. It now houses the faculty of letters of the University of Catania.

The nave has two aisles, separated from the central section by huge piers. In the transept is one of the largest sundials in Europe, restored in 1996. It was built in the mid-1800s by the German baron Wolfgang Sartorius von Waltershausen and is extremely precise. Twenty-four slabs of inlaid marble show the signs of the zodiac, days of the year and the seasons. At noon, sunlight falls on the spot from an opening in the roof, marking the day and month.

### Via Etnea

Catania's main street goes up a slight incline and connects the most important parts of the city. Partly closed to traffic, Via Etnea has the most elegant shops and cafés in town. Halfway along it lies **Piazza Stesicoro**, with the ruins of the Roman amphitheatre, built in the 2nd century AD. Nearby is the vast **Piazza Carlo Alberto**, where a bustling antiques market is held every Sunday morning. Back on Via Etnea is the **Collegiata**, a chapel built in the early 1700s and one of the most important late Baroque works in the city. The concave façade, designed by Stefano Ittar, is enlivened by columns, statues and niches. Near the end of Via Etnea is the **Villa Bellini**, a public garden with subtropical plants and busts of famous Sicilians.

The University building on Via Etnea, the most elegant street in Catania

Motta Sant'Anastasia, with its medieval tower dwarfed by Mount Etna

## Motta Sant'Anastasia ❷

**Road map** E3. 7,600.
*Ferrovia Circumetnea (095-541 250). Pro Loco, Piazza Umberto 42 (095-308 161).*

Mount Etna forms a constant backdrop to Motta. From the top of the village, with the massive tower of the 12th-century **Norman Castle**, the snow-capped volcano gleams through the winter, gradually darkening in spring and summer. Not far away is the **Chiesa Madre** (Cathedral), also built in Norman times. At the foot of the old town is the heart of Motta Sant'Anastasia with its *pasticcerie* (pastry shops), Baroque churches and bustling atmosphere, placed as it is on a major route through the Catania region.

## Paternò ❸

**Road map** E3. 46,000.
*Ferrovia Circumetnea (095-541 250). 095-797 01 11.*
*Carnival (before Lent).*

Surrounded by orchards of citrus fruit, this town lies at the foot of a **castle**, which has a stunning view of Mount Etna and the Simeto Valley. The massive square castle was built by Roger I in 1073, totally rebuilt in the 14th century and then restored twice in the 1900s. To get to the castle, go up Via Matrice, which will also take you to the **Chiesa Madre**, the Cathedral dedicated to Santa Maria dell'Alto. The church was originally Norman, but it was rebuilt in 1342.

The 12th-century Norman castle, dominating Paternò from above, with its wide-ranging views taking in the Simeto valley and Etna

## Centuripe ❹

**Road map** E3. 6,600. *from Catania or Enna, Romano (0935-73114). 0935-74755. Mon.*

Known as "the balcony of Sicily" because of the wide views, Centuripe is especially pretty in February and March, when snow-capped Mount Etna forms a striking contrast with the blossoms of orange and almond trees. An impor-

### THE CIRCUMETNEA RAILWAY

The picturesque carriages of the Ferrovia Circumetnea climb up the slopes of Mount Etna, passing through barren stretches of black lava alternating with luxuriant vegetation. This delightful route will take you back to the dawn of tourism, when the pace of travel was much slower than today. It takes about five hours to cover the 90 km (56 miles) or so between Catania and Riposto, the two termini, plus another hour to get back to Catania from Riposto via state rail. However, the rewards are magnificent views of terraced vineyards and almond and hazelnut groves, as well as the awe-inspiring volcano itself.

**Ferrovia Circumetnea**
Corso delle Provincie 13, Catania.
***Tel*** *095-541 250.* **www**.circumetnea.it

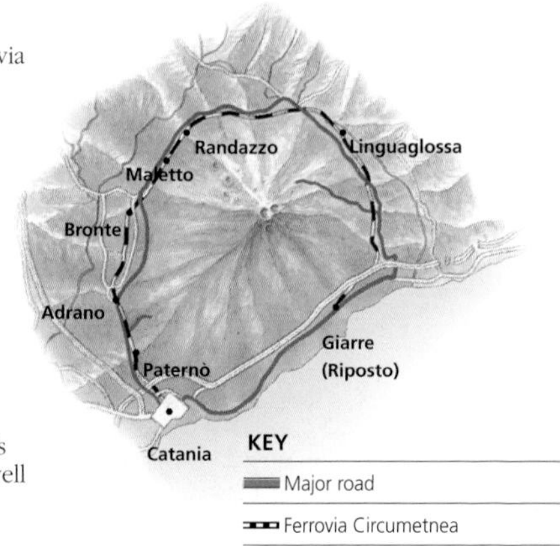

gira, perched on a sloping hillside, has preserved its fascinating Arab town plan

ınt Greek-Roman town, it ,as destroyed by Frederick II ıd rebuilt in the 16th entury. A long tree-lined venue leads to a viewing errace called **Castello di orradino**, with ruins of an nperial Roman mausoleum.

## Regalbuto ❺

**oad map** E3. *8,200.* *from atania.* *Pro Loco (0935-710 99).*

his town was destroyed ı 1261 by the inhabitants f Centuripe and rebuilt by Ianfredi. The heart of Regal-uto is **Piazza della Repub-lica**, with its multicoloured aving and **San Rocco**. **an Basilio** and **Santa Maria el Carmine** are also worth look. Nearby is the **Lake ozzillo dam**, the largest rtificial basin in Sicily, and a **anadian military cemetery** vith the graves of 490 soldiers vho were killed in 1943.

ne Saracen bridge on the Simeto river, near Adrano

## Agira ❻

**Road map** D3. *9,200.* *from Enna.* *Pro Loco, Largo Fiera 40 (0935-692 793).*

Because of its elevated position, Agira is clearly visible from a distance, with Mount Etna rising behind it. The ancient Siculan town of *Agyron* was colonized by the Greeks in 339 BC, and the ancient historian Diodorus Siculus was born here *(see p22)*. The most interesting aspect of Agyron's modern-day counterpart is its Arab layout, with Norman churches and patrician residences with Arab-style portals. Centrally located **Piazza Garibaldi** boasts **Sant'Antonio**, with a 16th-century wooden statue of San Silvestro and a painting on marble of *The Adoration of the Magi*. In the vicinity is **Santa Maria del Gesù**, with a crucifix by Fra' Umile da Petralia. In Piazza Roma is the lovely 16th-century façade of **San Salvatore**, with its bell tower covered with majolica tiles.

## Adrano ❼

**Road map** E3. *35,500.* *Ferrovia Circumetnea (095-541 250).* *Pro Loco, Via Roma 56 (095-769 94 23).* *Easter: the "Diavolata".*

A sanctuary dedicated to the local deity Adranos stood on a lava plateau facing the Valle del Simeto, where Sicilian hounds *(cirnecos)* were trained as hunting dogs *(see p170)*. The city was founded in the Greek period by Dionysius the Elder, who chose this natural balcony to build a military stronghold.

The centre of town is Piazza Umberto I, site of the **Norman Castle**, a massive, quadrilateral 11th-century construction. It houses the **Museo Archeologico**, with a collection of Neolithic pottery, Greek amphoras and mill-stones. A narrow stair, cut out of the Hohenstaufen wall in the Middle Ages, leads to the upper floors. Two have displays of archaeological items while the third houses the **Art Gallery**. The **Chiesa Madre**, built by the Normans and reconstructed in the 1600s, also stands in the same square.

### Environs

A byroad below the town leads to a dirt road that passes through citrus orchards for 1 km (half a mile) to the **Ponte dei Saraceni**, a 14th-century bridge on the Simeto river, with an **archaeological zone** nearby.

## Mascalucia 8

**Road map** E3. *24,500.* *from Catania.* *Pro Loco, Via Etnea 145 (095-727 77 90).*

On the eastern slopes of the volcano, just above Catania, to which it is connected by an uninterrupted series of villages and hamlets, is Mascalucia, a town of largish houses and villas. It is worth stopping here to visit the **Giardino Lavico**, at the Azienda Trinità farmstead, a small "oasis" surrounded by modern building development on the slopes of Etna. The "lava garden" consists of an organically cultivated citrus grove, a 17th-century house and a garden filled with prickly pears, yuccas and other plants that thrive in the lava soil. The orchard's irrigation canals were inspired by Arab gardens. For helicopter trips over Mount Etna, make inquiries at the Azienda.

**Giardino Lavico**
Azienda Agricola Trinità, Via Trinità 34. ***Tel*** *095-727 21 56.* *by appt.*

## Aci Castello 9

**Road map** E3. *18,000.*
*Corso Italia 302 (095-373 084).*
*AST (095-746 10 96 or 840-000 323).* *15 Jan: Festa di San Mauro.*

The name of this fishermen's village, a few kilometres from Catania, derives from the Norman **Castle** built on the top of a basalt rock jutting into the sea. It was built in 1076 from black lava and in 1299 was the base for the rebel Roger of Luria. The castle was subsequently destroyed by Frederick II of Aragón *(see p29)* after a long siege. Some rooms in the surviving parts are occupied by the **Museo Civico**, with archaeological and natural history collections relating to the Etna region (temporarily closed). There is also a small **Botanical Garden**. The town, with straight streets and low-rise houses, marks the beginning of the **Riviera dei Ciclopi**: according to Greek mythology, Polyphemus and his friends lived on Etna.

**The castle at Aci Castello, destroyed by Frederick II of Aragon**

## Aci Trezza 10

**Road map** E3.
*24 Jun: San Giovanni Battista.*

This picturesque fishing village, part of Aci Castello, was the setting for Giovanni Verga's novel *I Malavoglia* and for Luchino Visconti's film adaptation, *La Terra Trema (see p22 and p24).* The small harbour faces a pile of basalt rocks, the **Isole dei Ciclopi**, now a nature reserve. On the largest island there is a biology and oceanography station. According to Homer, Polyphemus hurled the rocks at the sea in an attempt to strike the fleeing Ulysses, who had blinded him.

**The Aci Trezza stacks, hurled by Polyphemus at Ulysses, according to Greek myth**

## Acireale ⓫

**Road map** E3. *48,500.* FS *Stazione FS (095-606 914 or 532 719).* *Messina–Catania.* *Via Scionti 15 (095-891 999).* *Carnival; Good Friday: Procession with traditional costumes; Jul: Santa Venere.*

Acireale stands on a lava terrace overlooking the Ionian Sea in the midst of citrus orchards. Since Roman times it has been famous as a spa town with sulphur baths. It is the largest town on the eastern side of Mount Etna and has been destroyed time and again by eruptions and earthquakes. It was finally rebuilt after the 1693 earthquake, emerging as a jewel of Sicilian Baroque architecture. The heart of town is **Piazza Duomo**, with its crowded cafés and ice-cream parlours. Acireale is dominated by its **Cathedral**, built in the late 1500s. The façade has two cusped bell towers covered with multicoloured majolica tiles. The Baroque portal leads to the vast interior with its frescoed vaults. In the right-hand transept is the Cappella di Santa Venera, the patron saint of the town. On the transept floor is a meridian marked out in 1843 by a Danish astronomer. Piazza Duomo also boasts the **Palazzo Comunale**, with a Gothic door and a fine wrought-iron balcony, and **Santi Pietro e Paolo**, built in the 17th century but with an 18th-century façade.

ue detail, :ireale

Close by is the **Teatro dei Pupi**, known for its puppet shows, and the **Pinacoteca dell'Accademia Zelantea**, with works by local painter Pietro Vasta, whose paintings also appear in the town's churches. The main street, **Corso Vittorio Emanuele**, has elegant shops and cafés and crosses squares such as Piazza Vigo, with **Palazzo Pennisi di Floristella** and **San Sebastiano**, decorated with a balustrade and statues.

The Chiesa Madre at Zafferana Etnea, on the eastern slopes of Etna

## Zafferana Etnea ⓬

**Road map** E3. *8,000.* *22 km (14 miles) from Catania.* *Pro Loco, Piazza L Sturzo 1 (095-708 28 25).*

Zafferana Etnea lies on the eastern slopes of Mount Etna and is one of the towns most frequently affected by recent lava flows. The most destructive eruptions occurred in 1852, when the lava reached the edge of town, and in 1992. The heart of Zafferana is its large tree-lined main square, dominated by the Baroque **Chiesa Madre**. The square is also the home of a permanent agricultural fair which, besides selling local wine and produce, has old farm implements on display.

**Environs**

Down the road towards Linguaglossa is **Sant'Alfio**, a town surrounded by vineyards and known for the huge 2,000 year-old tree called "Castagno dei cento cavalli" (Chestnut tree of 100 horses). According to legend, the leaves of this famous tree once protected Queen Jeanne d'Anjou and her retinue of 100 knights.

### *I MALAVOGLIA*

Published in 1881 in Milan, *I Malavoglia* (The House by the Medlar Tree) is a masterpiece by novelist Giovanni Verga *(see p22)* and of Italian *verismo*. Set on the Riviera dei Ciclopi at Aci Trezza, it describes the harsh life of fishermen and their constant struggle with the sea. The Toscano family, "I Malavoglia", are "all good seafaring people, just the opposite of their nickname" (*malavoglia* means ill-will). In 1947 Luchino Visconti made a film inspired by the book, *La Terra Trema*.

The beach at Aci Trezza, the setting for *I Malavoglia* (1881)

# Mount Etna ⓭

Mount Etna is fundamental to Sicily's nature and landscape. The Italian writer Leonardo Sciascia *(see p23)* called it "a huge house cat, that purrs quietly and awakens every so often". Etna is Europe's largest active volcano and dominates the whole of eastern Sicily. Feared and loved, Etna is both snow and fire, lush vegetation and black lava. Around the crater you can still see the remnants of numbers of ancient vents. Further down is the eerie, barren landscape of the Valle del Bove.

**Valle del Bove**
*Many recent lava flows have ended here. The craters Calanna and Trifoglietto I are of very ancient date. This is one of the most fascinating places in the Etna area.*

**The Sicilian Hound**
*The Sicilian hound or* cirneco *is a breed of dog native to the Etna area. In ancient times it was a hunting dog.*

**The 1983** eruption was the first that man was able to divert.

Ragalna

Nicolosi

Paternò

Catania

Acireale

2001 and 2002 eruptions

Zafferana

## THE LARGEST VOLCANO IN EUROPE

Etna, or Mongibello (from the Italian *monte* and the Arab *gebel*, both meaning "mountain"), is a relatively "recent" volcano that emerged two million years ago. It has erupted frequently in known history. Some of the most devastating eruptions were in 1381 and 1669, when the lava reached Catania. The most recent ones took place in 2001 and 2002. On these occasions the lava flow caused extensive damage to Rifugio Sapienza, destroyed the ski facilities and the cable-car apparatus and came within 4 km (2.5 miles) of the village of Nicolosi. Eruptions that have occurred in the last 20 years are shown here.

**Lowland Landscape**
*The breakdown of volcanic material in the valley below Mount Etna has resulted in very fertile land which supports almonds, olives, grapes, citrus fruit and vegetables below 1,000 m (3,280 ft).*

*For hotels and restaurants in this region see pp203–7 and pp218–21*

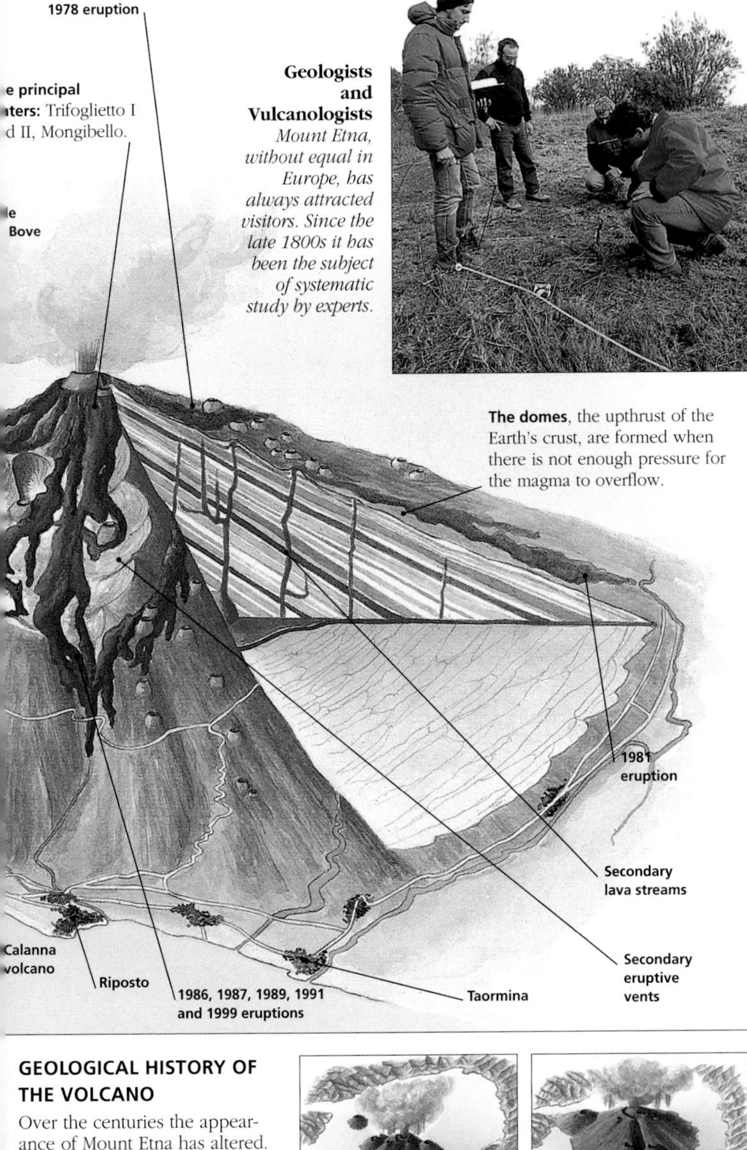


**Geologists and Vulcanologists** *Mount Etna, without equal in Europe, has always attracted visitors. Since the late 1800s it has been the subject of systematic study by experts.*

## GEOLOGICAL HISTORY OF THE VOLCANO

Over the centuries the appearance of Mount Etna has altered. In 1865 the summit was at 3,313 m (10,867 ft); in 1932 it was 3,263 m (10,703 ft); and today it is 3,320 m (10,892 ft) high. Eruptions in the central crater are rare, but they are frequent in the side vents, and here they create smaller secondary cones.

On the eastern slope of Mount Etna is a huge chasm known as the Valle del Bove, the result of an immense explosion.

**First stage, 200,000–100,000 years ago (Monte Calanna)**

**Second stage, 80,000 years ago (Vulcano Trifoglietto)**

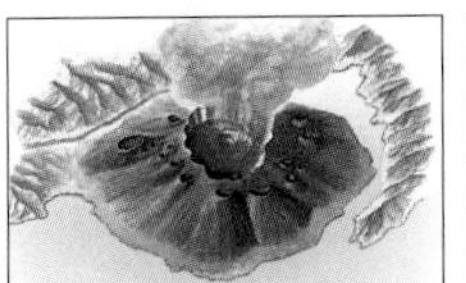

**Third stage, 64,000 years ago (the cone collapses)**

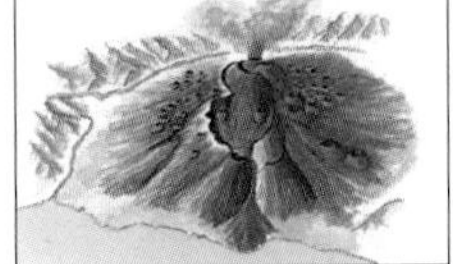

**Fourth, current stage (the Mongibello cone)**

# Exploring Mount Etna

A protected area 58,000 ha (143,260 acres) in size, Mount Etna offers many opportunities for excursions, and attracts thousands of visitors every year. A popular excursion is from Zafferana to the Valle del Bove, the spectacular hollow whose shape was changed by the 1992 eruptions. The hike up to the large craters at the summit is not to be missed. Start off at the Rifugio Sapienza and Rifugio Citelli hostels and Piano Provenzana (after suffering eruption damage, these hiker centres are now being rebuilt). A trip around the mountain is also thrilling: from the Sapienza to the Monte Scavo camp, Piano Provenzana and the former Menza camp. There are also several lava grottoes.

**The Effects of an Eruption**
*This chapel was one of many buildings destroyed in the massive lava flows caused by the 1983 eruptions.*

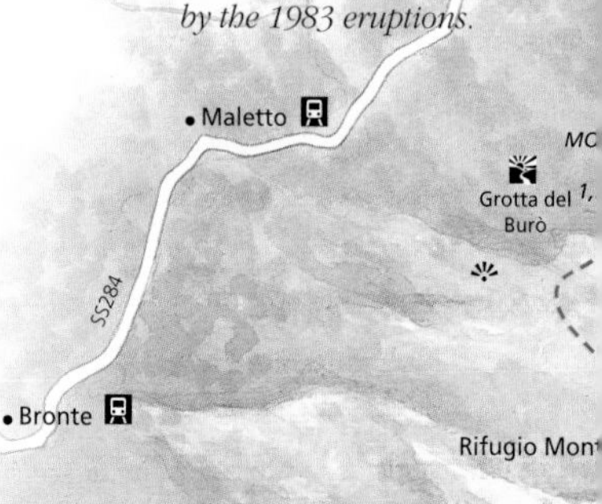

**Skiing on Etna**
*Although there are few chair lifts, skiing on Mount Etna is a unique experience. Besides the regular ski runs you can do cross-country skiing or mountain climbing in the snow.*

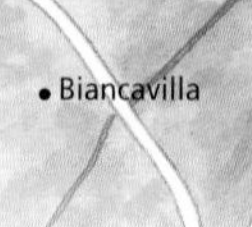


## NATURE ON MOUNT ETNA

Despite the many eruptions and the bitter cold that freezes the terrain in winter, many species of plants have succeeded in colonizing the lava soil. At high altitudes you can see small lichens, camomile and soapwort on the slopes. Poplars thrive in the more humid areas. Further down are woods of beech, birch, larch and Corsican pine. Centuries of hunting have reduced the animal population, though there are still rabbits, weasels, wildcats and foxes, while the main bird species are the Sicilian partridge and the *Dendrocopus* woodpecker.

**Pine forest on the slopes of Etna**

**Rifugio Sapienza**
*At over 1,800 m (5,904 ft), the Sapienza hostel is a base for hikers in the summer and for skiers in winter.*

## VISITORS' CHECKLIST

**Road map** E2, E3, F3. ✈ *095-723 91 11.* 🚌 *AST (095-746 10 96); SAIS (095-536 168).* FS *Catania (095-532 719).* 🚆 *Ferrovia Circumetnea (095-541 111).* **Parco dell'Etna** *(095-821 111).* **Italian Alpine Club (CAI)** *(095-715 35 15).* **Etna Alpine Guides** *(095-914 141).* **Rifugio Sapienza** *(hostel) (095-915 321).* **www**.parcoetna.ct.it

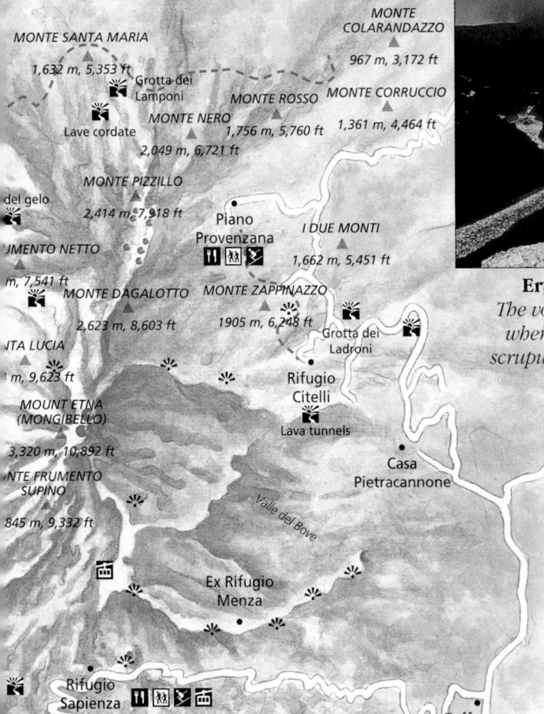


**Eruptions and Lava Flows**
*The volcano can be visited even when it is active, provided you scrupulously follow instructions. Above, the 1991 eruption.*

**KEY**

- Tourist information
- Major road
- Ferrovia Circumetnea
- Cable car
- Area of natural beauty, interest
- Restaurant
- Ski run
- Cross-country skiing
- Viewpoint
- Footpath (Trail)

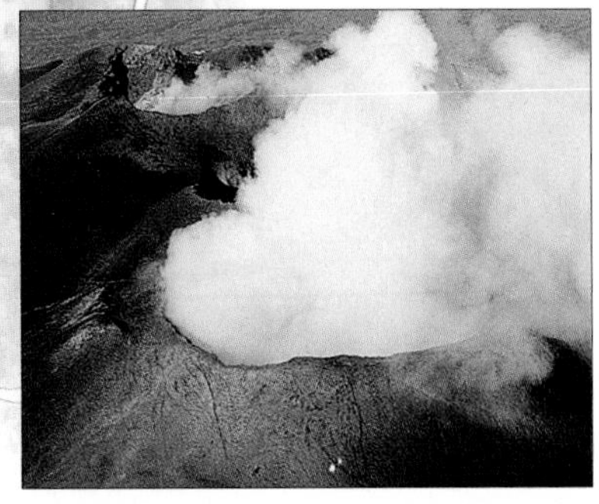

**Craters and Eruptions**
*At this stage in the history of Mount Etna, most of the eruptions occur in the side vents, while on the summit craters the occasional explosive eruption may take place.*

## Bronte ⓮

**Road map** E3. 18,500. *Ferrovia Circumetnea.* *Pro Loco, Via D'Annunzio 8 (095-774 71 11).* *Oct: Pistachio festival.*

Situated on a terraced lava slope, Bronte was founded by Charles V. In 1799 Ferdinand IV of Bourbon gave the town and surrounding estates to Admiral Horatio Nelson, who had helped him suppress the revolts in Naples in 1799. In 1860, after the success of Garibaldi's Red Shirts in Sicily, the peasants of Bronte rebelled, demanding that Nelson's land be split up among them, but their revolt was put down by Garibaldi's men. The episode was immortalized in a short story by Verga *(see pp22–3)*. The eruptions of 1651, 1832 and 1843 struck the centre of Bronte, which has however managed to retain its original character, with stone houses and steeply rising alleyways. The 16th-century **Annunziata** has a sandstone portal and, inside, an *Annunciation* (1541) attributed to Antonello Gagini *(see p53)* as well as some 17th-century canvases. In the village of Piana Cuntarati, the **Masseria Lombardo** farm has been converted into an Ethnographic Museum which, among many interesting objects, has an Arab paper mill dating from the year 1000. Today Bronte is famous for the production of pistachios.

**Environs**

Around 12 km (7 miles) from Bronte is **Castello di Maniace**, a Benedictine monastery founded by Margaret of Navarre in 1174, on the spot where the Byzantine general Maniakes had defeated the Arabs. Destroyed by the 1693 earthquake, the site became the property of Horatio Nelson. Today it looks like a fortified farm, with a garden of exotic plants. Nearby is the medieval **Santa Maria**, with scenes from the Book of Genesis sculpted on the capitals of the columns.

**Castello di Maniace**
***Tel*** *095-690 018.* *9am–1pm, 2:30–7pm (2:30–5pm Nov–Mar).*

## Randazzo ⓯

**Road map** E3. 11,500. *Ferrovia Circumetnea.* *Pro Loco, Piazza Municipio 17 (095-799 14 31).* *Easter Week, 15 Aug: Processione della "Vara", Jul–Aug: medieval festival.* *Sun.*

Built of lava stone 765 m (2,509 ft) above sea level, Randazzo is the town closest to the craters of Mount Etna, but it has never been inundated with lava. In the Middle Ages it was surrounded by a 3-km (2-mile) city wall, some parts of which have survived, such as the **Porta Aragonese** gate, on the old road to Messina.

Medieval window in central Randazzo

The major monument and symbol of the town is **Santa Maria**, a basilica built in 1217–39: the towered apses with the characteristic ribbing

The restored Via degli Archi with its cobbled lava paving

are all that is left of the original Norman construction, while the double lancet windows and portals are Catalan. The nave with its black lava columns has multicoloured marble altars and a marble basin sculpted by the Gagini school. **Corso Umberto**, the main street in Randazzo, leads to **Piazza San Francesco d'Assisi**, dominated by the **Palazzo Comunale**, once the monastery of the Minor Order, which has an elegant cloister with a cistern.

The narrow side streets have many examples of medieval architecture. The most characteristic of these is **Via degli Archi**, which has a lovely pointed arch and black lava cobblestone paving. In **Piazza San Nicolò** is the church of the same name, with a late Renaissance façade made of lava stone. In the interior there is a fine statue of San Nicola of Bari sculpted in 1523 by Antonello Gagini. The bell tower was damaged by an earthquake in 1783. Its reconstruction replaced the original cusp with a wrought-iron balcony. After a turn to the left, Corso Umberto crosses a square where **San Martino** stands. It has a beautiful bell tower with single lancet windows with two-coloured borders, and a polygonal spire.

The Castello di Maniace, the property of Lord Nelson's heirs until 1981

The Randazzo skyline, dominated by the bell tower of San Martino

Opposite is the **Castle**, which was a prison in the 1500s and will be the new home of the **Museo Archeologico Vagliasindi**, with interesting Greek finds from Tissa, such as the famous vase depicting the punishment of the Harpies.

## Linguaglossa ⓰

**Road map** E3. 6,000. *Ferrovia Circumetnea.* *095-643 094; APT Piano Provenzana (095-647 352); Pro Loco (095-643 094).* *Last Sun in Aug: Mount Etna festival.*

Linguaglossa is the largest village on the northeastern slopes of Etna as well as the starting point for excursions to the volcano summit and for the ski runs. Its name derives from a 17th-century lava flow that was called *lingua glossa* (big tongue). The town streets are paved with black lava and the houses have small wrought-iron balconies. The **Chiesa Madre**, dedicated to Santa Maria delle Grazie, is worth a visit for its Baroque decoration and fine coffered ceiling. Linguaglossa also boasts the **Museo delle Genti dell'Etna**, a museum with geological and natural history exhibits as well as everyday objects and craftsmen's tools.

**Museo delle Genti dell'Etna**
Piazza Annunziata. ***Tel*** *095-643 094.* *9am–1pm, 4–8pm Mon–Sat, 9:30am–12:30pm Sun.*

## Giarre ⓱

**Road map** F3. *27,200.* *Ferrovia Circumetnea.* *from Catania.* *095-963 111.*

This town lies in the middle of citrus groves extending down to the sea. Giarre is famous for its hand-made wrought-iron products. The heart of town is **Piazza Duomo**, dominated by the impressive Neo-Classical **Duomo**, built in 1794 and dedicated to Sant'Isidoro Agricola. The façade has two square bell towers with windows and a tambour. There are many delightful patrician residences made of lava stone in the old town. In the nearby village of Macchia is the **Museo degli Usi e dei Costumi delle Genti dell'Etna**, an ethnographic museum. One interesting exhibit here is a reproduction of a typical Etna farmhouse, with its old kitchen and bread oven, well and washtub. Also on display are farm implements, looms, and period photographs and daguerreotypes.

**Museo degli Usi e dei Costumi delle Genti dell'Etna**
***Tel*** *095-963 111.* *By appointment only; 9am–1pm Mon–Fri (4:30–6pm Mon & Thu).*

The rusticated façade of the late 18th-century Neo-Classical Duomo in Giarre

# Street-by-Street:Taormina ⓲

Byzantine mosaic

On a bluff above the Ionian Sea, at the foot of Monte Tauro, Taormina is Sicily's most famous tourist resort. Immersed in luxuriant subtropical vegetation, it was a favourite stop for those on the Grand Tour and the preferred summer residence of aristocrats and bankers, from Wilhelm II of Germany to the Rothschilds. In its time the town has been Siculan, Greek and Roman, but its medieval layout gives it today's look.

**Piazza IX Aprile**

*The second largest square in Taormina is home to the churches of San Giorgio and San Giuseppe, the Torre dell'Orologio and the Wünderbar Café.*

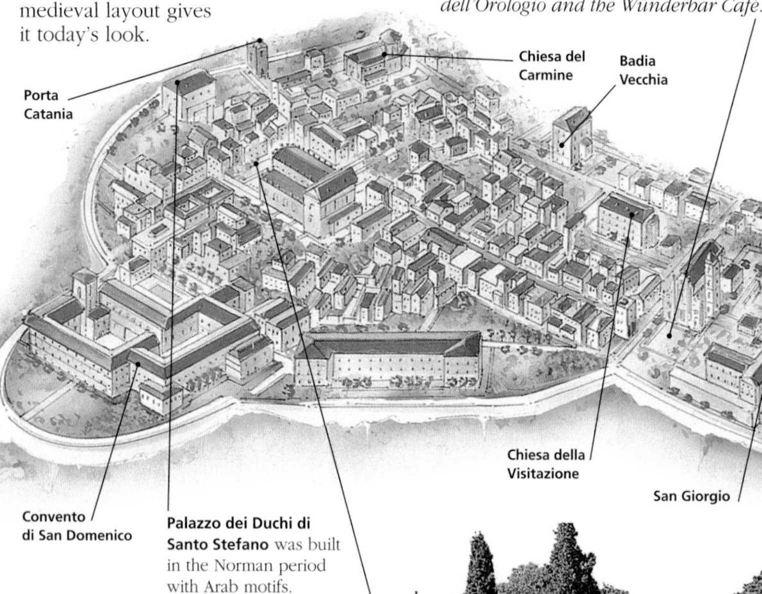


**Palazzo dei Duchi di Santo Stefano** was built in the Norman period with Arab motifs.

★ **Piazza del Duomo**

*This is the heart of town, at the western end of Corso Umberto I. In the middle of the square is a Baroque fountain, facing the Cathedral of San Nicolò and the Palazzo Comunale (Town Hall).*

**Villa Comunale**

*Located on a cliff with a stunning view, this lovely garden was donated to the town by a rich Englishwoman, an aristocrat who had fallen in love with Taormina.*

For hotels and restaurants in this region see pp203–7 and pp218–21

## VISITORS' CHECKLIST

**Road map** F2. *10,500.* *Catania Fontanarossa 70 km (43 miles).* *5 km (3 miles) from Giardini-Naxos.* *SAIS (0942-625 301).* *AAST (0942-232 43).* *Wed.* *June: Film Festival; Jul–Sep: Taormina Arte.*

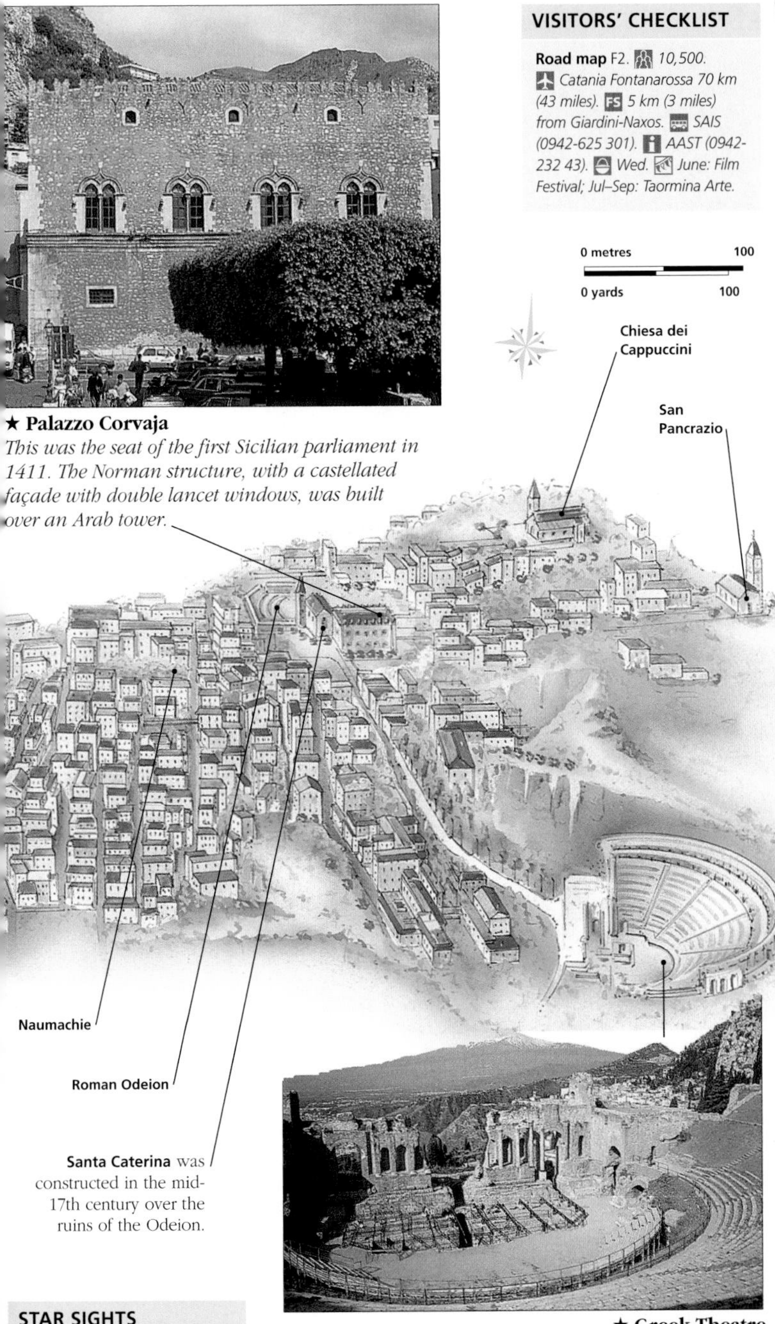


**★ Palazzo Corvaja**
*This was the seat of the first Sicilian parliament in 1411. The Norman structure, with a castellated façade with double lancet windows, was built over an Arab tower.*

**Santa Caterina** was constructed in the mid-17th century over the ruins of the Odeion.

**★ Greek Theatre**
*This is the second largest ancient theatre in Sicily after the one in Syracuse. It was originally built in the Hellenistic age (3rd century BC) and was almost entirely rebuilt by the Romans in the 2nd century AD. The theatre has a magnificent view of the sea and Mount Etna.*

### STAR SIGHTS

- ★ Piazza del Duomo
- ★ Palazzo Corvaja
- ★ Greek Theatre

# Exploring Taormina

From Easter to October Taormina is inundated with visitors, so if you prefer peace and quiet it is probably a good idea to go out of season. The climate is mild here even in the winter. The town is especially delightful in the spring, when the air is filled with the scent of orange and lemon blossoms, the gardens are in bloom and Mount Etna is still snow-capped. A regular shuttle bus links the car park to the centre of town, or you can park at Mazzarò and take the cable car to town.

**Corso Umberto I, running the length of the town**

### Corso Umberto I

The main street in Taormina begins at **Porta Messina** and ends at **Porta Catania**, a gate crowned by a building showing the municipal coat of arms. The street is lined with shops, *pasticcerie* and cafés famous for their glamorous clientele, like the **Wünderbar**, where you can try the cocktails that Liz Taylor and Richard Burton were so fond of. Halfway down the Corso is **Piazza IX Aprile**, a panoramic terrace with **Sant'Agostino** (now the Municipal Library) and **San Giuseppe**. A short distance away is the **Porta di Mezzo** gate with the 17th-century Torre dell'Orologio, or clock tower. Above and below Corso Umberto I there are stepped alleyways and lanes passing through quiet, characterful areas. One such alley leads to the **Naumachie**, a massive Roman brick wall dating back to the Imperial Age with 18 arched niches, which once supported a huge cistern.

**The Wünderbar has always been a favourite with film stars**

### Palazzo Corvaja

Piazza Vittorio Emanuele. ***Tel*** *0942-23243.* *9am–1pm, 4–6pm Tue–Sun.*

Taormina's grandest building dates from the 15th century, although it was originally an Arab tower. The austere façade topped by crenellation is made elegant by the three-mullioned windows and the limestone and black lava decorative motifs. The courtyard stairway decorated with reliefs of the *Birth of Eve* and *The Original Sin* takes you to the *piano nobile*, where the Sicilian parliament met in 1411 and where Queen Blanche of Navarre and her retinue lived for a short period. Some of the rooms are open to visitors. On the ground floor is the local tourist information bureau. Next to the palazzo are the Baroque **Santa Caterina** and the ruins of the **Odeion**, a small Roman theatre.

### Greek Theatre

Via Teatro Greco. ***Tel*** *0942-23220.* *9am–1 hr before sunset daily.*

Set in a spectacular position, this theatre is one of the most famous Sicilian monuments in the world. It was built in the Hellenistic age and then almost completely rebuilt in the Roman period, when it became an arena for gladiatorial combat.

From the cavea, carved from the side of a hill, the view takes in Giardini-Naxos *(see p180)* and Mount Etna. The upper part of the nine-section theatre is surrounded by a double portico. The theatre originally had a diameter of 109 m (358 ft) and a seating capacity of 5,000. Behind the stage area stood a wall with niches and a colonnade. Some of the Corinthian columns are still standing.

**The Greek Theatre in Taormina, capable of seating 5,000 spectators**

### Villa Comunale

Via Bagnoli Croci. *9am–one hour before sunset in summer; 8am–sunset in winter.*

Dedicated to Duke Colonna di Cesarò, this public garden was bequeathed to Taormina by an English aristocrat, Florence Trevelyan, who fell in love with the town. Situated on a cliff with a magnificent view of Etna and the coast, the garden is filled with Mediterranean and tropical plants. A characteristic part of the garden is the arabesque-decorated tower, similar to a Chinese pagoda, that the owner used for bird-watching.

A view of Piazza del Duomo: in the foreground, the Baroque fountain, which faces the Cathedral

### Cathedral

Piazza Duomo. **Tel** *0942-23123.*
*8am–1pm, 4–7pm.* *May–Sep: 7pm (Sun also 10am, 11:30am, 6pm); Oct–Apr: 6pm (Sun also 10am, 11:30am).*

The Cathedral (San Nicolò) was built in the 13th century and has been altered over the centuries. The austere façade is crowned by crenellation. The 17th-century portal is decorated with a medallion pattern, and over this are a small rose window and two windows with pointed arches. The nave has two side aisles and a wooden ceiling, as well as some interesting works of art: *The Visitation* by Antonio Giuffrè (15th century), a polyptych by Antonello Saliba of the *Virgin Mary and Child*, and an alabaster statue of the Virgin Mary by the Gagini school. In Piazza Duomo, in the middle of which is a lovely Baroque fountain, is the Town Hall, **Palazzo del Municipio**, with a storey lined with Baroque windows.

### Palazzo dei Duchi di Santo Stefano

Via De Spuches.
*8am–noon, 3–6pm.*

This 13th-century building near Porta Catania was the residence of the De Spuches, the Spanish dukes of Santo Stefano di Brifa and princes of Galati, two towns on the Ionian coast near Messina. In this masterpiece of Sicilian Gothic architecture the influence of Arab masons is clearly seen in the wide black lava frieze alternating with rhomboidal white Syracusan stone inlay. Note the tri-lobated arches and double lancet windows on the façade. The interior has a permanent exhibition of the works of sculptor Giuseppe Marzullo.

### Castelmola

A winding road of 5 km (3 miles) leads to this village perched on a rock. Today you only see the ruins of a medieval castle, but in antiquity this may have been the site of the ancient acropolis of Tauromenion. From Castelmola you can enjoy one of the most famous panoramic views in the world, especially fine at sunset.

Palazzo dei Duchi di Santo Stefano, influenced by Arab masons

View of Isola Bella from the steps that go from Taormina to the beach at Mazzarò

### Mazzarò

This small town is virtually Taormina's beach. It can be reached easily by cable car from Taormina or via the road leading to the Catania–Messina state road N144. An alternative is the steps which descend from the centre of Taormina through gardens of bougainvillea in bloom. From the **Bay of Mazzarò**, with its crystal clear water, you can go on excursions to other sights along the coast: **Capo Sant'Andrea**, with the **Grotta Azzurra**, a spectacular marine grotto, can be visited by boat; to the south are the stacks of **Capo Taormina** and the beach at **Villagonia**; and to the north are **Isola Bella**, one of the most exclusive places in the area, partly because of its clear waters, and the beaches at the **Baia delle Sirene** and the **Lido di Spisone**. Further on is the beach at **Mazzeo**, a long stretch of sand that leads as far as Letojanni and continues up to **Lido Silemi**.

### Letojanni

This small seaside resort is 5 km (3 miles) from Taormina. Busy and bustling in the summer, it is perhaps best seen in the spring or autumn. Locals and visitors alike come here to dine out in one of the many good fish restaurants by the water.

Ancient Silenic mask

The sea at Giardini-Naxos, the first Greek colony in Sicily

## Giardini-Naxos ⓳

**Road map** F3. 9,000. Catania Fontanarossa 66 km (41 miles). FS 095-532 719. Autolinee SAIS (0942-625 179). AAST, Via Tysandros 54 (0942-510 10).

Between Capo Taormina and Capo Schisò, Giardini-Naxos is a seaside resort near what was once the first Greek colony in Sicily. Thucydides relates that Naxos was founded in 735 BC by Chalcidians led by the Athenian Thucles, and Naxos became the base for all further colonization of the island. Naxos was destroyed by Dionysius of Syracuse in 403 BC. On the headland of Capo Schisò, amid lemon trees and prickly pears, are the **Naxos excavations**.

Of the two phases in the life of the city, the one which yielded the most important (if scarce) archaeological finds dates from the 6th and 5th centuries BC, with remains of the city walls and houses as well as stones from a temple that may have been dedicated to Aphrodite. In the village of **Giardini**, by the beach, there are still some fine mansions on the oldest streets.

**Naxos Excavations**

***Tel*** *09425-1001.* *9am–1 hr before sunset (to 4pm Nov–Mar).*

## Castiglione di Sicilia ⓴

**Road map** F3. 4,000. *Ferrovia Circumetnea.* *Giardini di Naxos.* *Town hall (0942-980 211 or 800-010 552).*

This pretty village lies on a crag dominating the **Alcantara Valley**. It was founded by the Greeks, then, many years later, it became a royal city under the Normans and the Hohenstaufens, and the fief of Roger of Lauria at the end of the 13th century.

Castiglione still retains its medieval layout, the narrow streets converging in central **Piazza Lauria**. From this point, moving up the hill, you will see many churches. The first is the **Chiesa Madre**, or San Pietro *(see p185)*, which still has a Norman apse; then there are the 17th-century **Chiesa delle Benedettine** and the Baroque **Sant' Antonio** and **Chiesa Della Catena**. At the top of the village is the medieval **Castel Leone**, built by the Normans over the Arab fortifications, where you have a view of the **medieval bridge** on the Alcantara River.

The Alcantara River flowing between basalt cliffs

### Environs

The **Alcantara ravine**, 20 m (66 ft) deep, cut out of black basalt by the rushing waters of the Alcantara river, is a marvellously compelling sight. If the weather is good, it is worth following the gorge for about 150 m (490 ft), but only if you can manage without raincoats and weatherproof gear. There is also a lift (elevator) that you can take to avoid the long flight of steps that leads from the parking area to the entrance of the ravine.

Forza d'Angrò, a medieval village with a 16th-century castle at the summit

### THE PELORITANI MOUNTAINS

The Monti Peloritani form a ridge between two seas peaking in **Monte Poverello** (1,279 m, 4,195 ft) and the **Pizzo di Vernà** (1,286 m, 4,218 ft). It is a marvellous area for excursions, often with stunning views of the sea and Mount Etna, in a landscape of knife-edge ridges and woods. On 4 August a major pilgrimage is made to the **Antennamare Sanctuary**, while 7 September is the day for festivities at the **Sanctuary of the Madonna del Crispino**, above the village of **Monforte San Giorgio**. Many of the mountain villages are interesting from a historical and artistic point of view. **Forza d'Angrò**, dominated by a 16th-century castle; **Casalvecchio I Siculo**, with the Arab-Norman Basilica dei Santi Pietro e Paolo; **Savoca**, with Capuchin catacombs and embalmed bodies; **Ali**, which has a strong Arab flavour; **Itala**, overlooking the Ionian Sea, with San Pietro e Paolo, built by Roger I as a thanks offering for a victory over the Arabs; and lastly **Mili San Pietro**, with the basilica-monastery of Santa Maria, which was founded in 1082 by Roger I.

# Messina ㉑

The position of this ancient city, founded by colonists from Messenia in Greece, has always been the key to its importance. Situated between the eastern and western Mediterranean, and between the two vice-royalties of Naples and Sicily, Messina has always been influenced by its role as a meeting point. Over the centuries it has been populated by Armenians, Arabs, Jews and other communities from the large maritime cities of Europe, becoming increasingly important up to the anti-Spanish revolt of 1674–78, after which the city fell into decline. Already damaged by the 1783 earthquake, Messina was almost totally razed in 1908.

The votive column at the entrance to the port of Messina

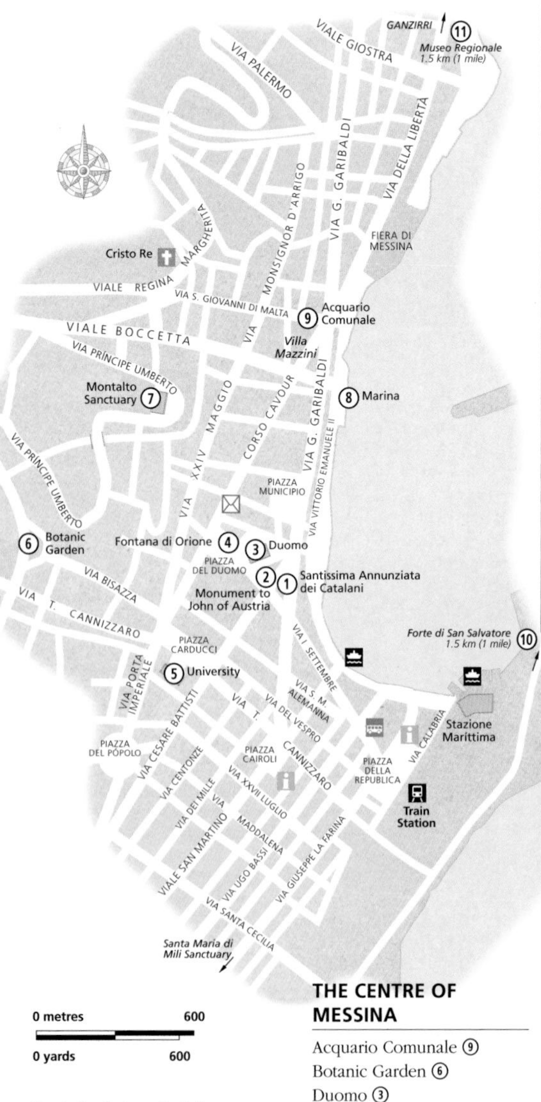


**Key to Symbols** *see back flap*

## THE CENTRE OF MESSINA

Acquario Comunale ⑨
Botanic Garden ⑥
Duomo ③
Fontana di Orione ④
Forte di San Salvatore ⑩
Marina ⑧
Montalto Sanctuary ⑦
Monument to John of Austria ②
Museo Regionale ⑪
Santissima Annunziata dei Catalani ①
University ⑤

## Exploring Messina

The city developed around the harbour and its layout is quite easy to understand if you arrive by sea. The defences of the **Forte San Salvatore** and the **Lanterna di Raineri**, on the peninsula of the same name that protects the harbour to the east, are your introduction to Messina, which lies on the gently sloping sides of the Peloritani Mountains. The main streets are **Via Garibaldi** (which skirts the seafront by the harbour) and **Via I Settembre**, which leads from the sea to the centre of town around **Piazza Duomo**. Interesting attractions such as the **Botanic Garden** and the **Montalto Sanctuary** are located on the hillside above the city.

### Santissima Annunziata dei Catalani

Piazza dei Catalani. ***Tel*** *090-661 691 or 360 585.* *by appointment only.*

Paradoxically, the devastating 1908 earthquake helped to "restore" the original 12th–13th-century structure of this Norman period church, as it destroyed almost all the later additions and alterations. The nave has two side aisles and leads to the apse with its austere brick cupola.

***For hotels and restaurants in this region see pp203–7 and pp218–21***

The Orion Fountain, with the Duomo and the Torre dell'Orologio in the background

### Monument to John of Austria

In the square in front of the Annunziata church is a statue of John of Austria, the admiral who won the famous Battle of Lepanto, with his foot on the head of the defeated Ottoman commander Alì Pasha. The work was sculpted in 1572 by Andrea Calamech.

The pedestal celebrates the formation of the Holy League and the defeat of the Turks in this historic naval battle. One of the sailors taking part was the great Miguel de Cervantes, author of *Don Quixote*, who recovered from his wounds in a Messina hospital.

### Duomo

The Cathedral is in Piazza Duomo, in the heart of town. Although it was reconstructed after the 1908 earthquake and the 1943 bombings, it has preserved its medieval aspect. It was built by Henry VI Hohenstaufen in 1197. The façade was totally rebuilt but you can still see the original central portal built in the early Middle Ages, decorated with two lions and a statue of the Virgin Mary and Infant Jesus. The side doors are decorated with statues of the Apostles and lovely inlay and reliefs. On the left-hand side of the façade is the large campanile, almost 60 m (197 ft) high, built to house a unique object – the largest astronomical clock in the world, built by a Strasbourg firm in 1933. Noon is the signal for a number of mechanical figures to move in elaborate patterns, geared by huge cogwheels. Almost all of the impressive interior is the result of fine post-war reconstruction. Some sculptures on the trusses in the central section of the two-aisle nave, a 15th-century basin and the 1525 statue of St John the Baptist by Gagini are part of the original decoration. The doorways in the right-hand vestibule leading to the Treasury are of note, as is the tomb of Archbishop Palmieri, sculpted in 1195. In the transept is an organ, built after World War II, with five keyboards and 170 stops. The side aisles house many works of art, especially Gothic funerary monuments, most of which have been reconstructed.

### Orion Fountain

This lovely 15th-century fountain stands next to the Duomo. It incorporates statues representing four rivers: the Tiber, Nile, Ebro and Camaro (the last of which was channelled into Messina via the first aqueduct in the city specifically to supply the fountain with water).

One of the two lions on the portal of the Duomo

## VISITORS' CHECKLIST

**Road map** F2. *236,000.*
*SNAV (090-364 044).*
FS *(090-532 719).*
*AAST, Piazza Cairoli 45 (090-293 5292); AAPT, Via Calabria 301b (090-674 236).*
*Carnival: procession of floats with tableaux; Aug: Cavalcata dei Giganti.*
**www**.aptmessina.it

### University

The University is in **Piazza Carducci**. It was founded in 1548, closed by the Spanish in 1679 and reconstructed at last in 1927. Besides the university faculties, the complex also includes the small **Museo Zoologico Cambria** (tel: 090-392 721), with its fine collections of vertebrates, shells and insects. Follow Viale Principe Umberto, and you come to the **Botanic Garden** and the **Montalto Sanctuary**, with the *Madonna of Victory*, built after the Battle of Lepanto, standing out against the sky.

## THE 1908 EARTHQUAKE

At 5:20am on 28 December 1908, it seemed that nature was intent upon destroying Messina: an earthquake and a tidal wave struck at the same time, bringing over 91 per cent of the buildings to the ground and killing 60,000 people. Reggio Calabria, on the other side of the Straits of Messina, was also destroyed. Reconstruction began immediately. Some of the remains of the old town were salvaged by being incorporated into a new urban plan, designed by Luigi Borzi. His scheme gives Messina its present-day appearance.

Messina the day after the earthquake

### Marina

After walking along the Marina in 1789, the author Frances Elliot wrote: "There is nothing in the world like the Messina seafront. It is longer and more elegant than Via Chiaia in Naples, more vigorous and picturesque than the Promenade in Nice…". Not far away is another focal point in Messina, **Piazza dell'Unità d'Italia**. The buildings that lined the marina before the earthquake were part of the "Palazzata" complex, also known as the **Teatro Marittimo**. The Teatro was a series of buildings that extended for more than a kilometre in the heart of the port area – the centre of commercial transactions – which also included the homes of the most powerful families in Messina.

### Forte San Salvatore

Beyond the busy harbour area, at the very tip of the curved peninsula that protects the harbour, is Forte San Salvatore, built in the 17th century to block access to the Messina marina. On top of one of the tall towers in this impressive fort is a statue of the *Madonna della Lettera*: according to tradition, the Virgin Mary sent a letter of benediction to the inhabitants of Messina in AD 42.

On **Via Garibaldi** is the bustling **Stazione Marittima**, the boarding point for the ferry boats that connect Messina to Calabria on the mainland of Italy.

**One of the five panels of Antonello da Messina's *St Gregory Polyptych* (1473)**

### Acquario Comunale

The garden of the **Villa Mazzini** is decorated with busts and statues, and is also home to the Municipal Aquarium. Next door is the **Palazzo della Prefettura**, in front of which is the **Fountain of Neptune**, sculpted in the mid-1500s by Giovanni Angelo Montorsoli. The statues are 19th-century copies and the originals are on display in the Museo Regionale.

***Madonna and Child*, Francesco Laurana**

### Museo Regionale

Viale della Libertà. ***Tel*** *090-361292.* *9am–1:30pm Mon–Sat (also Apr–Oct: 4–6:30pm Tue, Thu, Sat; Nov–Mar: 3–5:30pm Tue, Thu, Sat); 9am–12:30pm Sun & hols.*

This fascinating museum is close to Piazza dell'Unità d'Italia. It boasts a major collection of art works salvaged after the catastrophic 1908 earthquake. In fact, most of the works come from the Civico Museo Peloritano, which was in the now destroyed Monastery of St Gregory. The museum has 12 rooms that present an overview of the artistic splendour of old Messina and include a number of famous paintings. At the entrance there are 12 18th-century bronze panels depicting the *Legend of the Sacred Letter*. Some of the most important works include paintings from the Byzantine period and fragments from the Duomo ceiling (room 1); the Gothic art in room 2; the examples of Renaissance Messina in room 3; the *Polyptych* that Antonello da Messina *(see p23)* painted for the Monastery of St Gregory

### BRIDGING THE STRAITS OF MESSINA

Communications with the mainland have always been a fundamental issue for Sicily, and for over 30 years the question of building a bridge over the Straits of Messina has been debated. There has even been a proposal to build a tunnel anchored to the sea bed. This idea now seems to have been discarded, and work on the design of a bridge is under way. In 1981 the Società Stretto di Messina was established with the aim of designing a single-span suspension bridge over the straits to connect Torre Faro and Punta Pezzo – a distance of 3 km (2 miles). A multitude of problems still needs to be tackled, however, one of which is the constant danger of earth quakes.

**A 1997 design for the planned bridge over the Straits of Messina**

(room 4) and, in the same room, a *Madonna and Child* sculpture attributed to Francesco Laurana and a 15th-century oil on panel by an unknown Flemish artist.

Room 9 has two of the "pearls" of the museum, two masterpieces by Caravaggio, executed in 1608–1609: *The Raising of Lazarus* and *The Nativity*. This great artist's sojourn in Messina exerted an influence on other artists, giving rise to a local Caravaggesque school, as can be seen in the canvases by Alonso Rodriguez, *Supper at Emmaus and Doubting Thomas*, on view in room 10.

**The Pantano Grande lake at Ganzirri, used for shellfish farming**

**Environs**

By proceeding northwards along the coastline of the Straits, past the Museo Regionale, you will come to **Grotta** and then, about 7 km (4 miles) from Messina, the turn-off to **Ganzirri**. A short drive along the coastal road takes you to the **Pantano Grande** (or Lago Grande), a lagoon that measures 30 ha (74 acres) and is at most 7 m (23 ft) deep. One side of the lagoon consists of a long sandbar and it is connected to the sea by an artificial canal. The Pantano Grande is supplied with fresh water from underground streams and it is used for shellfish farming on a large scale. This point is quite close to the easternmost tip of Sicily: 3 km (2 miles) away is **Torre Faro**, a fishing village known for its excellent swordfish, facing the coast of Calabria. The panorama here is dominated by the pylon and electric power cable that crosses the Straits of Messina for 3,646 m (11,959 ft) in a single span, from the power stations in Calabria. **Capo Peloro**, a short distance from Torre Faro, is crowned by a 16th-century tower that has been used for centuries as a lighthouse. Further along the coastal road you will come to the second, smaller lagoon of Ganzirri, known as the **Pantano Piccolo**. The lake is a stone's throw away from the Tyrrhenian Sea and is linked to the Pantano Grande.

**The church of San Pietro e Paolo in Itala** ***(see p181)***

**Santa Maria di Mili**

If you head southwards from Messina for about 12 km (7 miles), you will reach the villages of **Mili San Marco** and, higher up in the Peloritani Mountains, **Mili San Pietro**. Not far from the latter, in an area of wild landscape characterized by the deep **Forra di Mili** (ravine), is the **Santa Maria di Mili Sanctuary**. The church is in a convent. It has been rebuilt several times and now has a 17th-century appearance. It was founded in 1090 by Roger I as proof of his recovered religious faith after taking Sicily from the Arabs. The Norman king later chose it as the burial site for his son.

The splendid 16th-century marble portal is crowned by a sculpture of the Madonna and Child. Above the two-aisle nave is a finely wrought wooden ceiling that dates from 1411. Once past the three arches marking off the apse area, this ceiling becomes a series of small domes, a characteristic feature of religious architecture of the Norman period.

# Tyndaris ㉒

**Road map** E2. *from Messina (090-675 184 or 662 244).* *0941-369 184.* *9am–1 hr before sunset daily.* *combined ticket with Roman House, Patti.* *8 Sep: Pilgrimage of the Madonna Nera.*

Ancient Tyndaris was one of the last Greek colonies in Sicily, founded by the Syracusans in 396 BC, when the Romans were beginning to expand their territory in the Mediterranean. The town also prospered under Roman rule and became a diocese during the early Christian period, after which time it was destroyed by the Arabs. A visit to the archaeological site is fascinating, partly because of the monuments but also because of the many details, which give you an idea of everyday life in the ancient city. The town is laid out in a classical grid plan consisting of two straight and parallel streets *(decumani)* intersected by other streets *(cardines)*.

Past the walls through the main city gate, not far from the **Madonna di Tindari Sanctuary** (which houses the famous Byzantine *Madonna Nera* or Black Madonna, honoured in a pilgrimage held every 8 September) is the **Greek Theatre**, situated on the slope of a rise and facing the sea; it has a diameter of more than 60 m (197 ft). Nearby is the **Agora**, which has, unhappily, been obscured by modern buildings.

In the theatre area are the remains of a **Roman villa** and **baths**. If you stroll through the streets of the ancient city you will see storehouses for food and the Greek-era drainage system. A large building known as **Ginnasio** or **Basilica** was probably used for public meetings during the Imperial Age. Next to the theatre is the **Museo Archeologico**, which has a large model of the Greek theatre stage, as well as Greek statues and vases, a colossal head of the Emperor Augustus and prehistoric finds. One unmissable sight is the splendid scenery under the **Promontory** of Tyndaris: the **Laguna di Oliveri**, the place celebrated by the poet and Nobel Prize winner Quasimodo *(see p23)*.

## THE NEBRODI MOUNTAINS

The Arabs occupied the Nebrodi Mountains for centuries and referred to them as "an island on an island". The name comes from the Greek word *nebros*, or "roe deer", because of the rich wildlife found in this mountain range, which separates the Madonie Mountains to the west from the Peloritani Mountains to the east. The Parco Regionale dei Monti Nebrodi is a nature reserve with extensive forests and some pastureland, which is covered with snow in the winter. In the middle of the park is the Biviere di Cesarò lake, a stopover point for migratory birds and an ideal habitat for the *Testudo hermanni* marsh turtle. The tallest peak is Monte Soro (1,850 m, 6,068 ft). Higher up, the maquis is replaced by oak and beech woods.

Horses grazing in the Parco Regionale dei Monti Nebrodi

**Parco Regionale dei Monti Nebrodi**
*Tel 0941-705 934.*
www.parcodeinebrodi.it

The unusual natural scenery at the Laguna di Oliveri, seen from the Promontory of Tyndaris

The sarcophagus of Roger I's wife Adelaide in Patti Cathedral

## Patti ㉓

**Road map** E2. *13,100.* *from Messina and Palermo (0941-361 081).* *AAST (0941-241 136).* **www**.pattietindari.it

On one of the stretches where the coastal scenery is most fascinating, just past the rocky promontory of **Capo Calavà** on the slopes overlooking the sea, is the town of Patti. Initially a fief of the Norman ruler Roger I, it was later destroyed during the wars with the Angevins and then frequently pillaged by pirates from North Africa.

Patti boasts an 18th-century **Cathedral** built over the foundations of the former Norman church. Inside is a sarcophagus with the remains of Queen Adelaide, Roger I's wife, who died here in 1118.

Along the road down to **Marina di Patti** are the ruins of a **Roman villa** which were brought to light during the construction of the Messina–Palermo motorway. This Imperial Age building measures 20,000 sq m (215,200 sq ft) and comprises a peristyle, an apse-like room, thermal baths and many well-preserved mosaics. The villa was destroyed by an earthquake; on the basis of various archaeological finds, historians have been able to date this event at the second half of the 4th century AD.

**Roman Villa**

Via Papa Giovanni XXIII, Marina di Patti. **Tel** *0941-361 593.* *hours vary; call ahead.* *combined with Tyndaris.*

## Capo d'Orlando ㉔

**Road map** E2. *11,300.* *AAST (0941-912 784).*

Forming part of a region known for the intensive cultivation of citrus fruits, the Nebrodi Mountains jut out into the sea at intervals. The coastal town of Capo d'Orlando lies at the foot of the **Rupe del Semaforo** cliff and the rocky hill after which the town was named.

A climb of about 100 m (328 ft) will take you to the top of the cliff. There, in a large open space, stand the remains of a 14th-century fortress and **Maria Santissima**, a church built in the late 1500s and now home to a number of interesting paintings. However, the main reward for climbing up the hill is the panoramic view of the sea and of the fishing boats moving about in the pretty harbour below.

## Milazzo ㉕

**Road map** F2. *30,000.* *from Messina & Palermo (091-616 18 06).* *AAST (090-922 28 65 or 922 27 90).*

Milazzo began to take its place in written history when *Mylai* was colonized by the Greeks in 716 BC. The Normans later chose it as their main coastal stronghold. Frederick II personally designed the castle built here in 1239. The town was divided into three distinct zones in the Middle Ages – the **walled town**, the **Borgo** and the **lower town** – and it was expanded in the 1700s. The **Salita Castello** leads up to the **ancient rock**, which affords access to the walled town via a covered passageway. A doorway opens into **Frederick II's Castle**, surrounded by a wall with five round towers and the great hall of the **Sala del Parlamento** (Parliament Hall). On the same rise are the remains of the old **Duomo**, the original 17th-century cathedral, now in a state of disrepair. Do not miss the chance of an excursion to **Capo Milazzo**, where you will be rewarded with towers, villas and, at the foot of the 18th-century lighthouse, a marvellous view of the Aeolian Islands, with Calabria beyond. This was the site of the 260 BC naval battle in which the Romans routed the Carthaginian fleet. Steps lead to the place where St Anthony is said to have taken refuge from a storm in 1221.

The castle at Milazzo, strengthened structurally by Alfonso of Aragon

# The Aeolian Islands 26

Three-colour clay vase, 4th century BC

Consisting of Strikingly beautiful volcanic cliffs separated by inlets, sometimes quite deep, the Aeolian Islands (in Italian, Isole Eolie) are unique for their extraordinary rock formations and volcanoes, and for their history. The islands attract hordes of visitors every summer who come to bathe and dive, yet despite the crowds, each island somehow manages to preserve its own individual character. Dominating the islands, especially in the winter, is the sea, with migratory birds nesting on the cliffs and frequent storms, which can reinforce a sense of isolation, even in this age of rapid communications.

**Filicudi**
*There are three villages on this island: Val di Chiesa, Pecorini and Filicudi Porto. On the Capo Graziano promontory are the ruins of a prehistoric village.*

**Alicudi**
*The 5 sq km (2 sq miles) of Alicudi do not leave room for many inhabitants. The highest peak is the Filo dell'Arpa – 675 m (2,214 ft).*

Pecorini

M a

**Lipari**
*The main island in the archipelago, Lipari has many hot springs and fumaroles, evidence of its volcanic origin. The old town, with a castle and cathedral, is built within walls. There is an important Museo Archeo-logico Eoliano here, with an excellent collection*

*For hotels and restaurants in this region see pp203–7 and pp218–21*

**Stromboli**
*The main attraction on this island is the climb up the volcano and the fine view from the "Sciara del Fuoco".*

## VISITORS' CHECKLIST

*FS Milazzo. [bus] from Catania airport, SAIS (090-771 914); from Messina to Milazzo Giunta (090-673 782 or 675 749). [ferry] Siremar, all year from Milazzo (892123) and Naples (081-551 90 96); SNAV, all year from Milazzo (090-9287821 and Naples (081-4285 555). In summer there are connections from Messina, Palermo, Reggio Calabria, Sant'Agata di Militello, Cefalù, Maratea, Riposto/Giardini and Salerno.* **Lipari** [i] *(090-988 00 95).* **Vulcano** *Jul–Sep* [i] *(090-985 20 28).* **Salina** [i] *at Malfa (090-984 43 26), at Leni (090-980 92 25).* **Stromboli** [i] *Jul–Sep (090-986 023).*

**KEY**

[ferry] Ferry port

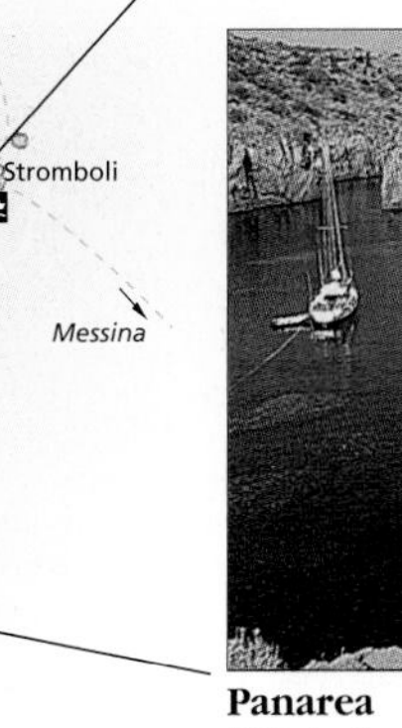


**Panarea**
*This is the smallest Aeolian island, surrounded by rocks and small islands. It was inhabited in prehistoric times.*

**Vulcano**
*According to ancient mythology, the fabulous island of Vulcano was the workplace of the god of fire and blacksmiths, Hephaestus.*

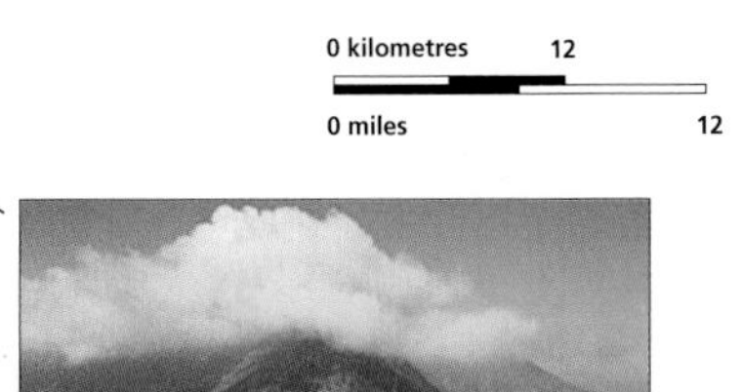

**Salina**
*The island, consisting of two volcanic cones, is the second largest in the group and was named after the ancient salt mine* (salina) *at Lingua, now closed.*

# Exploring the Aeolian Islands

Gold ring, 4th century BC

The best starting point for a visit to the varied Aeolian Islands is Lipari, because it is the largest of the islands and the boat service is good. Here you can decide what type of holiday you want – natural history excursions, including Vulcano and Stromboli, the exclusive tourist resort at Panarea among villas and yachts, or the timeless tranquillity of Alicudi.

The summit of the Vulcano crater, an hour's climb from the base

### Lipari

**Road map** E1. *11,000 (the municipality of Lipari includes all the other islands, except for Salina).*

The main Aeolian island is not large – a little less than 10 km (6 miles) long and barely 5 km (3 miles) wide, culminating in **Monte Chirica**, 602 m (1,974 ft) high. The volcanic activity of the past can be noted here and there in the hot springs and fumaroles. The town of Lipari has two landing places: **Sottomonastero** for ferry boats and **Marina Corta** for hydrofoils. Inevitably, this is the busiest stretch of the seafront.

The old **Cathedral** is worth a visit. Built by the Normans in the 11th century, it was rebuilt after a barbarous pirate raid completely destroyed the town in 1544. Next door to the Cathedral is the **Museo Archeologico Eoliano**, which takes up part of the **old castle**, built by the Spanish (who incorporated the ancient towers and walls) in order to put an end to the constant pirate raids.

The first rooms in the museum are devoted to prehistoric finds in Lipari. The adjoining rooms have objects from the same period, but from the other islands. Then there is a large section featuring classical archaeological finds, some discovered under water. Part of the museum has volcano-related exhibits, with interesting detailed descriptions of the geological configuration of each island. Three further sights are the **Belvedere Quattrocchi** viewpoint, the ancient **San Calogero thermal baths and Acquacalda beach**, which was once used as a harbour for the ships that came to load the local pumice stone. The best way to get about is by scooter or bicycle, both of which can be rented in the town of Lipari.

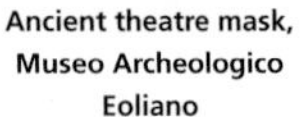
Ancient theatre mask, Museo Archeologico Eoliano

**Museo Archeologico Eoliano**
Via Castello 2. ***Tel*** *090-988 01 74.*
*9am–1pm, 3–6pm Mon–Sat, 9am–1pm Sun & hols.*

The archaeological zone at Lipari, home to many different cultures

### Vulcano

**Road map** E1.

Close to Lipari is the aptly named island of Vulcano. Dedicated to Vulcan, the Roman god of fire and metalworking, Homer described the island as the workshop of Hephaestus, the Greek god of fire. The only landing place is the **Porto di Levante**, from which a paved road leads to the **Faro Nuovo** (new lighthouse). Vulcano consists of three old craters. The first, in the south between **Monte Aria** and **Monte Saraceno**, has been extinct for centuries; the **Gran Cratere**, on the other hand, is still active, the last eruption occurring in 1890. **Vulcanello**, the third crater, is a promontory on the northeastern tip of the island created almost 2,000 years ago by an eruption. The climb up to the middle crater is particularly interesting, and you can reach the top in less than an hour. Once there, it is worthwhile going down the crater to the Piano delle Fumarole. Bathing and mud baths are available all year round at the spas near Porto di Levante, while hot springs heat the sea around the stack *(faraglione)*.

### Salina

**Road map** E1. *800.*

The second largest Aeolian island is 7 km (4 miles) long, 5.5 km (3 miles) wide, and 962 m (3,155 ft) high at its highest point, **Monte Fossa delle Felci**. There are three villages: **Santa Maria di Salina, Leni** and **Malfa**. Santa Maria overlooks the sea and is not far from a beach; it is connected to the other villages by an efficient minibus service which runs until late in the evening in the summer. Salina is also the site

*For hotels and restaurants in this region see pp203–7 and pp218–21*

of a nature reserve, created to protect the two ancient volcanoes of **Monte dei Porri** and **Fossa delle Felci**. The dominant vegetation here is maquis, as the inhabitants have almost exterminated the forests that grew here in antiquity. The starting point for a visit to the reserve is the **Madonna del Terzito Sanctuary**, the object of colourful pilgrimages. Salina, and, in particular, the steep walls of the Pizzo di Corvo is also a regular nesting ground for colonies of the rare Eleonora's falcon, which migrate to this spot every year from Madagascar.

Among the best-known local products is a highly prized sweet Malvasia wine.

Santa Maria di Salina, one of the three villages on the island

### Panarea

**Road map** E1.

The smallest Aeolian island is surrounded by cliffs and stacks. Visitors land at the small harbour of **San Pietro** (the other villages are **Drauto** and **Ditella**). At **Capo Milazzese**, in one of the most fascinating spots in the Aeolian Islands, archaeologists have uncovered the ruins of a Neolithic village, founded at **Cala Junco**. Interesting finds such as Mycenaean pottery, tools and other items are on display in the local museum. A half-hour walk will take you to the village, starting off from **San Pietro** and passing through **Drauto** and the **Spiaggia degli Zimmari** beach. This island now has luxury tourist facilities.

Typical Aeolian landscape at Cala Junco, on Panarea

The Stromboli volcano, active for 2,000 years

### Stromboli

**Road map** F1.

The still-active crater of the northeasternmost island in the archipelago has been described by travellers for more than 20 centuries. Italian volcanoes have always been both famous and feared. The ancient Greeks believed that Hephaestus, the god of fire (known as Vulcan to the Romans), lived in the depths of Mount Etna. Boats call either at **Scari** or **Ginostra**, but the island has other villages: **San Vincenzo, Ficogrande** and **Piscità**. The characteristic features of Stromboli are its stunning craggy coast (the deep waters are a favourite with swimmers and divers) and its famous volcano. For an excursion to the crater, start off from **Piscità**; you first come to the old **Vulcanological Observatory** and then the top of the **crater**. The best time to go is around evening, as the eruptions are best seen in the dark. The climb is not always accessible, and the volcano can be dangerous. It is best to go with a guide and to wear heavy shoes (or hiking boots) and suitable clothing. There are also boats offering evening excursions to take visitors close to the **Sciara del Fuoco** lava field for the unforgettable spectacle of lava flowing into the sea.

### Filicudi

**Road map** E1.

Halfway between Salina and Alicudi, this extremely quiet island has three villages: **Porto, Pecorini a Mare** and **Val di Chiesa**. You can make excursions into the interior or, even better, take a boat trip around the island and visit the **Faraglione della Canna** basalt stack, **Punta del Perciato, Grotta del Bue Marino** and **Capo Graziano**.

### Alicudi

**Road map** D1.

This island was abandoned for the entire Middle Ages and was colonized again only in the Spanish period. Tourism is a relatively recent arrival, and there are no vehicles. The steps and paths are covered on foot, and accommodation can be found in private homes. There is no nightlife, making this an ideal spot for those in search of a peaceful, relaxing break.

# TRAVELLERS' NEEDS

# WHERE TO STAY

Sicily has a wide range of accommodation available, from simple campsites to refurbished mansions. Many hotels have been converted from old palazzi or farmhouses. You may find a room with a view of the Valle dei Templi in Agrigento or of the multicoloured roofs of the churches of Palermo. The place with the most varied accommodation, in all categories, is Taormina, for over a century a favourite with international clients. The coastline of Sicily is lined with three- and four-star hotels, often with a pool or private beach. On the islands off the coast the hotels are often open only in the summer and half-board is obligatory. Alternatively you can stay in private homes or tourist villages. More adventurous visitors might opt for a farm holiday in the interior, which can be good value and often includes good local food. This section and the list of hotels on pages 198–207 provide further information on accommodation in Sicily.

Sign from a historic hotel *(see p206)*

The pool at Les Sables Noires on the island of Vulcano (see p207)

## HOTEL GRADING AND FACILITIES

In common with the rest of Italy, Sicilian hotels are classified by a star-rating system – from one for family-run pensions with simple, basic facilities to five stars for luxury hotels. Among the best hotels in Sicily in this latter category are the **Villa Igiea** *(see p199)* in Palermo and the **San Domenico** and **Grand Hotel Timeo** in Taormina *(see p207)*. All three are housed in historic buildings – the San Domenico is a former monastery – with spectacular views and beautiful gardens.

The four-star category offers first-class service without the very high prices of the luxury hotels. Four-star hotels include some lovely places, such as the **Baglio della Luna** in Agrigento *(see p201)*, the **Villa Sant'Andrea** *(p207)* in Taormina and the **Centrale Palace** in Palermo *(see p198)*. Visitors are sometimes pleasantly surprised at finding good value for money in three-star hotels, such as the **Atelier** by the sea at Castel di Tusa *(see p199)*, the **Domus Mariae** *(see p203)* in Syracuse or the **Baglio Santa Croce** *(see p201)* in Valderice.

In general, all Sicilian hotels have a restaurant, which is usually open to non-residents as well. Along the coast, all the four-star and most of the three-star hotels provide a swimming pool or a private beach. Facilities for the disabled and access for people in wheelchairs are usually available only in newer or recently renovated hotels.

## HOTEL CHAINS

Besides such large international chains as **Best Western** and **Sheraton**, there are Sicilian hotel chains as well. One of these is **Framon Hotels**, which is based in Messina. Their 11 hotels, at different locations throughout Sicily, are known for their good restaurants, as well as other facilities.

## PRICES

By law, every hotel room in Italy must carry, on the back of the door, the **Ente del Turismo** (Tourist Board) price for the room with the maximum charges during the year; these prices may not be exceeded. The displayed prices, or those quoted by the hotel when you book, usually include taxes and service. Breakfast is generally included as well, but you should check with the hotel beforehand. On the whole, you are expected to take half or full board in hotels on the coast.

Breakfast may be served outside in summer

◁ Shop window displaying baskets of marzipan fruits

A room at Kempinski Hotel Giardino di Costanza, Mazara del Vallo *(see p200)*

Extras are likely to include drinks taken with meals, room service, drinks and food taken from the minibar in your room, and telephone calls. Note, however, that hotel phone charges are usually extremely expensive.

In the off season you could try asking for a special bed and breakfast rate, rarely available in peak season.

## TOURIST SEASON

Most of the hotels on the offshore islands are open seasonally, from April to October, so that visiting the Aeolian or Egadi islands in the winter months may be difficult. Hotels in the cities are open all year round.

## BOOKING

Should you decide to go to Sicily in the summer, you need to book well in advance, especially for July and August and if you want to stay on the coast, as the island gets very busy in peak season. When you book, you will probably be asked to pay a deposit by international money order or by giving the hotel a credit card number.

## TOURIST VILLAGES

Holiday villages give you the chance to enjoy a seaside holiday in a less formal atmosphere than in a hotel. Most villages are sited on the islands and along the Sicilian coast, and many offer inclusive package deals. Accommodation may vary according to requirements, from rooms in a residence to small apartments with an outside terrace.

Each village offers a range of recreation and sports facilities. Besides one or more swimming pools, villages usually offer tennis courts and windsurfing, diving or sailing lessons. Some even provide baby-sitting. Among the best of these are the **Club Vacanze di Favignana e Pantelleria,** the **Club Méditerranée Kamarina** in the Ragusa area and the **Villaggio Valtur Pollina** in the province of Palermo.

Some villages offer all-inclusive holidays where the price even includes drinks at the bar. Charges in tourist villages are always calculated on a weekly basis.

Alternatively, you may choose to rent an apartment and select and pay for any further recreation and sports facilities as you go along. This enables you to be independent, and at the same time provides a range of possible facilities. For full details concerning the main tourist villages, make enquiries at a travel agent, or contact the major tour operators who manage these villages, listed on page 197.

## CAMPING

Spending your holiday on a camping site is a good way of keeping costs down. Almost all the camping sites in Sicily are on the coast, with direct access to a beach. In the interior there are only a few sites on the slopes of Mount Etna, well situated for excursions to the largest volcano in Europe. Camping outside official sites is prohibited, with camping on beaches particularly frowned upon. If you want to stay on private property you must ask the owner's permission.

In general, campsites are clean and well-managed. Besides an area for tents and/or caravans (trailers), most sites also provide bungalows with private bathrooms and a kitchen area. Facilities often include grocery shops, pizzerias (and, occasionally, restaurants), laundries and organized sports facilities.

For longer stays, book well ahead of time, and in high season, phone in advance even for a one- or two-night stop. If you are touring, start to look for a site by early afternoon. Most campsites are open from Easter to October. The main ones are listed on page 197.

The Hotel Grotta Azzurra in Ustica, built above the grotto *(see p201)*

## HOSTELS, REFUGES, B&BS AND PRIVATE HOMES

There are very few youth hostels in Sicily, but they do offer very cheap accommodation (roughly €9 per night for a bed in a dormitory). A membership card is needed to use hostels affiliated with the **Associazione Italiana Alberghi della Gioventù** (Italian Youth Hostel Federation), listed on page 197.

There are also mountain refuges, most on Mount Etna, but the **Club Alpino Italiano** has two on the Madonie and Nebrodi mountains.

**Bed & Breakfast Italia** provides a selection of accommodation in Sicily, while on the Aeolian and Egadi islands, near Taormina and at Scopello, you can rent a room in a private home. You may see road signs indicating such rooms, but you can also ask at the local Pro Loco tourist bureaux or in the bars and cafés.

## FARM HOLIDAYS

Spending your holiday on a working farm *(agriturismo)* can be both enjoyable and cheap. You may even be lucky enough to find accommodation in an orange grove with a view of Mount Etna or in a fortified farmstead in the vineyards around Marsala. This kind of holiday offers a good opportunity to become acquainted with local traditions. Farm holidays are not widely available in Sicily, but accommodation is well kept and hospitable, even if rooms are by no means as luxurious as the equivalent in Umbria or Tuscany. As well as rooms, usually with a private bathroom, some farms offer small apartments with a bathroom and kitchen area, perhaps in converted stables or buildings once used for wine-making.

**The Baglio Santacroce in Valderice, with many original features *(see p201)***

**The tower at the Foresteria Baglio della Luna, Agrigento *(see p201)***

Most of these farms offer half- or full-board and in the high season lodging is organized on a week-by-week basis. Meals consist of produce grown on the farm and standards are generally very good. Breakfast might include home-grown honey and jams made from the owners' fruit. Main meals may make use of vegetables from the kitchen garden, home-made cheese, or fish from local fishermen.

Meals are eaten at the owner's table together with the other guests, so if you are fussy about your privacy, this is not the type of holiday for you. But it is ideal for those who want to relax without the formalities of a hotel and for families with children, who will have space to play in. The owners will be only too happy to suggest the best excursions in the vicinity.

## SELF-CATERING (EFFICIENCY APARTMENTS)

Renting an apartment for two weeks or a month is undoubtedly the cheapest solution for a family or group of friends who want a reasonably priced holiday by the sea. If you have children, particularly small ones, self-catering is an excellent solution, as you are not tied in to formal meal-times. Renting an apartment for one week only is less advantageous economically, as cleaning costs can be high in proportion to the rent.

Self-catering options can be arranged through specialized agencies such as **Tailor-Made Tours, Individual Italy** and **Magic of Italy** before you leave for Italy, but be sure to book in advance as they can be booked up for months.

Another possibility, though more expensive, is to make enquiries through tour operators or travel agencies, who sometimes have lists of residential hotels. In these hotels charges are made on a weekly basis and a week's deposit is always required when making a booking.

If you decide to rent a private apartment, it is a good idea to find out the actual size of the property beforehand to make sure there is enough room. In some apartments, the living room is designed to double as a bedroom.

Before coming to an agreement on rental, be sure to ask whether electricity and gas are included in the rent or if they are extras. This also goes for other facilities such as swimming pools and use of gardens.

# DIRECTORY

## TOURIST INFORMATION

**Assessorato Regionale del Turismo, delle Comunicazioni e dei Trasporti**
Via Notarbartolo 9, Palermo. **Tel** *091-707 82 01.* **www**.regione.sicilia.it/turismo/web_turismo

## HOTEL CHAINS

**Framon Hotels**
Via Oratorio San Francesco 306, Messina.
**Tel** *090-228 22 66.*
**www**.framon-hotels.com

## TOURIST VILLAGES

**Club Mediterranée**
Largo Corsia dei Servi 11, Milan. **Tel** *02-778 61*
**www**.clubmed.it

**Club Vacanze**
Via Mentana 150, Parma.
**Tel** *0521-288 111.*
**www**.clubvacanze.it

**Valtur**
Via Milano 46, Rome.
**Tel** *06-482 10 00.*
**www**.valtur.it

## CAMPING

**Al Yag**
Via Altarellazzo, Pozzillo, Acireale (Catania).
**Tel** *095-764 17 63.*

**Baia dei Coralli**
Località Punta Braccetto, Santa Croce Camerina (Ragusa).
**Tel** *0932-918 192.*

**Baia del Sole**
Marina di Ragusa (Ragusa).
**Tel** *0932-230 344.*
**www**.baiadelsole.it

**Baia di Guidaloca**
Scopello, Castellammare del Golfo (Trapani).
**Tel** *0924-541 262 (summer); 323 59 (winter).*

**Baia Macauda**
Contrada Tranchina, Sciacca (Agrigento).
**Tel** *0925-997 001.*

**Baia Unci**
Località Canneto, Lipari (Messina).
**Tel** *090-981 19 09.*

**Bazia**
Contrada Bazia, Furnari (Messina).
**Tel** *0941-800 130.*

**Calanovella**
Contrada Calanovella, SS 113, km 90, (Messina).
**Tel** *0941-585 258.*
**www**.calanovella.it

**Capo Passero**
Contrada Vigne Vecchie, Portopalo di Capopassero (Syracuse).
**Tel** *0931-842 030.*

**Costa Ponente**
Contrada Ogliastrillo, Cefalù (Palermo).
**Tel** *0921-420 085. (summer); 0921-421 354 (winter).*

**El Bahira**
Contrada MaKari, San Vito Lo Capo (Trapani).
**Tel** *0923-972 577. (summer); 0923-972 231 (winter).* **www**.elbahira.it

**Eurocamping Due Rocche**
Contrada Faino, SS 115, km 241, Butera (Caltanissetta). **Tel** *0934-349 006.*

**Eurocamping Marmaruca**
Via Leto 8, Letojanni (Messina).
**Tel** *0942-366 76.*

**Fontane Bianche**
Località Fontane Bianche (Syracuse).
**Tel** *0931-790 333.*

**La Roccia**
Località Cala Greca, Lampedusa (Agrigento).
**Tel** *0922-970 964.*

**Mareneve**
Contrada Piano Grande, Milo (Catania).
**Tel** *095-708 21 63.*

**Miramare**
Contrada Costicella, Favignana (Trapani).
**Tel** *0923-921 330.*

**Rais Gerbi**
Contrada Rais Gerbi, Pollina Finale (Palermo).
**Tel** *0921-426 570.*
**www**.raisgerbi.it

## BED & BREAKFAST

**Bed & Breakfast Italia**
**Tel** *06-687 86 18.*
**www**.bbitalia.it

## FARM HOLIDAY ASSOCIATIONS

**Terranostra**
**Tel** *091-280 000.*
**www**.terranostra.it

## FARM HOLIDAYS

**Agriturismo.com**
**Tel** *0575-616 091.*
**www**.agriturismo.com

**Alcalà**
Masseria Alcalà, Misterbianco (Catania).
**Tel** *095-713 00 29.*

**L'Antica Vigna**
Contrada Montelaguardia, Randazzo (Catania). **Tel** *095-924 003 or 922 766.*

**Baglio Vajarassa**
Contrada Spagnola 176, Marsala. **Tel** *0923-968 628.*

**Borgo degli Olivi**
Località Aielli, Tusa (Messina). **Tel** *090-719 08.*

**Casa dello Scirocco**
Lentini (Syracuse).
**Tel** *095-44 77 09.* **www**.casadelloscirocco.it

**Casa Migliaca**
Località Migliaca, Pettineo (Messina).
**Tel** *0921-336 722.*

**Codavolpe**
Località Trepunti, Giarre (Catania). **Tel** *095-939 802.*
**www**.codavolpe.it

**Feudo Tudia**
Borgo Tudia, Castellana Sicula (Palermo).
**Tel** *0934-673 029.*

**Il Daino**
San Piero Patti (Messina).
**Tel** *0941-660 362.*
**www**.ildaino.com

**Il Limoneto**
Via Provinciale 195F, Acireale (Catania).
**Tel** *095-886 568.*
**www**.illimoneto.it

**Piccolo**
Fattoria di Grenne, Ficarra (Messina). **Tel** *0941-582 757.* **www**.grenne.com

**Savoca**
Contrada Polleri, Piazza Armerina (Enna).
**Tel** *0935-683 078.*
**www**.agrisavoca.com

**Tenuta di Roccadia**
Carlentini (Syracuse).
**Tel** *095-990 362.*
**www**.roccadia.com

**Trinità**
Via Trinità 34, Mascalucia (Catania).
**Tel** *095-727 21 56.*
**www**.aziendatrinita.it

**Valentina**
Contrada Piano Colla, Acate (Ragusa).
**Tel** *0932-989 539.*

## YOUTH HOSTELS

**Associazione Italiana Alberghi della Gioventù**
Via Cavour 44, Rome.
**Tel** *06-487 11 52.*
**www**.ostellionline.org

**Ostello Amodeo**
2nd km on the Trapani–Erice provincial road.
**Tel** *0923-552 964.*

**Ostello delle Aquile**
Salita Federico II d'Aragona, Castroreale (Messina). **Tel** *090-974 63 98.*

**Ostello Etna**
Via della Quercia 7, Nicolosi (Catania).
**Tel** *095-791 46 86.*

**Ostello Lipari**
Via Castello 17, Lipari (Messina). **Tel** *090-981 15 40 or 981 25 27.*

## SELF CATERING

**Individual Italy**
**Tel** *08700 772772.*
**www**.individualtravellers.com

**Magic of Italy**
**Tel** *0870 888 02 28.*
**www**.magicofitaly.co.uk

**Tailor-Made Tours**
**Tel** *020 8291 9736.*
**www**.tailormadeinitaly.com

# Choosing a Hotel

The hotels in this guide have been carefully selected across a wide price range for the quality of service, decor and location. They have been divided into five geographical areas and are listed by place and price category. Palermo hotels are listed according to the city zones shown in the chapter on Palermo.

**PRICE CATEGORIES**
The following price ranges are for a standard double room and taxes per night during the high season. Breakfast is not included, unless specified.

€ up to 85 euros
€€ 85–150 euros
€€€ 150–250 euros
€€€€ 250–350 euros
€€€€€ over 350 euros

## PALERMO

**EAST PALERMO Hotel Orientale** €

*Via Maqueda 26, 90133* ***Tel*** *091-616 57 27 or 616 35 06* ***Fax*** *091-616 11 93* ***Rooms*** *24* ***Map*** *2 D5*

The courtyard entrance speaks of the faded nobility that used to live in this 18th-century palazzo. The grand staircase leads to the "noble floor", with ceiling frescoes in the main salon (Mussolini once gave a speech from its balcony). A friendly, family-run hotel with pleasantly furnished rooms (not all are en suite). **www.albergoorientale.191.it**

**EAST PALERMO Villa Archirafi** €€

*Via Lincoln 30, 91034* ***Tel*** *091-616 88 27* ***Fax*** *091-616 863* ***Rooms*** *37* ***Map*** *2 E4*

Good for those who prefer a central location to size, the moderately priced Villa Archirafi is conveniently situated between Palermo's central train station and the botanical garden, and is a short walk from the Teatro Garibaldi, Santa Maria dello Spasimo and the museum of mineralogy. Comfortably furnished. **www.villaarchirafi.com**

**EAST PALERMO Excelsior Palace** €€€

*Via Marchese Ugo 3, 90134* ***Tel*** *091-790 90 01* ***Fax*** *091-342 139* ***Rooms*** *123*

Built in 1891 and remodelled in 1987, this hotel is still a favourite of visiting aristocracy and has a loyal following. It features some lovely stairways and conversation spaces – a gracious throwback to a Palermo from genteel days gone by. Some rooms have antiques and high ceilings. **www.excelsiorpalermo.it**

**EAST PALERMO Grand Hotel et des Palmes** €€€

*Via Roma 398, 90134* ***Tel*** *091-602 81 11* ***Fax*** *091-331 545* ***Rooms*** *180* ***Map*** *1 C1*

On a central street that runs from the train station to Piazza Sturzo, this historic Ingham-Whitaker palazzo became a hotel in 1874. With its grand entrance and marble lobby, the Grand Hotel caters particularly to business travellers: it has conference rooms and services for meetings, conventions and banquets. **www.grandhoteletdespalmes.it**

**WEST PALERMO Ai Cavalieri Hotel** €€€

*Via Sant'Oliva 8, 90141* ***Tel*** *091-583 282* ***Fax*** *091-612 65 89* ***Rooms*** *39* ***Map*** *1 A2*

This classic 1891 hotel faces Piazza Sant'Oliva, with its good choice of neighbourhood restaurants, and is an easy walk to the Teatro Massimo, Teatro Politeama and Palazzo Abatellis. A Best Western hotel, Ai Cavalieri caters mainly to business travellers (it has two conference rooms). Daily parking costs 15 euros. **www.aicavalierihotel.it**

**WEST PALERMO Centrale Palace** €€€

*Corso Vittorio Emanuele 327, 90134* ***Tel*** *091-336 666* ***Fax*** *091-334 881* ***Rooms*** *104* ***Map*** *1 C3*

On one of Palermo's lively main streets, this converted 18th-century noble palace is on all major transport routes, and a short walking distance to shops, museums, food markets and the Teatro Biondo. The hotel has a solarium and fitness centre and in good weather, guests can enjoy breakfast on the terrace. **www.centralepalacehotel.it**

**WEST PALERMO Massimo Plaza Hotel** €€€

*Via Maqueda 437, 90133* ***Tel*** *091-325 657* ***Fax*** *091-325 711* ***Rooms*** *15* ***Map*** *1 B2*

Opened in 1999, the Massimo Plaza faces the Teatro Massimo. In the heart of the city, close to shops and restaurants and on public transport lines, this intimate hotel has only 15 rooms, so be sure to reserve well in advance. Bedrooms have damask covers and small writing desks; some also feature a balcony. **www.massimoplazahotel.com**

**WEST PALERMO Palazzo Conte Federico** €€€€

*Via dei Biscottari 4, 90134* ***Tel*** *091-651 18 81* ***Fax*** *091-637 43 84* ***Rooms*** *1* ***Map*** *1 B4*

Count and Countess Federico graciously welcome guests in their torch-lit noble palace with its 12th-century tower. They offer a complimentary drink on arrival, plus breakfast. The medieval bedroom has interconnecting chambers: ideal for accommodating additional family members who do not need private entrances. **www.contefederico.com**

**FURTHER AFIELD Casena dei Colli** €€

*Via Villa Rosato 20, 90146* ***Tel*** *091-688 97 71* ***Fax*** *091-688 97 79* ***Rooms*** *93* ***Road Map*** *C2*

Once the home of Ferdinand of Bourbon's secretary, this residence is located near the Parco della Favorita and the Palazzina Cinese, and offers guests a patch of green in Palermo, away from the central bustle. In the summer months, breakfast is served in the garden. Rooms are comfortably furnished. **www.casenadeicolli.it**

**Key to Symbols** *see back cover flap*

**FURTHER AFIELD Hotel Gallery House** €€

*Via Mariano Stabile 136, 90139* **Tel** *091-612 47 58* **Fax** *091-612 47 79* **Rooms** *12* **Road Map** *C2*

Opened in 2005, this hotel benefits from the charming personal touch of the family who runs it. Conveniently located a short walk from the historic centre, the Gallery House features nicely appointed guest rooms, plus two apartments that are handy for families with children. Garage service on request. **www.hotelgalleryhouse.com**

**FURTHER AFIELD Splendid Hotel La Torre** €€

*Via Piano Gallo 11, Mondello, 90151* **Tel** *091-450 222* **Fax** *091-450 033* **Rooms** *168* **Road Map** *C2*

Mondello represents the centre of Palermo's beach action. This modern hotel is up above the crowd on a cliff with a luxuriant garden, tennis courts and sea-water swimming pool. Some rooms have a terrace with sea views for a slightly higher fee than a standard room. Large conference rooms host conventions. **www.latorre.com**

**FURTHER AFIELD Villa d'Amato** €€

*Via Messina Marina 180, 90121* **Tel/Fax** *091-621 27 67* **Rooms** *37* **Road Map** *C2*

On the busy coastal road east of Palermo's port, this modern villa welcomes leisure and business travellers, plus meetings in its conference centre. Rooms are furnished in a modern style and some have a view of the sea. Breakfast is served on the terrace. A shuttle service operates on request. **www.hotelvilladamato.it**

**FURTHER AFIELD Villa Esperia** €€

*Viale Margherita di Savoia 53, Mondello, 90151* **Tel** *091-684 07 17* **Fax** *091-684 15 08* **Rooms** *22* **Road Map** *C2*

The family atmosphere and smaller size of this hotel are draws if you seek a more intimate experience at the beach in Mondello. Rooms are attractively furnished, with rugs and iron-framed beds, some with canopies. Hedges around the hotel offer tranquillity in this busy area. The restaurant has garden dining. **www.hotelvillaesperia.it**

**FURTHER AFIELD Astoria Palace** €€€

*Via Montepellegrino 62, 90142* **Tel** *091-628 11 11* **Fax** *091-637 21 78* **Rooms** *326* **Road Map** *C2*

This modern hotel near the Fiera del Mediterraneo exhibition centre attracts a primarily business and convention clientele for the trade shows; it also hosts its own events in its conference centre. Rates tend to be lowest when the Fiera has no shows or events booked. Rooms are furnished in a standard modern style. **www.ghshotels.it**

**FURTHER AFIELD Baglio di Pianetto** €€€

*Santa Cristina Gela, Scorrimento Veloce, 90030* **Tel** *091-857 00 02* **Fax** *091-857 00 15* **Rooms** *13* **Road Map** *B2*

Count Marzotto produces high-quality wines, which inspired the countess to open an inn with views over the family vineyards, olive trees and nearby mountains. The chef's bounty comes from nearby fields and farms, and there is a wine tasting room as well as an outdoor swimming pool and a solarium. **www.bagliodipianetto.com**

**FURTHER AFIELD Grand Hotel Villa Igiea** €€€

*Salita Belmonte 43, 90142* **Tel** *091-631 21 11* **Fax** *091-547 654* **Rooms** *113* **Road Map** *C2*

Set above the west end of Palermo's harbour, the city's most romantic and deluxe hotel is a favourite of the international and political elite. Elegantly furnished, Villa Igiea has a beautiful garden with pool and a classical temple overlooking the harbour. Facilities include a fitness centre and tennis courts. **www.villaigieapalermo.it**

**FURTHER AFIELD Hotel Principe di Villafranca** €€€

*Via G. Turrisi Colonna 4, 90141* **Tel** *091-611 85 23* **Fax** *091-588 705* **Rooms** *34* **Road Map** *C2*

This hotel is located in an upscale neighbourhood that offers good dining and shopping opportunities. The lobby has a small bar and in winter the fireplace adds a perfect touch of cosiness. Bathrooms are smallish, so request a room with a tub. The drinks in the room fridge are free. **www.principedivillafranca.it**

**FURTHER AFIELD Mondello Palace** €€€

*Viale Principe di Scalea 2, Mondello, 90151* **Tel** *091-450 001* **Fax** *091-450 657* **Rooms** *83* **Road Map** *C2*

In the 1950s, this was the scene of dances and social events; now its main focus is conventions. The hotel has a historic bathhouse and retains a bygone allure throughout. Some of the pleasantly furnished rooms have a sea view. There is also a private beach with a range of water sports, such as sailing and scuba diving. **www.mondellopalacehotel.it**

## NORTHWESTERN SICILY

**CARINI Hotel Portorais** €€€

*Via Piraineto 125, 90044* **Tel** *091-869 34 81* **Fax** *091-869 34 58* **Rooms** *55* **Road Map** *B2*

West of Palermo, on the coast near the airport, this modern hotel attracts guests with its fitness centre, swimming pool, beach and other facilities, such as table tennis and billiards. Its conference centre draws the business clientele. Rooms are furnished in a modern style and some have a view over the Gulf of Carini. **www.hotelportorais.com**

**CASTEL DI TUSA L'Atelier sul Mare** €€

*Via Cesare Battisti 4, 98070* **Tel** *091-334 295* **Fax** *091-334 283* **Rooms** *40* **Road Map** *D2*

On the coast east of Cefalù, this hotel showcases the work of contemporary artists, turning itself into a sort of art gallery. The public areas have paintings and sculptures, as do some of the rooms. Those furnished by contemporary artists cost about 50 euros more than standard rooms. **www.ateliersulmare.com**

**CASTELLAMMARE DEL GOLFO Hotel Al Madarig** €€

*Piazza Petrolo 7, 91014* ***Tel*** *0924-33 533* ***Fax*** *0924-33 790* ***Rooms*** *38* ***Road Map*** *B2*

In the town centre, facing a square by the harbour, this hotel was built into abandoned port warehouses. The steps (*al madarig* in Arabic) lead down to the beach. It's a good base for excursions to the Zingaro nature reserve, which is a short drive northwest along the coast. Modern, functional rooms, some with sea views. **www.almadarig.com**

**CEFALÙ Baia del Capitano** €€

*Contrada Mazzaforno, 90015* ***Tel*** *0921-420 003/5* ***Fax*** *0921-420 163* ***Rooms*** *52* ***Road Map*** *D2*

Located near the beach, this pleasant, modern Mediterranean-style hotel has access to beach facilities as well as a swimming pool, tennis courts, bowling green, table tennis, windsurfing and a disco. Its two meeting rooms occasionally host small conferences. Dog-owners and their pets are welcome. **www.baiadelcapitano.it**

**CEFALÙ Gli Alberi del Paradiso** €€€

*Via dei Mulini 18–20, 90015* ***Tel*** *0921-423 900* ***Fax*** *0921-423 990* ***Rooms*** *55* ***Road Map*** *D2*

A historic manor house on a small hill was converted to an inn, then expanded with a modern wing. It is run by a friendly family who will arrange tennis, golf, horseback riding and a number of water sports for their guests. They are also particularly proud of their chef. Bedrooms are comfortable and pleasantly furnished. **www.alberidelparadiso.it**

**ERICE Hotel Elimo** €€

*Via Vittorio Emanuele 75, 91016* ***Tel*** *0923-869 377* ***Fax*** *0923-869 252* ***Rooms*** *21* ***Road Map*** *A2*

The lobby's warm colours, Oriental rugs and leather sofas are inviting, while in winter a fireplace becomes the room's focus. There is another large fireplace in the restaurant, which is an ideal spot for evening drinks. The rooms have red lacquer doors, nice drapes and comfortable furniture. Courtyard and terrace, too. **www.hotelelimo.it**

**ERICE Hotel Moderno Erice** €€

*Via Vittorio Emanuele 63, 91016* ***Tel*** *0923-869 300* ***Fax*** *0923-869 139* ***Rooms*** *40* ***Road Map*** *A2*

The friendly family who runs this hotel is very present – you'll see them working at the reception desk, eating in the restaurant or relaxing in the lounge. Rooms are simply furnished (some are located across the street in the annexe); four have antique or handcrafted furniture. The small terrace has a lovely view. **www.hotelmodernoerice.it**

**ERICE Torri Pepoli** €€€

*Giardini del Balio Viale Conte Pepoli, 91016* ***Tel*** *0923-860 117* ***Fax*** *0923-522 091* ***Rooms*** *7* ***Road Map*** *A2*

Restored in 1870 by Count Pepoli, this Norman castle was reopened in 2005 by his descendants as a deluxe hotel. Rooms have commanding views of Erice's countryside and the Count's Room is one of the suites. Enjoy an apéritif or cappuccino in the restaurant bar. A grand, quiet hideaway with a charming lookout point. **www.torripepoli.it**

**FAVIGNANA Aegusa** €€

*Via Garibaldi 11–17, 91023* ***Tel*** *0923-922 430* ***Fax*** *0923-922 440* ***Rooms*** *28* ***Road Map*** *A2*

A short hop on the ferry from Trapani is the island of Favignana. This small Mediterranean-style hotel, converted from an old palazzo, stands in the historic centre near the harbour. The lovely rooms are decorated simply and tastefully. The restaurant is open for lunch and dinner (except Tue lunch); alfresco dining is also available. **www.aegusahotel.it**

**MARSALA Hotel Carmine** €€

*Piazza Carmine, 16, 91025* ***Tel*** *0923-711 907* ***Fax*** *0923-717 574* ***Rooms*** *28* ***Road Map*** *A3*

This 17th-century former convent underwent a five-year renovation and is now a family-run hotel. All rooms have antique furniture, Oriental pattern rugs, good reading lights, pretty bath tiles and nice textiles; some also have a view of the square. A dining plan with three local restaurants can be arranged. **www.hotelcarmine.it**

**MARSALA La Finestra sul Sale** €€

*Contrada Ettore Infersa, 91025* ***Tel*** *0923-733 003* ***Fax*** *0923-733 142* ***Rooms*** *3* ***Road Map*** *A3*

"Window over the Salt" bed and breakfast offers a unique immersion into the culture of sea salt in Sicily. All bedrooms have a view of Mozia, its salt flats, the bay and a windmill. Bedrooms have terracotta floors, ceilings of wooden beams and bricks, and wood furniture. Salt is harvested from May to June, but this hotel is lovely year-round.

**MARSALA Agriturismo Baglio del Marchese** €€€

*Lungomare Mediterraneo, 91025* ***Tel/Fax*** *0923-951 115 or 348 002 20 70* ***Rooms*** *10* ***Road Map*** *A3*

This historic former manor house offers deluxe accommodation. Once a hunting reserve, the estate now cultivates vineyards, and wine tastings are available. Bedrooms have original antiques, marble floors, wood and volcanic-rock ceilings, and decorative tile baths. The beach and a nature reserve are nearby. **www.bagliodelmarchese.com**

**MARSALA Agriturismo Tenute Montalto** €€€€

*Lungomare Mediterraneo, Litoranea Sud, 91025* ***Tel/Fax*** *0923-951 115 or 348 002 20 70* ***Rooms*** *7* ***Road Map*** *A3*

This historic estate produces wine (Nero d'Avola, Grillo), olive oil and citrus fruit. The accommodation consists of two villas: the larger one sleeps seven people; the smaller villa, four. Bedrooms have Sicilian furniture, plus some family antiques. The public spaces are decorated in Art Nouveau style. **www.tenutemontalto.com**

**MAZARA DEL VALLO Kempinski Hotel Giardino di Costanza** €€€€

*Via Salemi, km 6.8, 91100* ***Tel*** *0923-675 000* ***Fax*** *0923-675 876* ***Rooms*** *8* ***Road Map*** *A3*

Formerly known as Villa Fontanasalsa, this hotel was bought by the Kempinski chain, enlarged and transformed into a luxury resort with a beauty and wellness centre. Pool, sauna, gym and tennis are all available and the hotel has its own private beach. Bedrooms are luxurious and spacious, with all modern conveniences. **www.kempinski-sicily.com**

**Key to Price Guide** *see p198* **Key to Symbols** *see back cover flap*

**SCOPELLO Albergo La Tavernetta** €€

*Via Diaz 3, 90414* ***Tel/Fax*** *0924-541 129* ***Rooms*** *11* ***Road Map*** *B2*

This small hotel is situated at the southern end of the Zingaro nature reserve, between San Vito and Castellammare del Golfo. Once an Arab enclave, this simply furnished former residence is intimate in size and ideal for nature lovers who don't want to resort to camping. A restaurant is conveniently located on site.

**SELINUNTE Hotel Miramare Selinunte** €

*Via Pigafetta 2, Marinella di Selinunte, 91022* ***Tel*** *0924-46 045* ***Fax*** *0924-46 744* ***Rooms*** *20* ***Road Map*** *B3*

Formerly known as Garzia, the hotel was renovated and repainted in 2006. The terrace and some of the guest rooms have a view of the sea and of the archaeological ruins. There is a restaurant/pizzeria on the premises, and the hotel also has a private beach. **www.hotelmiramareselinunte.com**

**TRAPANI Vittoria** €€

*Via Crispi 4, 91100* ***Tel*** *0923-873 044* ***Fax*** *0923-29 870* ***Rooms*** *65* ***Road Map*** *A2*

The exterior will not win it any architectural awards, but this hotel is right in the centre of Trapani, so it is a popular choice with businesspeople. The rooms are furnished in a simple, basic style, but they are comfortable, and some have a view of the historic centre or of the sea. Helpful staff. **www.hotelvittoriatrapani.it**

**TRAPANI Crystal Hotel** €€€

*Piazza Umberto 1, 91100* ***Tel*** *0923-20 000* ***Fax*** *0923-25 555* ***Rooms*** *68* ***Road Map*** *A2*

The modern white-and-glass exterior reflects the colour of the locally sourced sea salt. This hotel caters to the business traveller; its two meeting rooms often host conferences. Guest rooms are modern, most with a black-and-white colour scheme, and all have Wi-Fi Internet access. Located near the city centre. **www.framonhotels.com**

**USTICA Grotta Azzurra** €€€

*Contrada San Ferlicchio, 90010* ***Tel*** *0931-97 1018* ***Fax*** *0931-52 32 03* ***Rooms*** *52* ***Road Map*** *B1*

This white hotel stands out from the rocks and the natural blue cave in the hollow of the cliffs below. Most rooms face the sea and have a terrace. Lounge chairs are set out on platforms along the rocky shoreline. Facilities include a private beach, outside dining, a diving centre, windsurfing, boat taxi and boat rental. **www.framonhotels.com**

**VALDERICE Baglio Santa Croce** €€

*Contrada Santa Croce, 91019* ***Tel*** *0923-891 111* ***Fax*** *0923-891 192* ***Rooms*** *67* ***Road Map*** *A2*

A new wing constructed in 2006 more than doubled this hotel's capacity. The original 1637 farm building has stone walls, terracotta floors, wood-beamed ceilings and rustic furniture. The new wing has lighter, larger rooms with oak doors, wooden furniture, tile floors, and larger beds and bathrooms. **www.bagliosantacroce.it**

**VALDERICE Tonnara di Bonagia** €€€

*Piazza Tonnara, 91019* ***Tel*** *0923-431 111* ***Fax*** *0923-592 177* ***Rooms*** *121* ***Road Map*** *A2*

The 17th-century maritime quarter of Valderice has been sympathetically converted and expanded into a hotel and convention centre. The *mattanza*, the ancient ritual of catching tuna, still takes place nearby in May and June. Facilities include a fitness centre, pool, diving centre, boat rental and tennis courts. **www.framonhotels.com**

## SOUTHWESTERN SICILY

**AGRIGENTO Hotel Kaos** €€

*Villaggio Pirandello, 92100* ***Tel*** *0922-598 622* ***Fax*** *0922-589 770* ***Rooms*** *105* ***Road Map*** *C4*

Set above the beach, this restored aristocratic villa complex is delightful. The spacious pool curves graciously through the lovely garden, with its sea views and terrace dining. The interior is tastefully furnished and the staff are attentive. Tennis, soccer, bridge tournaments and cooking classes are all on offer. Beach shuttle. **www.athenahotels.com**

**AGRIGENTO Foresteria Baglio della Luna** €€€

*Contrada Maddalusa Valle dei Templi, 92100* ***Tel*** *0922-511 061* ***Fax*** *0922-598 802* ***Rooms*** *24* ***Road Map*** *C4*

This former country estate with an ancient lookout tower offers a garden with a panorama of the countryside and Baroque art in some of the rooms. Bedrooms are comfortably furnished with modern conveniences; some have a view of the temples. The restaurant features local produce in traditional recipes. **www.bagliodellaluna.com**

**AGRIGENTO Villa Athena** €€€

*Via dei Templi 53, 92100* ***Tel/Fax*** *0922-402 180* ***Rooms*** *40* ***Road Map*** *C4*

Savour the view of the majestic Temple of Concord from the garden (and most of the rooms), or head for the pool, set in a lovingly tended garden of luxuriant plants. Oriental carpets, antiques and tasteful art make for a pleasant stay in this lovely, well-managed hotel. **www.hotelvillaathena.com**

**CALTANISETTA Villa San Michele** €€

*Via Fasci Siciliani, 93100* ***Tel*** *0934-553 750* ***Fax*** *0934-598 791* ***Rooms*** *136* ***Road Map*** *D3*

Built to attract conventions in the hills of central Sicily, this modern hotel aims to keep abreast of business trends with its conference facilities, helipad and technical support. Guest rooms are large, with modern conveniences; some have a view of the hills. The restaurant is closed on Sunday and most of August. **www.hotelsanmichelesicilia.it**

**ENNA Sicilia** €€

*Piazza Colajanni 7, 94100* ***Tel*** *0935-500 850* ***Fax*** *0935-500 488* ***Rooms*** *80* ***Road Map*** *D3*

This centrally located hotel in Enna is convenient for visits to the Castello di Lombardia, Duomo, Torre and other local sights. Refurbished in 2003, it is unexceptional in design or facilities, but serves the purpose for a brief stay for business or tourism. Rooms are furnished in a modern style and have all conveniences. **www.hotelsiciliaenna.it**

**LAMPEDUSA I Dammusi di Borgo Cala Creta** €

*Contrada Cala Creta, 92010* ***Tel*** *0922-970 883* ***Fax*** *0922-970 590* ***Rooms*** *25* ***Road Map*** *B5*

Traditional, Arab-inspired *dammusi* are stone houses with white cupolas and small windows to keep the interior cool. Here, each one has its own patio and garden. There is a shuttle service, plus optional excursions and boat trips. Half-board is available and weekly stays may be required in mid-August. **www.calacreta.com**

**LAMPEDUSA Sirio** €€

*Via Antonello da Messina 5, 92010* ***Tel/Fax*** *0922-970 401* ***Rooms*** *10* ***Road Map*** *B5*

This small hotel faces Lampedusa island's harbour. Bedrooms are furnished in typical blue and yellow seaside colours. During mid-August guests are requested to take the half-board option, which includes dinner in the hotel restaurant. Boat excursions can be arranged.

**LAMPEDUSA Il Gattopardo** €€€€€

*Cala Creta, 92010* ***Tel*** *0922-970 051* ***Fax*** *0922-971 645* ***Rooms*** *12* ***Road Map*** *B5*

Accommodation at Il Gattopardo is in *dammusi*, traditional stone houses, in a tranquil seaside setting. Two boats take guests out on daily excursions with lunch, and there are seven small cars available to explore the island's interior independently. The chef prepares a delicious dinner in the evening. Weekly stays only. **www.equinoxe.it**

**PANTELLERIA Mursia** €€€

*Mursia, 91017* ***Tel*** *0923-911 217* ***Fax*** *0923-911 026* ***Rooms*** *74* ***Road Map*** *A5*

On the northwestern coast of Pantelleria, this hotel has two pools (salt- and freshwater), a children's pool, tennis courts and a piano bar. Bedrooms are furnished in handcrafted wood and neutral-colour fabrics, and they all have a terrace. Many rooms also have a vaulted ceiling with a cupola. **www.mursiahotel.it**

**PIAZZA ARMERINA Hotel Gangi** €

*Via Generale Ciancio 68, 94015* ***Tel*** *0935-682 737* ***Fax*** *0935-687 563* ***Rooms*** *18* ***Road Map*** *D4*

This family-run hotel in the centre of Piazza Armerina offers a pleasant stay. Two rooms are decorated in a retro style. In nice weather, breakfast is served on the terrace. The staff are happy to arrange excursions nearby or across Sicily. Ideally located for walks into town, to the shops and restaurants. **www.hotelgangi.it**

**PIAZZA ARMERINA La Casa sulla Collina d'Oro** €

*Via Mattarella snc, 94015* ***Tel/Fax*** *0935-89 680* ***Rooms*** *7* ***Road Map*** *D4*

This 1872 house is the most historic building on the southern hill. Rooms are tastefully decorated in natural materials such as stone, wood, terracotta, linen and cotton, and the terrace has a view over the medieval village. The owners are passionate historians and offer tours in Italian or German. Dinner by request. **www.lacasasullacollinadoro.it**

**PIAZZA ARMERINA Azienda Turistica Torre di Renda** €€

*Contrada Torre di Renda, 94015* ***Tel*** *0935-687 657* ***Fax*** *0935-687 821* ***Rooms*** *16* ***Road Map*** *D4*

This cosy wooded mountainside inn, enlarged from a 17th-century residence, was once a bishop's summer home. Bedrooms are simply furnished in wood. The restaurant is open to public; the half-board option (with either lunch or dinner) costs an extra 18 euros a day. Horse riding is available nearby. **www.torrerenda.it**

**SUTERA Piazza Bed & Breakfast** €

*Contrada Fosse, 93010* ***Tel/Fax*** *0934-954 125* ***Rooms*** *8* ***Road Map*** *C3*

A family-run hotel in this unique town carved into a rock near picturesque mountains, ruins and valleys. The spotless bedrooms are simply furnished in wood, and one has a balcony with a view of faraway Etna. Hot, substantial English breakfasts are on offer, as well as guided walks. **www.bedandbreakfastpiazza.it**

## SOUTHERN SICILY

**CALTAGIRONE Grand Hotel Villa San Mauro** €€€

*Via Porto Salvo 10, 95041* ***Tel*** *0933-26 500* ***Fax*** *0933-31 661* ***Rooms*** *92* ***Road Map*** *D4*

This hotel set among the hills aims to please both leisure and business travellers. It is decorated with beautiful local ceramics and most rooms have balconies with views of the surrounding countryside. The pool has a snack bar. The conference centre seats up to 160. One floor is reserved for non-smokers. **www.framonhotels.com**

**MARINA DI RAGUSA Hotel Terracqua** €€€

*Via delle Sirene 35, 97010* ***Tel*** *0932-615 600* ***Fax*** *0932-615 580* ***Rooms*** *77* ***Road Map*** *E5*

This hotel has a beautiful private beach across the road. Few rooms have a sea view, however, and the hotel is beginning to show signs of wear, but it continues to be a popular destination for receptions and conventions. Marina di Ragusa's continuing building boom might mean noise or unattractive surroundings. **www.shr.it**

**Key to Price Guide** *see p198* **Key to Symbols** *see back cover flap*

**MODICA L'Orangerie** €€

*Vico de Naro 5, 97015* **Tel** *3470-674 698* **Fax** *0932-754 840* **Rooms** *7* **Road Map** *E5*

This 19th-century neo-Renaissance palace in the heart of Modica is charming. Each room is decorated in a different elegant colour, and all have contemporary graphics. Enchanting period frescoes decorate some of the rooms and one of the halls. Breakfast is served in the traditional 19th-century kitchen. **www.lorangerie.it**

**RAGUSA Hotel Locanda Don Serafino** €€

*Via XI Febbraio 15, Ragusa Ibla, 97100* **Tel** *0932-220 065* **Fax** *0932-663 186* **Rooms** *10* **Road Map** *E5*

In the Baroque heart of town, this intimate hotel was constructed within an 18th-century palazzo. One room's Gothic arch dates to 1300, while another has a tub carved out of the rock. The furniture is handmade in early 19th-century style. The owners' restaurant a few blocks away also merits a visit. **www.locandadonserafino.it**

**RAGUSA Mediterraneo Palace** €€

*Via Roma 189, 97100* **Tel** *0932-621 944* **Fax** *0932-623 799* **Rooms** *92* **Road Map** *E5*

In the Baroque section of Ragusa, near the Museo Archeologico, is this hotel with comfortable, spacious rooms furnished in modern style with all conveniences. Baths are large, with marble floors, and some have a whirlpool, a good antidote to tired feet after a long day's sightseeing. **www.mediterraneopalace.it**

**RAGUSA Eremo della Giubiliana** €€€

*Contrada Giubiliana, 97100* **Tel** *0932-669 119* **Fax** *0932-669 129* **Rooms** *12* **Road Map** *E5*

This 12th-century monastery is an elegant retreat and its plateau position offers superb panoramic views. This makes a more tranquil base for beach excursions than any hotel in Marina di Ragusa. Rooms are in former monks' cells, all elegantly furnished. **www.eremodellagiubiliana.it**

**SYRACUSE Domus Maiae** €€

*Via Vittorio Veneto 76, 96100* **Tel** *0931-24 854* **Fax** *0931-24 858* **Rooms** *16* **Road Map** *F4*

Ursuline nuns efficiently run this hotel with spacious rooms; a room with a sea view costs an additional 15 euros. The hotel has a small library, where guests can dine during part of the year (the dining room is not open to outsiders). It all adds up to a pleasant and tranquil stay.

**SYRACUSE Hotel Il Podere** €€

*Contrada Torre Landolina 11, 96100* **Tel** *0931-449 390* **Fax** *0931-723 006* **Rooms** *26* **Road Map** *F4*

Inside the Fonte Ciane nature reserve, surrounded by citrus and olive groves, is this 19th-century farm complex, which has been elegantly converted to a hotel. Bedrooms are furnished with antiques and rugs. There are two pools, a playground, a private beach, horse riding and golf. Located near the Neapolis archaeological park. **www.ilpodere.it**

**SYRACUSE L'Approdo delle Sirene** €€

*Riva Garibaldi 15, 96100* **Tel** *0931-24 857* **Fax** *0931-483 764* **Rooms** *8* **Road Map** *F4*

This elegant historic two-storey building on the harbour channel has a roof terrace fragrant with jasmine and bougainvillea. Here you can have breakfast, admire the sunset or watch the action in the harbour. Some rooms have balconies overlooking the harbour. A light lunch is available on request. **www.apprododellesirene.com**

**SYRACUSE Palazzo Giaracà** €€

*Via dei Mille 34, 96100* **Tel** *0931-464 907* **Fax** *0931-480 419* **Rooms** *27* **Road Map** *F4*

This 1892 palace on the Ortygia harbour still has some original antiques. It is run by descendants of a noble family, whose personal touch creates a warm and inviting ambience. Floors are tiled or volcanic stone. The Count's Room has a fireplace, and there are down duvets. Some rooms have harbour views. **www.palazzogiaraca.it**

**SYRACUSE Hotel des Etrangers et Miramare** €€€

*Passagio Adorno 10–12, 96100* **Tel** *0931-319 100* **Fax** *0931-319 100* **Rooms** *80* **Road Map** *F4*

Reopened in 2005 after being closed for 30 years, this historic luxury hotel in central Ortygia faces a sandy beach. The hotel has two restaurants, one with a view of the coast and the other with a roof garden for alfresco dining. Sea-view rooms are more expensive. There is also a spa. **www.medeahotels.com**

**SYRACUSE Villa Lucia** €€€

*Trav. Mondello 1, Contrada Isola, 96100* **Tel** *0931-721 007* **Fax** *0931-721 587* **Rooms** *15* **Road Map** *F4*

Once the summer home of the family who runs it, this patrician villa is set back among the trees and boasts a nicely landscaped pool. Inside, their furniture and mementos give the interior a personal, homely touch. Rooms are spacious; the carriage house nearby has budget-priced mini-apartments with kitchens. **www.siracusavillalucia.it**

## NORTHEASTERN SICILY

**ACITREZZA Hotel Eden Riviera** €

*Via Litteri 57, 95026* **Tel** *095-277 760* **Fax** *095-277 761* **Rooms** *31* **Road Map** *F3*

This family-run hotel in the hills above the sea has a terrace with views of Lachea Island and unique rock formations. Its small, enchanting garden has an impressive prickly pear cactus and other Mediterranean plants that surround the swimming pool. Dinner supplement. Discounts available (not in August). **www.hoteledenriviera.com**

**CAPO D'ORLANDO La Tartaruga** €€

*Via Lido San Gregorio 70, 98071* **Tel** *0941-955 012* **Fax** *0941-955 056* **Rooms** *38* **Road Map** *E2*

Halfway between Milazzo and Cefalù, this small seaside hotel attracts a business clientele during most of the year. In summer, families enjoy its beach facilities, pool, pizzeria and disco. Rooms are simply furnished in yellow, blue or green. Bedroom terraces and balconies face the sea, pool or inner courtyard. **www.hoteltartaruga.it**

**CAPRILEONE Hotel Antica Filanda** €€

*Contrada da Raviola, 98070* **Tel** *0941-919 704* **Rooms** *16* **Road Map** *E2*

The hilltop vista from the terrace is of the Aeolian Islands. Guest rooms are spacious and decorated in an antique style with cherrywood furniture. Two suites have a fireplace and Jacuzzi. Sip afternoon cocktails on the terrace or by the pool, and enjoy homemade jams at breakfast (flavours include peach, orange and lemon). **www.anticafilanda.it**

**CATANIA Albergo Moderno** €

*Via Alessi 9, 95124* **Tel** *095-326 250* **Fax** *095-326 674* **Rooms** *18* **Road Map** *F3*

Opened in 1922 and run by the same family since 1955, the Moderno is an inexpensive option for those who prefer budget rates to chic or cutting-edge decor. Bedrooms have fluorescent lights and are rather spartan, but the hotel is clean and centrally located. **www.albergomoderno.it**

**CATANIA Hotel Centrale Europa** €

*Via Vittorio Emanuele, 167, 95124* **Tel** *095-311 309* **Fax** *095-317 531* **Rooms** *17* **Road Map** *F3*

Thanks to a recent facelift, this economical historic hotel has an inviting exterior. Inside, the rooms are pleasant, simple, and with new wooden furniture; most also have a terrific view of Piazza Duomo, so you can have fun watching the world go by. No lift (rooms are upstairs). Helpful staff. **www.hotecentraleuropa.it**

**CATANIA Garden** €€

*Trappeto, Via Madonna delle Lacrime, 95129* **Tel** *095-717 77 67* **Fax** *095-717 79 91* **Rooms** *95* **Road Map** *F3*

The hotel's large Mediterranean garden with local and exotic plants is especially appreciated when the pool opens in summer. Rooms are comfortably furnished, many with walnut furniture in antique style, and there is a fitness centre and sauna. Located west of Catania, a short distance away from Etna's small towns. **www.gardenhotel.ct.it**

**CATANIA Hotel del Duomo** €€

*Via Etnea 28, 95131* **Tel** *095-250 31 77* **Fax** *095-715 27 90* **Rooms** *12* **Road Map** *F3*

Step into the courtyard and leave the bustle of the city behind. Small, family-run and quiet, this hotel near Piazza Duomo opened in 2002. Rooms are pleasantly furnished, some with rooftop views; one room (Brancati) has a balcony. The patisserie downstairs (not part of the hotel) is handy for a sweet snack. **www.hoteldelduomo.it**

**CATANIA Castello di Xirumi-Serravale** €€€

*Castello di Xirume, Frazione Lentini, 95129* **Tel** *095-447 987* **Fax** *095-504 553* **Rooms** *10* **Road Map** *F3*

This 16th-century castle southwest of Catania, run by a noble family, is a link to Renaissance Sicily. The castle is furnished with antiques, and its atmosphere makes it a popular choice with locals for wedding receptions. A good base to see nearby Neolithic tombs, and the ceramics of Caltagirone are only half an hour away. **www.xirumi.com**

**CATANIA Hotel Royal** €€€

*Via A. Di Sangiuliano 337, 95124* **Tel** *095-250 33 47* **Fax** *095-250 33 60* **Rooms** *20* **Road Map** *F3*

This trendy hotel, with its contemporary architectural design, has a wine bar, restaurant and tearoom. It is located near the top of the hill and the street leads to the harbour below – a good base for city walks. Room balconies face the street or the courtyard. Facilities include a solarium, Jacuzzi, gym, sauna and Turkish bath. **www.hotelroyalcatania.it**

**CATANIA Il Principe Hotel** €€€

*Via Alessi 24, 95124* **Tel** *095-250 03 45* **Fax** *095-325 799* **Rooms** *25* **Road Map** *F3*

The flair of a contemporary architect shows in details like the lighting, wooden floors, luminous bathroom tiles and high-quality textiles in the guest rooms in this hotel. Services include a Turkish bath, Internet point, small bar and free parking. The Costanza Suite has a fireplace and skylight. **www.ilprincipehotel.com**

**CATANIA Katane Palace Hotel** €€€

*Via Finocchiaro Aprile 110, 95129* **Tel** *095-747 07 02* **Fax** *095-747 01 72* **Rooms** *58* **Road Map** *F3*

This lovely hotel attracts a business and tourist clientele that enjoys modern conveniences and style. From the bellboy to the manager, the staff here take great pride in the details: the salon has travel books and a grand piano for guests to play, and the flower-filled patio expands the dining area, which is run by a capable chef. **www.katanepalace.it**

**CATANIA Sheraton** €€€

*Via Antonello da Messina 45, Acicastello, 95020* **Tel** *095-711 41 11* **Fax** *095-271 380* **Rooms** *170* **Road Map** *F3*

This modern hotel caters primarily to the business and conference clientele. Summer visitors can take the underpass directly to the private beach, and there is a fitness centre, beauty centre and spa. The management is placing extra emphasis on developing an innovative quality restaurant, Il Timo, to also attract locals. **www.sheratoncatania.com**

**CATANIA Villa del Bosco Hotel** €€€

*Via del Bosco 62, 95125* **Tel** *095-733 51 00* **Fax** *095-733 51 03* **Rooms** *45* **Road Map** *F3*

This 19th-century villa opened as a hotel in 2001; four years later, it expanded into a modern wing. Some rooms are furnished with antiques, and the roof terrace has a view of the city. The hotel has non-smoking rooms, is well equipped for business meetings and can arrange car rental. **www.hotelvilladelbosco.it**

**Key to Price Guide** *see p198* **Key to Symbols** *see back cover flap*

**CATANIA Grand Hotel Baia Verde** €€€€
*Cannizaro, Via Musco 8–10, 95020* **Tel** *095-491 522* **Fax** *095-494 464* **Rooms** *162* **Road Map** *F3*

White-washed buildings at the sea's edge make this one of Catania's most attractive seaside resorts. The restaurant has a sea view and the terrace offers outdoor dining. The wellness centre is popular with locals too, who enjoy its many treatments and programmes. There is also a diving school. **www.baiaverde.it**

**GIARDINI-NAXOS Arathena Rocks** €
*Via Calcide Eubea 55, 98030* **Tel** *0942-51 349* **Fax** *0942-51 690* **Rooms** *50* **Road Map** *F3*

The sea-water swimming pool cut out of the rock is one of the main draws at this seaside hotel. Some bathrooms are decorated with Sicilian tiles. The hotel is open only during the warmer season, from April (sometimes earlier) to November. Half-board may be required during the month of August. **www.hotelarathena.com**

**GIARDINI-NAXOS Nike** €
*Via Calcide Eubea 27, 98030* **Tel** *0942-51 207* **Fax** *0942-56 315* **Rooms** *55* **Road Map** *F3*

Large terraces offer a panoramic view of the sea below. The hotel has a solarium, as well as its own private beach and a dock for pleasure boats. Some rooms do not have air conditioning, so specify which you prefer (the price difference is only a few euros). **www.hotelnike.it**

**LIPARI Giardino sul Mare** €€€
*Via Maddalena 65, 98055* **Tel** *090-981 10 04* **Fax** *090-988 01 50* **Rooms** *46* **Road Map** *E1*

This charming island hotel overlooks the sea and boasts its own private beach below. The terrace has magnificent views, and the garden has ancient plants and palm trees. All bedrooms were renovated in 2005; they are furnished in wood with blue-and-white floors and blue cotton bedcovers; most have sea views. **www.giardinosulmare.it**

**LIPARI Hotel A Pinnata** €€€
*Località Pignataro, 98055* **Tel** *090-981 16 97* **Fax** *090-981 47 82* **Rooms** *12* **Road Map** *E1*

From this hotel terrace the view to the island of Vulcano is breathtaking. Rooms are warm green or yellow, with mostly wooden furniture and iron beds. Guests have easy access to the beach. This hotel has no restaurant but there are many excellent eateries nearby. Closed Nov–Mar. **www.bernardigroup.it**

**LIPARI Hotel Tritone** €€€
*Via Mendolita, 98055* **Tel/Fax** *090-981 15 95* **Rooms** *39* **Road Map** *E1*

Volcanic spring water feeds the swimming pool at the Tritone; drinks and sandwiches are available pool-side. All rooms have a sea view, as does the breakfast room. The hotel, which has a health spa, is a short walk from the town centre and the sea. A shuttle service to the beach is provided. **tritone@CharmeRelax.com**

**LIPARI Villa Meligunis** €€€€
*Via Marte, 98055* **Tel** *090-981 24 26* **Fax** *090-988 01 49* **Rooms** *32* **Road Map** *E1*

Small and luxurious, this island hotel is located near Marina Corta in an 18th-century converted residence in a fishing village. The hotel has an established reputation for impeccable service, and in 2003 it added a swimming pool and a Turkish bath to its existing list of facilities. **www.villameligunis.it**

**MESSINA Grand Hotel Liberty** €€€
*Via I Settembre 15, 98122* **Tel** *090-640 94 36* **Fax** *090-640 93 40* **Rooms** *54* **Road Map** *F2*

Built in the Art Nouveau style, this classic hotel is located in the historic centre of Messina, near the train station and a short distance to the port for departures to the Aeolian Islands. In addition to the restaurant, services include tearoom, bar, conference rooms and Wi-Fi in the rooms, plus car and motorbike rentals. **www.framonhotels.com**

**MESSINA Royal Palace** €€€
*Via T. Cannizzaro 224, 98123* **Tel** *090-65 03* **Fax** *090-292 10 75* **Rooms** *116* **Road Map** *F2*

In the heart of Messina's shopping district and near the harbour, this hotel caters to both business and leisure travellers. The spacious rooms have plenty of light from big windows or terraces. Services include conference rooms and Wi-Fi in the guest rooms, plus car and motorbike rentals. **www.framonhotels.com**

**MILAZZO Petit Hotel** €€
*Via dei Mille 37, 98057* **Tel** *090-928 67 84* **Fax** *090-928 50 42* **Rooms** *9* **Road Map** *F2*

Zen furnishings, handcrafted Bourbon-style ceramics and original paintings decorate this 19th-century building in Milazzo. The owners installed natural-fibre mattresses, a filtered and ionized air system that removes dust, climatized wall panels to regulate temperature and other environment-improving technology. **www.petithotel.it**

**PANAREA Cincotta** €€€€
*Via San Pietro, 98050* **Tel** *090-983 014* **Fax** *090-983 211* **Rooms** *29* **Road Map** *E1*

Situated near Panarea's harbour and set into a cliff, this hotel offers a superb view of the sea from some of its rooms. The terrace has a sea-water swimming pool, and rooms are furnished in a warm Mediterranean style. From 7 to 27 August, the minimum stay is one week and half-board may be required. Closed Nov–Mar. **www.hotelcincotta.it**

**PANAREA Hotel Quartara** €€€€
*Via San Pietro 15, 98050* **Tel** *090-983 027* **Fax** *090-983 621* **Rooms** *13* **Road Map** *E1*

White-washed Aeolian-style architecture shapes this hotel with a terrace overlooking the sea. The luminous rooms feature teak furniture, handmade bedcovers and terraces. The terrace restaurant is known as much for its food as for its view. Garden, Jacuzzi and massages are all nice extras. **www.quartarahotel.com**

**PANAREA La Piazza** €€€€

*Via San Pietro, 98050* **Tel** *090-983 154* **Fax** *090-983 649* **Rooms** *33* **Road Map** *E1*

Set above the Calette Bay on Panarea's eastern coast, in a lovely Mediterranean garden, is La Piazza. In 2005, the sea-water swimming pool was supplemented by the island's only wellness centre. The season runs from April to October, but off-season a small annexe is open at bargain rates. **www.hotelpiazza.it**

**PANAREA Raya** €€€€€

*Panarea-Isole Eolie, 98050* **Tel** *090-983 013* **Fax** *090-983 103* **Rooms** *36* **Road Map** *E1*

The Raya has traditional Aeolian style combined with some modern architecture to maximize use of the space above the sea. Bedrooms are simply furnished, in light or dark wood, with white textiles; mirrors expand the light and create a double sea vista. Plush down duvets on the beds add a touch of luxury. Closed Mar–Oct. **www.hotelraya.it**

**SALINA L'Ariana** €€

*Via Rotabile 11, Rinella, 98050* **Tel** *090-980 90 75* **Fax** *090-980 92 50* **Rooms** *15* **Road Map** *E1*

This early Liberty villa in Rinella's small harbour has a spectacular view of Lipari and Vulcano. Guest rooms are spacious, decorated in yellow and white, each with an antique family chest; some have a sea view. In the summer dinner is served on the terrace. Prices are very reasonable in low season. **www.hotelariana.it**

**SALINA Hotel Signum** €€€

*Via Scalo 15, Malfa, 98050* **Tel** *090-984 42 22* **Fax** *090-984 41 02* **Rooms** *30* **Road Map** *E1*

An old hamlet of farmers' houses was entirely renovated to create this hotel complex. Three types of bedrooms are available, including some in the small houses among the gardens and vineyards. The outdoor swimming pool has a view of Stromboli. The restaurant serves traditional cuisine in a family atmosphere. **www.hotelsignum.it**

**SAN GIOVANNI LA PUNTA Villa Paradiso dell'Etna** €€€€

*Via per Viagrande 37, 95030* **Tel** *095-751 24 09* **Fax** *095-741 38 61* **Rooms** *34* **Road Map** *E3*

On the slopes of Etna, this 1927 villa has frescoed walls, *trompe-l'oeil* paintings, period furniture and fireplaces. The garden has trees that are centuries old and the swimming pool is heated. Non-smoking guest rooms. Services include a wellness centre, massages, tennis courts, bike rental and a private beach at Capomulini. **www.paradisoetna.it**

**STROMBOLI La Sciara Residence** €€€€

*Via S. Cincotta, 98050* **Tel** *090-986 004* **Fax** *090-986 284* **Rooms** *62* **Road Map** *F1*

Set in a garden filled with bougainvillea, this hotel features guest rooms decorated with white interiors and hand-crafted furniture, which reflects the rustic style of the island. Bedrooms have either a view of the sea or of the volcano; some also have a terrace and there is a tennis court. Half-board is required 4–24 Aug. Closed Oct–Apr. **www.lasciara.it**

**STROMBOLI La Sirenetta Park Hotel** €€€€

*Via Marina 33, 98050* **Tel** *090-986 025* **Fax** *090-986 124* **Rooms** *57* **Road Map** *F1*

This white hotel's flower-filled patio connects to a flight of steps and tiny alleyways that wind uphill towards a magnificent amphitheatre carved out of volcanic rock. Services include a sea-water swimming pool, dive centre, and boat and bicycle rentals. The restaurant features local fish and vegetable dishes. Closed Nov–Mar. **www.lasirenetta.it**

**TAORMINA Hotel Isabella** €€

*Corso Umberto 58, 98039* **Tel** *0942-23 153* **Fax** *0942-23 155* **Rooms** *32* **Road Map** *F2*

Set in the town centre amid local shops and restaurants, the Isabella offers comfortable, reasonably priced, cheerful rooms. The roof terrace has views over the rooftops, gardens, the sea and Etna. Some rooms share a terrace above an ancient Roman aqueduct; floors above have sea or street views. There is a shuttle to a private beach. **www.gaishotels.com**

**TAORMINA Hotel Villa Schuler** €€

*Piazzetta Bastione 16, 98039* **Tel** *0942-23 481* **Fax** *0942-23 522* **Rooms** *27* **Road Map** *F2*

This no-frills 19th-century villa will appeal to the budget-minded traveller who still wants to enjoy a central, family-run hotel. Rooms are simply furnished in wood; a garden view is less expensive than a sea view or balconied room. The terrace has a lovely vista and there is a large private garden. Shuttle service to the beach. **www.hotelvillaschuler.com**

**TAORMINA Hotel Villa Ducale** €€€

*Via Leonardo da Vinci 60, 98039* **Tel** *0942-28 153* **Fax** *0942-28 710* **Rooms** *16* **Road Map** *F2*

Flowers spill from everywhere here. The friendly owners and staff, who run this gem above Taormina, greet you with a welcome drink at check in. Rooms are cheerful, with tiles from Caltagirone, bright frescoes, wrought-iron beds and terraces that face Etna, the sea or Calabria. Garden, Jacuzzi, spa and bar. **www.hotelvilladucale.com**

**TAORMINA Hotel Villa Sirina** €€€

*Via Crocifisso 30, 98039* **Tel** *0942-51 776* **Fax** *0942-51 671* **Rooms** *16* **Road Map** *F2*

In the foothills below Taormina, surrounded by oleanders and citrus groves, is this early 20th-century family-run villa. Furnishings are homely and simple, with some antiques and crafts. Villa Sirina has a mountain and a sea view, and it is located only one kilometre from the Giardini (Taormina Gardens). **www.villasirina.com**

**TAORMINA Park Hotel La Plage** €€€

*Via Nazionale 107, Mazzarò, 98039* **Tel** *0942-626 095* **Fax** *0942-625 850* **Rooms** *66* **Road Map** *F2*

Fifty stone bungalows set in a pine forest that descends to the sea at Isola Bella provide a simple and somewhat more economical option than the major beach hotels. Most bungalows are decorated in a rustic style; the nicer ones are the eight junior suites, some furnished with antiques. There is also a spa. Closed Dec–Jan. **www.laplage.it**

**Key to Price Guide** *see p198* **Key to Symbols** *see back cover flap*

**TAORMINA Residence Villa Giulia** €€€

*Via Bagnoli Croce 75, 98039* ***Tel*** *0942-23 312* ***Fax*** *0942-23 391* ***Rooms*** *7* ***Road Map*** *F2*

These small apartments with kitchens are ideal for families and those who want to peruse markets and create their own dishes with local ingredients. Each sunny apartment has a terrace, wooden tables and cheerful ceramics. You have the use of a pool at a nearby hotel, a beach/health club shuttle service and a restaurant. **www.gaishotels.com**

**TAORMINA Villa Carlotta** €€€

*Via Pirandello 81, 98039* ***Tel*** *0942-626 058* ***Fax*** *0942-23 732* ***Rooms*** *27* ***Road Map*** *F2*

This lovely stone villa, with its quirky tower, striped awnings and stained glass, is a real charmer. Spacious guest rooms have cherrywood furniture and a balcony. The bright top room is ideal for reading or for evening drinks. There is also a small swimming pool, hot tub and Internet point. Closed Jan & Feb. **www.hotelvillacarlottataormina.com**

**TAORMINA Baia Taormina Hotel & Spa** €€€€

*Statale dello Ionio 39, Marina d'Agro, 98039* ***Tel*** *0942-756 292* ***Fax*** *0942-756 603* ***Rooms*** *60* ***Road Map*** *F2*

Set on a rocky slope above the bay a few kilometres north of Taormina, these villa-style buildings and terrace offer freshwater and saltwater swimming pools, private beach, gym, massages and a Turkish bath. Various sports can be arranged, including scuba diving, surfing, hang-gliding and tennis. Closed Nov–Mar. **www.baiataormina.com**

**TAORMINA Hotel Caparena and Wellness Club** €€€€

*Via Nazionale 189, Mazzarò, 98039* ***Tel*** *0942-652 033* ***Fax*** *0942-36 913* ***Rooms*** *88* ***Road Map*** *F2*

This tranquil beach hotel has its own garden for barbecues, a private beach, two rooftop restaurants, piano bar and year-round pool. The well-equipped wellness centre opened in 2004 and has massage therapists, gym, steam bath and various beauty treatments. The beach can be reached via an underground tunnel. Closed Nov–Mar. **www.gaishotels.com**

**TAORMINA Grand Hotel Atlantis Bay** €€€€€

*Via Nazionale 161, Mazzarò, 98039* ***Tel*** *0942-618 011* ***Fax*** *0942-23 194* ***Rooms*** *86* ***Road Map*** *F2*

Lavishly carved and decorated stone walls and a tropical aquarium give the impression of being in your own private grotto. The colour scheme is mostly white with natural fabrics; many rooms have sea views. Among the highlights are the pool, private beach and the wellness centre. Non-smoking rooms and Internet point. **www.atlantisbay.it**

**TAORMINA Grand Hotel Mazzarò Sea Palace** €€€€€

*Via Nazionale 147, Mazzarò, 98039* ***Tel*** *0942-612 111* ***Fax*** *0942-626 237* ***Rooms*** *88* ***Road Map*** *F2*

Modern and comfortable, this hotel hosts business conferences but also welcomes leisure travellers who enjoy its pool, fitness centre and private beach. Most rooms have terraces with sea view, and the hotel also offers a piano bar, pay parking and non-smoking rooms. Various water sports can be arranged. Open Mar–Nov. **www.mazzaroseapalace.it**

**TAORMINA Grand Hotel San Pietro** €€€€€

*Via Pirandello 50, 98039* ***Tel*** *0942-620 711* ***Fax*** *0942-620 770* ***Rooms*** *62* ***Road Map*** *F2*

This idyllic hotel harmonizes with Taormina's existing architecture and environment. Antiques adorn the lobby, while lovely prints and sumptuous textiles decorate the rooms; most have a sea view, some look towards Etna. The artist-in-residence gives painting lessons, and the chef prepares creative dishes. Shuttle to beach. **www.gaishotels.com**

**TAORMINA Grand Hotel Timeo e Villa Flora** €€€€€

*Via Teatro Greco 59, 98039* ***Tel*** *0942-23 801* ***Fax*** *0942-628 501* ***Rooms*** *84* ***Road Map*** *F2*

Located next to the ancient Greek theatre, Taormina's first hotel (1850) exudes historic charm. The elegant salons have large windows and are ideal for conversation, reading or evening piano. The Literary Terrace looks over a splendid garden, the sea and Etna. Guest rooms also have terraces. Bar and tearoom. **www.framonhotels.com**

**TAORMINA San Domenico Palace Hotel** €€€€€

*Piazza San Domenico 5, 98039* ***Tel*** *0942-613 111* ***Fax*** *0942-625 506* ***Rooms*** *111* ***Road Map*** *F2*

This former 15th-century Domenican convent matches its ancient grandeur with modern conveniences. The hotel has a lovely courtyard and inviting plush grand salons with some remaining frescoes. The garden terrace offers a sweeping vista of the sea and Etna. The stone fireplace is cosy and welcoming in winter. **www.sandomenico.thi.it**

**TAORMINA Villa Sant'Andrea** €€€€€

*Via Nazionale 137, Mazzarò, 98039* ***Tel*** *0942-625 837* ***Fax*** *0942-24 838* ***Rooms*** *83* ***Road Map*** *F2*

An aristocratic British family built this villa in 1830. Set in a sub-tropical garden on the beach, it still maintains the charm of a private residence. Services include a private beach, wellness centre with sauna and massages and an entertaining piano bar. Staff can arrange for bicycles, scuba diving, windsurfing and other sports. **www.framonhotels.com**

**VULCANO Hotel Conti** €€

*Località Ponte di Ponente, 98050* ***Tel*** *090-985 20 12* ***Fax*** *090-985 20 64* ***Rooms*** *67* ***Road Map*** *E1*

A modest hotel in Aeolian style that offers peace and tranquillity near Vulcano's famous black-sand beach. The restaurant features various regional cuisines; half-board options are available and may be required in August. Closed Nov–Apr. **www.contivulcano.it**

**VULCANO Les Sables Noires** €€€

*Ponte di Ponente, 98050* ***Tel*** *090-98 50* ***Fax*** *090-985 24 54* ***Rooms*** *48* ***Road Map*** *E1*

Named after the black volcanic sand on the beach, this hotel has modern, comfortable rooms – most with balconies. The interior colour scheme reflects the area's white-washed houses, while black accessories recall the island's sand. Most water sports can be arranged. Terrace restaurant. **www.framonhotels.com**

# WHERE TO EAT

Sicilians love good food and like nothing better than joining family and friends around a restaurant table, especially if the food is genuinely homemade. Fish is one of the highlights of Sicilian cuisine. Almost all restaurants serve freshly caught fish, grilled or fried according to local recipes, and fish is often an ingredient for pasta sauces as well. Pasta is widely available and so is couscous, an Arab legacy.

**A restaurant sign in a Sicilian village**

Restaurant opening hours are typical of the southern Mediterranean: in general places open from 1–3:30pm for lunch and from 9–12 midnight for dinner. Most restaurants generally close one day a week and may close for up to a month for annual holidays, so it is a good idea to check ahead to avoid disappointment. The restaurants listed on pages 212–21 have been selected from among the best on the island.

**Buffet at the Azienda Agricola Trinità, in Mascalucia *(see p168)***

## BREAKFAST AND SNACKS

Besides the traditional croissant, eaten with black coffee *(espresso)* or a milky coffee *(cappuccino)*, Sicilians also enjoy croissants stuffed with ice-cream and iced coffee and milk for breakfast. Bars and pastry shops *(pasticcerie)* stock a range of pastries, and Sicilian freshly squeezed fruit juices are excellent. If you are staying in a hotel where breakfast is included, it is likely to consist of coffee or tea with croissants and bread with fruit jam. More luxurious hotels will offer a buffet with yoghurt, breakfast cereal, fresh fruit, sliced ham and salami. For a mid-morning snack, or for lunch, you can go to a bar or *rosticceria*, where you will find a range of sandwiches *(tramezzini)* and filled rolls *(panini)*, *arancini* (rice and meat balls) and *impanate* (breadcrumb croquettes stuffed with aubergines (eggplant), spinach and cheese, or potatoes and onions). Favourite Palermo snacks are *pane ca meusa* (bread stuffed with spleen) or *pane e panelle* (chick pea fritters). These specialities are also sold in outdoor markets.

## TYPES OF RESTAURANT

In Sicily, even the smallest village is likely to have a trattoria serving local specialities. There is not much difference (in terms of price, cuisine and décor) between a restaurant proper and a trattoria, especially along the coast, where even quite sophisticated establishments are decorated with maritime paraphernalia. *Putie* are typically simple trattorias with home cooking and a set menu; they generally offer good value for money. Pizzerias are widespread and are ideal for cheap and fast meals. Another typical aspect of Sicilian tradition is the *rosticceria*, serving quick, hot meals from the roasting oven, and *focacceria*, where the Sicilian flat bread *focaccia* is used as a pizza base.

## READING THE MENU

Printed menus are still rare in Sicily, as it is the custom for the waiter to recite the day's list at your table. Good antipasti *(see pp210–11)* are vegetables (from olives to aubergines) in oil, seafood and fish salads and seafood soups (with mussels, clams, cuttlefish, squid). The first course is pasta, usually with vegetables or fish and often so hearty that it is as filling as a main course: try *pasta con le sarde*, with sardines *(see p210)*; *spaghetti alla Norma*, with tomato, basil, aubergine and ricotta, *cuscus alla trapanese*, couscous with onion, spices and a fish sauce; *pasta*

**The terrace at I Mulini on the island of Pantelleria *(see p216)***

The renowned Wünderbar in Taormina *(see p178)*

*n'casciata*, macaroni pie with meat sauce, sausage, cheese and hard-boiled eggs. The main course is often fish (typically tuna, swordfish, bream), freshly cooked and sold by weight (so ask for a rough price). Fresh fruit or dessert (*cannoli*, ricotta cheese and candied fruit rolls; *cassata*, cake with ricotta cheese, sugar, chocolate and candied fruit *(see p211)*; ice-cream) wind up the meal. For vegetarians there are excellent vegetables and a range of pasta dishes.

## WINE

Most restaurants, even the average ones, have a wine list with a good selection of Sicilian wines. Trattorias on the other hand tend to offer their house wine, locally produced, and inexpensive table wine, usually served in a carafe.

## FIXED-PRICE MENUS

Not many Sicilian trattorias and restaurants offer fixed-price menus. In general these are limited to the family-run trattorias which offer only one or two different dishes every day.

## PRICES AND PAYING

In trattorias a normal three-course meal will cost about €20–€25. In restaurants, a similar meal will cost upwards of €30. Even in a top restaurant you are unlikely to spend more than a maximum of €60 per person. Pizza is always good value, and rarely costs more than about €8–€10.

Your bill may be a simple total, without the different courses being itemized. If you do have an itemized bill, the total will include a cover charge (€1–€3) and a service charge. Tipping is not obligatory, but if you decide to leave a tip, calculate 8–10 per cent. Italian law requires all eating establishments to issue a bona fide printed receipt *(ricevuta fiscale)* to clients when they pay. Anything else is illegal. Make sure you get a receipt as you may receive a hefty fine if you cannot produce a *ricevuta fiscale* if requested by a police officer.

Waiter with a tray of desserts

Most Sicilian restaurants and trattorias accept a range of credit cards, including MasterCard and Visa. Bars, cafés and smaller, family-run establishments may only accept cash, so check you have enough.

## OPENING HOURS

All restaurants are closed one day during the week, with the possible exception of the high season, in July and August. This closing day is shown in the listings on pages 212–21. Restaurants and trattorias also close for about one month for annual holidays. In large cities like Palermo this usually occurs in August, whereas on the coast almost all restaurants are closed in the winter months. Island restaurants generally open according to the needs of the tourist season.

## MAKING RESERVATIONS

In the evening, especially in the summer, restaurants often get very crowded and you may find it difficult to get a table. It is always a good idea to book a table in advance, even in trattorias. An alternative is to arrive early, about 8pm, to avoid standing in line.

Phoning ahead is also advisable if you want to make sure that a restaurant's specialities will be available.

## CHILDREN

Children are always welcome in restaurants, particularly family-run places which are only too happy to prepare special dishes or half-portions for youngsters. Sophisticated restaurants may be less geared for children, so telephone beforehand.

## SMOKING

Smoking in restaurants is no longer allowed. Though many establishments might turn a blind eye, it is within your rights to ask someone not to smoke near you.

Sicilian ice-cream, almost always locally made

# The Flavours of Sicily

Sicilian cuisine is Italy's most varied and exotic, influenced by the different settlers who have grown flavourful ingredients in the lava-enriched soil and hot sunshine. Homer's *Odyssey* describes the island's bounty of apples, pomegranates and grapes. The Normans brought their way of curing fish with salt and the Spanish imported tomatoes and peppers. But it was the Arabs' introduction of almonds, aubergines (eggplants), saffron and sugar cane that defines much of Sicilian cooking. Their traditions of stuffing vegetables, making sweet pastries and using rice, couscous and sweet-sour combinations are still used today.

Fresh herbs

Local farmer with a basket of freshly made ricotta

## NORTHWESTERN SICILY

Cooking in northwestern Sicily is often highly spiced, revealing a strong eastern influence, not least in the capital, Palermo, where the food markets have the feel of Arabian souks.

Blossom and fruits from the orange and lemon groves of La Conca d'Oro near Palermo perfume the air and feature in many dishes, while the vineyards around Marsala produce wines that are used in both savoury dishes and desserts. *Insalata d'arance* – orange salad – refreshingly combines oranges, mint and marsala.

Historically, villages along the northwest coast thrived on tuna fishing, and Mazaro del Vallo has one of the Mediterranean's largest deep-sea fishing fleets.

## SOUTHWESTERN SICILY

Inland the traditional fare is poultry, meat and offal. Liver is often cooked in a sweet-and-sour sauce while rabbit or goat is simmered with vegetables, herbs and spices. Fruits are made into preserves and pastes, almonds into marzipan treats. The speciality in Agrigento, where there is an almond festival each spring, is a sweet *cuscus* with

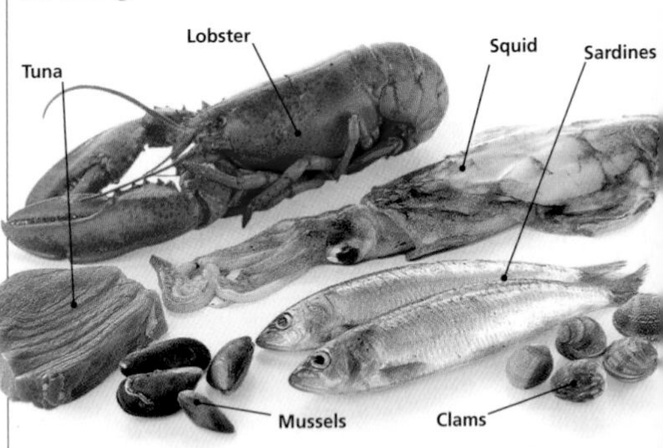


Selection of seafood from the clear waters of Sicily's coastline

## SICILIAN DISHES AND SPECIALITIES

Local figs

Antipasti include carpaccio of tuna or swordfish; *caponata* – aubergines (eggplant) in a rich sweet-and-sour tomato sauce with capers, olives, pine nuts and basil; and *frittedda* of artichokes, peas and broad (fava) beans. *Arancini* are small stuffed, fried balls of golden risotto rice, named for the little oranges they resemble.

Fresh ricotta melds with aubergine and tomato as a sauce for *pasta alla norma*. Seafood and shellfish are also added to pasta, such as *pasta al nero di sepia* (with cuttlefish ink) and *pasta con aragosta* (with lobster). Sardines, squid and mullet are cooked in myriad ways, like *calamari in umido* (squid and anchovies in tomato sauce) and *triglie di scoglio* (red mullet in a sweet-sour onion sauce).

**Maccheroncini con le sarde** *is Sicilian macaroni with sardines, fennel, pine nuts, raisins, breadcrumbs and saffron.*

Farmer selling fruit from the back of his truck in Taormina, Sicily

chocolate, pistachios and almonds. A savoury *cuscus*, cooked with fish or chicken stock, cloves and nutmeg in a terracotta pot, is found on Pantelleria, the closest point to the North African coast.

## NORTHEASTERN SICILY

Dominated by Mount Etna and its fertile slopes, the east has fields, orchards, citrus groves and vines. Local dishes use herbs rather than spices.

On the coast, Messina is known for swordfish, often served simply grilled with herbs and lemon, and Catania for *risotto nero* using dark cuttlefish ink (sometimes topped with tomato sauce to resemble an Etna eruption).

Mountain snow, mixed with sugar and flower essence or juice, began the Sicilian tradition of sorbets and ice creams.

## SOUTHERN SICILY

In Ragusa province, vast greenhouses dot the landscape, enabling the year-round production and export of fruit and vegetables. Yellow peppers, plump

Freshly harvested olives ready to be pressed into rich oil

aubergines (eggplants), courgettes (zucchini) and tomatoes are the basis for pasta sauces like *vermicelli alla siracusana* (of Syracuse), which also uses black olives, capers and anchovies.

Pork from the pigs farmed inland has the distinctive taste of the prickly pears on which they feed, and the local sausages are often flavoured with wild herbs.

Milk from cows, sheep and goats is made into cheeses such as pecorino, and is sometimes studded with peppercorns or olives. Ricotta is crumbled onto stews, pasta and rice dishes and is an essential ingredient in many desserts.

## WHAT TO DRINK

High quality wines include Faro and Cerasuolo di Vittoria (both reds), Contea di Sclafari, Erice, Nero d'Avola and Etna wines from the slopes of the volcano (dry reds and whites).

Marsala, a fortified wine created by 18th-century English merchants, may be dry *(secco)* or sweet *(dolce)*.

Sweet *moscato* (muscat) comes from Noto, Syracuse and Pantelleria. Rare Malvasia from Lipari is known as "drinkable gold".

There are liqueurs made from almonds, lemon, prickly pears, and herbs and roots.

**Pesce spada**, *swordfish steak, may be cooked in an orange sauce, or pan-fried or grilled with lemon and herbs.*

**Pollo alla marsala** *is pan-fried chicken (veal may also be used) with marsala, lemon juice, capers and parsley.*

**Cassata** *is Sicily's famous sponge cake, with ricotta, nuts, marsala, chocolate, candied fruit and marzipan.*

# Choosing a Restaurant

The restaurants in this chart have been selected across a wide price range for the high quality of their service and decor and their location. They have been divided into five areas and are listed by price category. Palermo restaurants are listed by price category and according to the city zones shown in the chapter on Palermo.

**PRICE CATEGORIES**
The following price ranges are for a three-course meal, including beverage (except for wine), tax and service.

€ under 20 euros
€€ 20–30 euros
€€€ 30–40 euros
€€€€ 40–50 euros
€€€€€ over 50 euros

## PALERMO

### EAST PALERMO Trattoria Il Maestro del Brodo €€

*Via Pannieri 7, 90133* ***Tel*** *091-329 523* **Map** *1 C3*

At the entrance of the Vucciria market is this economical hole-in-the-wall eatery, where the "master of broth" specializes in boiled veal. The most popular pasta dish on the menu is made with swordfish, tiny shrimp and courgette (zucchini). Fish is served fried, grilled or poached in seawater. Closed dinner (except Fri and Sat); Mon.

### EAST PALERMO Antica Focacceria San Francesco €€€

*Via Alessandro Paternostro 58, 90133* ***Tel*** *091-320 264* **Map** *2 D3*

Fragrant breads lure patrons into this historic, lively bakery opposite the church of San Francesco. Traditional dishes include *sfinciani* (stuffed flat bread), *u pani ca' meusa* (a type of stuffed bread) and lightly fried *panelle* (fritters made from chickpea flour). A good place to pick up a meal to take away. Closed Tue.

### EAST PALERMO Capricci di Sicilia €€€

*Via Istituto Pignatelli 6, at Piazza Sturzo, 90139* ***Tel*** *091-327 777* **Map** *1 B1*

Near the Galleria d'Arte Moderna and the Teatro Politeama, this trattoria is handy for lunch after visiting the museum or for dinner before or after a theatre performance. Most dishes revolve around meat and fish, and are traditionally Sicilian, sometimes with an elaborate, innovative twist. Closed Mon and 2 weeks Aug.

### EAST PALERMO Hanami €€€

*Via Alessandro Paternostro 56, 90133* ***Tel*** *091-320 264* **Map** *2 D3*

At this stylish restaurant you can dine on sushi and other international food trends that inspire the chef. Interesting seating areas, nice lighting and stylish architectural details attract Palermo's smart set for drinks and nibbles at the bar, or for a complete meal. The tables outside have a view of San Francesco. Open for dinner only. Closed Tue.

### EAST PALERMO Mi Manda Picone €€€

*Via Alessandro Paternostro 59, 90133* ***Tel*** *091-616 06 60* **Map** *2 D3*

When its neighbour Hanami is filled to overflowing, this restaurant is an easy back-up option. Mi Manda Picone does catering around Palermo, for large groups as well as private residences. One of its specialities is the *degustazione*, a wine-tasting menu that is matched to particular dishes on the menu. Closed Sun and Christmas.

### EAST PALERMO Osteria dei Vespri €€€

*Piazza Croce dei Vespri 6, 90133* ***Tel*** *091-617 16 31* **Map** *2 D4*

Once the historic Gangi Palace stables, this cosy restaurant balances exceptional cuisine and lovely presentations with attentive service and a great wine list. Try the superb raw fish, the *anneletti* (pasta rings) with octopus and Nero d'Avola sauce, or the sublime desserts. There is also a generous selection of premium wines by the glass. Closed Sun.

### EAST PALERMO Santandrea €€€

*Piazza Sant'Andrea 4, 90133* ***Tel*** *091-334 999* **Map** *1 C3*

The interior of this restaurant near the Vucciria market is all calm, neutral tones and simple lines – a striking contrast to the Baroque square outside and the colours of the market. Focus is on traditional cuisine, from antipasti to pasta and fish. Santandrea attracts a well-dressed crowd. Closed lunch; Tue; Jan.

### WEST PALERMO Pasticceria Mazzara €

*Via Generale Magliocco 19, 90141* ***Tel*** *091-321 443* **Map** *1 B2*

Located near the Teatro Massimo, this lovely patisserie with its attractive bars is known primarily for its sweets. However, they also serve a basic, economical lunch from 12:30pm to 3pm: it includes oven-baked pastas, salads and traditional Sicilian dishes. Try the pastries or the pistachio gelato for dessert. Opens at 7:30am.

### WEST PALERMO Ai Vecchietti €€

*Piazza S Oliva 10, 90141* ***Tel*** *091-585 606* **Map** *1 A1*

The gregarious owner sets the friendly tone here. Mixed antipasti feature *pannella* (fried bread) and olives. Try the *pappardelle cantalupo* (wide pasta ribbons with cantaloupe melon and prawns) or the squid, which is fried expertly and lightly. The 18th-century *cassata* recipe was procured from cloistered nuns. Folk music plays in the background.

**Key to Symbols** *see back cover flap*

**WEST PALERMO Cin-Cin Ristorante** €€

*Via Manin 22, 90139* ***Tel*** *091-612 40 95*

Vintage jazz plays softly in this restaurant where the elaborate 18th-century Baroque dishes have intriguing pungent notes. Try the fettucine with fresh oysters, and the perfectly cooked vegetables. Authentic Cajun meals can also be prepared (only on advance request) – the chef spent 20 years in Baton Rouge. Closed Sat lunch.

**WEST PALERMO Cucina Papoff** €€€€

*Via Isidoro La Lumia 32, 90139* ***Tel*** *091-586 460*

This place is elegant through and through: from the ceiling's intricate woodwork to the well-dressed crowd of professionals and aristocrats that receive attentive service. Popular dishes include purée of fava beans, linguine with red mullet, risotto with citrus fruit, a casserole of tiny meatballs, plus meat or fish dishes. Closed Sat lunch, Sun; Aug.

**FURTHER AFIELD Café Centro Città** €

*Via Archimede 184C, 90139* ***Tel*** *091-335 093* ***Road Map*** *C2*

An ordinary coffee bar that expands between noon and 3:30pm to offer a no-frills lunch for local office workers. The choice includes pastas, rice moulds (either traditional, with tomato sauce, or in variations like courgette (zucchini) and Emmenthal), meat dishes or salads. Closed evening; Sun.

**FURTHER AFIELD Caflisch** €

*Mondello, 90151* ***Tel*** *091-684 04 44* ***Road Map*** *C2*

Palermo's most outstanding patisserie is also one of Sicily's undisputed best. They also serve an informal express lunch, and diners can experience the pleasure of eating under the trees near Mondello beach. In the summer, don't miss the sublime *gel di melone* (watermelon gel). Extensive wine list. Closed Tue in winter.

**FURTHER AFIELD Pasticceria Bar Aluia** €

*Via Libertà 27, 90139* ***Tel*** *091-583 087* ***Road Map*** *C2*

Sweets are this patisserie's primary business, but at lunchtime Aluia also offers hot meals of oven-baked pasta, vegetables and other options. Local office workers and shoppers come for the low prices and traditional fare. By late afternoon the pasta disappears, and it's back to the pastry-and-coffee clientele. Closed Mon.

**FURTHER AFIELD Il Delfino** €€

*Via Torretta 80, Sferracavallo, 90148* ***Tel*** *091-530 282* ***Road Map*** *B2*

A short ride west of Mondello, this restaurant is known for its reasonable prices and its good fish and seafood menu. Specialities include pasta with sardines and fennel, seafood risotto or fettuccine with shrimp and clams. For the main course, indecisive diners are often directed towards the outstanding *sarde a beccaficu* (stuffed sardines).

**FURTHER AFIELD La Dispensa dei Monsù** €€

*Via Principe di Villafranca 59, 90141* ***Tel*** *091-609 04 65* ***Road Map*** *C2*

A French chef (*monsù*) and a well-stocked pantry (*dispensa*) were obligatory in any Sicilian noble household. Here you will find excellent cheeses: fresh ricotta with pistachios, *caprino Robiola* (goat's cheese), *piacentu ennese* (with saffron and peppercorn), *pecorino ubriaco* (wine-aged), plus Sicilian prosciutto and salami. Open for dinner only and closed Sun.

**FURTHER AFIELD La Tonnara** €€

*Piazza Tonnara 18, Arenella, 90142* ***Tel*** *091-363 055* ***Road Map*** *C2*

The name of this restaurant in the tiny Arenella harbour indicates that tuna is the main speciality, although other fish and seafood are also on the menu. Dishes such as ravioli filled with grouper or crabmeat are worth the trip out of town. Local wine is available by the carafe; other wines, by the bottle. Closed Wed; 2 weeks Aug.

**FURTHER AFIELD Sapori di Mare** €€

*Via Mondello 52, Mondello, 90151* ***Tel*** *091-684 06 23* ***Road Map*** *C2*

Right in the midst of Mondello's beach scene, near the aquamarine sea, is this fish restaurant. Its signature dish is linguine with lobster, but other delicious specialities include ravioli stuffed with fish and topped with shrimp or lobster sauce, fish cous cous, seafood risotto and spaghetti with sea urchins. Closed Tue in winter.

**FURTHER AFIELD La Botte 1962** €€€

*SS186 km10, Contrada Lenzitti 20, Monreale, 90046* ***Tel*** *091-414 051* ***Road Map*** *B2*

Plan your visit to this well-stocked wine shop in advance if you wish to dine here: they serve food only at lunchtime on Sunday and during the holidays. Regional fare, based on fish and meat, is highlighted. As you would expect, the wines are always superbly matched to the food on offer to enhance the flavours. Closed Mon–Thu; Jun–20 Sep.

**FURTHER AFIELD Bye Bye Blues** €€€€

*Via del Garofalo 23, Mondello, 90149* ***Tel*** *091-684 14 15* ***Road Map*** *C2*

The excellent, refined food made here receives national attention. A main course may take the shape of pasta with sea urchins and puréed fava, potato and basil pie with fish soup, pork with onion marmalade, or snapper with lemon marmalade. Exquisite pistachio cake or ice cream. Closed lunch (except holidays); Tue; part of Nov.

**FURTHER AFIELD Graziano** €€€€

*Frazione Bolognetta, Villafrati, 90030* ***Tel*** *091-872 48 70* ***Road Map*** *C2*

Start a meal at this intimate spot on the road to Agrigento (SS121) with cream of fava beans with shrimp and ricotta, or soup with shrimp and basil. Recommended main courses are potatoes with *cernia* (grouper) and light pesto, or fish fillet covered with breadcrumbs and pistachios. Finish off with almond cake covered with dark-chocolate sauce. Closed Mon.

**FURTHER AFIELD Baglio di Pianetto** €€€€€

*Contrada Pianetto, Scorrimento Veloce, San Cristina Gela, 90030* ***Tel*** *091-857 00 02* ***Road Map*** *B2*

Surrounded by vineyards and olive groves, the Baglio di Pianetto winery opened this eatery in 2006. The chef's bounty comes from nearby fields and farms – lightly fried wild borage, lamb in delicate sauce, wild salad greens. You can sample the winery's excellent Merlot, Nero d'Avola, Viognier and other wines in the wine-tasting room. Book ahead.

**FURTHER AFIELD Il Ristorantino** €€€€€

*Piazzale De Gasperi 19, 90146* ***Tel*** *091-670 2999* ***Road Map*** *C2*

Expect a new take on Sicilian cuisine in "the little restaurant" near the Parco della Favorita. Squid is served with salt and basil as an appetizer; *maltagliati* (irregularly shaped pasta) might have a sauce of bitter chocolate, aubergine (eggplant) and swordfish; fish might come in a potato crust with cous cous on the side. Closed Mon; early Jan, Aug.

**FURTHER AFIELD La Scuderia** €€€€€

*Via del Fante 9, 90146* ***Tel*** *091-520 323* ***Road Map*** *C2*

The light open room, wood panel walls and fireplace offer understated comfort in this haven for power brokers. Tradition reigns with some innovations, food presentations are lovely and there are 500 wines on the list. The stadium is next door, so make sure your arrival does not coincide with a game (the restaurant staff will advise). Closed Sun.

## NORTHWESTERN SICILY

**CASTELBUONO Nangalarruni Ristorante** €€€

*Via Alberghi 5 (formerly Via delle Confraternite), 90013* ***Tel*** *0921-671 428* ***Road Map*** *D2*

In the hills southeast of Cefalù, Nangalarruni is ideal for sampling wild mushrooms, including *basilisco*, the "king of mushrooms", which is prepared with tagliatelle. Wild herbs season the dishes, like Nebrodi pork with almonds and pistachios. Desserts include ricotta pastry and chocolate flan. About 600 international wines on the list. Closed Wed.

**CASTELLAMMARE DEL GOLFO Torre Bennistra** €€€

*Via Natale di Roma 19, Località Scopello, 91014* ***Tel*** *0924-541 128* ***Road Map*** *B2*

Reopened in 2005 after an extensive four-year renovation, Torre Bennistra has a homely family atmosphere. Antipasti include tuna *carpaccio* (thin, raw slices), shrimp with lemon and *sarde a beccaficu* (stuffed sardines). The inn overlooks the village of Scopello and the rocks.

**CEFALÙ La Brace** €€€

*Via XXV Novembre 10, 90015* ***Tel*** *0921-423 570* ***Road Map*** *D2*

At this restaurant near the cathedral, one can enjoy local specialities like stuffed aubergines (eggplant). Ethnic theme nights on Wednesdays offer Spanish paella, while on Fridays the menu includes *cous cous mezzo Tunisino* (half-Tunisian), the other half being the chef's own interpretation. Mostly Sicilian wines. Closed Mon, Tue lunch; Christmas.

**CEFALÙ Taverna del Presidente** €€€

*Via Lungomare G Giardina 163, 90015* ***Tel*** *0921-921 359* ***Road Map*** *D2*

On Cefalù's seafront, this restaurant offers views of the sea and the town, as well as terrace dining in warm weather. The fish, meat and vegetables are all locally sourced. Try the cod salad with citrus fruit, fish *carpaccio* (thin, raw slices), *pappardelle* (wide pasta ribbons) with rabbit and wild asparagus, tuna steak or braised pork. Closed Tue.

**ENNA Centrale** €€

*Piazza VI Dicembre 9, 94100* ***Tel*** *0935-500 963* ***Road Map*** *D3*

Try a 15th-century pasta dish made with wild fennel and fresh ricotta, or ravioli with lemon cream. Vegetarians will appreciate the wide assortment of seasonal vegetables, while meat eaters can turn to steak or local boiled beef with oranges or peaches, depending on the season. Two tasting menus and 49 Sicilian wines. Closed Sat lunch.

**ERICE Monte San Giuliano** €€

*Vicolo San Rocco 7, 91016* ***Tel*** *0923-869 595* ***Road Map*** *A2*

Located in the medieval centre, the menu here offers excellent seafood, veal roulades with prosciutto in Marsala and mushroom sauce, or pasta with fresh *pesto trapanese* (aubergines/eggplant, tomatoes, almonds, garlic, basil and breadcrumbs). Thirty Sicilian wines; the house red is a lovely Nero d'Avola. Closed Mon; Jan, 2 weeks Nov.

**FAVIGNANA La Bettola** €€

*Via Nicotera 47, 91023* ***Tel*** *0923-921 988* ***Road Map*** *A2*

Enjoy dining on the veranda or indoors at this small, informal trattoria. Regional specialities include cous cous with various types of fish; fresh *busiati* pasta with swordfish and aubergine (eggplant); a cooked pesto of tuna, tomatoes, basil and anchovies; fish grilled over lava rocks; octopus salad and fried squid. Closed Thu; Dec.

**FAVIGNANA Egadi** €€€€

*Via Cristoforo Colombo 17, 91023* ***Tel*** *0923-921 232* ***Road Map*** *A2*

One of the best spots for dining in the Egadi Islands. Fresh fish is served grilled, poached or marinated, but the speciality is raw fish, including tuna *tartare*, or marinated in a variety of ways, including fresh herbs. Lobster soup is a signature dish, as is cous cous with crustaceans. The cellar holds 50 different wines. Closed Oct–Apr.

**LEVANZO Paradiso** €€€

*Via Lungomare 8, 91023* **Tel** *0923-924 080* **Road Map** *A2*

Paradiso cooks fish as it comes off the boats in the nearby port, views of which can be enjoyed from the veranda. Specialities include pasta with *pesto trapanese* (garlic, almonds, tomatoes, basil, olive oil), with tuna and fresh mint, or with mussels and sea urchins, and cous cous with fish. There is a good list of Sicilian wines. Closed mid-Nov–Mar.

**MARETTIMO Il Veliero** €€

*Via Umberto 22, 91023* **Tel** *0923-923 274* **Road Map** *A2*

This trattoria on Marettimo, the westernmost of the Egadi Islands, offers diners a superb sea view. A dozen or so main courses include lobster served with pasta in its own broth and pasta with sardines. Tuna is especially popular, as is Trapani-style cous cous. The list of wines is limited, with about ten regional labels on offer.

**MARSALA Ristorante Mamma Laura** €

*Contrada Ettore Infersa, 91025* **Tel** *0923-966 036* **Road Map** *A3*

This cute rustic café at the edge of the salt flats offers a view of brilliant salt crystals and of the small boats that arrive and depart for Mozia. Outside, a thatched roof offers shady respite from the heat. No gourmet cuisine, but a few simple hot dishes and sandwiches at lunch. An ideal spot for a morning cappuccino or an apéritif while the sun sets.

**MARSALA La Bottega del Carmine** €€

*Via Carturca 20, 91025* **Tel** *0923-719 055* **Road Map** *A3*

This hip newcomer sets the ambience with a dramatically lit courtyard, gauzy drapes and contemporary music. The fish roulades with rocket and cherry tomatoes are particularly delicious, and there is a good roast-meat platter. Bar snacks, like *arancini* (rice balls) or cheese bites, plus a glass of wine won't cost very much. Closed lunch.

**MARSALA Tiburon Beach Lido Signorino** €€

*Via Berbaro 278, 91025* **Tel** *0923-998 441* **Road Map** *A3*

This lively beach restaurant attracts everyone from wine executives and importers to teenagers who opt for pizza from their wood-burning oven. The antipasti plate, which includes *cannonichio* (a local mollusc), fried tiny octopus, shrimp in mayonnaise, sea urchins and other delights, can be a light summer meal on its own. Great value.

**MARSALA Eubes** €€€

*Contrada da Spagnola 228, 91025* **Tel** *0923-996 231* **Road Map** *A3*

A sandy lane across from Mozia's salt flats leads to Eubes's tempting variety of seafood dishes. Try the excellent smoked tuna, fried tuna with sweet-and-sour sauce or the fish balls. Pasta with shrimp is flavourful, as is the perfectly fried squid. The chef skilfully gives traditional dishes a delightfully inventive twist.

**MARSALA Trattoria Garibaldi** €€€

*Piazza Addolorato 35, 91025* **Tel** *0923-953 006 or 989-100* **Road Map** *A3*

In summer the wooden tables expand into the lovely square. The generous antipasti buffet includes local fish, vegetables and meat. *Busiati* (sliced pasta tubes) with shellfish is particularly recommended. Select your fish from the display, and it will be cooked to order (fried, broiled or steamed). Closed Sat lunch, Sun dinner.

**MARSALA Villa Favorita** €€€

*Via Favorita 27, 91025* **Tel** *0923-989 100* **Road Map** *A3*

Once a wine estate, this early 19th-century villa is a favourite of locals for its quality cuisine and the pretty setting. Its historic buildings, renovated in 2006, and its Mediterranean garden are popular for wedding receptions and other important occasions. The fish dishes are particularly good, whether as antipasti, with pasta or as a main course.

**MAZARA DEL VALLO Trattoria del Pescatore** €€€

*Via Lozzani 11, 91026* **Tel** *0923-947 580* **Road Map** *A3*

Fish is the star here. For starters, try the *arancini di mare* (seafood rice balls), a tasty variation on the traditional meat or cheese *arancini*. Much of the cuisine has a strong Tunisian influence, so look for fish cous cous and other North African dishes. A tasting menu is also available. Closed Mon.

**SAN VITO LO CAPO Gna Sara** €€

*Via Duca degli Abruzzi 8, 91010* **Tel** *0923-972 100* **Road Map** *B2*

This busy trattoria has outside seating – some with sea view – and offers traditional fare with a twist. Popular dishes include cous cous with fish; home-made pasta with Trapani-style pesto (tomatoes, aubergine/eggplant, almonds, pecorino cheese, basil); pasta with fish in lemon-wine sauce and pizza. About 120 wines on the list. Closed Nov–Dec.

**SAN VITO LO CAPO Tha'am** €€€

*Via Abruzzi 32, 91010* **Tel** *0923-972 836* **Road Map** *B2*

*Tha'am* is Arabic for "food". In the local dialect, the word is also sometimes used to mean cous cous. The speciality here is Tunisian cuisine, plus there is a good choice of local dishes. The list also features 40 Sicilian wines. The interior has some Arabic touches, and some outdoor tables have a view of the port. Closed Wed (except Jun–Sep); Jan.

**TRAPANI Da Peppe** €€

*Via Spalti 50, 91100* **Tel** *0923-282 46* **Road Map** *A2*

Peppe's dishes place a special emphasis on fresh vegetables. *Pesto trapanese*, made with fresh tomato, almonds, basil and garlic, dresses pasta like *busiate* (sliced tubes), or you can try the fish cous cous or fish soup. There is also much to satisfy vegetarians. The summer tasting menu is a bargain. Closed Mon in winter; Christmas–mid-Jan.

**TRAPANI Trattoria del Porto** €€

*Via Ammiraglio Staiti 45, 91100* ***Tel*** *0923-547 822* ***Road Map*** *A2*

Trapani is proud of this family-run trattoria near the ferries for the Egadi Islands. Fish cous cous is its most popular dish; indeed, some claim this trattoria's version is the area's best. Other main courses include pasta with swordfish, aubergine (eggplant) and shrimp, seafood lasagna, and cuttlefish with nuts. Closed Mon in winter; Christmas.

## SOUTHWESTERN SICILY

**AGRIGENTO Leon d'Oro** €€€

*Viale Emporium 102, San Leone, 92100* ***Tel*** *0922-414 400* ***Road Map*** *C4*

On the road that links the Valle dei Templi to the sea, this local favourite offers meat and fish dishes. The popular antipasti platter includes mussels with lemon liqueur and fava purée. Those who need a break from seafood could try the filet steak with capers and olives. About 300 types of wine from Sicily and beyond. Closed Mon; mid-Oct–mid-Nov.

**AGRIGENTO Trattoria del Pescatore** €€€€

*Via Lungomare 20, Lido di San Leone, 92100* ***Tel*** *0922-414 342* ***Road Map*** *C4*

Fish, and only fish, is on the menu at this trattoria: raw, cooked or with pasta. The tranquil interior (no TVs, no family receptions or events) suits the clientele of local politicos, couples, businesspeople and tourists. The tables outside have a view of seaside amusement rides and the crowded seaside pavement in summer. Closed Mon in winter; Jan, Nov.

**AGRIGENTO Villa Athena** €€€€

*Via dei Templi 53, 92100* ***Tel*** *0922-596 288* ***Road Map*** *C4*

The view alone is reason enough to come here. Enjoy your dinner alfresco, in the carefully tended Mediterranean garden with its citrus trees, exotic flowers, pool and spectacular view of the Temple of Concord. Arrive in time for the sunset or in evening, when the temple is illuminated. The menu and wine list are somewhat limited.

**CALTANISSETTA Cortese** €€

*Viale Sicilia 166, 93100* ***Tel*** *0934-591 686* ***Road Map*** *D3*

Regional cooking with a focus on meat and local vegetables is offered at this restaurant. *Ditalini* (small pasta tubes) with broad beans and salted, aged ricotta is a speciality, as is *cravatte* (pasta bow ties) served with aubergine (eggplant) and tomato. Don't miss the *cannoli* and other desserts. The wine list includes about 80 labels. Closed Mon; Aug.

**LAMPEDUSA I Gemelli** €€

*Via Cala Pisana 2, 92010* ***Tel*** *0922-970 699* ***Road Map*** *B5*

The island of Lampedusa is close to the North African coast, so it is no surprise to learn that the fare here is influenced by the cuisine of Tunisia. Look for spicy dishes, including octopus, aubergine (eggplant) and sausage, and a Tunisian version of paella. Closed lunch; Nov–May.

**LICATA La Madia** €€€€

*Via Filippo Re Capriata 22, 92027* ***Tel*** *0922-771 443* ***Road Map*** *C4*

This elegant and tranquil restaurant is decorated with frescoes that show town scenes. The chef experiments with original recipes but maintains some traditional touches, like home-made pasta and bread. This is baked twice daily: first at lunch, then a new batch at dinner. The fishermen's catch determines the day's fish specials. Closed Tue.

**PANTELLERIA I Mulini** €€

*Contrada Tracino, 91017* ***Tel*** *0923-915 398* ***Road Map*** *A5*

On the island of Pantelleria, near an old mill, is this restaurant in a traditional *dammuso* (a house with small windows to keep the interior cool). Dinner is served on the terrace, from which there is a splendid view. Look for dishes that feature locally grown capers, and finish with a *passito* wine, for which the island is famous. Closed Tue; Nov–Feb.

**PANTELLERIA La Risacca** €€

*Via Milano 65, 91017* ***Tel*** *0923-912 975* ***Road Map*** *A5*

Pantelleria's harbour is the backdrop for this restaurant that prepares island specialities. Start with *caponata* (aubergine stew), then, for your main course, choose between ravioli with ricotta and mint, and fish cous cous. The menu also features various types of fish, including deep-water fish. They have about 15 local and Sicilian wines on the list. Closed Mon.

**PIAZZA ARMERINA Al Fogher** €€€

*Contrada Bellia, SS 117 bis (towards Aidone), 94015* ***Tel*** *0935-684 123* ***Road Map*** *D4*

A rustic, cosy tavern with elegantly appointed tables and refined cuisine. *Gnocchetti* (tiny pasta dumplings) with porcini mushrooms, braised veal with truffles and mushrooms, or Nebrodi pork coated with pistachios and tuna *bottarga* (roe) are some of the divine flavour combinations. Closed Mon, Sun dinner; usually mid-Aug.

**SCIACCA Hostaria del Vicolo** €€€

*Vicolo Sammaritano, 92019* ***Tel*** *0925-230 71* ***Road Map*** *B3*

Located in Sciacca's historic centre, this rustic eatery specializes in fish-based cuisine. Some dishes are traditional, while the chef has creatively reinterpreted others. Popular choices include fresh tagliatelle with prawns and courgette (zucchini), as well as angler fish in wine sauce. The cellar offers about 150 wines. Closed Sun & Mon.

**Key to Price Guide** *see p212* **Key to Symbols** *see back cover flap*

**SCIACCA Villa Palocla** €€€

*Contrada Raganella Ovest, 92019* ***Tel*** *0925-902 812* **Road Map** *B3*

Set in an 18th-century villa, this restaurant specializes in fish, often grilled as a main course. Pasta like local *busiati* (sliced tubes) might be combined with sardines or with *bottarga* (roe), sea urchins and eggplant. At lunch or dinner, you can dine inside or in the garden, which has citrus trees and a view of the mountains. Closed lunch in winter.

**SUTERA Ristorante Civiletto** €€€

*Via San Giuseppe 7, 93010* ***Tel*** *0934-954 587* **Road Map** *C3*

In the former Arab quarter, this beloved restaurant showcases local ingredients, all creatively transformed into new variations that show great international flair. There are two tasting menus available where you can sample a range of dishes. The chef-sommelier stocks 100 regional and national wines, plus international wines based on demand. Closed Mon.

## SOUTHERN SICILY

**AUGUSTA Donna Ina** €€€

*Contrada Faro Santa Croce, 96011* ***Tel*** *0931-983 422* **Road Map** *F4*

Diners at Donna Ina select fish from a market-style display to be grilled, steamed in seawater or poached with oranges. Antipasti include raw fish, grilled shrimp or classic mixed fried-fish platter. For main course, try the lasagne with swordfish sauce, the fish ravioli or the penne with vegetables. There are 70 Sicilian wines on the list. Closed lunchtimes & Mon.

**BUCCHERI U Locale** €€

*Via Dusmet 14, 96010* ***Tel*** *0931-873 923* **Road Map** *E4*

A handy spot for sustenance for those who are visiting the Akrai or Pantalica archaeological sites, this family-run trattoria offers meals using seasonal produce and game typical of the hillside forests, like wild boar. *Pappardelle* (broad pasta ribbons) with roast peppers and tomatoes is another popular choice. Closed Tue; Jul.

**CHIARAMONTE GULFI Il Tegamino** €€

*Contrada Ponte 35, 97010* ***Tel*** *0932-921 333* **Road Map** *E4*

"The Casserole Pot" has a casual atmosphere and offers mainly fresh fish. The *tagliatelle all'astice* (pasta ribbons with lobster) is perfect, with just the prawns' own juices as pasta sauce to enhance the flavours. They also make a good mixed roast-fish and shellfish platter. Pizza serves as a hearty starter or a simple dinner. Closed Tue.

**CHIARAMONTE GULFI Majore** €€

*Via Martiri Ungaresi 12, 97010* ***Tel*** *0932-928 019* **Road Map** *E4*

Set up on the hill in the town of Chiaramonte Gulfi, this restaurant is unique in that, from appetizers to desserts, the main theme on the menu is pork in all its forms: as salami, in aspic, roasted and sliced, in sauces, in a risotto. No doubt, pork ends up as *strutto* (shortening) in dessert crusts or cookies, or as gelatin. Closed Mon.

**MARINA DI RAGUSA Da Serafino** €€€

*Lungomare Doria, 97010* ***Tel*** *0932-239 522* **Road Map** *E5*

A beach restaurant since 1953, Da Serafino is a summer tradition in Marina di Ragusa. The restaurant has its own private beach facilities, so one can rent chairs and an umbrella for the day and enjoy some of the loveliest water in Sicily. The menu of fish-based courses is simple but expertly prepared. They also make pizza. Closed Oct–Mar.

**MODICA Fattoria delle Torri** €€€€

*Vico Napolitano 14, 97015* ***Tel*** *0932-751 286* **Road Map** *E5*

This former 18th-century warehouse is now a restaurant, wine bar and cellar offering dishes like terrine of aubergine (eggplant) with basil; ravioli with fava beans and herbed ricotta; and rabbit with truffles. Some desserts are based on the chocolate of Modica, a relative of Mexican chocolate. Extensive wine list. Closed Mon; late Jun–early Jul.

**NOTO Del Carmine** €€

*Via Ducezio 1, 96017* ***Tel*** *0931-838 705* **Road Map** *E5*

The menu in this simple family-run trattoria is based on the bounty of southern Sicily's hills. Pasta dishes include ricotta-filled ravioli with pork sauce, and *tagliatelle capricciose* (pasta with fresh vegetables). Rabbit *alla stimpirata* has sweet-and-sour sauce with seasonal vegetables. *Cannoli* or cake are two of the dessert options. Closed Mon.

**PALAZZOLO ACREIDE Anapo da Nunzio** €€

*Corso Vittorio Emanuele* ***Tel*** *0931-882 286* **Road Map** *E4*

This trattoria in the centre of town is a handy stop after touring the archaeological excavations at Akrai. Cheese is a local speciality, so begin or end your meal with a cheese platter to sample *provola* and pecorino (sheep's cheese, fresh or aged). Ravioli filled with ricotta is an excellent menu staple. Closed Mon.

**RAGUSA Baglio La Pergola** €€€€

*Piazza Luigi Sturzo 6, 97100* ***Tel*** *0932-686 430* **Road Map** *E5*

This elegant restaurant in the Baroque part of town features traditional cuisine with some new twists, like antipasti of grilled cheese with peppers and cinnamon, or macaroni made from spelt flour, pistachios and shrimp. Fish might be served with lemon and mint, and accompanied by *caponata* (aubergine/eggplant stew). Closed Tue; mid-Aug.

**RAGUSA IBLA Duomo** €€€€€

*Via Capitano Bocchieri 31, 97100* ***Tel*** *0932-651 265* ***Road Map*** *E5*

One of Italy's top restaurants is located in a Baroque palazzo near the Duomo. Tradition informs contemporary and innovative dishes with international flair: cous cous with pistachios and mint paired with fish soup and harissa (a spicy North African sauce); or pork in a sauce of cocoa beans, legumes and spinach. Closed Mon, Sun eve; Oct.

**RAGUSA IBLA Locanda Don Serafino** €€€€€

*Via Orfanotrofio 39, 97100* ***Tel*** *0932-248 778* ***Road Map*** *E5*

An 18th-century palazzo hosts one of Ragusa's best restaurants. Contemporary variations on traditional recipes include red mullet stuffed with courgette (zucchini), baked ricotta with fried chicory, and lasagne made with cocoa filled with ricotta. There are also elaborate desserts, flavourful mini-cookies and 1,000 wines on the list. Closed Tue.

**ROSOLINI Locanda del Borgo** €€€

*Via Controscieri 11, 97100* ***Tel*** *0931-850 514* ***Road Map*** *E5*

This restaurant occupies the former offices of the 18th-century Prince of Platamone, with their two cupolas and original frescoes. The covered terrace offers a view of the hills, and the cuisine uses traditional ingredients that had almost been forgotten in new, imaginative ways. About 300 wines feature on the list. Closed Tue, some Sun.

**SYRACUSE La Medusa da Kamel** €€

*Via Santa Teresa 21, 96100* ***Tel*** *0931-614 03* ***Road Map*** *F4*

Near the ancient spring of Fonte Aretusa, in Ortygia's historic centre, this restaurant specializes in Sicilian seafood. On Thursday evenings the Tunisian chef offers a menu that features fish or lamb cous cous with other traditional North African accompaniments; there are also various fish pastas and mixed grilled fish. Closed Mon.

**SYRACUSE La Spiaggetta** €€

*Viale del Lido 473, Fontane Bianche, 96010* ***Tel*** *0931-790 334* ***Road Map*** *F4*

All dining rooms, terrace and garden have a magnificent view of the sea. Fish is prepared in various forms, and specialities include *zuppa di pesce* (fish soup), spaghetti with sea urchins, linguine with lobster, swordfish *involtini* (roulades) or fish with Syracuse-style sauce of tomatoes, capers, olives and garlic. Closed Tue Oct–Mar.

**SYRACUSE Jonico 'a rutta 'e ciauli** €€€

*Riviera Dionisio il Grande 194, 96100* ***Tel*** *0931-655 40* ***Road Map*** *F4*

This restaurant is perched on a cliff and offers alfresco dining. One of their specialities comes from a humble tradition: *pasta ca muddica* is pasta mixed with olive oil, breadcrumbs, anchovies and red peppers – a tasty option today, but a necessity in days gone by, when no meat, cheese, eggs or other fish were easily available. Closed Tue.

**SYRACUSE Don Camillo** €€€€

*Via Maestranza 46, 96100* ***Tel*** *0931-671 33* ***Road Map*** *F4*

Barrel-vaulted ceilings and stone walls stacked with wine bottles set the stage for the refined cooking here. Soup of newborn red mullet in a delicate broth, spaghetti with sea urchins and shrimp, and grilled tuna encrusted with black pepper are some of the dishes on offer. Excellent selection of cheeses. Closed Sun; mid-Feb, mid-July, Christmas.

**VITTORIA Sakalleo** €€

*Piazza Cavour 12, Località Scoglitti, 97019* ***Tel*** *0932-871 688* ***Road Map*** *D5*

*Sakalleo* is the name of a boat that was used for sponge fishing. Recipes at this restaurant on the coast south of Gela maintain the old culinary traditions and are based on fish brought in from one of the owner's three boats. There is no menu as such, just what is caught that morning. The wine list includes about 80 labels. Closed Mon.

## NORTHEASTERN SICILY

**ACI CASTELLO Alioto** €€€€

*Via Mollica 24–26, 95021* ***Tel*** *095-494 444* ***Road Map*** *E3*

This seaside village restaurant offers a wide selection of fresh fish and shellfish. Main courses include *risotto pescatore* (rice with fish and seafood); *linguine al cartoccio* (pasta and seafood steamed inside paper wrapping); and pasta with lobster. End your meal with a delicious strawberry cake or *cassata*. Closed Tue; 2 weeks Aug.

**ACIREALE A'Cumarca** €

*Via Timone Zaccanazzo 87, 95024* ***Tel*** *095-886 200* ***Road Map*** *E3*

The main attraction here is the terrace with its view of Etna, the mountains and the sea. The food is traditional and reasonably priced, with antipasti, *caponata* (aubergine/eggplant stew), pizza and light snacks being the most popular fare. Open only for dinner, but until late (about 1am). Closed Mon.

**ACIREALE La Grotta** €€€

*Via Scalo Grande 46, 95024* ***Tel*** *095-764 81 53* ***Road Map*** *E3*

Built inside a grotto by the sea, this small restaurant sits only 25 people inside, but the outside area more than doubles that number. Fish is the speciality and prices are reasonable. La Grotta's most popular dishes are the seafood salad and mixed grilled fish. There is also a limited selection of Sicilian wines. Closed Tue; mid-Oct–mid-Nov.

**Key to Price Guide** *see p212* **Key to Symbols** *see back cover flap*

**ACI TREZZA Verga da Gaetano** €€€€
*Via Provinciale 119, 95021* ***Tel*** *095-276 342* ***Road Map*** *E3*

Near a small harbour, this restaurant has walls hung with photographs from the Luchino Visconti film *La Terra Trema*, in which the owner's wife had a role. Outside, the view is of the sea, the Cyclops Island and a lighthouse. The small trattoria (70 seats) specializes in fish and offers 20 Sicilian and Italian wines. Closed Thu; Jan.

**CAPRILEONE L'Antica Filanda** €€€€
*Contrada Raviola SS 157, 98070* ***Tel*** *0941-919 704* ***Road Map*** *E2*

This elegant hillside restaurant offers excellent meat dishes as well as local cheeses. Nero dei Nebrodi pork is prepared in a variety of ways, as are lamb and goat. Local wild field greens and mushrooms are used liberally, and bread is made in their wood-burning oven. Impressive selection of cheeses and wines. Closed Mon.

**CATANIA Al Gabbiano** €€
*Via Giordano Bruno 128, 95100* ***Tel*** *095-537 842* ***Road Map*** *E3*

This economical classic trattoria features only fish. Antipasti include mixed fried fish, shrimp with rocket, and octopus salad, as well as potato fritters. Spaghetti with clams is a popular first course. Fish can be roasted, fried, baked in salt, poached in seawater or steamed in paper. Seventeen local wines appear on the list. Closed Sun; Aug.

**CATANIA Antica Marina** €€
*Via Pardo 29 (Pescheria di Catania), 95100* ***Tel*** *095-348 197* ***Road Map*** *E3*

This is the ideal place to come for those who want to dine in the midst of Catania's fish market. It is best at lunch when the action is in full swing (except Sunday, when the market is closed). Recommended dishes are the mixed seafood starter and the spaghetti with sea urchins, but check to see what is being offered on the day. Closed Wed & Aug.

**CATANIA I Vicerè** €€
*Via Grotte Bianche 97, 95021* ***Tel*** *095-320 188* ***Road Map*** *E3*

The chef at this restaurant close to the 11th-century Norman castle is fond of inventing his own recipes. As one would expect from a coastal village, seafood is strongly featured. Pasta with fish and pine nuts or with clams often appears on the menu. A good choice of meat is available too, including steak, pork, lamb and rabbit. Open dinner only.

**CATANIA Menza** €€
*Viale Mario Rapisardi 143–153, 95100* ***Tel*** *095-350 606* ***Road Map*** *E3*

This rotisserie is a good spot to try a variety of specialities from Catania, such as *arancini* (rice balls), which are usually eaten as an appetizer or snack, or *crispelle* (rice fritters) with honey for dessert. One can put a satisfying meal together here with baked pasta and roasted meats. Closed Mon.

**CATANIA Sicilia in Bocca Piazza Pietro Lupo** €€
*Piazza Pietro Lupo 16, 95100* ***Tel*** *095-746 13 61* ***Road Map*** *E3*

This trattoria dates back to the early 20th century. The speciality is seafood at reasonable prices. Try the fish-stuffed ravioli or one of the many pasta dishes with a fish sauce. Choose from the day's catch, which might be swordfish, snapper or grouper, and accompany it with one of the 50 wines on offer. Friendly service. Closed Mon, Wed; 2 weeks Aug.

**CATANIA Dell'Hotel Poggio Ducale – Da Nino** €€€
*Via Gaifami 7, 95100* ***Tel*** *095-330 016* ***Road Map*** *E3*

This family-run restaurant attracts a business clientele who appreciate the personal attention, professional service and excellent fish preparations. The raw fish is served in a variety of interesting combinations, including with mandarin, garlic and olive oil. The refreshing lemon-mint sorbet provides a light finish. Closed Mon lunch, Sun eve; Aug.

**CATANIA Le Tre Caravelle** €€€
*Via Catania Savoca 2, San Gregorio, 95100* ***Tel*** *095-717 74 34* ***Road Map*** *E3*

Since 1998 this restaurant has been serving traditional local food, well prepared and simple. One of the most popular dishes is spaghetti with clams and shrimp. For the main course, diners select fish from the display and have it cooked in one of several different ways. The wine list includes a vast selection of Sicilian wines.

**CATANIA Sicilia in Bocca alla Marina** €€€
*Via Dusmet 35, 95100* ***Tel*** *095-250 02 08* ***Road Map*** *E3*

This atmospheric trattoria in a 14th-century palazzo attracts a young crowd. You can enjoy the pizza and lively outdoor dining scene downstairs, or dine on the terrace upstairs, which offers a great view of the cupola of the Duomo and the Museo Diocesano. Closed Mon.

**CATANIA Azienda Vinicola Benanti** €€€€
*Via Garibaldi 475, Viagrande, 95029* ***Tel*** *095-789 35 33* ***Road Map*** *E3*

The prestigious Benanti winery offers a tour of its wine cellar and vineyards followed by a wine tasting. By advance reservation only, a lunch with wine tasting will be prepared for a minimum of five (and a maximum of 100) people. Diners can finish with cigars and spirits from Benanti's select collection. Ask about dining outside during the summer.

**CATANIA La Siciliana** €€€€
*Viale Marco Polo 52A, 95126* ***Tel*** *095-376 400* ***Road Map*** *E3*

One of Catania's most popular restaurants. The food prepared includes some inventive dishes, as well as plenty of traditional favourites, like *pasta alla Norma* (pasta with fried aubergine (eggplant), aged ricotta and tomato sauce), cuttlefish risotto black from its ink, and local ricotta cheese. Closed Mon and Sun evening.

**CATANIA Osteria Tre Bicchieri** €€€€

*Via San Giuseppe al Duomo, 31, 95100* ***Tel*** *095-715 35 40* **Road Map** *E3*

In a 19th-century palazzo, this wine bar is elegant to the last detail: Rosenthal porcelain, Riedel glasses and silver cutlery make dining here a truly special occasion. The selection of over 500 wines, good cheese and salami platters, and creative Mediterranean cuisine also contribute to the fine dining experience. Closed lunch; Sun, Mon; most of Jul–Aug.

**FILICUDI Nino Santamaria** €€

*Filicudi Porto, 98050* ***Tel*** *090-988 99 84* **Road Map** *E1*

Here one can dine on a terrace that overlooks the brilliant, clear waters of the Tyrrhenian Sea. Specialities include octopus salad, fried calamari (squid) and pasta with swordfish, which you can accompany with some nice local wines. Prices offer some of the best value anywhere. Cash only. Closed Oct–Mar.

**LETOJANNI Nino** €€€

*Via Rizzo 29, Letojanni, 98037* ***Tel*** *0942-361 47* **Road Map** *F2*

Begin with the heavenly antipasti: small fish cakes, squid with artichokes, octopus with home-pickled garlic, blood orange stuffed with shrimp and wild fennel, large shrimp stuffed with mashed fennel potatoes. The main courses are equally creative. If you are still hungry, end your meal with the home-made ice cream. Closed Tue in winter; Dec–Feb.

**LIPARI E Pulera** €€€€

*Via Diana, 98055* ***Tel*** *090-981 11 58* **Road Map** *E1*

Considered one of Lipari's top restaurants. Here you can dine on a terrace surrounded by a lush garden; each table is covered with vividly coloured ceramic tiles that represent different islands in the Aeolian archipelago. The cuisine is traditional Aeolian prepared with a refined touch, and the atmosphere is elegant. Closed lunch; 10 Oct–10 May.

**LIPARI La Nassa** €€€€

*Via Franza 36, 98055* ***Tel*** *090-981 11 39* **Road Map** *E1*

Diners can reach La Nassa by walking up the hill. The reward for this effort is a meal on the lovely terrace, in the welcome shade of the garden. This restaurant specializes in traditional Aeolian cuisine, with the emphasis on fish. Try some of the Malvasia and other regional wines. Closed Thu in spring; Nov–Mar.

**MESSINA Trattoria Anselmo** €€€

*Via Lago Grande 29, Ganzirri, 98100* ***Tel*** *090-393 225* **Road Map** *F2*

Ganzirri is at the northeast tip of Sicily, where the island almost touches Calabria, in the windy Strait of Messina. Some say the strong sea currents make the fish taste even better, and this restaurant certainly provides ample proof of such outstanding quality. Located in a rebuilt area, Trattoria Anselmo specializes in shellfish. Closed Mon in winter.

**MESSINA Da Piero** €€€€

*Via Ghibellina 119, 98100* ***Tel*** *090-718 365* **Road Map** *F2*

Locals, many of whom consider this to be Messina's best restaurant, come here for its classic local cuisine, which is a tradition since 1962. Seafood and meat dishes are featured, as well as some lighter vegetable or salad plates. Attentive, professional service is the norm. Open for dinner only, closed Sun; Aug.

**MILAZZO Piccolo Casale** €€€€

*Via R D'Amico 12, 98057* ***Tel*** *090-922 479* **Road Map** *F2*

This former 19th-century country home is tastefully furnished and inviting. On the menu are mostly fresh local fish and vegetables, with some meat options, and imaginative pasta dishes like cocoa ravioli filled with ricotta and almonds. There are over 800 wines on the list. Summer terrace dining takes place among the rooftops of Milazzo. Closed Mon.

**PANAREA Da Francesco** €€

*Via San Pietro (Porto), 98050* ***Tel*** *090-983 023* **Road Map** *E1*

This trattoria near the port serves reliable food at economical prices, and the terrace offers a lovely view. Main fare is fish, usually grilled, but there are also good vegetable options: *spaghetti alla disgraziata*, for example, with tomatoes, aubergine (eggplant), peppers, chilli peppers, capers and olives. The baby squid in Malvasia wine is very tasty.

**PANAREA Da Pina** €€€

*Via San Pietro 3, 98050* ***Tel*** *090-983 032* **Road Map** *E1*

Pina offers reliably good dining, which includes typical traditional dishes from the island as well as their own innovative specialities. Try the home-made *tagliolini* (thin pasta strands) with delicate lemon sauce, which marries happily with fish dishes like the swordfish *involtini* (lightly braised roulades).

**PANAREA Hycesia** €€€€€

*Via San Pietro, 98050* ***Tel*** *090-983 041* **Road Map** *E1*

This intimate restaurant is only minutes from the port and the menu reflects the daily catch. Scorpion fish *tartare* (raw), linguine with asparagus and shrimp, and crustaceans in a cream sauce are some favourites. Reserve ahead – even VIPs compete to score one of the 12 tables. Vast wine list and tastings of olive oil and spirits, too. Closed Nov–Mar.

**SALINA Porto Bello** €€€€

*Via Bianchi 1, Santa Marina, 98050* ***Tel*** *090-984 31 25* **Road Map** *E1*

This restaurant is known as much for its gracious service as for its fine cuisine, which one can enjoy on the shaded terrace. Most dishes here are traditional, but there is also some innovative fare. Try the tuna in olive oil, sea perch baked with potatoes, or squid with onions and Malvasia wine. Closed Wed (Oct–May); Nov.

**Key to Price Guide** *see p212* **Key to Symbols** *see back cover flap*

**SAN GIOVANNI LA PUNTA Giardino di Bacco** €€€

*Via Piave 3, 95037* ***Tel*** *095-751 27 27* ***Road Map*** *E3*

Dine on the southeast slope of Europe's largest volcano, Mount Etna. This cheerful, well-run restaurant is in the former gatehouse to a grand villa and makes for elegant dining in the evening. The emphasis is on local cuisine, which is prepared expertly. Closed lunch (except on holidays); Mon; Jan.

**SANT'ALFIO Azienda Agricola Casa Perrotta** €€€

*Via Andronico 2, 95010* ***Tel*** *095-968 928* ***Road Map*** *E3*

On Etna's slope, this 16th-century monastery offers views of the volcano and the sea. The menu offers more than 40 antipasti, meat or vegetable, hot or cold. Try the spicy pork with sweet-and-sour sauce or the beef *involtini* (roulades) in lemon leaves. Desserts include *Gelo di cannella*, a cinnamon-based sweet. Closed lunch (Mon–Fri); Mon in winter.

**TAORMINA A'Zammara** €€

*Via Fratelli Bandiera 15, 98039* ***Tel*** *0942-244 08* ***Road Map*** *F2*

The rustic wooden furniture, nostalgic prints on the walls, and family atmosphere give diners a sense of stepping back into a Taormina of years ago. Unpretentious and hearty food includes meatballs wrapped in lemon leaves or veal *involtini* (roulades). Good selection of regional wines. Closed Wed in winter; 10 Jan–10 Feb, 20 Nov–20 Dec.

**TAORMINA La Botte** €€

*Piazza San Domenico, 98039* ***Tel*** *0942-241 98* ***Road Map*** *F2*

One of Taormina's rare budget restaurants, La Botte is frequented by locals, as well as by tourists and the Hollywood set when it's in town (Woody Allen was a regular when filming in the area). There are lots of colourful ceramics and a sense of fun about this casual and cosy place, which is decorated with wooden wine barrels (*botti*). Closed Mon.

**TAORMINA Al Duomo** €€€

*Vico Ebrei 11, 98039* ***Tel*** *0942-625 656* ***Road Map*** *F2*

The owner of this intimate, friendly, colourful restaurant across from the cathedral takes pride in preserving historic recipes, some of which date back 1,000 years and reflect Arabic and French traditions. Some are staples of the *cucina povera* ("humble cuisine"), with wild field greens, bread and beans. Closed Wed and Feb.

**TAORMINA Casa Grugno** €€€€€

*Via Santa Maria dei Greci, 98039* ***Tel*** *0942-212 08* ***Road Map*** *F2*

In the heart of medieval Taormina, this 16th-century palazzo highlights its architectural features with modern decor and candlelight. Traditional and historic recipes are given modern interpretations by the chef, who keeps the flavours very Mediterranean in style. Excellent wine selection. Closed Sun; part of Feb and Nov.

**TAORMINA La Baronessa** €€€€€

*Corso Umberto, 98039* ***Tel*** *0942-620 163 or 628 191* ***Road Map*** *F2*

The lovely 19th-century decor creates an elegant Victorian ambience. Anchovy and wild mint *timballo* (soufflé), pasta with lobster, *canule* (roulades) with artichokes and broad beans, the signature *sformatino* (layered pie) with ricotta and aubergine (eggplant), or *millefoglie* (paper-thin layers) of swordfish are all good main courses. Closed lunch.

**TAORMINA La Giara Ristorante e Pianobar** €€€€€

*Vico La Floresta 1, 98039* ***Tel*** *0942-625 083 or 233 60* ***Road Map*** *F2*

A splendid example of that vanishing species of elegant supper and dancing club, La Giara draws an upmarket clientele for drinks, dining, music at the piano bar and dancing. Expect to see a well-heeled, traditional crowd with the occasional jet-setter stopping by. Closed winter (except for special events).

**TAORMINA Maffei's** €€€€€

*Via San Domenico de Guzman 1, 98039* ***Tel*** *0942-240 55* ***Road Map*** *F2*

This Taormina chef has an extraordinary refined, subtle touch – his sauces enhance flavours without ever being heavy or dominating. Try the fresh oysters from Messina, the light and flavourful spaghetti with sea urchins, or the delicious sea snails in tomato sauce. Great service and a superb wine selection. Closed Tue; 7 Jan–20 Feb.

**TAORMINA Ristorante Vicolo Stretto** €€€€€

*Via Vicolo Stretto 6, 98039* ***Tel*** *0942-838 19* ***Road Map*** *F2*

This gem of a restaurant is tiny (30 seats inside) and features traditional Sicilian cuisine with creative variations. Start with raw fish, fish salads or delicious vegetable antipasti. *Gnocchi* (potato dumplings) with shrimp and pistachios are tasty. Fish cous cous or grouper *involtini* (roulades) are popular. International wine selection. Closed Mon; Dec–Feb.

**TAORMINA (BEACH) La Capinera** €€€

*Via Nazionale (under Autostrada Spisone), 98039* ***Tel*** *0942-626 247* ***Road Map*** *F2*

Right on the beach, with a sea view as well as indoor dining, this place run by the chef and his sisters has something for everybody. The seafood menu changes by the season and there is also a good vegetarian selection. There are three tasting menus: meat, fish and the so-called Chef's Inspiration. Closed Mon.

**TRECASTAGNI All'Angolo** €€€

*Via Catania 37, 95039* ***Tel*** *095-780 69 88* ***Road Map*** *E3*

Set at the foot of Mount Etna, west of Acireale and north of Catania, this old farmhouse offers an Italian (rather than Sicilian) menu in an intimate setting with just 20 seats. The interior is furnished in part with antiques and you can dine in the garden in the summer. The list of 180 wines includes some international labels. Closed lunch (open by request only).

# SHOPS AND MARKETS

All the most well-known fashion designer shops can be found in the larger Sicilian cities (such as Palermo, Catania and Syracuse), together with smart chain stores stocking household articles and furniture. In tourist resorts it is possible to find shops specializing in Sicilian handicrafts, in particular ceramics, although the best items are sold in the places where they are made. Sicilian pastry shops sell delicious cakes, *cannoli* pastries, *cassata* cakes and *torroncini* (almond nougat). Keep an eye out for the delicatessens selling local specialities, such as spiced capers, *ventresca* (tuna in oil), tuna (*tonno*), salted mullet roe *(bottarga)* and aubergine *caponata*. You can also buy excellent produce such as organic fruit, olive oil, honey and fruit jam at farmhouses offering accommodation for visitors. Another good and typically Sicilian purchase is salt.

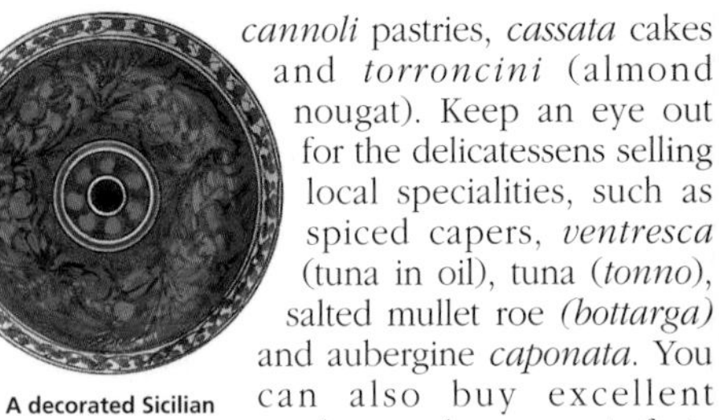

A decorated Sicilian terracotta dish

A shop specializing in wrought-iron products

## OPENING HOURS

Generally, shops, boutiques and department stores are open from 8 or 9am to 1pm, and in the afternoon, opening hours are 4–8pm. In the summer these hours may be extended, particularly in tourist resorts. In the cities, most shops close for two or three weeks in August. Seaside resort towns, on the other hand, usually operate on a seasonal basis, opening only from June to September.

## HOW TO PAY

In the larger cities, the leading shops and department stores accept major credit cards, especially Visa and MasterCard, whereas in the towns and villages many shops still prefer cash payment. In Palermo, Catania and Syracuse, some top hotels have deals with shops and restaurants for discounts of up to 40 per cent. The concierge will be able to tell you if your hotel takes part in this scheme.

## HANDICRAFTS

In Caltagirone, Sciacca and Santo Stefano di Camastra, the main production centres for striking Sicilian ceramics, there are shops and workshops selling plates, jugs, tiles, vases, mugs and statuettes. The **Laboratorio Branciforti** in Caltagirone makes jugs, vases and dishes with traditional decorative motifs.

At Sciacca, stylish ceramics can be found in the studio of **Giuseppe Navarra**, who has exhibited his works in New York and Montreal. The **Artigianato del Sole** also has a good range: as well as dinner services, jugs and ornamental plates, they make furniture, such as tables made of lava stone, and majolica tiles. Many artisans work in wrought iron. Among the good workshops near Giarre and Giardini Naxos is the **Laboratorio Patanè**.

Two traditional puppet-makers still active in Palermo are **Piero Scalisi** and **Vincenzo Argento**, whose studios are open to the public.

Another typical gift is the *coppola*, the traditional Sicilian cap.

## OPEN-AIR MARKETS

If you want to experience the atmosphere of the old quarters of Sicilian towns and buy local produce, you have to go to the outdoor markets. In Palermo, the **Vucciria** market, immortalized by artist Renato Guttuso, is at its most atmospheric in the evening, when it is illuminated by thousands of lights. In Via Argenteria pause at the stall of **Antonino Giannusa**, who offers an amazing range of preserves as well as an excellent Palermo-style pesto sauce. Another market worth visiting is the **Ballarò**,

Renato Guttuso, *La Vucciria* (1974)

between Piazza del Carmine and Piazza Ballarò, which is busiest around noon. Every day, just by the Porta Uzeda, there is an **antiques market** *(mercantino dell'antiquariato)* where furniture sellers and second-hand dealers offer items costing from a few cents to thousands of euros. In Catania, by Piazza Duomo, there is a colourful **fish market** every morning (stalls selling vegetables and meat stay open until the evening). On Sundays Piazza Carlo Alberto fills with an **antiques market** with second-hand items as well as rare pieces of Sicilian craftsmanship.

### ICE CREAM PARLOURS AND PASTRY SHOPS

Popular pastry shops include **Alba** and **Caflisch** in Palermo, **Castorina** in Acireale or **Colicchia** in Trapani, where you can enjoy coffee or an aperitif. Sicilian pastry shops are a delight for the eye and tastebuds with their *cannoli, cassata* and almond paste cookies. Some cake shops offer their own specialities. These include the marzipan sweets with citron filling at the **Antica Pasticceria del Convento** in Erice; ricotta puff pastries at **Scivoli** in Caltagirone; vanilla- or cinnamon-flavoured chocolate at the **Antica Dolceria Bonaiuto** in Modica; ricotta and pistachio *cannoli* at **Savia** in Catania; chestnuts filled with citrus fruit jam and topped with dark chocolate at the **Caffè Sicilia** in Noto; and nougat at **Geraci**, in Caltanissetta.

Marzipan figure, an Erice speciality

Sicily is a paradise for ice cream buffs. The **Caffè del Corso**, in Acireale, sells traditional ice creams in all flavours. In Taormina **Niny Bar** is the place to go, and in Catania it is **Saint Moritz**.

A stall with Sicilian cheese in the varied market in Catania

### REGIONAL SPECIALITIES

Delicatessens and farms with accommodation *(agriturismo)* are ideal places for regional specialities. Smoked swordfish and tuna in oil can be found at the **Casa del Pesce** in Syracuse; salted mullet roe at **Quartana** in Trapani; on Mount Etna the **Azienda Luigi Conti** sells olive oil, bottled olives, artichokes, cream of artichoke, wild asparagus and pumpkin. The **Azienda Agricola Trinità** has tangerines, olive oil, honey and wine, and the **Azienda Agricola Alcalà** offers a mail order service for all products, including fresh fruit. Both firms are based in Catania.

## DIRECTORY

### CERAMICS

**Artigianato del Sole**
Via Santa Margherita 72, Misterbianco (Catania).
***Tel*** *095-398 472.*

**Laboratorio Branciforti**
Scala S. Maria del Monte 3, Caltagirone (Catania).
***Tel*** *0933-244 27.*

**Studio Navarra**
Corso Vittorio Emanuele 38, Sciacca (Agrigento).
***Tel*** *0925-850 00.*

### WROUGHT IRON

**Laboratorio Patanè**
Via Regina Margherita 111, Giardini-Naxos (Messina).
***Tel*** *0942-511 49.*

### PUPPETS

**Piero Scalisi**
Via Federico De Maria 30, Palermo.
***Tel*** *091-488 898.*

**Vincenzo Argento**
Corso Vittorio Emanuele 445, Palermo. **Map** 1 B4.
***Tel*** *091-661 36 80.*

### PASTRY SHOPS

**Alba**
Piazza San Giovanni Bosco 7d, Palermo.
***Tel*** *091-309 016.*

**Antica Dolceria Bonaiuto**
Corso Umberto I 159, Modica (Ragusa).
***Tel*** *0932-941 225.*

**Antica Pasticceria del Convento**
Via Guarnotta Gian Filippo 1, Erice (Trapani).
***Tel*** *0923-869 777.*

**Caffè Sicilia**
Corso Vittorio Emanuele 125, Noto (Syracuse).
***Tel*** *0931-835 013.*

**Caflisch**
Viale Margherita di Savoia 2, Palermo.
***Tel*** *091-684 04 44.*

**Castorina**
Corso Savoia 109, Acireale.
***Tel*** *095-601 546.*

**Colicchia**
Via delle Arti 6, Trapani.
***Tel*** *0923-547 612.*

**Geraci**
Via Niscemi 253, Caltanissetta.
***Tel*** *0934-581 570.*

**Savia**
Via Etnea 302, Catania.
***Tel*** *095-322 335.*

**Scivoli**
Via Milazzo 123, Caltagirone (Catania).
***Tel*** *0933-231 08.*

### ICE CREAM PARLOURS

**Caffè del Corso**
Corso Umberto 165, Acireale. ***Tel*** *095-604 626.*

**Niny Bar**
Via Vittorio Emanuele 216, Letojanni-Taormina (Messina).
***Tel*** *0942-361 04.*

**Saint Moritz**
Viale Raffaello 10, Catania.
***Tel*** *095-437282.*

### REGIONAL SPECIALITIES

**Azienda Alcalà**
Statale 192, km 78, Misterbianco (Catania).
***Tel*** *095-713 00 29.*

**Azienda Luigi Conti**
Contrada Pozzillo, Biancavilla (Catania).
***Tel*** *095-981 132.*

**Azienda Trinità**
Via Trinità 34, Mascalucia (Catania).
***Tel*** *095-727 21 56.*
**www**.aziendatrinita.it

**Casa del Pesce**
Via Emanuele De Benedictis 9, Syracuse.
***Tel*** *0931-691 20.*

**Quartana**
Via 30 Gennaio 17, Trapani. ***Tel*** *0923-206 86.*

# What to Buy in Sicily

In general, Sicilian artisans now concentrate on ceramics and lava stone products. The prices are by no means low, but the objects are often beautifully handcrafted. However, historically, the most classic creations are the traditional Sicilian rod puppets and carts. They have become rarities because there are so few people left who know how to make and repair them. Some shops offer drab reproductions for tourists; but in the antique shops you can still find fine – if expensive – examples of these ancient crafts. When it comes to food and wine, Sicily excels: citrus fruit such as oranges, lemons and grapefruit ripen well in the sunny climate, and you can buy wonderful fruit preserves, wine, nougat, almond paste sweets (candies) and Sicilian pastries such as *cannoli* and *cassata*.

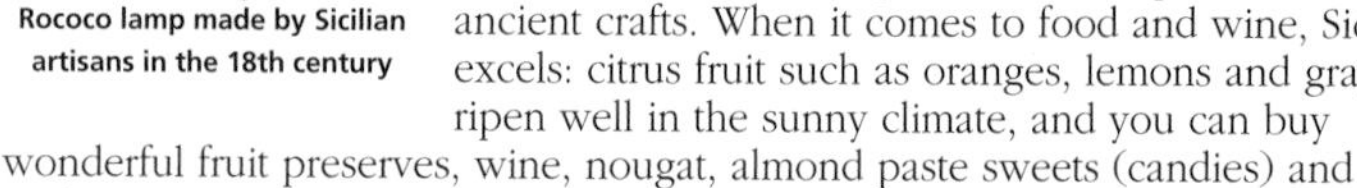

**Rococo lamp made by Sicilian artisans in the 18th century**

**Marzipan fruit**

**Sicilian confectionery** *Buy* cannoli *and cassata just before going back home – they should be eaten within 12 hours. Marzipan fruit will last up to three months.*

**Sicilian oranges**

**Citrus fruit** *Delicious tangerines, blood and navel oranges, grapefruit, lemons and mandarins – superior to those sold elsewhere in Italy – can be purchased in any market. You can also order them directly from the producer, who will send them to your home address.*

**Wines from Pantelleria**

**Wine** *Buy sweet Malvasia from Lipari, sweet Passito wine from Pantelleria, Nero d'Avola from Noto and dry red or white Corvo from Salaparuta or Bianco d'Alcamo. Buy directly from the producers or from wine shops, which also provide shipment to an onward destination.*

**Fillets of tuna**

**Tuna and vegetables in oil** *Tuna fillets, salted mullet roe* (bottarga*), spiced capers in extra virgin olive oil, spiced black olives, aubergines (eggplant) in oil and chilli pepper – are all regional specialities that can be purchased in leading Sicilian delicatessens.*

**Olive oil** *The best comes from the Valle del Belice; it is heavy, almost salty, with a peppery flavour. Ragusa oil is green and fragrant, and Taormina oil is more delicate.*

**Preserves and honey** *Organic fruit jams, prepared on the spot in the "agritourist" farms, have an unmistakable flavour. The fragrant and rare orange and lemon blossom honey also has therapeutic properties.*

## SICILIAN CERAMICS

This is probably the most highly appreciated handicrafts product of all. Light blue, yellow and green are the dominant colours in the lovely ceramics made in Caltagirone; they are richly decorated with volutes, flowers and geometric motifs. You can purchase vases, jugs, plates, mugs, jars and statuettes. Terracotta plaques with house numbers are also very much in demand. In the ceramics made in Sciacca – less famous but just as lovely as those from Caltagirone – the lemon is the prevailing decorative motif. Tiles also come in a variety of styles. The multicoloured majolica tiles bear 19th-century motifs and can be used for floors or simply as decorative objects to be set on an elegant table.

**Elaborately decorated 19th-century tiles**

**Ceramic mask**

**Carts** *Once used to transport heavy loads, traditional Sicilian carts – covered with paintings of religious or historical scenes – are now purely decorative objects. There are very few originals left, and sadly this ancient, noble craft is dying out.*

**Sicilian cart**

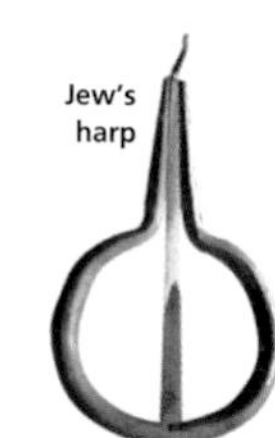

**Jew's harp**

**Jew's harp** *This typical musical instrument consists of an iron frame in the shape of a lyre around a thin flexible metal tongue that produces the sound.*

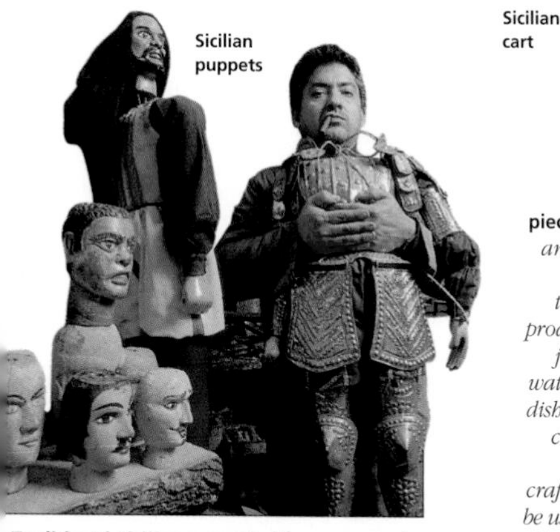

**Sicilian puppets**

**Traditional Sicilian puppets** *The armoured knights errant and the Saracens with round shields and turbans are characters from the puppet plays about Charlemagne. These small masterpieces can be purchased at the few puppet makers' workshops or in antique shops.*

**Terracotta pieces** *Simple and elegant Sicilian terracotta products – oil jars and huge water storage jars, dishes, jugs and oil cruets – are still made by local craftsmen and can be used as decorative objects for your home.*

**Terracotta jar**

# ENTERTAINMENT IN SICILY

The entertainment on offer in Sicily is wide-ranging and varied, and the programmes for cultural, musical and theatrical events are particularly imaginative. In the cities, the theatres put on a long and eclectic winter season, while in the spring and summer the ancient sites become the venues for top-level ancient Greek theatre and symphony concerts. There are also many cultural events connected with artists and personalities who have contributed to Sicily's colourful history. Added to this, there are numerous folk festivals and vibrant carnival celebrations. Far from being performed for the benefit of tourists, these are genuine expressions of the spirit of Sicily. The nightlife is lively in the main towns and the seaside resorts also stay active until the small hours.

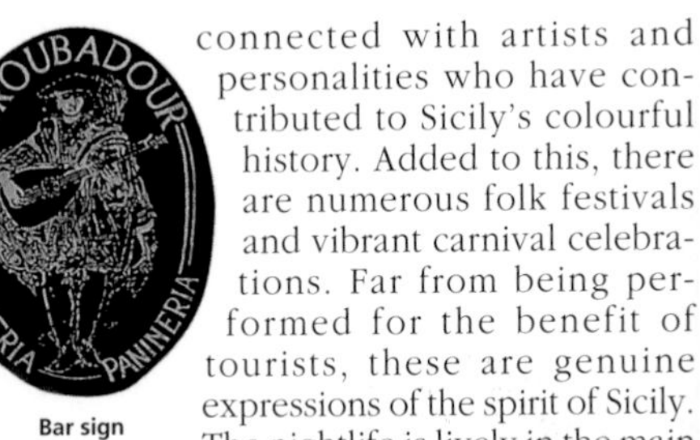

Bar sign

## PRACTICAL INFORMATION

Information in English about what is on in Sicily is difficult to find, but there are several excellent Italian-language websites that offer up to date details on events. The most informative for the island as a whole is www.lasicilia.com/eventi_sicilia.cfm, which lists events in all nine provinces for any particular day. For Palermo, www.palermoweb.com provides a comprehensive guide to entertainment in Sicily's largest city.

The site www.sicilycinema.it offers a complete guide to what is playing in all of the island's cinemas.

## BOOKING TICKETS

There are several nationwide booking agencies operating in Sicily, including **Box Office** and **Ricordi Media Store**. Each of these has offices in the main Sicilian centres. The more prominent theatres and music venues also have their own websites where you can book online.

## OPERA, THEATRE, CLASSICAL MUSIC

Palermo's **Teatro Massimo** stages a year-long opera programme that includes favourites such as Verdi and Puccini alongside more contemporary composers, like Samuel Barber. The theatre's orchestra readily embraces an eclectic mix of music, including tribute bands to The Beatles. The **Teatro Politeama**, home to the Sicilian Symphony Orchestra, hosts classical music concerts throughout the year, as well as artisits such as Paolo Conte.

Palermo's main playhouse is the **Teatro Biondo**, the repertoire of which ranges from popular Greek tragedies and Tennessee Williams to August Strindberg and Eduardo De Filippo.

Outdoor performances are always popular in the summer months

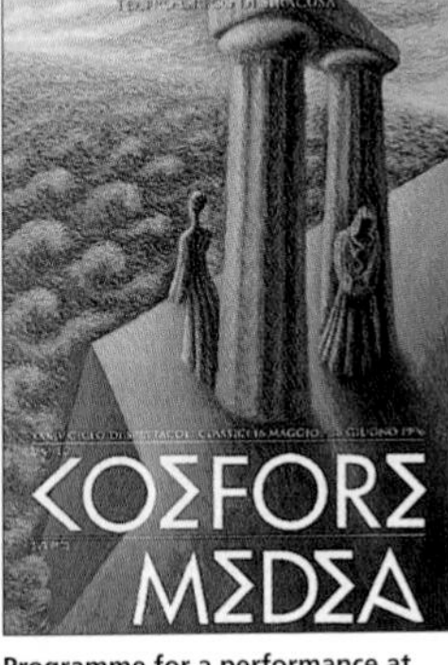

Programme for a performance at the Teatro Greco in Syracuse

With its excellent acoustics, Catania's **Teatro Massimo Bellini** is a favourite with performers. The opera season lasts all year, while the Bellini Orchestra's concert season runs from October to June. The 477-seat **Teatro Sangiorgi**, owned by Teatro Bellini, stages contemporary music, chamber music, operetta, prose and experimental theatre. Catania's chief theatre is the **Teatro Stabile**, which presents mainstream drama by the likes of Shakespeare, Molière and Pirandello.

Sicily's ancient Greek and Roman outdoor theatres come into their own in the warmer months, providing spectacular settings for traditional and modern drama. One of the best known is the **Teatro Greco** in Syracuse, a large and well-preserved monument dating back to the 5th century BC. A classical theatre season is held here biennially in May and June *(see p38)*.

The **Ortygia Festival**, at the Archaeological Park and the Castello Maniace, showcases some of the most innovative Italian theatre and also attracts international artists.

In odd-numbered years, Segesta's temple is the atmospheric backdrop for both traditional and modern plays *(see p38)*, while Taormina's ancient Greek theatre plays host to music and drama during **Taormina Arte** *(see p39)*, a series of events running from April to October. In early June, the theatre stages La Kore, the fashion world's equivalent of the Academy Awards.

Each year Agrigento pays a double tribute to Luigi Pirandello. In summer, during the Rappresentazioni Pirandelliane *(see p39)*, plays are performed in front of the house where the great Sicilian novelist and playwright was born; and in December, the Rassegna di Studi Pirandelliani *(see p41)*, held at the **Centro Nazionale Studi Pirandelliani**, provides an opportunity for students to visit the places that inspired him.

You don't need to understand Italian to appreciate a good puppet show. Puppet theatre reached the height of its popularity in the mid-1800s, but there has been renewed interest in this traditional art. Based on local folklore and comedy and usually involving one of Charlemagne's knights, Orlando, fighting the Saracens, puppet theatre is performed throughout Sicily. In Palermo the **Museo delle Marionette** puts on tourist performances, but for a more authentic experience, visit the **Cuticchio Puppet Theatre**. Puppet shows can also be enjoyed in Acireale, Taormina and Syracuse.

The scenic setting of a classical production at the Teatro Greco in Syracuse

A traditional Sicilian puppet in full armoured suit

## CINEMA

Taormina's annual **FilmFest** in June might not be as important as the Venice Film Festival, but its location makes it an attractive destination for film fans. Movies are screened in the ancient Greek theatre, against the dramatic backdrop of Mount Etna. At over 50 years old, this is the longest lasting film festival in Italy after Venice. Today its focus is predominantly on new directors and films from developing countries.

Lipari, in the Aeolian Islands, hosts its own film festival, **Un Mare di Cinema**, in the first week of August. Since 1990, directors and actors have vied for the festival's prestigious Efesto d'Oro prize.

Sicily is also a popular film location *(see p24)*. Sicilian director Giuseppe Tornatore filmed his Academy Award-winning *Cinema Paradiso* (1989) around Palermo, and his wartime film *Malena* (2000) was also shot in various locations on the island, including Messina, Siracusa, Noto and Taormina. Filmed almost completely on the Aeolian island of Salina, Michael Radford's poignant *Il Postino* (1994) features some splendid scenes shot around the village of Pollara.

## CARNIVALS AND FOLK FESTIVALS

February is carnival time in Italy, and this period is also celebrated with enthusiasm in many Sicilian towns. One of the most spectacular events is the **Carnevale di Acireale** *(see p41)*, blending poetry, games and a procession of colourful floats through the town centre. The famous **Carnevale di Sciacca** *(see p41)* is symbolized by a huge puppet and a procession of floats through the town's streets. In the same month, the people of Catania worship the memory of **Sant'Agata** *(see p41)*, whose relics, including a veil that the faithful believe once shielded Catania from lava erupting out of nearby Mount Etna, are carried through the town.

In Agrigento, the imminent arrival of spring is celebrated each February with the **Sagra del Mandorlo in Fiore** *(see p41)*. As fragrant almond blossoms fill the air, a procession makes its way to the lovely Valle dei Templi. Coinciding with this is the **Folklore Festival** *(see p41)*, featuring dance, traditional costumes and music.

**Carnival time in Sicily spells a week of crowds and colour**

Noto also welcomes spring, but not until the third week in May, with **L'Infiorata** *(see p38)*, which sees the laying down of a carpet of flowers depicting religious or mythological themes.

Easter is an important time for religious festivals. In Caltanissetta, a week is given over to processions, including the Good Friday carrying of a crucifix made of black wood, which was found in a cave in 1625 *(see p38)* . A week-long festival held in Enna culminates on Easter Sunday, when images of Christ and the Madonna are brought together in the Piazza Duomo *(see p38)*. Trapani's **Mystery Procession** *(see p38)* is almost 400 years old. Winding its way through the town, it showcases 20 wooden and fabric sculptures embellished with silver, and each of one is carried on the shoulders of at least ten men.

Caltigirone produces a dazzling spectacle for the feast of its patron saint, the **Festa di San Giacomo** *(see p39)*, with 4,000 candles illuminating the 142 steps of the Scala di Santa Maria del Monte.

In July, the feast day of the patron saint of Palermo, **Santa Rosalia** *(see p39)*, involves actors and musicians recreating the arrival of the Flemish painter Antony van Dyck, who visited Palermo in 1624 and painted Saint Rosalia interceding to rescue the town from the plague.

In August, Piazza Armerina celebrates its French heritage with the **Palio dei Normanni** *(see p39)*. The three days of festivities begin with a re-enactment of Roger's entrance into the town and culminate in a medieval tournament.

Christmas is the occasion for a number of festivals. The town of Agira, near Enna, is the setting of the only **Presepe Vivente** (Nativity play) in Italy to take place on Christmas night. More than 100 players in period costume take part in the festival, which also features ancient crafts such as spinning, carpentry and pasta-making.

Another fascinating **Presepe Vivente** is played out in the northwestern town of Custonaci, in a cave called Grotta Mangiapane, named after the family that lived in it from the 1800s until 1945.

## TRADITIONAL AND POPULAR MUSIC

Traditional Sicilian folk music has a loyal following. Among the best-known exponents are Carmelo Salemi and Giancarlo Parisi, players of the *zampogna* (bagpipes), *friscalettu* and other Sicilian wind instruments. They are regular performers at festivals such as Agrigento's **Folklore Festival** *(see p41)*, Taormina's **Womad**, Palermo's **World Festival on the Beach** and the **Ortygia Festival**.

Jazz also finds a dedicated audience. The Palermo-based Brass Group, an association that promotes this genre of music, has its headquarters in a historic building called **Lo Spasimo**, which is also home to the Sicilian Jazz Orchestra.

In Catania the best place for live music is **La Chiave**, where they play blues on Thursdays and jazz on Sundays.

## NIGHTLIFE

Sicily's lively nightlife centres on the cities in winter and the tourist resorts in summer. Discos often charge a cover fee that can be as high as €20.

Palermo has its share of pubs, including **Au Domino, Agricantus**, **Cambio Cavalli** and **Crazy Bull**; the latter offering live Italian, American, English and South American music. New musical talent is showcased at the **Biergarten** and **Malox**. Popular discos in the inner city are **Tonnara Florio**, in the ancient district of Arenella, the **Anticlea Pub**, **Kursaal Kalesa Club** and the **Country Club**, whose large dance floors become open-air in summer. Outside central Palermo are well-known discos like **La Conchiglia**.

Located just out of Catania is **Banacher**, an outdoor club that attracts a mix of locals and tourists; here you can dance amid a maze of plants. **Il Bagatto** is a popular watering hole offering live music on the island of Ortygia, the ancient heart of Syracuse.

Buzzing Taormina caters for all tastes, from casual cafés to late night discos. **La Giara** is a popular apéritif and after-dinner drink spot that does not get crowded until after 10pm. **Bar Morgana** is for the young and fashionable and is open till late. In the seaside town of Giardini Naxos is **Marabù**, a beautiful open-air disco where you can dance until the early hours.

**Catania boasts one of the most vivacious nightlife scenes in Sicily**

# DIRECTORY

## BOOKINGS

**Box Office**
Via Cavour 133, Palermo. **Map** 1 C2. ***Tel*** *091-335 566.*
Via G Leopardi 95, Catania. ***Tel*** *095-722 53 40.*

**Ricordi Media Store**
Via Sant'Euplio 38, Catania.

**Ticket One**
**www**.ticketone.it

## OPERA, THEATRE, CLASSICAL MUSIC

**Centro Nazionale Studi Pirandelliani**
Via Santa Lucia 27, Agrigento. ***Tel*** *0922-290 52.* **www**.cnsp.it

**Cuticchio Puppet Theatre**
Via Bara all'Olivella 95, Palermo. **Map** 1 B2. ***Tel*** *091-323 400.* **www**.figlidartecuticchio.com

**Museo delle Marionette**
Via Butera 1, Palermo. **Map** 2 E3. ***Tel*** *091-328 060.* **www**.museomarionettepalermo.it

**Ortygia Festival**
Via Agatocle 51, Syracuse. ***Tel*** *0931-483 648.* **www**.ortigiafestival.it

**Taormina Arte**
***Tel*** *0942-211 42.* **www**.taormina-arte.com

**Teatro Biondo**
Via Teatro Biondo 11, Palermo. **Map** 1 C3. ***Tel*** *091-743 43 00.*

**Teatro delle Marionette**
Via Nazionale per Catania 195, Acireale. ***Tel*** *095-764 80 35.*

**Teatro delle Marionette**
Via Giudecca 5, Syracuse. ***Tel*** *093-146 55 40.*

**Teatro delle Marionette**
Via di Giovanni, Taormina. ***Tel*** *0942-628 644.*

**Teatro Greco**
Corso Gelone 103, Syracuse. ***Tel*** *0931-465 831 or 0931-674 15.* **www**.indafondazione.org

**Teatro Massimo**
Piazza Giuseppe Verdi, Palermo. **Map** 1 B2. ***Tel*** *091-605 31 11.* **www**.teatromassimo.it

**Teatro Massimo Bellini**
Via Perrota 12, Catania. ***Tel*** *095-730 61 11.* **www**.teatromassimobellini.it

**Teatro Politeama**
Piazza Ruggero Settimo, Palermo. **Map** 1 A/B1. ***Tel*** *091-605 34 21.*

**Teatro Sangiorgi**
Via A di Sangiuliano 233, Catania. ***Tel*** *095-730 61 11.*

**Teatro Stabile**
Via Fava 39, Catania. ***Tel*** *095-354 466.* **www**.teatrostabilecatania.it

## CINEMA

**Taormina FilmFest**
***Tel*** *094-223 243.* **www**.taorminafilmfest.it

**Un Mare di Cinema**
Lipari. ***Tel*** *090-981 29 87.*

## CARNIVALS AND FOLK FESTIVALS

**Carnevale di Acireale**
Acireale. ***Tel*** *095-891 19 99.* **www**.carnevaleacireale.com

**Carnevale di Sciacca**
Sciacca. ***Tel*** *0925-245 37.* **www**.carnevaledisciacca.it

**Festa di San Giacomo**
Caltagirone. ***Tel*** *093-353 809.*

**Festa di Sant'Agata**
Catania. ***Tel*** *095-760 62 33.* **www**.comune.catania.it/portale/

**Festa di Santa Rosalia**
Palermo. ***Tel*** *091-583 847.* **www**.palermoweb.com/santarosalia

**Folklore Festival**
Agrigento. **www**.mandorloinfiore.net

**L'Infiorata**
Noto. **www**.infioratadinoto.it

**Mystery Procession**
Trapani. ***Tel*** *092-354 55 11.* **www**.processionemisteritp.it

**Palio dei Normanni**
Piazza Armerina. ***Tel*** *0935-682 501 or 0935-686 063.* **www**.paliodeinormanni.com

**Presepe Vivente**
Agira. ***Tel*** *0935-691 111.*

**Presepe Vivente**
Custonaci. ***Tel*** *0923-973 553.* **www**.mcsystem.it/presepe

**Sagra del Mandorlo in Fiore**
Agrigento. ***Tel*** *092-220 454.* **www**.mandorloinfiore.net

## TRADITIONAL AND POPULAR MUSIC

**La Chiave**
Via Landolina, Catania. ***Tel*** *347-948 09 10.* **www**.lachiave.it

**Ortygia Festival**
Syracuse. **www**.ortigiafestival.it

**Lo Spasimo**
Via Giuseppe La Farina, Palermo. ***Tel*** *091-348 751.* **www**.thebrassgroup.it

**Womad**
Taormina. **www**.womad.org

**World Festival on the Beach**
Palermo. **www**.wwfestival.com

## NIGHTLIFE

**Agricantus**
Via XX Settembre 82, Palermo. ***Tel*** *091-487 117.*

**Anticlea Pub**
Viale Galatea 6, Palermo. ***Tel*** *091-346 772.*

**Au Domino**
Via Principe di Belmonte 88, Palermo. **Map** 1 C1.

**Il Bagatto**
Piazza San Giuseppe, Ortygia, Syracuse. ***Tel*** *093-122 040.*

**Banacher**
Via Vampolieri 2, Aci Castello. ***Tel*** *095-27 12 57.*

**Bar Morgana**
Scesa Morgana 4, Taormina. ***Tel*** *094-262 00 56.*

**Biergarten**
Viale Regione Siciliana 6469, Palermo. ***Tel*** *091-688 97 27.*

**Cambio Cavalli**
Via Patania 54, Palermo. ***Tel*** *091-581 418.* **Map** 1 C2.

**La Conchiglia**
Via del Mare, Balestrate, Palermo. ***Tel*** *091-878 69 96.*

**Country Club**
Via dell'Olimpo 5, Palermo. ***Tel*** *091-453 782.*

**Crazy Bull**
Via Atenasio 8a, Palermo. ***Tel*** *091-685 05 27.*

**La Giara**
Vico La Floresta 1, Taormina. ***Tel*** *094-223 360.*

**Kursaal Kalesa Club**
Foro Italico 21, Palermo. **Map** 2 E3. ***Tel*** *091-616 22 82.*

**Malox**
Piazzetta della Canna 8–9, Palermo. **Map** 1 B3. ***Tel*** *091-612 47 12.*

**Marabù**
Via Iannuzzo, Giardini Naxos, Taormina. ***Tel*** *094-265 30 29.*

**Tonnara Florio**
Via Discesa Tonnara, Palermo. ***Tel*** *091-637 56 11.* **www**.tonnaraflorio.com

# SPECIALIST HOLIDAYS AND OUTDOOR ACTIVITIES

For most visitors to Sicily, sporting activities tend to be water-based: swimming, fishing, windsurfing and diving in the crystal-clear waters off the extensive coast and the many islands that dot the Tyrrhenian and Mediterranean seas. Sailing enthusiasts have a vast choice of enticing routes on a variety of charter craft. There are plenty of other outdoor activities to enjoy too, such as hiking along old pathways in the Madonie and Nebrodi mountains or on Mount Etna. In the winter, the snowy slopes of the imposing volcano provide good conditions for downhill as well as cross-country skiing. Horse riding, including organized programmes of long-distance trekking, is also becoming increasingly popular in Sicily. Visitors can embark on many of these activities under their own steam, though an ever-growing number of local and overseas agencies offer a good choice of all-inclusive outdoor and sporting holidays.

**Sport fishing**

**Sailing has become an increasingly popular activity in Sicily**

## SAILING

The coastline and inlets of Sicily and the region's wonderful islands are a paradise for sailing aficionados, and the sport is especially popular along the island's northern coast. True to their name – derived from the Greek god of wind – the Aeolian Islands *(see pp188–91)* guarantee a constant stiff breeze, as does the distant Pelagie archipelago *(see pp124–5)* off the southwestern coast.

In 2005, the international races held in the waters off the coast of Trapani as part of the prestigious America's Cup trials represented a landmark event for Sicily. This, along with the coming and going of yachts from all over Europe, has had a very positive influence of late, triggering a series of improvements in nautical tourism facilities in the many port towns along the coast.

Yachts of varying sizes and degrees of comfort are available for charter at ports all around the island through companies such as **Onda Eoliana**. Many nautical centres hold sailing courses for the uninitiated, including **Centro Vela** in Lampedusa, though qualified multilingual crews can always be requested to transport passengers who desire a thoroughly relaxing sailing experience. **Syracruse Sailing Team** offers a number of trips around Sicily's islands and **EtnaSail** can arrange an unusual trip in a traditional Turkish-style *caicco* boat.

The **Velalinks** website (www.velalinks.it) is helpful in locating charter companies and instructors. There are also several UK-based companies that organize all-inclusive sailing holidays.

## WINDSURFING

This energetic sport can be practised at most Sicilian seaside resorts thanks to conditions that guarantee constant winds. Virtually every beach in Sicily offers rental facilities. Mondello beach *(see p72)*, just outside Palermo, is well-served by **Albaria Windsurfing Club**. However, expert windsurfers claim that the best places for the sport are the Aeolian Islands and the Capo Passero area *(see p148)* in the south where the Ionian and Mediterranean seas merge. This same area is also favoured by kitesurfers. The popular beach location of Pozzallo has rental facilities, and expert instruction for different abilities is also available. The **Kitesicilia** website (www.kitesicilia.it) offers suggestions on the island's hot spots and a list of local contacts.

**Windsurfers can often be spotted in the waters around Sicily**

## DIVING

The sea beds around Sicily are the delight and joy of scuba- and free-divers, who head for the offshore islands – especially the Aeolians *(see pp188–91)*, which are of volcanic origin. The island of Ustica *(see p109)* has a marvellous marine reserve making it an ideal spot for underwater sports. Agencies here include **Alta Marea**, which offers diving courses for all levels of experience, and **Barracuda**. Almost in Tunisian waters, the Pelagie islands of Pantelleria *(see p124)* and Lampedusa *(see p125)* offer superb diving in brilliantly clear waters. As well as fish, you may spot some historical artifacts such as Roman amphorae from an ancient shipwreck on the sea bed. **Dibex Centro Subacqueo** has a particularly good range of diving trips from Pantelleria.

The rugged coastline in the Riserva dello Zingaro, ideal for hiking

The crystalline waters around the Aeolian Islands favour snorkelling and scuba diving

Generally speaking, most seaside resorts offer at least basic diving facilities, including refills of your oxygen cylinder. The resort of Terrasini, on the coast west of Palermo, offers both instructors and facilities.

If you are planning to dive independently, always make sure that someone knows of your whereabouts and plans. The Italian website **Dive Italy** has useful information and a number of operators, such as **The Sicilian Experience**, can organize diving holidays.

## WALKING & TREKKING

There is an impressive range of rewarding walking itineraries all over Sicily. The choice includes hills, mountains, coastal districts and fantastic limestone gorges such as the ones at Pantalica *(see p157)* and Cava d'Ispica *(see p149)* in the Monti Iblei (Hyblaei Hills). The protected park area around Mount Etna *(see pp170–73)* offers marvellous opportunities for high-altitude trips among the lava fields and grottoes. Qualified leaders from **Etna Guides** escort thrilling climbs to the smoking summit craters. To the east is the Alcantara River valley *(see p181)*, which offers easy routes through old settlements and a fascinating basalt ravine gouged out by the impetuous watercourse.

The rugged Madonie mountains and park feature spectacular panoramas, marked paths and rare vegetation in the Vallone Madonna degli Angeli, near Piano Battaglia *(see p94)* and the Pizzo Carbonara summit.

Highlights of the vast rolling Nebrodi mountain chain *(see p186)*, another protected area, include the Biviere di Cesarò, a pretty lake and important staging point for migratory birds. **Parco Regionale dei Monti Nebrodi** provides extensive and helpful information about the area. Close by, and towering over the village of Alcara Li Fusi, is the dramatic Rocche di Crasto, home to the griffon vulture. These impressive rock formations are accessible on clear paths. Other interesting areas for walkers include Piana degli Albanesi *(see p96)* and the divine coastline of the **Riserva dello Zingaro** *(see p97)*.

Several islands have unusual walking opportunities, such as the Aeolians *(see pp188–91)*, with ascents of volcanoes, both extinct and active, on Stromboli (where a guide is essential), Vulcano, Salina and Lipari. **Magma Trek's** tour leaders are particularly knowledgeable about the science and history of Stromboli's active volcano.

In both the interior and main cities of Sicily, visitors can find a number of sports associations and guesthouses offering trekking holidays and excursions. **Club Alpino Italiano** also organizes excursions on a regular basis as does **Explore Worldwide**.

The awesome ravine gouged out of the basalt rock by the course of the Alcantara River

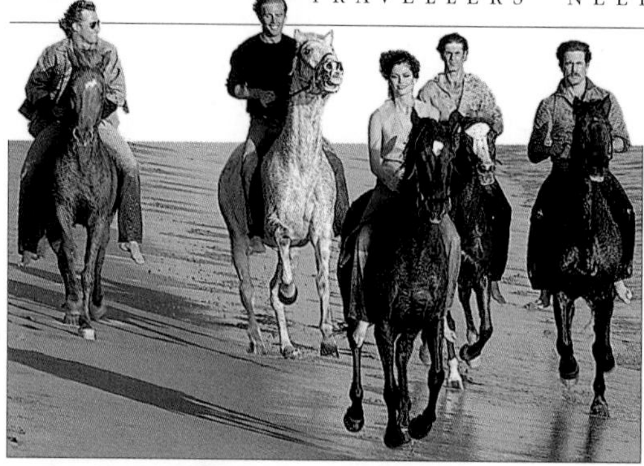

**A group of friends horse riding on a Sicilian beach**

## HORSE RIDING

This popular activity is gathering an increasingly loyal following, especially among local inhabitants. Sicily's rugged, mountainous interior is perfectly suited to horse riding enthusiasts, featuring numerous routes that are easily accessible from village centres.

One particularly interesting multi-day itinerary is the one that stretches for 70 km (43.5 miles) and runs east to west along the central ridge of the Nebrodi mountain range *(see p186)*, following age-old droving routes. This region is home to 5,000 native horses, a pretty, dark variety known as San Fratellino. Believed to descend from an ancient breed known to the Greeks and Romans, the horses are left to graze freely.

Many *agriturismo* farms and some of the larger holiday villages have riding schools that cater to varying levels of ability. Tucked away in the divine Anapo Valley *(see p157)*, near a wild gorge, **Pantalica Ranch** arranges horse riding trips. **Centro Ippico Amico del Cavallo** is an equestrian centre based in Misterbianco, close to Catania, which offers one-day trips as well as longer treks on horseback. There are also many establishments dotted around the slopes of Mount Etna offering various horse riding excursions.

For further information on the most important horse riding centres in Sicily, contact the **Associazione Nazionale Turismo Equestre** (ANTE) in Rome.

## SKIING

If the weather is good, the panorama from the slopes of Mount Etna *(see pp170–73)* is simply awe-inspiring, with the sea at Taormina mirroring the sunlight and the volcano's fumes rising lazily above you.

However, do not expect to find state-of-the-art skiing facilities here. There is no artificial snow (the perennial drought in Sicily precludes anything of the kind), and the heat of the volcano tends to melt the snow in a hurry, so the skiing season is limited to a few months, from late December until March. Thanks to a cable-car and four ski lifts, you can ski up to 3,000 m (9,850 ft) above sea level on the runs around **Rifugio Sapienza** and the old Montagnola crater.

On the northern flank of the mountain, reconstruction of both facilities and runs continues in the wake of destructive 2002 eruptions that all but wiped out the small-scale resort of Piano Provenzana *(see p172)*.

Perfect for all age groups, the thrill of tobogganing is another good, fun activity.

Mount Etna is not only for downhill-skiing enthusiasts, though their numbers continue to grow with each year. There is also a beaten track near the Grande Albergo, just below **Rifugio Sapienza**, which is ideal for cross-country skiing.

The volcano also attracts lovers of alpine techniques, telemarking and even the increasingly popular pursuit of snowshoeing; real off-the-beaten-track activities.

The wonderfully wild Nebrodi range *(see p186)* also gets a decent snow cover and offers many opportunities for exploration with cross-country skis and snowshoes.

**Making the most of the brief skiing season on Mount Etna**

Piano Battaglia *(see p94)*, in the Madonie mountains, attracts weekenders from Palermo for its lovely, if limited, pistes and lifts.

Finally, thrill-seekers will enjoy the uniquely Sicilian sport of travelling down the black volcanoes of the Aeolian Islands *(see pp188–91)* on a snowboard. But be warned, the dry lava surface is much harder than snow.

**Snowboarding on a lava field on Vulcano, one of the Aeolian Islands**

# DIRECTORY

## SAILING

**Centro Nautica**
(charter & rental)
Baia Levante, Vulcano.
**Tel** *090-982 21 97.*
**www**.baialevante.it

**Centro Vela**
(courses)
Lampedusa.
**www**.centrovelalampedusa.com

**Etnasail**
Catania
**Tel** *095-712 69 52.*
**www**.etnasail.com

**Gulliver**
(rental & courses)
Favignana.
**www**.arteutile.net/gulliver

**Harbour Office**
Lipari.
**Tel** *090-981 32 22.*
**www**.lipari.guardiacostiera.it

**Harbour Office**
Ustica.
**Tel** *091-844 96 52.*

**Nauta**
(charter & rental)
Lipari.
**Tel** *090-982 23 05.*

**Nautica Levante**
(charter & rental)
Salina.
**Tel** *090-984 30 83.*
**www**.nauticalevante.it

**Onda Eoliana**
(rental)
**Tel** *090-984 40 10.*
**www**.ondaeoliana.com

**Rinauro**
(charter & rental)
Stromboli.
**Tel** *090-986 156.*

**Sailing Information**
**www**.lampedusa.to

**Sopravvento**
(rental & courses)
Pantelleria.
**www**.sopravvento.net

**Syracuse Sailing Team**
(charter)
**Tel** *0931-608 08.*
**www**.sailingteam.biz

**Trinacria Sailing**
**Tel** *090-641 34 38.*
**www**.trinacriasailing.com

**Velalinks**
**www**.velalinks.it

**Vulcano Consult**
**Tel** *800-090 541.*
**www**.vulcanoconsult.it

## WINDSURFING

**Albaria Windsurfing Club**
**Tel** *091-684 44 83.*

**Kitesicilia**
**www**.kitesicilia.it

## DIVING

**Alta Marea**
Ustica.
**Tel** *091-625 40 96.*
**www**.altamareaustica.it

**Barracuda**
Ustica.
**Tel** *091-844 91 32.*
**www**.barracudaustica.com

**Centro Immersioni Lo Verde**
Lampedusa.
**Tel** *0922-970 181.*

**Dibex Centro Subacqueo**
Pantelleria.
**www**.pantelleria.it/divex

**Dive Italy**
**www**.diveitaly.com

**Diving Cala Levante**
**Tel** *0923-915 463.*
**www**.calalevante.pantelleria.it

**Diving Center Manta Sub**
Lipari.
**Tel** *090-981 10 04*

**Green Divers**
**Tel** *0923-918 209.*
**www**.greendivers.it

**Hospital**
(hyperbaric chamber)
**Tel** *090-988 51*

**La Sirenetta Diving Center**
Stromboli.
**Tel** *090-986 338.*
**www**.lasirenettadiving.it

**Lipari Diving Centre**
**Tel** *339-647 22 72.*

**Profondo Blu**
**Tel** *091-844 96 09.*
**www**.ustica-diving.it

**Ricarica ARA**
Filicudi.
**Tel** *090-988 99 84.*

**Ricarica ARA**
Diving Center La Gorgonia
**Tel** *090-981 26 16.*
**www**.lagorgoniadiving.it
Salina.
**Tel** *090-984 30 92.*

**Ricarica ARA di Rosalia Ailara**
**Tel** *091-844 96 05.*
**www**.ustica.ara.it

**Salina Diving**
**Tel** *338-495 90 80.*
**www**.salinadiving.com

**Scubaland**
**Tel** *091-844 96 36.*
**www**.scubaland.it

**The Sicilian Experience**
6 Palace Street,
London SW1E 5HY.
**Tel** *020-7828 9171.*
**www**.thesicilianexperience.co.uk

**Sotto l'Acqua del Vulcano**
**Tel** *090-986 025.*

**Terrasini Dive Center**
**Tel** *091-868 76 95.*
**www**.divecompanie.com

**Vulcano Mare**
Vulcano.
**Tel** *090-985 31 05.*
**www**.vulcanomare.com

## WALKING & TREKKING

**Club Alpino Italiano**
Catania.
**Tel** *095-715 35 15.*
**www**.caicatania.it
Palermo.
**Tel** *091-329 407.*
**www**.palermoweb.com/caipalermo

**Etna Guides**
**Tel** *095-791 47 55.*
**www**.etnaguide.com

**Explore Worldwide**
**www**.explore.co.uk

**Magma Trek**
Stromboli.
**Tel** *090-986 57 68.*
**www**.magmatrek.it

**Parco dell'Etna**
Nicolosi. **Tel** *095-821 111.*
**www**.parks.it/parco.etna

**Parco Fluviale dell'Alcantara**
Francavilla di Sicilia.
**Tel** *0942-98 99.*
**www**.parcoalcantara.it

**Parco delle Madonie**
Petralia Sottana.
**Tel** *0921-923 327.*
**www**.parcodellemadonie.it

**Parco Regionale dei Monti Nebrodi**
Caronia.
**Tel** *0921-333 211.*
**www**.parcodeinebrodi.it

**Riserva dello Zingaro**
**Tel** *0924-351 08.*
**www**.riservazingaro.it

## HORSE RIDING

**Associazione Nazionale Turismo Equestre**
Rome. **Tel** *06-3265 0230.*
**www**.fiteec-ante.it

**Centro Guide Equestri Ambientali Sanconese**
**Tel** *0933-970 883.*
**www**.geasanconese.it

**Centro Ippico Amico del Cavallo**
Misterbianco.
**Tel** *095-461 882.*
**www**.amicodelcavallo.com

**Pantalica Ranch**
**Tel** *0931-942 069.*
**www**.pantalicaranch.it

**Rifugio Villa Miraglia**
Portella Femmina Morta,
Nebrodi.
**Tel** *095-773 21 33.*
**www**.villamiraglia.it

## SKIING

**Funivia dell'Etna**
**Tel** *095-911 158.*
**www**.funiviaetna.com

**Rifugio Ostello della Gioventù**
Piano Battaglia.
**Tel** *0921-649 995.*

**Rifugio Sapienza**
**Tel** *095-915 321.*

# SURVIVAL GUIDE

# PRACTICAL INFORMATION

In recent years, there has been renewed interest in caring for and revitalizing the unique historic, artistic and natural heritage of Sicily, and the island is no longer a destination solely for the adventurous. The Sicilian coastline, one of the most beautiful in Italy, attracts thousands of visitors every year. The island's long history and numerous monuments are as much an attraction – if not a greater one – than its marvellous landscape. Those who are interested in Sicilian history and culture would do well to plan their visit for a time other than the crowded – and very hot – months of July and August. But whenever you choose to visit the island known to the ancients as Trinacria, there is always something exciting to explore. Everyone comes expecting to enjoy the island's food and wine, coastline and art treasures. But there are also inland areas to explore, including Mount Etna, the Madonie Mountains and Riserva dello Zingaro nature reserves, as well as sports activities and spas.

**The Trinacria, ancient symbol of Sicily, now regional coat of arms**

**Ferry boats, connecting the island of Sicily with mainland Italy**

## OPENING HOURS

In Sicily shops are generally open from 8 or 9am until 1pm and then from 3:30 or 4pm (in the winter) or 5pm (in the summer) to 7 or even 8pm from Monday to Saturday. They are closed on Sundays and for one afternoon during the week.

Banks are open from 8:30am to 1:30pm and 3:30 to 4:30pm from Monday to Friday. Restaurants are closed one day a week and for annual holidays, usually in the winter. Off season most hotels, especially those along the coast, will be closed, so that if you travel in the winter months you should book accommodation ahead to avoid complications.

One of the special characteristics of Sicilian life is that people dine later than on the mainland, particularly in the summer when the weather can be very hot. The midday meal may begin as late as 2pm, and evening meals may not be served until 10pm.

## MUSEUMS AND MONUMENTS

Normally Sicilian museums and archaeological sites are open every day in the morning except for Monday. Many sites are also open in the afternoon. Opening hours tend to be longer during the summer. Apart from particularly important places such as Agrigento, admission to archaeological areas is free.

Entrance fees for museums vary from €1 to €5. Youngsters and senior citizens are usually either allowed a reduction or enter free of charge. Church opening hours can be erratic, and you will need both luck and patience if you want to see every interior, especially in smaller villages. Most churches are open to the public during morning and evening mass. Should a church be closed, you can always try asking the priest or sacristan if he will let you in for a brief visit.

## COMMUNICATIONS

It is easy enough to find a post office or phone booth in the larger towns, but they are rare, if not non-existent, in the interior and small villages. Reception on a mobile phone might not be good, especially on the islands. It is wise to carry an Italian phrasebook as English is not always spoken.

**Telephone booths, quite rare in the interior of Sicily**

◁ **Horse riding in the hilly countryside**

## NEWSPAPERS

The leading local papers are *Il Mediterraneo* and *Giornale di Sicilia* in Palermo, *Gazzetta del Sud* in Messina, *Gazzettino di Sicilia* in Syracuse, and *La Sicilia* in Catania. All are useful for local events information. The leading Italian daily newspapers are sold in Sicily. English-language newspapers are sold in the larger towns.

**Italian and foreign daily newspapers sold in Sicily**

## IMMIGRATION AND CUSTOMS

European Union (EU) residents and visitors from the United States, Canada, New Zealand and Australia, for example, need no visa for a stay of up to three months. Information concerning visas can be obtained in advance at your nearest Italian consulate. Non-EU citizens must carry a valid passport, while for EU citizens an ID will suffice. By law you must carry your ID with you at all times, as it may be needed – during a road block *(see p238)* for instance. Any customs formalities are completed at the first Italian arrival point (usually the mainland). Non-EU citizens can claim back sales tax (IVA) on purchases costing over €336.

## TOURIST INFORMATION

The provincial capitals of Sicily have an official tourist board, the **Ente Provinciale per il Turismo** (it might also be called **Azienda Autonoma Provinciale per l'Incremento Turistico** or **Azienda Provinciale Turismo)**, where information and brochures are available. Larger towns have an **Azienda Autonoma di Soggiorno**. In the small towns and villages, make enquiries at the **Pro Loco** or the Town Hall. You can get the addresses and phone numbers of smaller bureaus at the **Azienda Provinciale Turismo**. You can obtain information on how to organize your trip from the **Enti Provinciali per il Turismo** or the **Assessorato al Turismo della Regione Sicilia** in Palermo. The web site www.sicilia.com is useful.

## DIRECTORY

### TOURIST BOARDS

**Assessorato al Turismo Regione Sicilia**
Via Notarbartolo 11, Palermo.
**Tel** *091-696 11 11.*
**www**.regione.sicilia.it/turismo

**Agrigento**
**AAPIT Tel** *0922-401 352.*
**AAST Tel** *0922-204 54.*

**Caltagirone**
**AAST Tel** *0933-538 09.*

**Caltanissetta**
**AAPIT Tel** *0934-530 411 or 530 403.* **www**.aapit.cl.it

**Catania**
**AAPIT Tel** *095-730 62 22 or 730 62 33.* **www**.apt.catania.it

**Cefalù**
**AAST Tel** *0921-921 990 or 421 458.* **www**.cefalu-tour.pa.it

**Enna**
**AAPIT Tel** *800-221 188.*
**www**.apt-enna.com
**AAST Tel** *0935-261 19/500 875.*

**Erice**
**AAST Tel** *0923-869 388/522 021.*

**Gela**
**AAST Tel** *0933-923 268.*

**Giardini Naxos**
**AAST Tel** *0942-510 10.*
**www**.aastgiardininaxos.it

**Isole Egadi**
**Tel** *0923-922 121.*
**www**.isoleegadi.it

**Lampedusa**
**www**.enteturismolampedusa.it

**Lipari**
**Tel** *090-988 00 95.*

**Messina**
**AAPIT Tel** *090-674 236.*
**AAST Tel** *090-293 52 92.*
**www**.azienturismomessina.it

**Noto**
**APT Tel** *0931-836 744/573 779.*

**Palermo**
**APT Tel** *091-605 81 11.*
Azienda Autonoma Turismo Palermo e Monreale
**Tel** *091-540 122.*
**www**.palermotourism.com

**Ragusa**
**AAPIT Tel** *0932-221 511 or 663 094.* **www**.ragusaturismo.it

**Sciacca**
**AAST Tel** *0925-227 44.*
**www**.aziendaturismosciacca.it

**Syracuse**
**AAPIT Tel** *0931-481 200.*
**www**.apt-siracusa.it
**AAST Tel** *0931-652 01/464 255.*

**Taormina**
**AAST Tel** *0942-232 43 or 239 12.*
**www**.gate2taormina.com

**Trapani**
**AAPIT Tel** *0923-545 511.*
**www**.apt.trapani.it
**AAST Tel** *0923-290 00.*

### UK TOURIST OFFICE

Italian State Tourist Office (ENIT) UK
1 Princes Street, London W1R 2AY.
**Tel** *020-7408 1254.*
**www**.enit.it

### ITALIAN EMBASSIES AND CONSULATES

**United Kingdom**
38 Eaton Place, London SW1.
**Tel** *020-7235 9371.*
**www**.amblondraesteri.it

**United States**
690 Park Avenue, New York.
**Tel** *212-737 9100.*
**www**.italyemb.org

**Australia**
6–9 Macquarie Street, Sydney 2000, NSW. **Tel** *02-247 84 42.*
**www**.ambitalia.org.au

# Personal Security and Health

On the whole, Sicily is safe for visitors. At busy tourist spots, such as the ferry ports and main stations, it is wise to keep a close eye on your belongings. Also, avoid leaving valuables in your car if the parking lot is unattended. However, in the smaller towns and villages, petty crime is rare. The rural areas are even safer, and if you speak a little Italian, getting to know people will increase your personal security. The summer heat can leave the countryside susceptible to fires. Visitors and residents alike are asked to do all they can to prevent fires from breaking out.

In the event of fire, follow the firemen's instructions carefully

A *carabinieri* patrol boat on duty off the coast of Sicily

## PERSONAL PROPERTY

It is not really a good idea to carry large sums of money on you. Major credit cards such as Visa and MasterCard are accepted by most businesses throughout the island. There are automatic cash dispensers *(bancomat)* in all larger towns and you may choose to buy travellers' cheques in addition.

In general, parking is safe. However, in large cities it is best not to leave your car unattended for too long.

State policeman City policeman

In the event of a theft, make sure you report it immediately to the local police or *carabinieri* stations (you have to do this in order to make an insurance claim).

## ROADBLOCKS

Generally speaking, travelling on Sicilian roads poses few problems apart from some reckless drivers. However, because of the presence of the Mafia, you may be stopped at a police or army roadblock *(posto di blocco)*, particularly around the Palermo area. Officers usually check your ID and the vehicle, but it is possible that they might ask to search your car. Simply stay calm and cooperate with the police – there should be no cause for alarm.

## IN THE EVENT OF FIRE

Sadly, fires are a scourge in Sicily – and in the rest of Southern Italy, for that matter. Some of them are natural occurrences, some are genuine accidents, but most are cases of arson. Fire can spread rapidly, especially in the dry summer vegetation, and the wind may carry the fire for long distances in a very short time. Firefighting is usually entrusted to the local fire departments and forest rangers, volunteers and specially equipped firefighting planes, which are located at strategic points around the island.

### FIRE PREVENTION RULES

1. Do not throw cigarettes out of your car.
2. Never light a fire except in areas where this is explicitly permitted.
3. If you see a fire, call 1515 at once.
4. Do not stop or park your car to watch a fire; you may block the road and interfere with the firefighting operations.
5. Pay attention to the wind direction: it is extremely dangerous to be downwind of a fire, as it may spread rapidly and catch you unawares.

The coastguards at Lampedusa

## HEALTH

Emergency medical care is free for all EU citizens in Italy, with a European Health Insurance Card (EHIC). The form is available from main post offices in the UK. Only emergencies are covered, and private medical insurance is needed for all other situations. Non-EU citizens should get comprehensive medical insur-

**EMERGENCY NUMBERS**

**General Emergencies**
*Tel* 113.

**Police**
*Tel* 112.

**Fire Department**
*Tel* 115.

**Road Emergencies**
*Tel* 116.

**Telephone Information**
*Tel* 12.

**Nautical Information**
*Tel* 196.

**Ambulance & Mountain Emergencies**
*Tel* 118.

**Forest Fires**
*Tel* 1515.

ance before their arrival. Sicily has a network of hospitals and first-aid stations *(pronto soccorso)*. All tourist resorts operate seasonal emergency treatment centres *(guardia medica)*. Pharmacies are normally open from Monday to Friday at 9am–1pm and 4–7pm and on Saturday morning. However, for emergencies, a list of the night and holiday opening rotas will always be posted on or near the shop door.

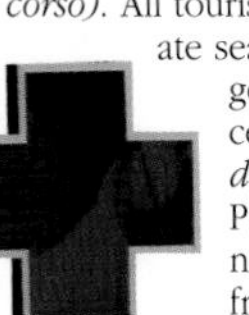

Italian pharmacy sign

Police car

Carabinieri car

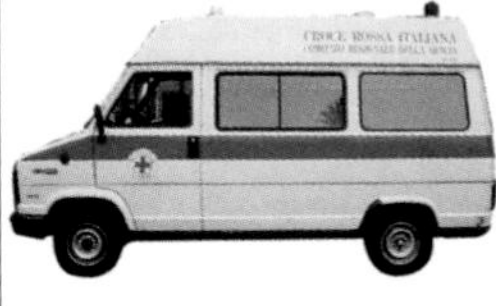

Red Cross ambulance

## SAFETY OUTDOORS

During your stay in Sicily, whether you go in the summer or winter, you will be spending a good deal of time outdoors, so you must be prepared for the various problems outdoor life can pose in the different seasons. In the summer, whether you are at the seaside or in the interior, do not overdo sunbathing, as it may cause serious burns and sunstroke. The wind can be very deceptive, often making you think the temperature is lower than it actually is.

While exploring among the tumbled stones of the ancient cities of Magna Graecia, or during a hike in the mountains, be on the lookout for snakes, which can be quite common in the summer.

Although camping just anywhere is not allowed, you can make private arrangements with landowners to put up your tent outside an official camp site. Remember, however, that you must take away all rubbish and must not light fires. While on a walk or hiking, keep your distance from sheepdogs, because they are trained to chase away all intruders.

Sicilians are very hospitable but are also reserved, so out of respect you should always ask permission before you cross over private property, go through a gate or a fenced area. On unpaved roads or paths you may come across closed gates or fences. It is always a good idea to ask whether in fact you can go through. Having done so, remember to close the gate or fence so that any animals in the field cannot escape.

An automatic cash dispenser (ATM)

## CURRENCY

Sixteen countries – Austria, Belgium, Cyprus, Finland, France, Germany, Greece, Ireland, Italy, Luxembourg, Malta, The Netherlands, Slovakia, Slovenia, Portugal and Spain – have replaced their traditional currencies, such as the Italian lire, with a single European currency, the euro, which came into circulation on 1 January 2002. All euro notes and coins can be used anywhere inside the participating member states. You can exchange currency when you arrive, at an automatic cash dispenser (ATM), at the airport or at a bank, but it is best to have some euros with you beforehand. The best exchange rates are offered by the banks, where commission charges are lower. Euro banknotes have seven denominations. The €5 note (grey in colour) is the smallest, followed by the €10 note (pink), €20 note (blue), €50 note (orange), €100 note (green), €200 note (yellow) and €500 note (purple). All notes show the stars of the European Union. The euro has eight coin denominations: €1 and €2 (silver and gold in colour), 50 cents, 20 cents, 10 cents (gold), 5 cents, 2 cents and 1 cent (bronze). If you prefer travellers' cheques, choose a well-known name or a bank. There is a minimum commission charge for each transaction, so avoid changing small amounts. Bureaux de change have the same opening hours as shops. Credit card holders can draw money directly from ATMs, found throughout Sicily.

Euro notes

# TRAVEL INFORMATION

The two main airports in Sicily are at opposite ends of the island, one at Palermo and one at Catania. In the holiday season, charter flights may land directly at one of these, but the majority of travellers flying to Sicily will fly first to a mainland airport, usually Milan or Rome, before changing to a connecting flight. A good ferry service links Sicily with the mainland (connecting Reggio Calabria and Messina). The state railway, Ferrovie dello Stato, runs regular trains using this ferry link. The smaller offshore islands are also easy to reach by ferry and some of them, for example Lampedusa, even have a small airport. There are plans to build a road bridge connecting Sicily to the mainland across the Straits.

Riding a scooter

## AIRPORTS

There are regular flights from the Italian mainland to Palermo and Catania. Direct charter flights from European cities operate all year round, linking, for example, London Gatwick to Catania or Palermo. The island's main airport is **Palermo Punta Raisi**. It handles domestic flights to and from Rome, Naples, Bologna, Milan, Pisa, Genoa, Turin, Verona, Cagliari, and the Sicilian islands Pantelleria and Lampedusa. **Catania Fontanarossa** airport serves the eastern side, with domestic flights to and from Rome, Milan, Turin, Naples, Verona, Genoa and Pisa. The small **Trapani Birgi** airport offers connections only to and from Palermo and the islands of **Pantelleria** and **Lampedusa** (the latter has a tiny airport linked to Rome, Milan and Verona). The airports on the islands all connect to Trapani and Palermo airports, and to other mainland towns.

## FLIGHT CONNECTIONS

In April 2004, **British Airways** began a London–Catania service, while **Ryanair** flies daily between Stansted and Palermo. Italian state airline **Alitalia** has no direct London–Sicily flights.

**Alitalia, Meridiana, Air One, Alpieagles** and **Volare/Air Europe** offer frequent services from the Italian mainland. The latter company also offers flights to Sicily's neighbouring islands (especially in the summer).

**American, Continental** and **Delta Airlines** offer direct flights from the United States to Rome, where you can catch a connecting flight to Sicily.

## TRAINS

The Italian state railway (FS) operates services throughout Italy, with regular links to Sicily. If you plan to travel to Sicily by train, reserve a seat (the trains are crowded in high season) and be prepared for a long journey.

The train station in Palermo

By way of compensation, the coastline as you travel south of Rome is stunningly beautiful. If possible, book a berth or couchette (sleeping compartment) before you travel.

## BUS SERVICES

Given the varied and often mountainous topography of Sicily, not everywhere is accessible by train, and even where there are lines, services can be slow. In recent years local investment in infrastructure has focussed on developing the roads rather than the railway. An extensive network of local bus services connects even the smallest villages, and there are good long-distance bus links to the most important resorts.

## FERRIES

Reggio Calabria is the principal mainland port with ferry connections to Sicily. In the summer there are also ferries between Palermo and Genoa, Livorno and Naples, and car ferries between Messina and Naples.

Catania airport, the main point of arrival for visitors to eastern Sicily

The hourly summer ferry service connecting Reggio Calabria and Messina

## CONNECTIONS TO THE SMALLER ISLANDS

Ferry services to the Sicilian islands are well organized and operate regularly. Several ferry companies, such as **Siremar**, **Alilauro**, **Ustica**, **SNAV** and **Covemar**, operate on different routes (for more information, visit www.ferriesonline.com). Ferries *(traghetti)* and hydrofoils *(aliscafi)* can get quite crowded in the summer, but services continue all year round. In the archipelagoes, such as the Aeolian Islands, local ferry companies operate services alongside the larger ones: information about these companies and timetables can be obtained from the local tourist information bureaux and Pro Loco offices.

## DIRECTORY

### AIRLINE INFORMATION

**Air One (Italy)**
**Tel** *199-207 080.*
**www**.flyairone.it

**Alitalia (UK)**
**Tel** *0871-424 14 24.*
**www**.alitalia.co.uk

**Alitalia (US)**
**Tel** *800-223 5730.*
**www**.alitaliausa.com

**Alpieagles (Italy)**
**Tel** *899-500 058.*
**www**.alpieagles.com

**American Airlines (US)**
**Tel** *800-433 73 00.*
**www**.aa.com

**British Airways (UK)**
**Tel** *0844-493 0787.*
**www**.britishairways.com

**Continental (US)**
**Tel** *800-231 08 56.*
**www**.continental.com

**Delta Airlines (US)**
**Tel** *800-241 41 41.*
**www**.delta.com

**Meridiana (Italy)**
**Tel** *078-952 682.*
**www**.meridiana.it

**Ryanair**
**Tel** *0871-246 00 00* (UK) *899-678 910* (Italy).
**www**.ryanair.com

**Volare/Air Europe**
**Tel** *899-65 65 45.*
**www**.volareweb.com

### AIRPORTS

**Catania Fontanarossa**
**Tel** *095-405 05.*
**www**.aeroporto.catania.it

**Lampedusa**
**Tel** *0922-971 548.*

**Palermo Punta Raisi**
**Tel** *091-702 07 18.*
**www**.gesap.it

**Pantelleria**
**Tel** *0923-911 817.* **www**.pantelleriaairport.it

**Trapani Birgi**
**Tel** *0923-842 502.* **www**.airgest.com

### TRAIN INFORMATION

**Citalia (UK)**
**Tel** *(Italian State Railways) 0870-901 40 13.*
**www**.citalia.co.uk

**Disabled Assistance**
**Tel** *Rome 06-6821 9168.*

**Trenitalia (Italy)**
**Tel** *(Italian State Railways) 892 021 (24-hr info line).*
**www**.trenitalia.com
*(timetables, info in English.)*

### MAINLAND CONNECTIONS

**Caronte & Tourist**
**Tel** *Messina 090-572 65 04.*
**www**.carontetourist.it

### AEOLIAN ISLANDS CONNECTIONS

**Blue Lines – Agenzia Chidas**
**Tel** *from Sant'Agata (August only) Militello 0941-701 318.*

**Siremar**
**www**.siremar.it
**Tel** *Milazzo 090-928 32 42.*
**Tel** *Naples 081-551 90 96.*

**SNAV**
**www**.snav.it
**Tel** *Cefalù 0921-421 595.*
**Tel** *Messina 091-362 114.*
**Tel** *Naples 081-428 55 55.*
**Tel** *Palermo 091-362 114.*
**Tel** *Reggio Calabria 0965-295 68.*

### EGADI ISLANDS CONNECTIONS

**Siremar**
**Tel** *Favignana 0923-921 368.*
**Tel** *Levanzo 0923-924 128.*
**Tel** *Marettimo 0923-923 144.*
**Tel** *Trapani 0923-545 411.*

### PANTELLERIA CONNECTIONS

**Siremar**
**Tel** *0923-911 120.*

**Ustica Lines**
**Tel** 0923-911 078.
**www**.usticalines.it

### USTICA CONNECTIONS

**Siremar**
**Tel** *Naples 081-580 03 40.*
**Tel** *Palermo 091-582 403.*
**Tel** *Ustica 091-844 90 02.*

**Ustica Lines**
**Tel** *Trapani 0923-222 00.*
**www**.usticalines.it

# Getting Around Sicily

No-parking sign

The heart of the largest island in the Mediterranean is rugged and mountainous. You will notice this as soon as you begin to travel around Sicily. Roads become steep and winding the further you go inland. What may look like a short journey on the map may in fact take quite a long time. Networks of railways and buses connect most towns and villages, but you may need a car for the more inaccessible areas. Sicily's rail network includes a full circuit of Mount Etna, a journey that takes five hours.

## GETTING AROUND BY TRAIN

The two major railway lines run south from Messina to Catania and Syracuse, and west in the direction of Palermo. A secondary route branches off from the Messina–Palermo line at Termini Imerese and goes – fairly slowly – to Agrigento.

Another line connects Palermo with Trapani, Marsala, Mazara, Castelvetrano and Ribera.

North of Catania, the privately run Ferrovia Circumetnea railway line *(see p166)*, describes a huge circle around Mount Etna through fertile lava fields filled with vines and fruit trees.

The state-run railway network (FS) offers frequent connections between Sicily and the mainland *(see p240)*, but the long-distance trains to and from the island win no prizes for quality and comfort.

## GETTING AROUND BY CAR OR MOTORCYCLE

If you want to get to know the real Sicily, travelling around by car, or even by motorcycle if you are brave, is probably the best way. The main roads and motorways linking the major towns are generally in good condition. This includes the Messina–Palermo, Messina–Catania and Catania–Palermo roads.

When planning your trip, bear in mind that on some of these routes, including long stretches of the southern coast, the roads may be busy with traffic and therefore quite slow, and that the mountain roads may be even slower. As a precaution, it is a good idea to buy a good up-to-date road map, such as the ones published by the Touring Club Italiano with a 1:200,000 scale. A road map of Sicily is provided on the back endpaper of this guide.

A fast, straight road crossing a valley in the interior of Sicily

## ARRIVING BY CAR

Car ferries go regularly across the Straits of Messina *(see pp240–41)*, and taking a car to Sicily should not present any particular problems. You need a valid driving licence to drive anywhere in Italy, and it may be a good idea to carry a translation of your licence.

## CAR HIRE

Almost all the major car hire companies have branch offices throughout Sicily, including the seaports of Palermo and Catania and the airports of Palermo Punta Raisi, Catania Fontanarossa and Trapani Birgi. You can also find an office in every provincial capital. If you choose a major firm such as Hertz or Rent a Car *(see*

**The Ferrovia Circumetnea *(see p166)*, offering a scenic route around Europe's largest volcano**

*Directory)*, check the rental conditions in advance to see what is included and whether you need additional insurance. A number of holiday companies offer inclusive fly-drive deals, enabling you to pick up your car on arrival at the airport. This is normally cheaper than renting a car on the spot. On some of the offshore islands you can find scooters as well as motorcycles and cars for hire. Island roads are often in poor condition, and you may find travelling by two-wheeled transport is a more comfortable way of getting around.

## ROAD REGULATIONS

The rules of the road are the same as in the rest of Italy, including driving on the right, speed limits (50 km/h, 30 mph in towns) and compulsory seat belts in cars and helmets for motorcyclists. Parking is a real problem in the larger cities (especially Palermo), and also in historic centres. Petrol *(benzina)* is generally expensive.

## BICYCLES AND MOUNTAIN BIKES

The roads in the interior are fairly quiet and are therefore suitable for cycling and even for touring by bicycle. As a result, some travel agencies have begun to offer bike excursions, with the added convenience of vans to carry

**Using a rented bicycle, the best way to see the small islands**

**Buses, the best way of getting around larger cities such as Palermo**

your luggage for you from place to place. Sicilian drivers are not used to seeing cyclists on the road, however, so stay alert at all times.

Mountain biking is becoming more popular as a sport in Sicily, particularly in the Peloritani, Nebrodi and Madonie mountain areas.

Cycling with a group of mountain bike riders is increasingly popular, and it is not uncommon to see a cavalcade on the cattle tracks and paths that run through the various parks and nature reserves on the island.

## GETTING AROUND IN THE CITIES

Public transport is quite reliable, and easy to use in the main cities in Sicily – Palermo, Catania and Messina. In other towns, such as Trapani, Syracuse and Agrigento, and in the smaller towns, the best way to get around is on foot. Public transport in Palermo is run by the **AMAT** (tel: 848-800 817). The service connects all the most interesting sights, including Monreale and Mondello. The 101 bus runs north to south.

Tickets can be purchased at tobacconists *(tabaccaio)* and newsagents *(giornalaio)*, or in the AMAT kiosks, which also provide transport maps. Tickets are valid for two hours and cost €1; all-day tickets are also available. Note that there is a fine for riding without a valid ticket.

All of Catania's most interesting sights can be reached on foot. However, should you need a bus to go from the centre to the airport take the Alibus (no. 457). The network of buses that go between the train station and the centre is run by **AMT** (tel: 801-018 696). Tickets are valid for 90 minutes, but there is also a 24-hour tourist ticket available. In Messina, public transport is handy if you want to visit the Museo Regionale *(see pp182–3)*, which is 45 minutes' walking distance from the centre of town; the stops for buses going in this direction are in Piazza Castronovo, which is also the terminus for buses to Ganzirri (Nos. 78, 79 and 81). Tickets can be purchased from tobacconists.

**A Palermo transport system tourist ticket**

## DIRECTORY

### CAR HIRE

**Avis**
***Tel*** *Palermo 091-591 684.*
***Tel*** *Catania 095-340 500.*
**www**.avisworld.com

**Europcar**
***Tel*** *Palermo 091-301 825.*
***Tel*** *Catania 095-348 125.*
**www**.europcar.com

**Hertz**
***Tel*** *Palermo 091-213 112.*
***Tel*** *Catania 095-341 595.*
**www**.hertz.com

**Rent a Car (Maggiore)**
***Tel*** *Palermo 091-591681.*
***Tel*** *Catania 095-340 594.*
***Tel*** *Syracuse 0931-66548.*
**www**.maggiore.it

# General Index

Page numbers in **bold** refer to main entries

## G



## H

## T

# Acknowledgments

Dorling Kindersley would like to thank the following people, museums and organizations, whose contributions and assistance have made the preparation of this book possible. Dorling Kindersley would also like to thank all the people, organizations and businesses, too numerous to mention individually, for their kind permission to photograph their establishments.

Alessandra Arena; Ms Puleo, Assessorato al Turismo Regione Sicilia; AAPT Caltanissetta, Egidio Cacciola, AAST Acireale; Grazia Incorvaia, AAST Agrigento; AAST Caltagirone; AAST Capo D'Orlando; Ms Lidestri, AAST Catania and Acicastello; AAST Cefalù; Ms Petralia, AAST Enna; AAST Giardini Naxos; AAST Messina; AAST Milazzo; Salvatore Giuffrida, AAST Nicolosi; AAST Palermo and Monreale; AAST Patti; Ivana Taschetta, AAST Piazza Armerina; AAST Sciacca; AAST Syracuse; AAST Taormina; Mario Cavallaro, APT Syracuse; Ms Mocata, APT Trapani; Carlo Rigano, Associazione Culturale Sicilia '71 di Mascalucia, Paolo Mazzotta, Biblioteca "E Vittorietti", Palermo; Barbara Cacciani; Franco Conti, Carthera Aetna; Nicolò Longo; Prof Giorgio De Luca, Istituto Europeo di Scienze Antropologiche; Giorgia Conversi; EPT Agrigento; Nello Musumeci, EPT Catania; Dr Ragno, EPT Messina; Dr Majorca, EPT Palermo; Manilo Peri, Fondazione Culturale Mandralisca, Cefalù; Dr Rosano, Framon Hotels; Galleria Regionale di Sicilia – Palazzo Abatellis (Palermo); Domenico Calabrò, Gazzetta del Sud; Gisella Giarrusso; Ernesto Girardi; Salvo Amato, Giuliano Rotondi Freelance Studio, Acireale; Carmelo Guglielmino; Mr Altieri, Hotel Baglio della Luna; Hotel Baglio Santa Croce; Hotel La Tonnara di Bonagia; Col Girardi; Hotel Villa Paradiso dell'Etna; Luigi Lacagnina and his family; Maggiore Budget Autonoleggi; Prof Gaetano Maltese; Emma Marzullo; Meridiana; Museo Archeologico Regionale Paolo Orsi (Syracuse); Museo Etnostorico dei Nebrodi; Prof Iberia Medici, Museo-Laboratorio Village, Giarre; Ignazio Paternò Castello; Società Aerofotogrammetrica Siciliana (Palermo); Sandro Tranchina; Teatro Massimo (Palermo); Teatro Biondo (Palermo); Prof Amitrano Svarese, Faculty of Anthropological Sciences, University of Palermo; Mara Veneziani; Pia Vesin.

### Additional Assistance

Emily Anderson, Claire Baranowski, Maria Carla Barra, Tessa Bindloss, Michelle Clark, Lucinda Cooke, Michelle Crane, Conrad van Dyk, Gadi Farfour, Rhiannon Furbear, Katharina Hahn, Gerard Hutching, Giuliano Rotondi, Sands Publishing Solutions, Ellie Smith, Mary Sutherland, Stewart J Wild.

### Picture Credits

Key: t = top; tl = top left; tlc = top left centre; tc = top centre; trc = top right centre; tr = top right; cla = centre left above; ca = centre above; cra = centre right above; cl = centre left; c = centre; cr = centre right; clb = centre left below; crb = centre right below; cb = centre below; bl = bottom left; br = bottom right; b = bottom; bc = bottom centre; bcl = bottom centre left; bcr = bottom centre right.

Every effort has been made to trace the copyright holders. The publisher apologizes for any unintentional omissions and would be pleased, in such cases, to add an acknowledgment in future editions.

All the photographs reproduced in this book are from the Image Bank, Milan, except for the following:

Alamy Images: Claudio H. Artman 10cl; CuboImages srl/Alfio Garozzo 11tl, 11bc; CuboImages srl/Enrico Fumagalli 10tc; CuboImages srl/Enzo Signorelli 227bl; David Norton Photography/David Norton 10br; nagelestock.com 11cr. Fabrizio Ardito: 2, 3, 17b, 83br, 84, 100tl, 102bl, 110, 113tl, 114tl, 115br, 116tr, 116cl, 117cr, 118tr, 118bl, 119cr, 120tl, 120br, 121br, 122t, 122c, 123tl, 123b, 126cl, 128bl, 129cl, 129clb, 130tl, 131bl, 143tl, 143br, 144bl, 149tl, 149br, 153tl, 153cr, 154tl, 156c, 156b, 157br, 166tl, 166cr, 196, 209c. Archivio APT Siracusa: 136tl, 137bl, 139br. Archivio APT Trapani: 86tl, 87b. Archivio EPT Palermo: 109cr. Archivio Framon Hotels: 194cl, 195tl, 195br. Cephas Picture Library: Lehmann 224br. Corbis: Dave Bartruff 210cl; 211tl; Owen Franken 211c; Mimmo Jodice 227tr. Fabio De Angelis: 48tl, 48cl, 48bl, 49cr, 50tl, 50bc, 53br, 55cr, 56tl, 60tr, 60b, 61tr, 61br, 63tr, 65br, 66cr, 67tl, 68br, 69br, 73bl, 74tl, 90c, 210br, 224cl, 236tc, 236br, 237tl, 238cl, 238crb, 238bl, 239tl, 239tr, 239cra, 239crb, 240tc, 240cr, 240br, 242tl. Il Dagherrotipo: 230br, 231tr. DK Images: 20br, 29bl, 35tr, 35tl, 36–7c, 44tr, 46, 57br, 62, 72cr, 76–7, 146br, 192–3, Ian O'Leary 210-211. European Commission: 239br. Cristina Gambaro–Gino Frongia: 69bl, 85, 86bl, 90cl, 91b, 92b, 93tl, 94c, 95, 97bc, 98cl, 98bl, 102tl, 104, 106tl, 106b, 107tl, 117bl, 133, 146c, 177br, 208cr. Leonardo Media Ltd: 195tl. Nicolò Longo: 18crb, 19crb. Reculez: 210–11. Ronald Grant Archive: 24cla/tr. Marka, Milan: Sante Malli 231br; Danilo Donadoni 232cr. Giuliano Rotondi: 3c, 17tr, 22tr, 22cl, 22bc, 23tr, 23cl, 23bc, 24, 25tl, 25tc, 25c, 26, 27tc, 28tr, 28c, 28br, 29tl, 29tc, 29cl, 29br, 30tl, 30cl, 30cb, 30br, 31tl, 31cla, 31bla, 31bl, 32tl, 32ca, 32clb, 32bl, 32bc, 33cr, 33bc, 34tl, 34cl, 34br, 35cr, 35bl, 35br, 36ar, 36cl, 36cla, 36cb, 36bl, 36br, 36clb, 37cla, 37cra, 37tr, 37bl, 37br, 45tr, 51c, 51br, 54t, 66tr, 66cl, 67tc, 67cr, 69t, 72bl, 75tl, 92tc, 92c, 94tl, 99tr, 99cl, 102br, 103cr, 103br, 105cr, 106cl, 106cr, 128tr, 128br, 129tr, 129br, 134bc, 145bl, 150tr, 151cr, 152b, 154cl, 154br, 155tl, 156tl, 157cr, 160bl, 163tl, 164tl, 167t, 167bl, 169br, 172tr, 173tl, 175br, 176bl, 178cl, 183br, 185tr, 185bl, 210tr, 222tc, 224tl, 224tr, 225tr, 225cla, 225cra, 225clb, 225crb, 225b, 226cr, 226bl, 228br, 240cl, 242bl. Sbriglio: 137tl, 138, 142c, 144tl, 144cl, 144br, 145cr, 145bl, 146tl, 146tr, 147tr, 147cl, 147br, 148c, 148br, 160tr. Marco Scapagnini: 142tr, 145tr, 147cr, 208tc, 226tc.

Jacket

Front – Corbis: Zefa/Manfred Mehlig main image; Giuliano Rotondi clb. Back – Alamy Images: Anthony Collins bl; nagelestock.com clb; Corbis: Jose Fusta Raga tl; DK Images: John Heseltine cla. Spine – Alamy Images: Peter Horree b; Corbis: Zefa/Manfred Mehlig, t.

# Phrase Book

## In Emergency

| | | |
|---|---|---|
| Help! | Aiuto! | eye-yoo-toh |
| Stop! | Fermati! | fair-mah-tee |
| Call a doctor. | Chiama un medico. | kee-ah-mah oon meh-dee-koh |
| Call an ambulance. | Chiama un' ambulanza. | kee-ah-mah oon am-boo-lan-tsa |
| Call the police. | Chiama la polizia. | kee-ah-mah lah pol-ee-tsee-ah |
| Call the fire department. | Chiama i pompieri. | kee-ah-mah ee pom-pee-air-ee |
| Where is the telephone? | Dov'è il telefono? | dov-eh eel teh-leh-foh-noh? |
| The nearest hospital? | L'ospedale più vicino? | loss-peh-dah-leh pee-oo vee-chee-noh? |

## Communication Essentials

| | | |
|---|---|---|
| Yes/No | Si/No | see/noh |
| Please | Per favore | pair fah-vor-eh |
| Thank you | Grazie | grah-tsee-eh |
| Excuse me | Mi scusi | mee skoo-zee |
| Hello | Buon giorno | bwon jor-noh |
| Goodbye | Arrivederci | ah-ree-veh-dair-chee |
| Good evening | Buona sera | bwon-ah sair-ah |
| morning | la mattina | lah mah-tee-nah |
| afternoon | il pomeriggio | eel poh-meh-ree-joh |
| evening | la sera | lah sair-ah |
| yesterday | ieri | ee-air-ee |
| today | oggi | oh-jee |
| tomorrow | domani | doh-mah-nee |
| here | qui | kwee |
| there | la | lah |
| What? | Quale? | kwah-leh? |
| When? | Quando? | kwan-doh? |
| Why? | Perchè? | pair-keh? |
| Where? | Dove? | doh-veh? |

## Useful Phrases

| | | |
|---|---|---|
| How are you? | Come sta? | koh-meh stah? |
| Very well, thank you. | Molto bene, grazie. | moll-toh beh-neh grah-tsee-eh |
| Pleased to meet you. | Piacere di conoscerla. | pee-ah-chair-eh dee coh-noh-shair-lah |
| See you later. | A più tardi. | ah pee-oo tar-dee |
| That's fine. | Va bene. | va beh-neh |
| Where is/are ...? | Dov'è/Dove sono...? | dov-eh/doveh soh-noh? |
| How long does it take to get to ...? | Quanto tempo ci vuole per andare a ...? | kwan-toh tem-poh chee voo-oh-leh pair an-dar-eh ah ...? |
| How do I get to ...? | Come faccio per arrivare a ...? | koh-meh fah-choh pair arri-var-eh ah...? |
| Do you speak English? | Parla inglese? | par-lah een-gleh-zeh? |
| I don't understand. | Non capisco. | non ka-pee-skoh |
| Could you speak more slowly, please? | Può parlare più lentamente, per favore? | pwoh par-lah-reh pee-oo len-ta-men-teh pair fah-vor-eh? |
| I'm sorry. | Mi dispiace. | mee dee-spee-ah-cheh |

## Useful Words

| | | |
|---|---|---|
| big | grande | gran-deh |
| small | piccolo | pee-koh-loh |
| hot | caldo | kal-doh |
| cold | freddo | fred-doh |
| good | buono | bwoh-noh |
| bad | cattivo | kat-tee-voh |
| enough | basta | bas-tah |
| well | bene | beh-neh |
| open | aperto | ah-pair-toh |
| closed | chiuso | kee-oo-zoh |
| left | a sinistra | ah see-nee-strah |
| right | a destra | ah dess-trah |
| straight ahead | sempre dritto | sem-preh dree-toh |
| near | vicino | vee-chee-noh |
| far | lontano | lon-tah-noh |
| up | su | soo |
| down | giù | joo |
| early | presto | press-toh |
| late | tardi | tar-dee |
| entrance | entrata | en-trah-tah |
| exit | uscita | oo-shee-ta |
| toilet | il gabinetto | eel gah-bee-net-toh |
| free, unoccupied | libero | lee-bair-oh |
| free, no charge | gratuito | grah-too-ee-toh |

## Making a Telephone Call

| | | |
|---|---|---|
| I'd like to place a long-distance call. | Vorrei fare una interurbana. | vor-ray far-eh oona in-tair-oor-bah-nah |
| I'd like to make a reverse-charge call. | Vorrei fare una telefonata a carico del destinatario. | vor-ray far-eh oona teh-leh-fon-ah-tah ah kar-ee-koh dell dess-tee-nah-tar-ree-oh |
| Could I speak to... | Potrei parlare con... | po-tray par-lah-reh con |
| I'll try again later. | Ritelefono più tardi | ree-teh-leh-foh-noh pee-oo tar-dee |
| May I leave a message? | Posso lasciare un messaggio? | poss-oh lash-ah-reh oon mess-sah-joh? |
| Hold on. | Un attimo, per favore. | oon ah-tee-moh, pair fah-vor-eh |
| Could you speak up a little, please? | Può parlare più forte? | pwoh par-lah-reh pee-oo for-teh? |
| local call | telefonata locale | te-leh-fon-ah-tah loh-cah-leh |

## Shopping

| | | |
|---|---|---|
| How much does this cost? | Quant'è, per favore? | kwan-teh pair fah-vor-eh? |
| I would like ... | Vorrei ... | vor-ray... |
| Do you have ...? | Avete ...? | ah-veh-teh...? |
| I'm just looking. | Sto soltanto guardando | stoh sol-tan-toh gwar-dan-doh |
| Do you take credit cards? | Accettate carte di credito? | ah-chet-tah-teh kar-teh dee creh-dee-toh? |
| What time do you open/close? | A che ora apre/ chiude? | ah keh or-ah ah-preh/kee-oo-deh? |
| this one | questo | kweh-stoh |
| that one | quello | kwell-oh |
| expensive | caro | kar-oh |
| cheap | a buon prezzo | ah bwon pret-soh |
| size, clothes | la taglia | lah tah-lee-ah |
| size, shoes | il numero | eel noo-mair-oh |
| white | bianco | bee-ang-koh |
| black | nero | neh-roh |
| red | rosso | ross-oh |
| yellow | giallo | jal-loh |
| green | verde | vair-deh |
| blue | blu | bloo |

## Types of Shop

| | | |
|---|---|---|
| antique dealer | l'antiquario | lan-tee-kwah-ree-oh |
| bakery | il forno/ il panificio | eel forn-oh/ eel pan-ee-fee-choh |
| bank | la banca | lah bang-kah |
| bookstore | la libreria | lah lee-breh-ree-ah |
| butcher | la macelleria | lah mah-chell-eh-ree-ah |
| cake shop | la pasticceria | lah pas-tee-chair-ee-ah |
| delicatessen | la salumeria | lah sah-loo-meh-ree-ah |
| department store | il grande magazzino | eel gran-deh mag-gad-zee-noh |
| pharmacy | la farmacia | lah far-mah-chee-ah |
| fishseller | il pescivendolo | eel pesh-ee-ven-doh-loh |
| florist | il fioraio | eel fee-or-eye-oh |
| greengrocer | il fruttivendolo | eel froo-tee-ven-doh-loh |
| grocery | alimentari | ah-lee-men-tah-ree |
| hairdresser | il parrucchiere | eel par-oo-kee-air-eh |
| ice-cream parlour | la gelateria | lah jel-lah-tair-ree-ah |
| market | il mercato | eel mair-kah-toh |
| newsstand | l'edicola | leh-dee-koh-lah |
| post office | l'ufficio postale | loo-fee-choh pos-tah-leh |
| shoe shop | il negozio di scarpe | eel neh-goh-tsioh dee skar-peh |
| supermarket | il supermercato | eel su-pair-mair-kah-toh |
| tobacconist | il tabaccaio | eel tah-bak-eye-oh |
| travel agency | l'agenzia di viaggi | lah-jen-tsee-ah dee vee-ad-jee |

## Sightseeing

| | | |
|---|---|---|
| art gallery | la pinacoteca | lah peena-koh-teh-kah |
| bus stop | la fermata dell'autobus | lah fair-mah-tah dell ow-toh-booss |
| church | la chiesa/ la basilica | lah kee-eh-zah/ lah bah-seel-i-kah |
| closed for holidays | chiuso per le ferie | kee-oo-zoh pair leh fair-ee-eh |
| garden | il giardino | eel jar-dee-no |
| library | la biblioteca | lah beeb-lee-oh-teh-kah |
| museum | il museo | eel moo-zeh-oh |
| train station | la stazione | lah stah-tsee-oh-neh |
| tourist information | l'ufficio di turismo | loo-fee-choh dee too-ree-smoh |

## Staying in a Hotel

| | | |
|---|---|---|
| Do you have any vacant rooms? | **Avete camere libere?** | ah-**veh**-teh **kah**-mair-eh **lee**-bair-eh? |
| double room | **una camera doppia** | oona **kah**-mair-ah **doh**-pee-ah |
| with double bed | **con letto matrimoniale** | kon **let**-toh mah-tree moh-nee-**ah**-leh |
| twin room | **una camera con due letti** | oona **kah**-mair-ah kon **doo**-eh **let**-tee |
| single room | **una camera singola** | oona **kah**-mair-ah **sing**-goh-lah |
| room with a bath, shower | **una camera con bagno, con doccia** | oona **kah**-mair-ah kon **ban**-yoh, kon **dot**-chah |
| porter | **il facchino** | eel fah-**kee**-noh |
| key | **la chiave** | lah kee-**ah**-veh |
| I have a reservation. | **Ho fatto una prenotazione.** | oh **fat**-toh oona preh-noh-tah-tsee-**oh**-neh |

## Eating Out

| | | |
|---|---|---|
| Do you have a table for ...? | **Avete una tavola per ... ?** | ah-**veh**-teh oona **tah**-voh-lah pair ...? |
| I'd like to reserve a table | **Vorrei riservare una tavola** | vor-**ray** ree-sair-**vah**-reh oona **tah**-voh-lah |
| breakfast | **colazione** | koh-lah-tsee-**oh**-neh |
| lunch | **pranzo** | **pran**-tsoh |
| dinner | **cena** | **cheh**-nah |
| The bill, please | **Il conto, per favore.** | eel **kon**-toh pair fah-**vor**-eh |
| I am a vegetarian. | **Sono vegetariano/a.** | **soh**-noh **veh**-jeh-tar-ee-ah-noh/nah |
| waitress | **cameriera** | kah-mair-ee-**air**-ah |
| waiter | **cameriere** | kah-mair-ee-**air**-eh |
| fixed-price menu | **il menù a prezzo fisso** | eel meh-**noo** ah **pret**-soh **fee**-soh |
| dish of the day | **piatto del giorno** | pee-**ah**-toh dell **jor**-no |
| appetizer | **antipasto** | an-tee-**pass**-toh |
| first course | **il primo** | eel **pree**-moh |
| main course | **il secondo** | eel seh-**kon**-doh |
| vegetables | **il contorno** | eel kon-**tor**-noh |
| dessert | **il dolce** | eel **doll**-cheh |
| cover charge | **il coperto** | eel koh-**pair**-toh |
| wine list | **la lista dei vini** | lah **lee**-stah day-ee **vee**-nee |
| rare | **al sangue** | al **sang**-gweh |
| medium | **al puntino** | al poon-**tee**-noh |
| well done | **ben cotto** | ben **kot**-toh |
| glass | **il bicchiere** | eel bee-kee-**air**-eh |
| bottle | **la bottiglia** | lah bot-**teel**-yah |
| knife | **il coltello** | eel kol-**tell**-oh |
| fork | **la forchetta** | lah for-**ket**-tah |
| spoon | **il cucchiaio** | eel koo-kee-**eye**-oh |

## Menu Decoder

| | | |
|---|---|---|
| **l'acqua minerale gassata/naturale** | lah-**kwah** mee-nair-**ah**-leh gah-**zah**-tah/ nah-too-**rah**-leh | mineral water fizzy/still |
| **aceto** | ah-**cheh**-toh | vinegar |
| **aglio** | **al**-ee-oh | garlic |
| **l'agnello** | lah-**niell**-oh | lamb |
| **al forno** | al **for**-noh | baked/roasted |
| **alla griglia** | ah-lah **greel**-yah | grilled |
| **l'aragosta** | lah-rah-**goss**-tah | lobster |
| **arrosto** | ar-**ross**-toh | roast |
| **basilico** | bah-**zee**-lee-koh | basil |
| **la birra** | lah **beer**-rah | beer |
| **la bistecca** | lah bee-**stek**-kah | steak |
| **il brodo** | eel **broh**-doh | broth |
| **il burro** | eel **boor**-oh | butter |
| **il caffè** | eel kah-**feh** | coffee |
| **i calamari** | ee kah-lah-**mah**-ree | squid |
| **i carciofi** | ee kar-**choff**-ee | artichokes |
| **la carne** | la **kar**-neh | meat |
| **la cipolla** | la chip-**oh**-lah | onion |
| **i contorni** | ee kon-**tor**-nee | vegetables |
| **le cozze** | leh **coh**-tzeh | mussels |
| **i fagioli** | ee fah-**joh**-lee | beans |
| **il fegato** | eel **fay**-gah-toh | liver |
| **il finocchio** | eel fee-**nok**-ee-oh | fennel |
| **il formaggio** | eel for-**mad**-joh | cheese |
| **le fragole** | leh **frah**-goh-leh | strawberries |
| **il fritto misto** | eel free-toh **mees**-toh | mixed fried dish |
| **la frutta** | la **froot**-tah | fruit |
| **frutti di mare** | **froo**-tee dee **mah**-reh | seafood |
| **i funghi** | ee **foon**-ghee | mushrooms |
| **i gamberi** | ee **gam**-bair-ee | shrimp |
| **il gelato** | eel jeh-**lah**-toh | ice cream |
| **l'insalata** | leen-sah-lah-tah | salad |
| **il latte** | eel **laht**-teh | milk |
| **lesso** | **less**-oh | boiled |
| **la melanzana** | lah meh-lan-**tsah**-nah | aubergine (eggplant) |
| **la minestra** | lah mee-**ness**-trah | soup |
| **l'olio** | loh-lee-oh | oil |
| **il pane** | eel **pah**-neh | bread |
| **le patate** | leh pah-**tah**-teh | potatoes |
| **le patatine fritte** | leh pah-tah-**teen**-eh **free**-teh | French fries |
| **il pepe** | eel **peh**-peh | pepper |
| **la pesca** | lah **pess**-kah | peach |
| **il pesce** | eel **pesh**-eh | fish |
| **il polipo** | eel **poh**-lee-poh | octopus |
| **il pollo** | eel **poll**-oh | chicken |
| **il pomodoro** | eel poh-moh-**dor**-oh | tomato |
| **il prosciutto cotto/crudo** | eel pro-**shoo**-toh **kot**-toh/**kroo**-doh | ham cooked/cured |
| **il riso** | eel **ree**-zoh | rice |
| **il sale** | eel **sah**-leh | salt |
| **la salsiccia** | lah sal-**see**-chah | sausage |
| **le seppie** | leh **sep**-pee-eh | cuttlefish |
| **secco** | **sek**-koh | dry |
| **la sogliola** | lah **soll**-yoh-lah | sole |
| **i spinaci** | ee spee-**nah**-chee | spinach |
| **succo d'arancia/ di limone** | **soo**-koh dah-**ran**-chah/ dee lee-**moh**-neh | orange/lemon juice |
| **il tè** | eel **teh** | tea |
| **la tisana** | lah tee-**zah**-nah | herbal tea |
| **il tonno** | eel **ton**-noh | tuna |
| **la torta** | lah **tor**-tah | cake/tart |
| **l'uovo** | loo-**oh**-voh | egg |
| **vino bianco** | vee-noh bee-**ang**-koh | white wine |
| **vino rosso** | **vee**-noh **ross**-oh | red wine |
| **il vitello** | eel vee-**tell**-oh | veal |
| **le vongole** | leh **von**-goh-leh | clams |
| **lo zucchero** | loh **zoo**-kair-oh | sugar |
| **gli zucchini** | lyee dzu-**kee**-nee | zucchini |
| **la zuppa** | lah **tsoo**-pah | soup |

## Numbers

| | | |
|---|---|---|
| 1 | **uno** | **oo**-noh |
| 2 | **due** | **doo**-eh |
| 3 | **tre** | **treh** |
| 4 | **quattro** | **kwat**-roh |
| 5 | **cinque** | **ching**-kweh |
| 6 | **sei** | **say**-ee |
| 7 | **sette** | **set**-teh |
| 8 | **otto** | **ot**-toh |
| 9 | **nove** | **noh**-veh |
| 10 | **dieci** | dee-**eh**-chee |
| 11 | **undici** | **oon**-dee-chee |
| 12 | **dodici** | **doh**-dee-chee |
| 13 | **tredici** | **tray**-dee-chee |
| 14 | **quattordici** | kwat-**tor**-dee-chee |
| 15 | **quindici** | **kwin**-dee-chee |
| 16 | **sedici** | **say**-dee-chee |
| 17 | **diciassette** | dee-chah-**set**-teh |
| 18 | **diciotto** | dee-**chot**-toh |
| 19 | **diciannove** | dee-chah-**noh**-veh |
| 20 | **venti** | **ven**-tee |
| 30 | **trenta** | **tren**-tah |
| 40 | **quaranta** | kwah-**ran**-tah |
| 50 | **cinquanta** | ching-**kwan**-tah |
| 60 | **sessanta** | sess-**an**-tah |
| 70 | **settanta** | set-**tan**-tah |
| 80 | **ottanta** | ot-**tan**-tah |
| 90 | **novanta** | noh-**van**-tah |
| 100 | **cento** | **chen**-toh |
| 1,000 | **mille** | **mee**-leh |
| 2,000 | **duemila** | **doo**-eh **mee**-lah |
| 5,000 | **cinquemila** | **ching**-kweh **mee**-lah |
| 1,000,000 | **un milione** | oon meel-**yoh**-neh |

## Time

| | | |
|---|---|---|
| one minute | **un minuto** | oon mee-**noo**-toh |
| one hour | **un'ora** | oon **or**-ah |
| half an hour | **mezz'ora** | medz-**or**-ah |
| a day | **un giorno** | oon **jor**-noh |
| a week | **una settimana** | oona set-tee-**mah**-nah |
| Monday | **lunedì** | loo-neh-**dee** |
| Tuesday | **martedì** | mar-teh-**dee** |
| Wednesday | **mercoledì** | mair-koh-leh-**dee** |
| Thursday | **giovedì** | joh-veh-**dee** |
| Friday | **venerdì** | ven-air-**dee** |
| Saturday | **sabato** | **sah**-bah-toh |
| Sunday | **domenica** | doh-**meh**-nee-kah |

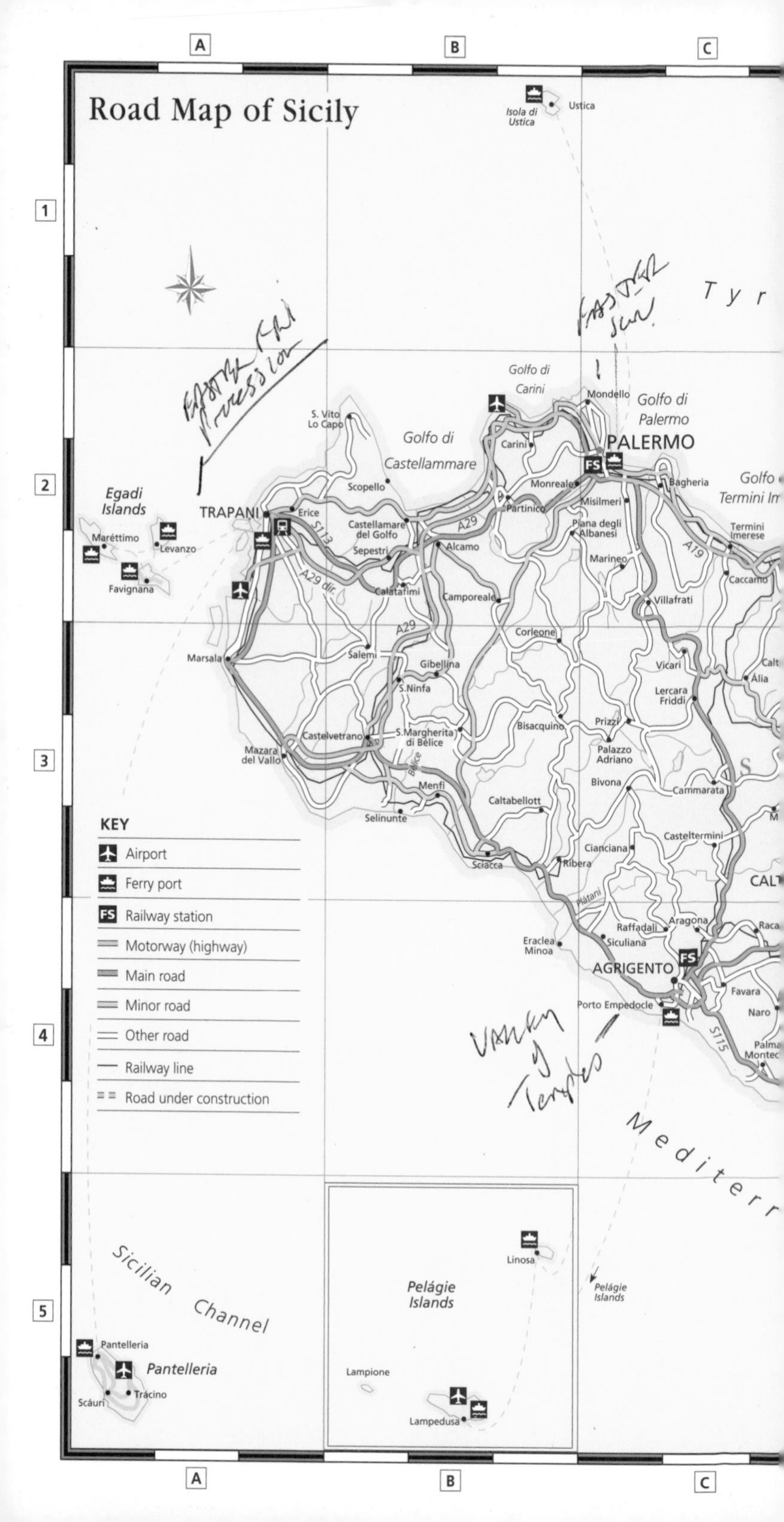

Road Map of Sicily
A
B
C
1
2
3
4
5
Isola di Ustica
Ustica
Tyr
Golfo di Carini
Mondello
Golfo di Palermo
PALERMO
S. Vito Lo Capo
Golfo di Castellammare
Carini
Bagheria
Golfo
Termini Im
Egadi Islands
TRAPANI
Erice
Scopello
Monreale
Misilmeri
Maréttimo
Levanzo
Favignana
Castellamare del Golfo
Partinico
Piana degli Albanesi
Termini Imerese
Sepestri
Alcamo
Marineo
Caccamo
Calatafimi
Camporeale
Villafrati
Corleone
Marsala
Salemi
Gibellina
Vicari
Alia
S.Ninfa
Lercara Friddi
Castelvetrano
S.Margherita di Bélice
Bisacquino
Prizzi
Palazzo Adriano
Mazara del Vallo
Bivona
Cammarata
Menfi
Caltabellott
Selinunte
Casteltermini
Cianciana
Sciacca
Ribera
CALT
Plátani
Raffadali
Aragona
Eraclea Minoa
Siciliana
AGRIGENTO
Favara
Porto Empedocle
Naro
Palma Montec
A29
A29 dir.
A19
S113
S115
Bélice
Mediterr
KEY
Airport
Ferry port
Railway station
Motorway (highway)
Main road
Minor road
Other road
Railway line
Road under construction
Sicilian Channel
Linosa
Pelágie Islands
Pantelleria
Tràcino
Scàuri
Lampione
Lampedusa